VICTORIA PHILPOTT

Celebrate!

THE GREATEST FESTIVALS AROUND THE WORLD
RAUSCHENDE FESTE RUND UM DIE WELT

teNeues

Introduction

As you travel through life and the world, I strongly recommend you visit a few festivals along the way. A local festival is the quickest way to get under the skin of a destination and uncover the history, culture, and beliefs that make it so unique. They're a fascinating insight into a group of individuals, bound by a common understanding.

As well as being visually incredible, festivals like Las Fallas in Valencia, Spain, offer a glimpse into the current world and a country's issues of the day—you just need to look deep into the meaning of those colorful statues. On the other hand, festivals like the Edinburgh Fringe in Scotland and Lake of Stars Festival in Malawi lay it all out with poetry, songs, and performances the artists produce.

Our earliest celebrations date back to 586 BCE, to the Pythian Games in Ancient Greece, which are generally considered mankind's first festival. With a combination of a banquet, sports, music, and horse racing to entertain the crowd, the Pythian Games set the standard for festivals to progress from then on.

Today's sports festivals follow this formula—with the Calgary Stampede in Canada serving up the country's best rodeo performances along with a wide selection of food and top music artists. And there's the Naadam Festival in Ulaanbaatar, Mongolia, which pits the "strongest men" against each other alongside great food and music.

Celebrations are an ancient ritual. They've forever addressed our need to commemorate and thank the seasons, our harvest, traditions, faith, life processes, art, and achievements. They also satisfy our need to celebrate ourselves, what we believe and how we interact. Festivals are a chance for tribes and groups to get together—whether it's their religion, social beliefs, or interests that bind them.

As you'll read in *Celebrate*, there's a festival around the world for everyone and everything. Some of the more unique ones I want to introduce within the pages of this book include the Lemon Festival in Menton, France; the Dragon Boat Festival in China; and the impressive Butter Lamp Festival in Tibet.

These festivals are a chance to pass on important traditions, rituals, and ceremonies that are vital to keeping a culture alive in an increasingly homogenized world. They're a time to honor traditions from the past and to applaud their importance in the modern day. The large carnivals around the world, our seasonal festivals, and our national holiday celebrations have shifted with the times but still pay respect to their heritage.

Other prolific festivals are more recent, particularly music festivals. It wasn't until around the 1970s that the world's biggest music festivals were established, with the USA's huge Summerfest in 1968, Woodstock in 1969, the UK's Glastonbury in 1970, and Denmark's Roskilde in 1971. From then on, music festivals have multiplied to the plethora we have to choose from now.

So, why go to festivals?

In today's computer-based, fast-paced world, festivals are an opportunity to put your tech down, look up, and enjoy what's around you. They're your chance to disconnect from normal daily life, to be present in the moment, and to celebrate shared interests with friends new and old. Festivals are an opportunity to let loose, clear and expand your mind, and learn something along the way. They're also a lot of fun.

In this book, I'll introduce you to some of the biggest celebrations in the world—how they began, and how they're celebrated today—to help you decide which one to travel to next.

Victoria Philpott

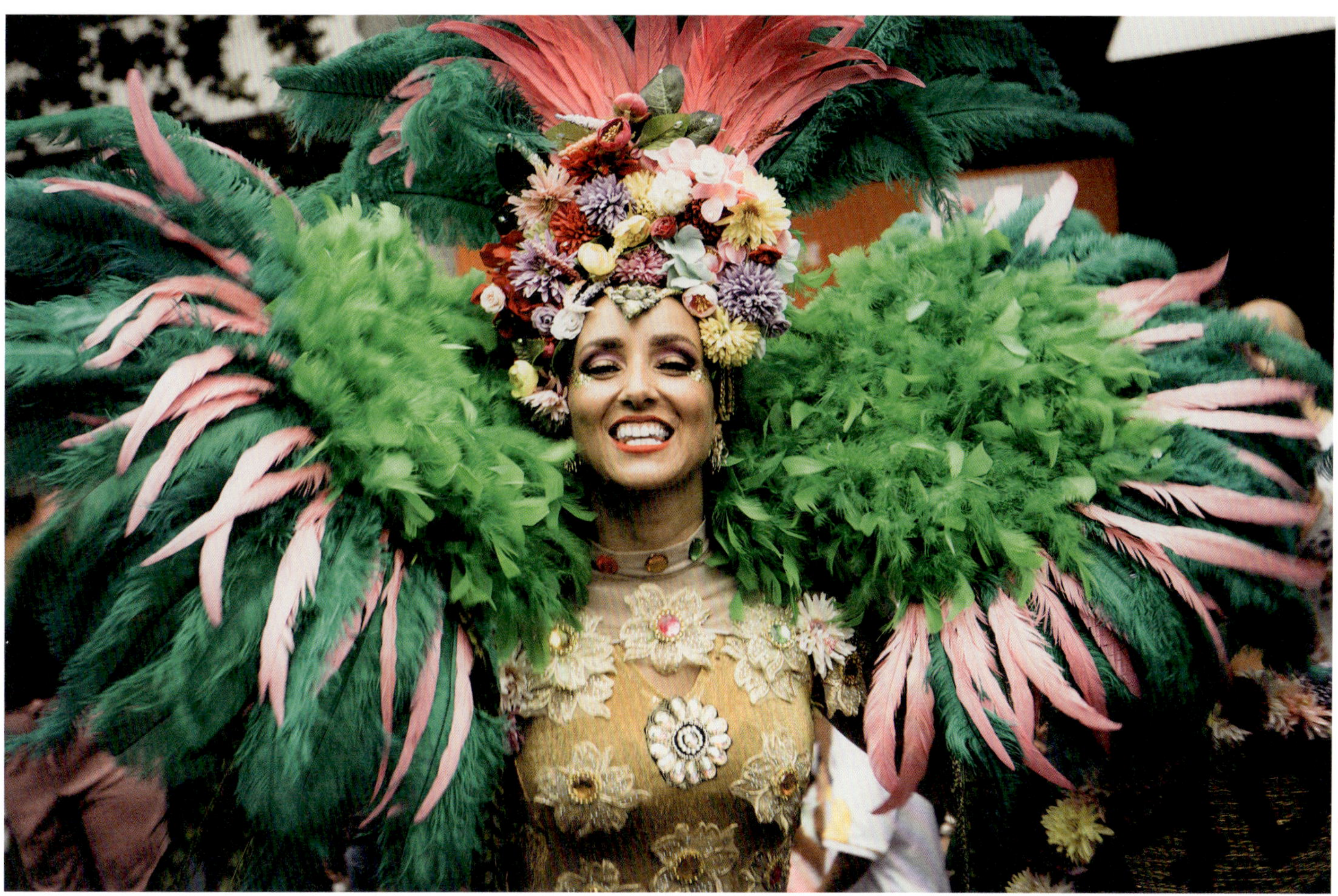

Einleitung

Ich empfehle Menschen immer, auf ihrer Reise durch die Welt und durchs Leben auch ein paar Festivals zu besuchen. Auf einem lokalen Fest taucht man sofort in einen fremden Ort ein und entdeckt die Geschichte, Kultur und Spiritualität, die ihn ausmachen. Traditionelle Feste und Zeremonien bieten faszinierende Einblicke in die Lebensräume anderer Menschen.

Ein Fest wie Las Fallas im spanischen Valencia ist nicht nur visuell spektakulär, sondern vermittelt auch einen Eindruck von den tagesaktuellen Themen, die das Land umtreiben – man muss nur die Bedeutung der bunten Figuren interpretieren. Auf Festivals wie dem Edinburgh Fringe in Schottland oder dem Lake of Stars Festival in Malawi verpacken die Künstler politische Themen hingegen in ihre Poesie, Lieder und Performances.

Die Pythischen Spiele im Griechenland der Antike um 586 v. Chr. gelten allgemein als das erste Festival der Menschheit. Mit ihrer Mischung aus Bankett, Sport, Musik und Pferderennen setzten sie den Standard für alle zukünftigen Festivals.

Heutige Sportfeste kopieren diese gelungene Formel. So serviert die kanadische Calgary Stampede zu den besten Rodeo-Vorführungen des Landes auch eine große Auswahl an kulinarischen Köstlichkeiten sowie Auftritte musikalischer Top Acts. Und auf dem Naadam-Fest im mongolischen Ulaanbaatar werden die „stärksten Männer" ebenfalls von gutem Essen und Musik flankiert.

Festivitäten und Feierlichkeiten sind uralte Rituale. Sie befriedigen unser Bedürfnis, uns zu erinnern und Dank zu sagen für Jahreszeiten, Ernte, Traditionen, Glauben, Leben, Kunst und Errungenschaften. Mit ihnen feiern wir aber auch uns selbst, das, an was wir glauben, und wie wir miteinander interagieren. Feste bieten Stämmen und Gruppen, die durch Religion, soziale Ansichten oder andere gemeinsame Interessen verbunden sind, regelmäßig die Möglichkeit zusammenzukommen.

Auf den folgenden Seiten werden Sie erfahren, dass es auf der Welt für alle und alles ein Fest gibt. Einige der ungewöhnlichsten möchte ich vorstellen, darunter das Zitronenfest im französischen Menton, das Drachenbootfest in China und das beeindruckende Butterlampenfest in Tibet.

Diese Feste sind Gelegenheiten, um wichtige Traditionen, Rituale und Zeremonien weiterzugeben, die in einer zunehmend homogeneren Welt einzigartige Kulturen am Leben erhalten. Auf Festen werden altehrwürdige Traditionen nicht nur als Verbeugung an die Vergangenheit gepflegt, sondern auch als Teil des modernen Lebens zelebriert. Die großen Karnevalsfeiern weltweit, unsere jahreszeitlichen Festivitäten und Nationalfeiertage haben sich zwar mit der Zeit gewandelt, aber sie respektieren immer noch ihre Ursprünge.

Andere Feierlichkeiten sind jüngeren Datums, vor allem Musikfestivals. Die größten wurden erst um 1970 herum ins Leben gerufen: das gigantische Summerfest in den USA 1968, Woodstock 1969, das britische Glastonbury-Festival 1970 und das Musikevent im dänischen Roskilde 1971. Seitdem schossen Musikfestivals wie Pilze aus dem Boden, sodass wir heute die Qual der Wahl haben.

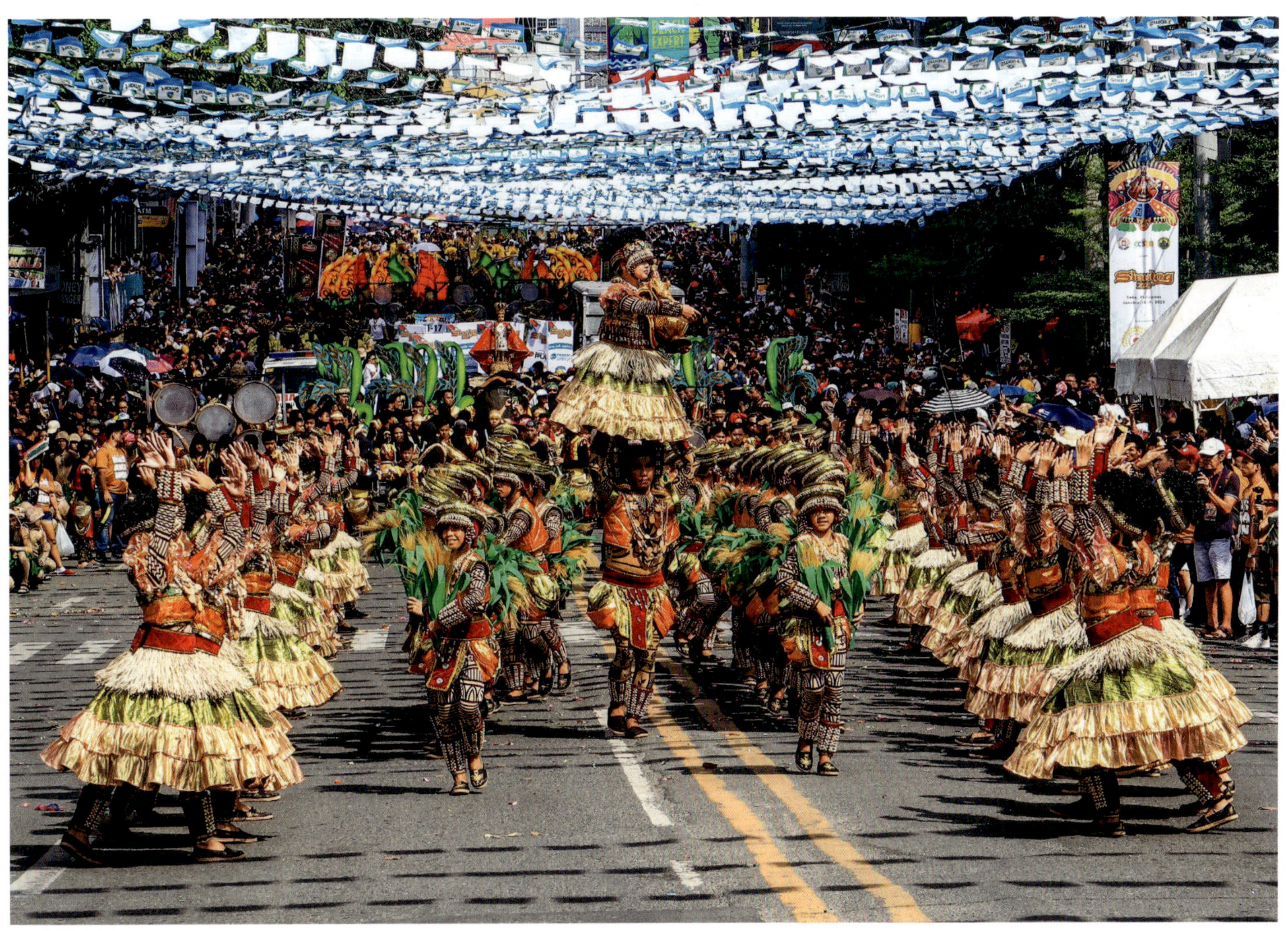

Aber warum sollten wir überhaupt Festivals besuchen?

In der heutigen digitalisierten schnelllebigen Welt bieten Festivals uns die Gelegenheit, elektronische Apparaturen abzulegen, den Blick zu heben und das zu genießen, was um uns herum passiert. Wir können eine Auszeit vom Alltag nehmen, ganz in den Augenblick eintauchen und mit alten und neuen Freunden gemeinsame Interessen zelebrieren. Auf Festivals kann man loslassen, den Kopf durchpusten, den Geist schweifen lassen oder etwas Neues lernen. Und auch einfach jede Menge Spaß haben.

In diesem Buch werden Sie einige der besten Feste der Welt kennenlernen – ihre Ursprünge, Besonderheiten und wie sie heute gefeiert werden. Entscheiden Sie dann selbst, an welchem Sie als Nächstes teilnehmen wollen.

Victoria Philpott

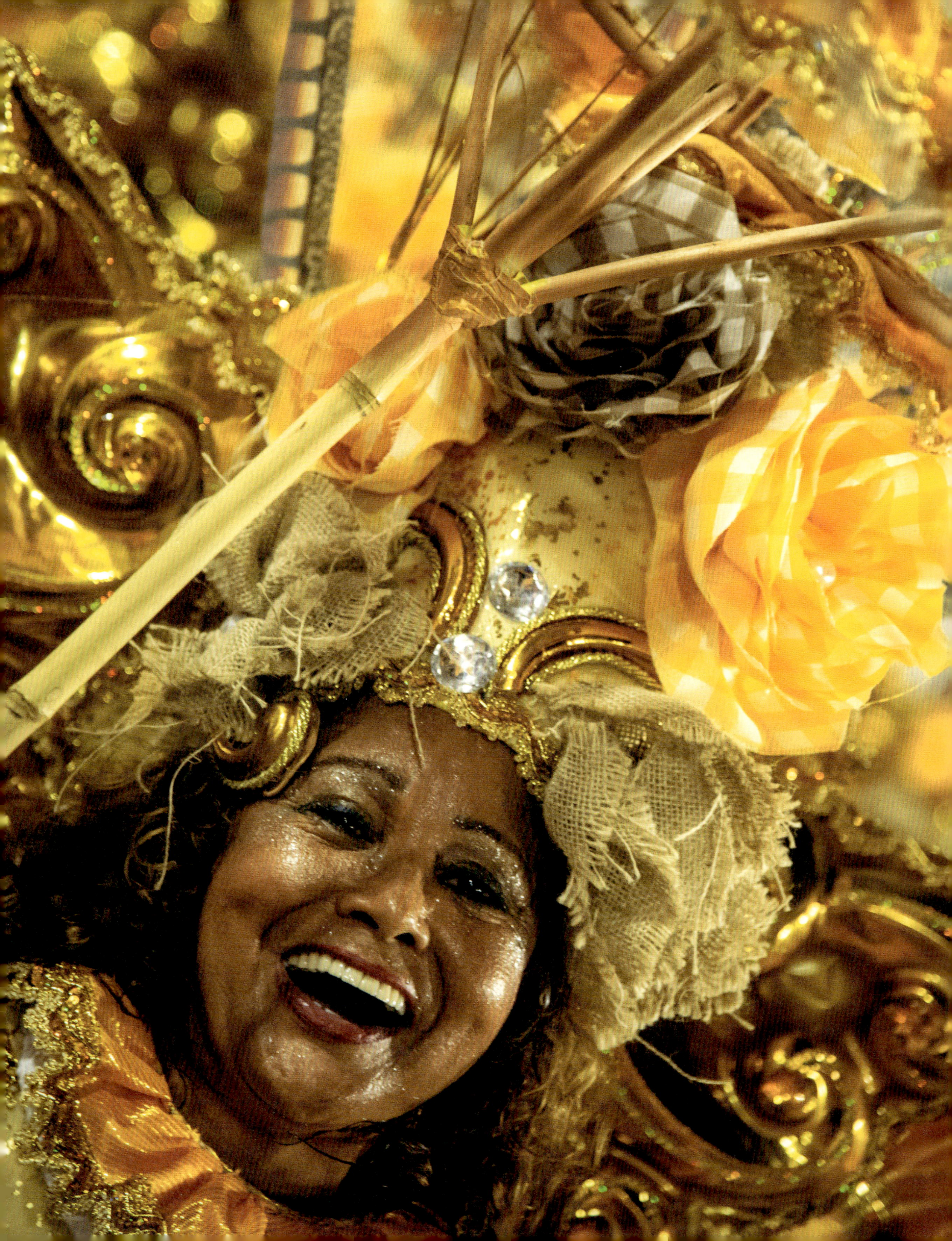

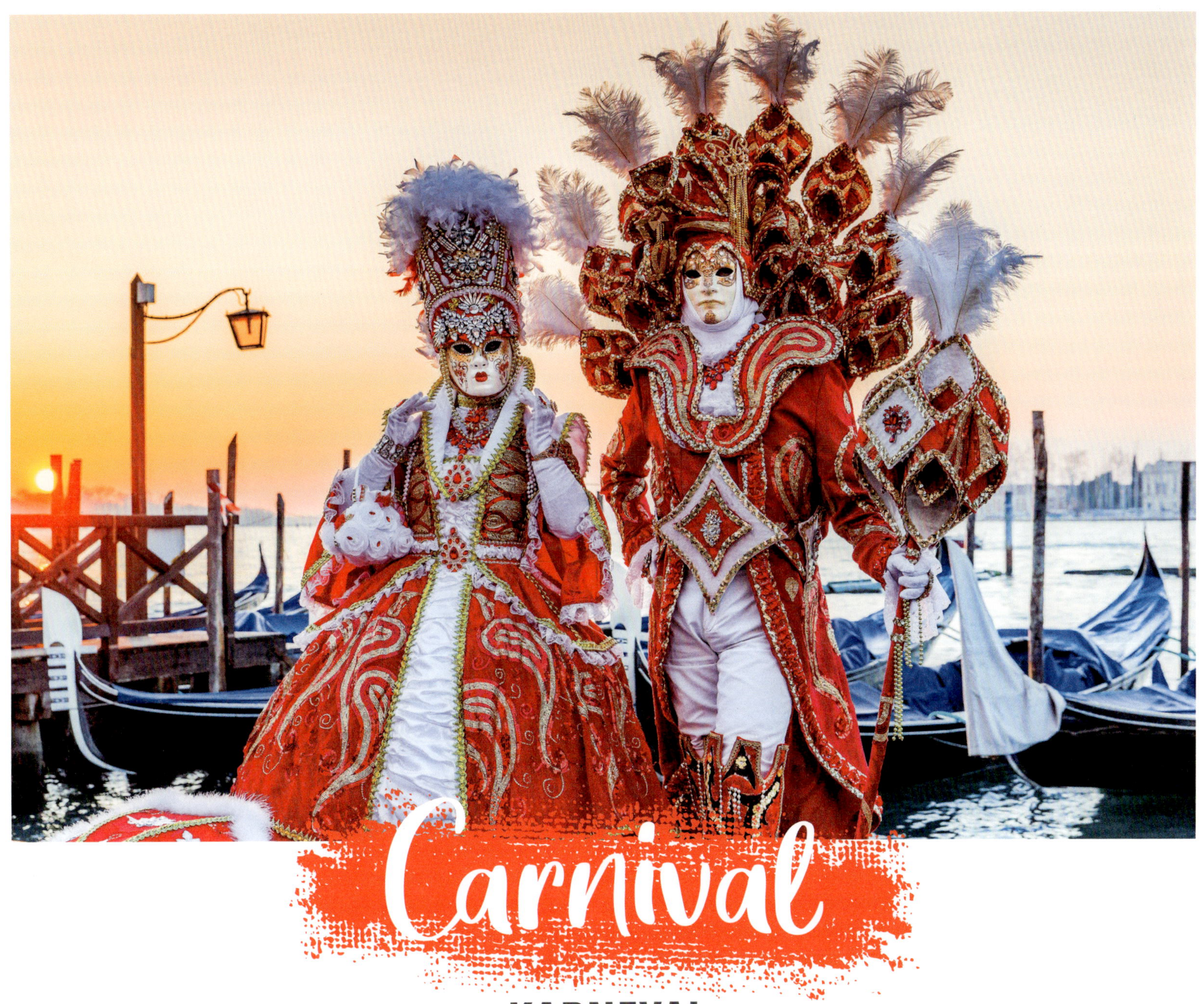

Carnival

KARNEVAL

The beginnings of the Venetian Carnival date back to the
11th century. It is most famous for its grand costume balls,
stunning masks, and sophisticated appeal.

Der venezianische Karneval lässt sich bis ins 11. Jahrhundert
zurückverfolgen. Bekannt ist er vor allem für prächtige Kostümbälle,
atemberaubende Masken und seine mondäne Wirkung.

A performer from the famous Portela samba school dances at the
parade during Rio de Janeiro Carnival. Portela is one of the most
traditional schools and has won the competition more than 20 times.

Tänzerin der berühmten Sambaschule Portela während der Karnevalsparade in Rio de Janeiro. Portela ist eine der traditionellsten Schulen
und hat den Sambawettbewerb über 20 Mal gewonnen.

Think "carnival" and you think feathered headpieces, colorful costumes, majestic parades, and joyful photos all around. *This* is why people travel across countries to visit the largest carnivals in the world. Humans are tribal, and we want to celebrate with people who share our passion and joy. To be part of such a big celebration, and either watch the parades in the streets, or even join in, is enough to make you book that ticket—however far.

Carnivals mark the Christian tradition of Lent. All the excitement wraps up by Fat Tuesday, aka Shrove Tuesday, Carnival Tuesday, or Pancake Tuesday—essentially, the Tuesday before the more subdued Ash Wednesday, and the beginning of Lent.

The most well known carnival has to be Rio Carnival in Brazil, with over two million attendees each year. The size of the floats and the parades *have* to be seen to be believed. Top samba schools compete in the procession to be crowned the champions by the many judges tasked with this difficult choice. An incredible celebration to see, whether you're religious or not!

In Europe, Venice Carnival in Italy thrives on sophistication—there aren't revealing costumes here! Instead, attendees wear specially created decorative masks and cloaks, and parade calmly in the streets. There's even a competition for *la maschera più bella*, or "the most beautiful mask," in St. Mark's Square. You can see plays and local craft displays, but it's the grand Venetian balls that entertain festivalgoers by night.

People flock to the wild Mardi Gras in New Orleans, in the United States, for the impressive floats, OTT costumes, and all-night parties. You know it's Mardi Gras when the people and streets are covered with the famous Mardi Gras beads. This French Catholic celebration has attendees leaning from balconies to join in on the fun in packed streets, while the Krewes on the floats throw out prized treats to attendees (think coconuts, food, and stuffed toys). (opposite, bottom)

Beim Wort Karneval denkt man an bunte Kostüme, prunkvolle Paraden, ausladenden Feder-Kopfschmuck und Fotos von fröhlichen Menschen. Deshalb locken diese Events so viele Besucher von Nah und Fern an. Wir Menschen sind Herdentiere und feiern nun mal gerne mit anderen. Teil einer solchen rauschhaften Feier zu sein – ob als Beobachter am Straßenrand oder mittenmang –, ist auf jeden Fall eine Reise wert.

Der Karneval markiert in der christlichen Tradition den Start der Fastenzeit. Er beginnt am Gründonnerstag und endet in der Nacht vor Aschermittwoch.

Der bekannteste Karneval ist der brasilianische in Rio de Janeiro, an dem jährlich über zwei Millionen Menschen teilnehmen. Prunk und Größe der Wagen und Paraden sind einfach überwältigend. Die besten Sambaschulen des Landes treten auf den Paraden leicht bekleidet gegeneinander an und werden von zahlreichen Juroren bewertet, der Sieger wird am Aschermittwoch gekrönt. Ein grandioses Spektakel!

Der Karneval in Venedig könnte nicht unterschiedlicher sein. Statt offenherziger Kostüme sieht man hier ausladende historische Gewänder, Umhänge und Masken, in denen man gesetzt durch die Straßen schreitet. Am Markusplatz wird *la maschera più bella* („die schönste Maske") gekürt. Es gibt Theateraufführungen und Präsentationen lokaler Handwerkskunst. Das Highlight sind nachts die prächtigen venezianischen Bälle.

Der wilde Mardi Gras in New Orleans lockt Besucher mit beeindruckenden Wagen, verrückten Kostümen und ausgelassenen Partys. Man weiß, dass der Mardi Gras tobt, wenn Menschen und Straßen mit den berühmten Perlenketten bedeckt sind. Bei diesem Fest französisch-katholischen Ursprungs feiern viele Bewohner auf ihren Balkonen, während die Krewes (soziale Organisationen) von den Wagen Kokosnüsse, Stofftiere und andere begehrte Geschenke in die dichtgedrängte Menge werfen (rechte Seite, unten).

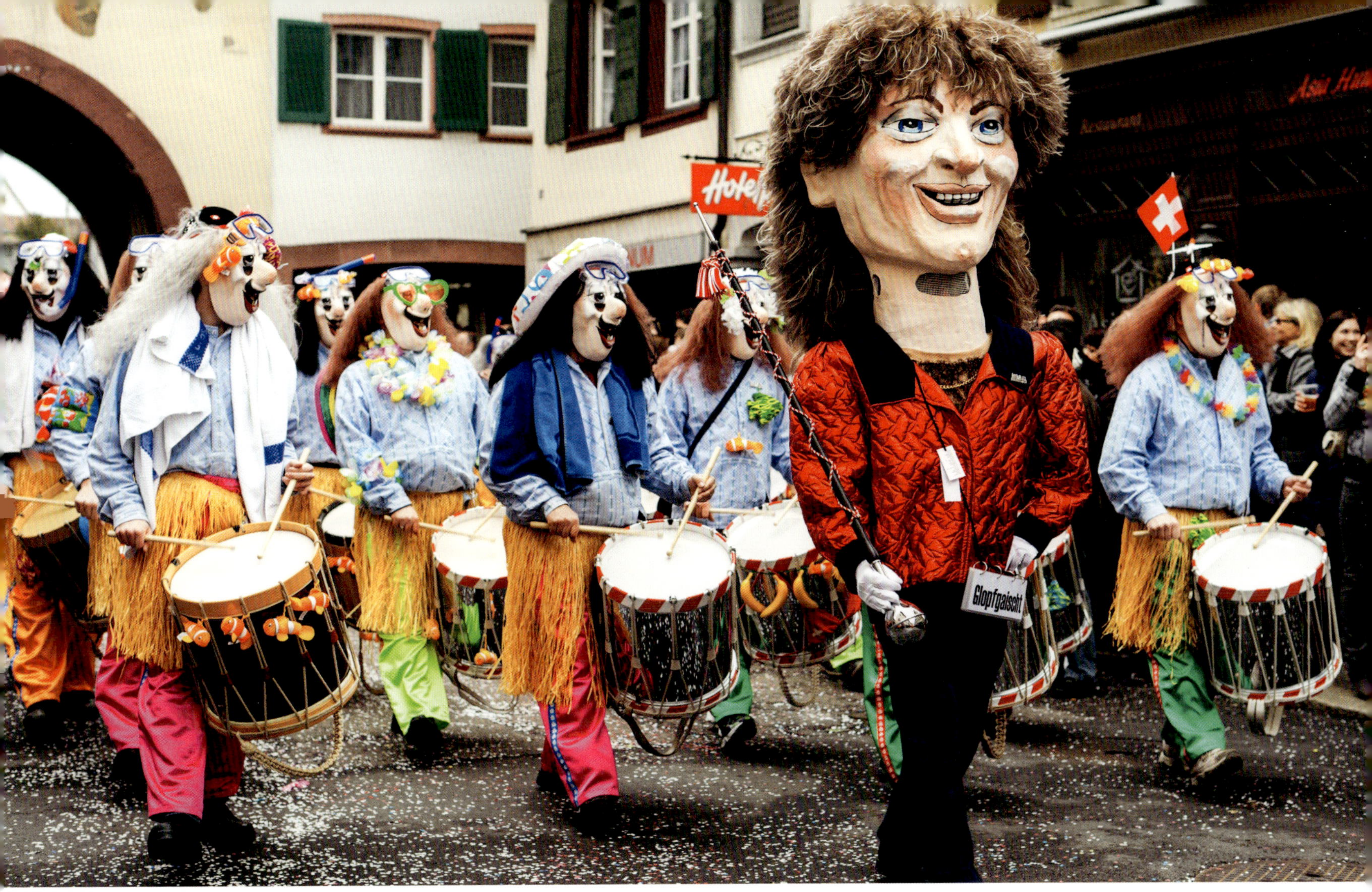

Glopfgaisch
MARCHING CLUB

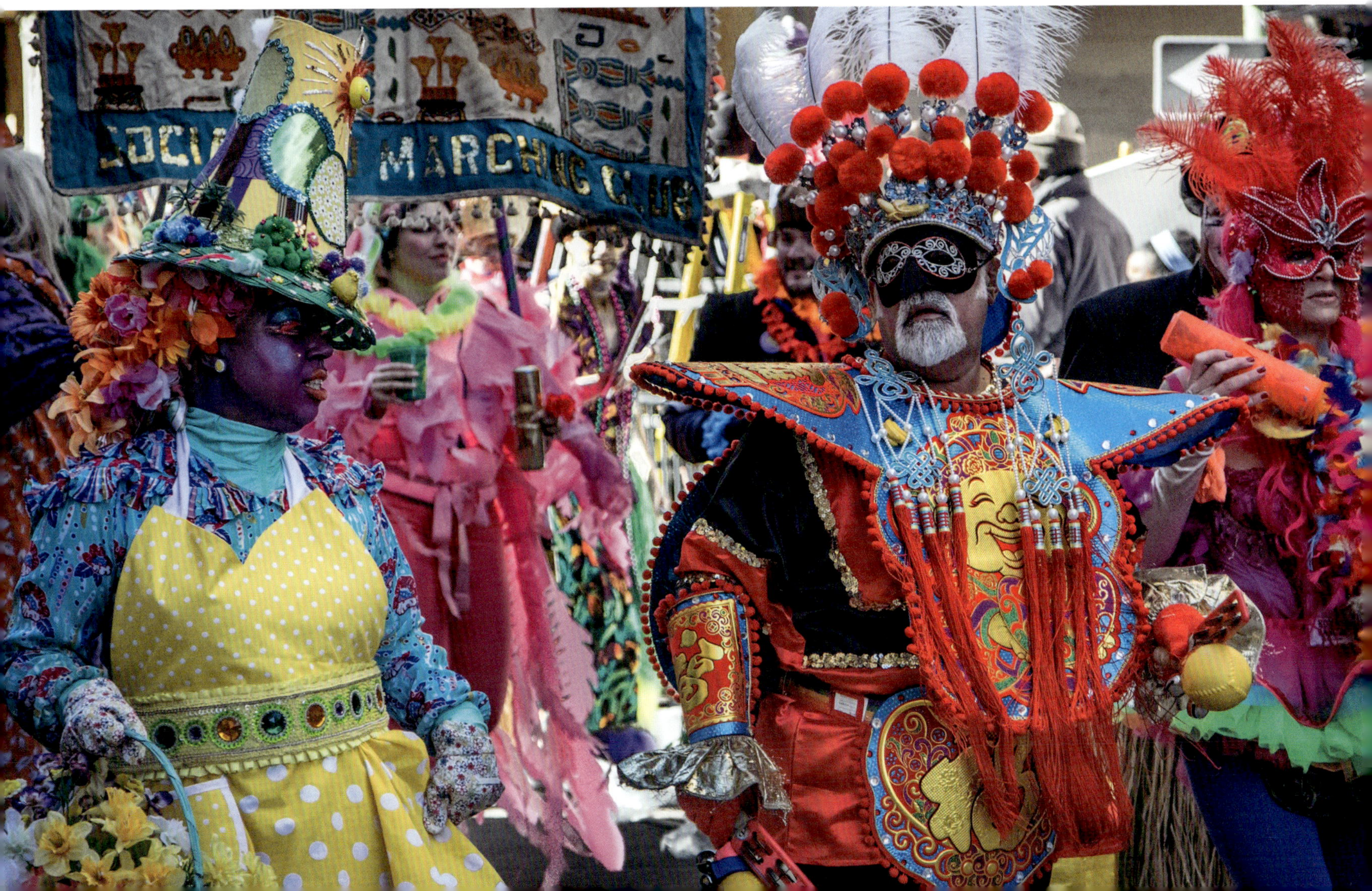

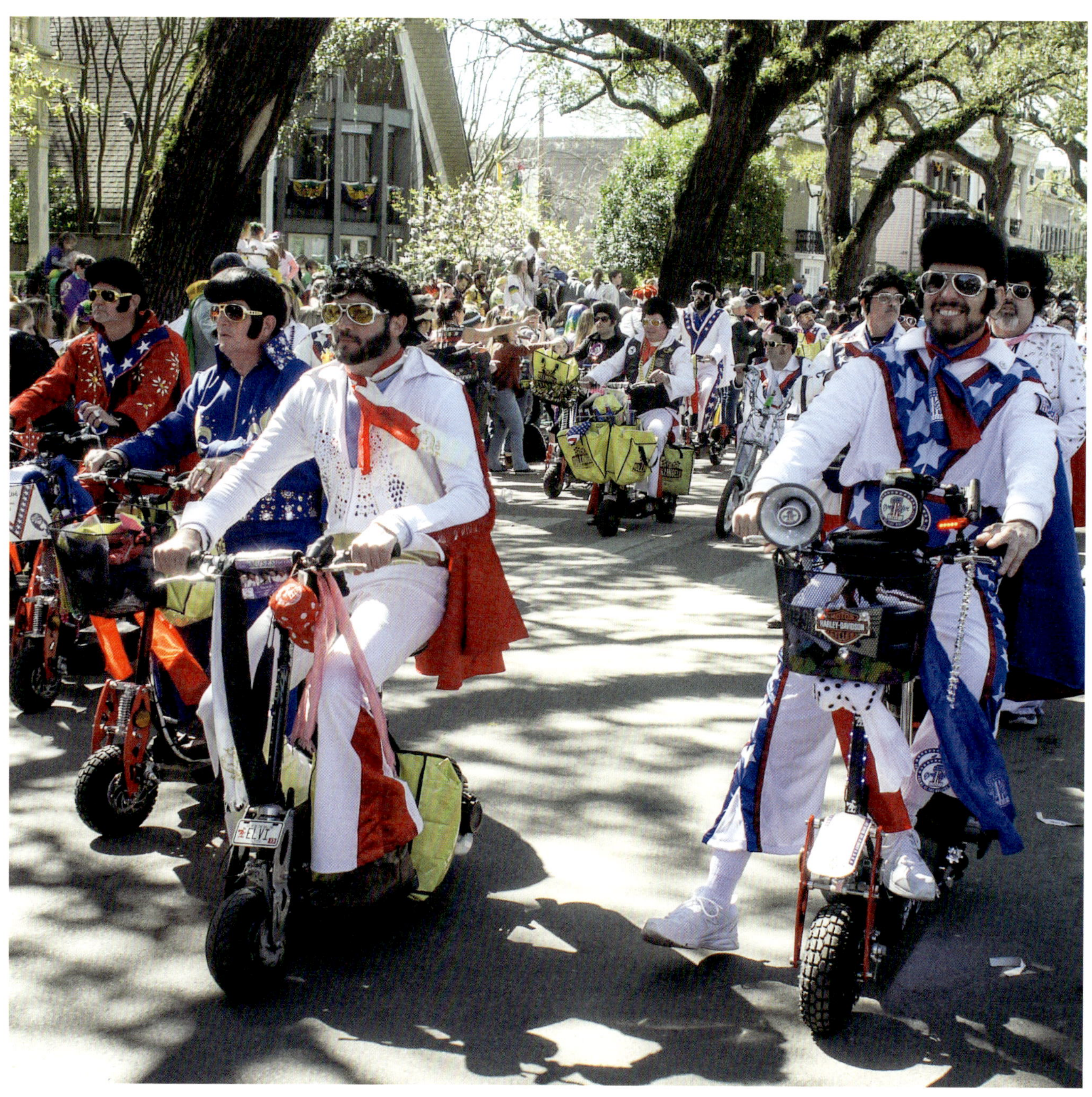

The Krewe of the Rolling Elvi rolls in the
Iris parade down St. Charles Avenue for
Mardi Gras in New Orleans, USA.

Die Krewe of the Rolling Elvi bei der Mardi-Gras-Parade
auf der St. Charles Avenue in New Orleans, USA.

New Orleans has almost 80 so-called "krewes."
These carnival organizations arrange balls and parades,
and build floats during the Mardi Gras season.

In New Orleans gibt es fast 80 sogenannte „Krewes".
Diese Karnevalsorganisationen veranstalten Bälle und Paraden
und bauen Umzugswagen für die Karnevalssaison.

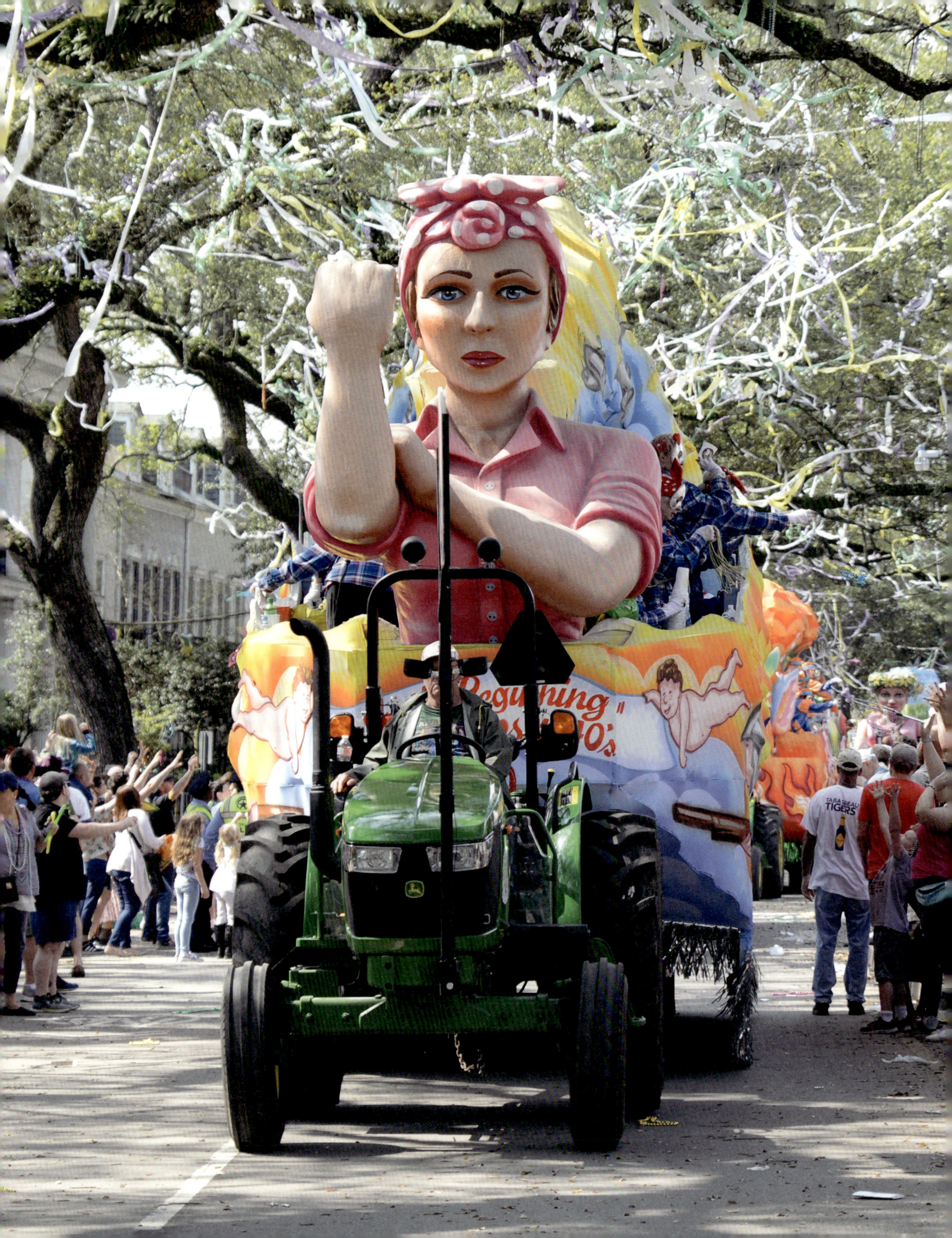
Beginning "
40's

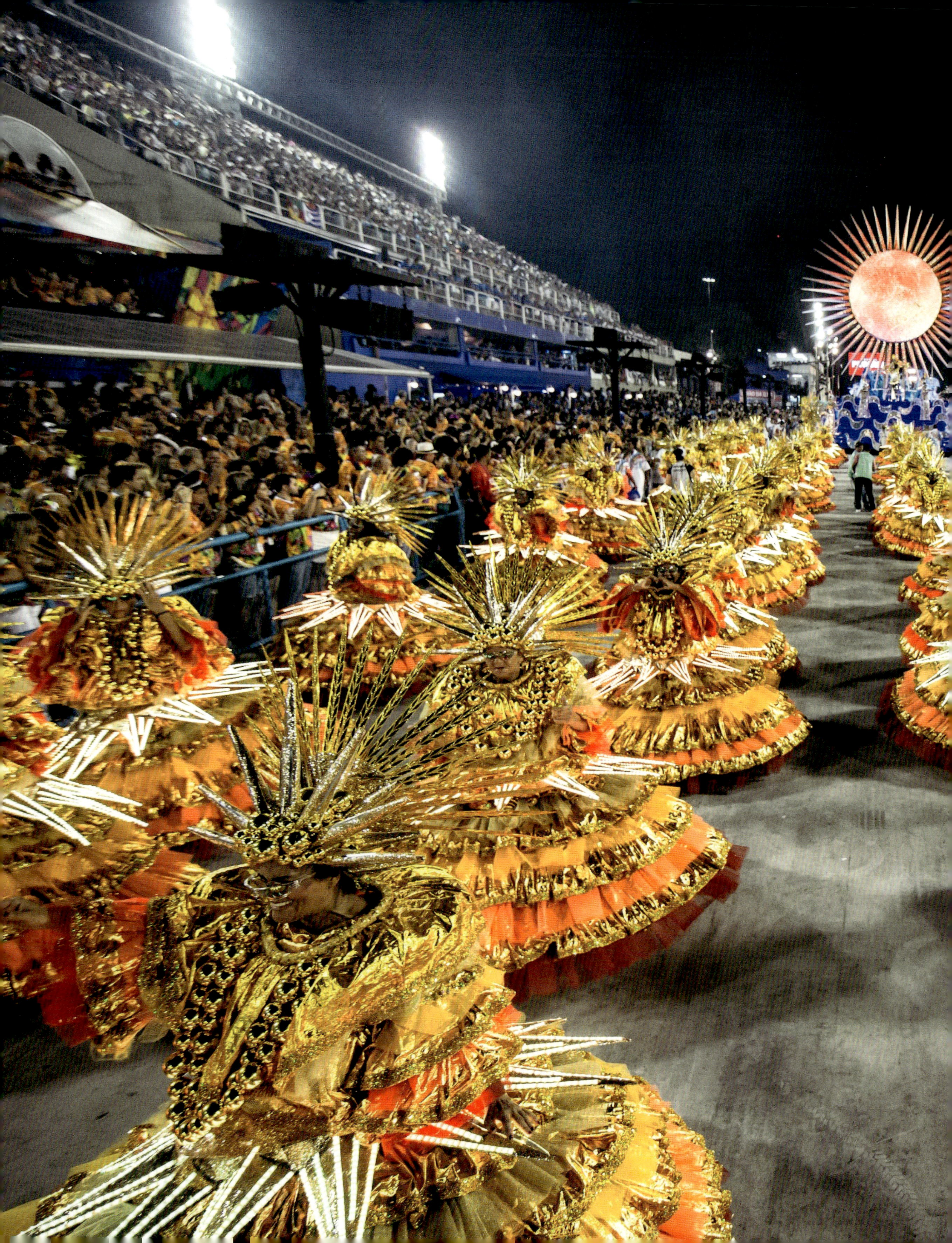

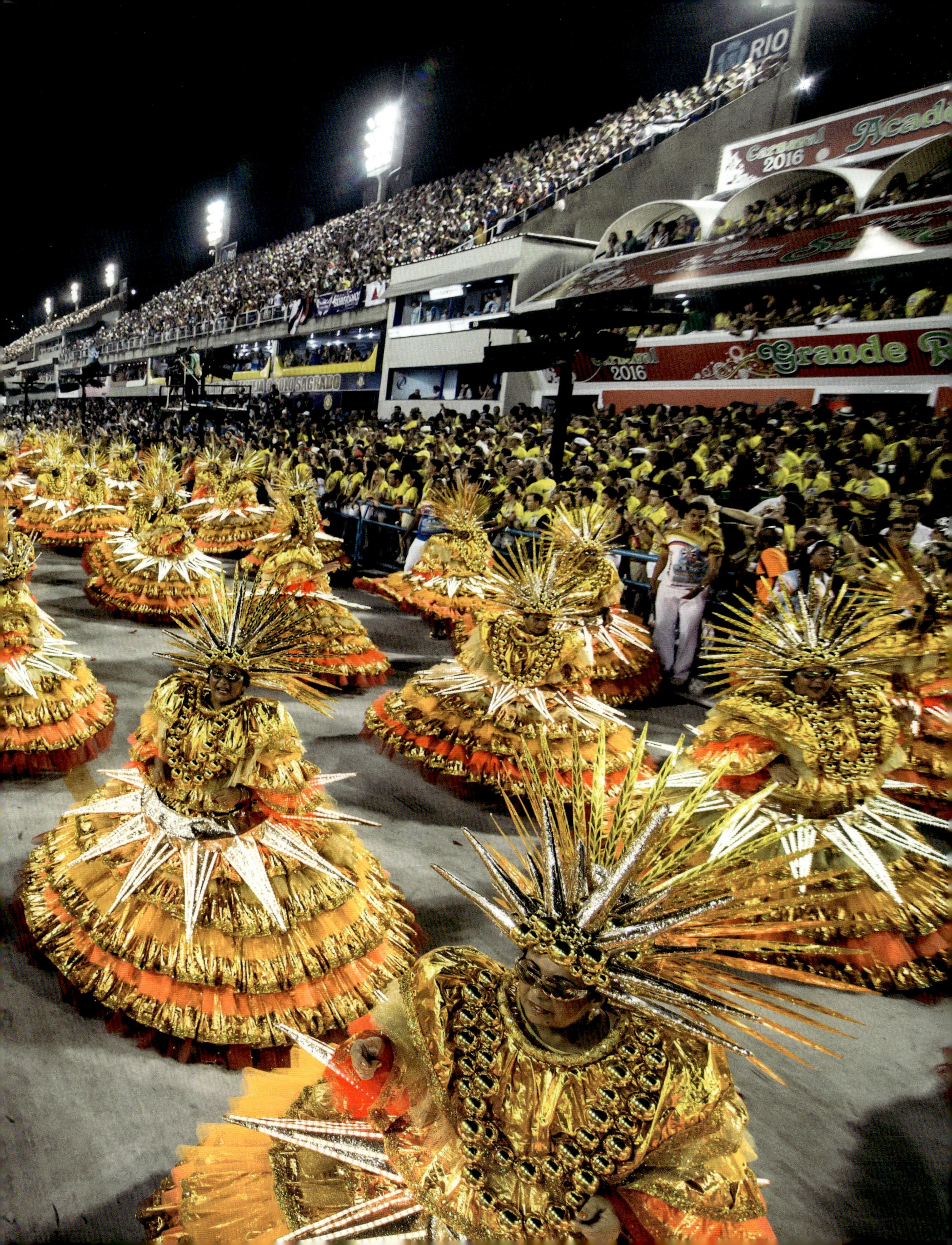

RIO
Carnaval 2016 Academ
Carnaval 2016 Grande R

Performers of the Mocidade Independente de Padre
Miguel samba school offer a spectacular show at
Rio's Sambódromo.

Tänzerinnen der Sambaschule Mocidade Independente
de Padre Miguel bieten eine spektakuläre Show im
Sambódromo von Rio.

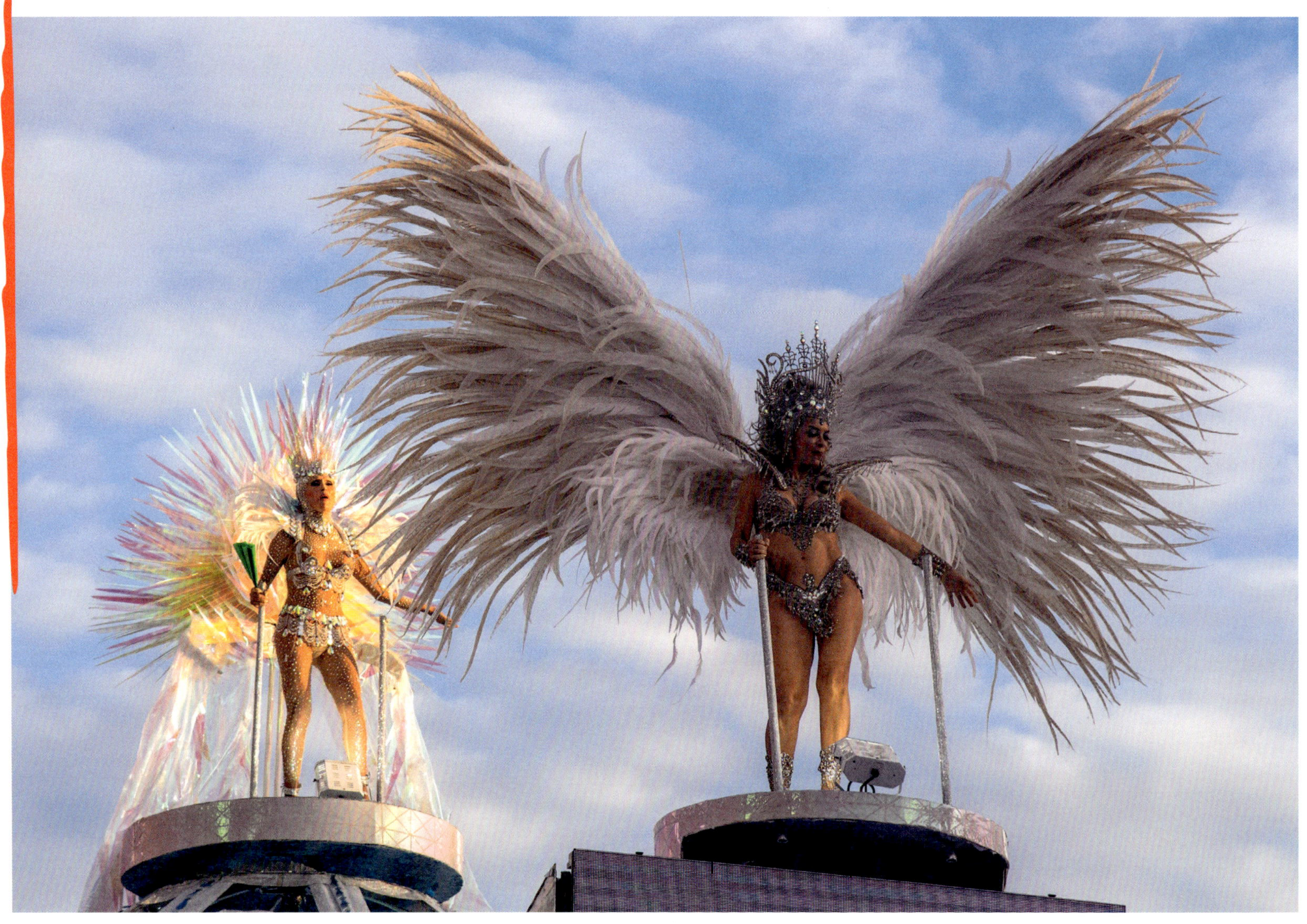

Rio de Janeiro's carnival parade is extraordinary,
with its jaw-dropping costumes and elaborate floats
presented by more than 200 samba schools.

Die brasilianische Karnevalsparade ist mit ihren atemberau-
benden Kostümen und aufwendigen Wagen, die von mehr als
200 Sambaschulen präsentiert werden, außergewöhnlich.

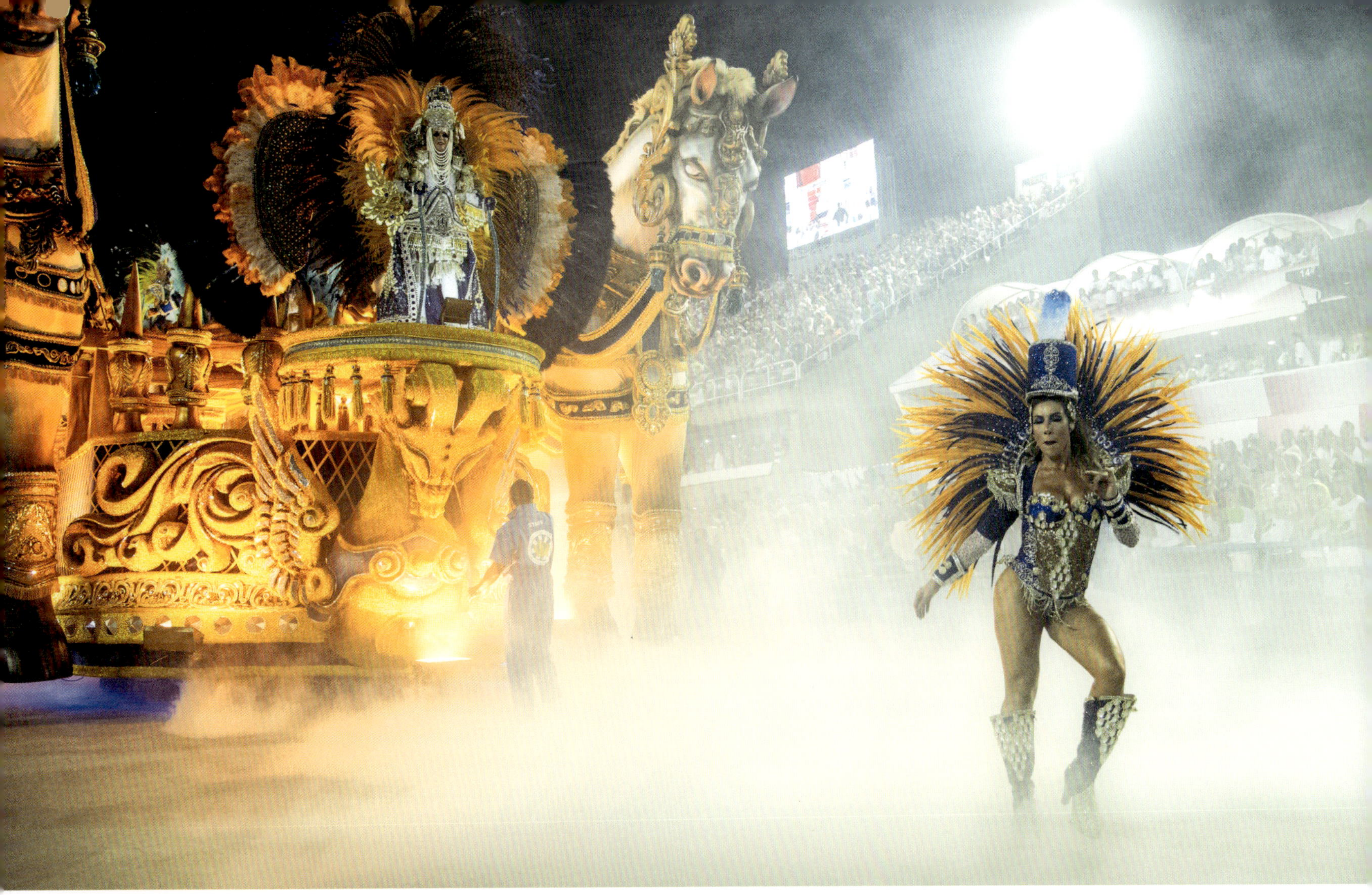

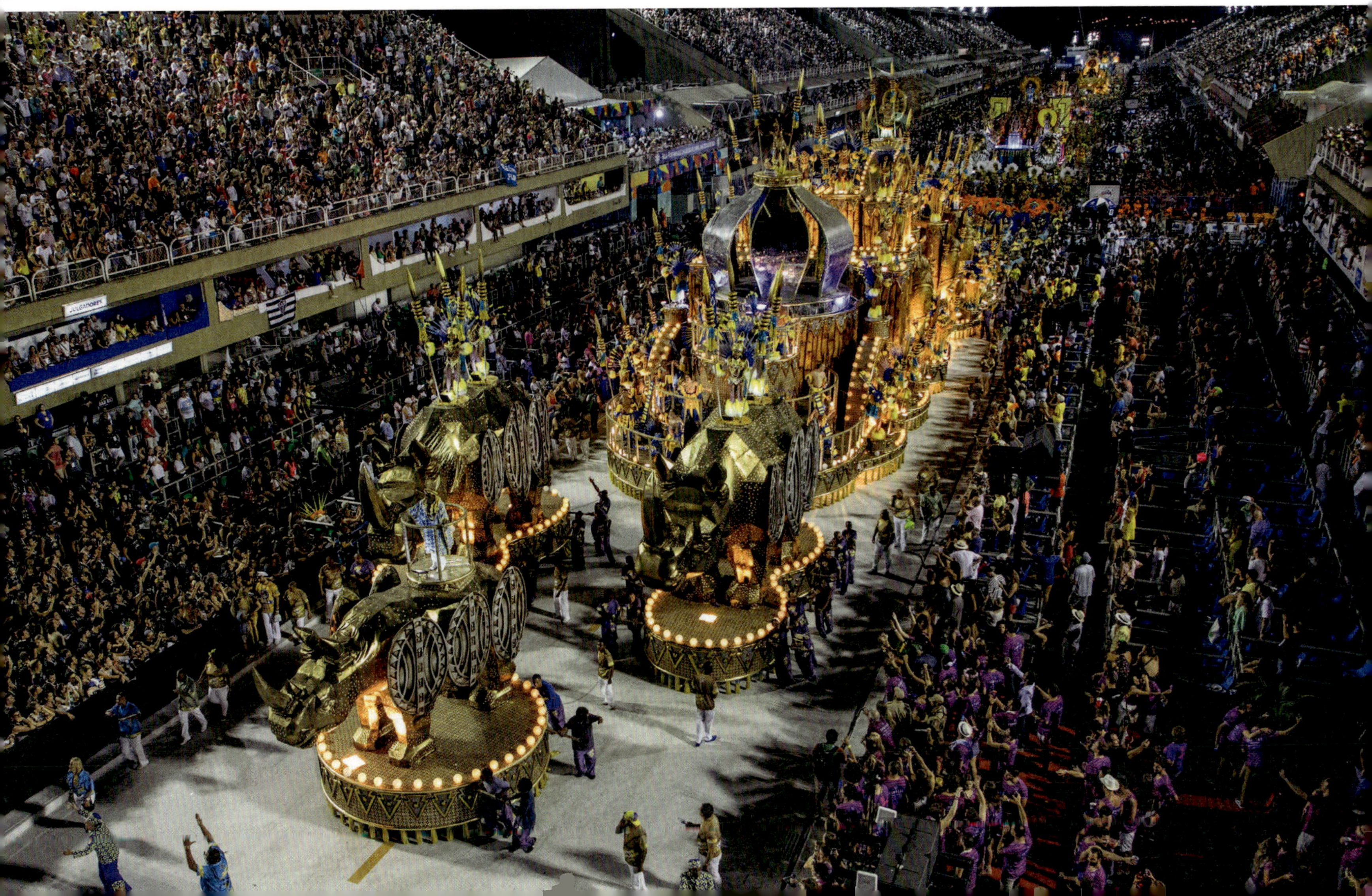

During Basler Fasnacht in Basel, Switzerland, groups of masked men and women join the great procession, playing music. Basler Fasnacht lasts exactly 72 hours and is included in UNESCO's intangible cultural heritage.

Während der Basler Fasnacht schließen sich Cliquen von maskierten Männern und Frauen zusammen, um beim großen Umzug zu musizieren. Die Karnevalsveranstaltung dauert genau 72 Stunden und gehört zum immateriellen Kulturerbe der UNESCO.

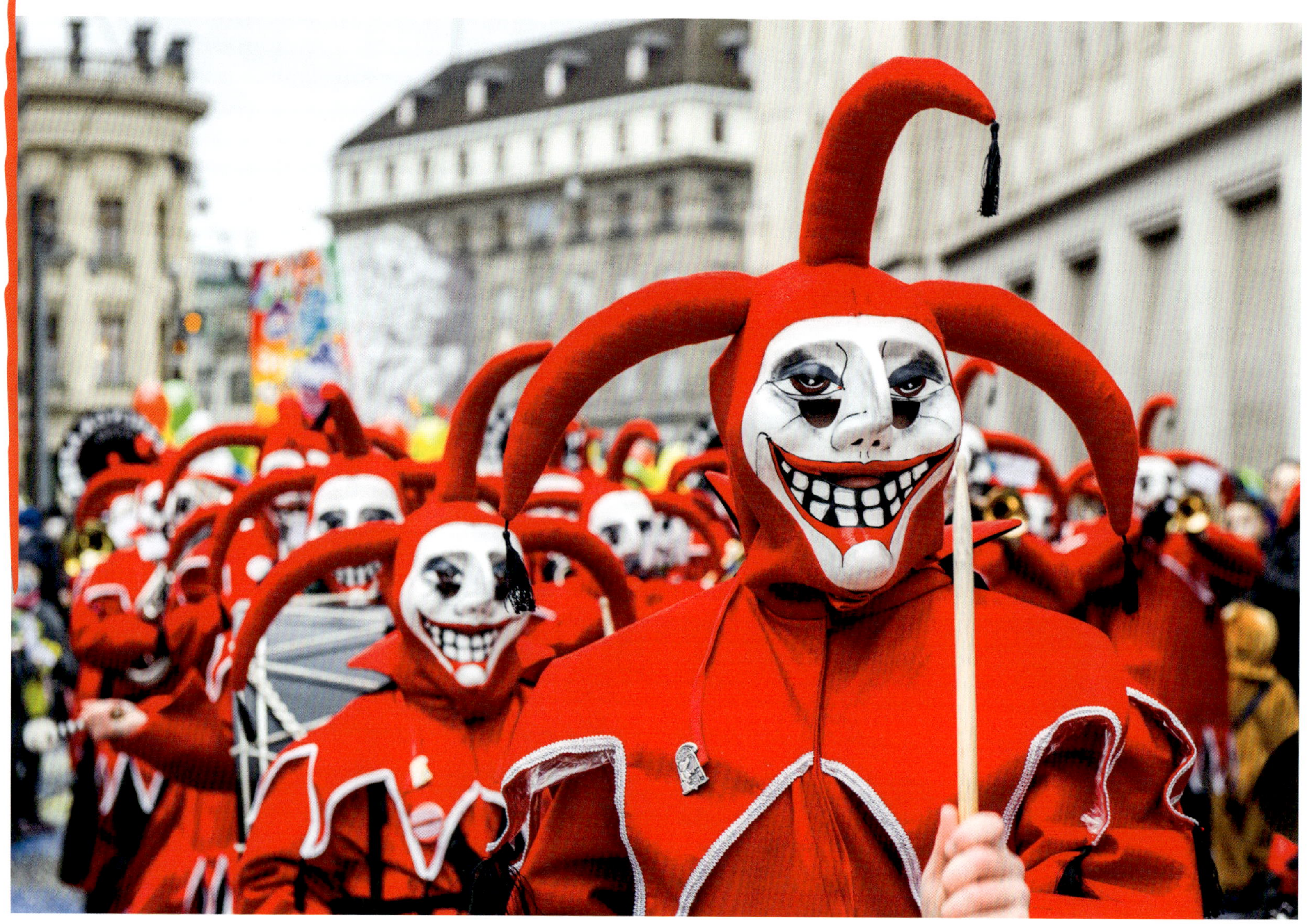

Top: The *Morgestraich* marks the beginning of Basler Fasnacht. At 4 a.m. hundreds of colorful lanterns are lit and carried through the streets. Bottom: The night before *Morgestraich*, carriers loaded with bundles of burning wood are pulled through town at the *Chienbäse*.

Oben: Der *Morgestraich* markiert den Beginn der Basler Fasnacht. Um 4 Uhr morgens werden Hunderte von bunten Laternen erleuchtet und durch die Straßen getragen. Unten: In der Nacht vor dem *Morgestraich* werden beim *Chienbäse*-Umzug mit Brennholz beladene Wagen durch die Stadt gezogen und große Fackeln entzündet.

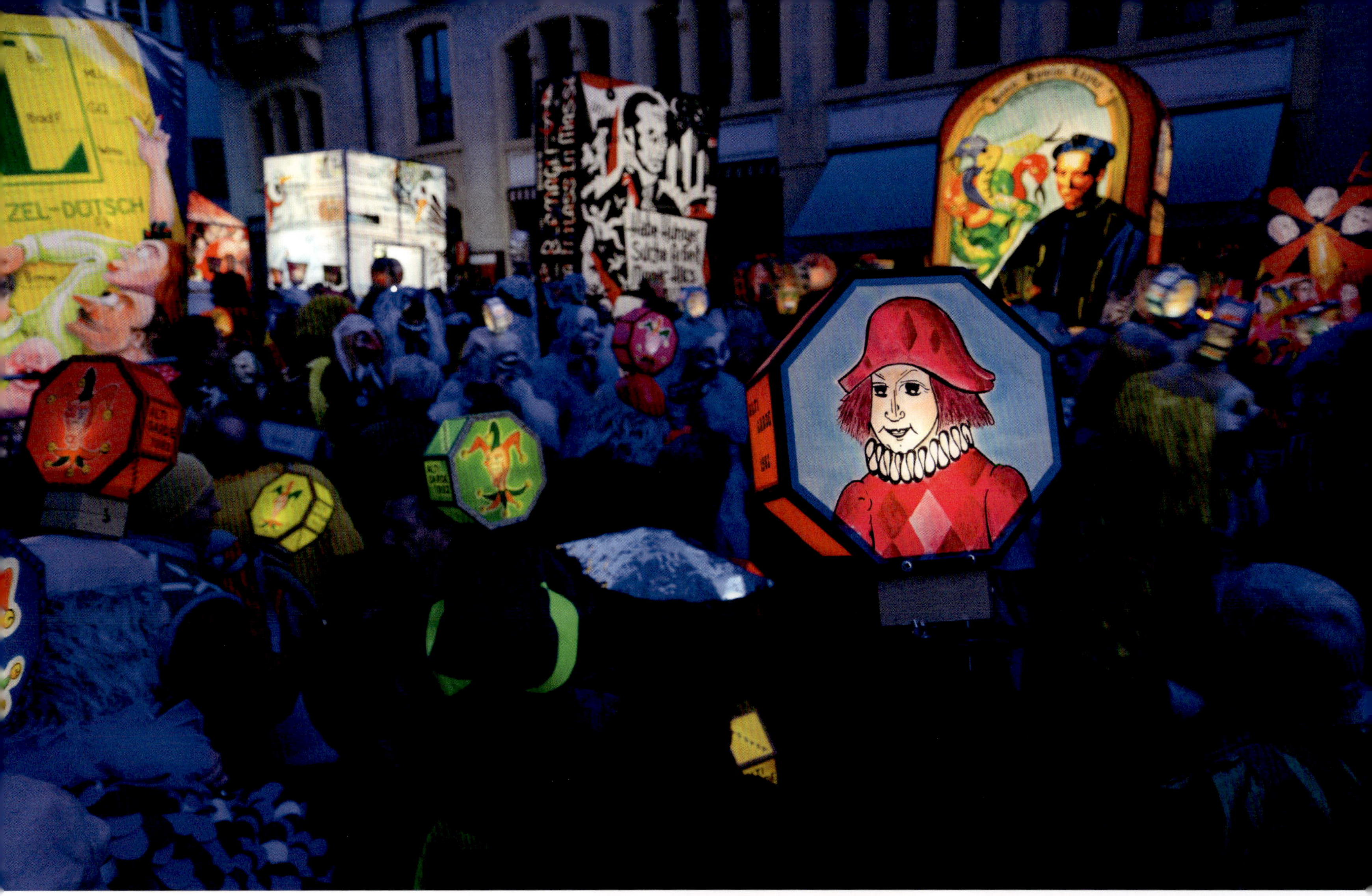

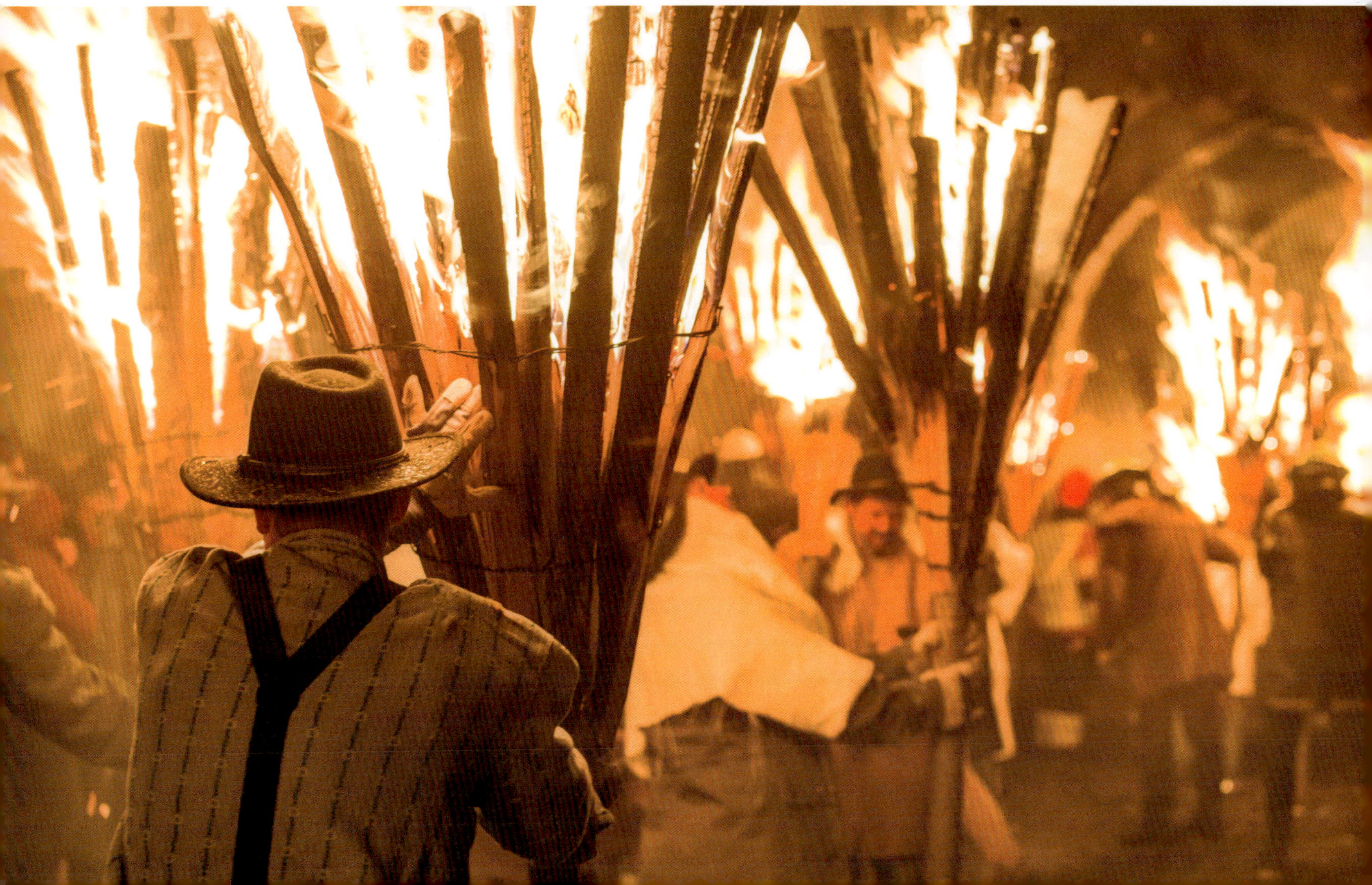

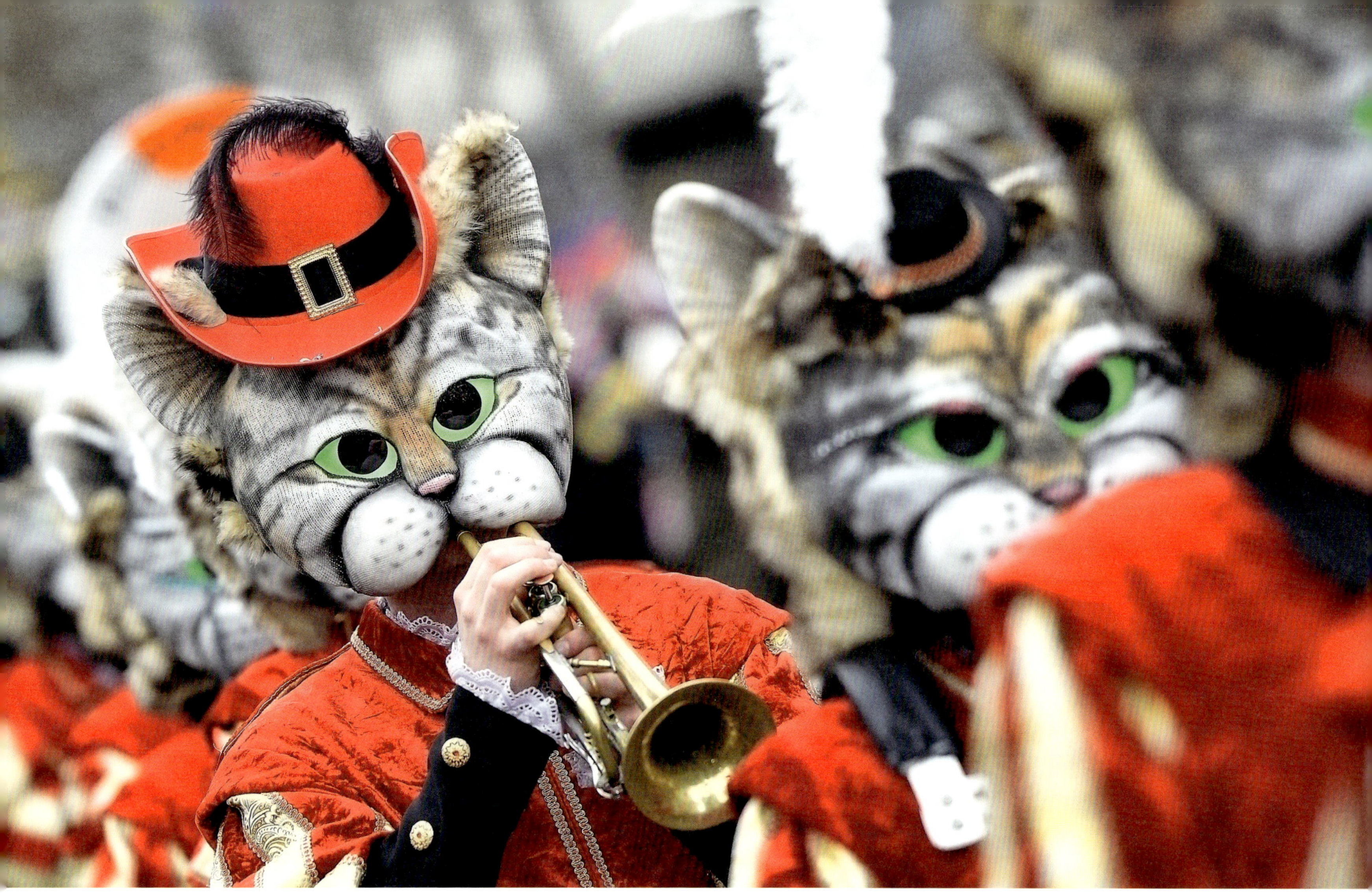

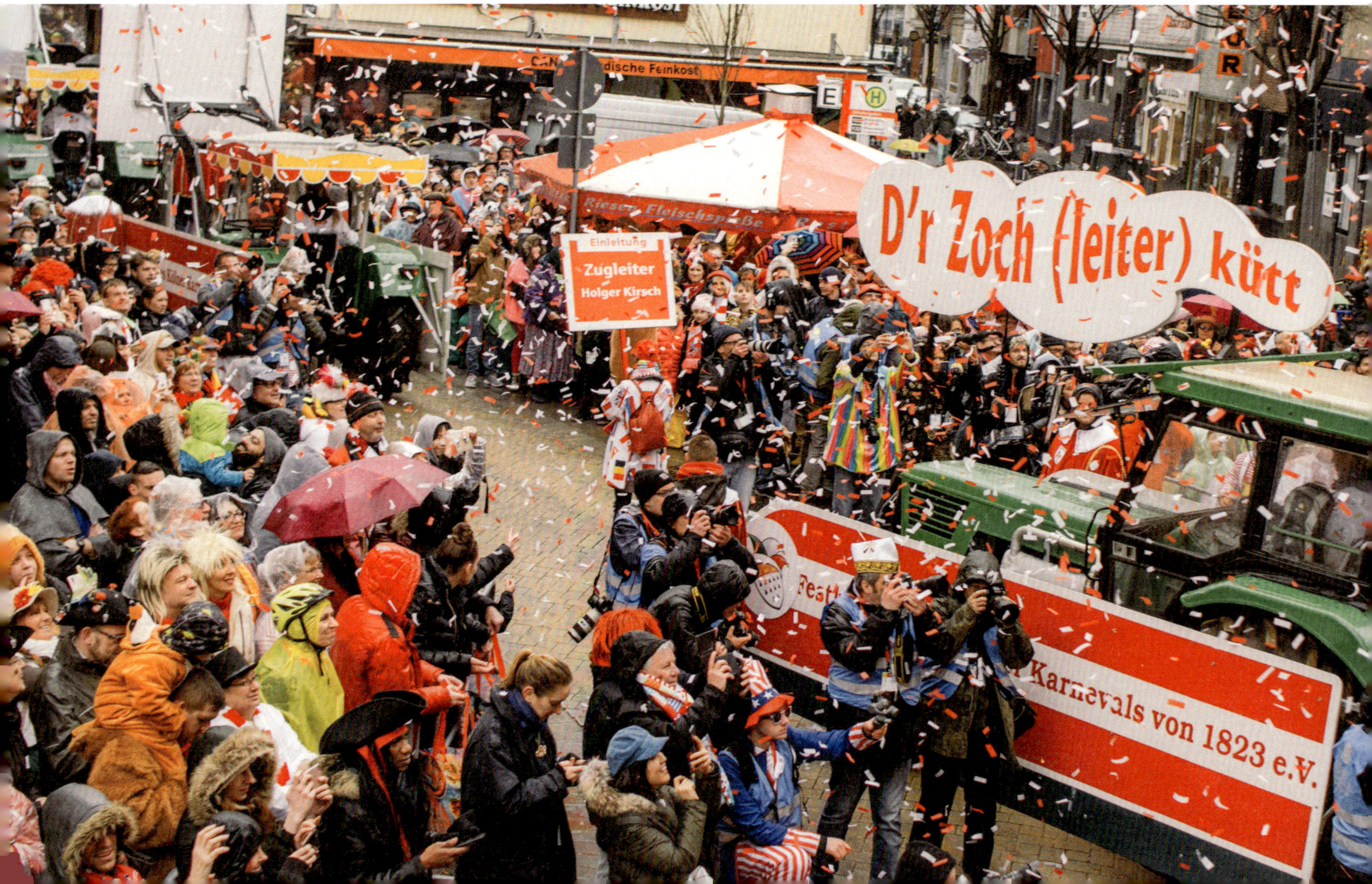

CAN... ...dische Feinkost

Einleitung
Zugleiter
Holger Kirsch

D'r Zoch (leiter) kütt

Fest...

Karnevals von 1823 e.V.

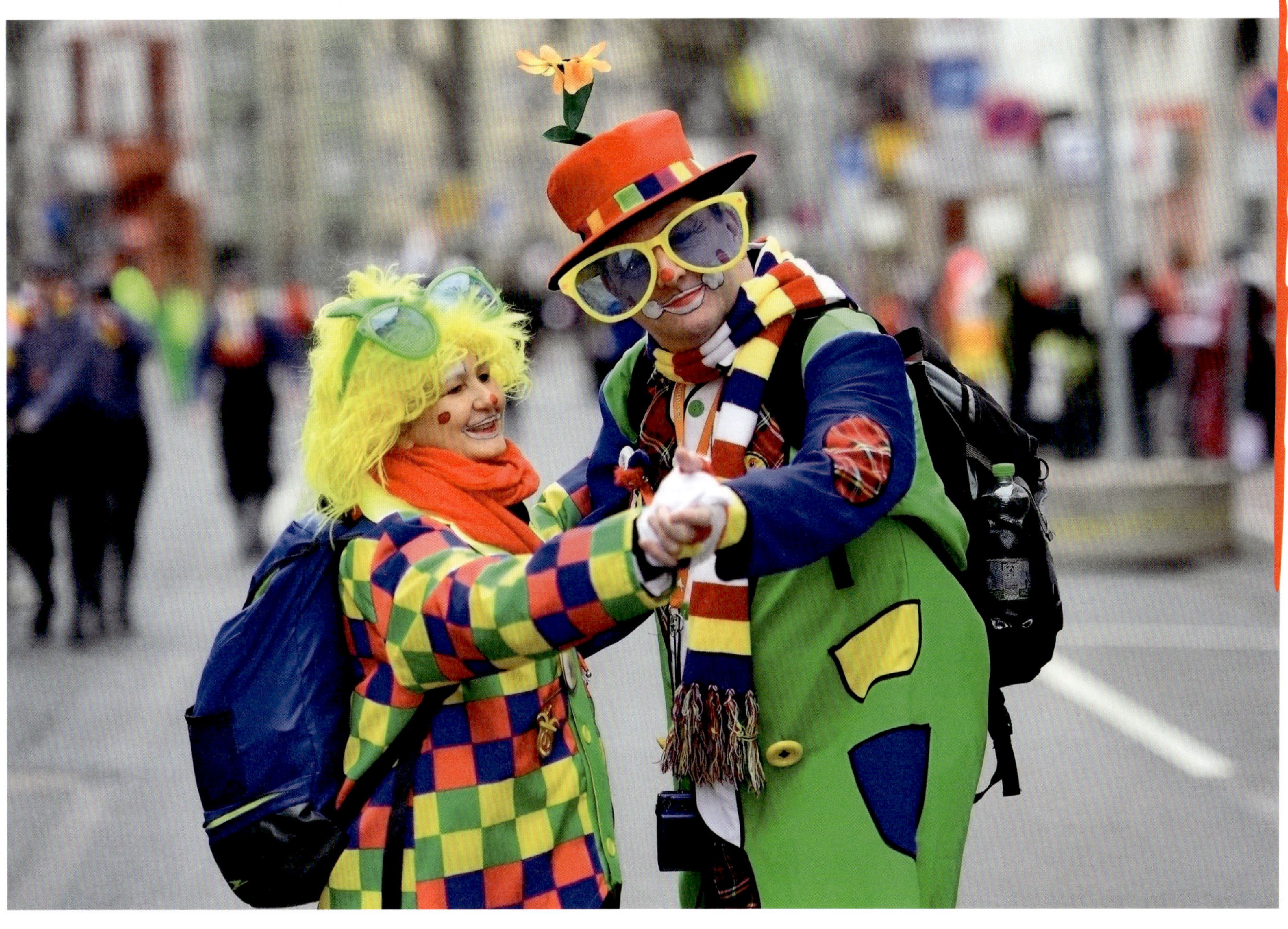

Political satire is a traditional cornerstone of the annual German
carnival parades: complex floats, music, and *Kamelle* (sweets thrown
from the floats) delight the spectators.

Politische Satire ist ein traditioneller Eckpfeiler der jährlichen
deutschen Karnevalsumzüge: Aufwendig gestaltete Wagen, Musik und
Kamelle erfreuen die Zuschauer.

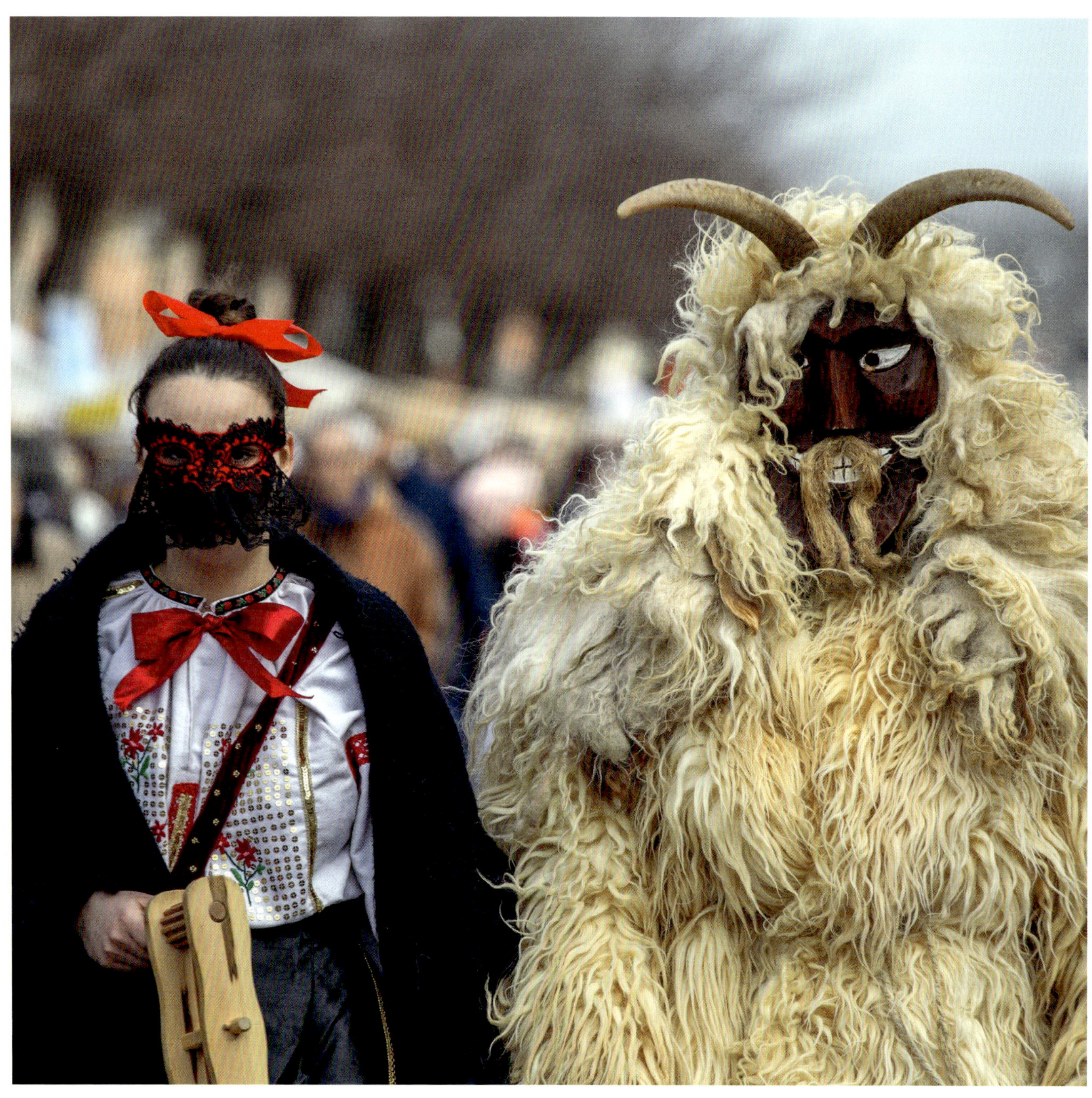

Busójárás is an annual six-day celebration held in Mohács, Hungary, by the Šokci ethnic group. The festivities feature the so-called Busós (traditional wooden masks), folk music, parades, and masquerading.

Das jährlich stattfindende ungarische Karnevalsfest Busójárás wird über sechs Tage von den Šokci in Mohács veranstaltet. Im Mittelpunkt der Feierlichkeiten stehen die sogenannten Busós (traditionelle Holzmasken), Volksmusik, Umzüge und Maskerade.

Busójárás is Hungary's oldest and best-known carnival tradition. The scary Busós date back to the Turkish occupation of Hungary, when the Mohács villagers tried to chase away the opposing army by wearing them.

Busójárás ist Ungarns älteste und bekannteste Karnevalstradition. Die furchteinflößenden Busós gehen bis auf die türkische Besetzung Ungarns zurück. Damals versuchten die Bewohner Mohács die gegnerische Armee mithilfe der Masken fernzuhalten.

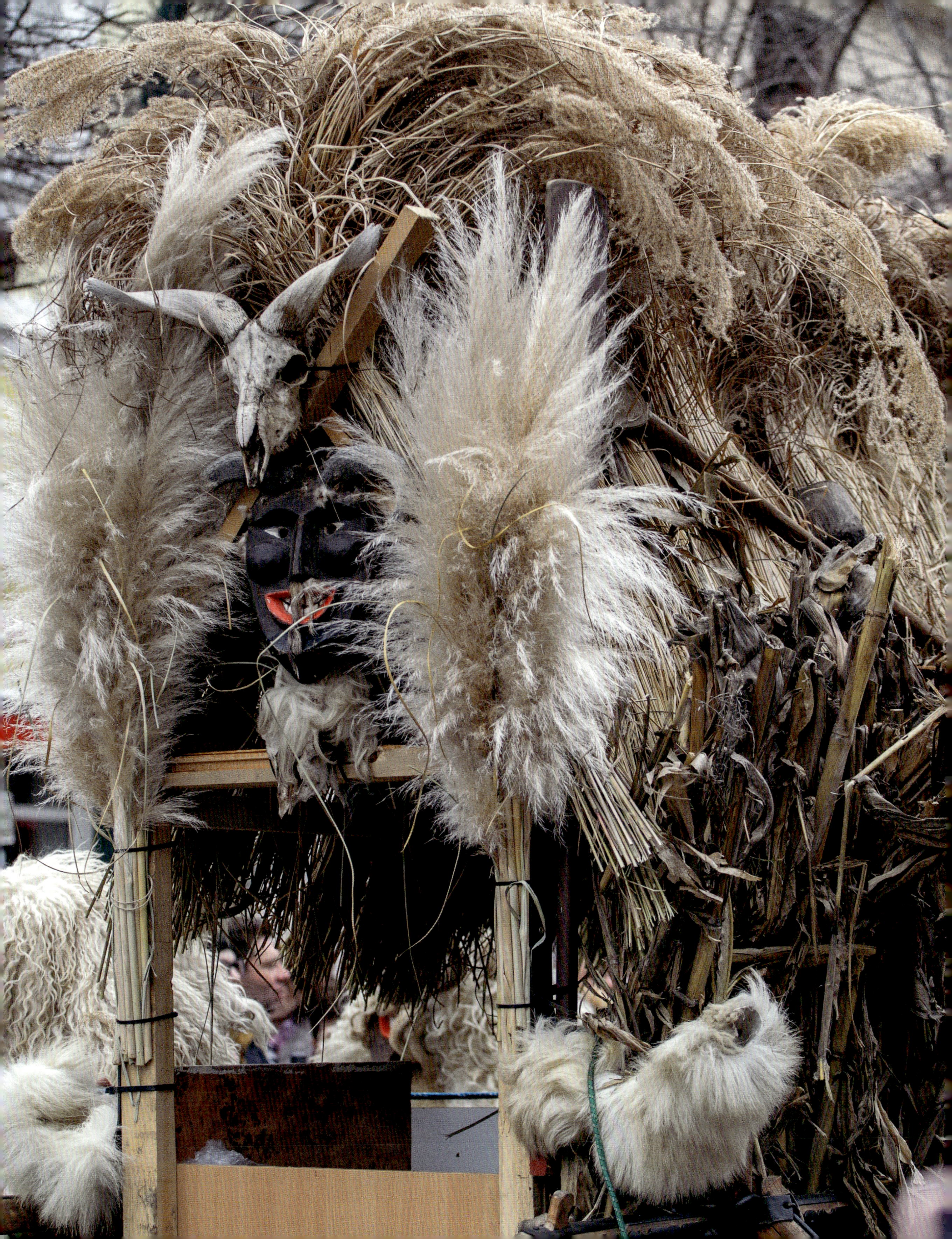

The traditional regatta marks the opening of the annual Venice Carnival. The theme or motto changes every year.

Mit der traditionellen Regatta wird der Karneval von Venedig eröffnet. Das Thema oder Motto ändert sich jedes Jahr.

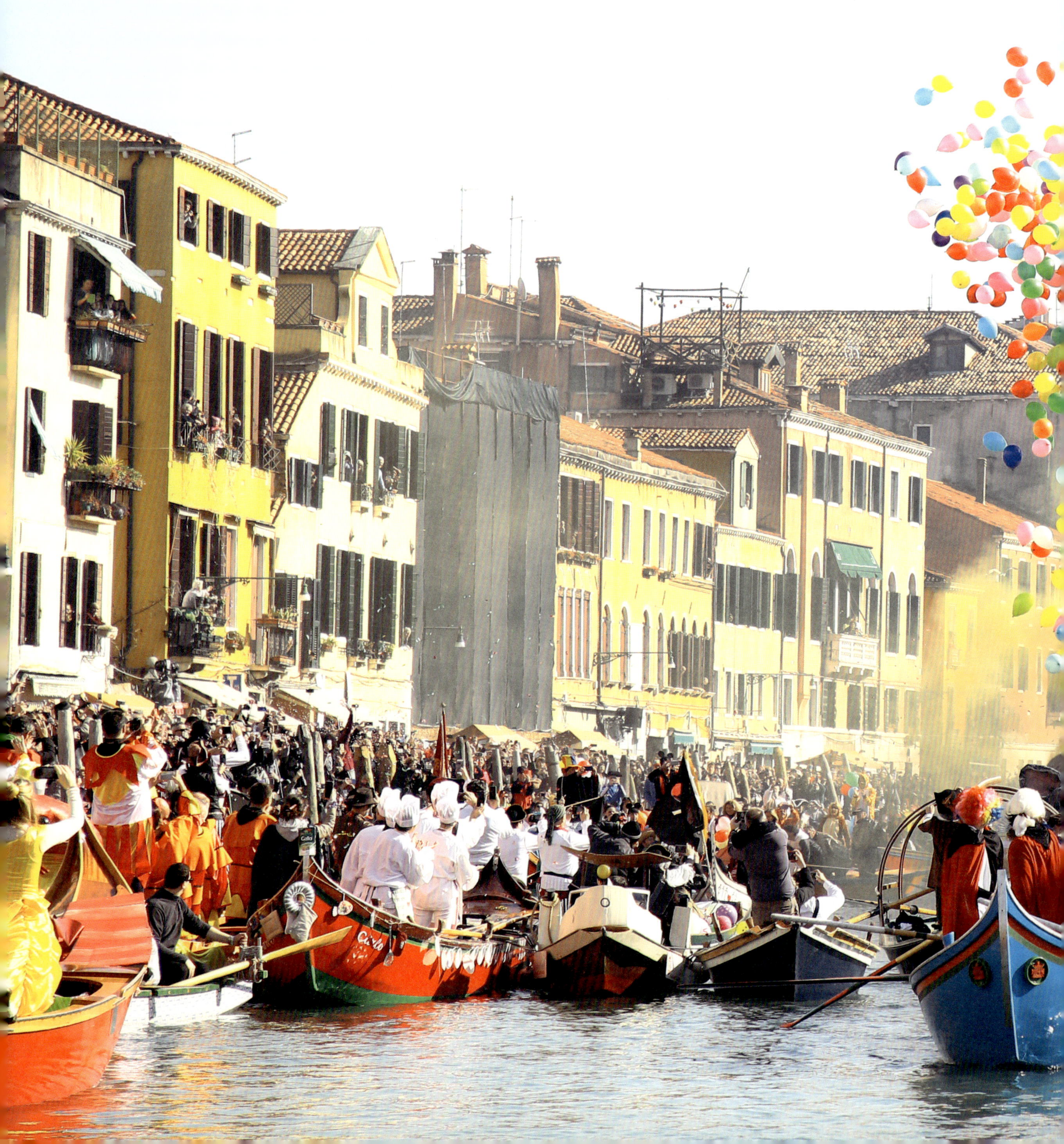

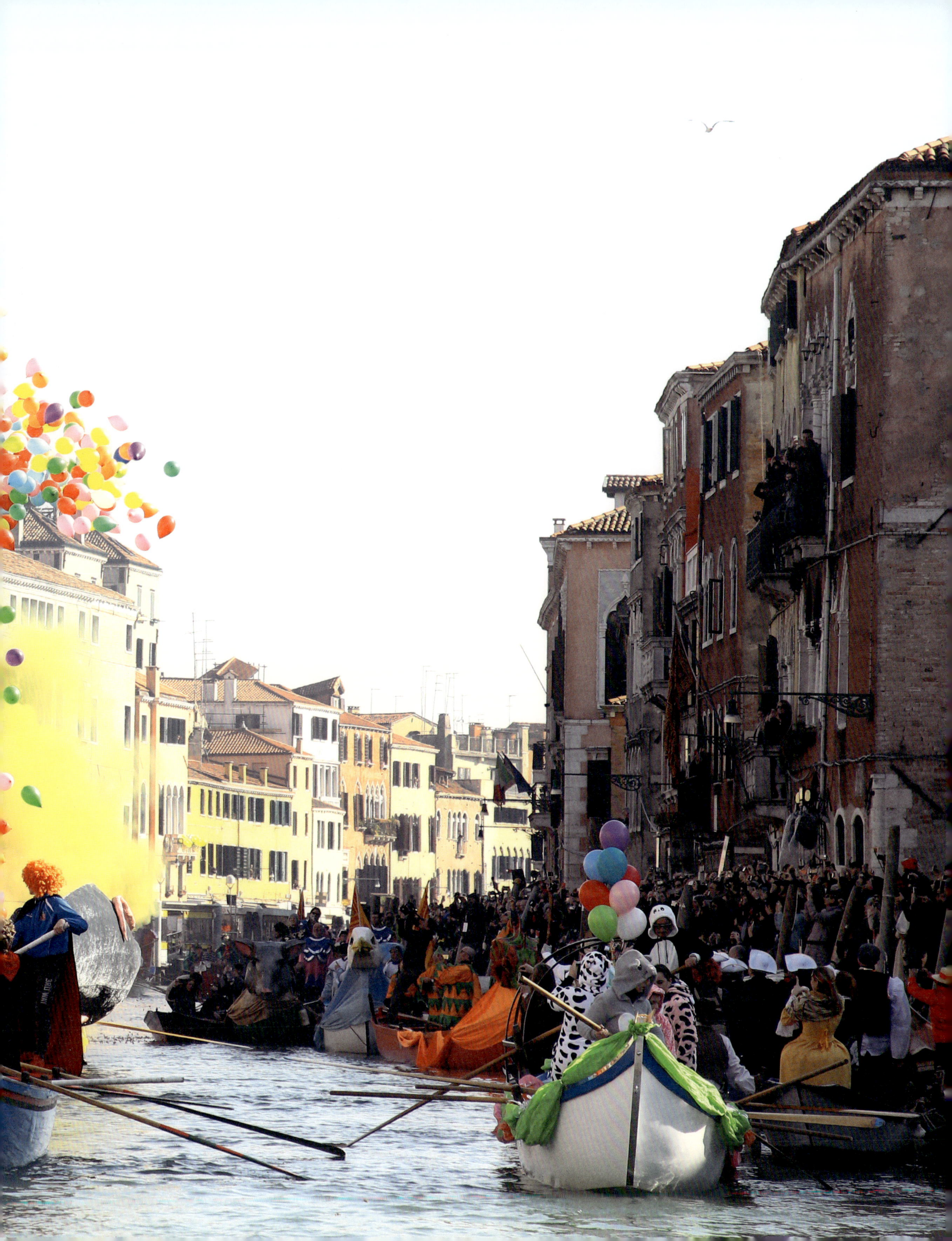

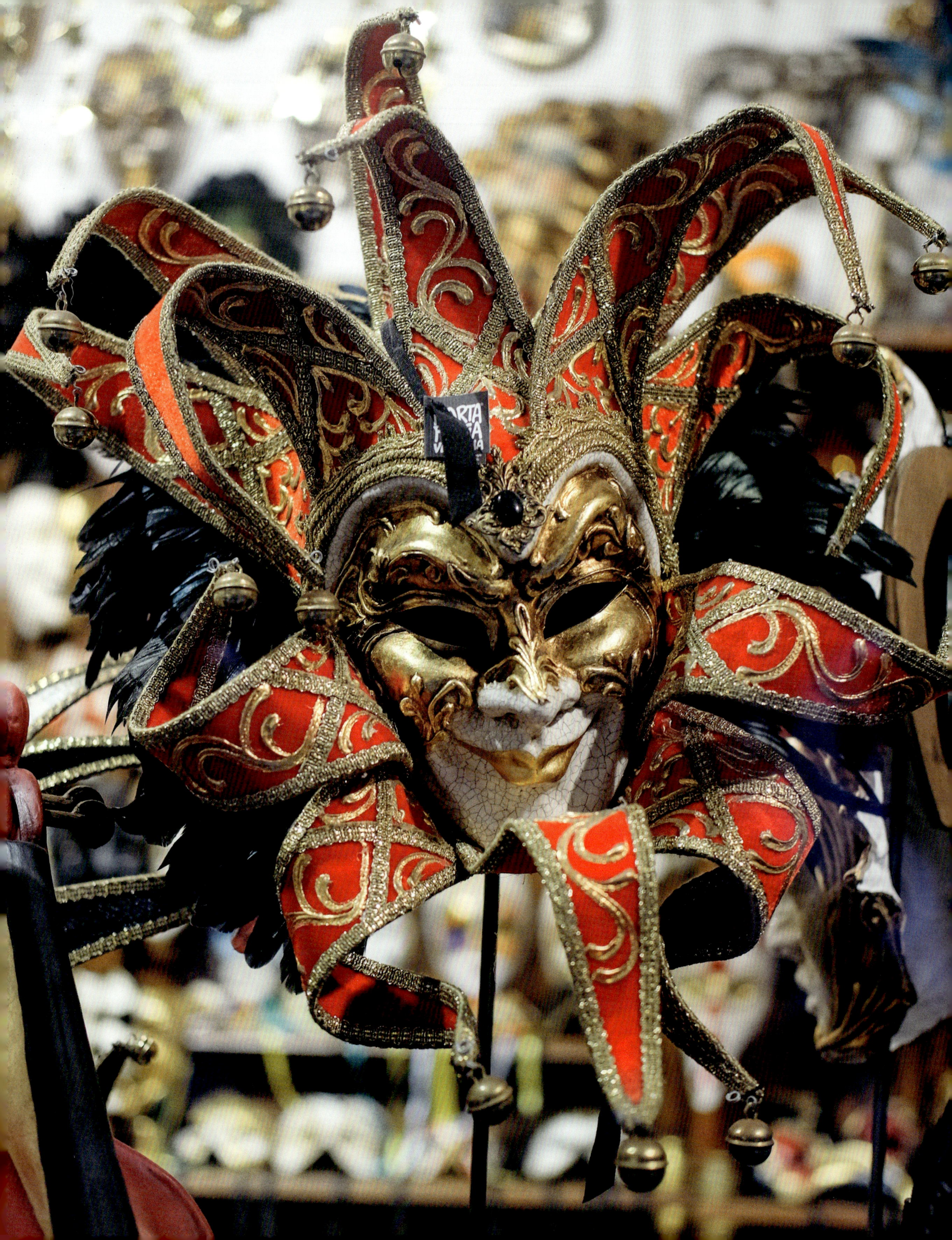

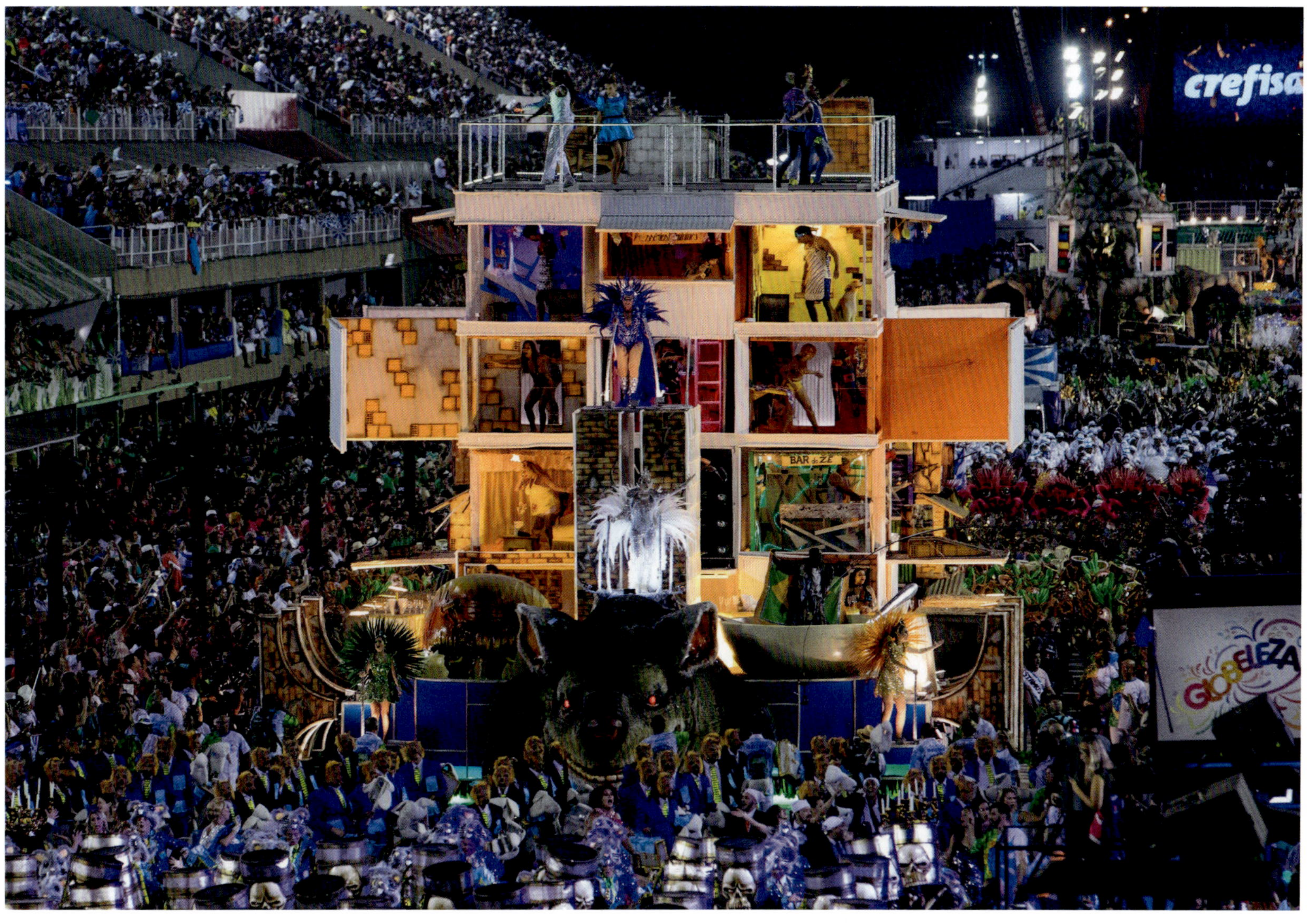

Rio Carnival is the largest in the world. It even has its own entry in the *Guinness Book of World Records*, with 400,000 foreign visitors in 2004.

Der Karneval von Rio ist der größte der Welt. In Bezug auf ausländische Besucher hat er sogar einen Eintrag im *Guinnessbuch der Rekorde*, im Jahr 2004 waren es 400 000.

Good to know
WISSENSWERTES

There are several types of Venetian masks, including the *bauta*, the mask of the city council (gilded or stark white, covering the entire face with a protruding chin); *colombina* (half-mask, covering the eyes and nose); and *volto* (made from porcelain or thick plastic, covering the whole face), is the most common mask (see page 9). The model opposite is called *jolly*.

Es gibt verschiedene Arten venezianischer Masken, darunter die *Bauta*, die Maske des Stadtrats (vergoldet oder ganz weiß, das ganze Gesicht bedeckend, mit vorstehendem Kinn), die *Colombina* (Halbmaske, die Augen und Nase bedeckt) und die *Volto* (aus Porzellan oder dickem Kunststoff, das ganze Gesicht bedeckend), ist die am häufigsten getragene Maske (siehe Seite 9). Das Modell links wird übrigens *Jolly* genannt.

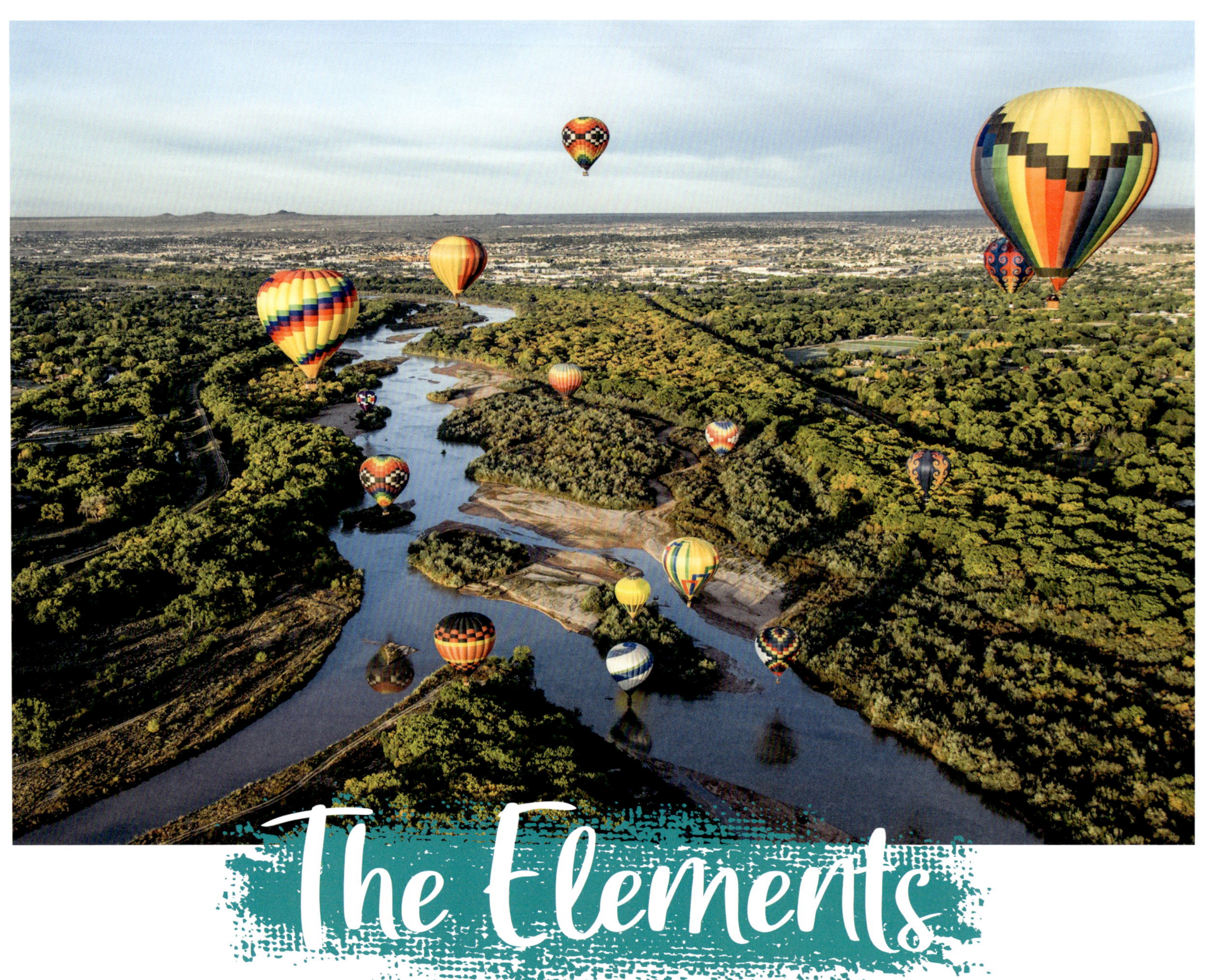

The Elements

FEIERN MIT DEN ELEMENTEN

This page: Hot air balloons over the Rio Grande in New Mexico, USA.
Opposite page, top: People celebrate on ghats and
in the Ganges River in Varanasi, India.
Bottom right: Boryeong Mud Festival, South Korea.

Diese Seite: Heißluftballons über dem Rio Grande in New Mexico, USA.
Rechte Seite, oben: Menschen feiern am und im Ganges in Varanasi, Indien.
Unten rechts: Boryeong-Schlammfestival, Südkorea.

Opposite page, bottom left: Los Escobazos Festival in Jarandilla de la Vera, Spain, is an
ancient annual celebration on December 7. At night, villagers burn brooms and
hit each other with them to celebrate the Immaculate Conception.

Rechte Seite, unten links: Los Escobazos findet jährlich am 7. Dezember in Jarandilla de
la Vera, Spanien, statt. Dabei verbrennen die Dorfbewohner nachts Besen und schlagen
sich gegenseitig mit den „Besenfackeln", um die Unbefleckte Empfängnis zu feiern.

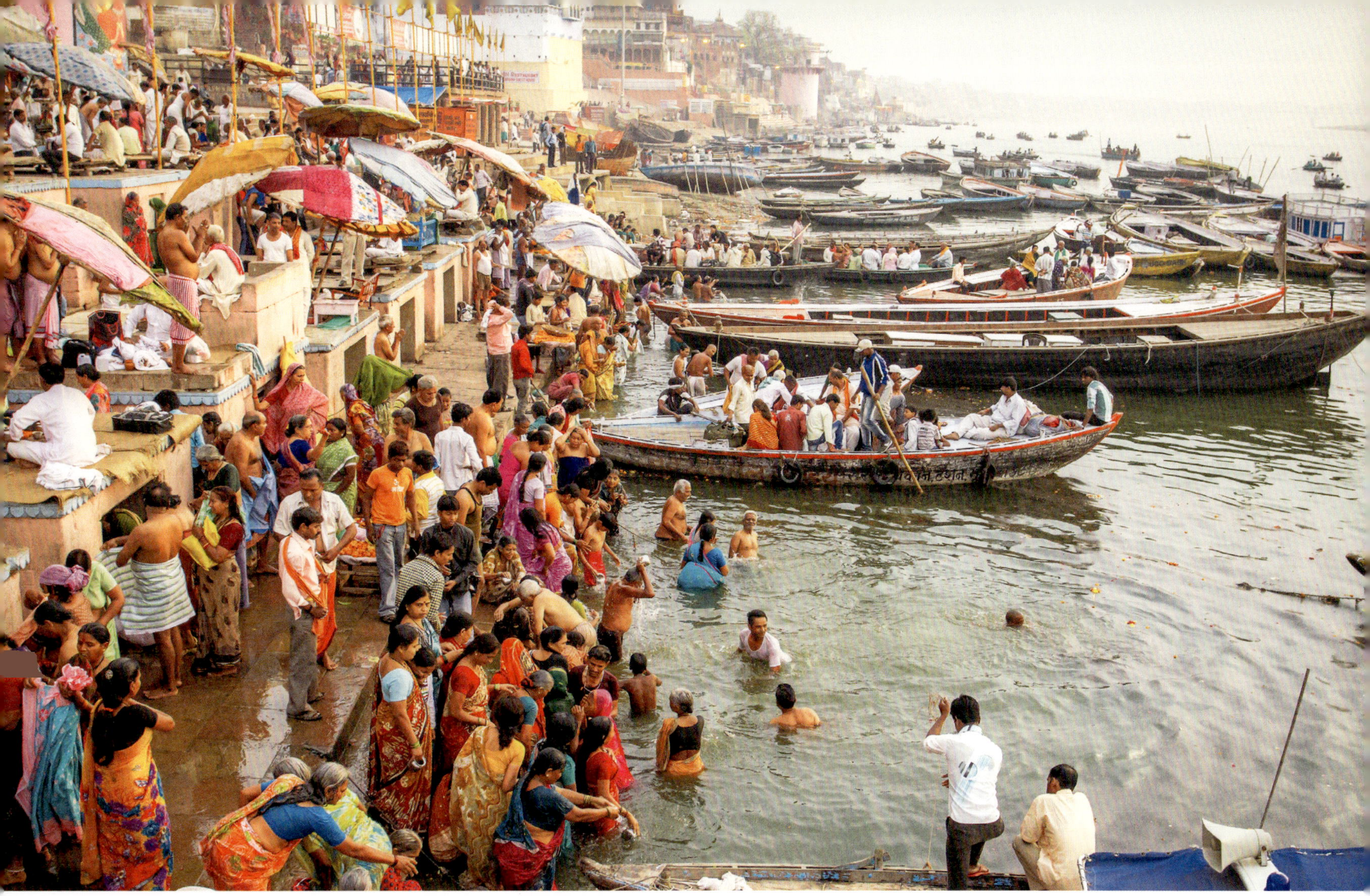

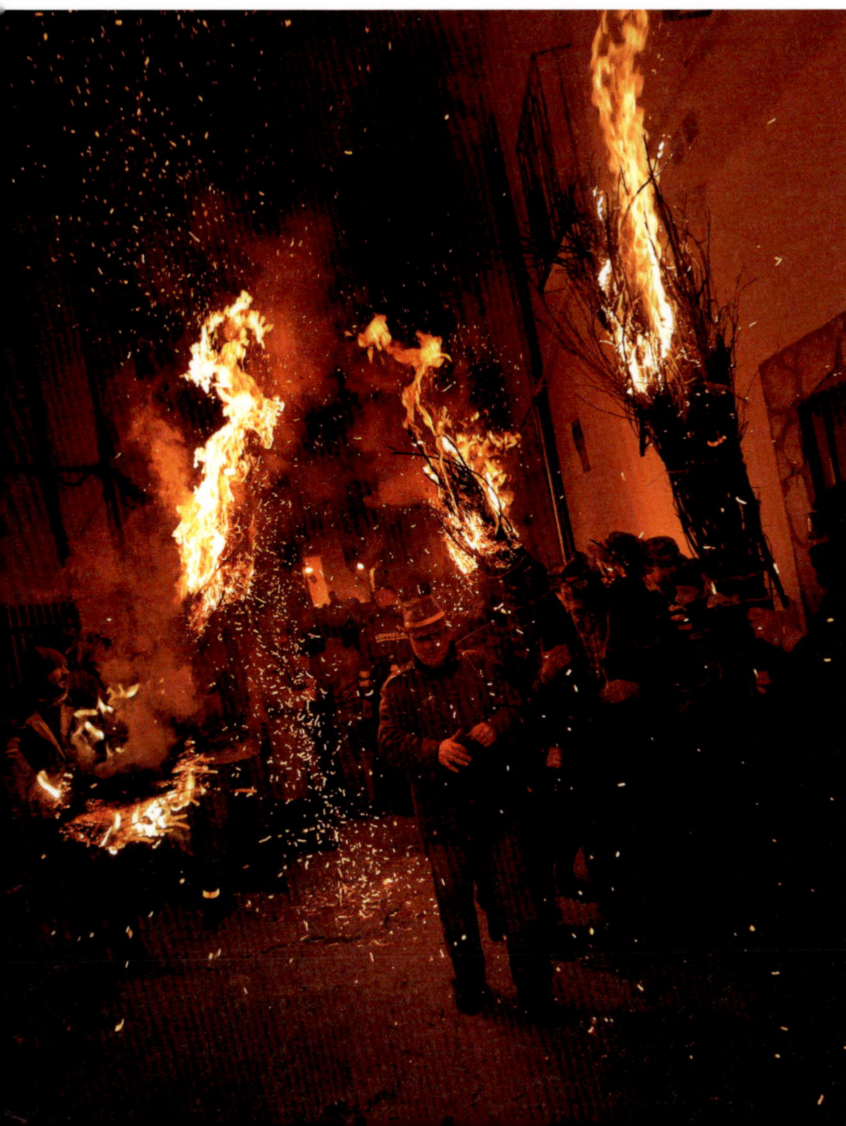
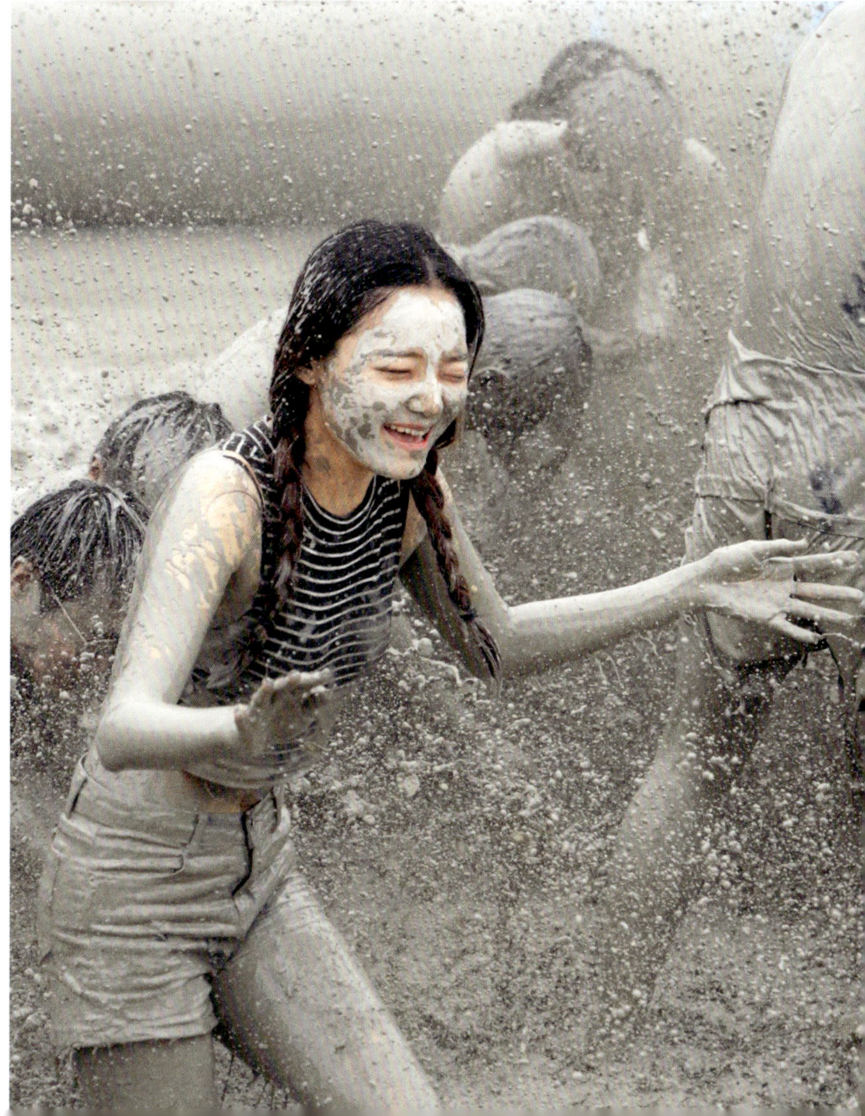

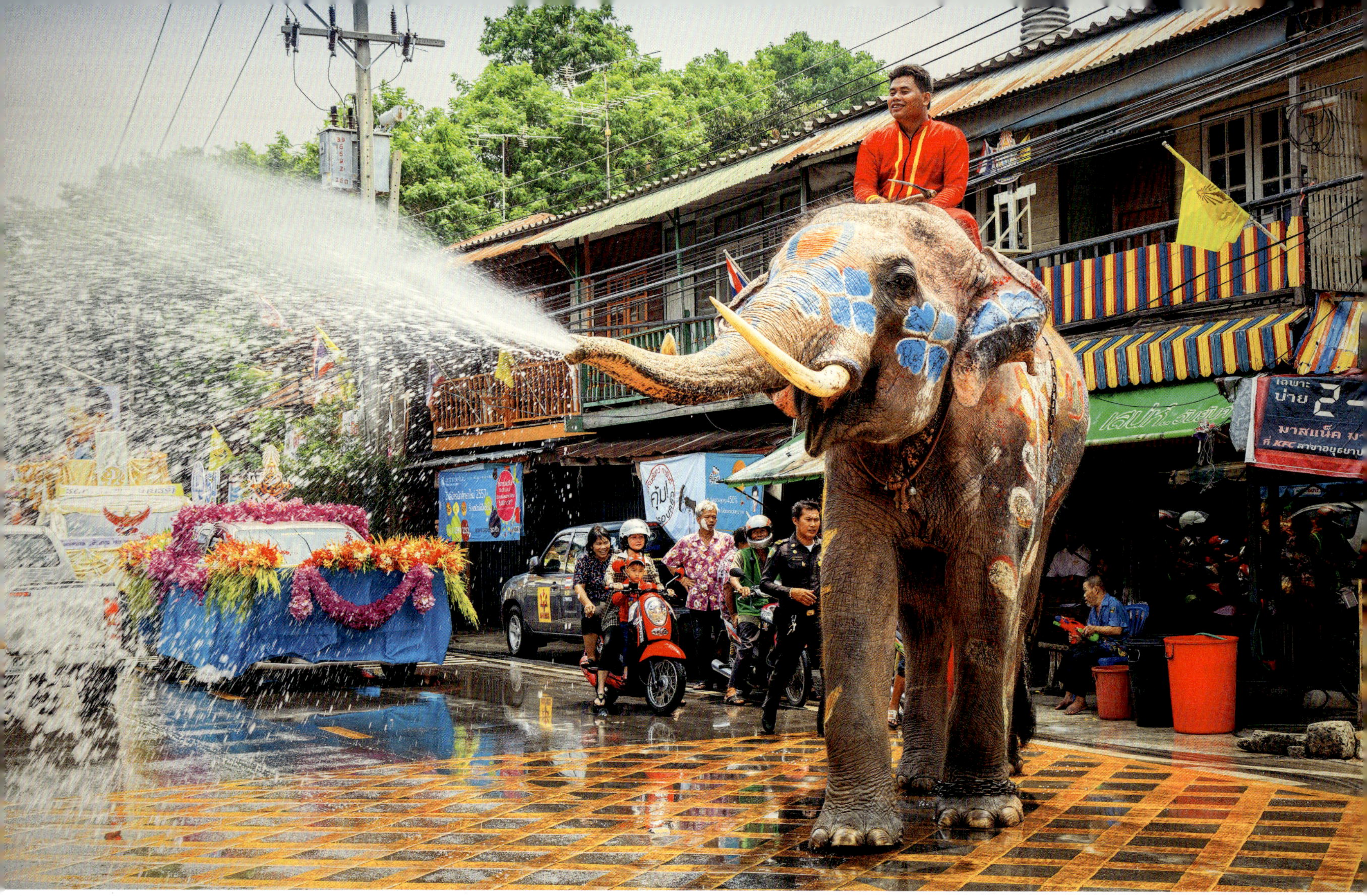

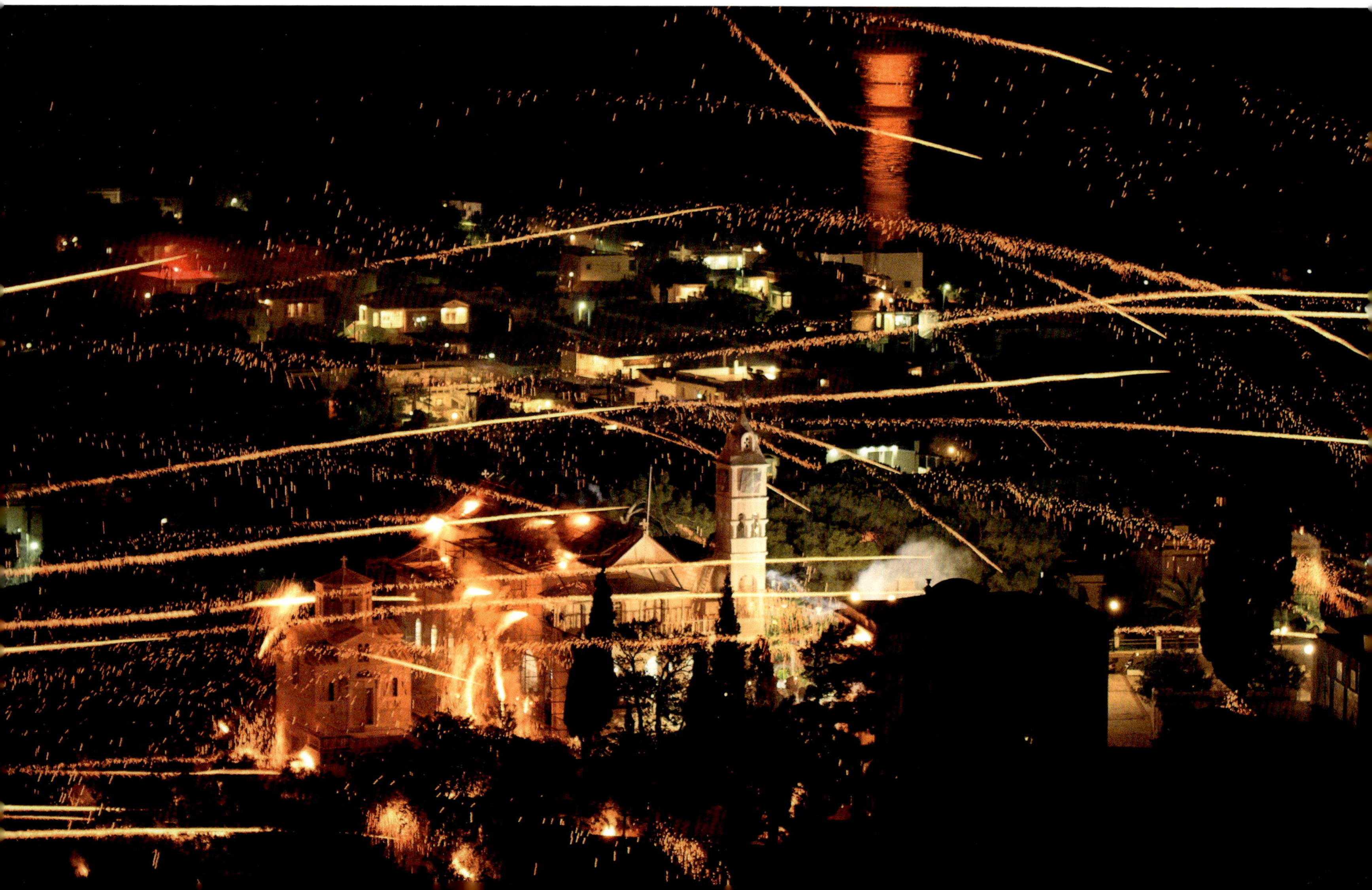

Festivals were born from a need to celebrate what's dearest to us and what makes us happy. The four elements are one of the earliest examples of this: water to drink; fire to cook and to warm us; the air we breathe; and the earth to help build shelter and walk on.

Many festivals around the world hark back to these simpler days of celebrating our essential needs. Is there anything more mesmerizing than standing around a fire, watching the flames flicker and engulf what they're fed? Now imagine that on an epic level, like in Valencia, Spain, at Las Fallas Festival. Artists spend a year building 20-foot (6-meter) statues, knowing that their artwork's inevitable and intended end is to be set alight in front of thousands of festivalgoers in the name of celebration.

At hot air balloon festivals, we stand around watching balloons fill with hydrogen or helium so they can glide between the clouds. And when the amount of hot air balloons is multiplied by tens, or even hundreds, as at the Albuquerque International Balloon Fiesta in the United States, the hypnotizing result is a colorful menagerie in the sky above our heads.

Water festivals are always fun. Songkran is one of the most famous, with thousands of Thai people and international visitors spending the weekend chasing each other with water guns and buckets of water. The spring festival marks the start of the Thai New Year, and it was originally based on the Lunar New Year. It is definitely a great chance to cool off in the hot Thai climate (opposite, top).

The Boryeong Mud Festival in Korea sees festivalgoers wrestling on the ground to cover each other in mud. There's no deep meaning to this festival, which started in 1998 as a way to promote cosmetics made from the mud in Boryeong!

Feste entstanden aus dem Bedürfnis heraus, das zu feiern, was zum Leben essenziell ist. Deshalb wurden auf den frühesten Festen der Menschheitsgeschichte die vier Elemente zelebriert. Wasser brauchen wir zum Trinken, Feuer zum Kochen und um uns zu wärmen, Luft zum Atmen und die Erde, um darauf zu gehen und Schutz zu finden.

Viele Feste auf der ganzen Welt berufen sich auf dieses ursprüngliche Zelebrieren ureigener Bedürfnisse. Was gibt es Faszinierenderes, als um ein Feuer herum zu stehen und zuzusehen, wie die Flammen das verschlingen, was man ihnen überlässt? Und nun stellen Sie sich das Ganze in epischem Ausmaß vor, wie beim Las-Fallas-Fest im spanischen Valencia. Künstler verbringen das ganze Jahr damit, sechs Meter hohe Statuen zu bauen, wohl wissend, dass ihre Werke dazu bestimmt sind, vor Tausenden von Besuchern in Flammen aufzugehen.

Auf Heißluftballon-Festivals sehen wir gebannt zu, wie Ballons mit Wasserstoff oder Helium gefüllt werden, um zwischen den Wolken zu schweben. Und wenn die Anzahl der Heißluftballons in die Hunderte geht, wie bei der Albuquerque International Balloon Fiesta in den USA, dann hat die bunte Himmels-Menagerie eine geradezu hypnotisierende Wirkung.

Wasserfeste machen oft besonders viel Spaß. Eines der berühmtesten ist das thailändische Neujahrsfest Songkran, bei dem Tausende von Besucher aus aller Welt sich ein Wochenende lang mit Wassereimern und -pistolen nassspritzen. Das im Frühling stattfindende Fest basierte ursprünglich auf dem Mondkalender und bietet im heißen Klima Thailands immer eine willkommene Abkühlung (linke Seite, oben).

Auf dem koreanischen Schlammfest Boryeong wälzen sich die Besucher im Matsch. Das Festival, das erst 1998 entstand, hat keine tiefere traditionelle Bedeutung, sondern dient lediglich dazu, Kosmetik aus dem Schlamm von Boryeong zu bewerben.

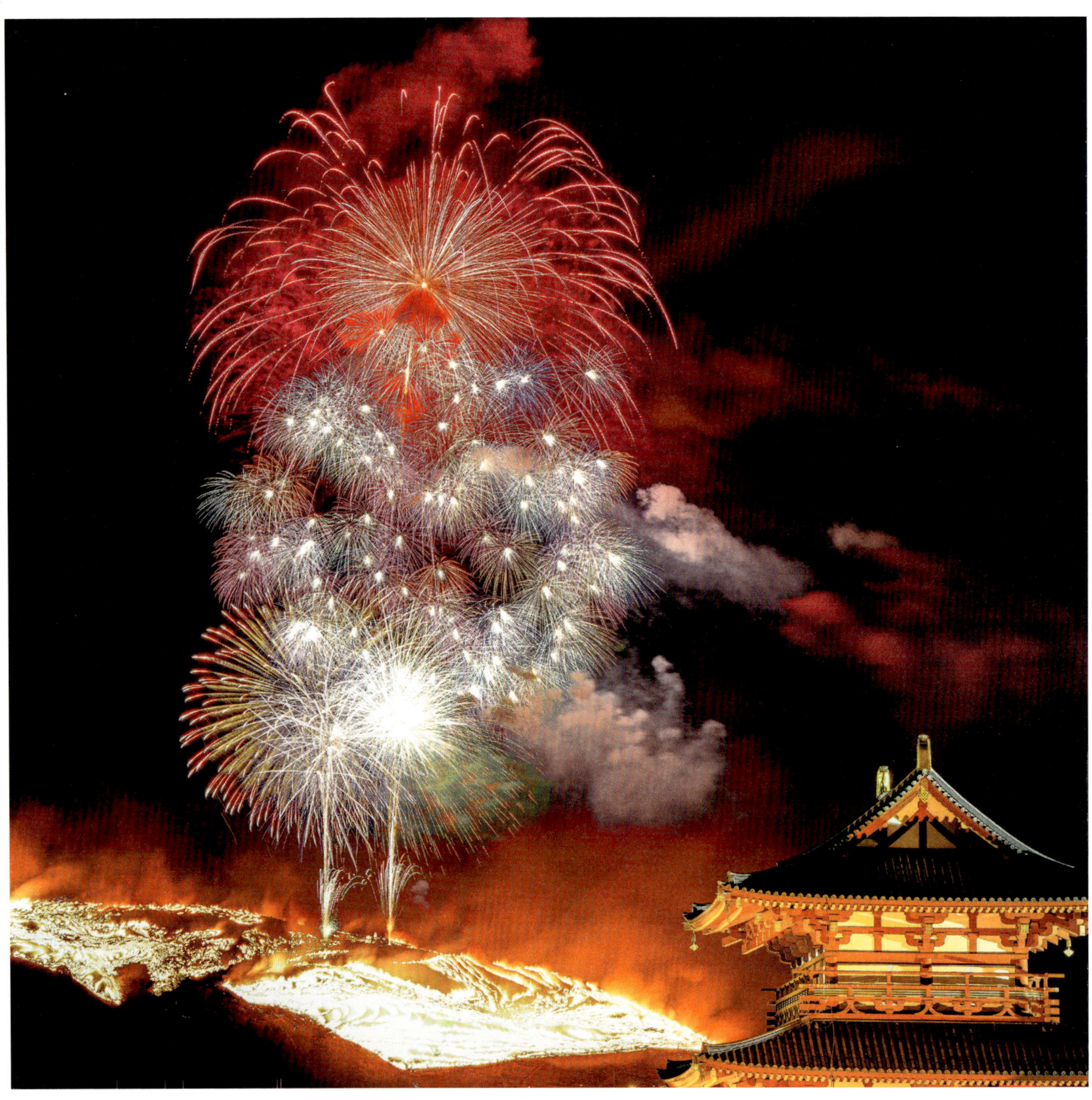

Previous page, bottom: Rouketopolemos, in Greece. The Easter event takes place in the town of Vrontados, where the congregations from two rival churches launch a "rocket war," attempting to hit the bell tower of the opposing church with tens of thousands of homemade rockets.
This page: At the Wakakusa Yamayaki Festival in Japan, the dead grass on the hillside of Mount Wakakusa is set on fire—alongside a stunning fireworks display.

Vorherige Seite, unten: Bei der Osterveranstaltung Rouketopolemos in Vrontados, Griechenland, begehen die Gemeinden zweier rivalisierender Kirchen einen „Raketenkrieg", indem sie versuchen, den Glockenturm der gegnerischen Kirche mit Tausenden selbst gebauter Raketen zu treffen.
Diese Seite: Beim Wakakusa-Yamayaki-Festival in Japan wird das abgestorbene Gras am Hang des Berges Wakakusa in Brand gesetzt – zeitgleich mit einem beeindruckenden Feuerwerk.

Up Helly Aa in Scotland is the largest fire festival in the world. Once a year, men dressed as Vikings parade through Lerwick, Shetland, and celebrate their Scandinavian roots. At the end, a Viking boat is burned.

Up Helly Aa in Schottland ist das größte Feuerfest der Welt. Einmal im Jahr ziehen als Wikinger verkleidete Männer durch Lerwick, Shetland, und feiern ihre skandinavischen Wurzeln. Zum Ende der Feierlichkeiten wird ein Wikingerboot verbrannt.

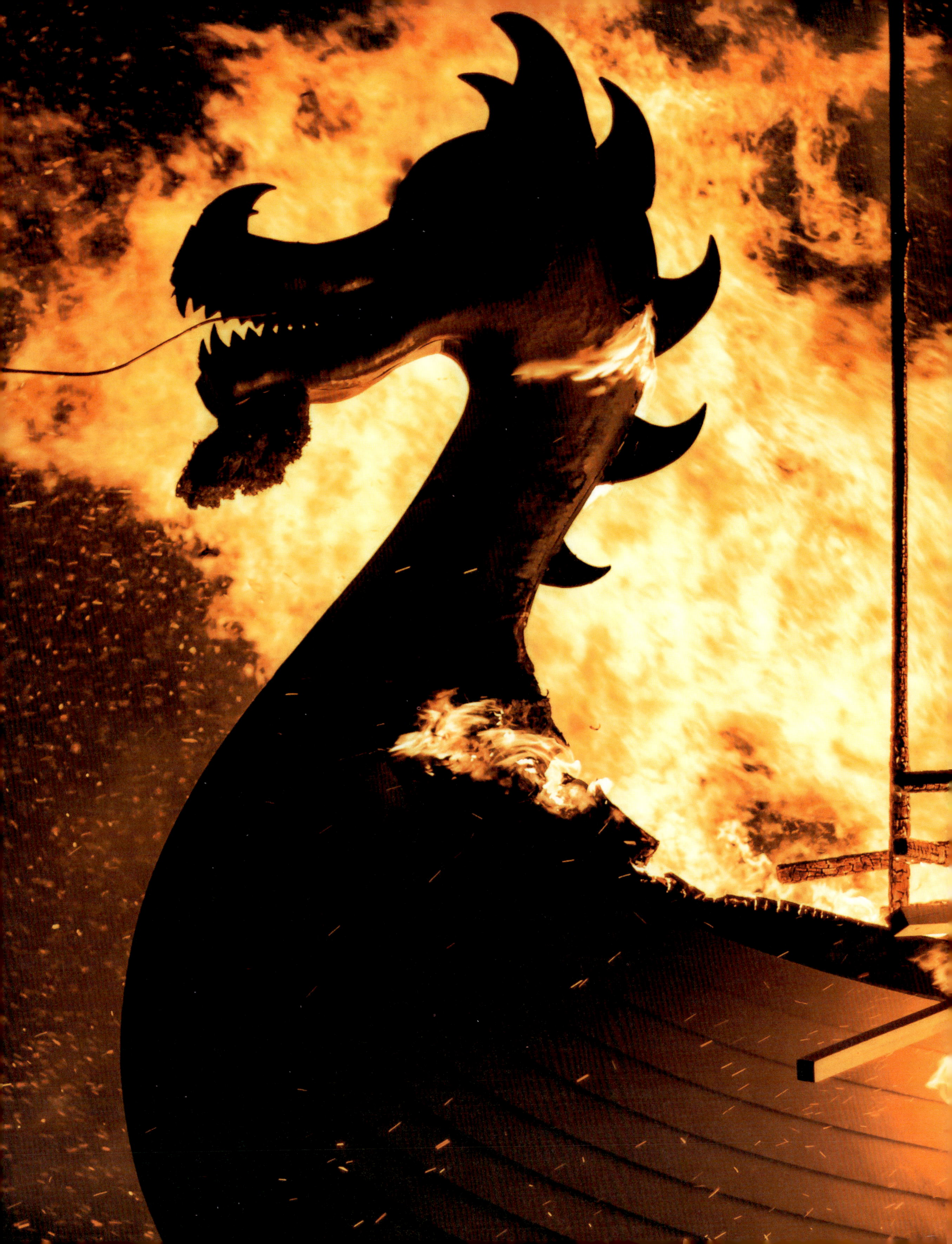

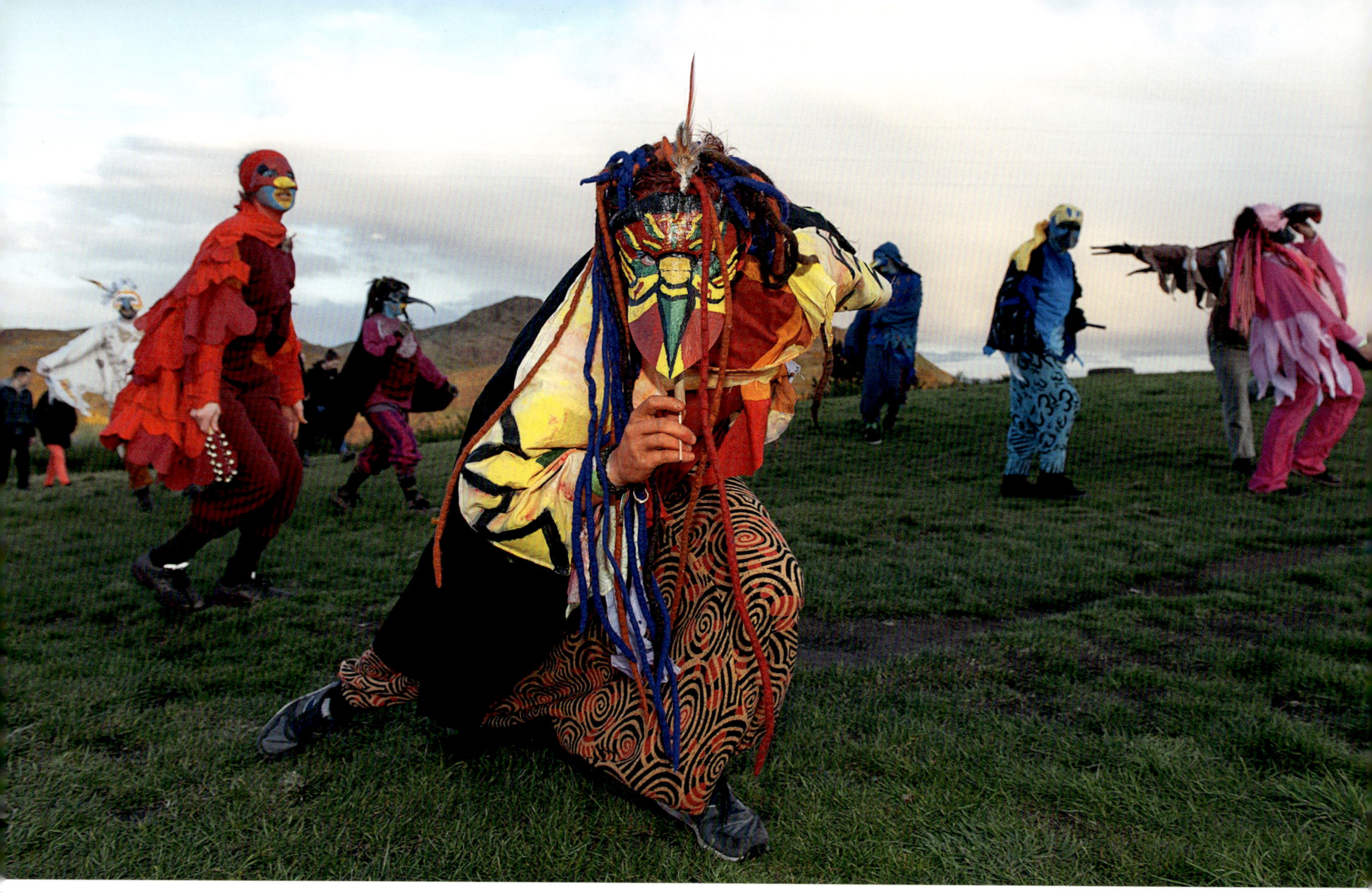

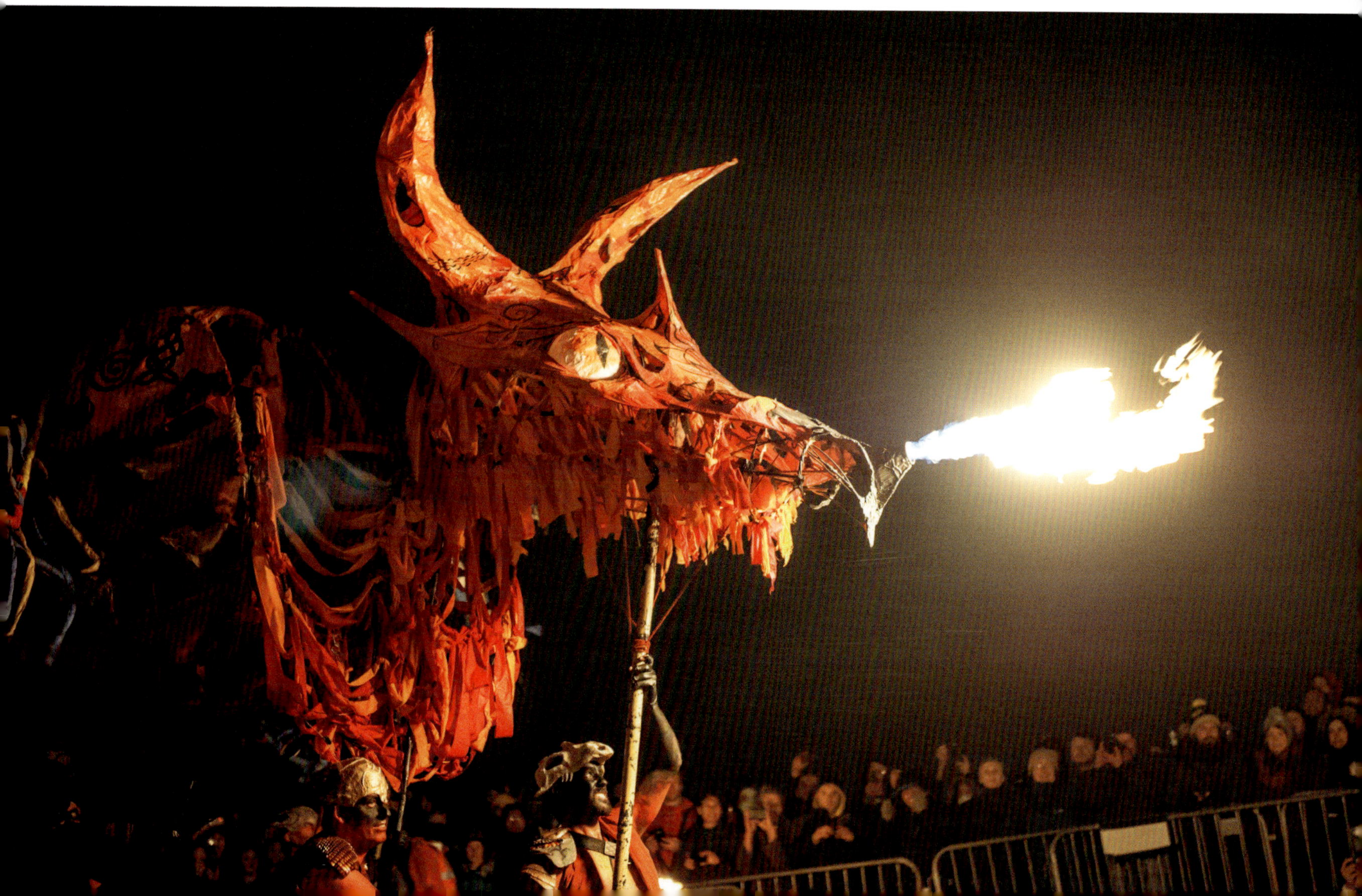

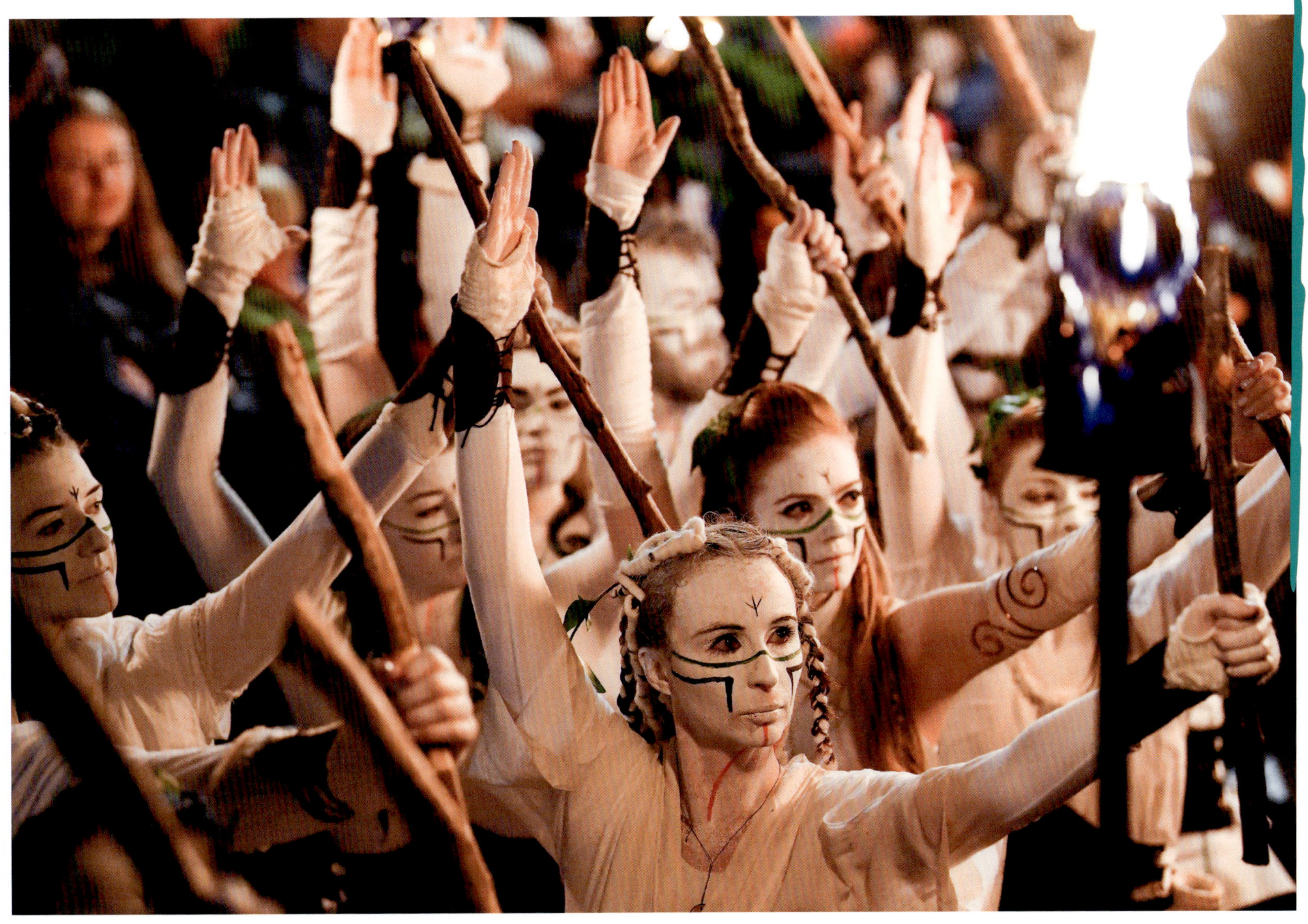

Beltane Fire Society performers celebrate the coming of summer.

Die Mitglieder der gemeinnützigen Beltane Fire Society feiern den
Beginn des Sommers.

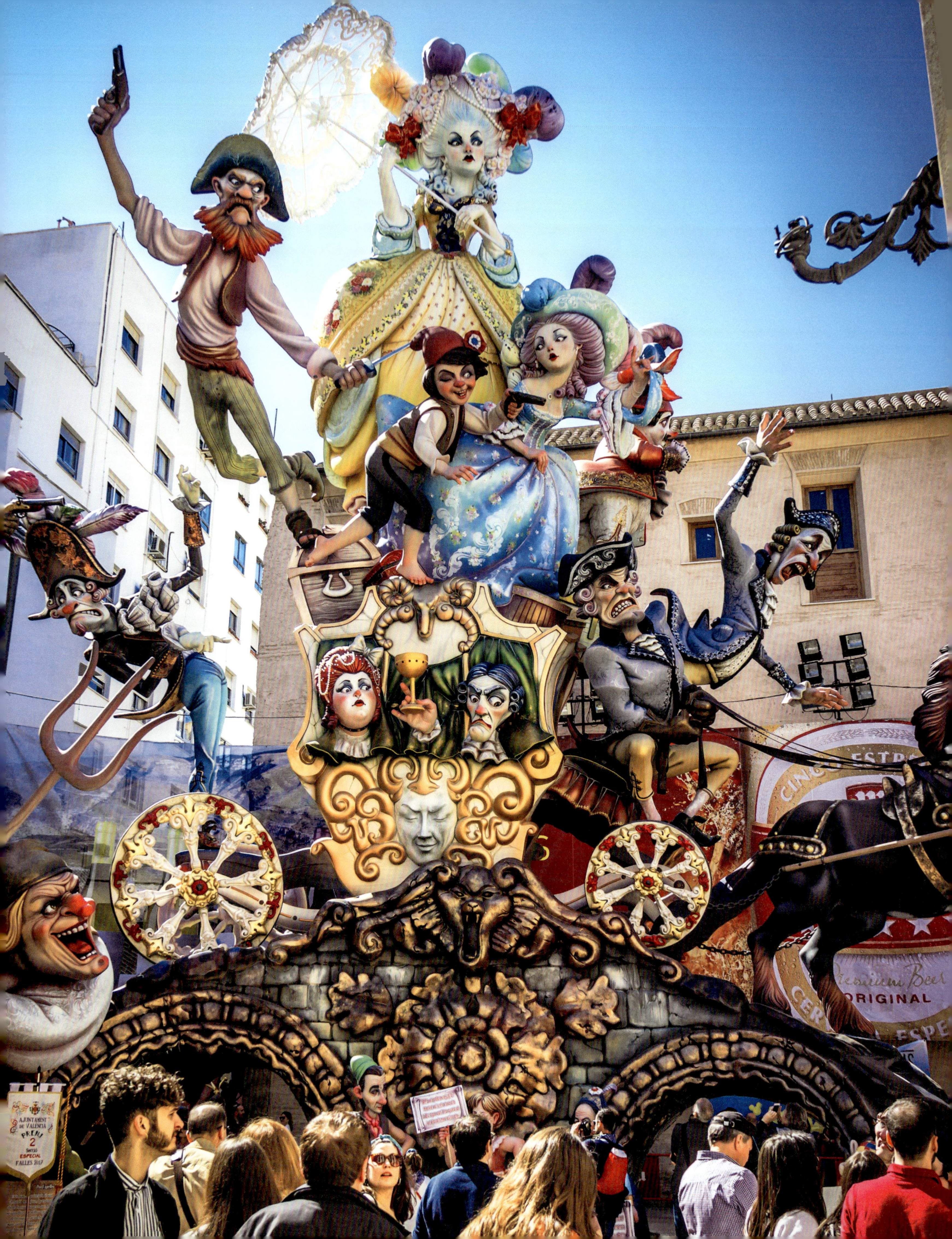

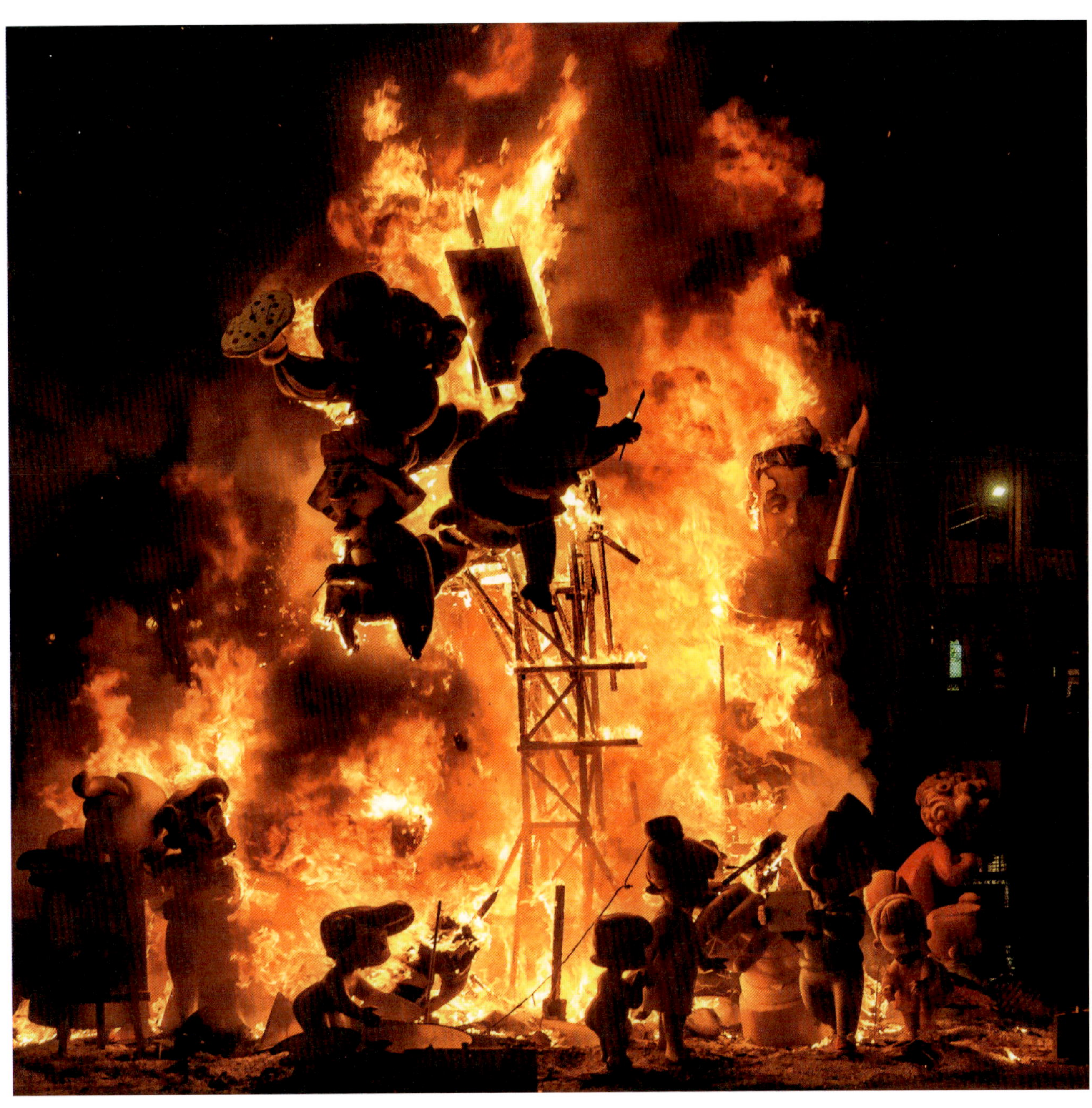

Fireworks start in Valencia well before the official
Las Fallas festival week. On the final night, the
sculptures are set ablaze.

Das Feuerwerk beginnt schon einige Zeit vor
der offiziellen Las-Fallas-Festwoche.
Die kunstvollen Skulpturen werden aber erst in der
letzten Nacht des Festes in Brand gesteckt.

The iconic Las Fallas sculptures are handmade by neighborhood *falla*
organizations—there are around 350 in the city—and paraded during the
official five-day festival.

Die ikonischen Las-Fallas-Skulpturen werden von den etwa 350 *Falla*-
Organisationen in den einzelnen Stadtteilen Valencias handgefertigt und
während des offiziellen fünftägigen Festes präsentiert.

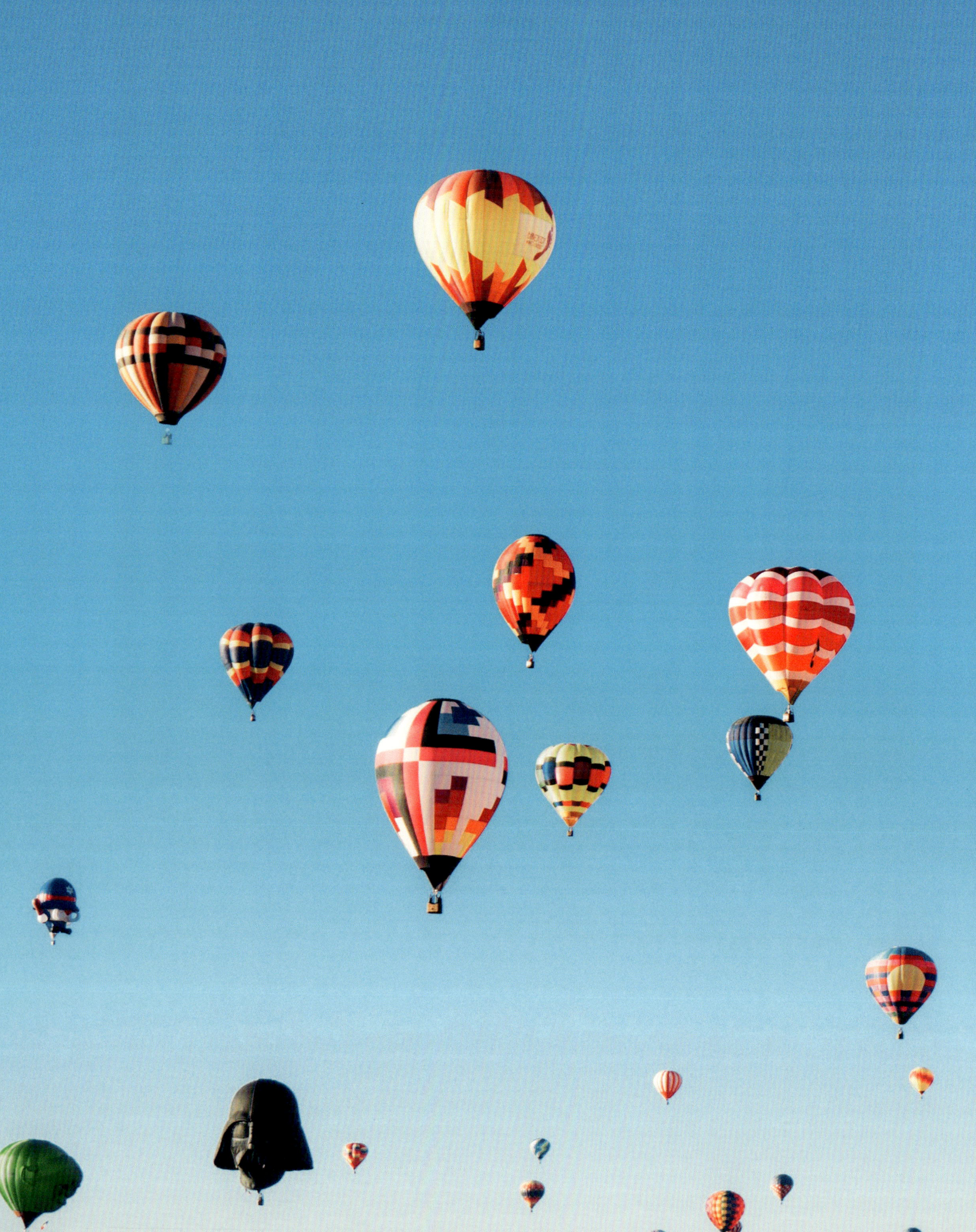

The Albuquerque International Balloon Fiesta is a
nine-day event with around 600 balloons and 750,000
visitors from all over the world.

Die Albuquerque International Balloon Fiesta ist eine
neuntägige Veranstaltung mit rund 600 Heißluftballons
und 750 000 Besuchern aus aller Welt.

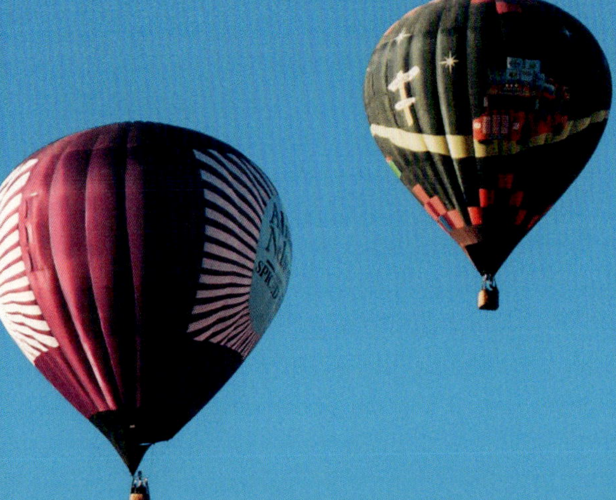
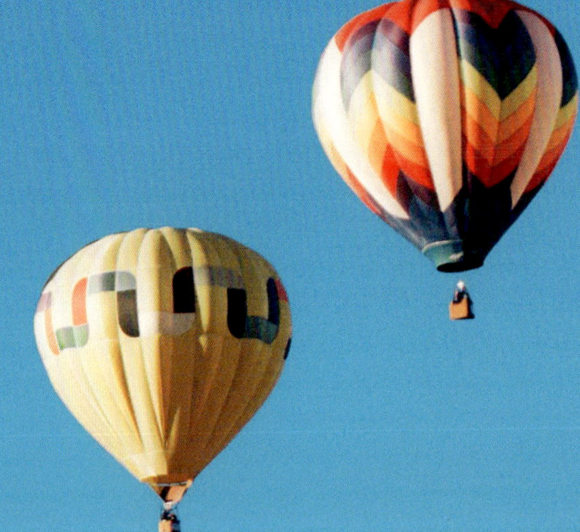
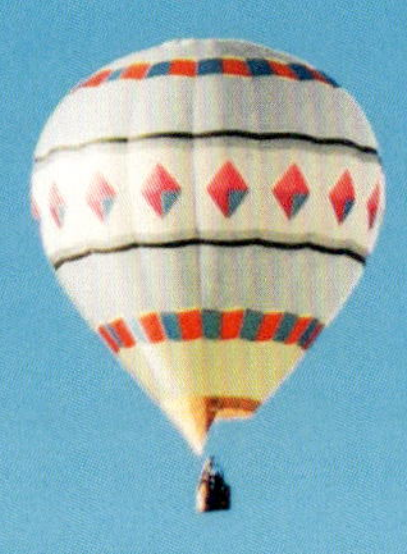
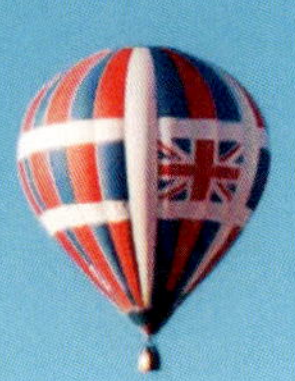
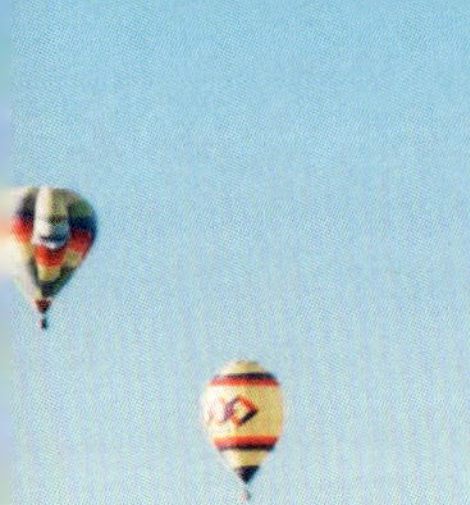
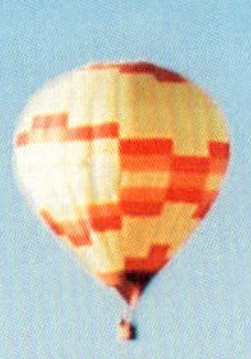
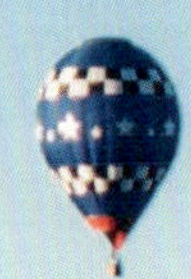
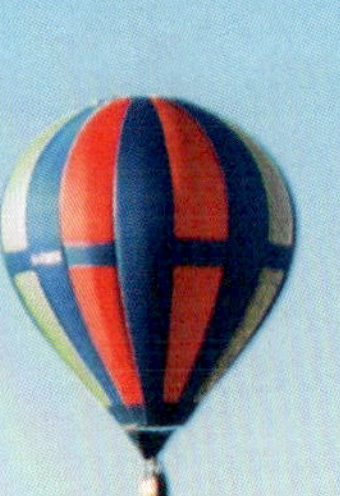
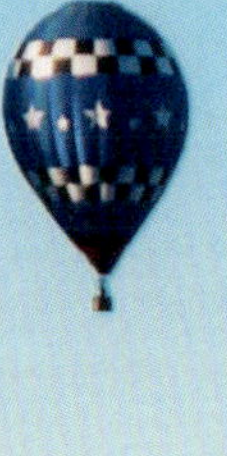
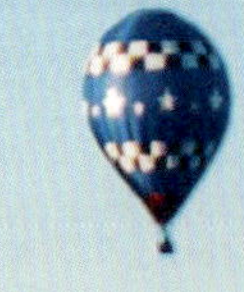

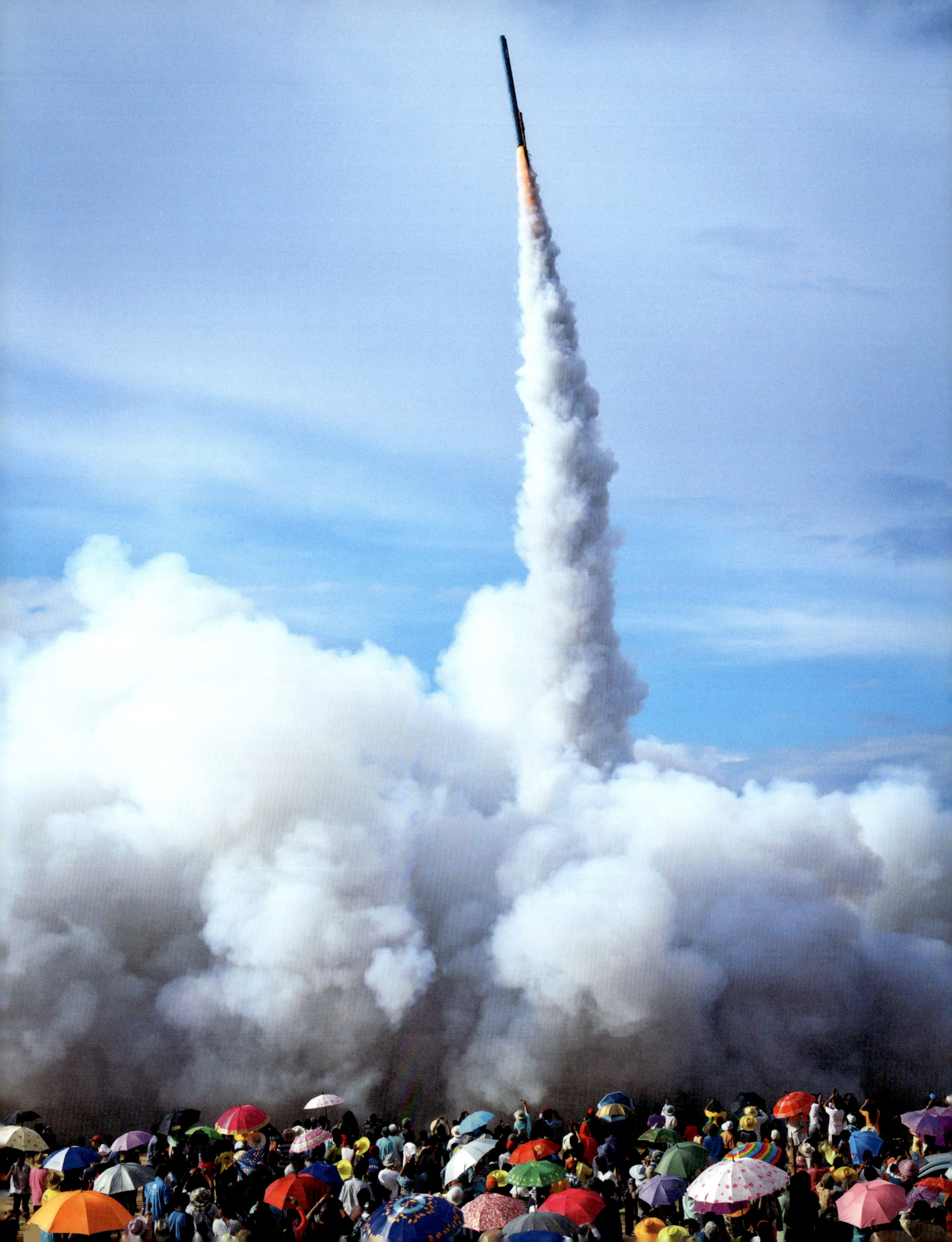

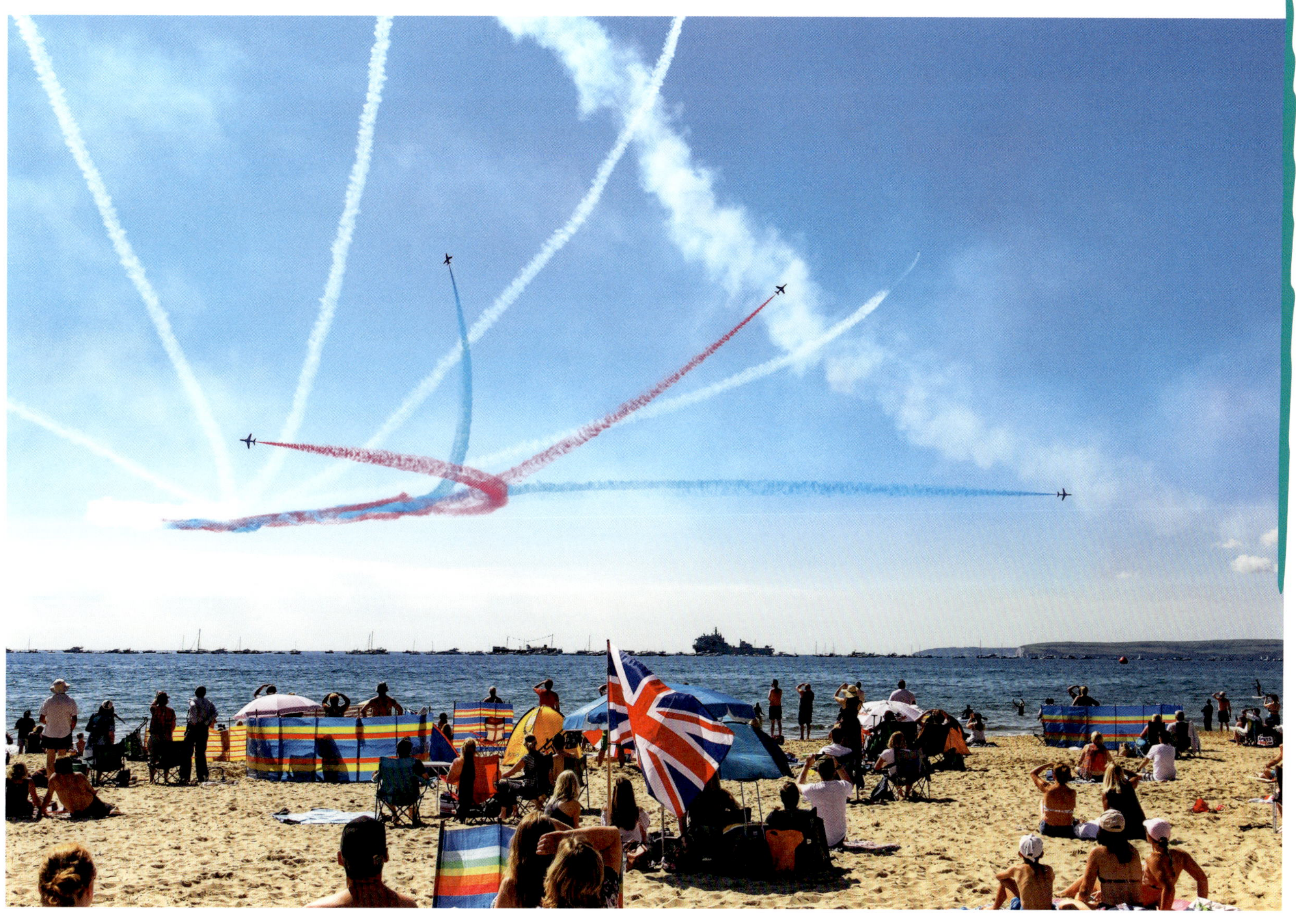

At the Bun Bang Fai Rocket Festival, celebrations include music and dance performances, float parades, and the competitive ignition of homemade rockets.

Das Bun-Bang-Fai-Raketenfest bietet Besuchern Paraden, Musik- und Tanzvorführungen, das Highlight ist aber wohl das Zünden der selbstgebauten Raketen, mit denen Tüftler gegeneinander antreten.

Chhath Puja is a Hindu Vedic festival dedicated to the solar deity
Surya, and includes rituals such as holy bathing and standing in
water while praying for long periods of time.

Chhath Puja ist ein hinduistisch-vedisches Fest, das der Sonnen-
gottheit Surya gewidmet ist und Rituale wie heilige Bäder beinhaltet,
bei denen man einige Zeit betend im Wasser verbringt.

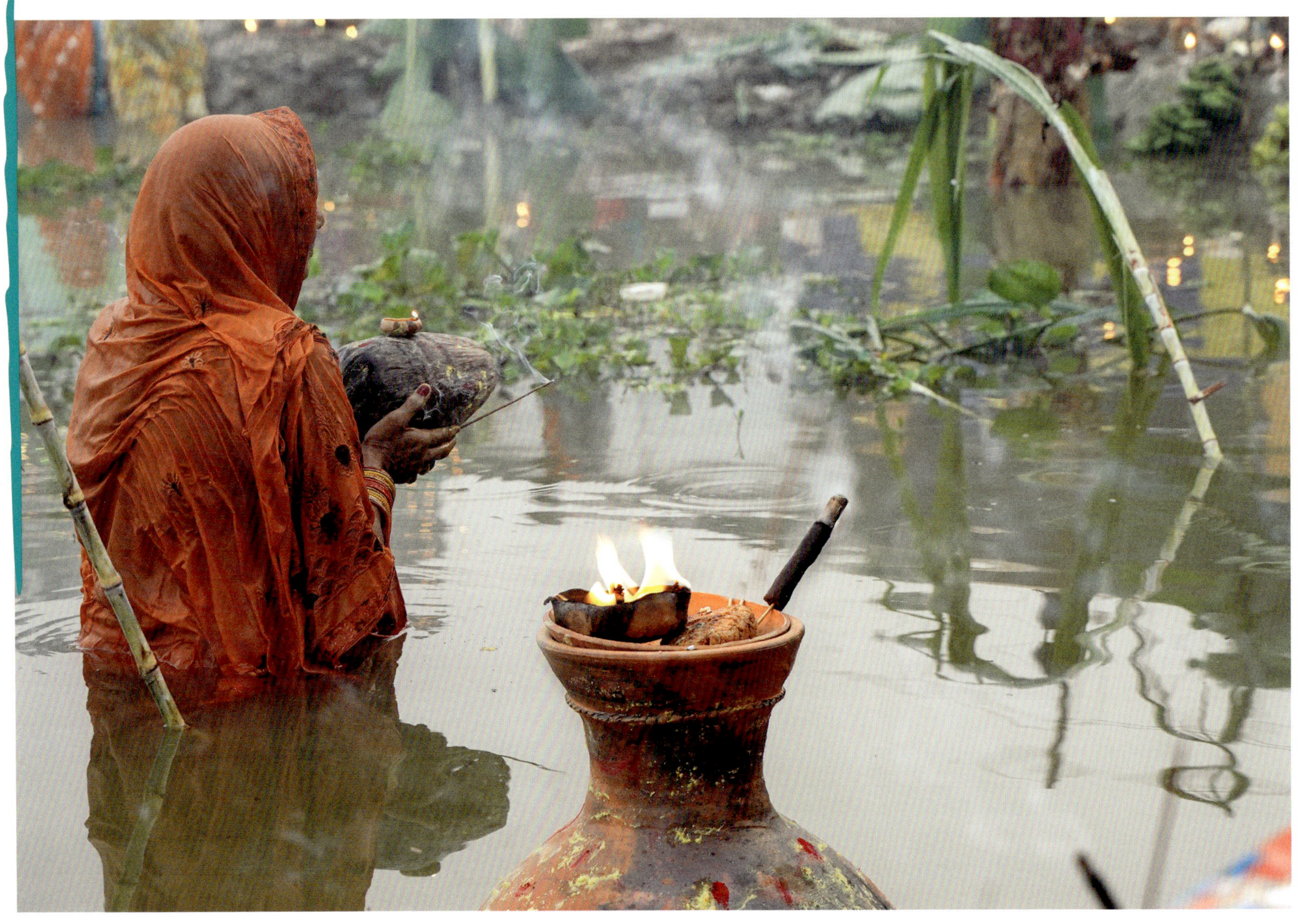

The Boryeong Mud Festival in South Korea was initially a marketing
tool to promote the local cosmetics industry. Nowadays the festival
attracts up to four million visitors per year.

Das Schlammfestival Boryeong war ursprünglich eine Marketingstra-
tegie zur Förderung der lokalen Kosmetikindustrie. Heutzutage zieht
das Festival jährlich bis zu vier Millionen Besucher an.

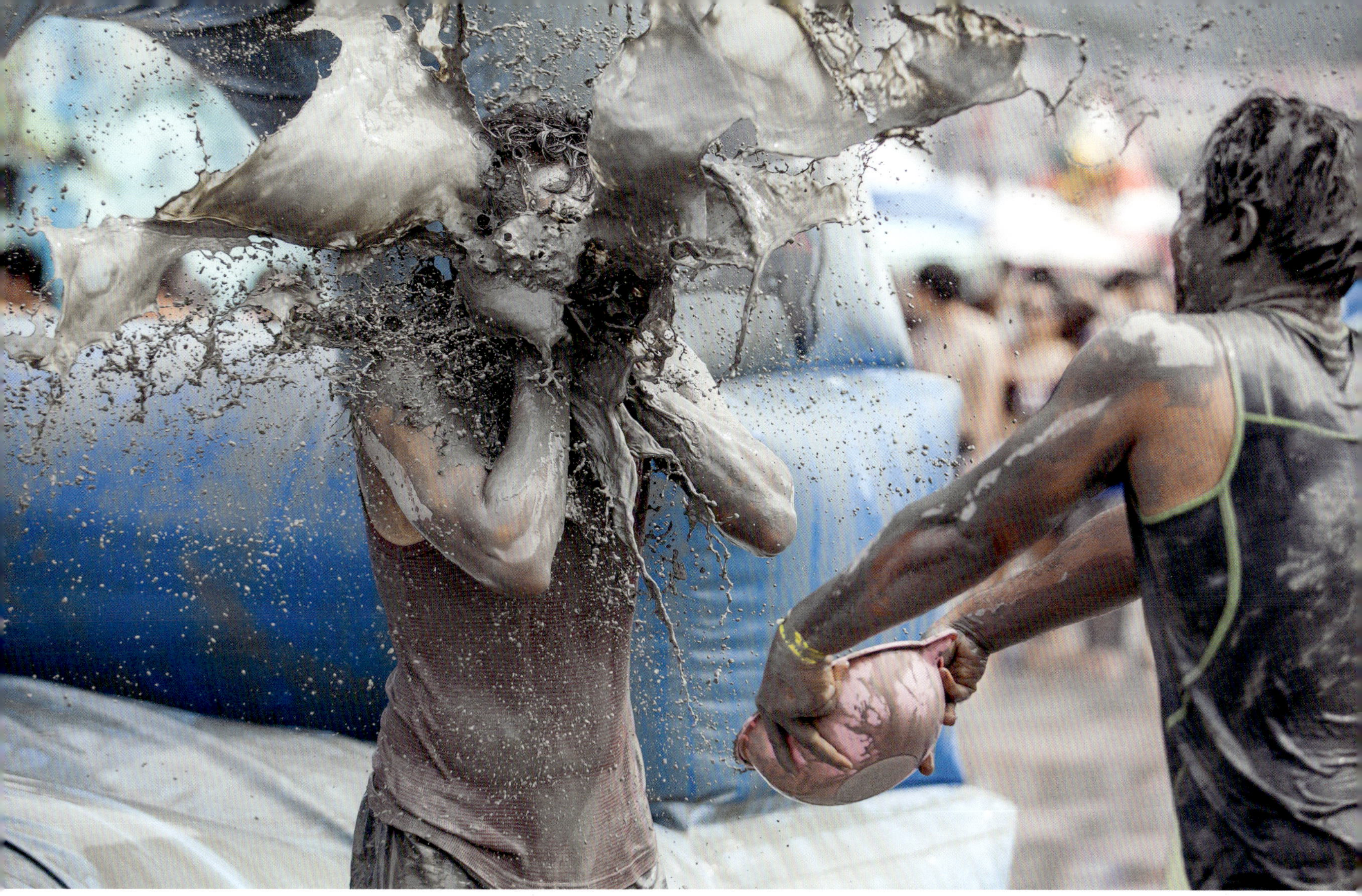

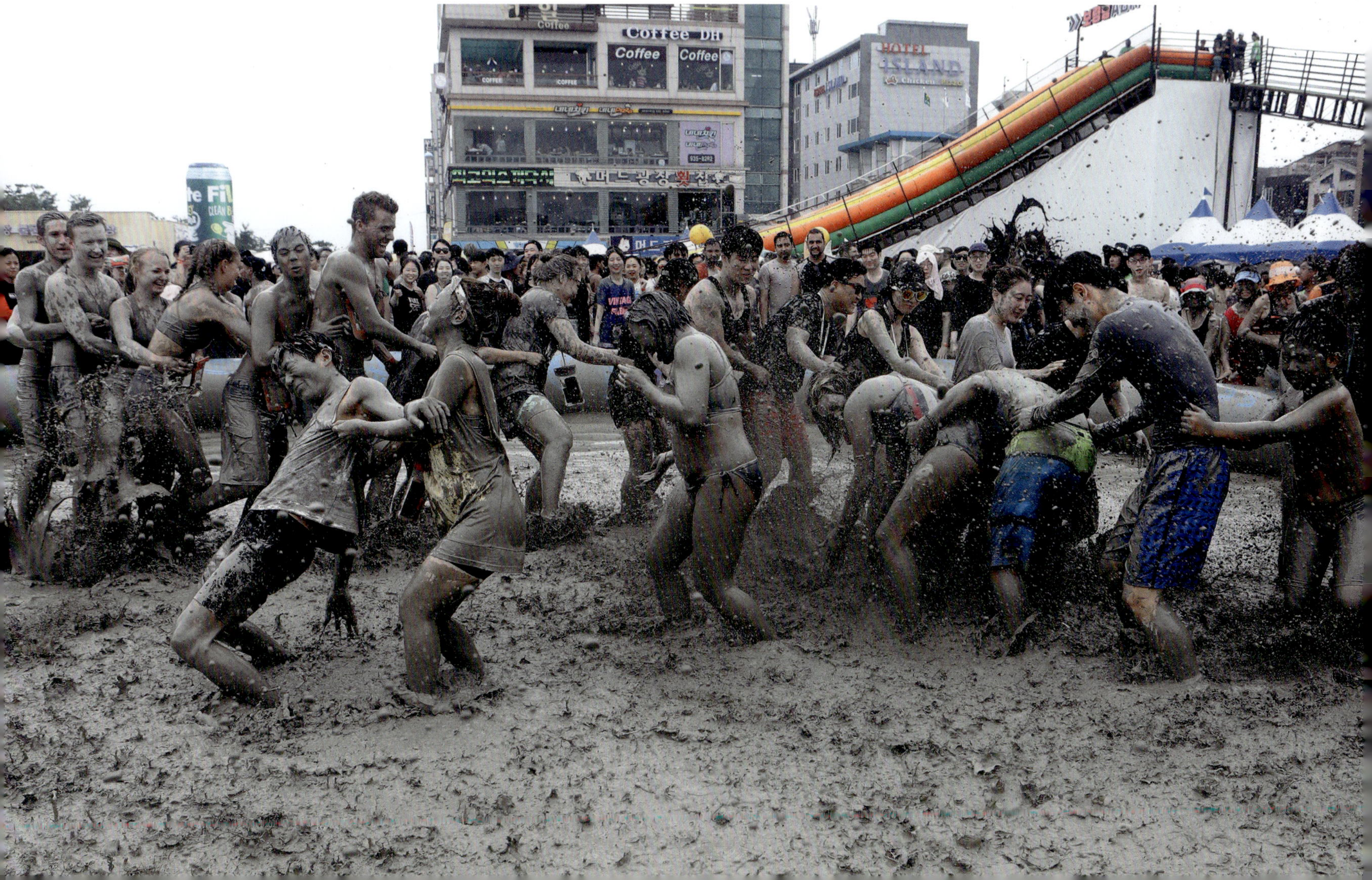
Coffee
Coffee DH
Coffee
Coffee
COFFEE
COFFEE
HOTEL
ISLAND

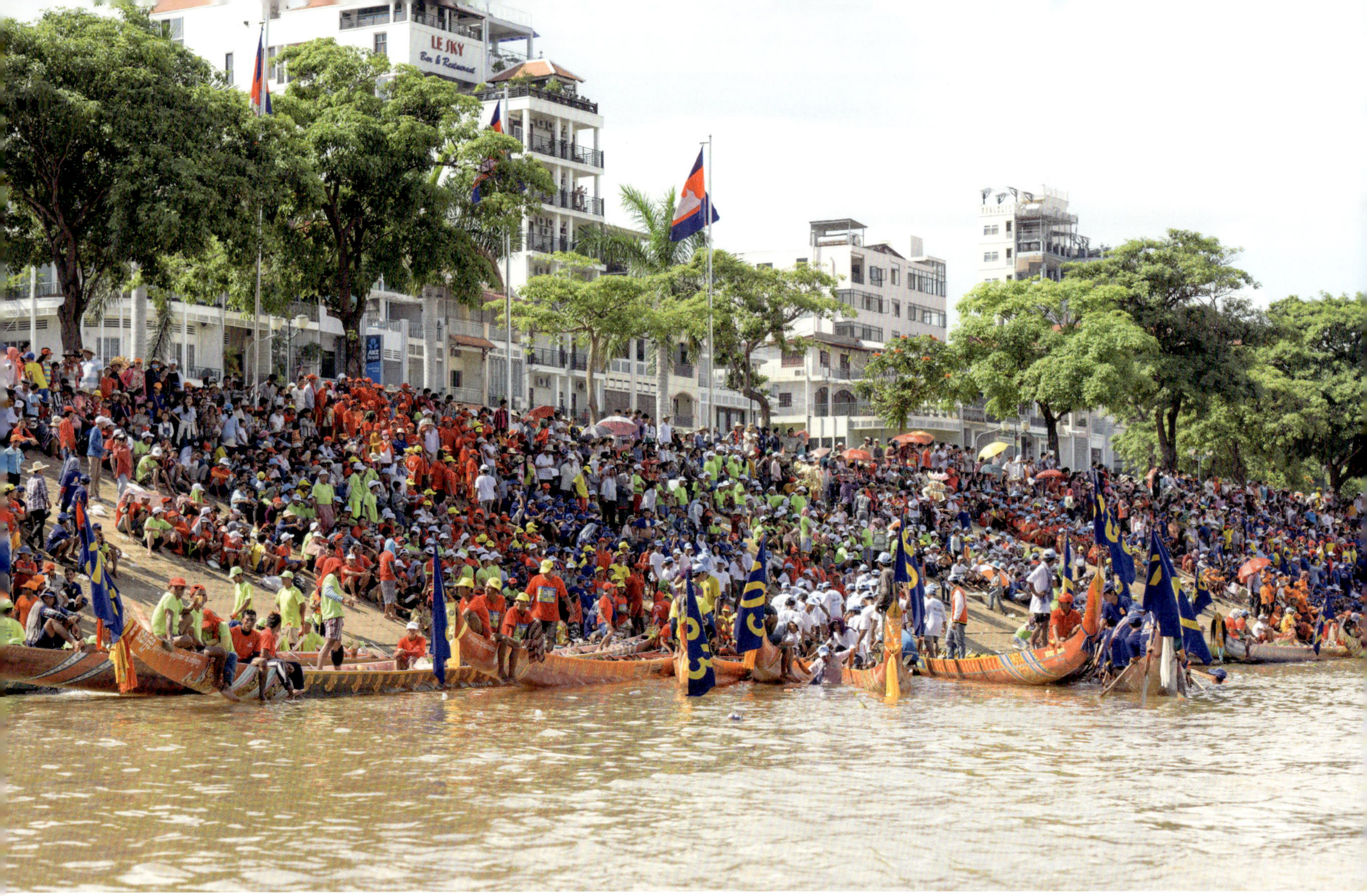

LE SKY
Bar & Restaurant

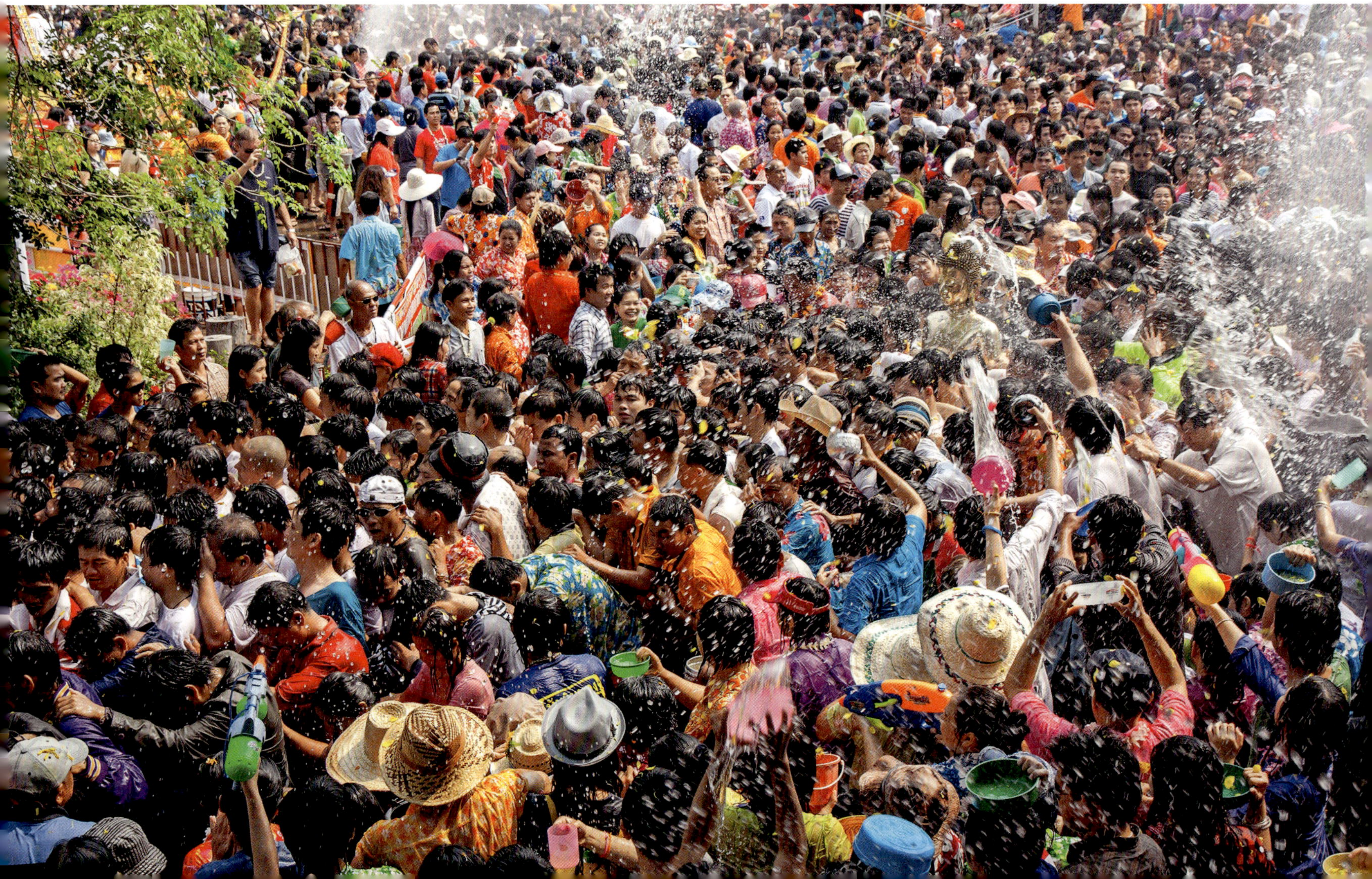

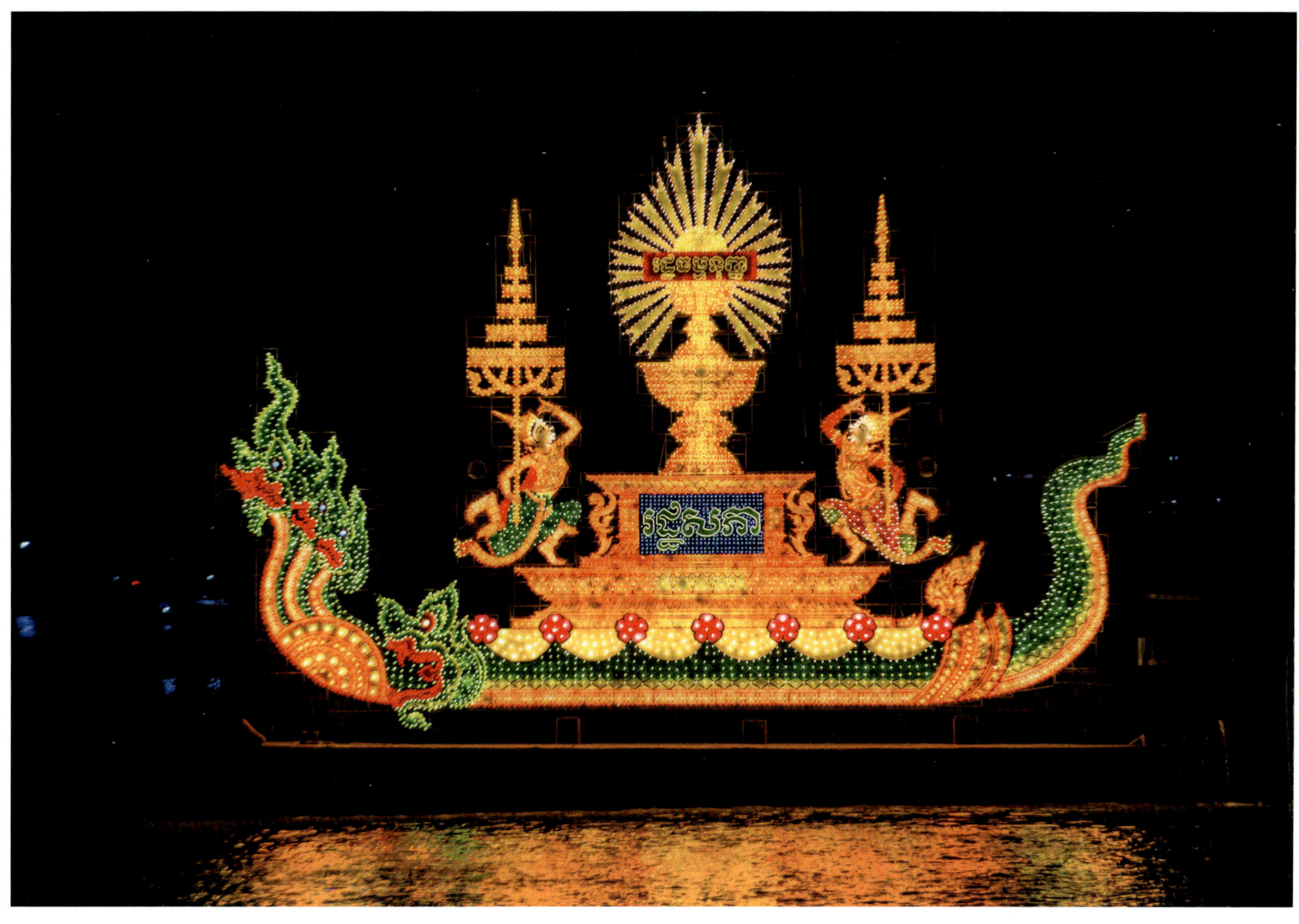

Opposite page, bottom: Songkran Festival, Thailand
Opposite page, top and this page: Bon Om Touk marks the end of the monsoon season. The highlights of this three-day Cambodian festival include dragon boat races and nightly processions of illuminated floats.

Linke Seite, unten: Songkran-Festival, Thailand
Linke Seite, oben und diese Seite: Das kambodschanische Wasserfestival Bon Om Touk markiert das Ende der Monsunzeit. Zu den Höhepunkten dieses dreitägigen Festes gehören Drachenbootrennen und nächtliche Paraden beleuchteter Festzugsboote.

Good to know
WISSENSWERTES

The origin of one of Cambodia's most important festivals is a unique natural phenomenon. With the end of the rainy season in October / November, the flow direction of the Tonlé Sap River, which flows into the Tonlé Sap Lake and is fed by the Mekong River during the rainy season, also changes.

Bon Om Touk celebrates the diminishing water of the lake and thus the beginning of the fishing season.

Der Auslöser für eines der wichtigsten Feste Kambodschas ist ein einzigartiges Naturphänomen. Denn mit dem Ende der Regenzeit im Oktober / November ändert sich auch die Fließrichtung des Tonlé-Sap-Flusses, der in den Tonlé-Sap-See mündet und in der Regenzeit vom Mekong gespeist wird. Bon Om Touk feiert das abnehmende Wasser des Sees und damit den Beginn der Fischfangsaison.

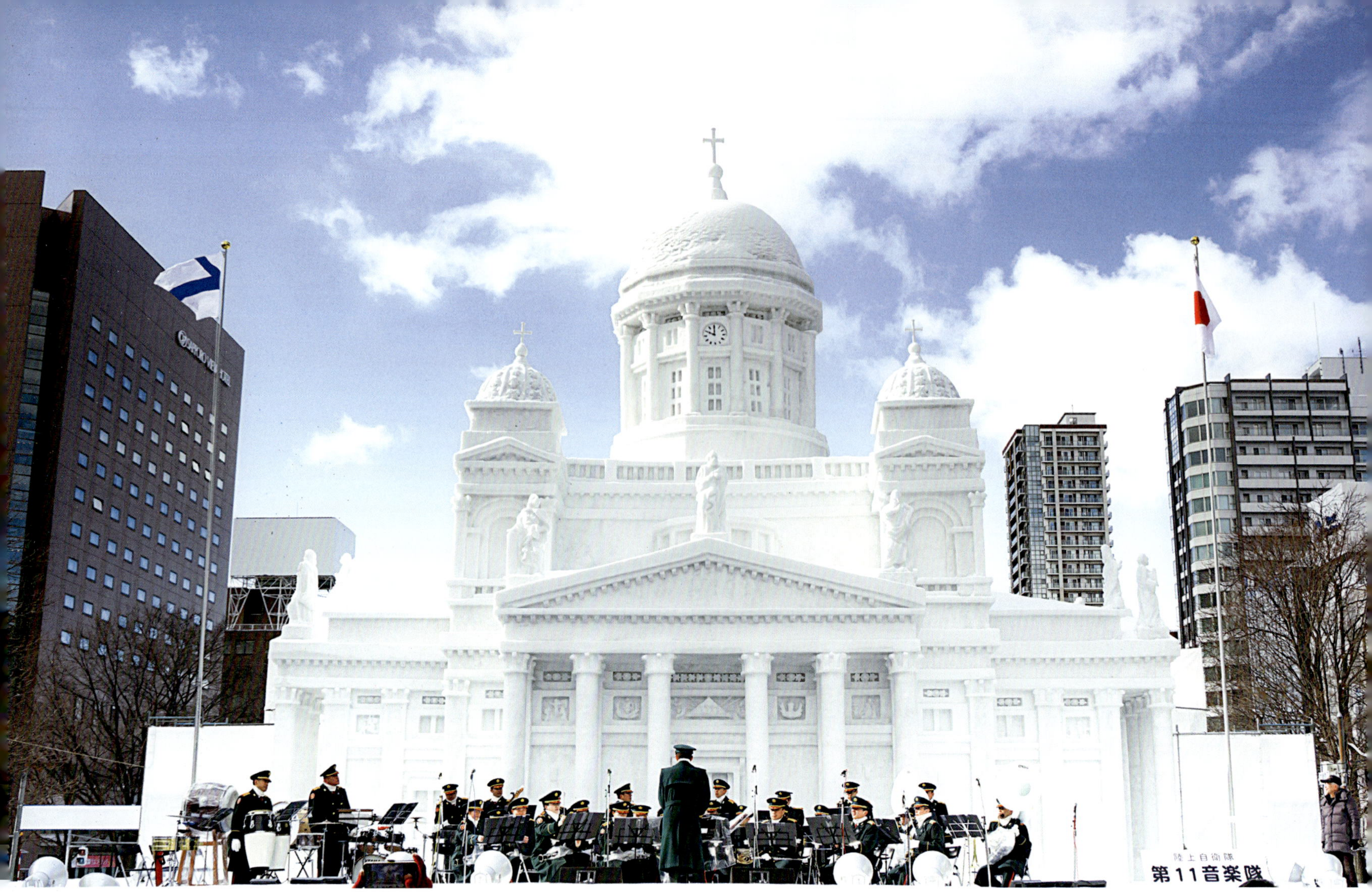

陸上自衛隊
第11音楽隊

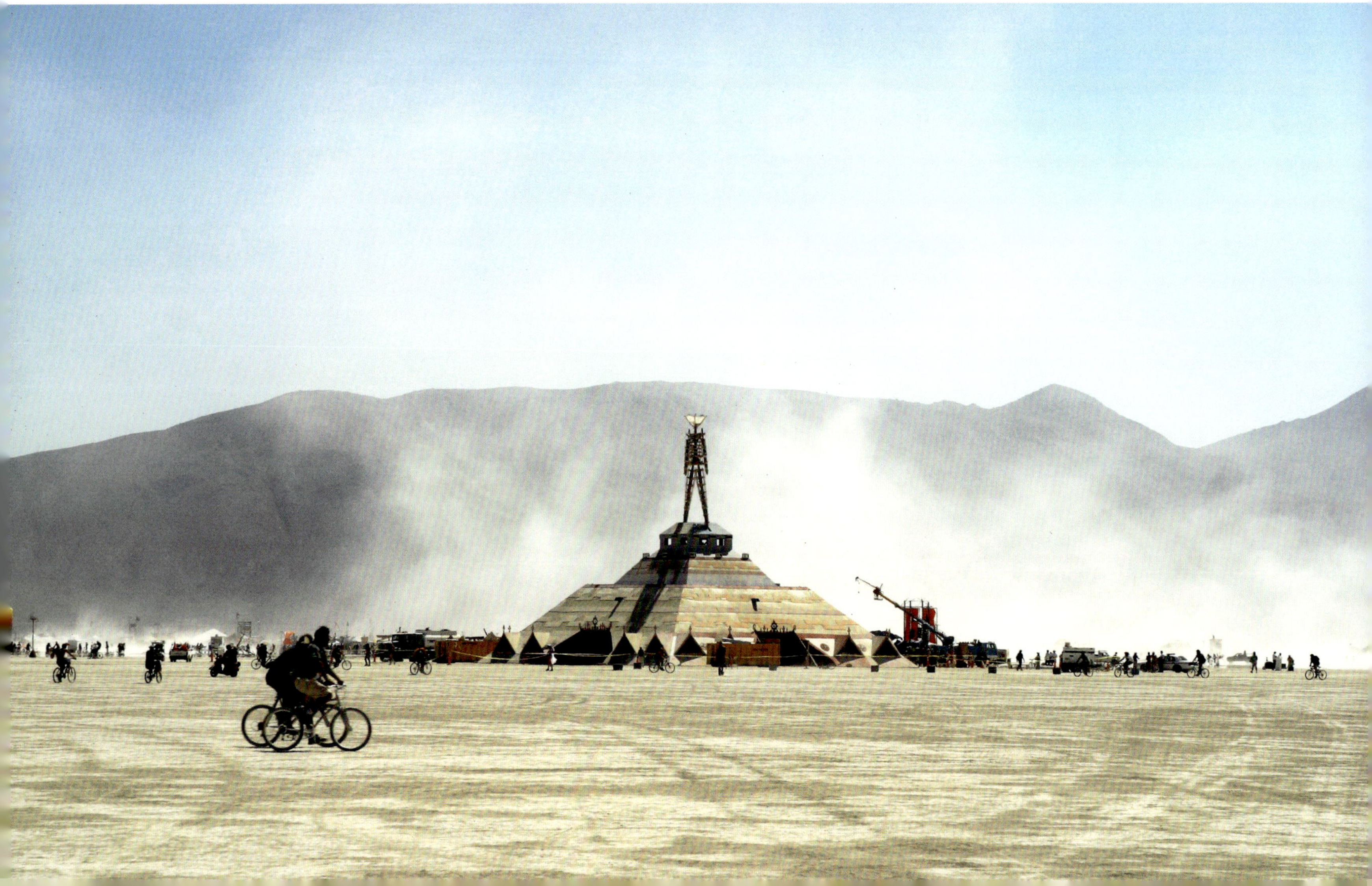

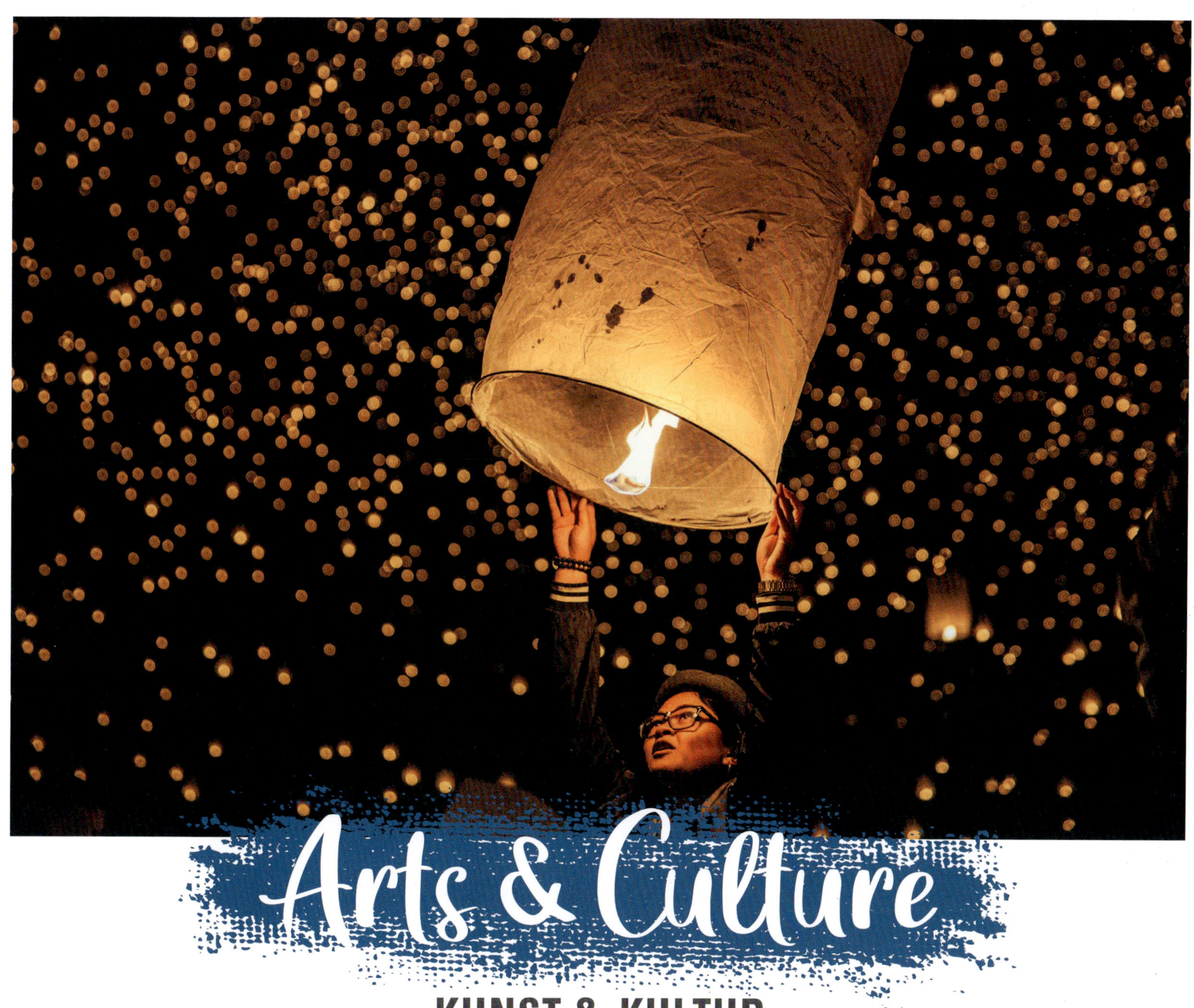

Arts & Culture

KUNST & KULTUR

This page: Yi Peng Lantern Festival in Thailand
Opposite page, top: Ice sculpture and concert at the
Sapporo Snow Festival in Japan.

Diese Seite: Yi-Peng-Laternenfest, Thailand
Linke Seite, oben: Konzert vor riesiger Eisskulptur,
Sapporo Snow Festival, Japan

Opposite page, bottom: Burning Man, USA. On the sixth
night of the event a wooden sculpture referred to as
"the Man" is set on fire, hence the name.

Linke Seite, unten: Burning Man, USA. Am sechsten Tag
der neuntägigen Veranstaltung wird eine Holzskulptur,
der sogenannte „Burning Man", in Brand gesetzt.

Festivals are tribal. They're representative of a unique way of life, of personal expression, and they offer a safe space for people to explore and welcome this part of their identity. Going to cultural festivals taps into the zeitgeist of the time and destination. Go to any poetry slam or improv or comedy performance at a festival and you'll soon find out the issues of the day from what you see on stage and the audience's reactions.

The Sapporo Snow Festival in Japan is one of the biggest art festivals in the world. Humongous sculptures are crafted from ice in the north of the country, in Hokkaido, for you to wander around. It all started in 1950 with high school students building a few snow statues in a park. Now you can expect over 400 unique statues—some more than 49 feet (15 meters) high and 82 feet (25 meters) wide—a Susukino Queen of Ice pageant, and more than two million visitors a year enjoying the ice rink, skiing, concerts, and food and drink in this snow-filled paradise.

The Edinburgh Festival Fringe in Scotland celebrates every facet of performance art possible. It's one of the world's largest arts events, with more than 3,000 shows, 50,000 performances, and 300 venues over 25 days. With so much going on, you really need to be prepared to make the most of it and see the most popular shows. If you don't get in, there's always the beautiful Edinburgh to enjoy! (opposite)

One of the most talked about festivals in the western world, Burning Man in Nevada, is often thought of as a music festival, but in fact it has its roots in art and describes itself as a "community." Huge interactive art installations are erected in the desert while over 80,000 "Burners" dress up to watch the Burning Man set on fire on the sixth night. Black Rock City becomes a community that everyone is expected to contribute to, and Burners practice radical inclusion and self-reliance, meaning you have to bring everything you could possibly need, and be nice to everyone!

Festivals repräsentieren bestimmte Gruppen, geben einem Lebensgefühl Ausdruck und bieten Menschen ein sicheres Umfeld, um ihre Identität auszuleben. Wer Kulturfestivals besucht, schnuppert in den Zeitgeist von Ort und Zeit hinein. Auf den dort stattfindenden Veranstaltungen wie Poetry Slams oder Comedy-Aufführungen erfährt man schnell, welche Themen gerade aktuell sind.

Das Sapporo-Schneefestival in Japan ist eines der größten Kunstfestivals der Welt. Gigantische Skulpturen werden in der Präfektur Hokkaido aus Eis gehauen und zur Schau gestellt. Das Ganze begann 1950, als Schüler in einem Park ein paar Schneestatuen schufen. Heute erwarten die über zwei Millionen Besucher des Festivals über 400 einmalige Skulpturen (einige über 15 Meter hoch und 25 Meter breit), der Eiskönigin-Susukino-Schönheitswettbewerb, Eislauf- und Skibahnen, Konzerte und jede Menge kulinarische Köstlichkeiten. Willkommen im Schneeparadies!

Auf dem schottischen Edinburgh Festival Fringe wird jede nur erdenkliche Performance-Kunst zelebriert. Mit über 3 000 Stücken und 50 000 Aufführungen verteilt auf 300 Spielorte und 25 Tage ist es eines der bedeutendsten Kunstevents der Welt. Bei diesem Überangebot ist gute und rechtzeitige Planung angesagt. Und wenn man irgendwo nicht reinkommt, kann man immer noch das wunderschöne Edinburgh erkunden! (rechte Seite)

Eine der coolsten Veranstaltungen der westlichen Welt, das Burning Man Event im US-amerikanischen Nevada, halten viele für ein Musikfestival, doch tatsächlich steht hier die bildende Kunst im Fokus und die Veranstalter beschreiben sich selbst als „Community". Gewaltige interaktive Installationen werden in der Black-Rock-Wüste errichtet und über 80 000 „Burner" verkleiden sich und sehen am sechsten Abend dabei zu, wie die riesige Statue eines Mannes in Flammen aufgeht. Für kurze Zeit entsteht in Black Rock City eine Gemeinschaft, zu der jeder etwas beitragen sollte. Als Burner wird von Ihnen erwartet, dass Sie sich selbst versorgen, keinen Abfall hinterlassen und zu jedem freundlich sind.

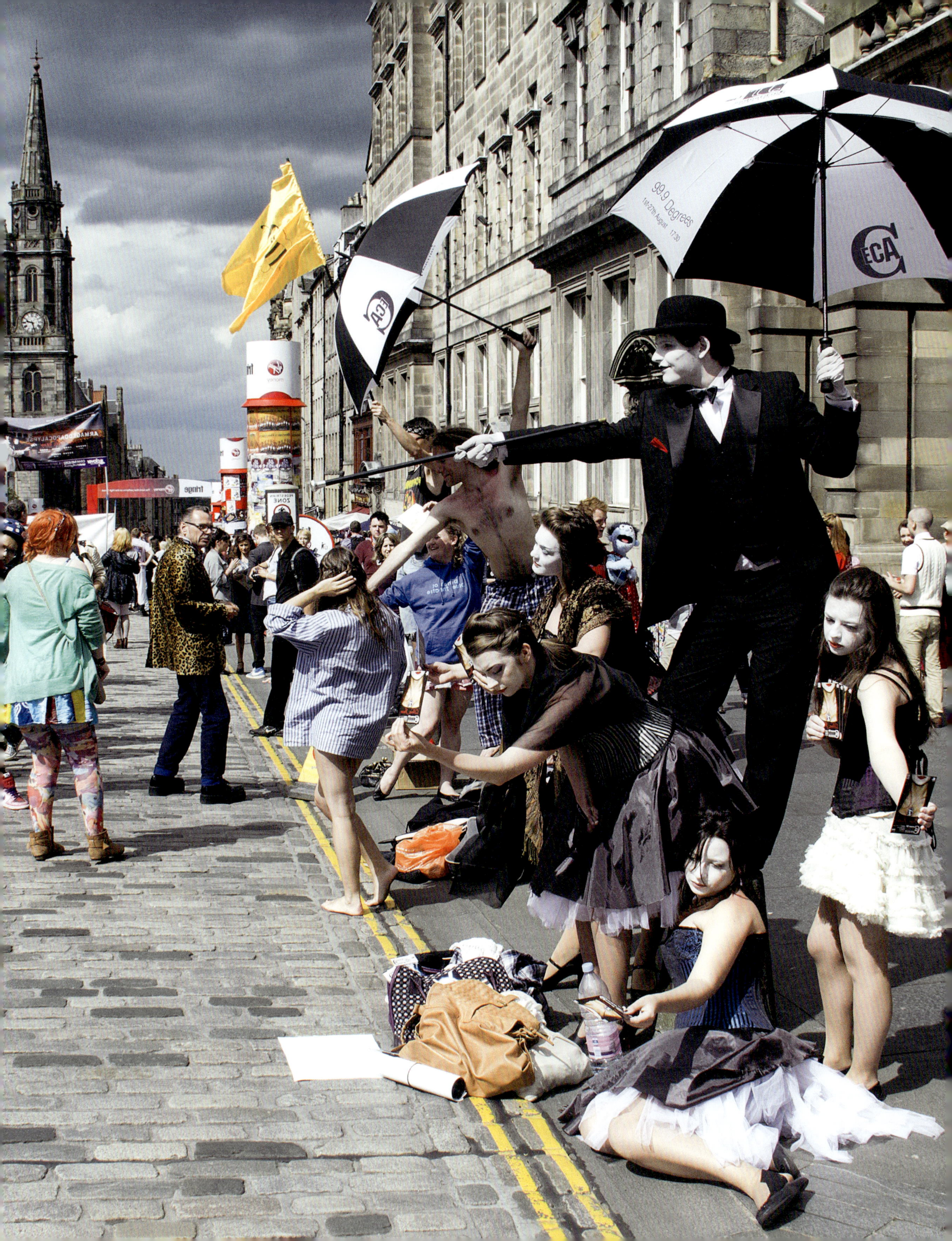

ECA
99.9 Degrees
18th-27th August 17:30
ECA
fringe
ARMAGEDDONCALYPSE
fringe

The Harbin Ice and Snow Festival in China is the largest of its kind in the world. The most impressively sized sculpture was built in 2007 by an international team of 600 sculptors—it was 656 feet (200 meters) long, 115 feet (35 meters) tall, and consisted of 120,000 cubic feet (3,398 cubic meters) of snow.

Das Harbin Ice and Snow Festival in China ist das größte seiner Art auf der Welt. Die imposanteste Schneeskulptur wurde 2007 von einem internationalen Team von 600 Eisbildhauern gebaut – sie war 200 Meter lang, 35 Meter hoch und bestand aus 3 398 Kubikmetern Schnee.

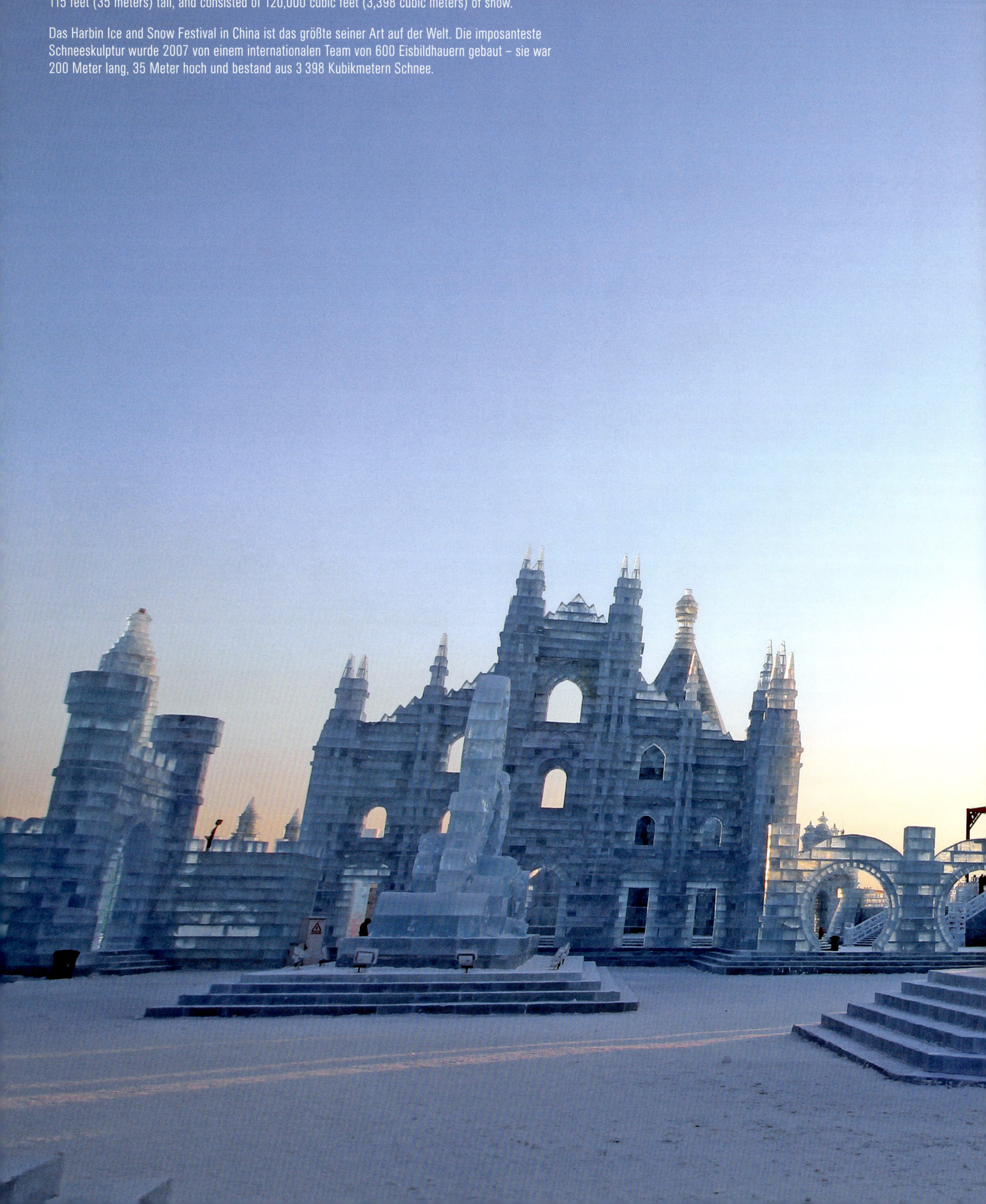

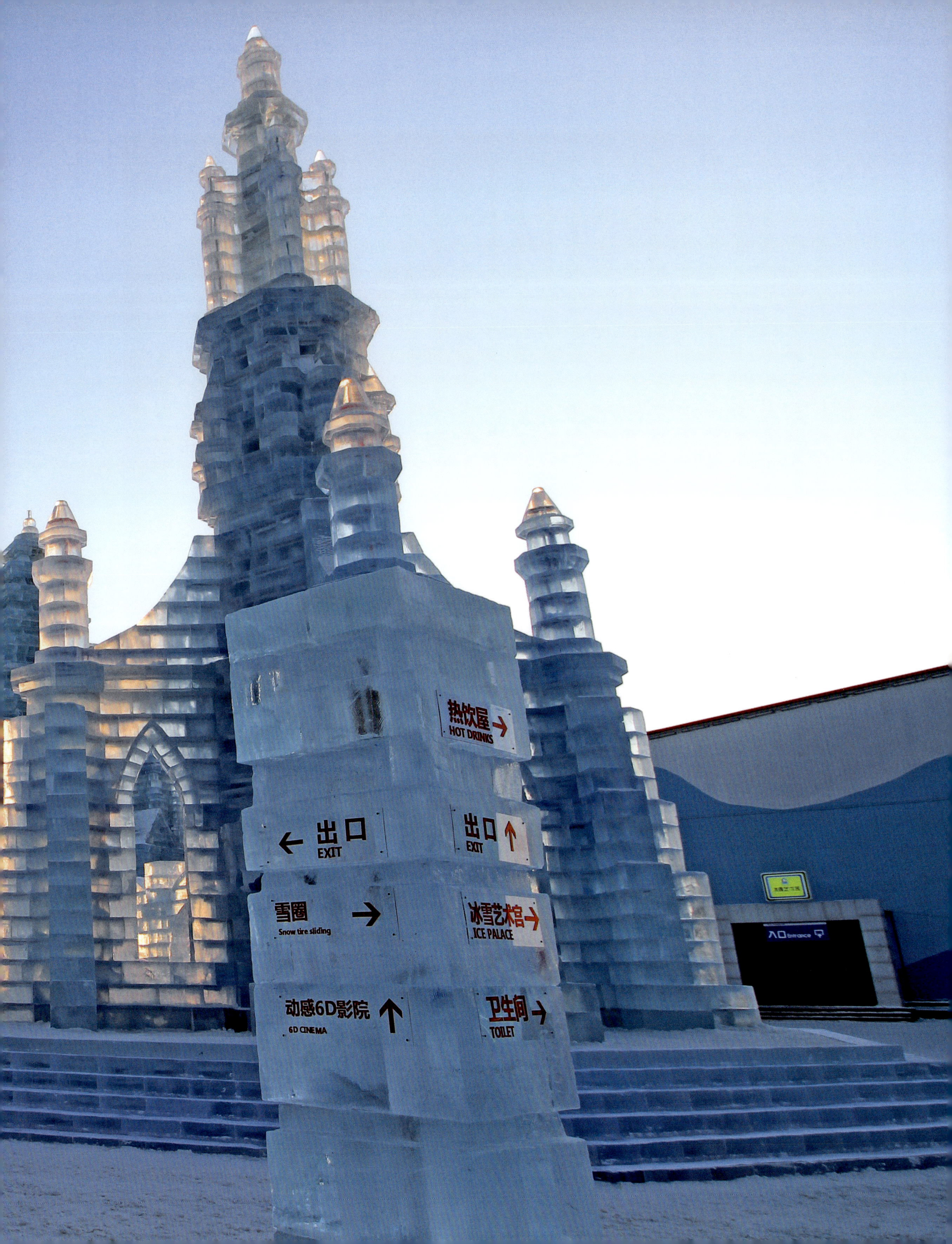
热饮屋 →
HOT DRINKS
← 出口
EXIT
出口 ↑
EXIT
雪圈 →
Snow tire sliding
冰雪艺术宫 →
ICE PALACE
动感6D影院 ↑
6D CINEMA
卫生间 →
TOILET
入口 Entrance

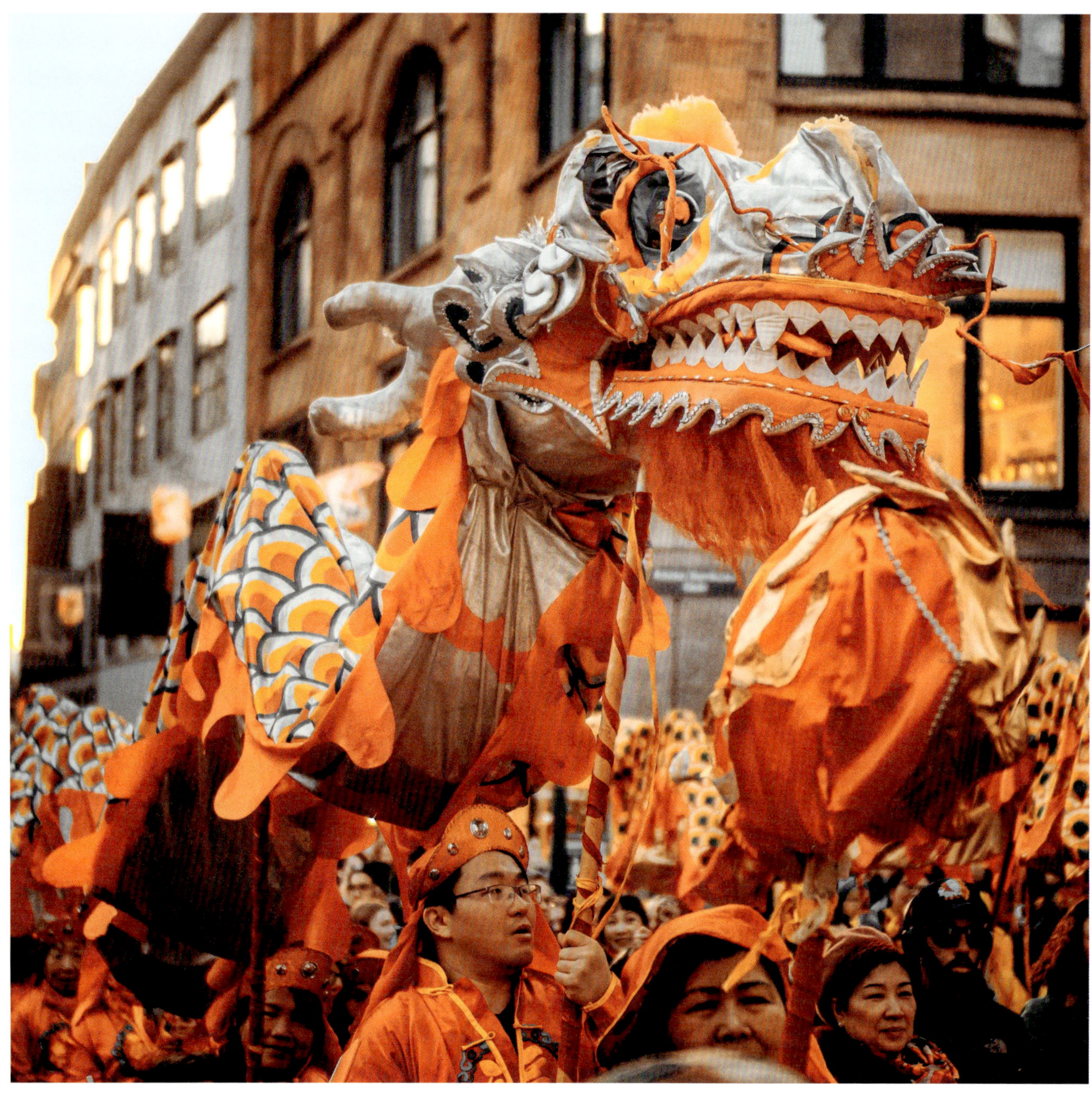

Lion and dragon dances, as well as a lantern festival,
are part of the Chinese New Year celebrations.

Löwen- und Drachentänze gehören ebenso zu den chinesischen Mond-Neujahrsfeierlichkeiten wie Laternenfeste.

The color red is considered lucky in China, and thus many red lanterns adorn temples for
Chinese New Year. It's one of the most important holidays in China and
is celebrated by Chinese expats around the world.

Die Farbe Rot gilt in China als Glücksbringer, und so schmücken zahlreiche rote Laternen
die Tempel zum Anlass des Mond-Neujahrsfestes. Einer der wichtigsten chinesischen
Feiertage wird auch von im Ausland lebenden Chinesen rund um die Welt zelebriert.

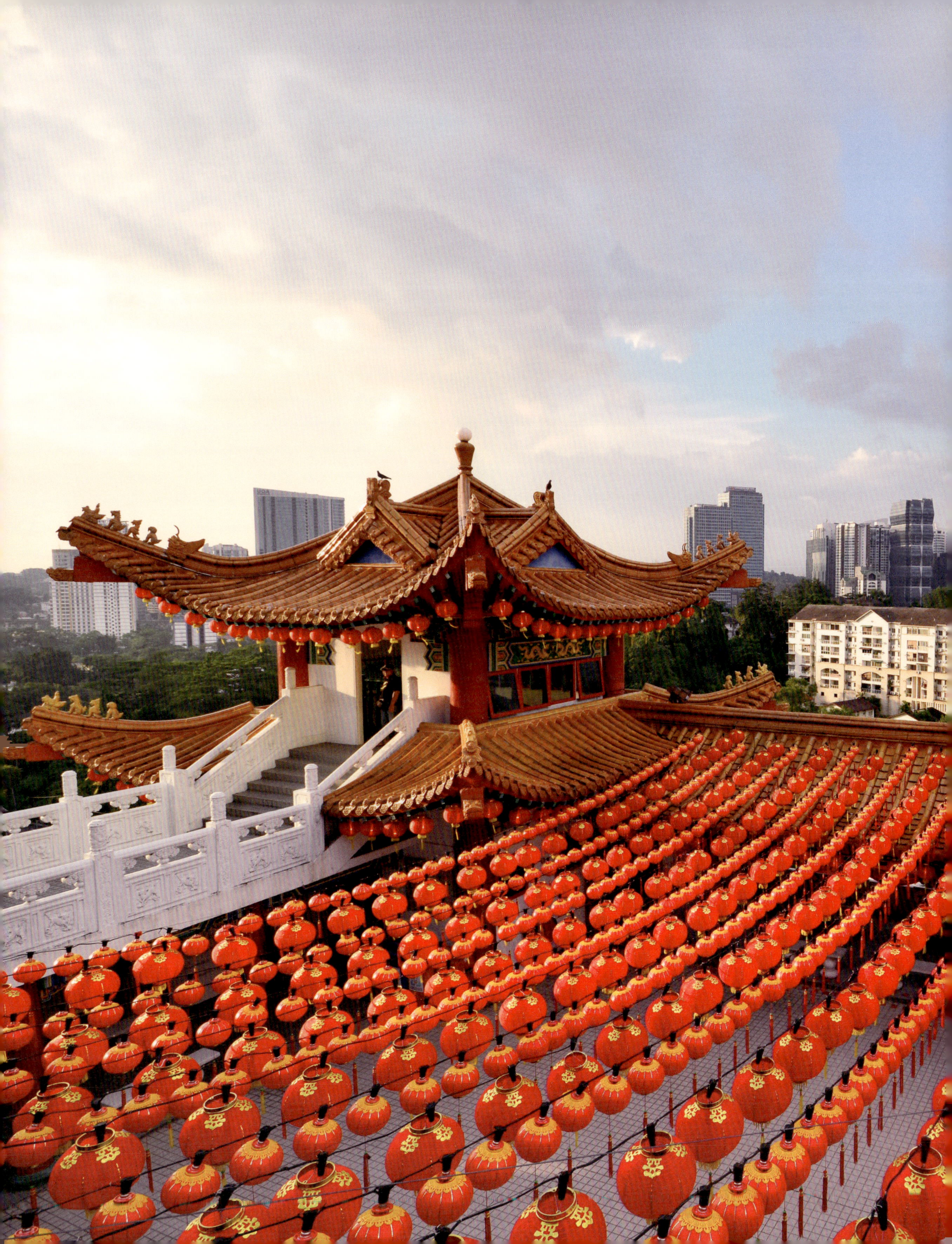

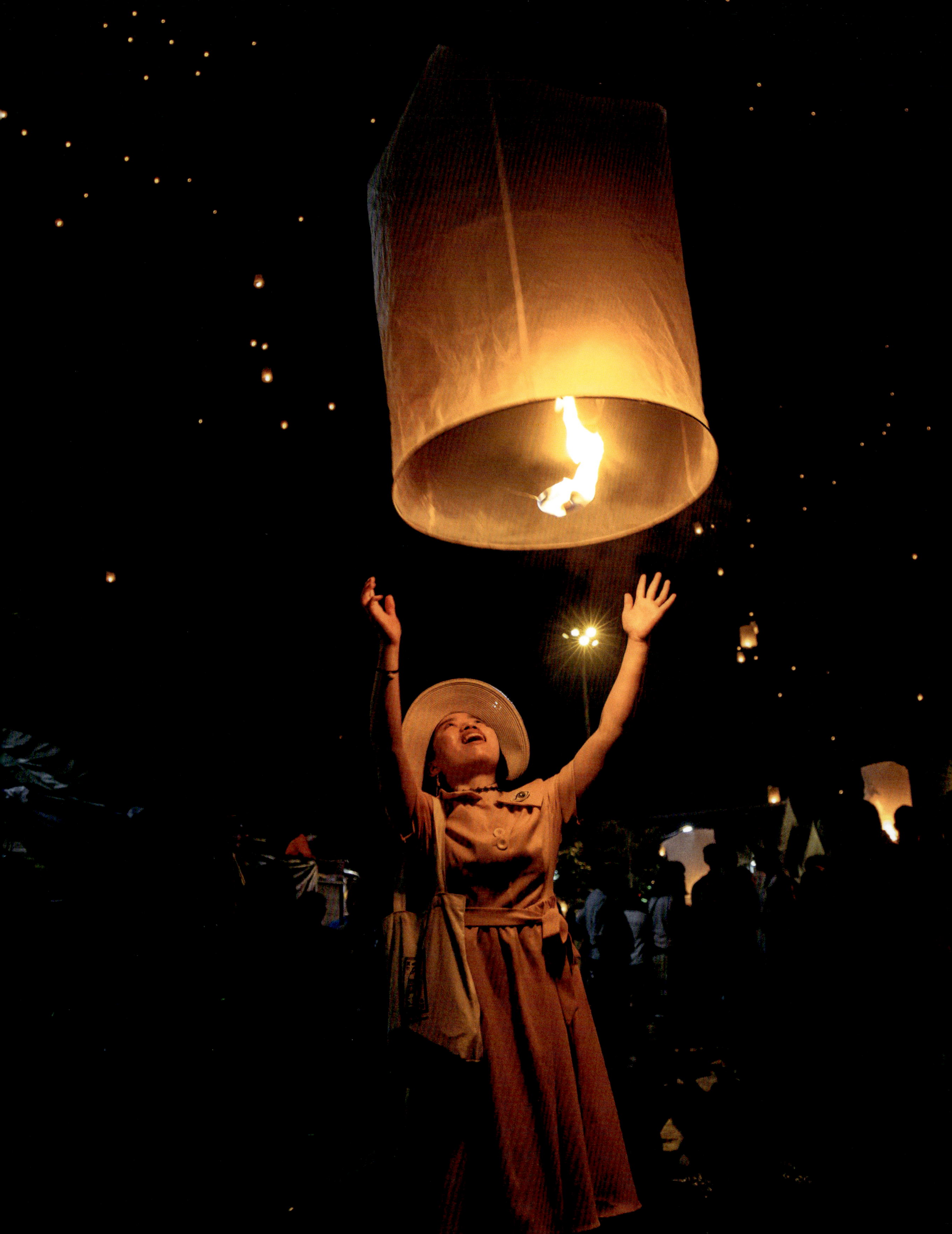

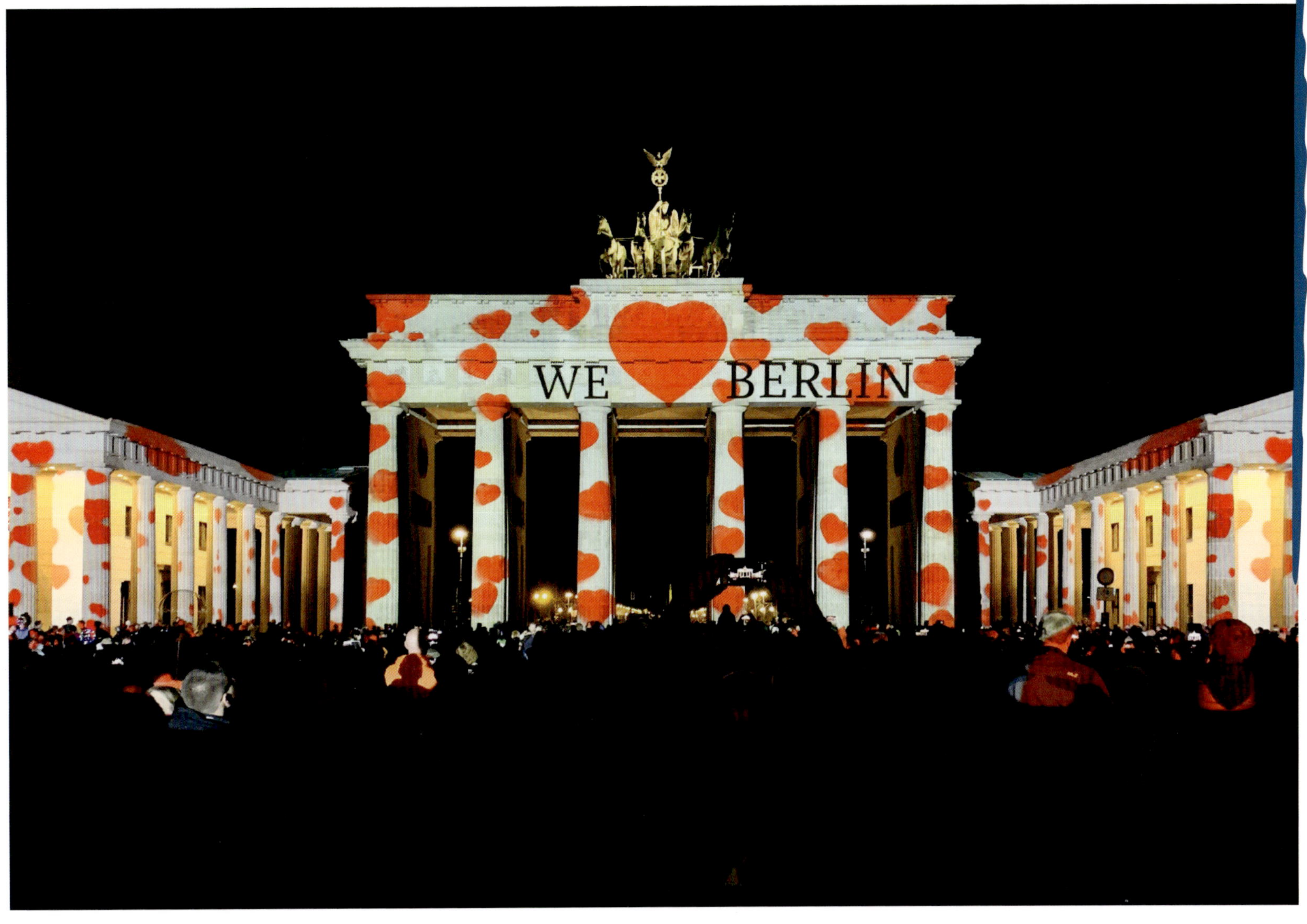

The lanterns launched into the sky at Yi Peng Festival in Thailand are called *khom loi* and are made from rice paper; a small candle or fuel cell of flammable material is attached to its frame. The lanterns are a fire hazard, so their use is increasingly restricted.

Die Laternen, die beim Yi-Peng-Festival in Thailand in den Himmel steigen, werden *khom loi* genannt und bestehen aus Reispapier; an ihrem Rahmen ist mittig eine kleine Kerze oder mit brennbarer Flüssigkeit getränkter Stoff befestigt. Von den Laternen geht erhebliche Brandgefahr aus, weshalb ihre Verwendung zunehmend eingeschränkt ist.

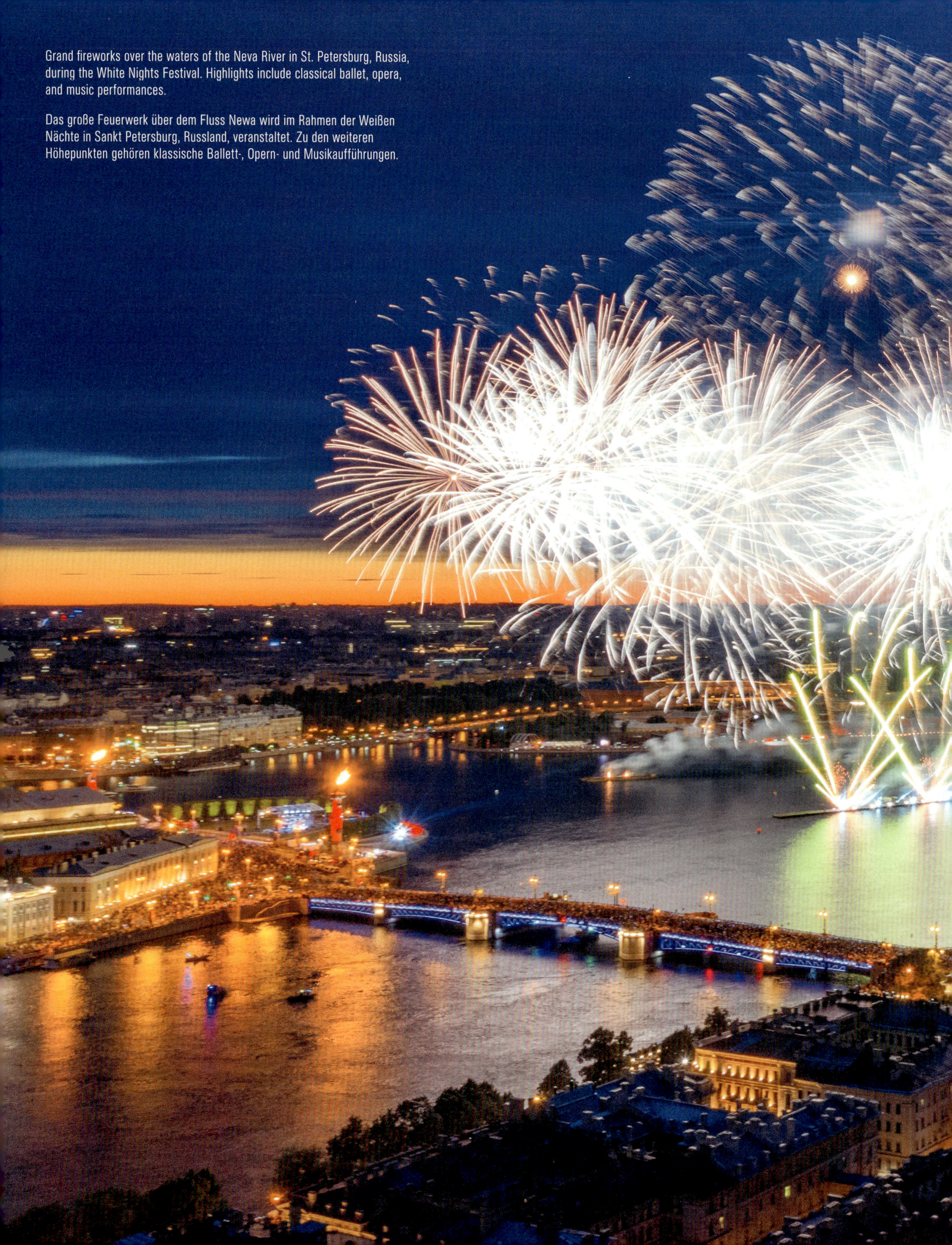

Grand fireworks over the waters of the Neva River in St. Petersburg, Russia, during the White Nights Festival. Highlights include classical ballet, opera, and music performances.

Das große Feuerwerk über dem Fluss Newa wird im Rahmen der Weißen Nächte in Sankt Petersburg, Russland, veranstaltet. Zu den weiteren Höhepunkten gehören klassische Ballett-, Opern- und Musikaufführungen.

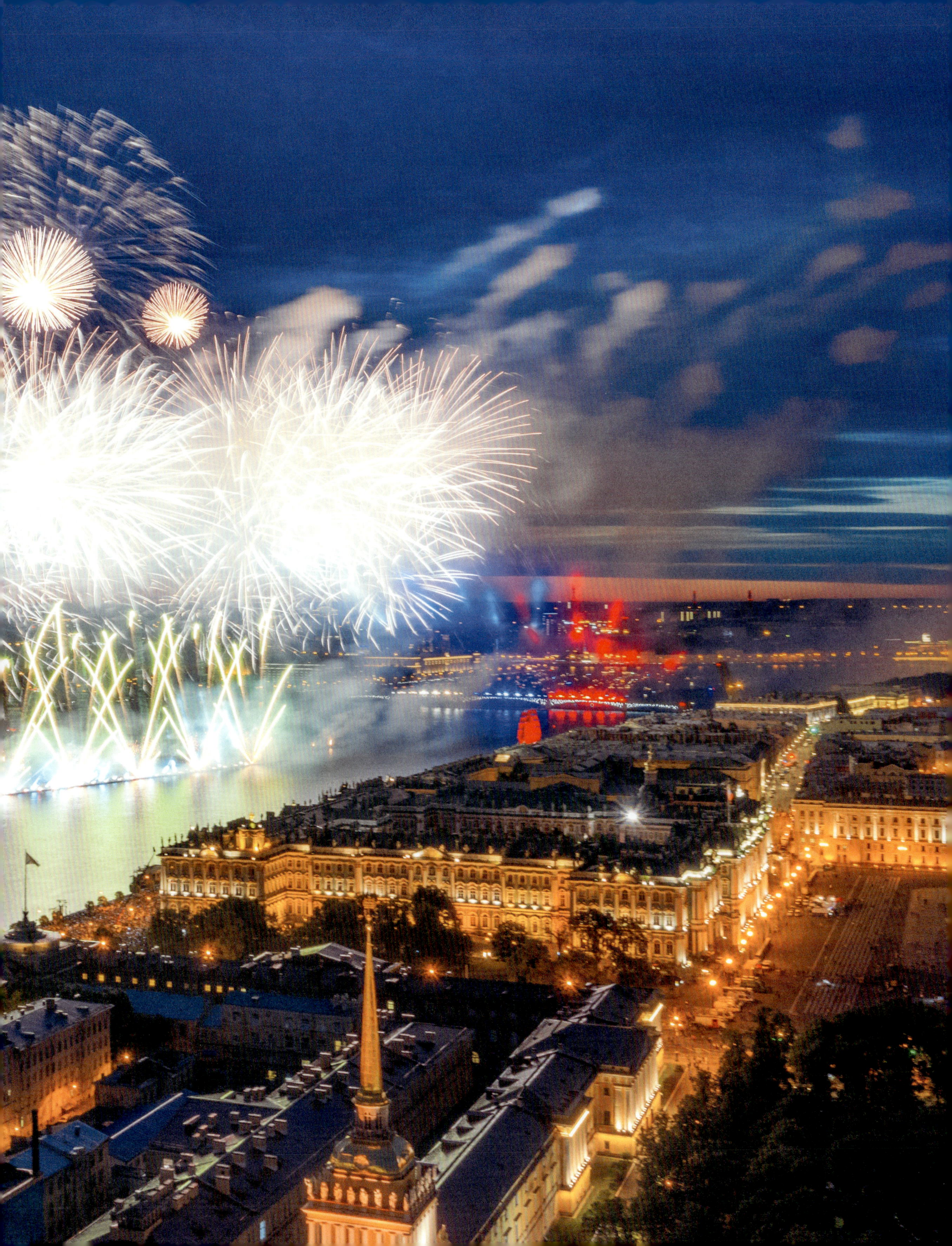

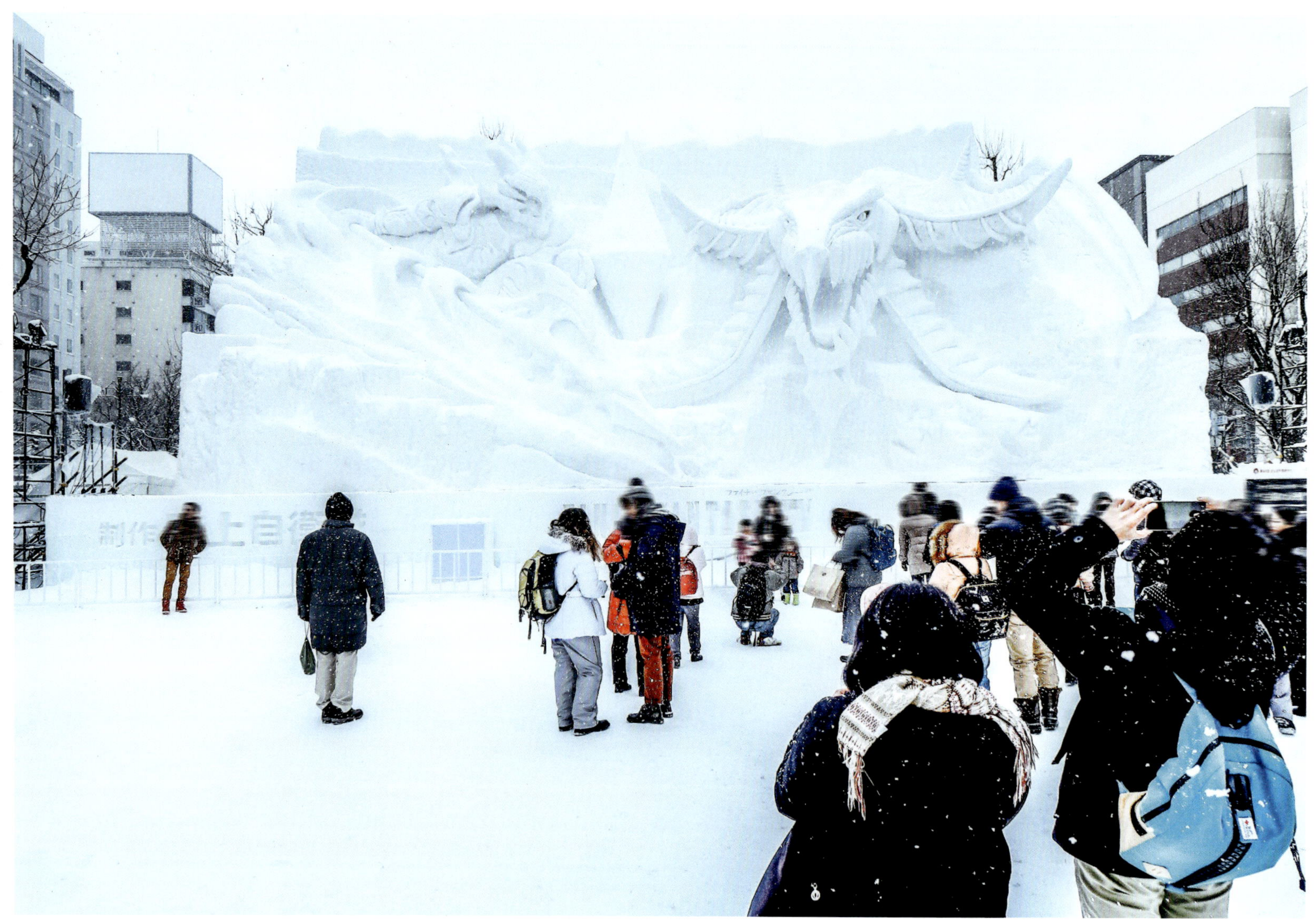

The prerequisites could not be more different:
art presented at 25.2°F (−3.8°C) at the Sapporo
Snow Festival in Japan, and at over 100°F (40°C)
at Burning Man, USA.

Die Voraussetzungen könnten unterschiedlicher
nicht sein: Kunst bei −3,8°C beim Sapporo Snow
Festival in Japan und bei über 40°C beim Burning
Man in den USA.

Good to know
WISSENSWERTES

Visit the Sapporo Snow Festival at night as well as during the day. The sculptures are illuminated at dusk, to give a whole new experience to the event. The nighttime view over the festival from the observatory at the Sapporo TV Tower is magical!

Besuchen Sie das Sapporo Snow Festival sowohl tagsüber als auch nachts. Die Skulpturen werden in der Abenddämmerung beleuchtet, und sehen so nochmal ganz anders aus. Der nächtliche Blick von der Aussichtsplattform des Fernsehturmes von Sapporo ist ebenfalls magisch!

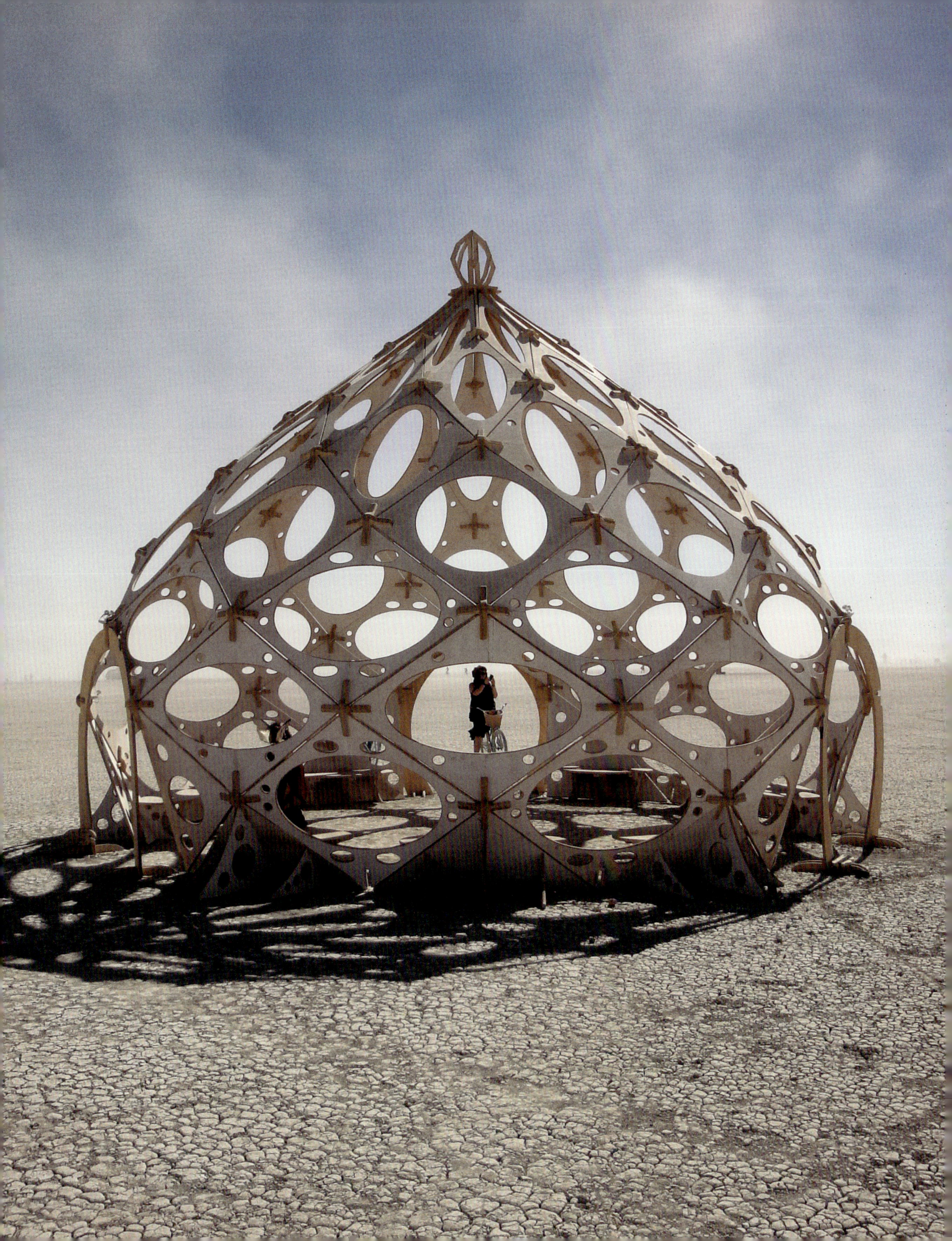

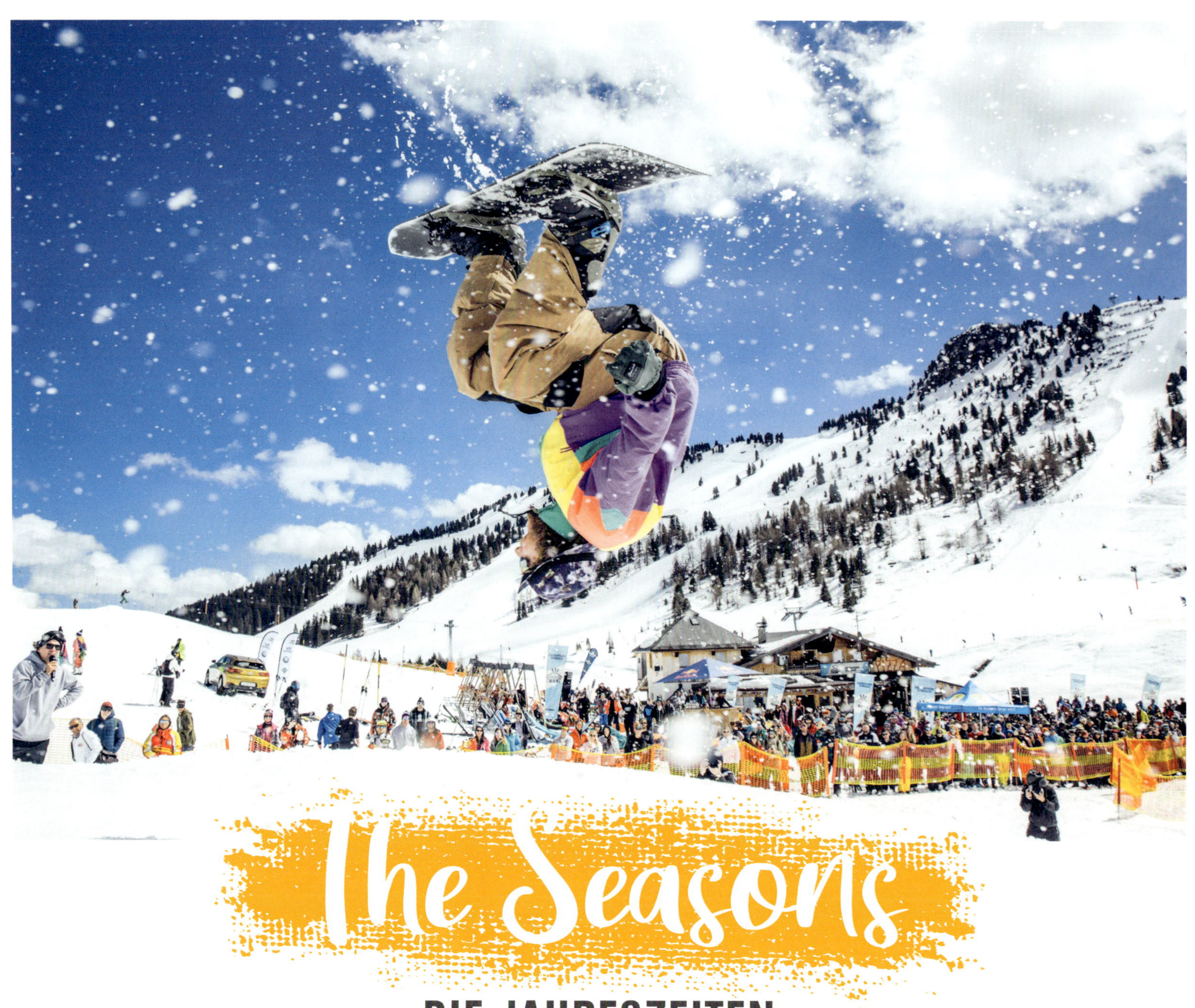

The Seasons

DIE JAHRESZEITEN

This page: Professional snowboarding competition at Snowbombing, Mayrhofen, Austria.
Opposite, top: People climb the Pyramid of the Sun in Mexico during the spring equinox to receive its energizing properties.

Diese Seite: Snowboarding-Wettbewerb beim Snowbombing-Festival in Mayrhofen, Österreich
Rechte Seite, oben: Während der Frühjahrs-Tagundnachtgleiche die Sonnenpyramide in Mexiko zu besteigen, soll einen Energieschub verleihen.

Opposite, bottom: Crowds enjoy the beginnings of spring by sitting under cherry blossoms and partaking in seasonal nighttime *hanami* festivals in Maruyama Park, Japan.

Rechte Seite, unten: Im japanischen Maruyama-Park genießen Menschen beim nächtlichen *Hanami*-Fest den Frühlingsanfang unter blühenden Kirschbäumen.

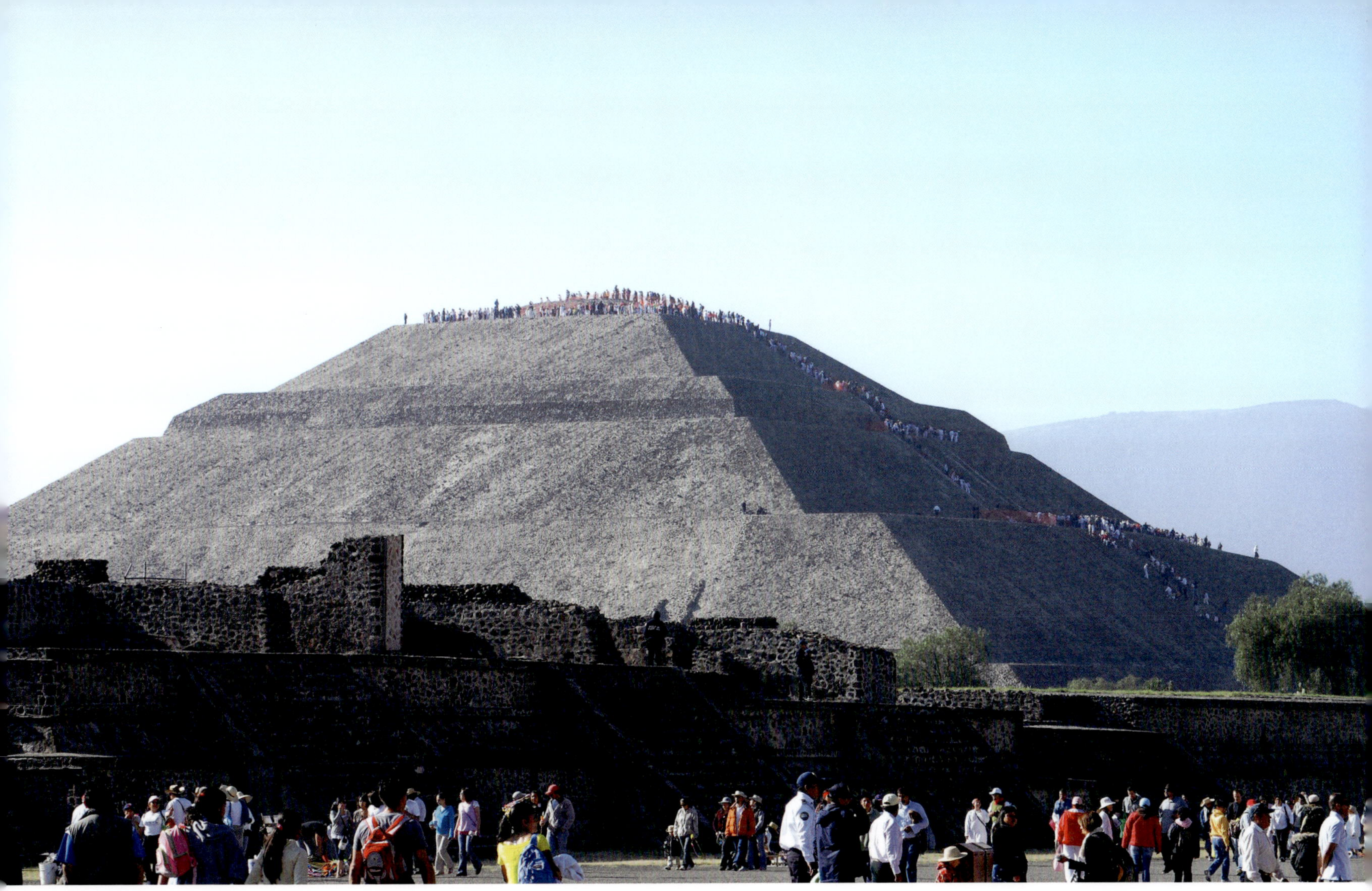

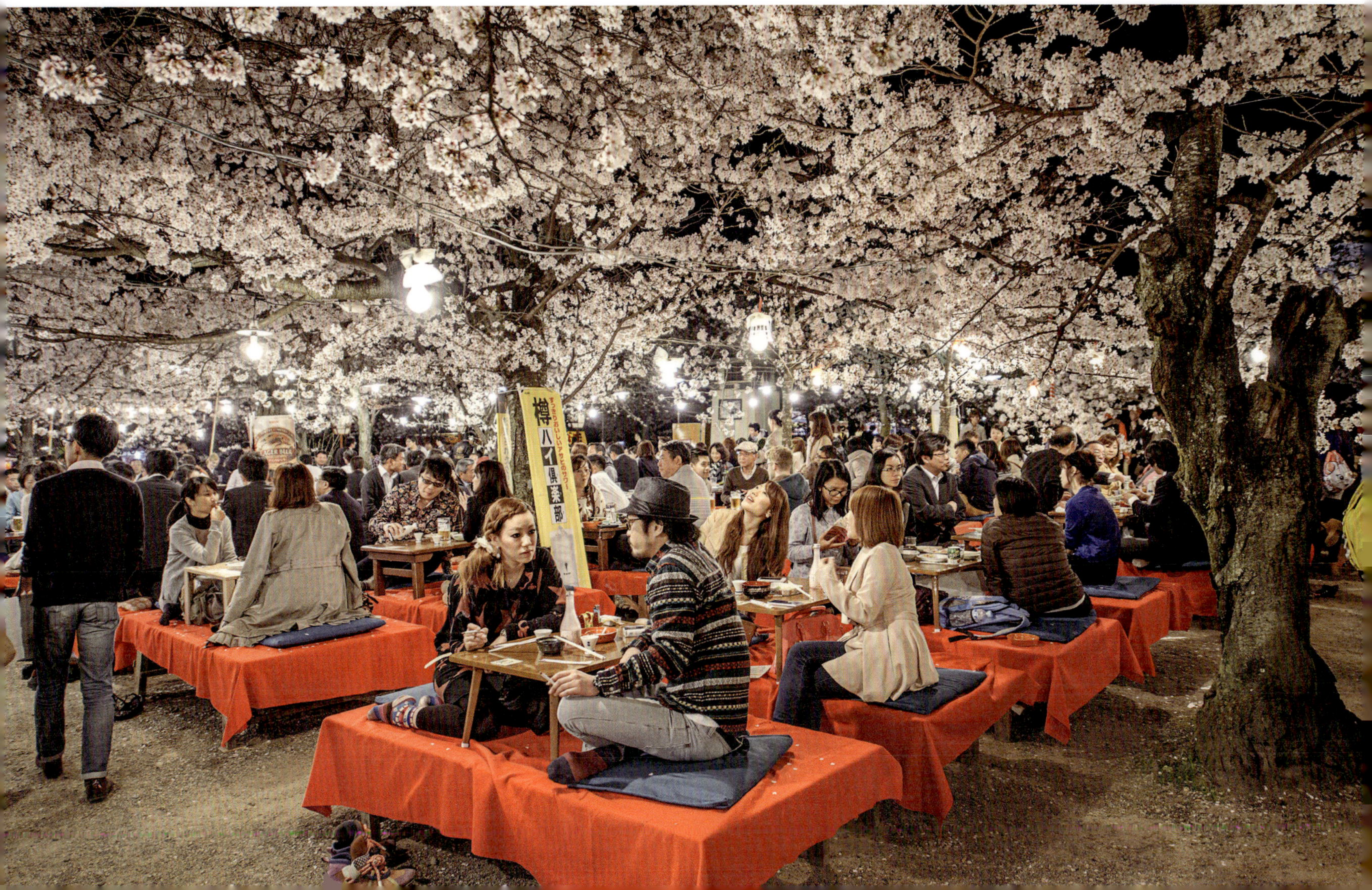

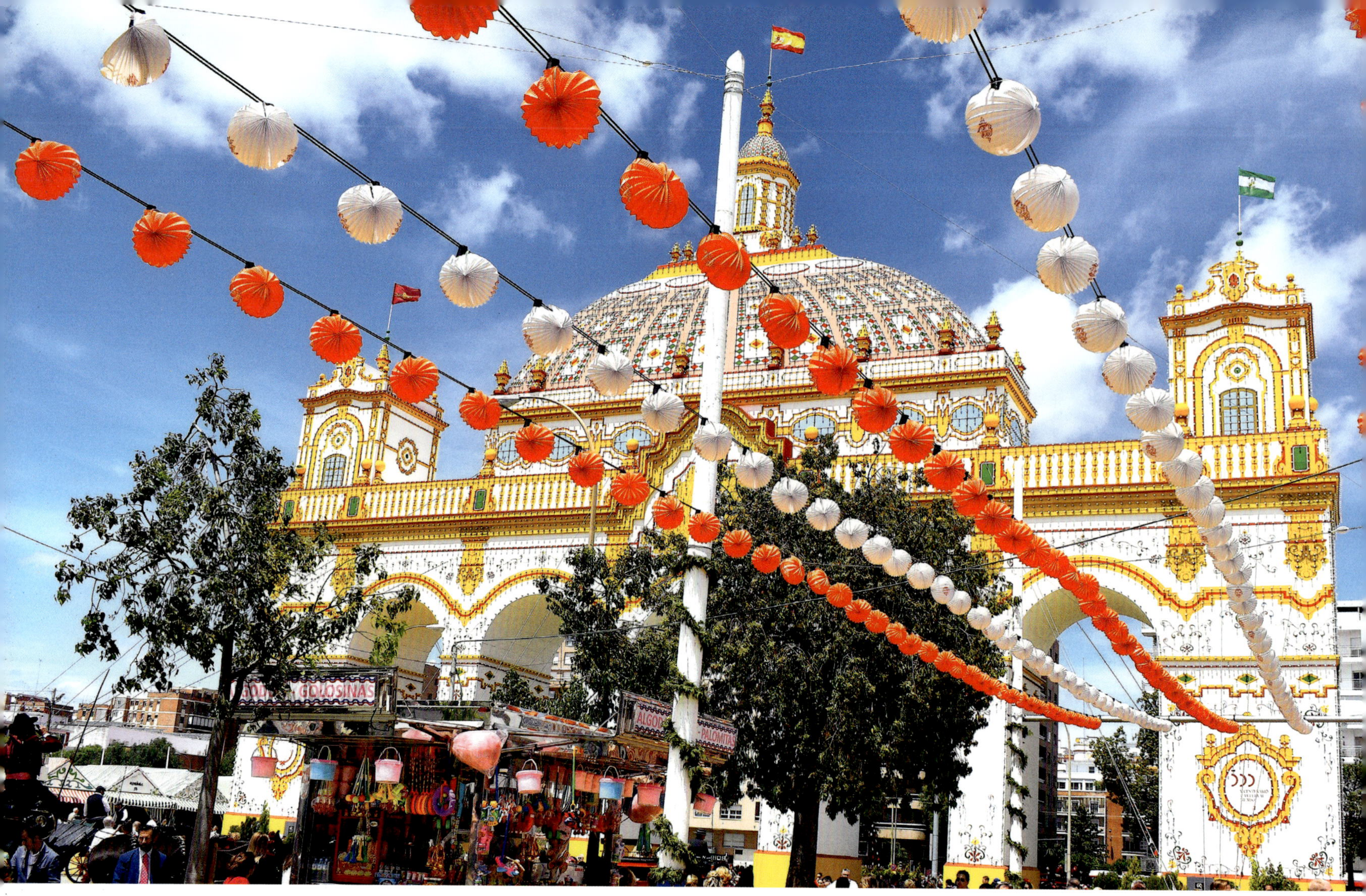

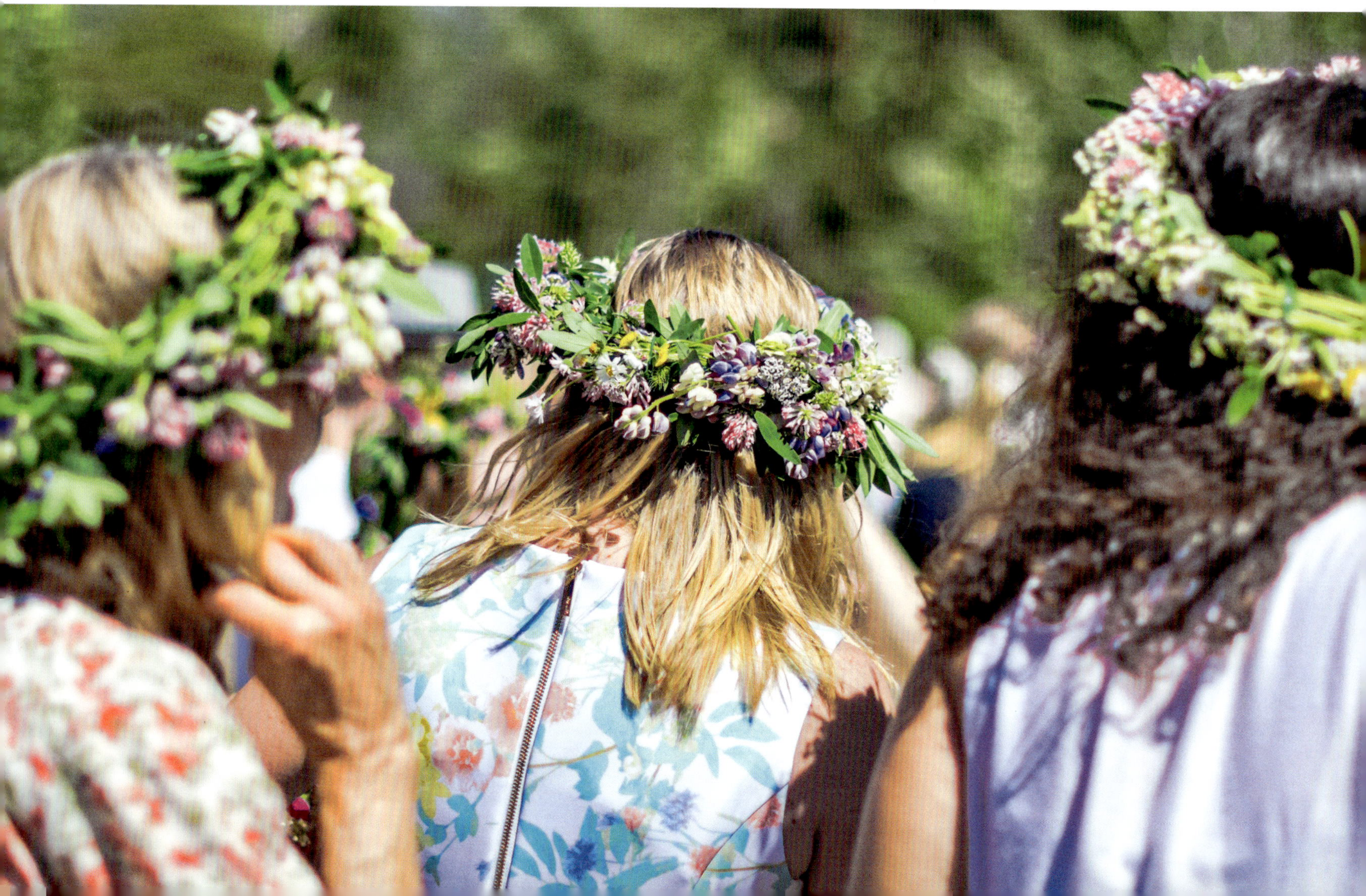

*O*ur reliance on nature is coming back to the forefront with the current emphasis on climate change. In the past, day to day life was dictated by the seasons—reaping the fruits of the last season, dealing with the current one, and preparing for the next. With help from overseas trade and updated growing methods, we're no longer as dependent as we were on local agriculture, but old habits die hard and the seasons are part of our being. They connect us to our culture and landscape.

Spring welcomes festivals of abundance. The Seville Fair, or Feria de Abril, in Spain is one of the most lively. Beginning in 1847 as a cattle trading fair, the festival is now a huge celebration of the harvest that spring brings. Expect fairground lights by night, local women in flamenco dresses, huge fireworks displays over the Guadalquivir River, and carriage parades. There are over 1,000 vibrant tent booths of people having fun—some open to visitors, and others privately organized months in advance (opposite, top).

As the long nights draw out, the increased daylight is observed around the world. The Summer Solstice in the UK is one of the most deep-rooted celebrations of this, with druids gathering at Stonehenge to see the sun shine through the heart of the stones. This incredible World Heritage Site dates back to 2,500 BCE!

Autumn brings all the celebrations of the harvest around the world. The Great Jack O'Lantern Blaze in the United States is one of the biggest celebrations of this time, with over 7,000 jack-o'-lanterns hand-carved along Croton-on-Hudson in New York. There are immersive displays and synchronized lighting to a spooky soundtrack, too.

And then winter is here! The Krampusnacht Festival in Austria and other countries of the Eastern Alps region is one of the most unique winter festivals. According to legend, Krampus is a demon who doles out coal and punishes those on the naughty list. On December 5, the people celebrate this evil man by dressing up as him and competing in the Krampus Run race. With alcohol as liquid fuel, this parade soon turns into a Krampi party, terrifying any child who might be around!

*A*ngesichts der Folgen des Klimawandels wird uns zunehmend bewusster, wie abhängig wir von der Natur sind. Früher wurde der Alltag der Menschen von den Jahreszeiten und deren Bedeutung für die Landwirtschaft bestimmt – im ewigen Rhythmus von Säen und Ernten. Dank des internationalen Handels und moderner Anbaumethoden sind wir heute nicht mehr so abhängig von lokaler Landwirtschaft, doch die Jahreszeiten sind für uns noch immer wichtige Eckpfeiler. Sie verbinden uns mit unserer Kultur und der uns umgebenden Natur.

Vor allem der Anbruch des Frühlings wird von zahlreichen Festen begrüßt. Die Feria de Abril (Aprilmesse) im spanischen Sevilla, die 1847 als Viehmarkt ins Leben gerufen wurde, ist eine der lebendigsten mit bunt beleuchteten nächtlichen Jahrmärkten, Frauen in Flamenco-Kleidern, spektakulären Feuerwerken über dem Rio Guadalquivir und Kutschenparaden. In über 1 000 Zelten – von denen manche für alle zugänglich sind und andere schon Monate im Voraus privat gebucht wurden – vergnügen sich Einheimische und auswärtige Besucher (linke Seite, oben).

Auch die zunehmend längeren Tage im Sommer werden gerne gefeiert. Das Fest der Sommersonnenwende in Großbritannien ist eines der traditionsreichsten. In Stonehenge versammeln sich dazu Druiden, um zu beobachten, wie die Sonnenstrahlen auf das Herz der Steinformation treffen. Dieses beeindruckende UNESCO-Weltkulturerbe ist über 4 500 Jahre alt.

Im Herbst wird weltweit das Einfahren der Ernte zelebriert. Die Great Jack O'Lantern Blaze in den USA ist eines der größten Feste in dieser Zeit: Über 7 000 handgeschnitzte Kürbislaternen erleuchten Croton-on-Hudson im Bundesstaat New York. Dazu gibt es Dekorationen, die einen in den Bann ziehen und eine Lightshow mit gruseligem Soundtrack.

Und dann ist der Winter da! Die Krampusnacht in Österreich und anderen Ländern des Ostalpenraumes ist eines der originellsten Winterfeste. Der Legende nach ist der Krampus ein Dämon, der Kohle verteilt und unartige Kinder bestraft. Am 5. Dezember feiern die Teilnehmer den Krampus, indem sie sich als Schreckgestalt verkleiden und beim sogenannten Krampuslauf reichlich Rutenschläge an Umstehende austeilen. Ein schaurig-schöner Spaß.

Established in 1999, Snowboming is the pioneering mountain music festival. Taking place each spring in one of the finest ski resorts in Europe—Mayrhofen, Austria—and showcasing 100+ world-class artists in the most unique venues imaginable; think enchanted forest parties, mountain top raves, Austria's wildest open-air street party, pop-up butcher's shop parties and so much more.

Snowbombing fand 1999 erstmalig statt und ist damit der Pionier unter den Musikfestivals in den Bergen. Jedes Frühjahr treten über 100 Weltklasse-Künstler in Mayrhofen, Österreich, einem der schönsten Skigebiete Europas, auf. Die Veranstaltungen und Locations sind ebenso einzigartig: Partys im Märchenwald, Raves auf Berggipfeln, Österreichs wildeste Open-Air-Straßenparty, Pop-up-Metzgerei-Partys und so geht es munter weiter.

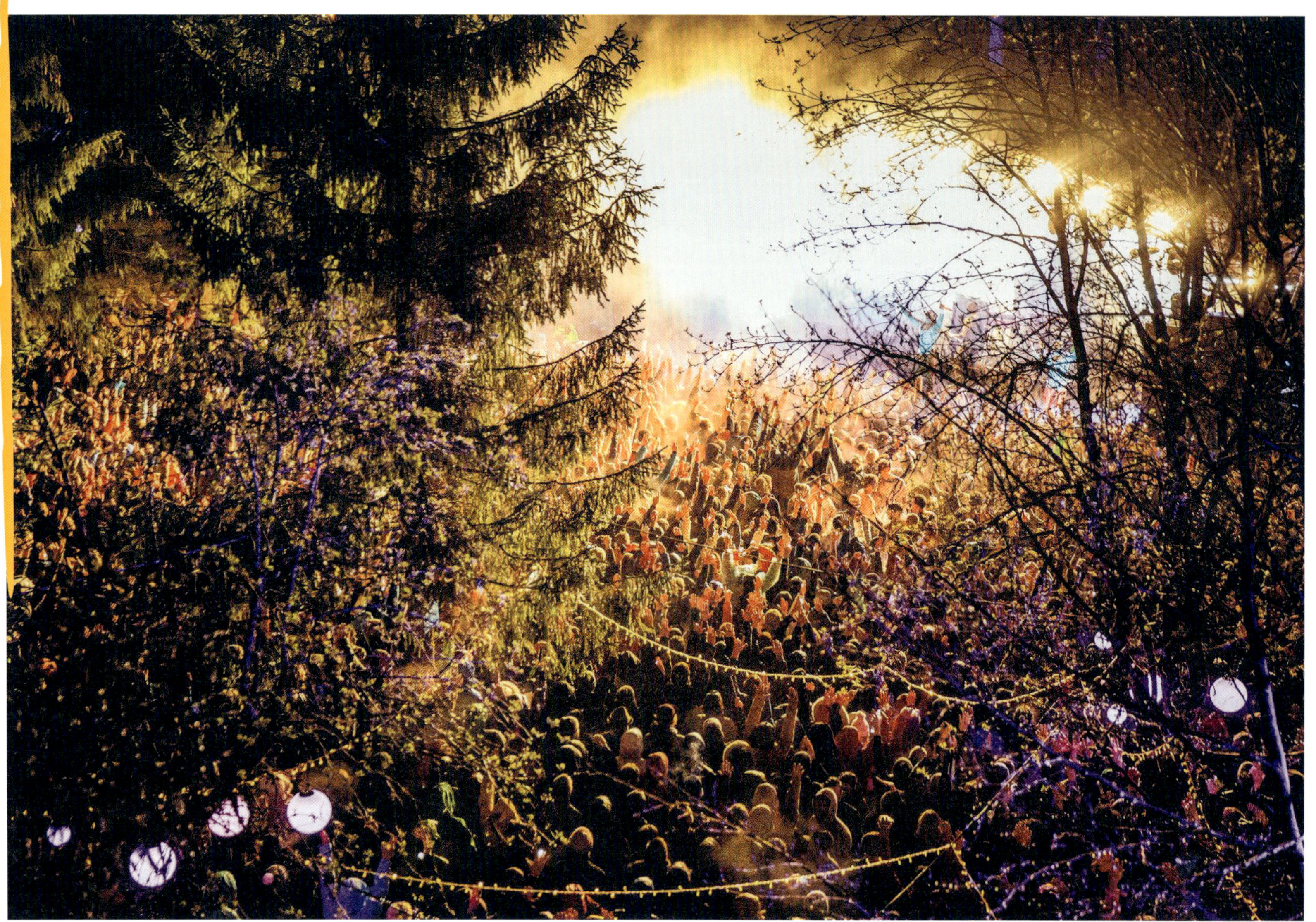

Opposite, top: Snowboxx in Avoriaz, France, is a huge winter music festival with international DJs on open-air stages in the mountains of the French Alps. The epic week of skiing, raving, and repeating includes legendary apres parties, hilarious bottomless brunches, igloo parties, slope-side games, and spa sessions by day and amazing performances by world-class acts by night.
Opposite, bottom: Barehanded fishing is the highlight of the Hwacheon Sancheoneo Ice Festival in South Korea. Attendees get into the icy waters to catch the freshest, tastiest trout to cook later.

Rechte Seite, oben: Snowboxx in Avoriaz, Frankreich, ist ein Wintermusikfestival mit internationalen DJs in den Bergen der französischen Alpen. Legendäre Apres-Partys, ausgelassene Brunches, Iglu-Partys, Pistenspiele und Spa-Sessions am Tag und Auftritte von Weltklasse-Acts auf den Open-Air-Bühnen in der Nacht machen das einwöchige Erlebnis unvergesslich.
Rechte Seite, unten: Mit bloßen Händen Fische fangen ist das Highlight des Hwacheon Sancheoneo Ice Festival in Südkorea. Die Teilnehmer steigen ins eiskalte Wasser, um sich eine Forelle zu schnappen, die sie dann später fangfrisch auftischen.

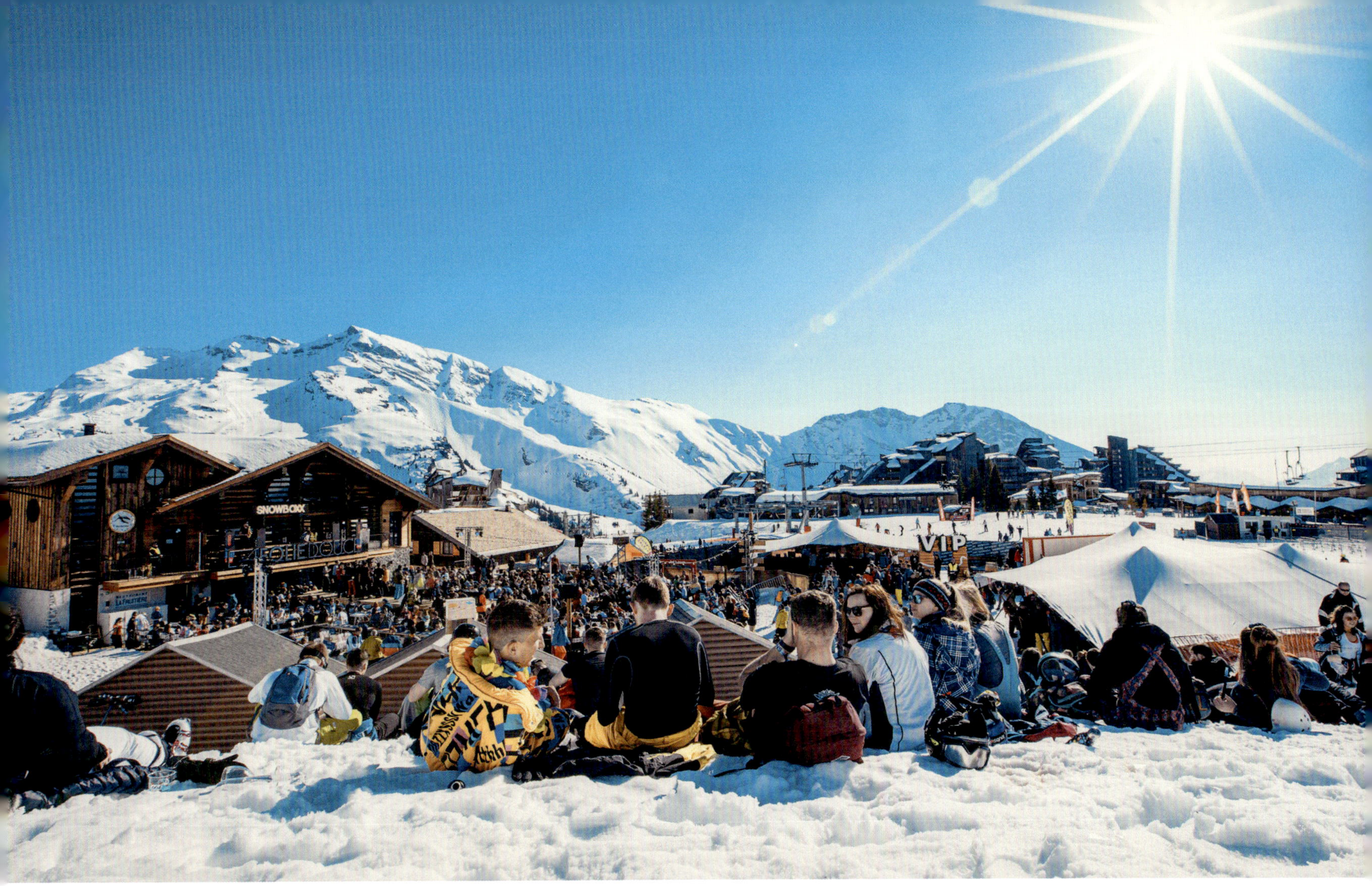
SNOWBOX
VIP

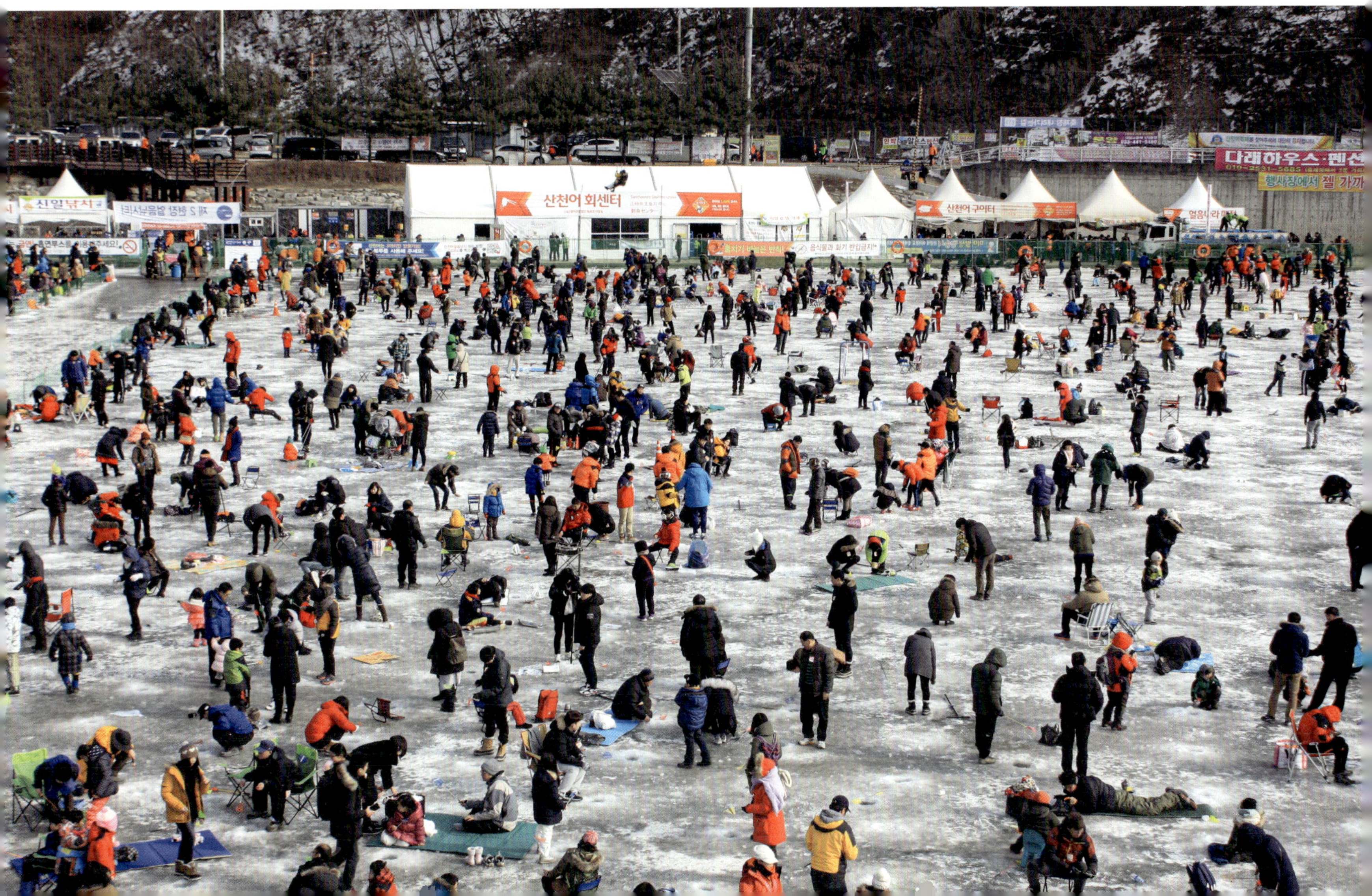
산천어 회센터
다래하우스·펜션

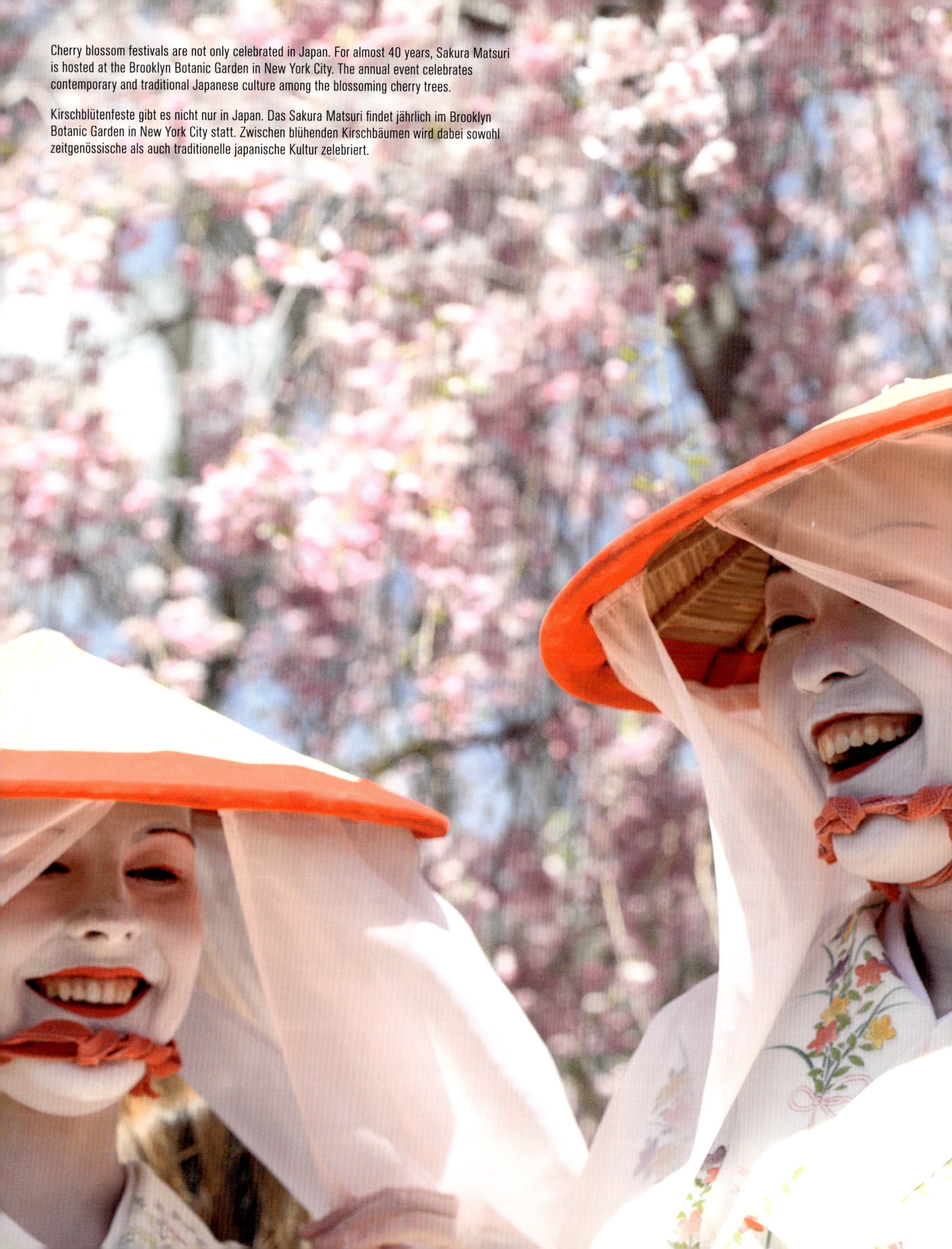

Cherry blossom festivals are not only celebrated in Japan. For almost 40 years, Sakura Matsuri is hosted at the Brooklyn Botanic Garden in New York City. The annual event celebrates contemporary and traditional Japanese culture among the blossoming cherry trees.

Kirschblütenfeste gibt es nicht nur in Japan. Das Sakura Matsuri findet jährlich im Brooklyn Botanic Garden in New York City statt. Zwischen blühenden Kirschbäumen wird dabei sowohl zeitgenössische als auch traditionelle japanische Kultur zelebriert.

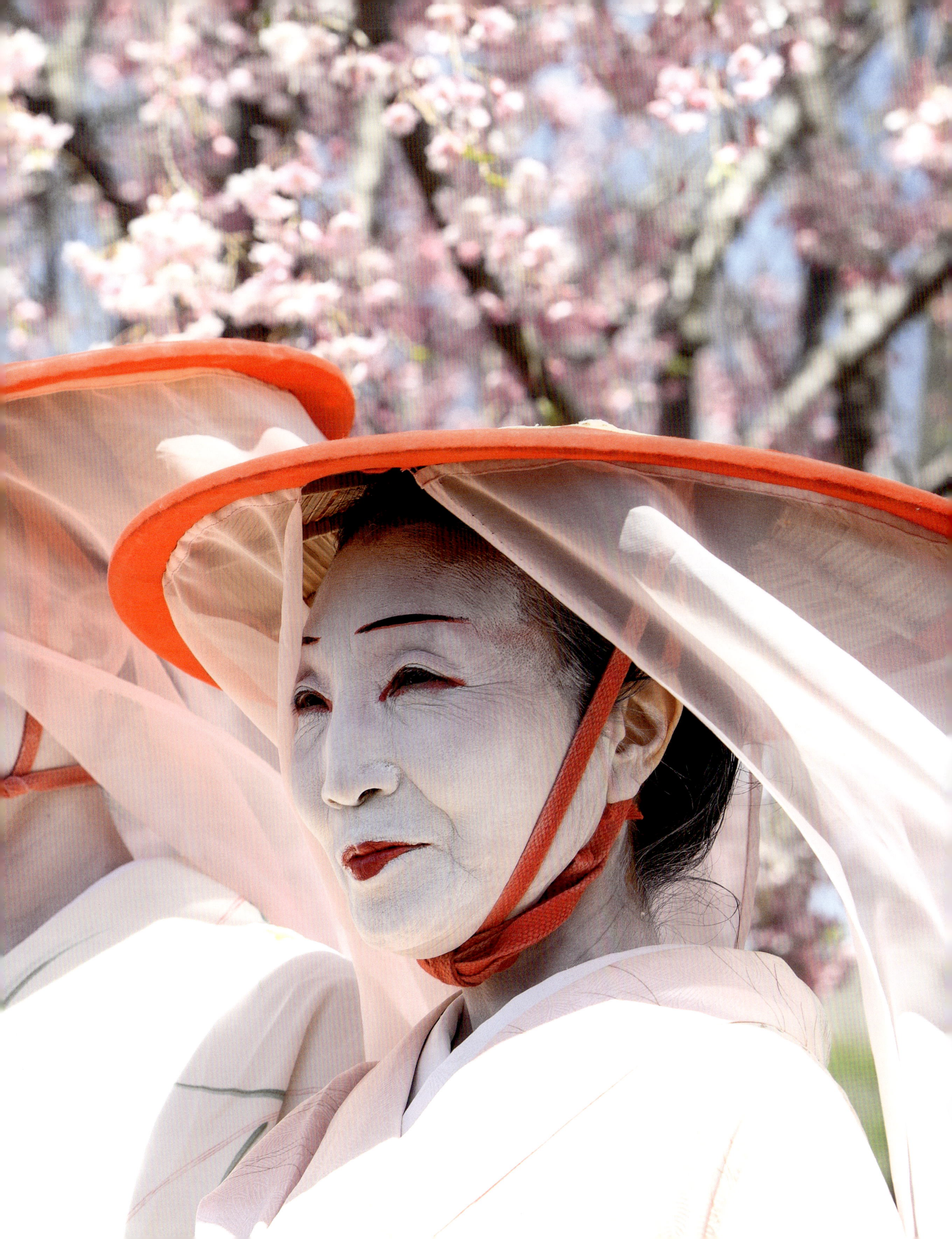

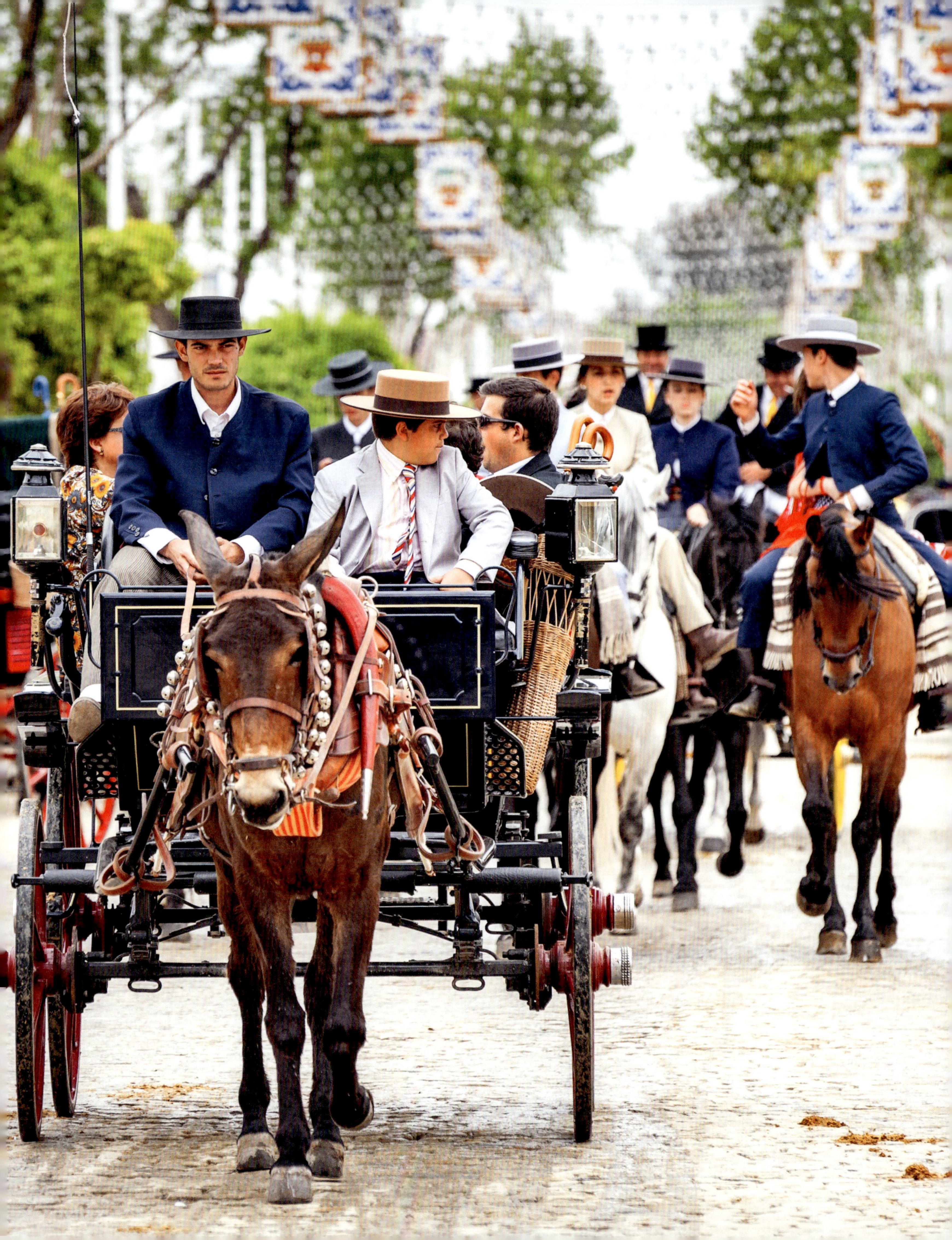

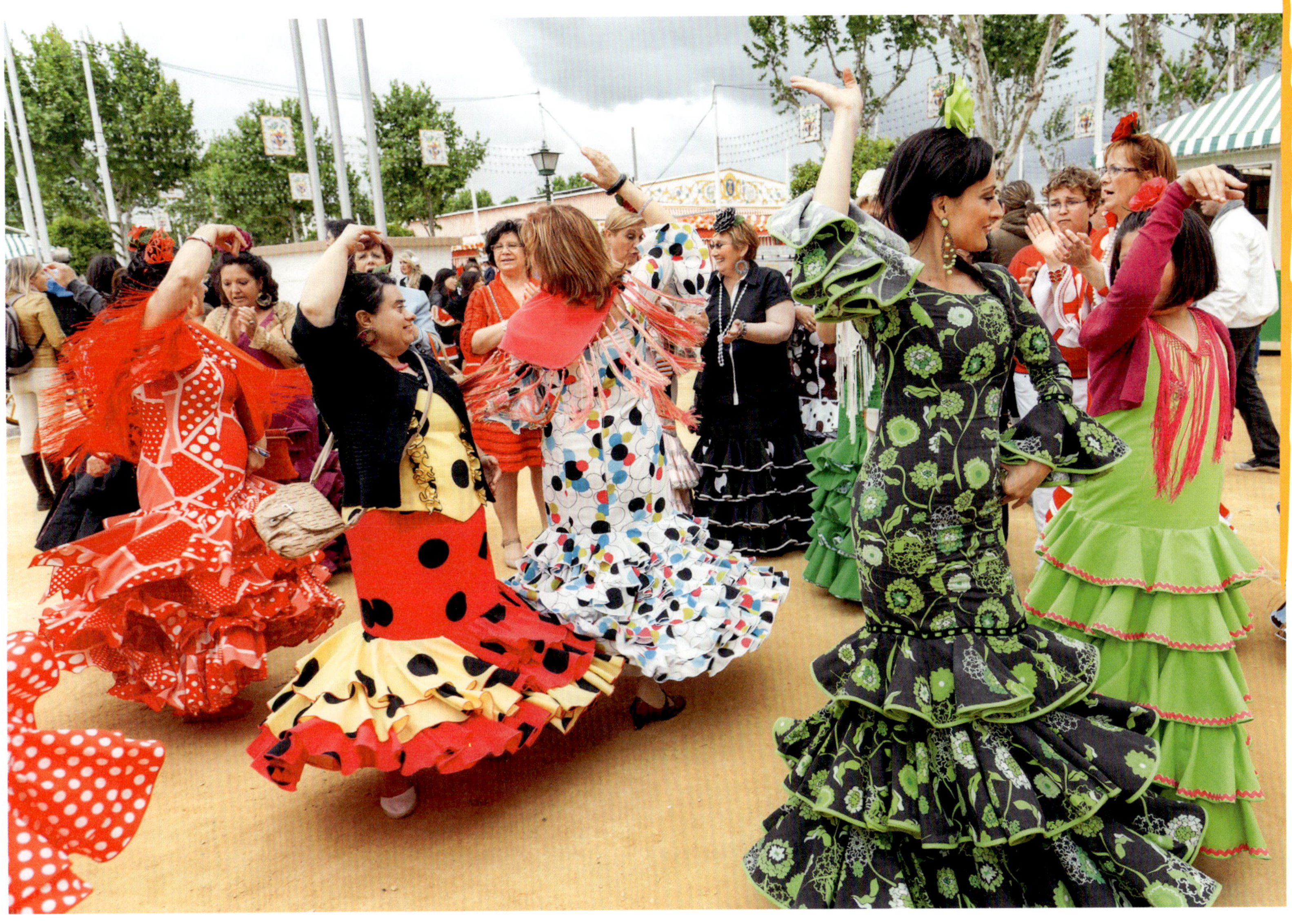

The *portada* (as seen on page 62), is a temporary gate that marks the main entrance to the *feria* grounds. Its decoration also changes every year.

Die *portada* (zu sehen auf Seite 62) ist ein provisorisches Tor zum Festivalgelände. Ihre Dekoration verändert sich auch von Jahr zu Jahr.

Families and friends in traditional Swedish dresses dance
around the maypole for midsummer celebration in
Gunnebo Castle, Gothenburg.

Freunde und Familien in traditioneller schwedischer
Tracht tanzen zum Mittsommerfest in Schloss Gunnebo
bei Göteborg um den Maibaum herum.

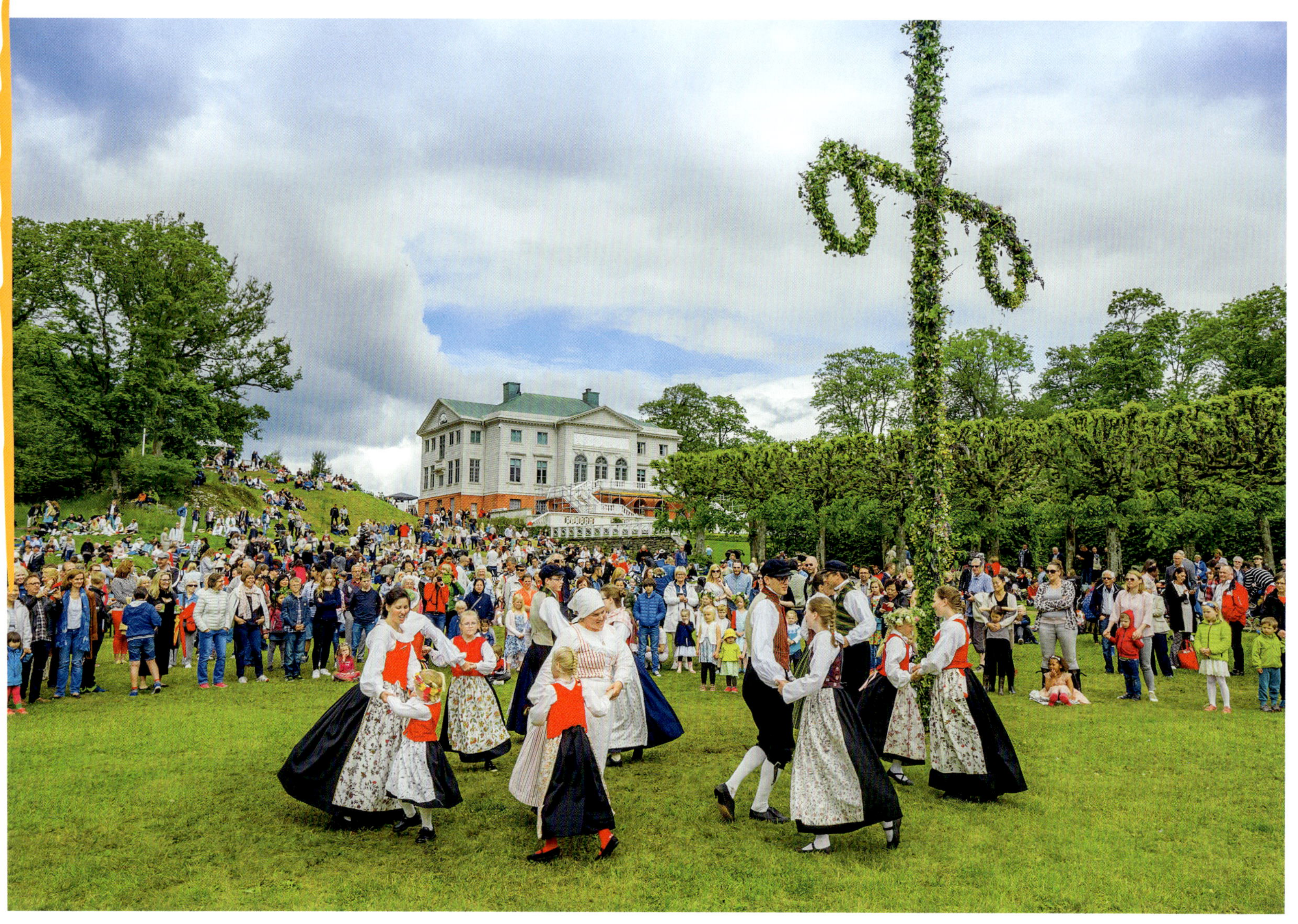

Raising of the traditional *majstång* or *midsommarstång* in
a small Swedish town.

Das Aufstellen der traditionellen *majstång* oder
midsommarstång auf dem Land

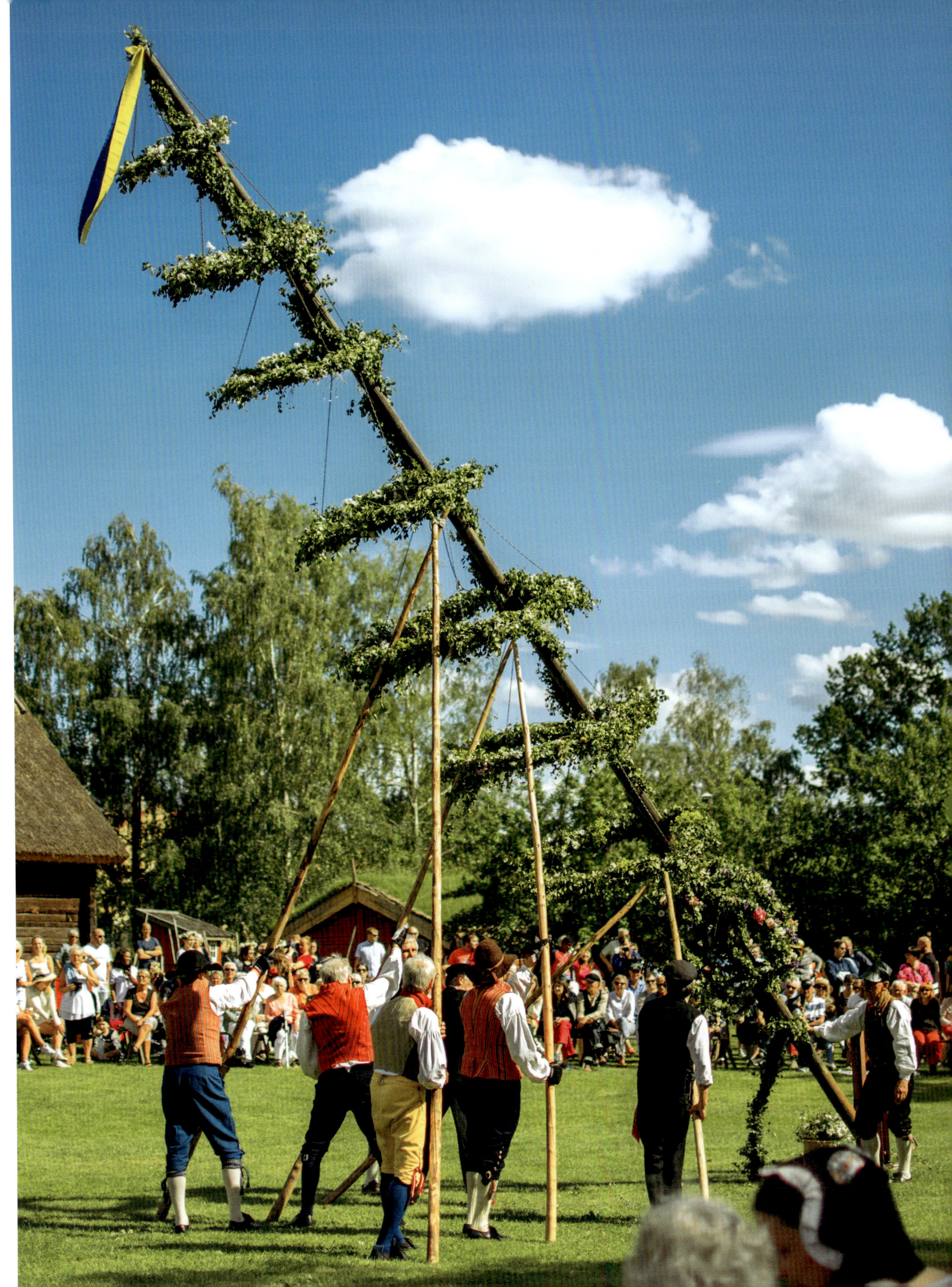

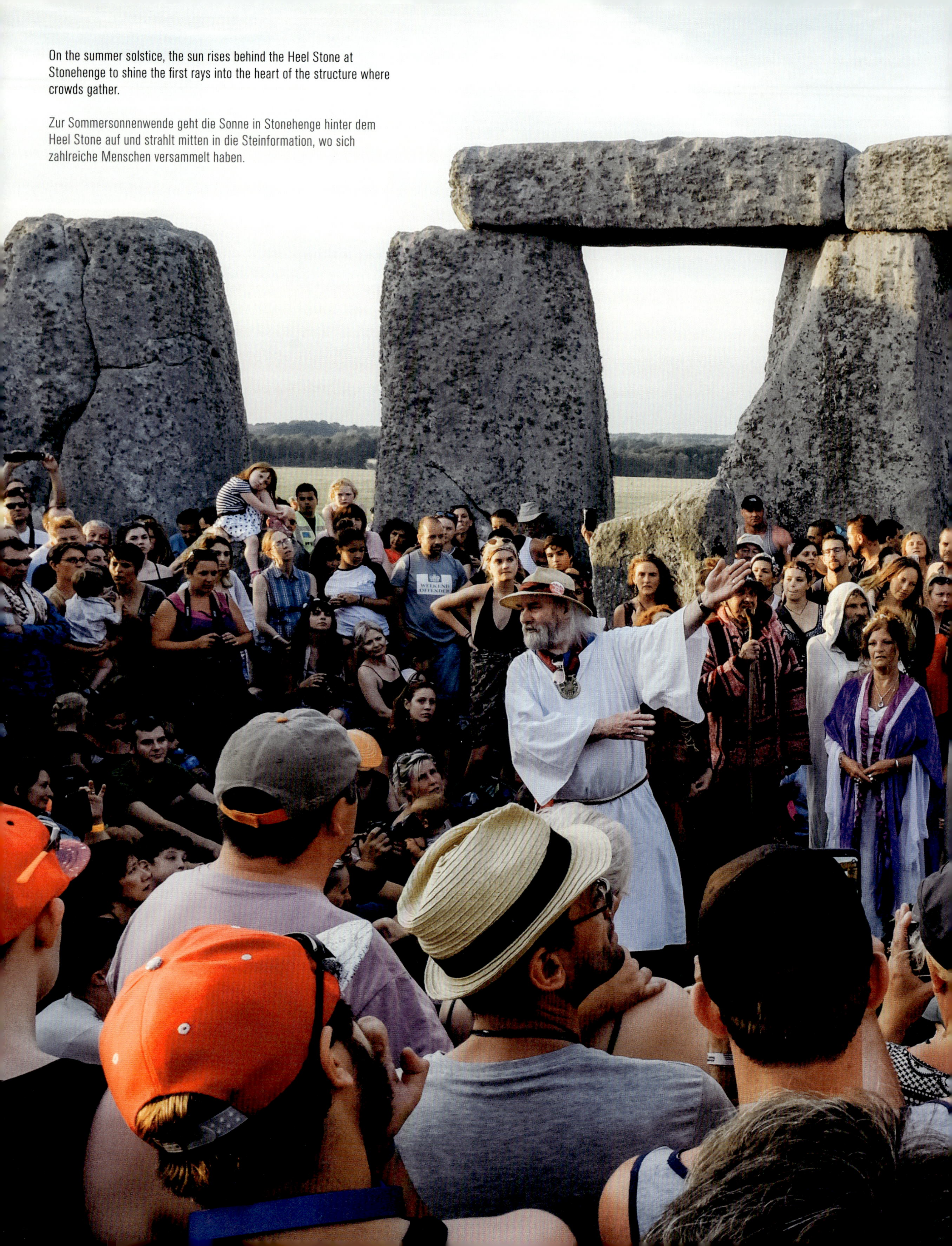

On the summer solstice, the sun rises behind the Heel Stone at Stonehenge to shine the first rays into the heart of the structure where crowds gather.

Zur Sommersonnenwende geht die Sonne in Stonehenge hinter dem Heel Stone auf und strahlt mitten in die Steinformation, wo sich zahlreiche Menschen versammelt haben.

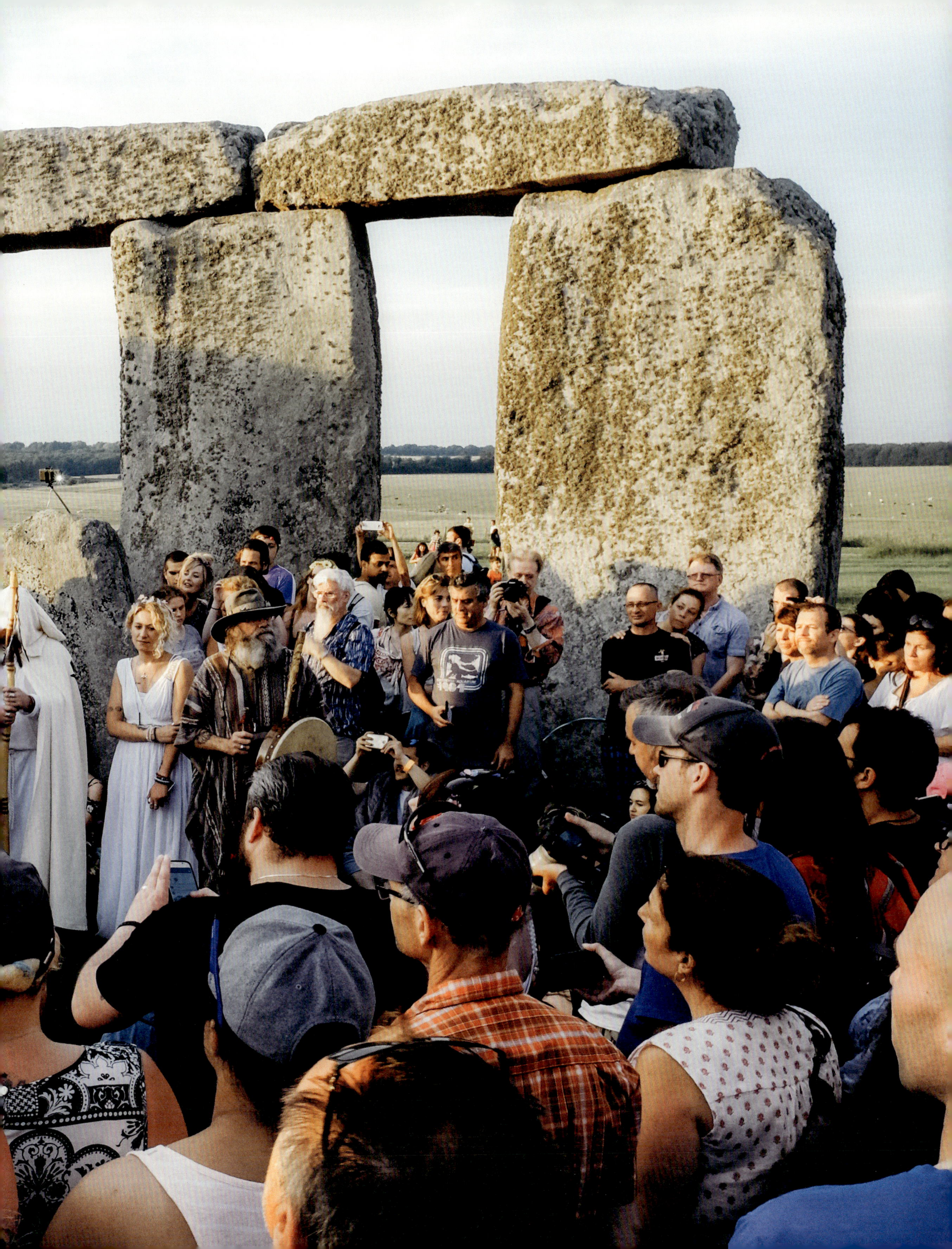

Inti Raymi was initially the celebration of the winter
solstice and the Incan New Year, and was first celebrated
in the 15th century in Peru.

Mit Inti Raymi wurden ursprünglich die Wintersonnen-
wende und das Neujahr der Inka zelebriert. Es entstand
im 15. Jahrhundert in Peru.

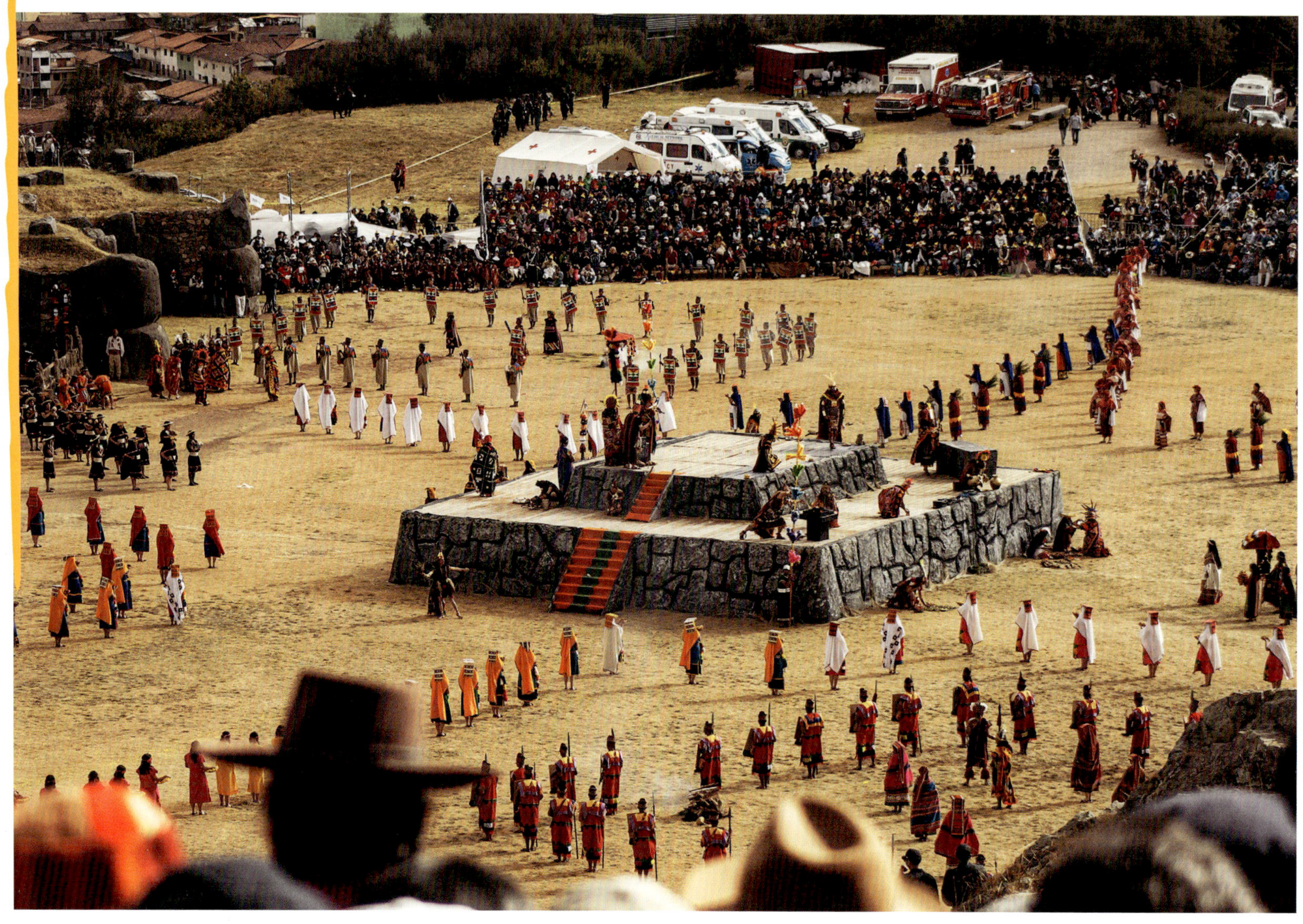

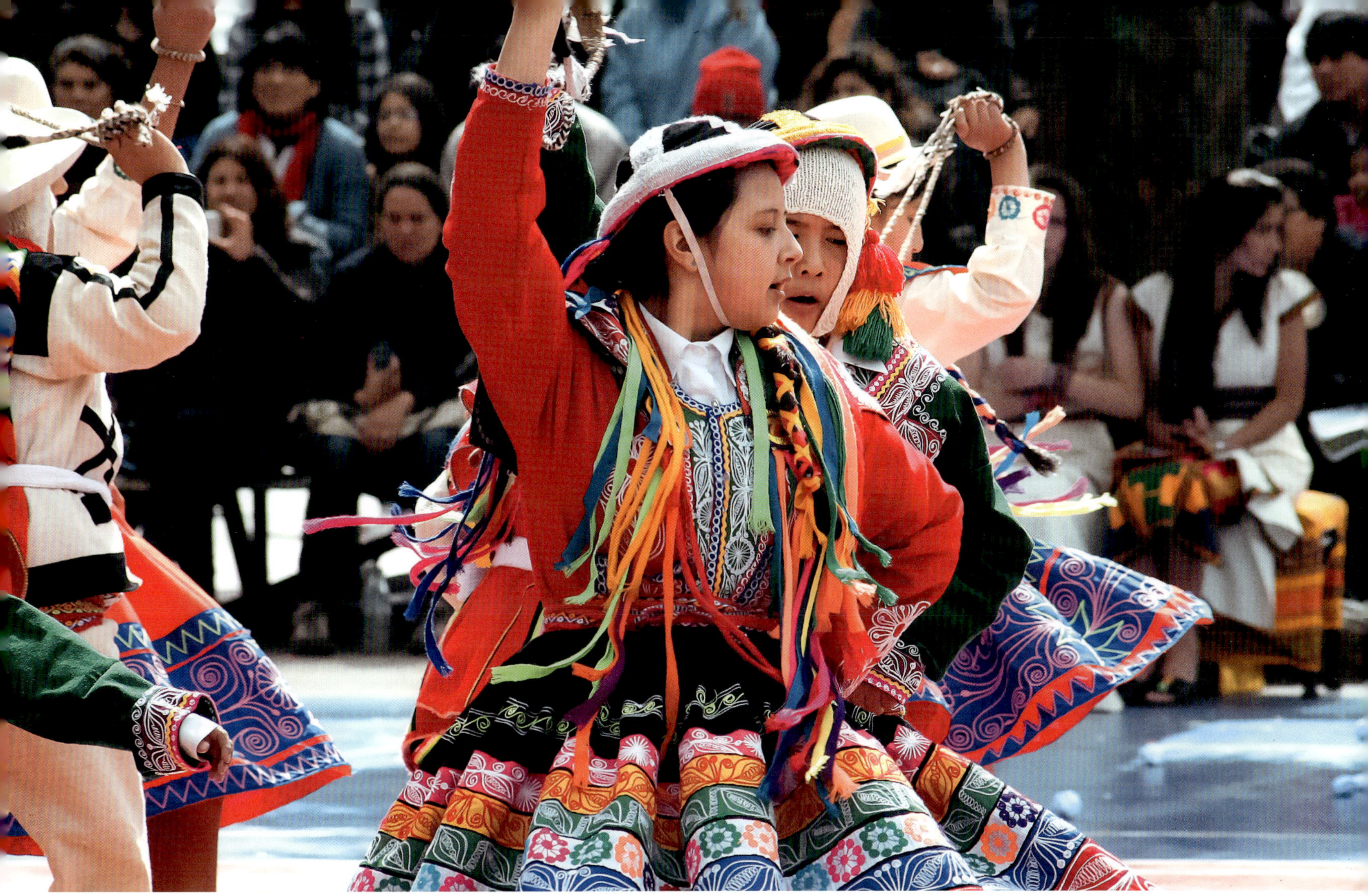

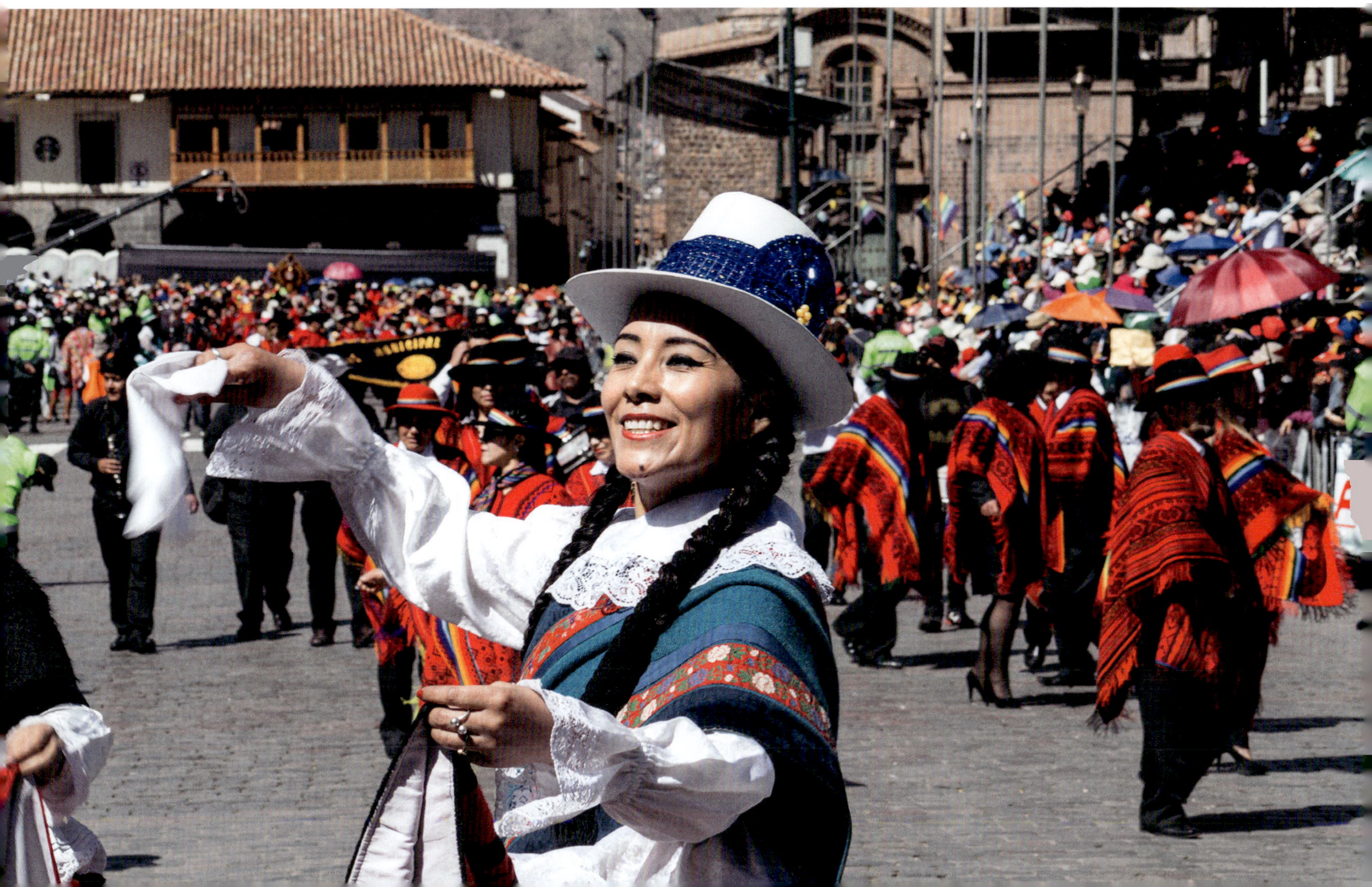

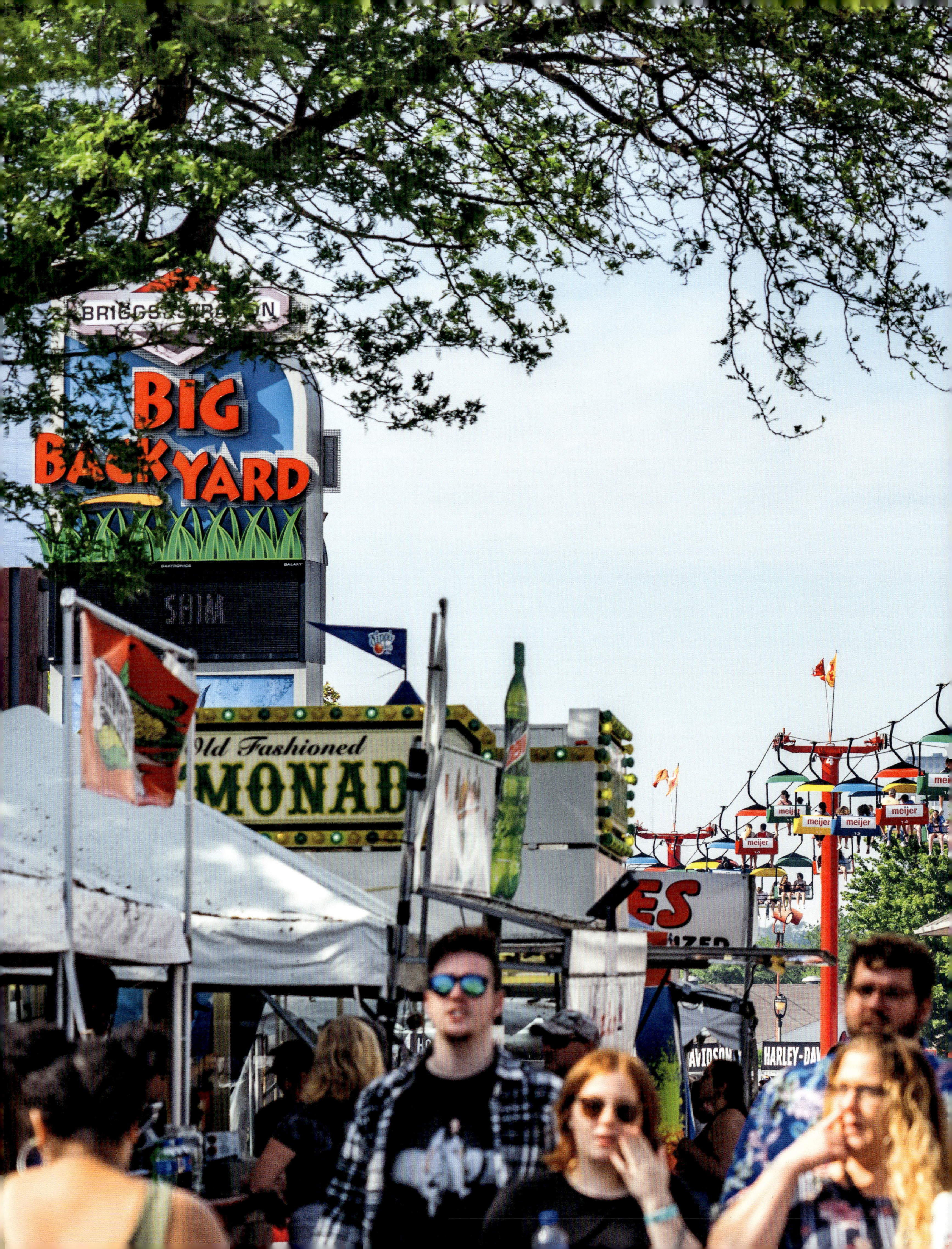

BRIGGS & STRATTON
BIG
BACKYARD
DAKTRONICS
GALAXY
SHIM
Old Fashioned
LEMONADE
meijer
meijer
meijer
meijer
meijer
HARLEY-DAV
HARLEY-DA
ES
IZED

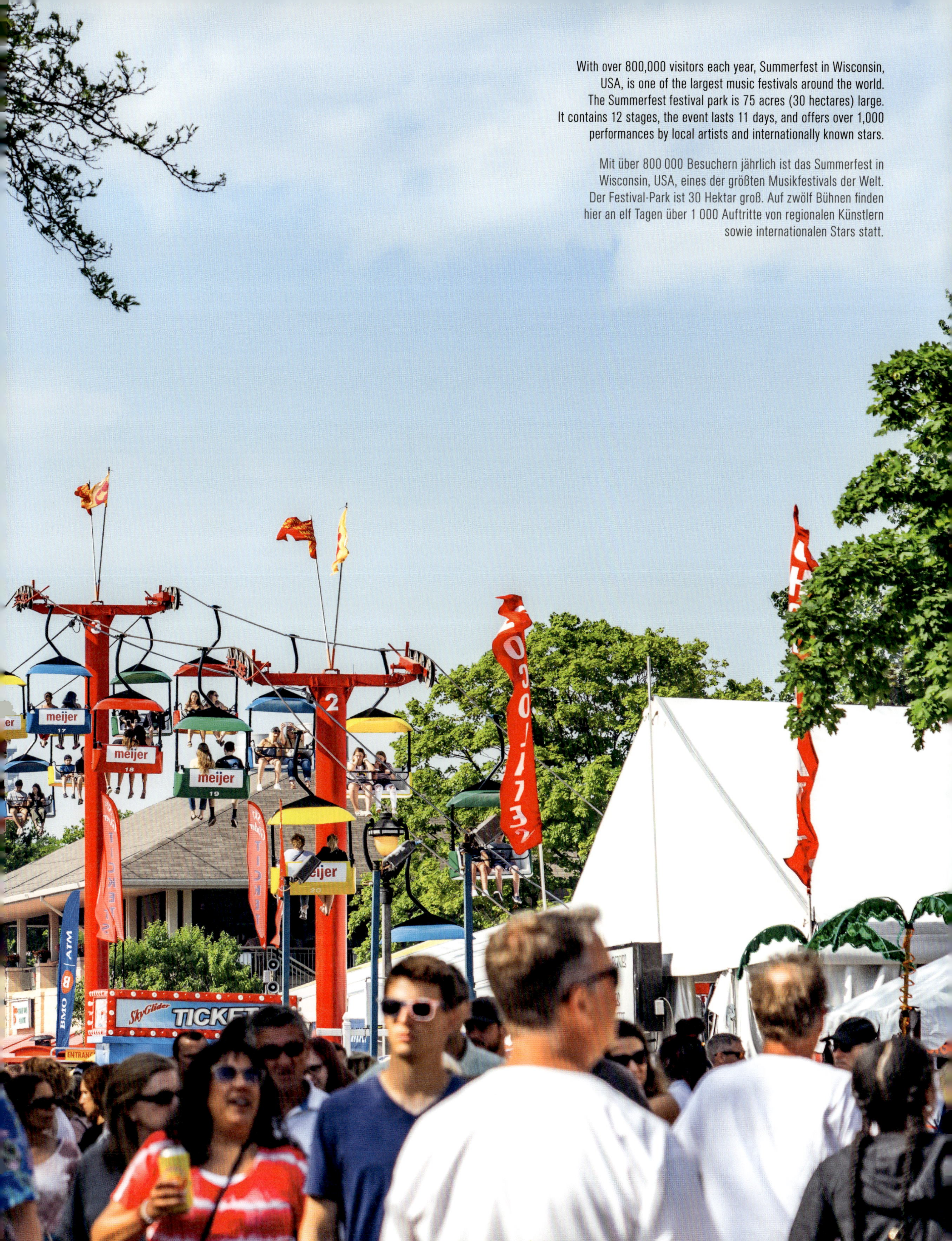

With over 800,000 visitors each year, Summerfest in Wisconsin, USA, is one of the largest music festivals around the world. The Summerfest festival park is 75 acres (30 hectares) large. It contains 12 stages, the event lasts 11 days, and offers over 1,000 performances by local artists and internationally known stars.

Mit über 800 000 Besuchern jährlich ist das Summerfest in Wisconsin, USA, eines der größten Musikfestivals der Welt. Der Festival-Park ist 30 Hektar groß. Auf zwölf Bühnen finden hier an elf Tagen über 1 000 Auftritte von regionalen Künstlern sowie internationalen Stars statt.

The "Street Witch of Salem" watches the action on the Essex Street pedestrian mall during the October-long pre-Halloween Haunted Happenings celebration in Salem, Massachusetts. Events include a grand parade, a street fair, costume balls, ghost tours, and music and theater performances.

Die „Straßenhexe von Salem" beobachtet während des im Oktober vor Halloween stattfindenden Festivals Haunted Happenings das Treiben in der Fußgängerzone Essex Street in Salem, Massachusetts. Neben einer großen Parade, Marktständen, Kostümbällen und Geistertouren, kann man während des Events Musik- und Theatervorstellungen erleben.

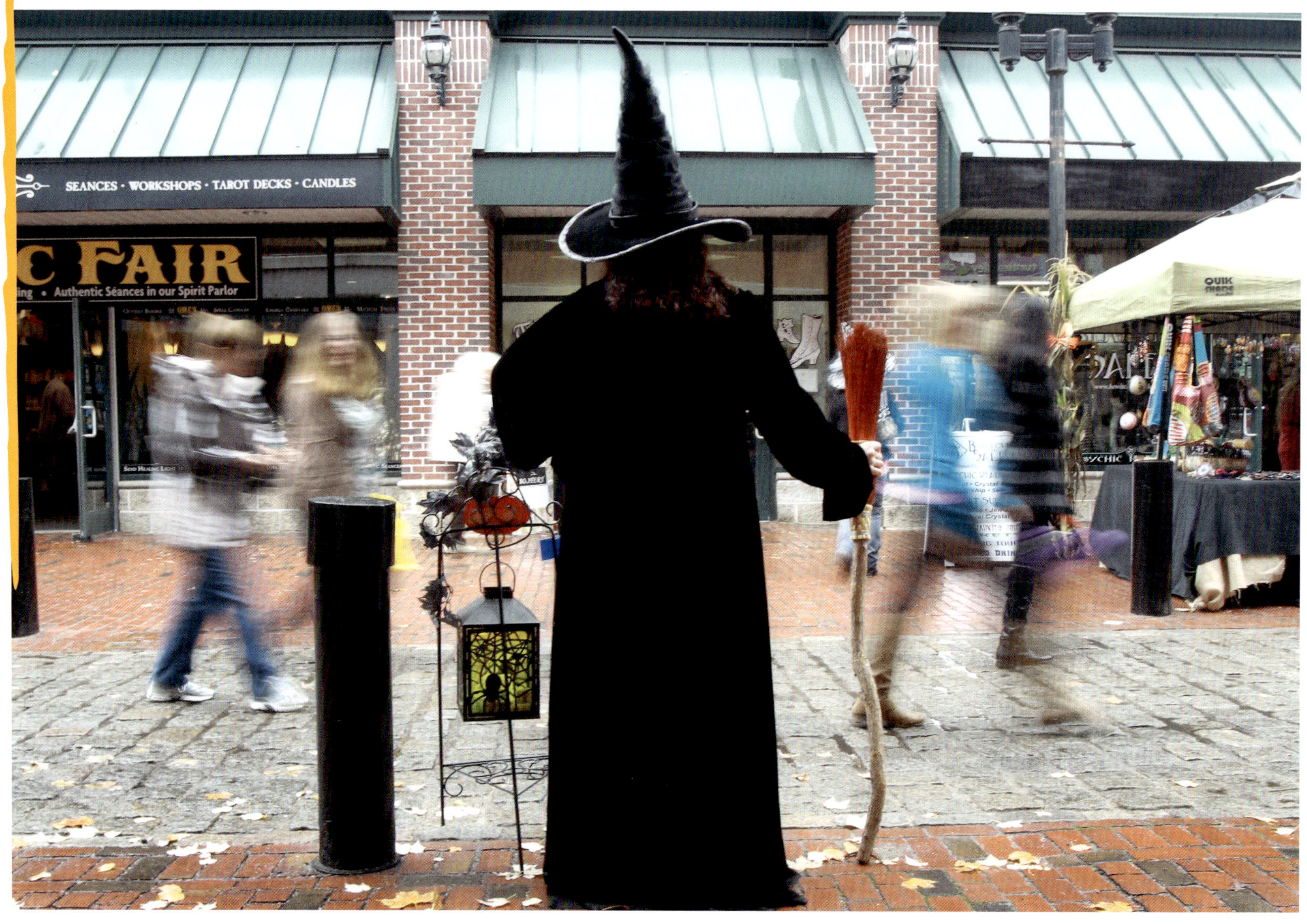

Ever wondered what it's like to walk through a tunnel of over 7,000 Jack-o'-lanterns? Find out in Hudson Valley, New York!

Wollten Sie schon immer durch einen Tunnel aus über 7 000 Kürbislaternen spazieren? Dann nichts wie auf ins Hudson Valley, New York!

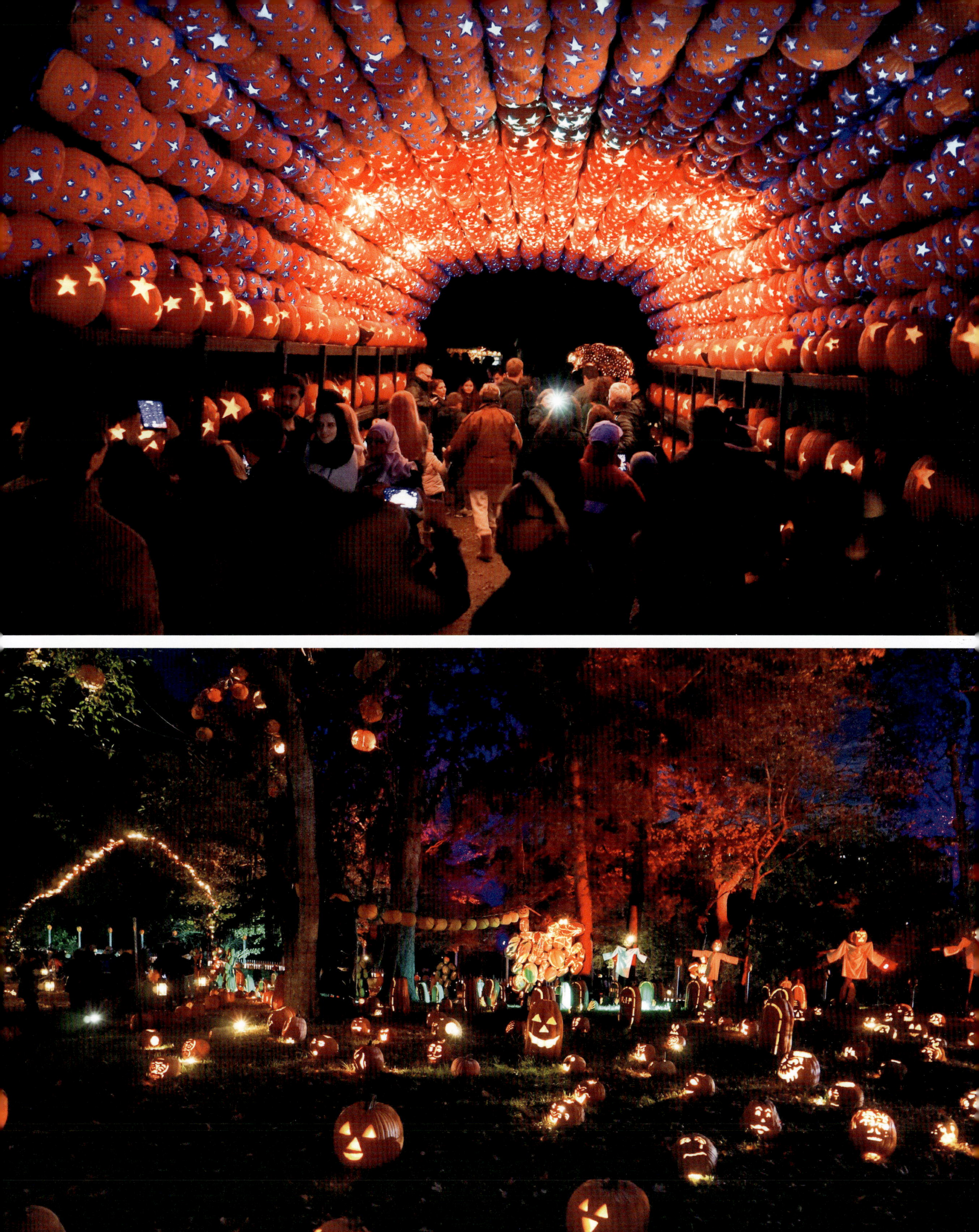

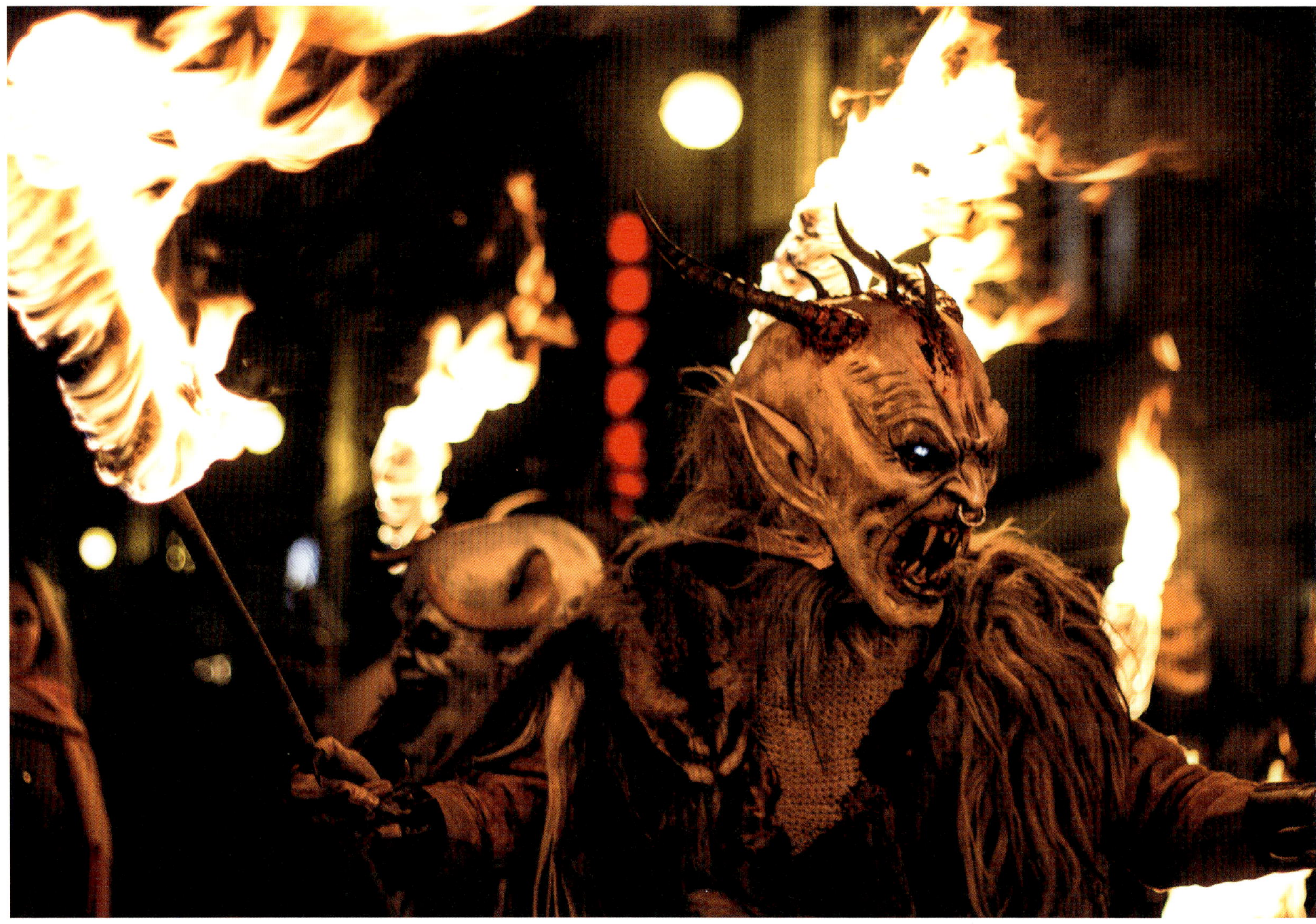

On Krampusnacht, on December 5, frightening Krampus figures like these half men / half goats roam the streets looking for naughty children to "drag to hell."

In der Krampusnacht durchstreifen am 5. Dezember Schreckgestalten wie diese Ziegenmenschen die Straßen auf der Suche nach unartigen Kindern, die sie „in die Hölle ziehen" wollen.

Good to know
WISSENSWERTES

"Krampus" dates back to Pagan mythology. Traditional costumes are made from sheep or goat skin, with a scary hand-carved wooden mask and a cowbell worn around the hips. Terrifying!

Der „Krampus" hat seinen Ursprung in der heidnischen Mythologie. Die traditionellen Kostüme werden aus Schafs- oder Ziegenhäuten hergestellt. Dazu gehört eine gruselige handgeschnitzte Holzmaske und eine an den Hüften befestigte Kuhglocke. Ziemlich furchterregend!

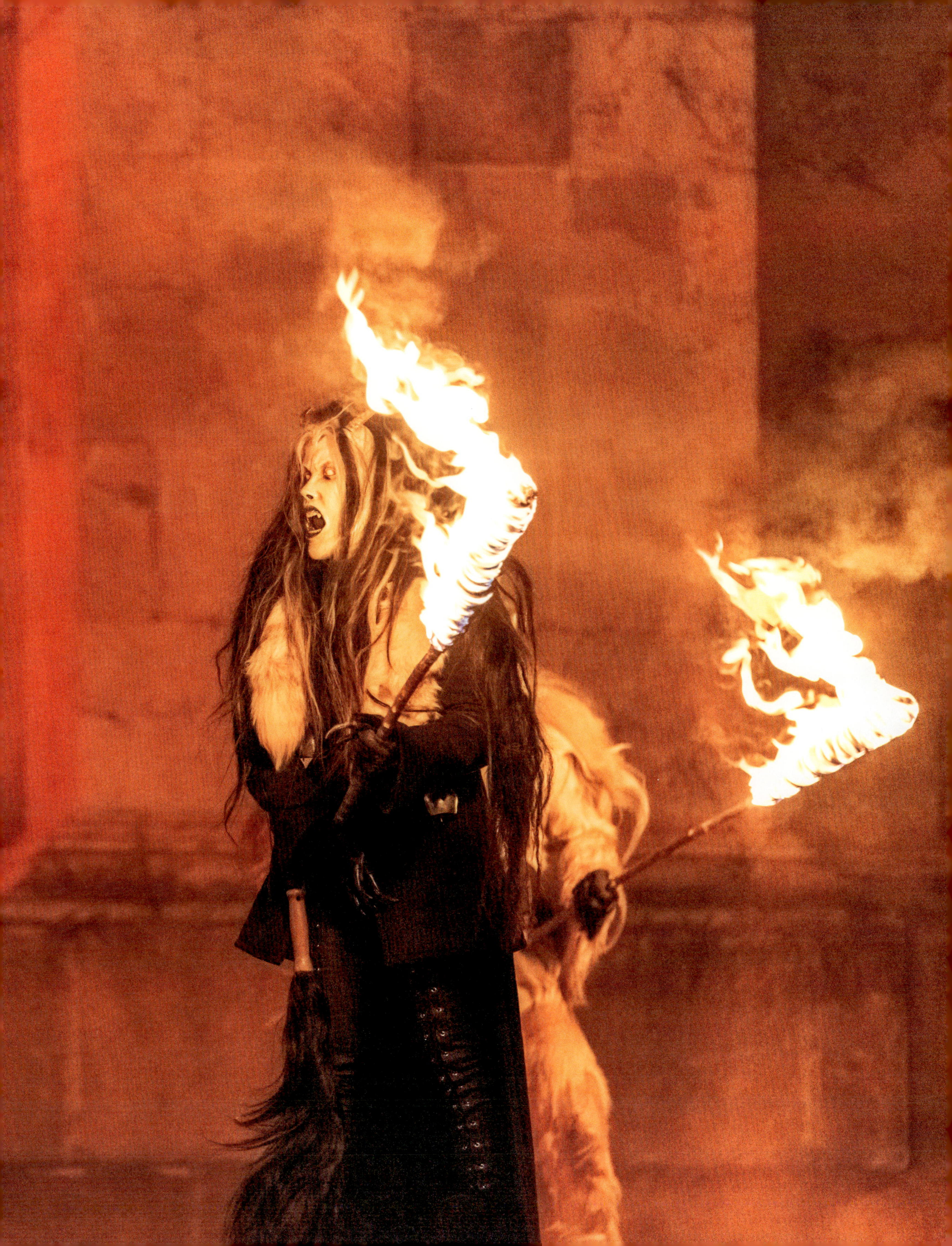

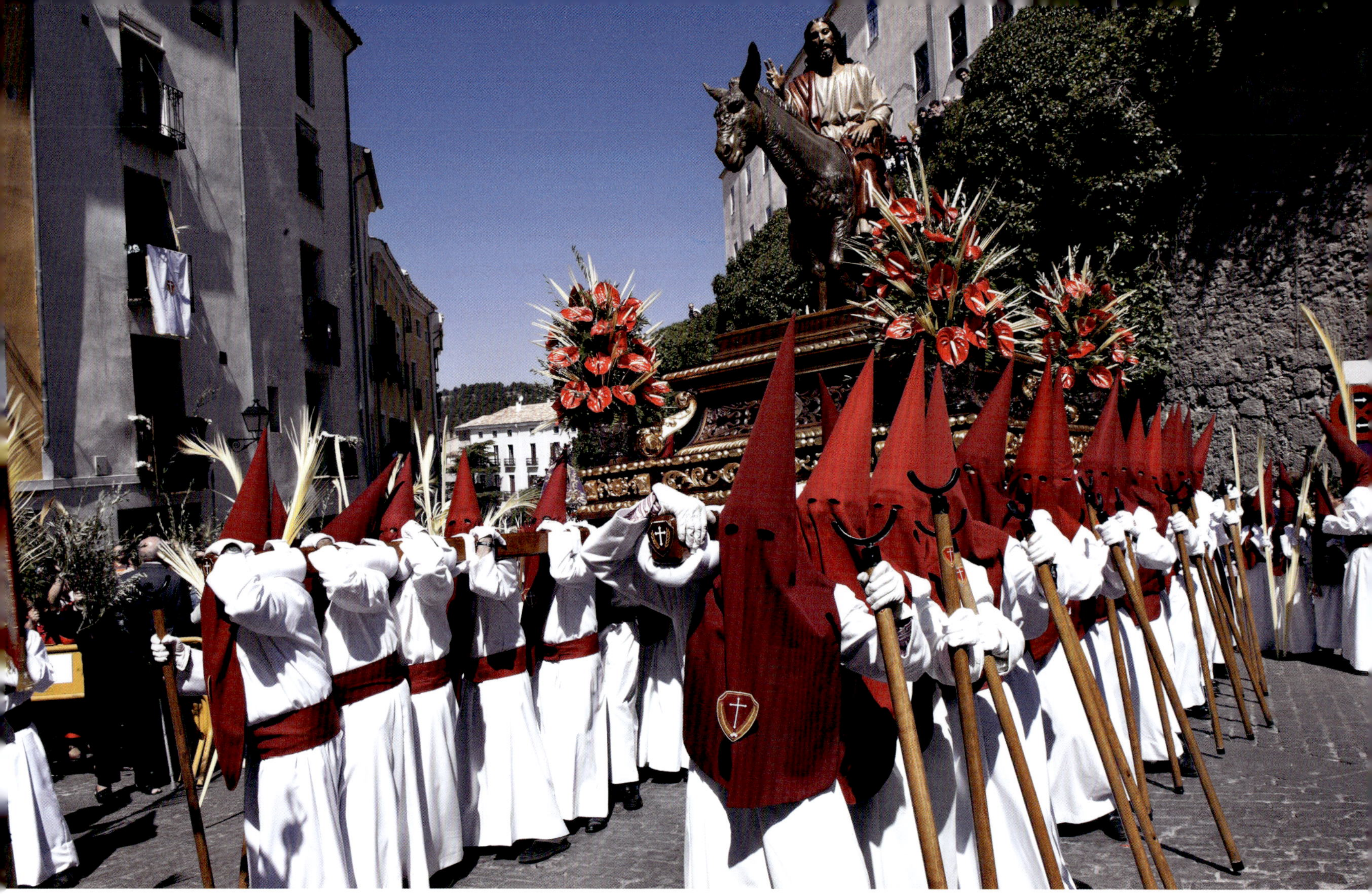

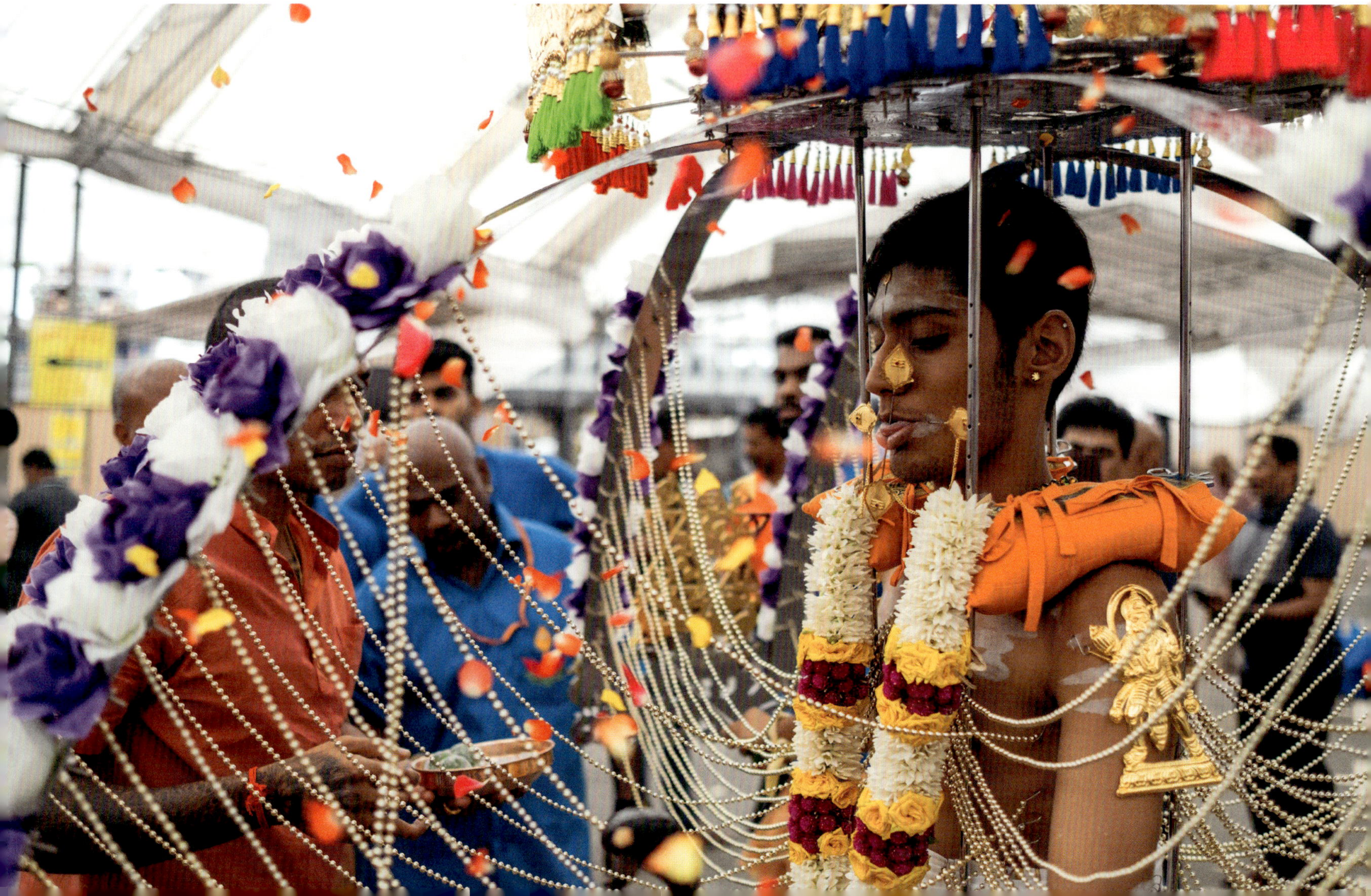

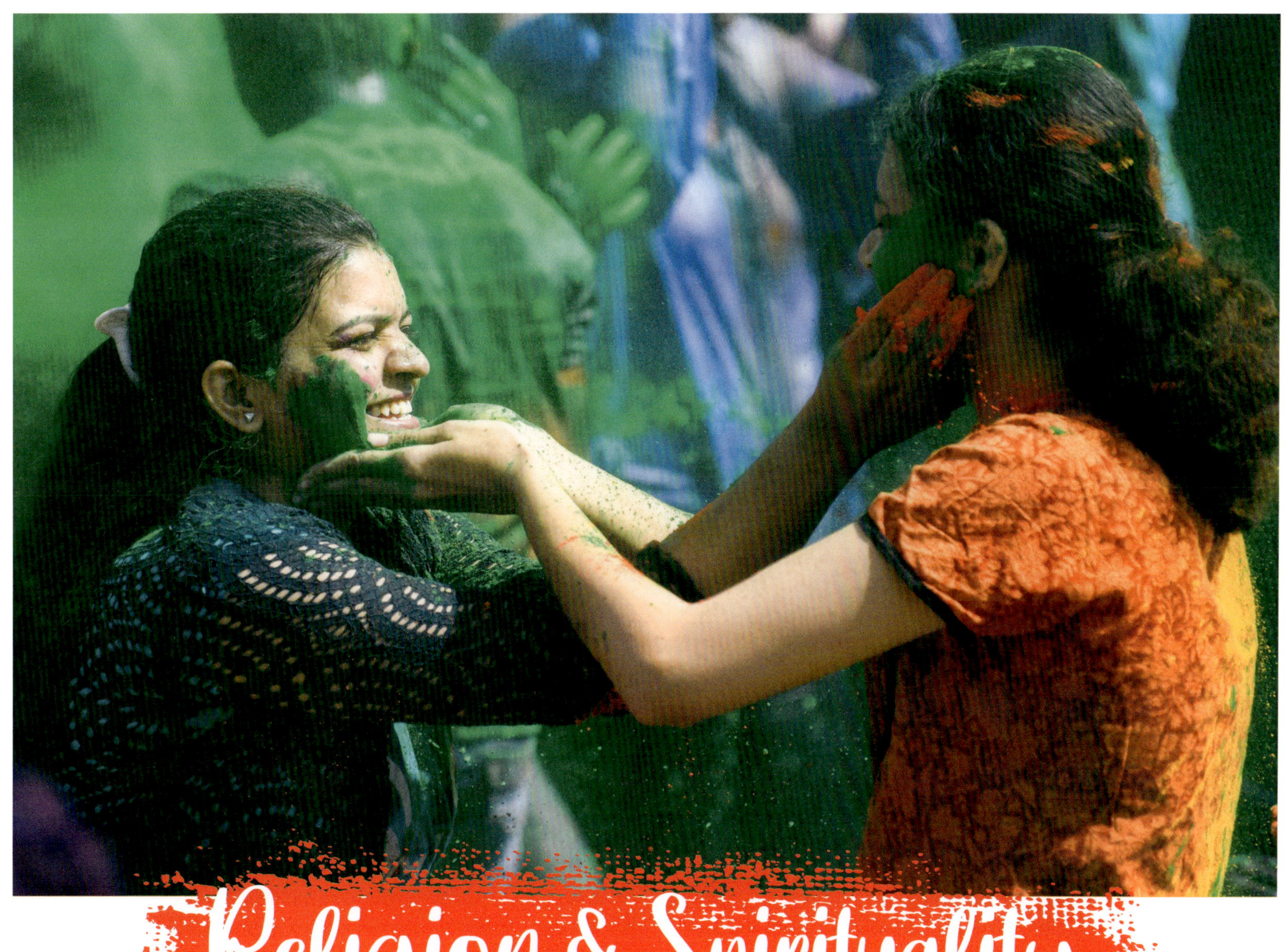

Religion & Spirituality

RELIGION & SPIRITUALITÄT

This page: Holi is one of the most popular Indian festivals;
it celebrates the beginning of spring, the harvest, and the
eternal love of the gods Radha and Krishna.

Diese Seite: Holi ist eines der beliebtesten Feste Indiens.
Man feiert damit den Frühlingsanfang, die Ernte und die
ewige Liebe der Götter Radha und Krishna.

Opposite, top: Christian procession during Semana
Santa, Spain.
Bottom: The Hindu festival of Thaipusam, Singapore.

Linke Seite, oben: Eine christliche Prozession
während der Semana Santa in Spanien
Unten: Das hinduistische Fest Thaipusam in Singapur

Religious gatherings are the earliest recorded festivals. And now, hundreds, even thousands of years later, spiritual festivals are still the most popular reason for these celebratory events. They are a chance to relax into the comfort of being around people with the same mindset and beliefs as you.

The largest of these pilgrimages, the Kumbh Mela in India, brings over 110 *million* people together to dip in the Triveni Sangam in Prayagraj—where the Ganges meets the Yamuna and the mythical Saraswati Rivers—over a 49-day period. Hindus believe bathing at this place will help them break free from the cycle of birth and death. Visit and you can see the holy sadhus who've come down from the mountains, take part in prayers, and know that you've participated in a major world gathering. Kumbh Mela takes place every three years at one of four sacred locations where, according to legend, four drops of immortality nectar fell to earth, these include Prayagraj, Haridwar, Nashik, and Ujjain (opposite, top).

The Tamil Hindu festival, Thaipusam, encourages followers to take time to express their thanks to one of their gods, Lord Murugan. It's also a time to pay penance for any bad they may have done. One of the main celebrations happens just outside Kuala Lumpur at the Batu Caves in Malaysia, where it's taken place since 1888. The alignment of the sun, moon, and planets has to be just right. Then, on the day before, thousands gather early for the morning charity procession featuring a wooden statue of Lord Murugan. It's a vibrant event, with devotees wearing Murugan's colors of yellow and orange, and holding up bowls of fruit, gifts, and even babies to be blessed by the procession (opposite, bottom).

Die ersten dokumentierten Feste der Menschheit waren religiöse Versammlungen. Heute, Tausende von Jahren später, gehören Feste mit spirituellem Hintergrund noch immer zu den beliebtesten Veranstaltungen. Schließlich kann man auf ihnen im Kreise von Gleichgesinnten entspannen.

Zum größten Fest dieser Art, der Kumbh Mela in Indien, strömen über 100 *Millionen* Menschen zusammen, um über einen 49-tägigen Zeitraum an der Stelle einzutauchen, wo die Flüsse Ganges, Yamuna und der mythische Saraswati in Prayagraj zusammentreffen. Hindus glauben, dass sie dadurch ihre Sünden abwaschen und schneller den Kreislauf der Wiedergeburt verlassen können. Besucher können auf dem Fest auch Sadhus begegnen, heiligen Männern, die von den Bergen hinabgestiegen sind, um an den Gebeten teilzunehmen. Kumbh Mela findet alle drei Jahre an einem von vier heiligen Orten statt, an denen laut einer Legende, vier Tropfen Unsterblichkeitsnektar auf die Erde niederfielen, dazu gehören neben Prayagraj auch Haridwar, Nashik und Ujjain (rechte Seite, oben).

Das tamilische Hindu-Fest Thaipusam wird zu Ehren des Gottes Lord Murugan begangen und bietet Gläubigen Gelegenheit, schlechte Taten zu bereuen. Eine der Hauptfeiern findet schon seit 1888 nahe Kuala Lumpur an den Batu-Höhlen in Malaysia statt. Sonne, Mond und Planeten müssen dabei in einer ganzen bestimmten Konstellation zueinander stehen. Am Tag vorher nehmen Tausende frühmorgens an einer Prozession mit einer Holzstatue von Lord Murugan teil. Bei diesem fröhlichen Ereignis tragen die Feiernden Murugans Farben Gelb und Orange und halten Schalen mit Obst und Gaben (und sogar Babys) hoch, damit diese gesegnet werden (rechte Seite, unten).

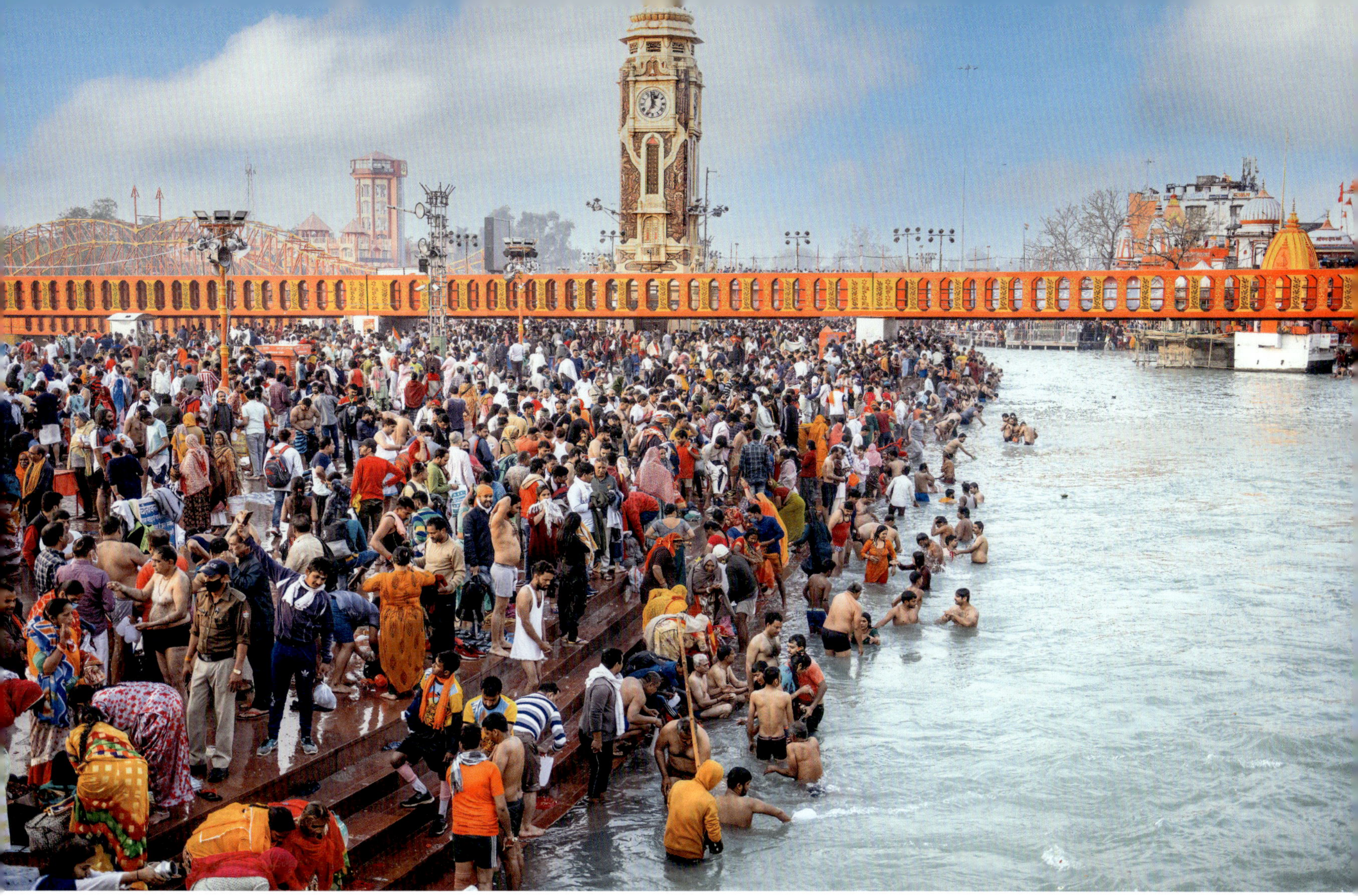

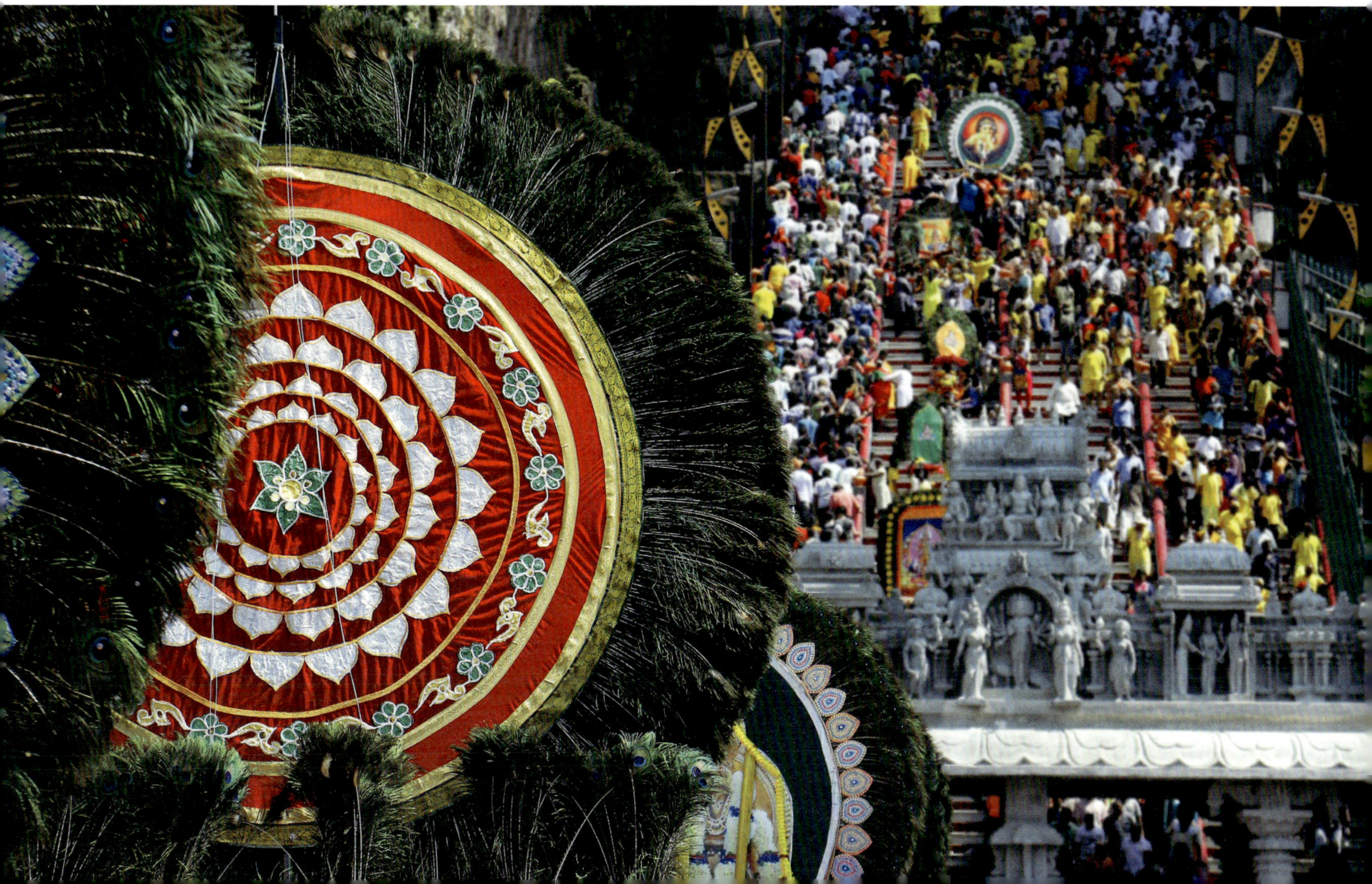

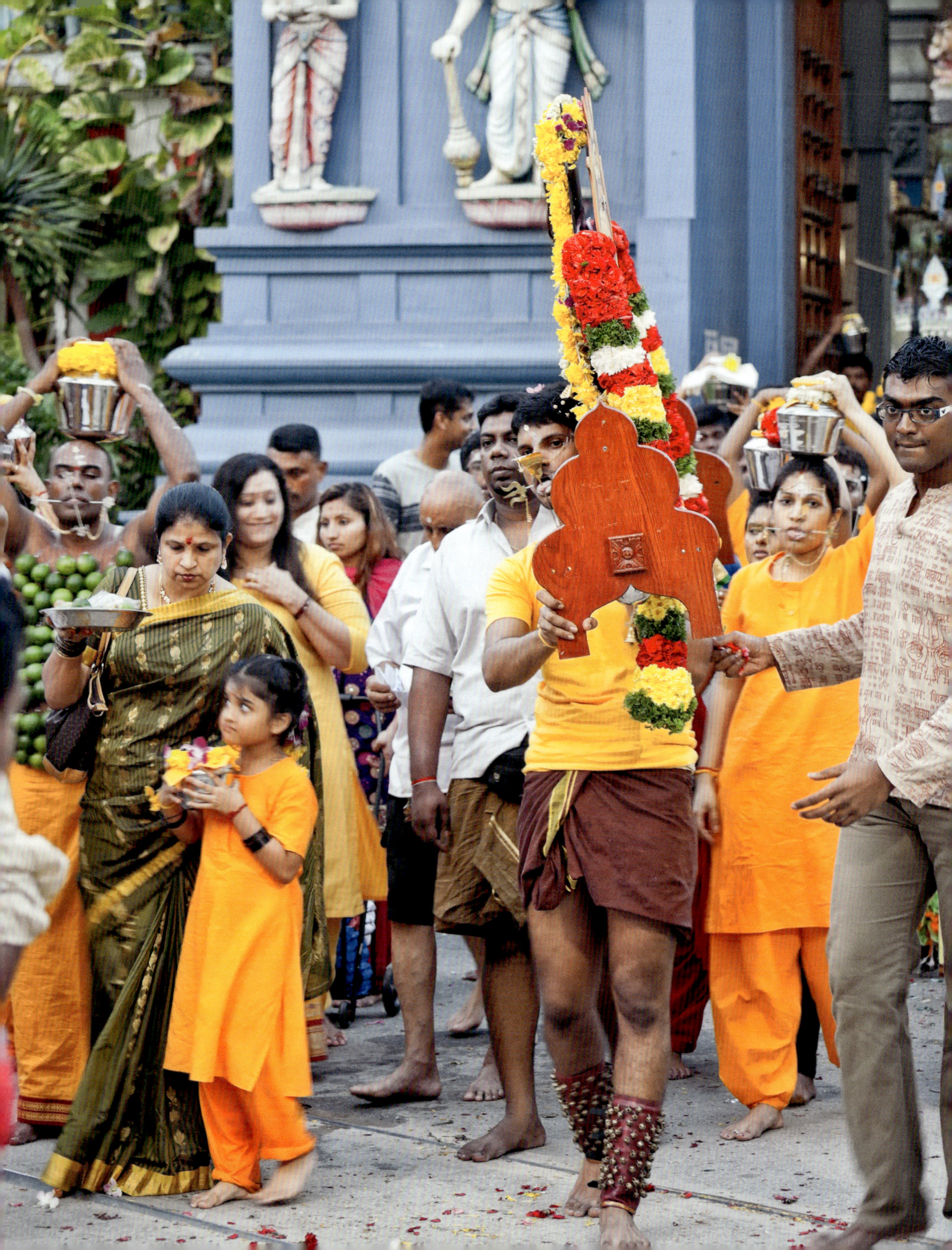

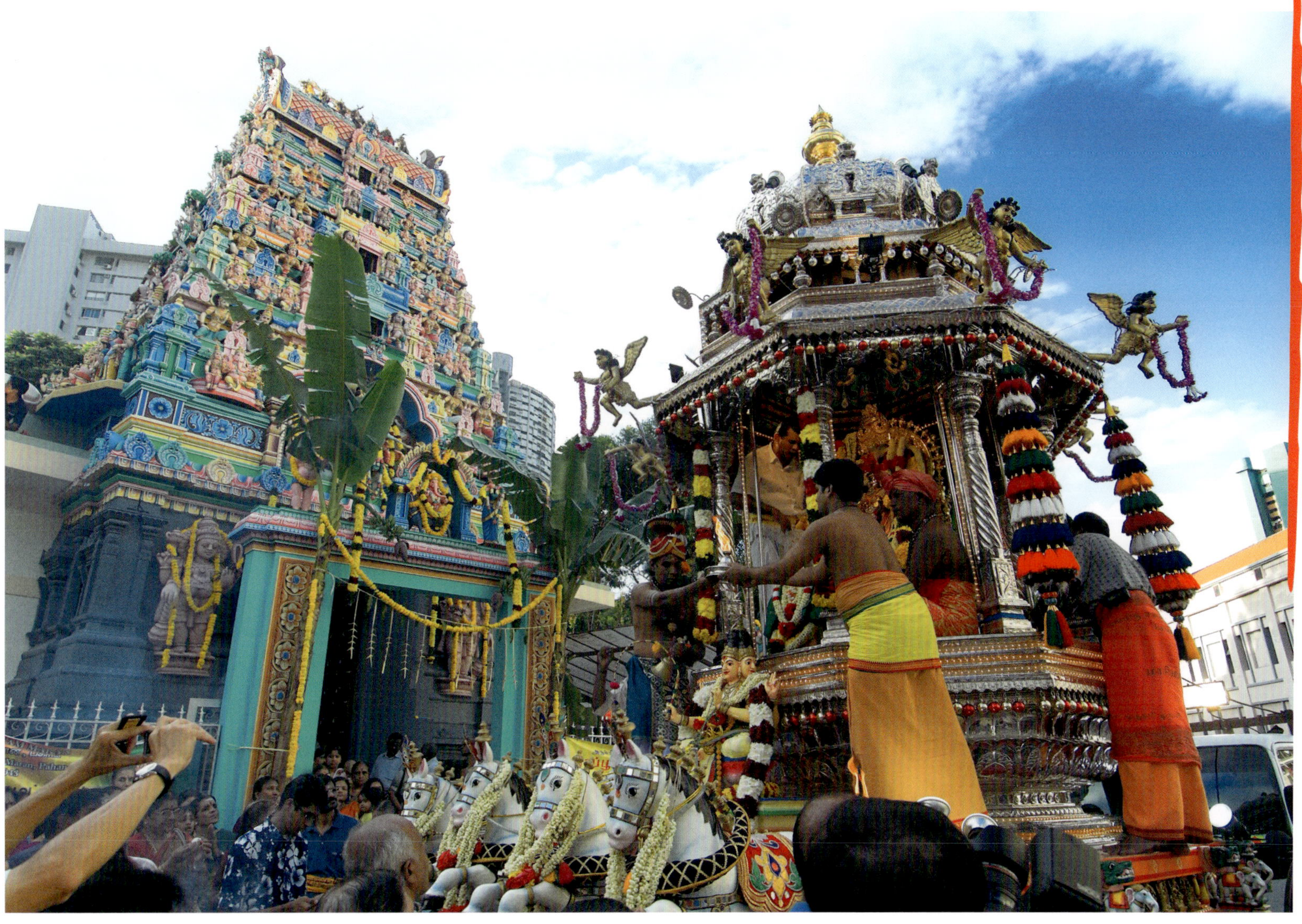

The name Thaipusam combines the words *thai*, the Tamil month of
January/February, and *pusam*, the name of a star that is at its highest
position during the festival.

Der Name Thaipusam ist aus den Wörtern *thai* (dem tamilischen Monat
Januar/Februar) und *pusam* (dem Namen eines Sterns, der während des
Festes an seinem höchsten Punkt steht) zusammengesetzt.

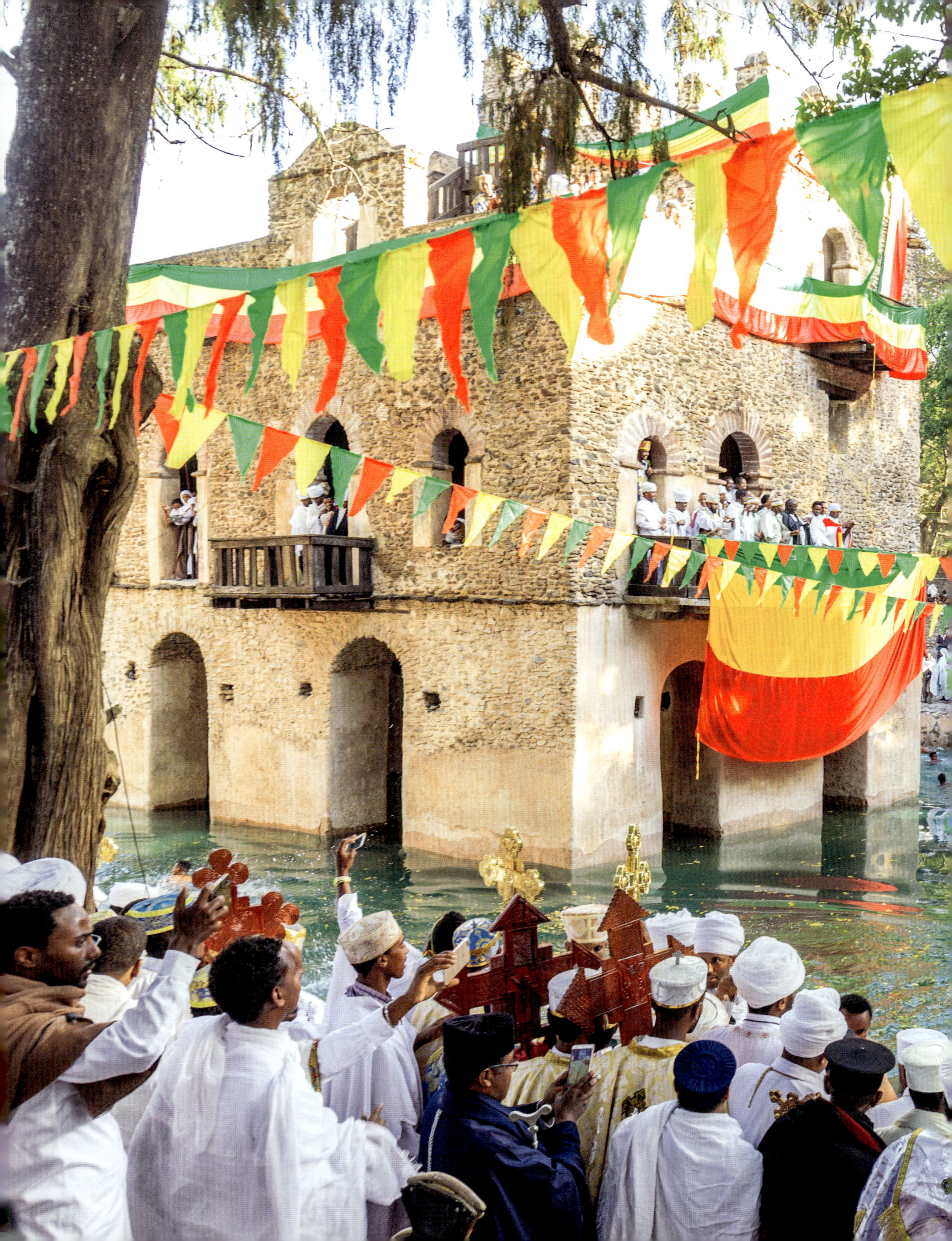

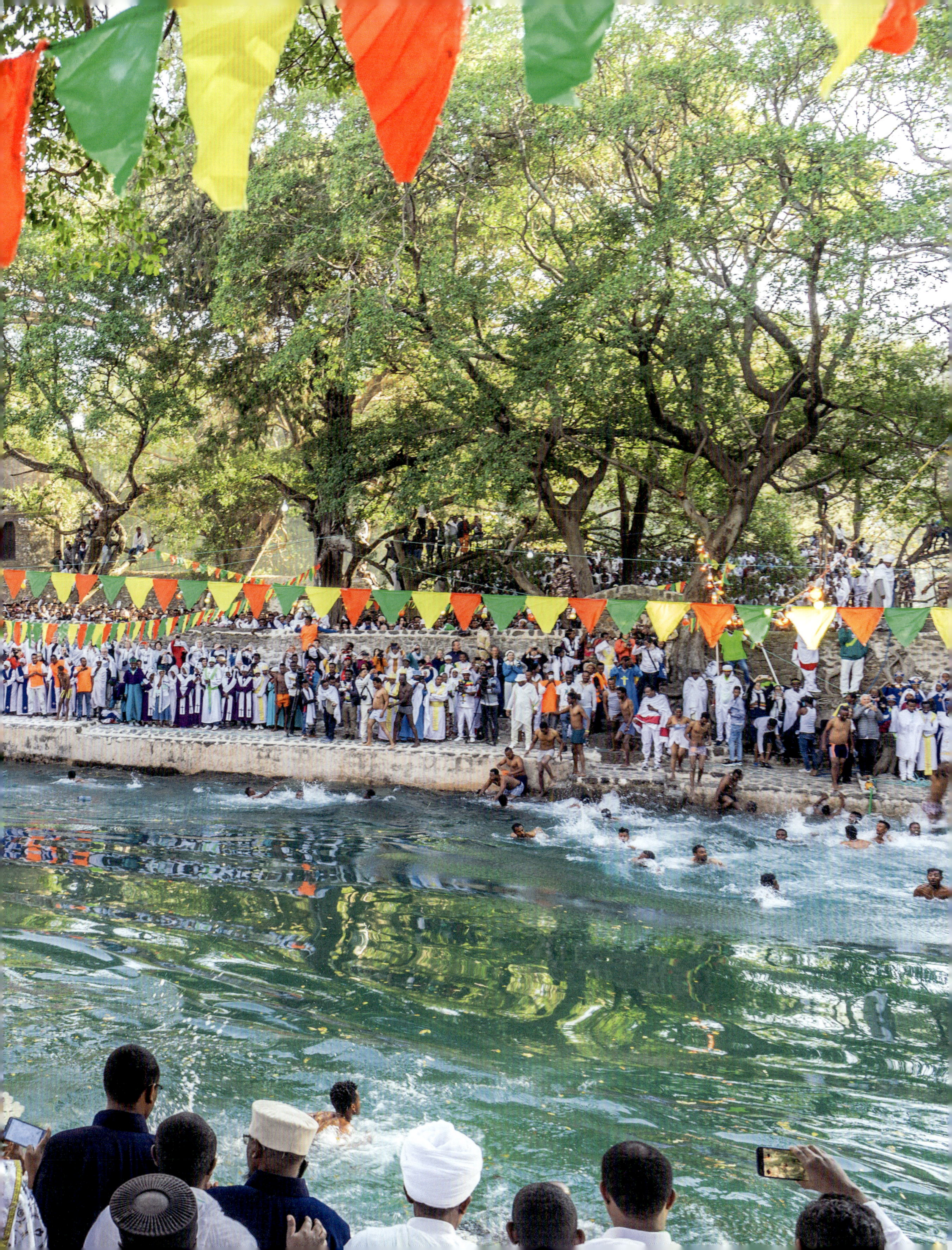

Previous pages: Fasilides' Bath during Timkat, in Gondar, Ethiopia.
Timkat is an Ethiopian-Orthodox festival that celebrates the epiphany
and the baptism of Jesus in the River Jordan.

Vorherige Seiten: Das Fasilides-Bad während des Timkat-Festes im
äthiopischen Gondar.
Timkat ist ein äthiopisch-orthodoxes Fest, das die Epiphanie und die
Taufe Jesus' im Jordan feiert.

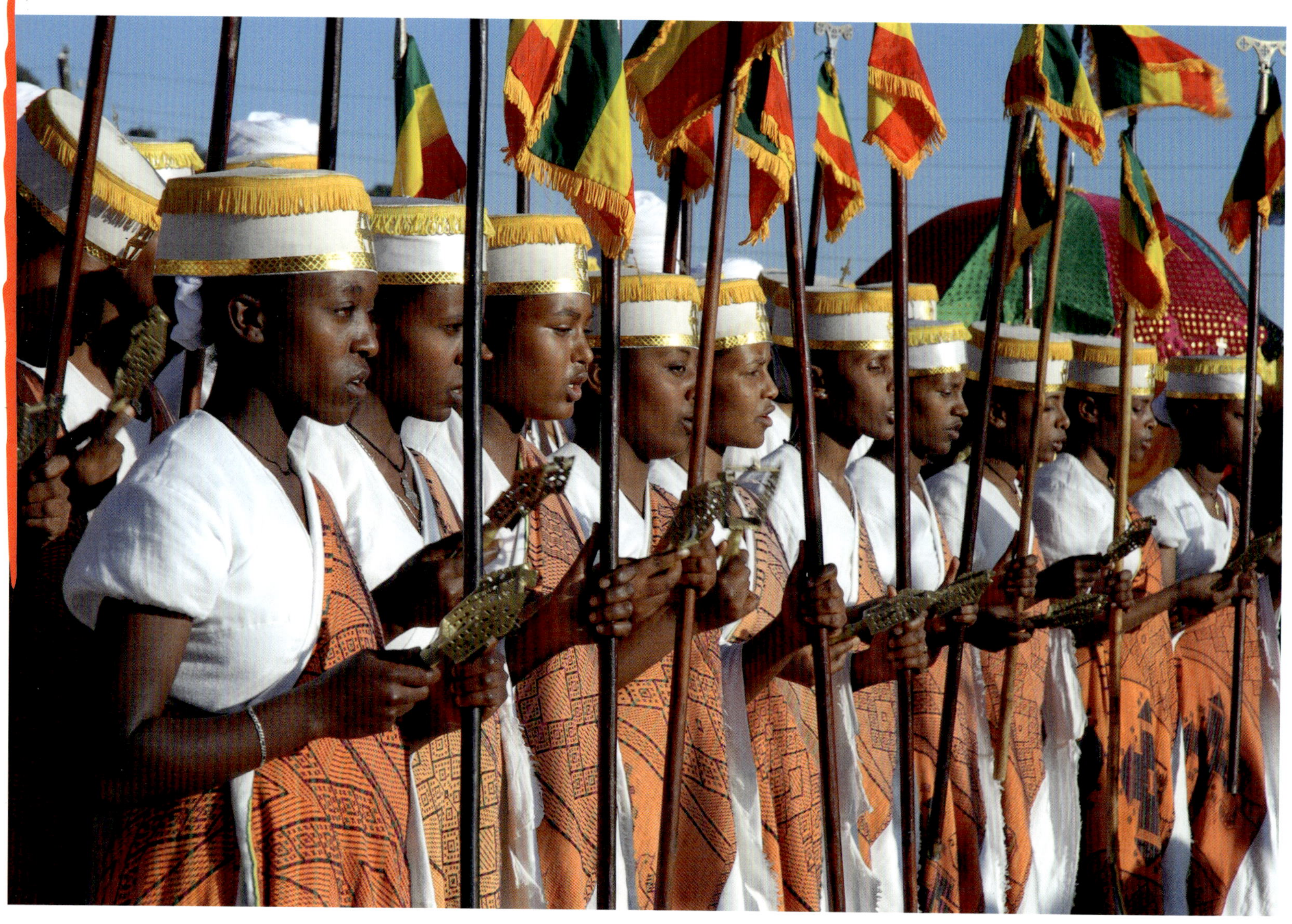

Pilgrims bear wooden crosses and are invited to leap into
the pool for a second baptism. Singing and dancing
are also part of the festivities.

Pilger tragen Holzkreuze und können für eine zweite
Taufe ins Becken springen. Gesang und Tanz sind
ebenfalls Bestandteil des Festes.

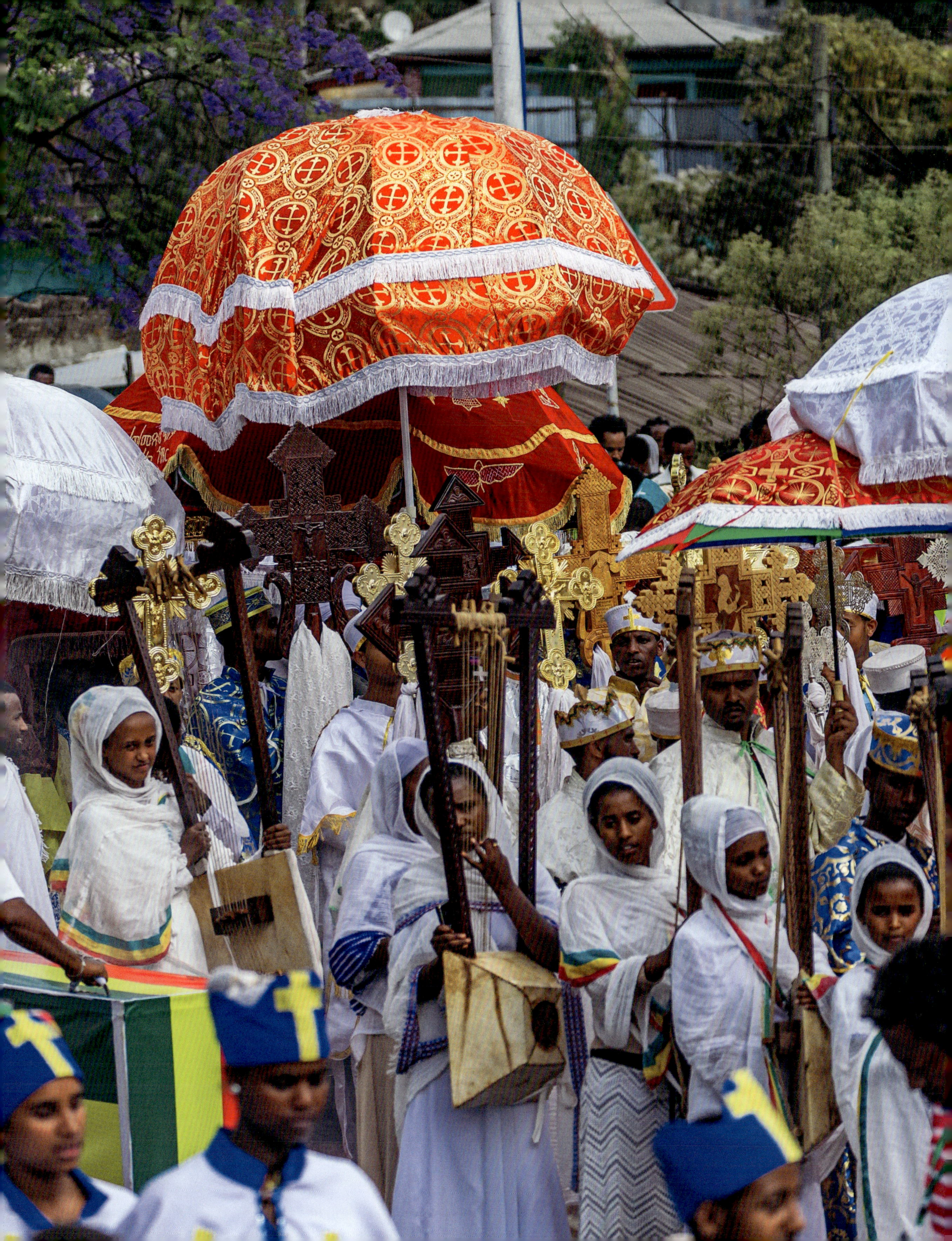

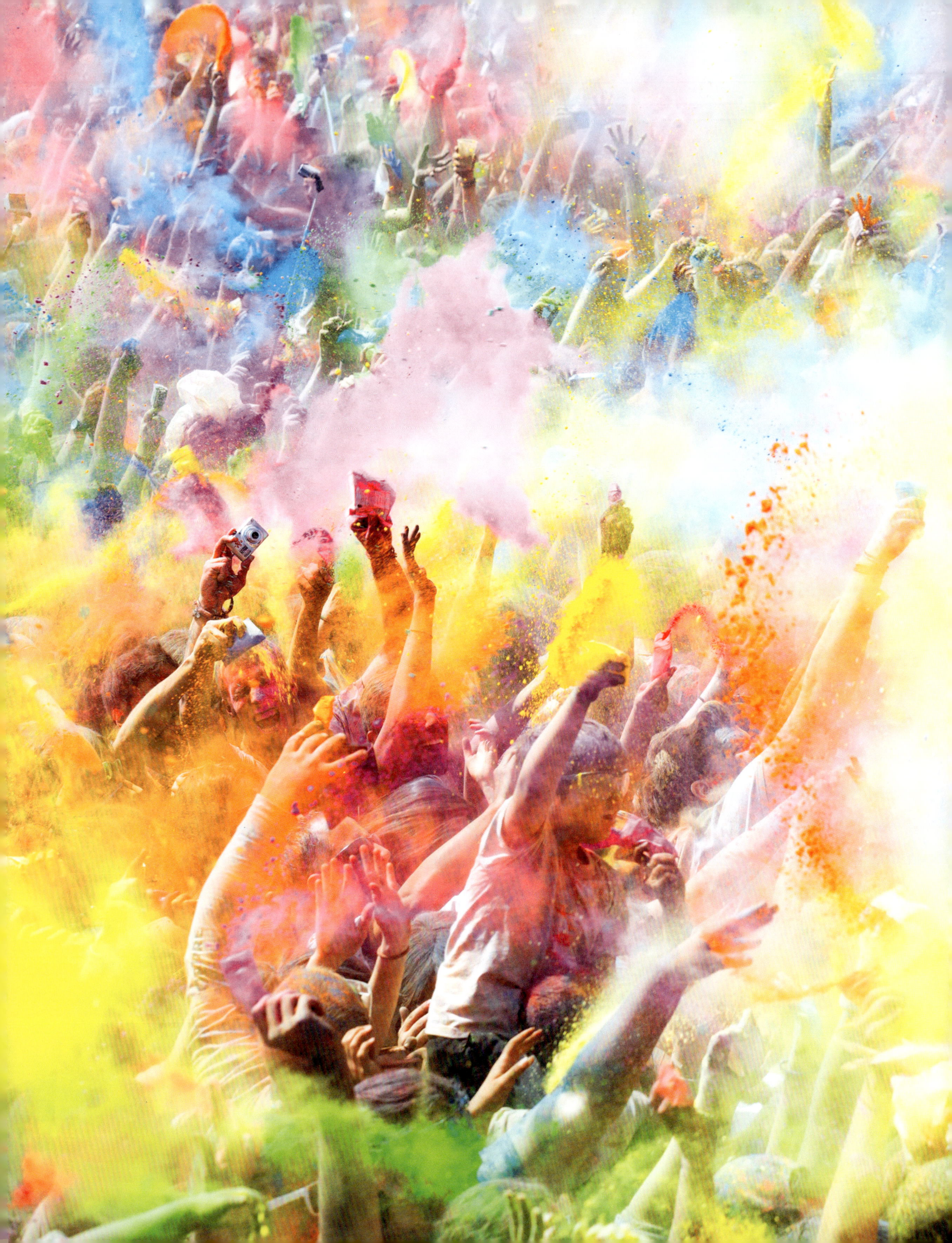

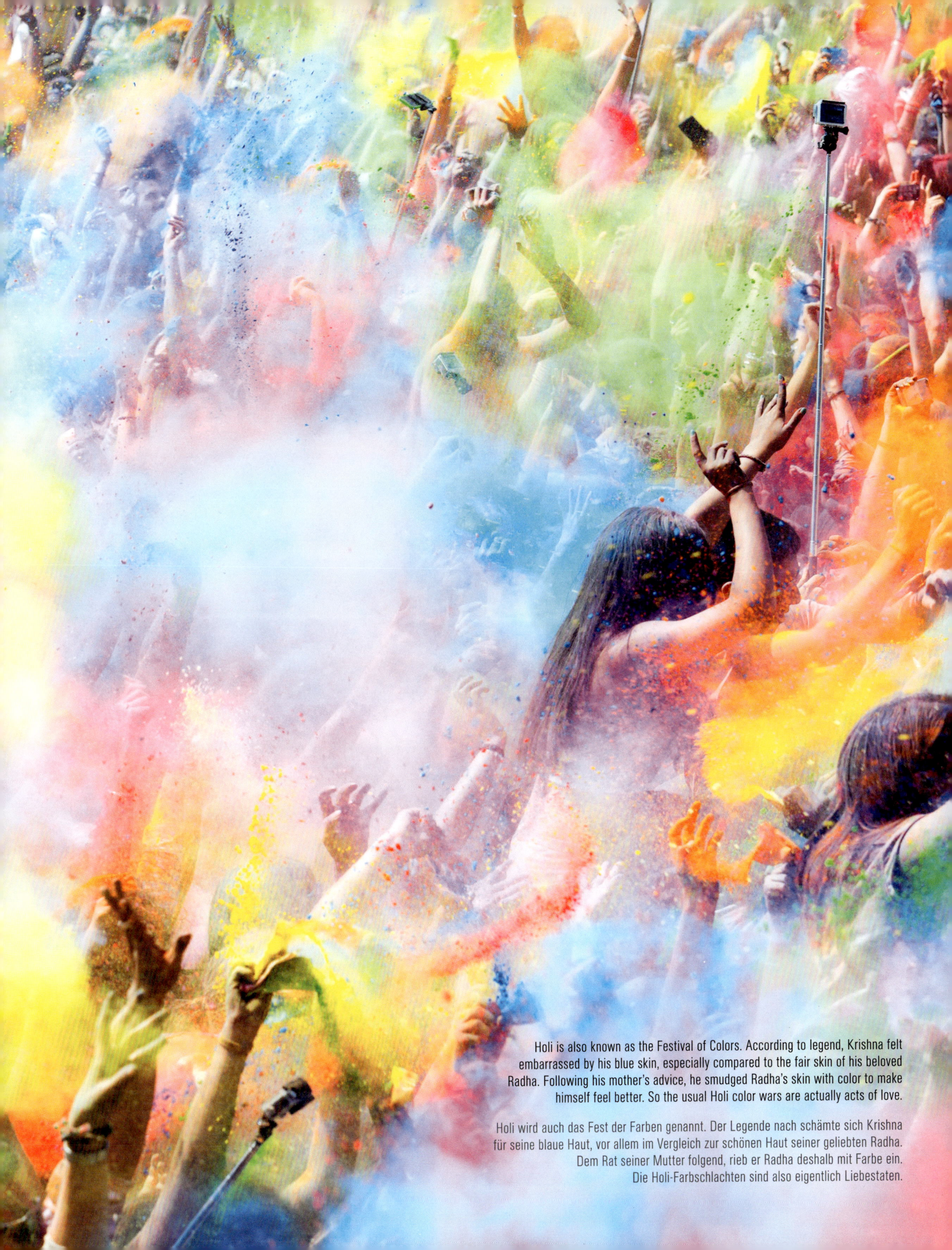

Holi is also known as the Festival of Colors. According to legend, Krishna felt embarrassed by his blue skin, especially compared to the fair skin of his beloved Radha. Following his mother's advice, he smudged Radha's skin with color to make himself feel better. So the usual Holi color wars are actually acts of love.

Holi wird auch das Fest der Farben genannt. Der Legende nach schämte sich Krishna für seine blaue Haut, vor allem im Vergleich zur schönen Haut seiner geliebten Radha. Dem Rat seiner Mutter folgend, rieb er Radha deshalb mit Farbe ein. Die Holi-Farbschlachten sind also eigentlich Liebestaten.

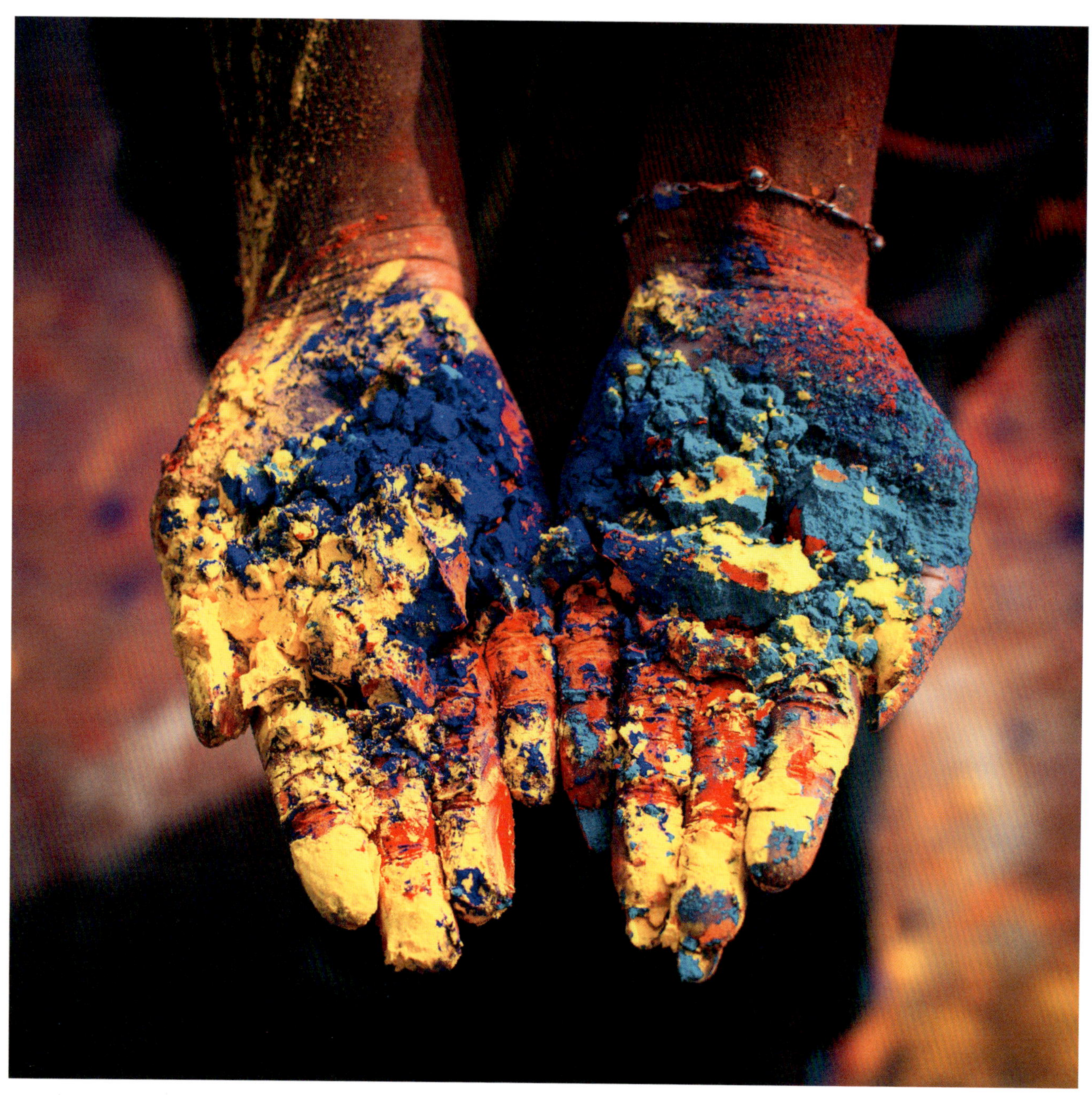

The colored powder, *gulal*, was originally made from flowers, spices, and roots. Today it is mainly synthetic.

Das Farbpulver *gulal* wurde ursprünglich aus Blüten, Gewürzen und Wurzeln gemacht. Heute wird es vorwiegend synthetisch hergestellt.

During the up to ten-day celebrations, barriers of caste, gender, skin color, age, and origin seem to dissolve.

Während der bis zu zehn Tage dauernden Feierlichkeiten scheinen sich die Barrieren zwischen Kasten, Geschlechtern, Hautfarbe, Alter und Herkunft aufzulösen.

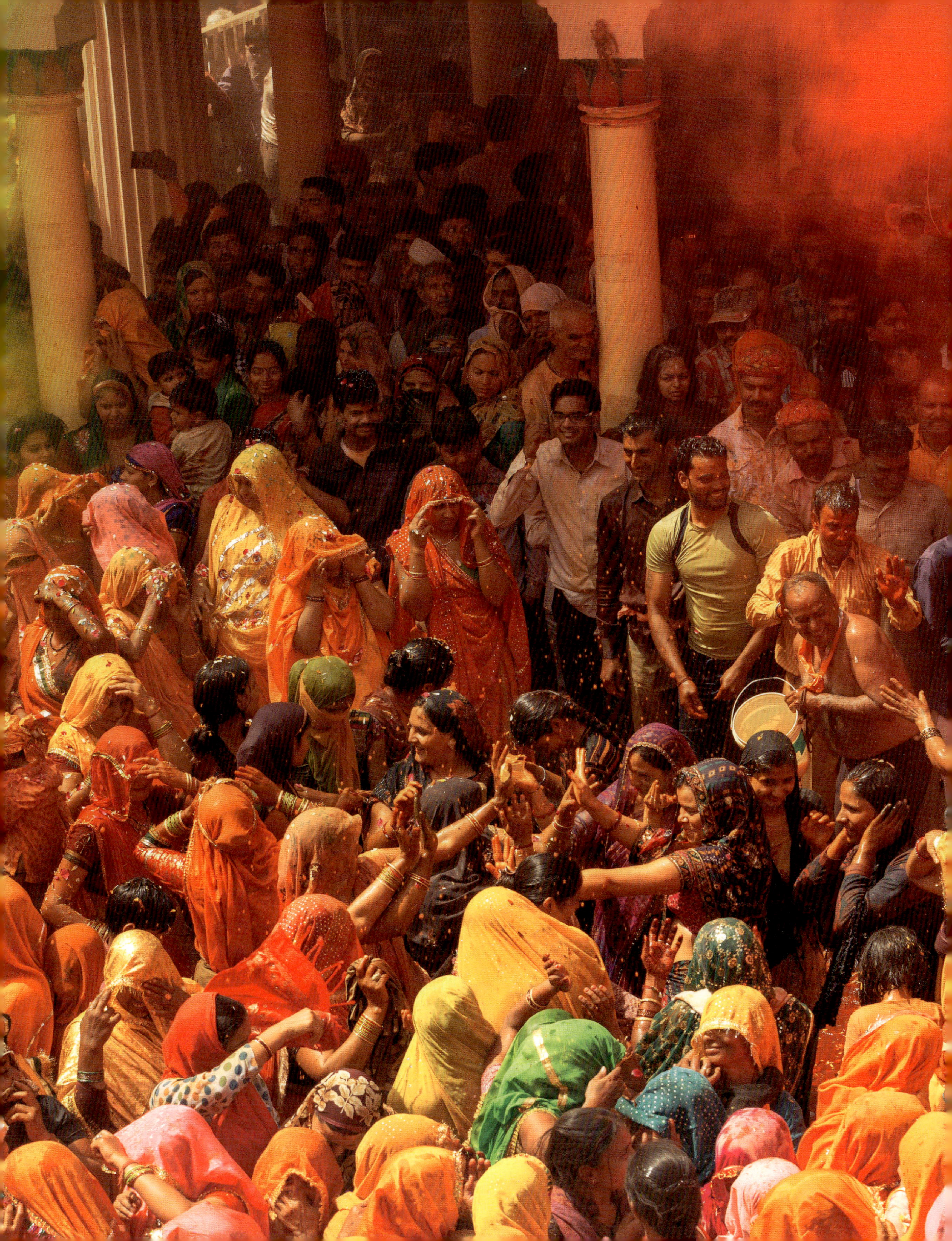

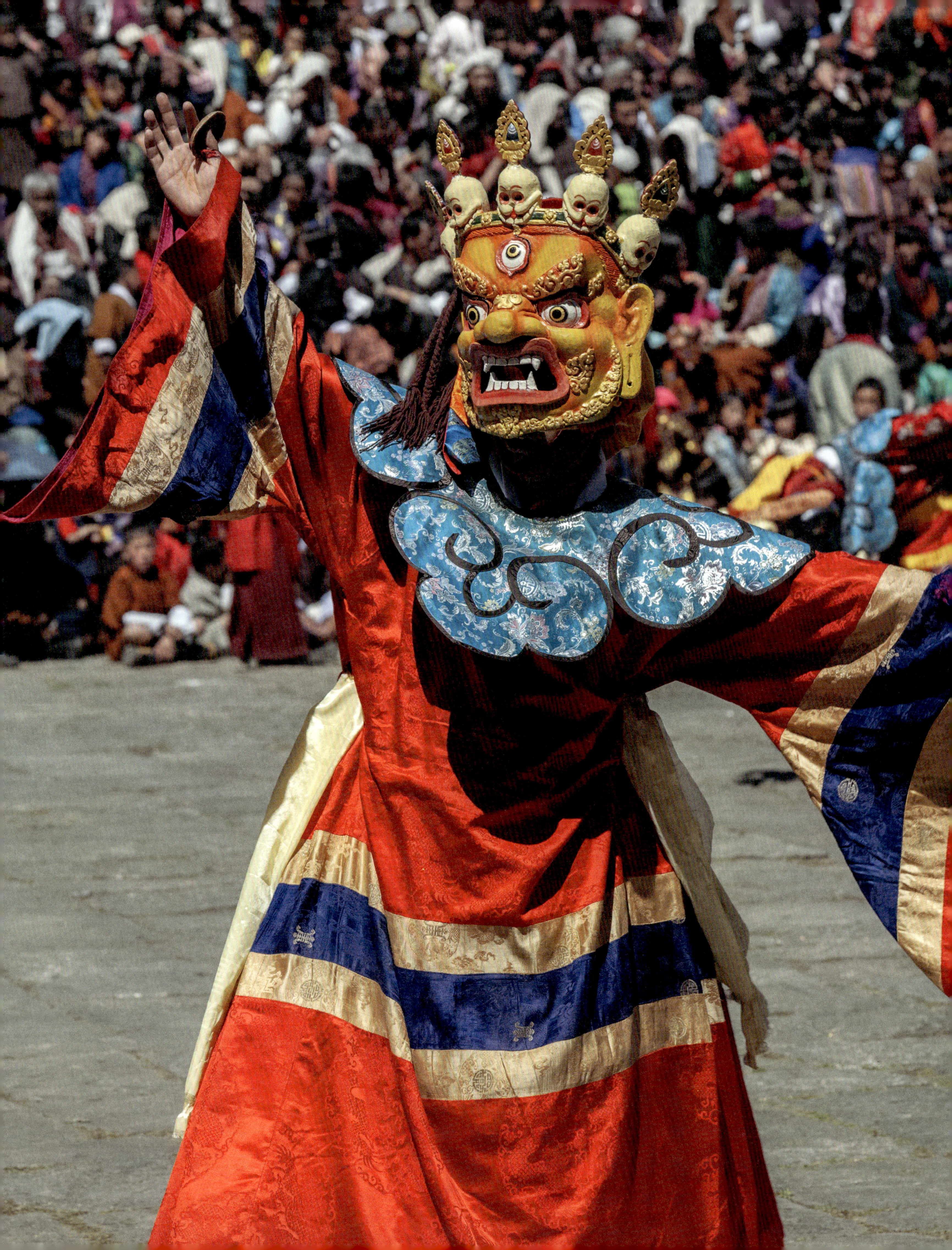

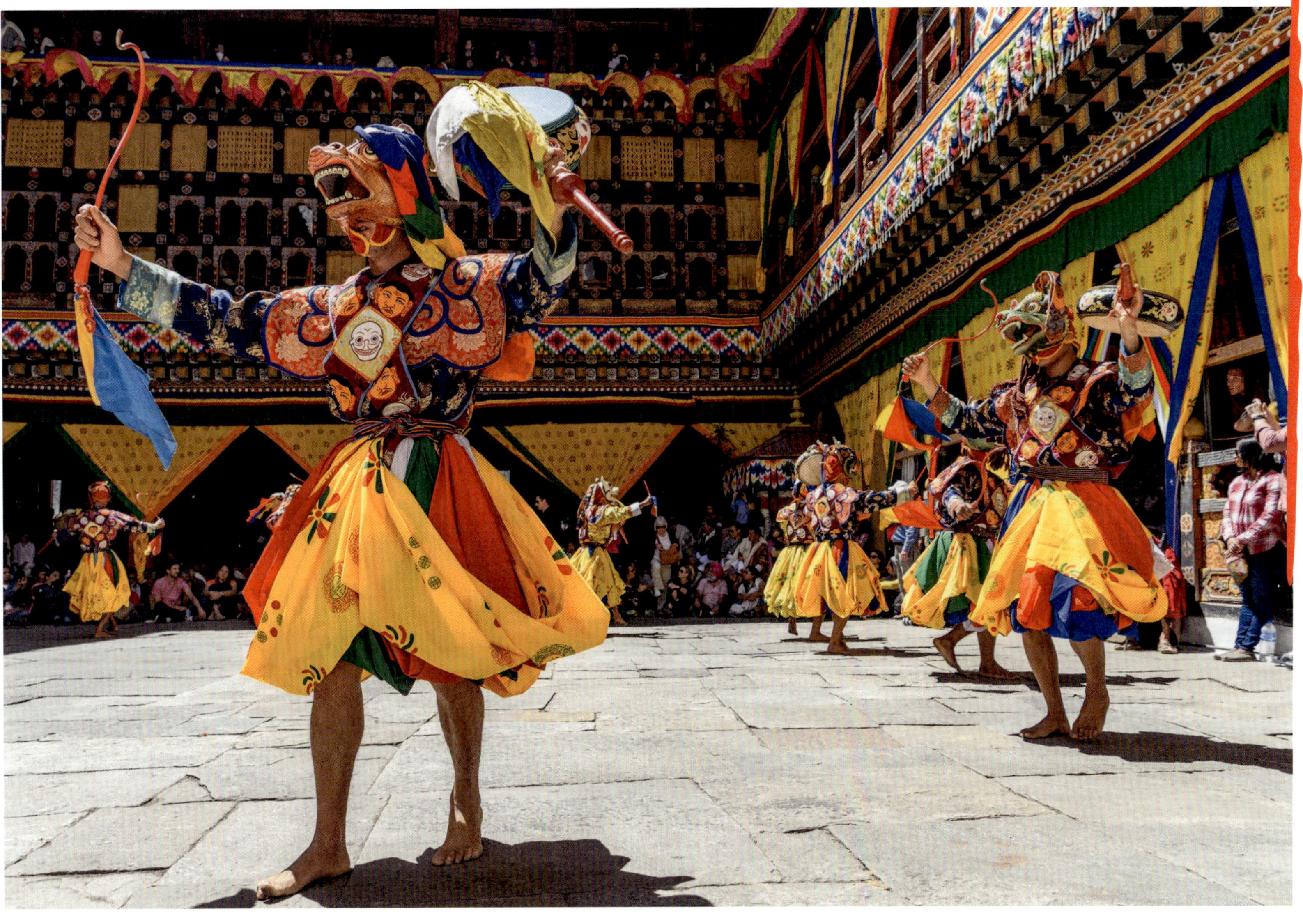

Paro Tshechu is one of the most famous annual Tibetan
Buddhist festivals in Bhutan.

Paro Tshechu ist eines der berühmtesten jährlichen,
tibetisch-buddhistischen Feste in Bhutan.

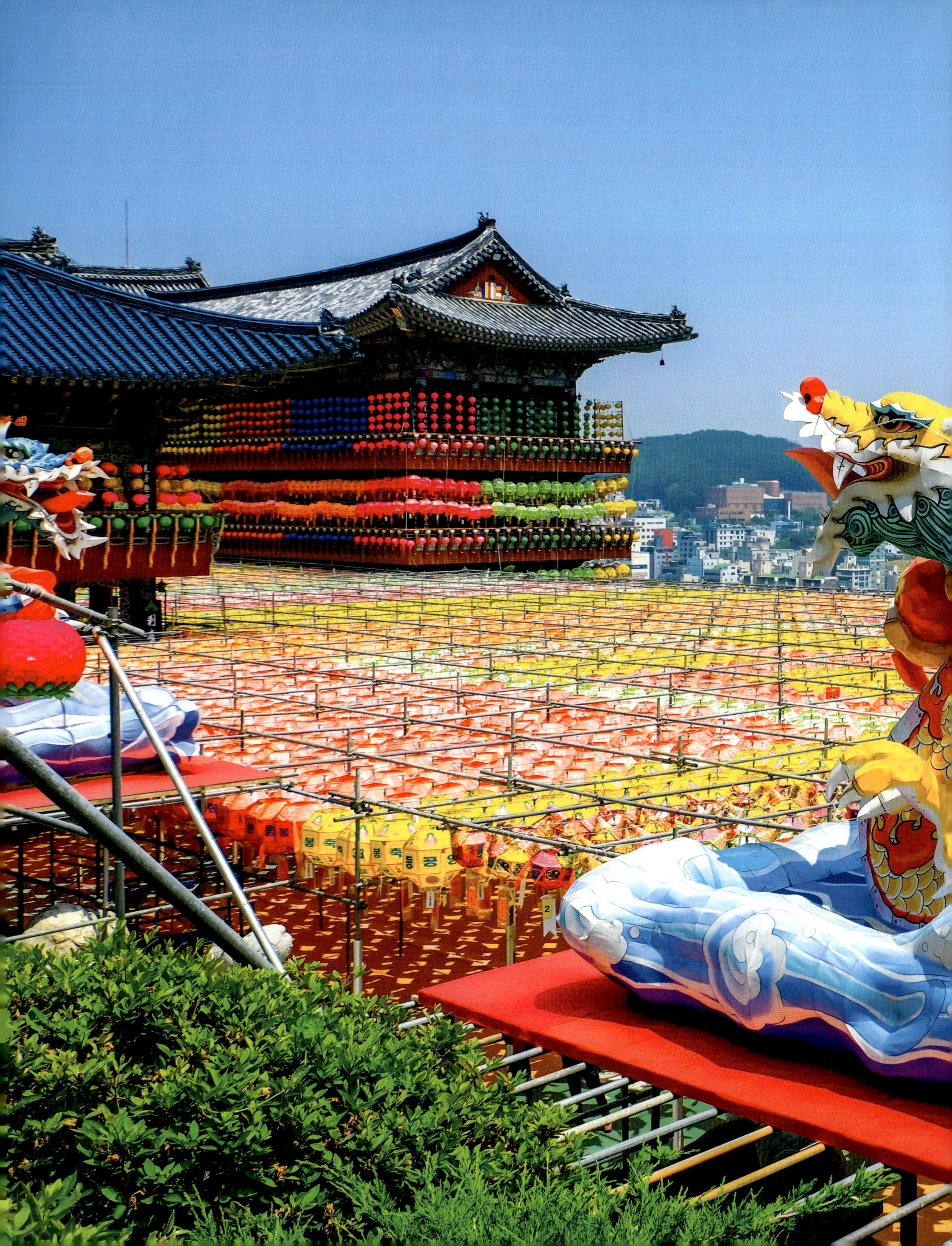

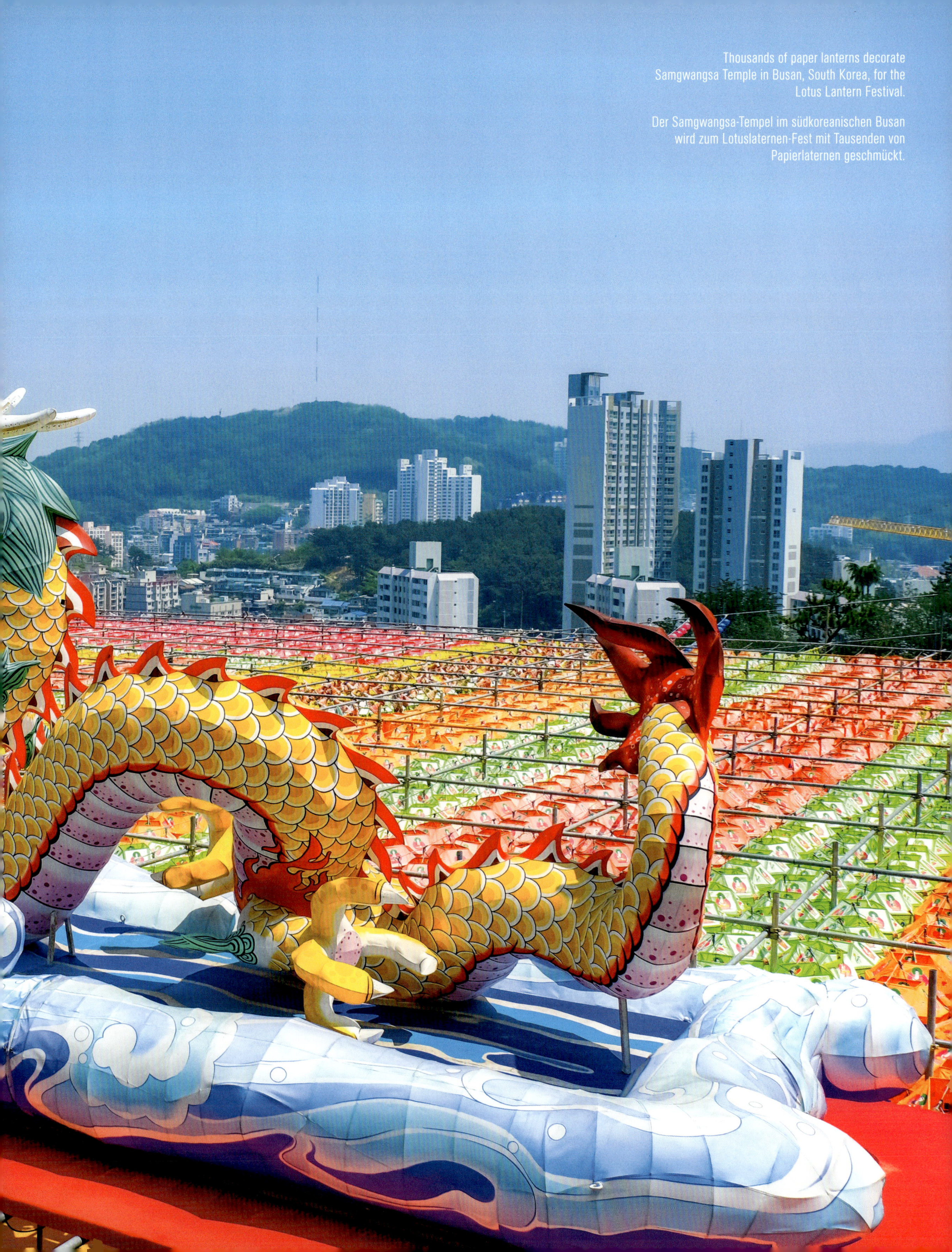
Thousands of paper lanterns decorate
Samgwangsa Temple in Busan, South Korea, for the
Lotus Lantern Festival.

Der Samgwangsa-Tempel im südkoreanischen Busan
wird zum Lotuslaternen-Fest mit Tausenden von
Papierlaternen geschmückt.

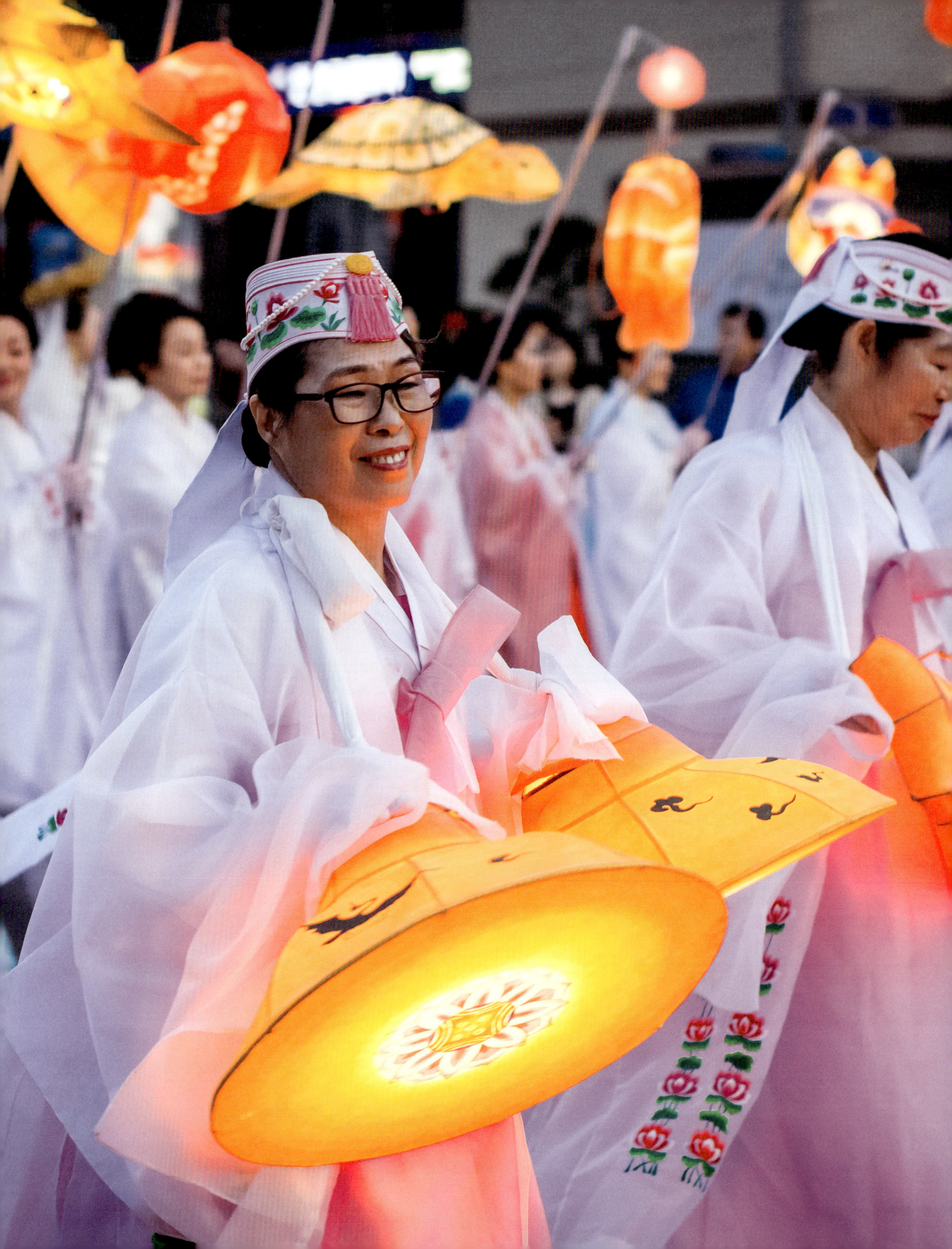

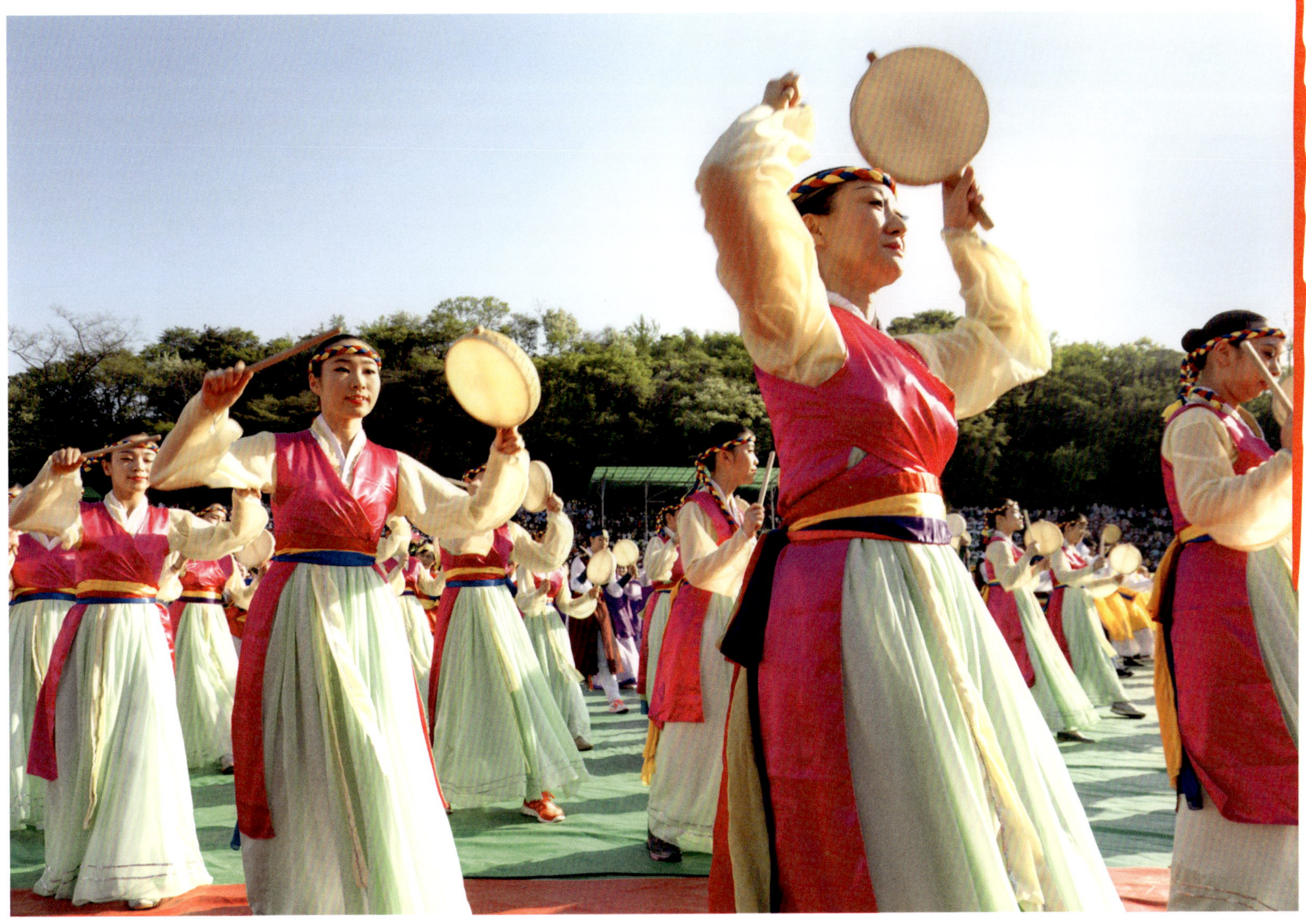

Yeon Deung Hoe (Lotus Lantern Festival) is an annual
South Korean event that celebrates Buddha's birthday.
It originated during the Silla dynasty (57 BCE–935 CE).

Mit dem Lotuslaternen-Fest Yeon Deung Hoe wird in Südkorea
jedes Jahr Buddhas Geburtstag gefeiert.
Es entstand während der Silla-Dynastie (57 v. Chr.–935 n. Chr.).

Semana Santa, "Holy Week" in English, is one of Spain's most traditional
religious festivals. The week-long celebration leads up to Easter Sunday and is
particularly popular in Andalusia.

Die Semana Santa (heilige Woche) ist eines der traditionellsten religiösen Feste
Spaniens. Die in Andalusien besonders beliebten Feierlichkeiten dauern eine
Woche und gipfeln im Ostersonntag.

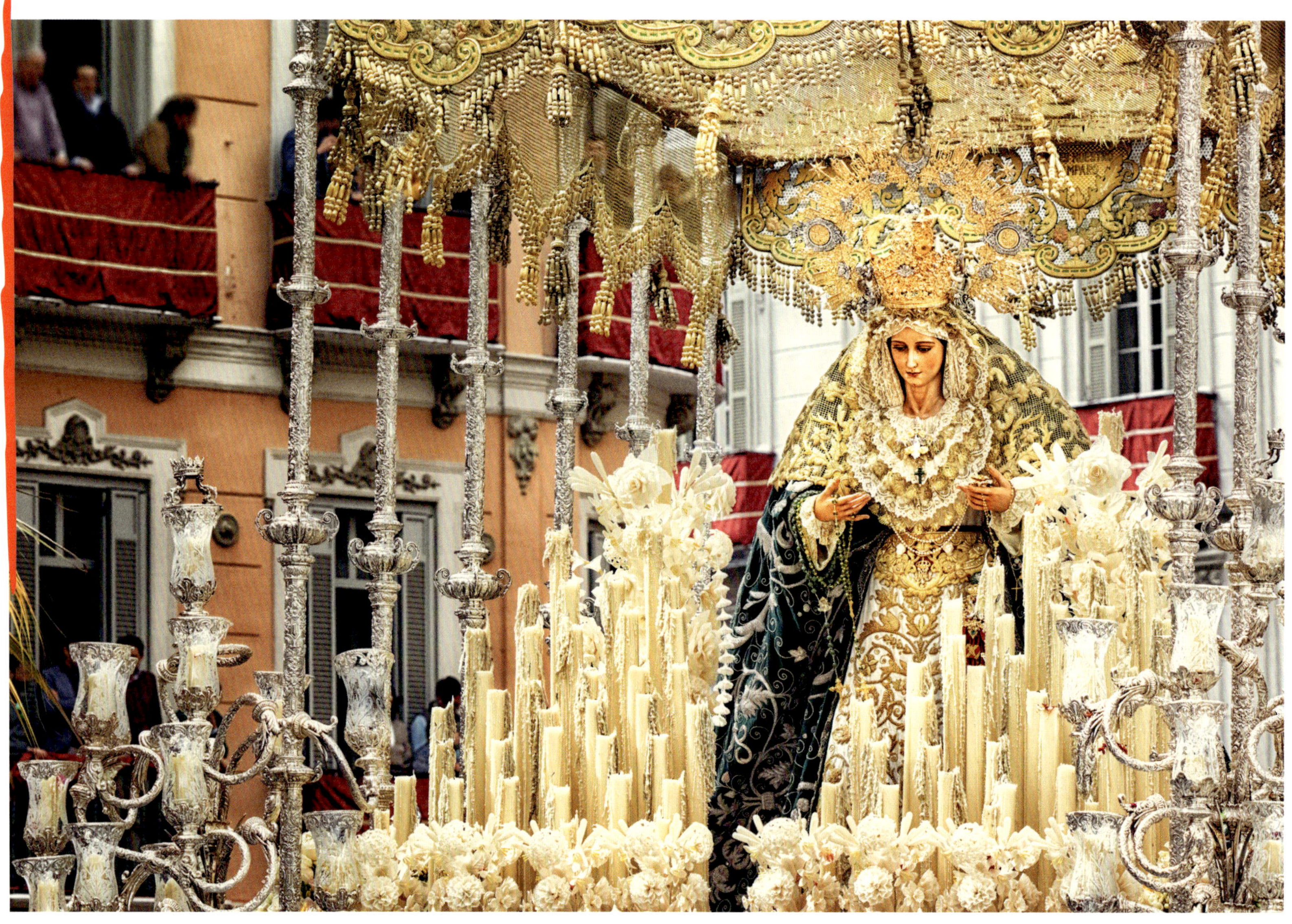

During the processions, massive floats carrying religious statues—mainly
effigies of Jesus Christ or the Virgin Mary—are brought to the church.
Accompanying marching bands play religious music.

Auf den Prozessionen werden riesige religiöse Statuen – hauptsächlich
Darstellungen von Jesus Christus und der Jungfrau Maria – auf Wagen zur
Kirche gebracht. Begleitet werden sie dabei von Marschkapellen,
die religiöse Musik spielen.

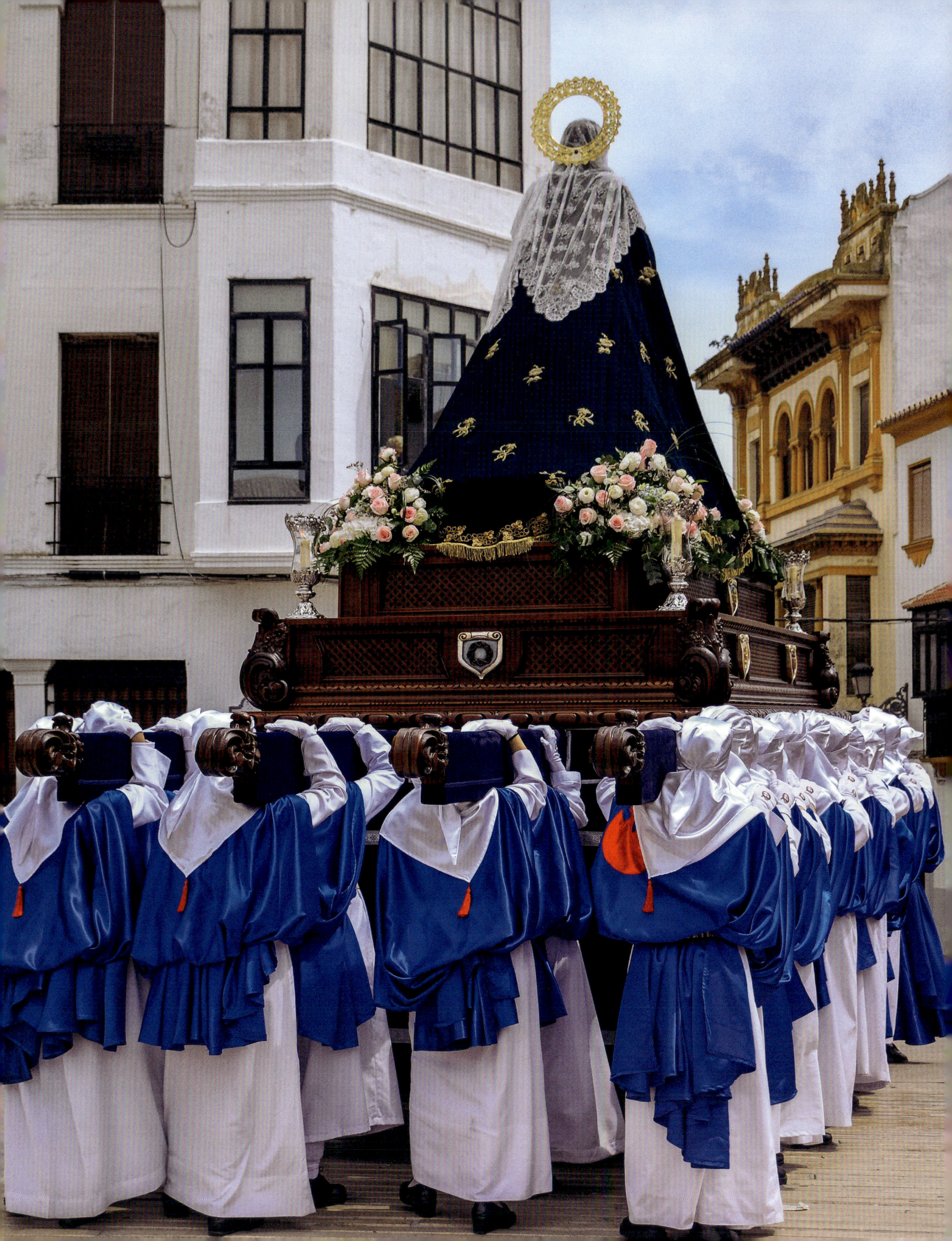

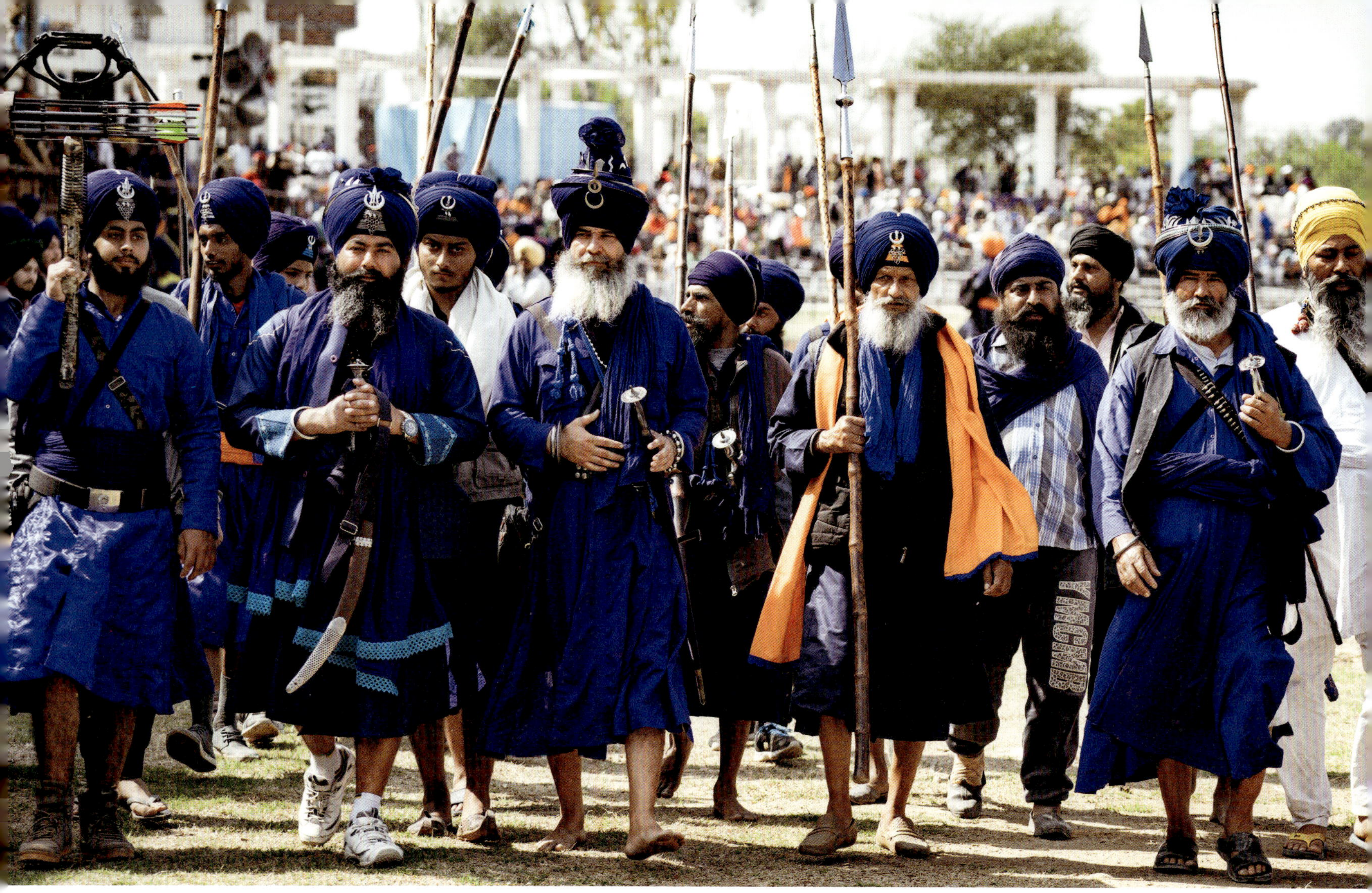

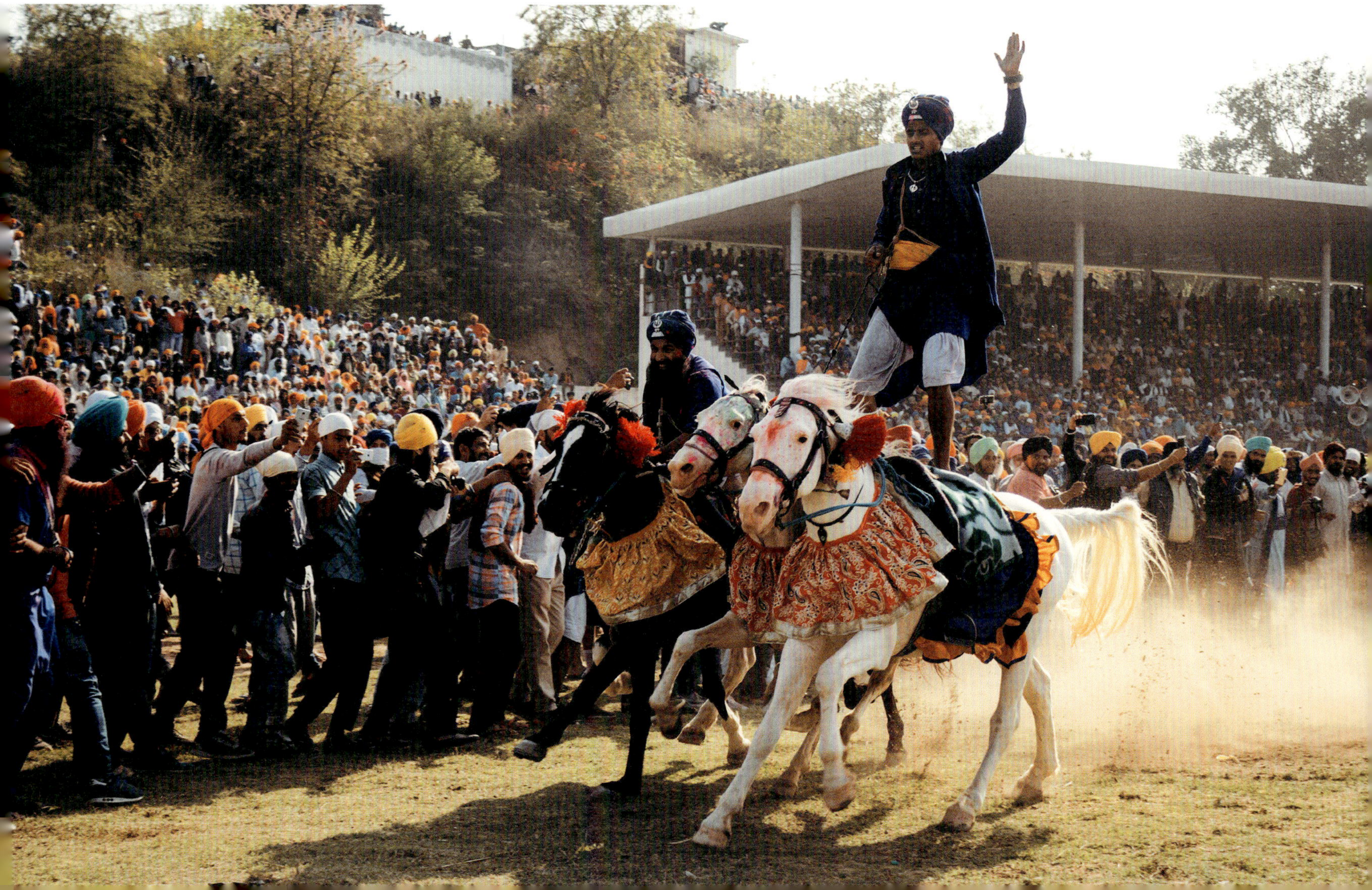

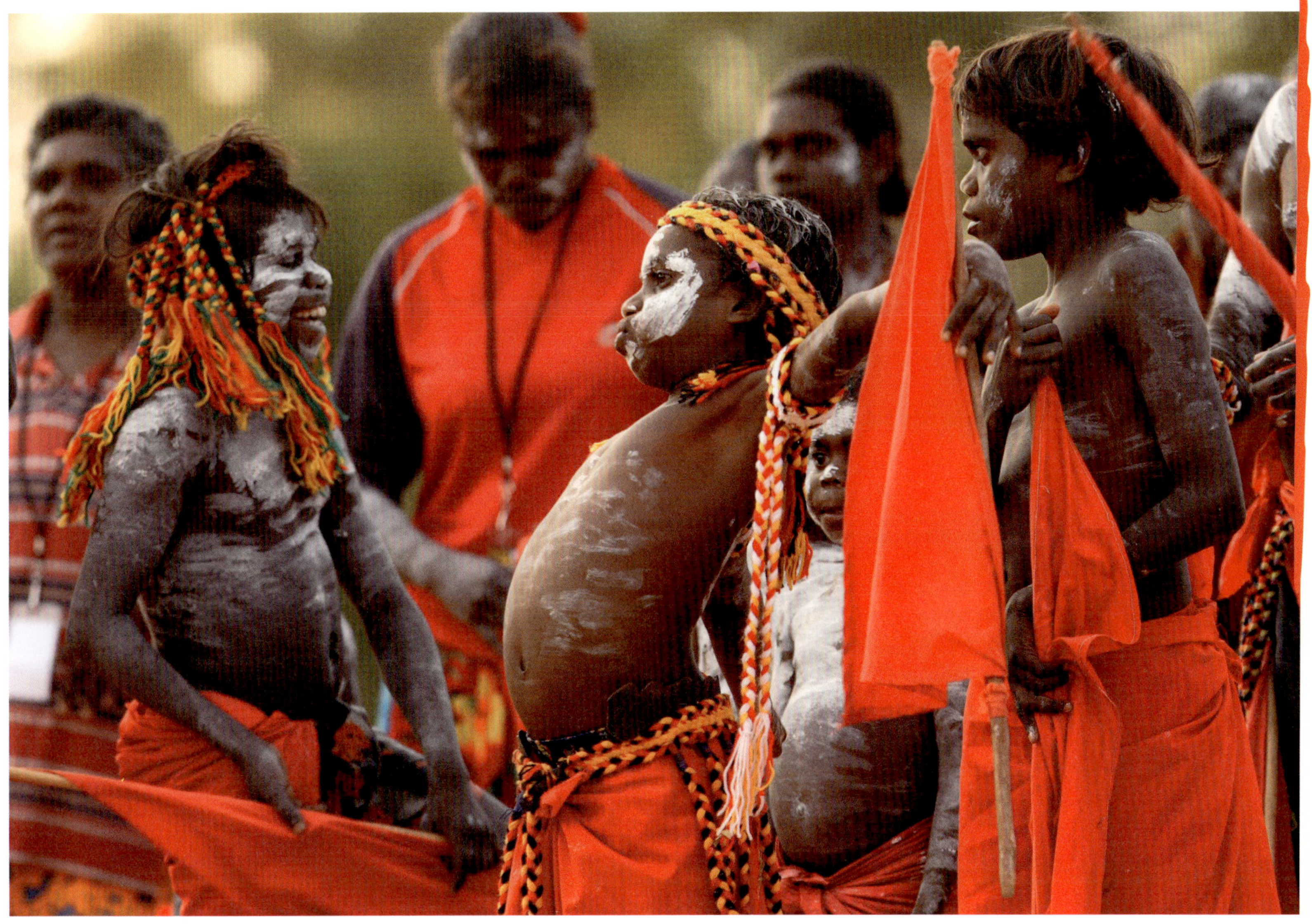

The Sikh festival Hola Mohalla was originally started as an event to practice
military exercises. Nowadays, it features various displays of fighting prowess
and bravery. It also includes the performance of *kirtans* (devotional songs),
as well as religious lectures, music, and poems.

Das Sikh-Fest Hola Mohalla war ursprünglich eine Veranstaltung für Militär-
übungen. Heutzutage werden dort verschiedene Kampfdisziplinen und Mutproben
präsentiert. Dazu kommen Aufführungen von *kirtans* (fromme Lieder), religiöse
Vorträge, musikalische und poetische Darbietungen.

People light up butter lamps to pray for good luck during the Chotrul Düchen Butter Lamp Festival in Lhasa, Tibet, a traditional celebration in Tibetan Buddhism. Chotrul Düchen, the "great day of miraculous manifestations," commemorates the historical Buddha performing one miracle each over 15 days to strengthen the faith of his disciples. On this day, the consequences of all positive and negative actions are multiplied by millions.

Beim Butterlampenfest Chotrul Düchen in Lhasa werden Lichter angezündet – eine Tradition des Tibetischen Buddhismus. Chotrul Düchen, der „große Tag wundersamer Manifestationen" erinnert daran, dass der historische Buddha über 15 Tage je ein Wunder vollbrachte, um den Glauben seiner Jünger zu stärken. An diesem Tag multiplizieren sich die Folgen aller positiven und negativen Handlungen für die Gläubigen um ein Millionenfaches.

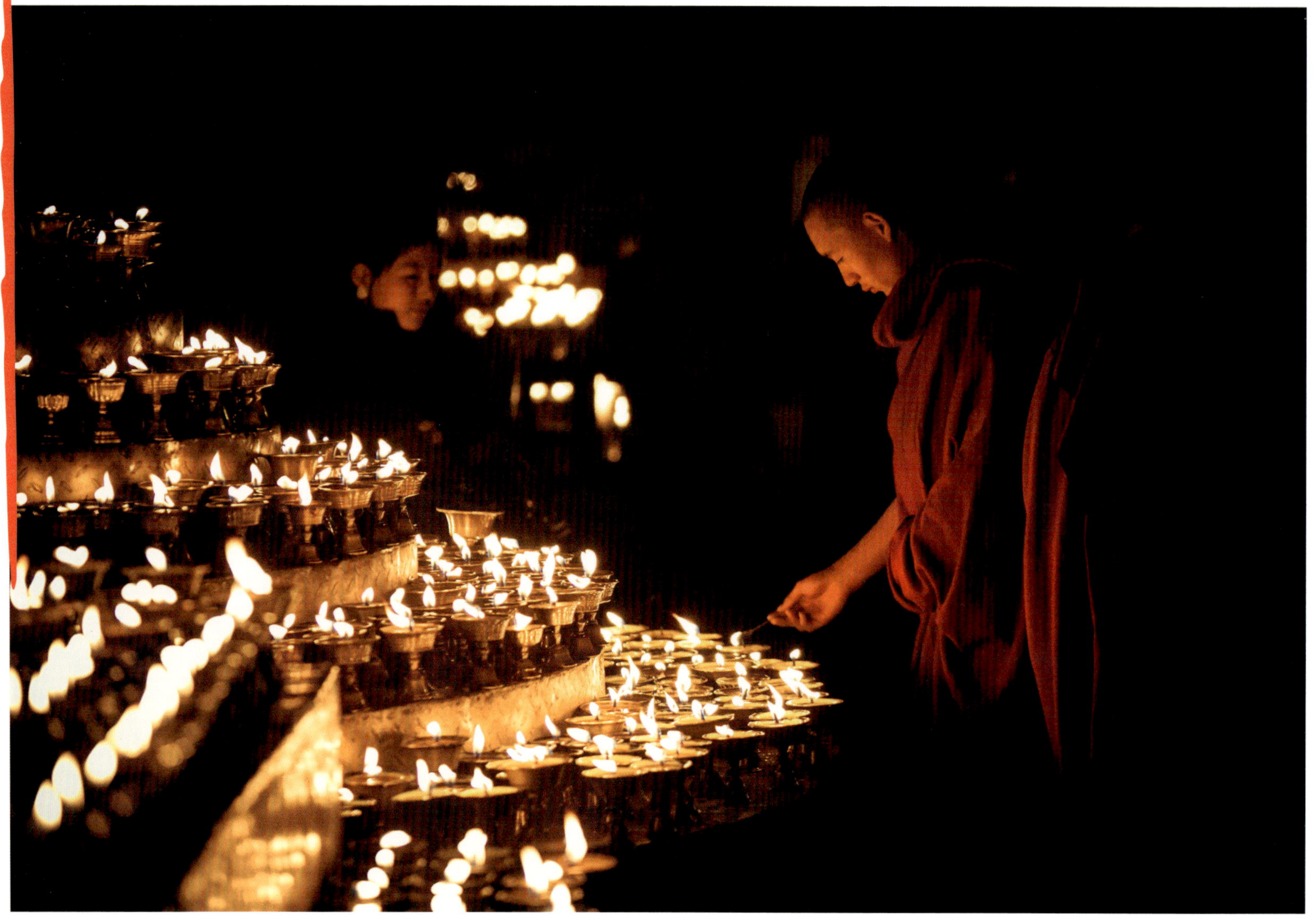

Diwali, the festival of lights, is a major celebration for Hindus, Sikhs, and Jains. During the five-day festival, everything is illuminated with *diyas* (oil lamps) and decorated with *rangoli* (elaborate mixed material ornaments). Offerings are presented to Lakshmi, the goddess of prosperity and wealth. Sweets and gifts are shared, too.

Das Lichterfest Diwali ist für Hindus, Sikhs und Jainas besonders wichtig. Während der fünftägigen Feierlichkeiten wird alles mit *diyas* (Öllampen) beleuchtet und mit *rangoli* (prächtigen Mustern aus verschiedenen Materialien) geschmückt. Man bringt Lakshmi, der Göttin des Wohlstands und der Gesundheit, Opfer dar und überreicht einander Süßigkeiten und Geschenke.

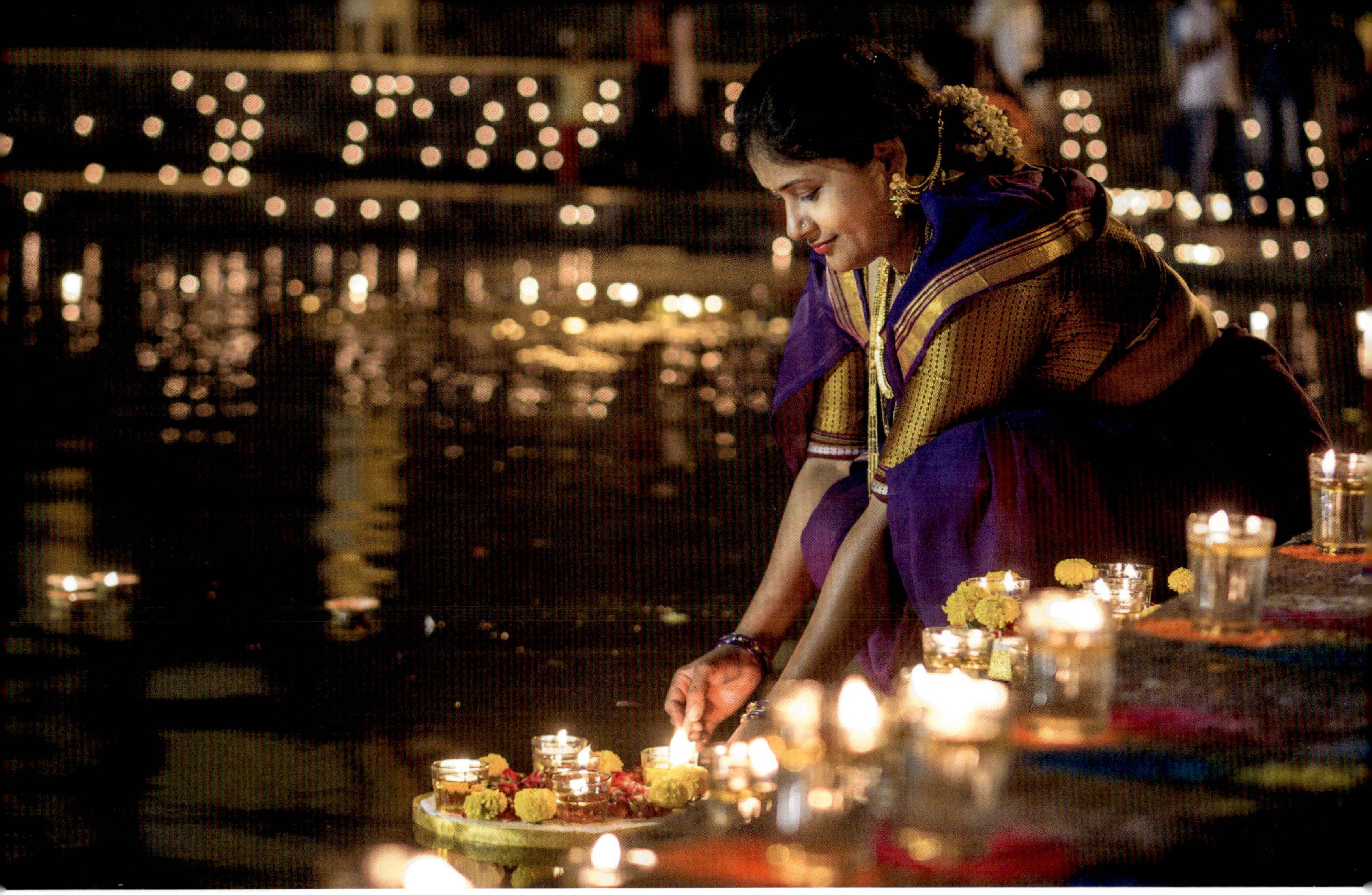

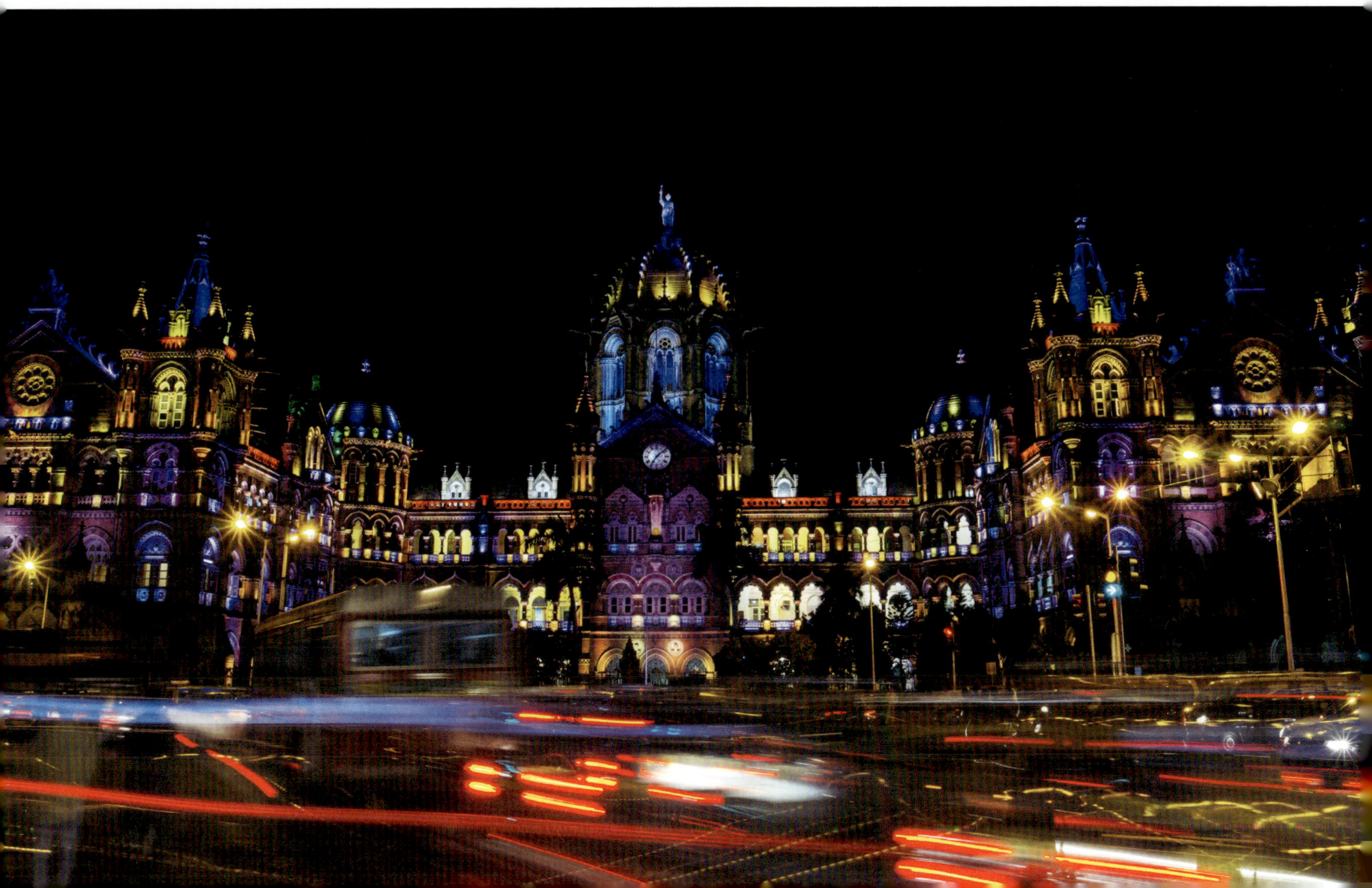

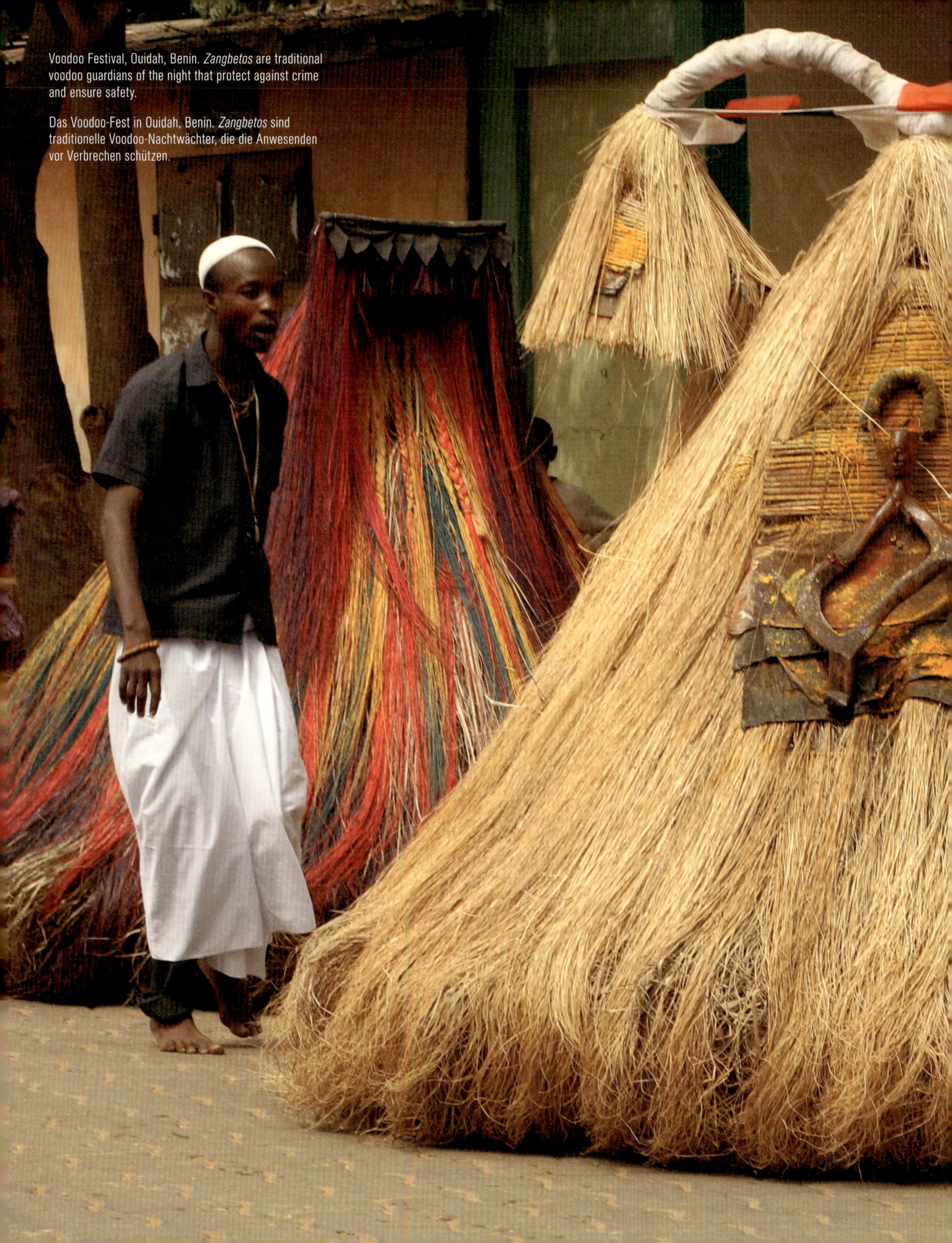

Voodoo Festival, Ouidah, Benin. *Zangbetos* are traditional voodoo guardians of the night that protect against crime and ensure safety.

Das Voodoo-Fest in Ouidah, Benin. *Zangbetos* sind traditionelle Voodoo-Nachtwächter, die die Anwesenden vor Verbrechen schützen.

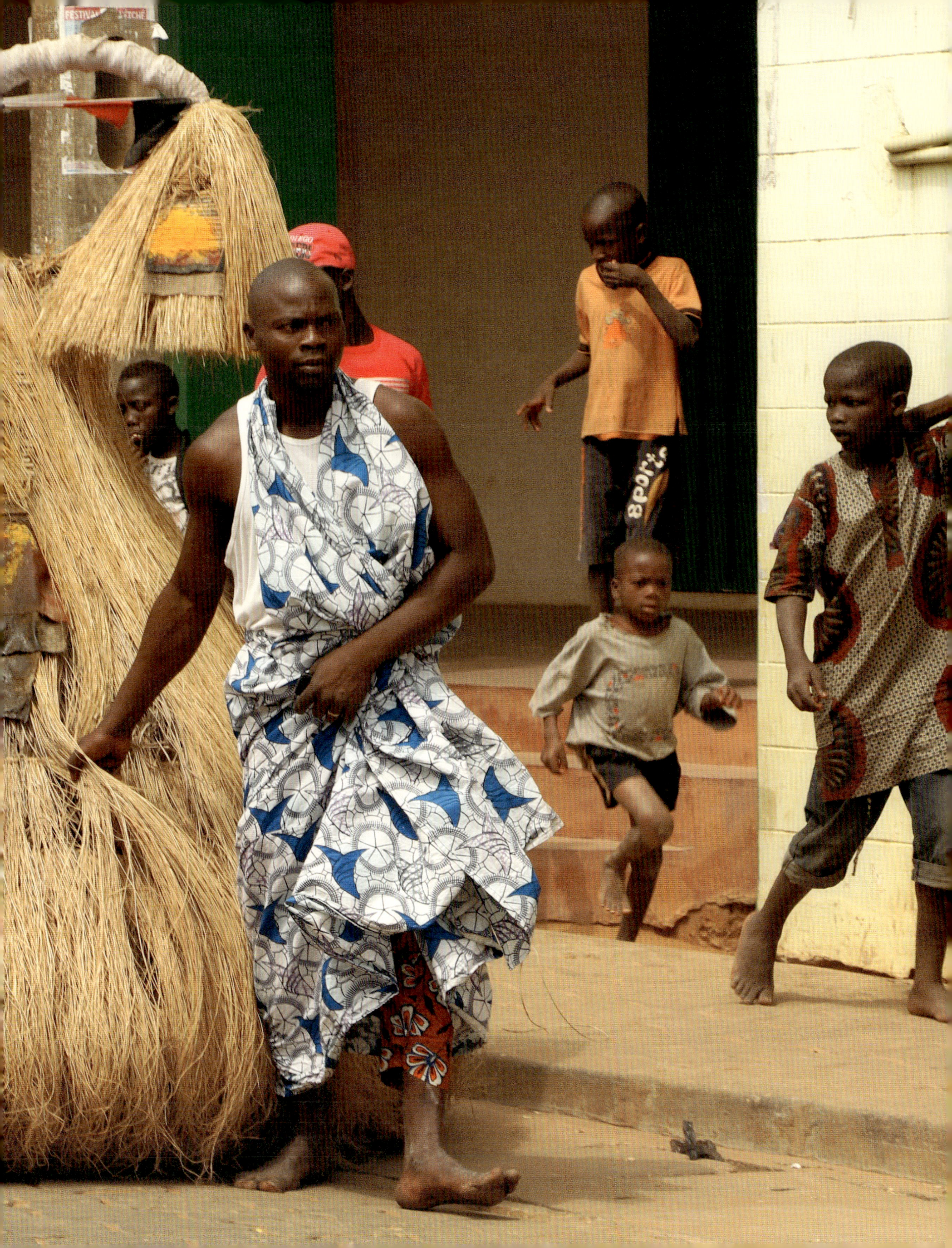

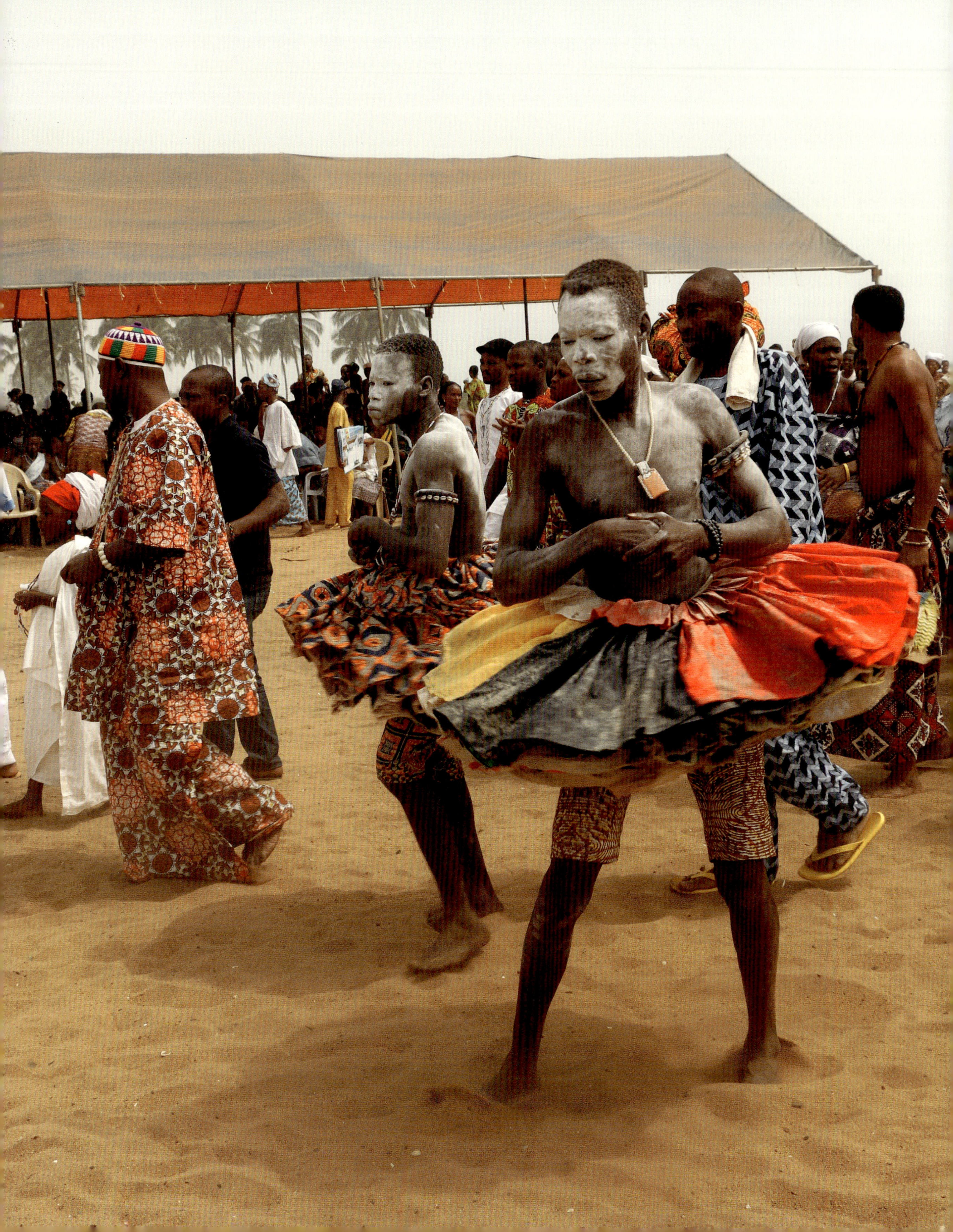

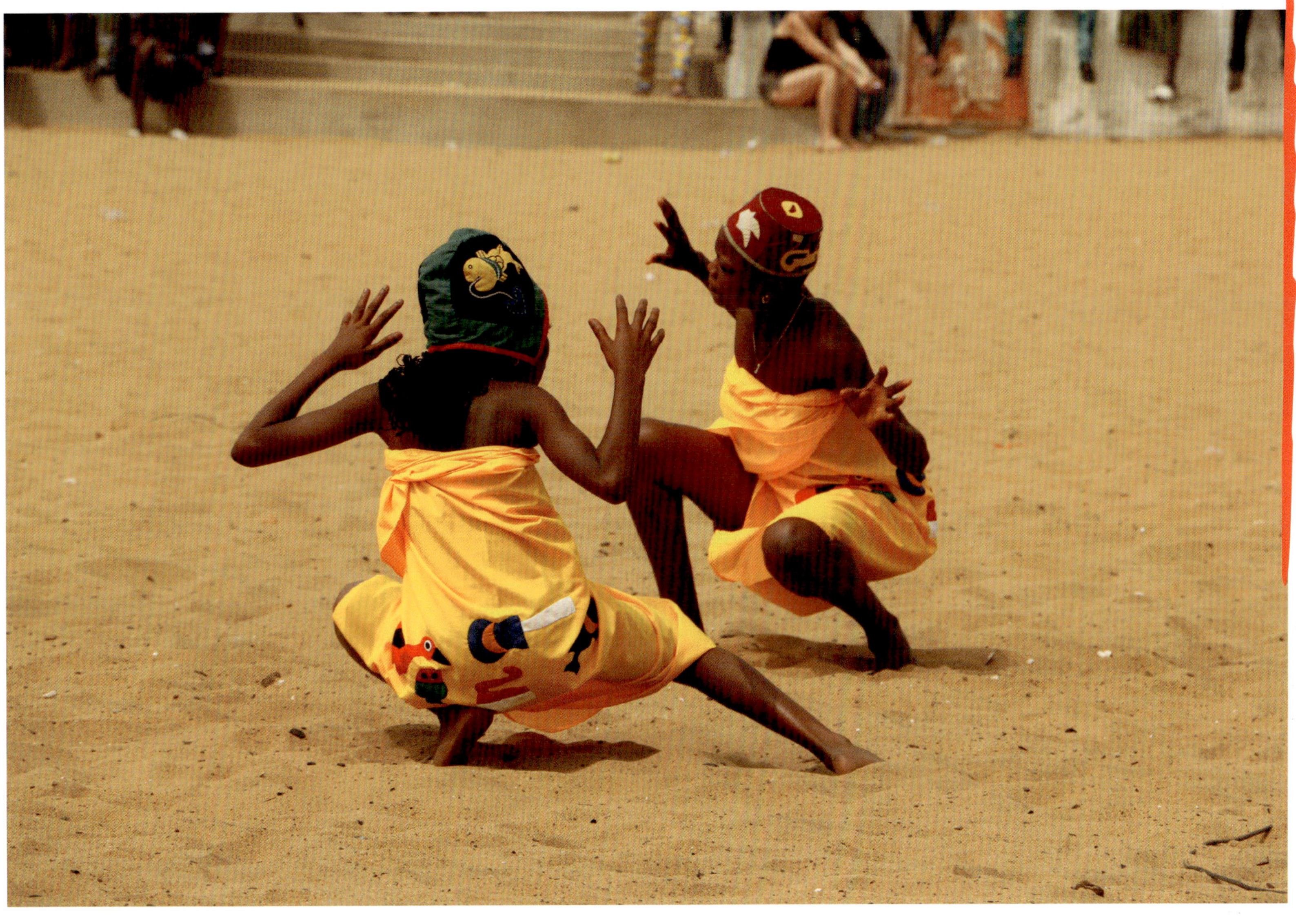

Benin celebrates the voodoo cult. The Voodoo Festival is
even an official holiday in the country.

Benin zelebriert den Voodoo-Kult. Das Voodoo-Fest ist
hier sogar ein gesetzlicher Feiertag.

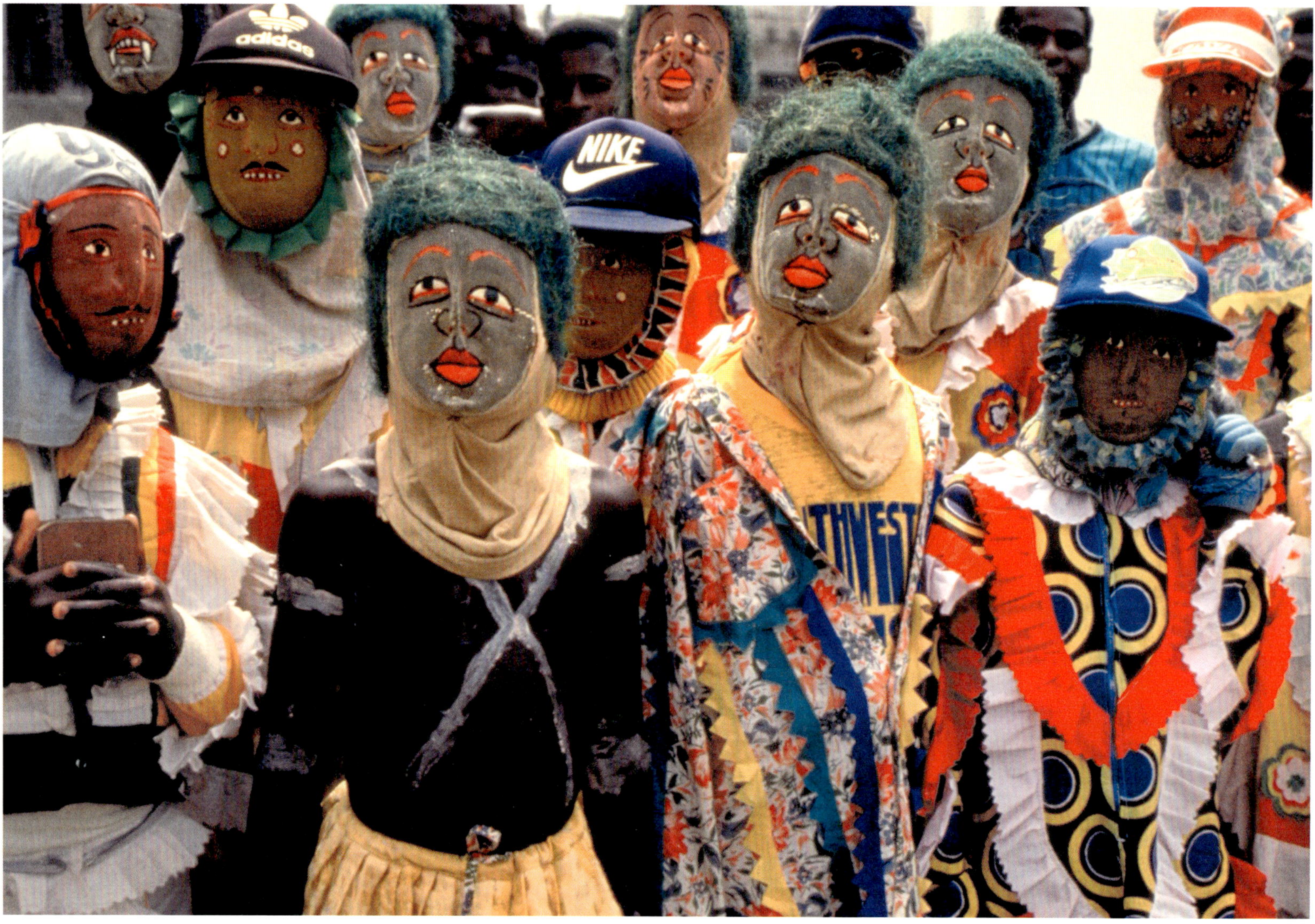

This page: Ghana's Fetu Afahye marks the change of the farming and harvesting season and celebrates health, cleansing, and keeping its people free from illness.
Opposite, top: Red Earth Festival in Oklahoma celebrates Native American culture and traditions.
Bottom: At the Mount Hagen Cultural Show in Papua New Guinea, numerous ethnic groups come together to celebrate their rituals and traditions to prevent their extinction.

Diese Seite: Fetu Afahye in Ghana markiert den Beginn der Erntesaison und feiert Gesundheit, Reinigung und die Vermeidung von Krankheiten.
Rechte Seite, oben: Das Red Earth Festival in Oklahoma zelebriert die Kultur und Traditionen der Native Americans.
Unten: Auf der Mount Hagen Cultural Show in Papua-Neuguinea kommen zahlreiche ethnische Gruppen zusammen, um ihre Riten und Traditionen zu feiern und deren Aussterben zu verhindern.

Good to know
WISSENSWERTES

The Sing-sing at Mount Hagen in Papua New Guinea is one of the biggest gatherings in the country. It's a chance for as many as 100 different tribes to show off their unique cultures through dance, body paint and decoration, music, and food. The event was originally intended to promote peaceful interactions between rival tribes and was not planned as a tourist event.

Das Sing-sing-Festival in Mount Hagen in Papua-Neuguinea ist eine der größten Zusammenkünfte des Landes. Es bietet den um die 100 verschiedenen Stämmen die Gelegenheit, ihre einmalige Kultur in Form von Tanz, Körperbemalung und -schmuck, Musik und Speisen zu präsentieren. Die Veranstaltung diente ursprünglich dazu die friedliche Interaktion rivalisierender Stämme zu fördern und war nicht als Touristenevent geplant.

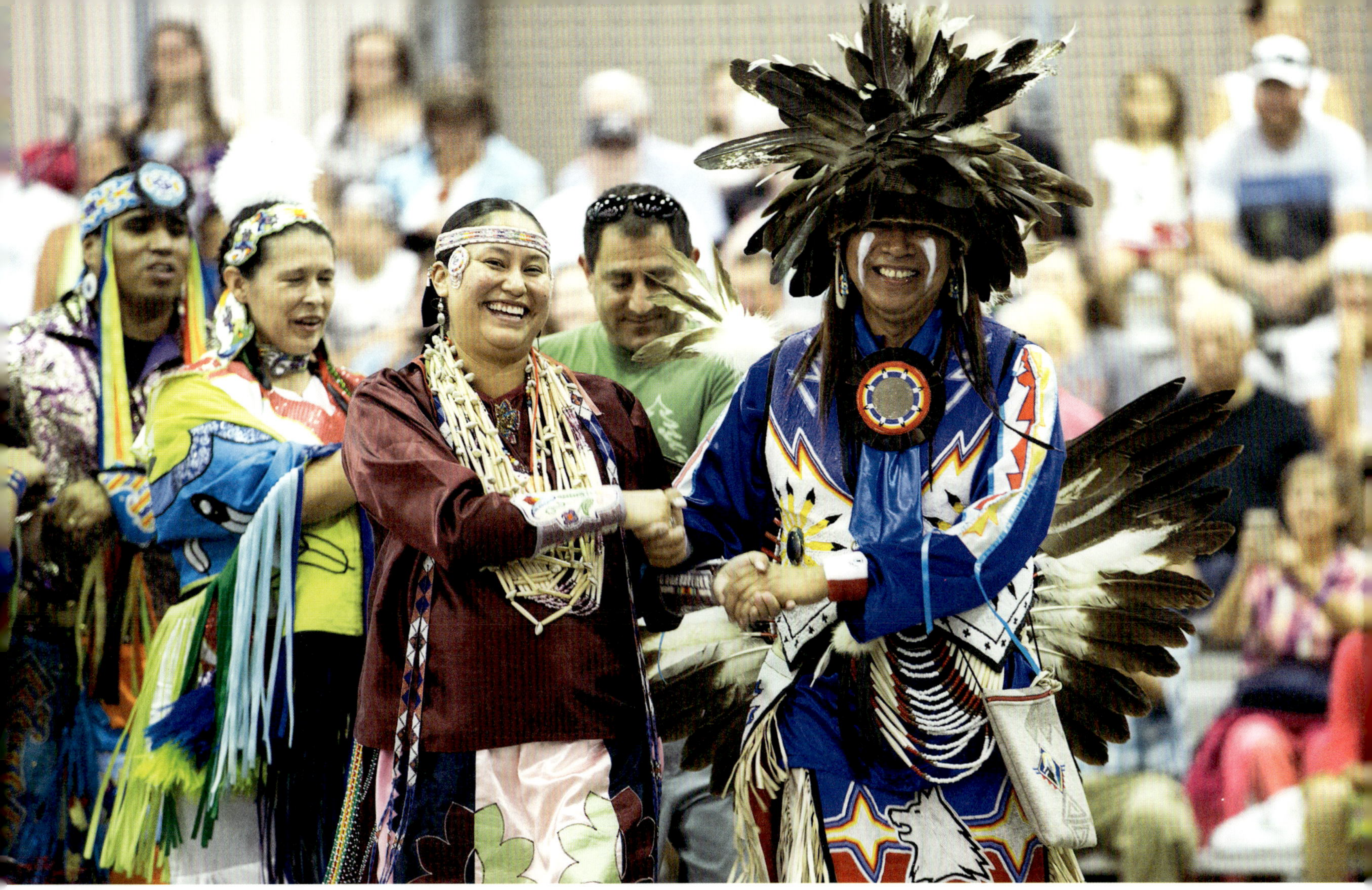

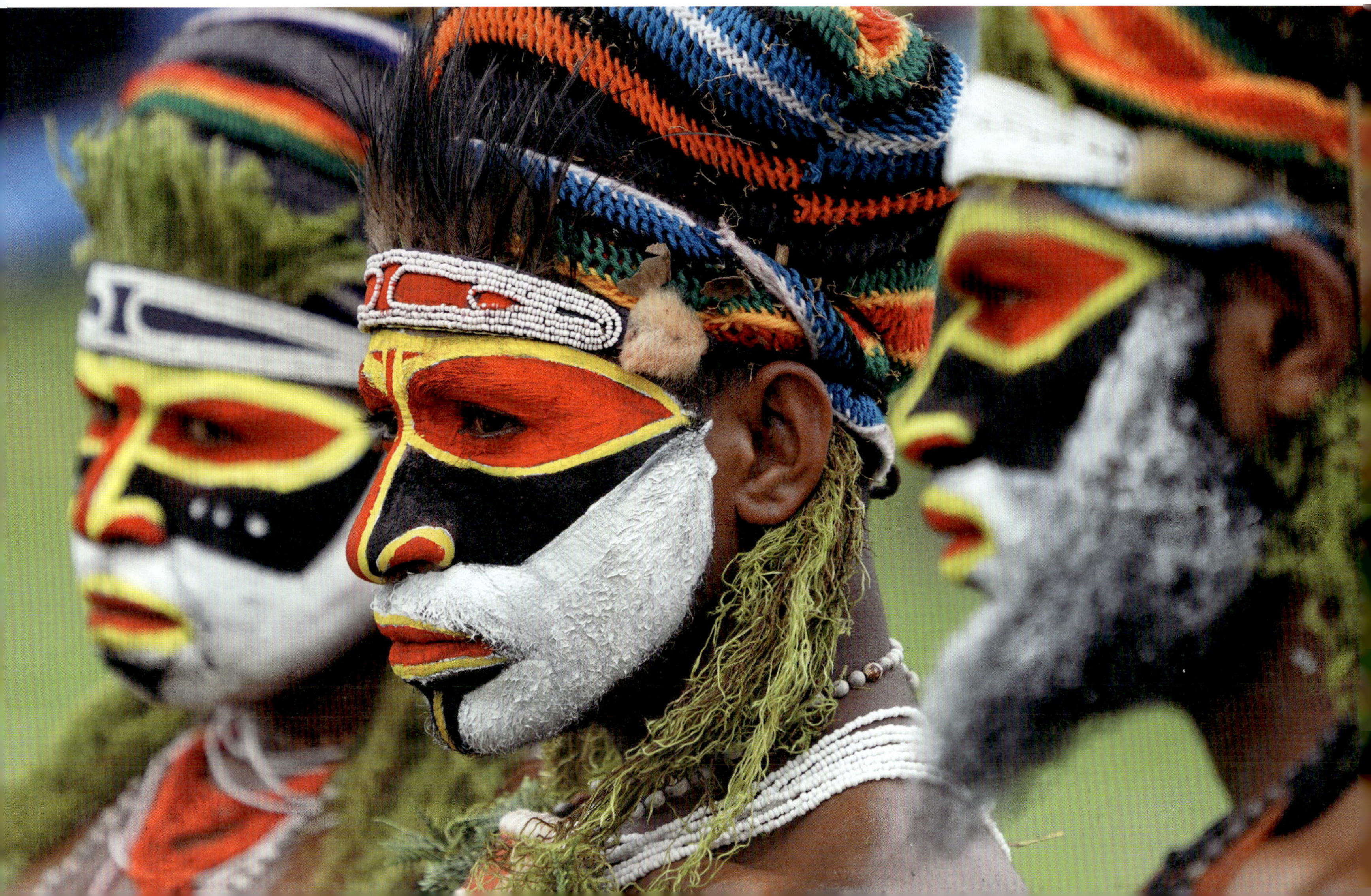

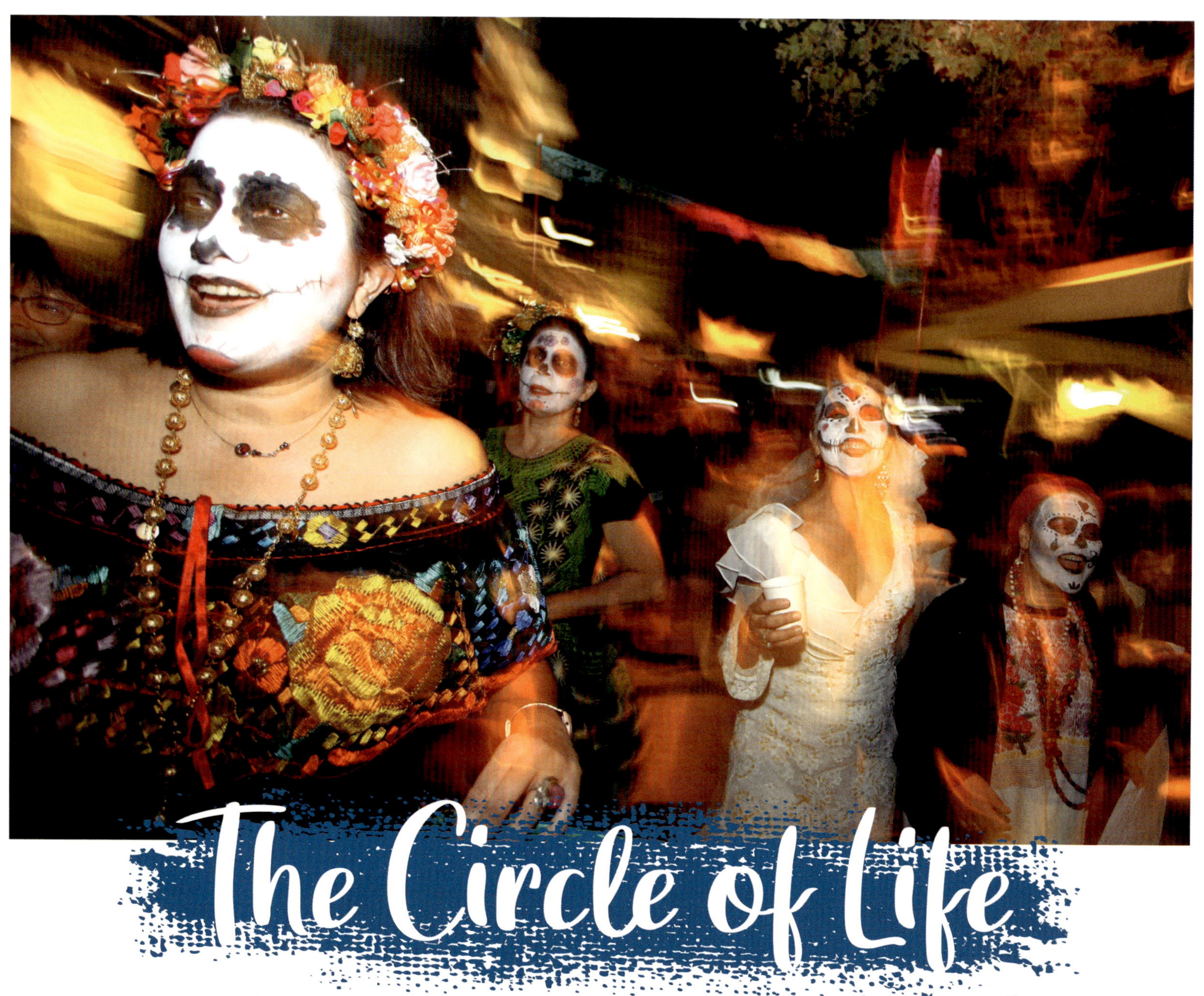

The Circle of Life

DER KREISLAUF DES LEBENS

The Día de los Muertos (Day of the Dead) is a colorful and diverse tradition in Mexico to celebrate friends and family members who have passed away.

Der Día de los Muertos (Tag der Toten) wird in Mexiko bunt und vielfältig begangen, um verstorbener Freunde und Familienmitglieder zu gedenken.

Next page: Scary costumes, pumpkins, and sweets–it must be Halloween in the USA!

Folgende Seite: Gruselkostüme, Kürbisse und Süßigkeiten – untrügliche Zeichen, dass in den USA Halloween gefeiert wird!

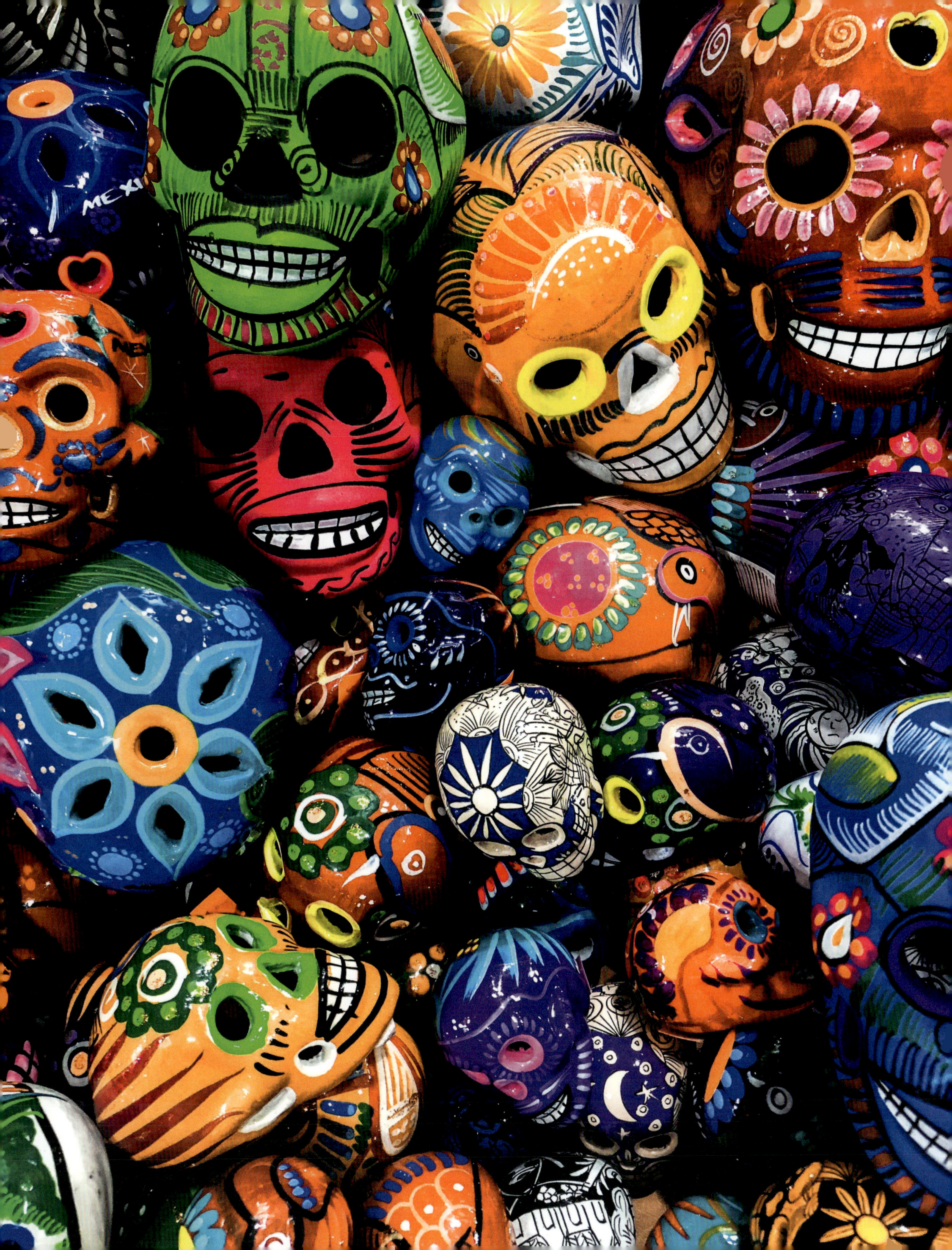

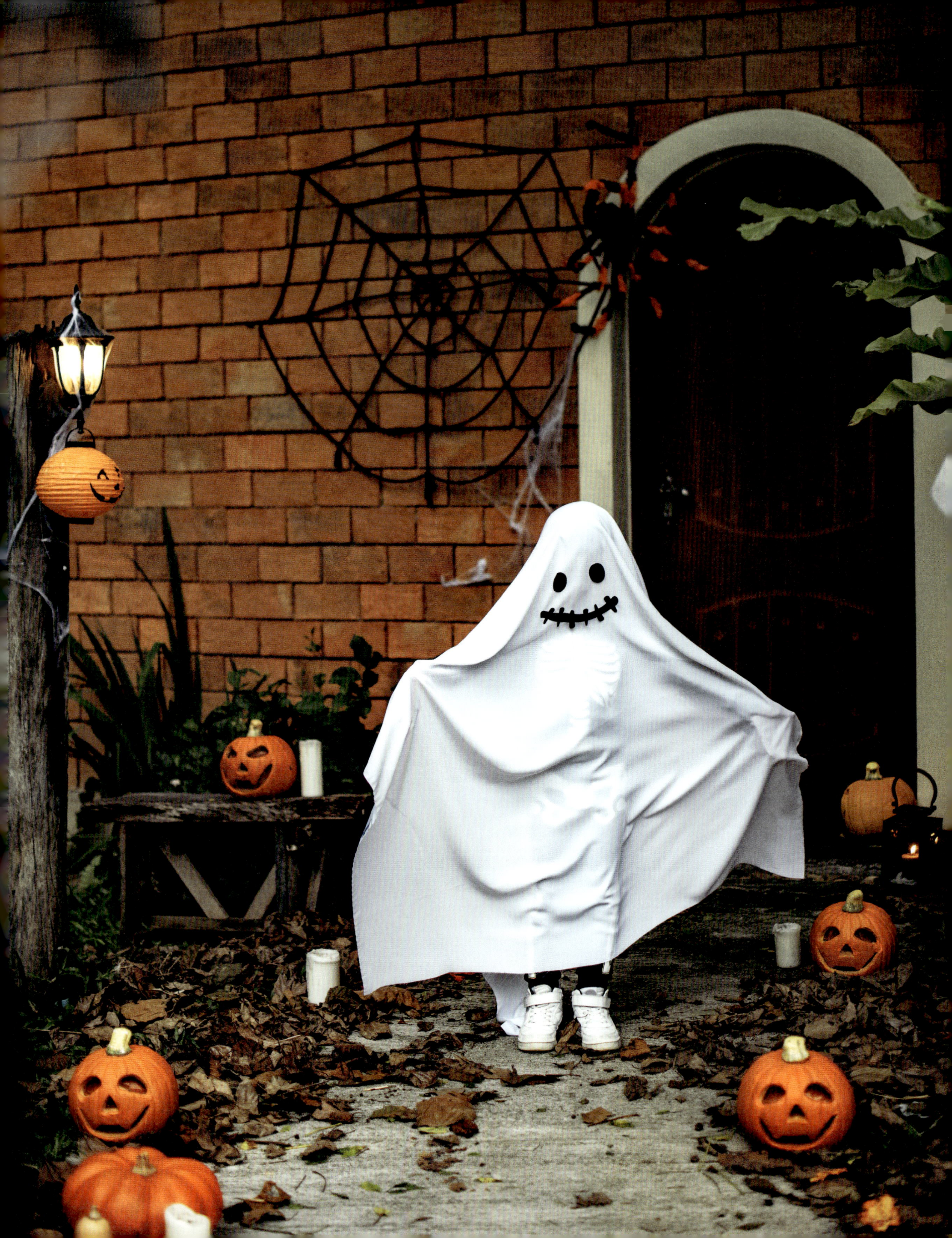

As you'll see in this book, there's a celebration for *every* aspect of life, but the most important processes any of us will ever go through are birth and death. And of course, there are festivals for both. Festivals like Tet in Vietnam, and Día de los Muertos in Mexico, celebrate the latter, while Kanamara Matsuri in Japan and Janmashtami in many Hindu countries, the former. And Halloween celebrates the afterlife and undead.

Kanamara Matsuri in Japan is also known as the "Penis Festival" and celebrates male fertility. It's easy for outsiders to just enjoy the overt novelty of this festival, but behind every phallic-shaped lollipop and penis parade, there's an important tradition. *This* is the time to celebrate sex and fertility in Japan, a country normally associated with mild manners and conservatism. Celebrated in Tokyo in April, over 50,000 people turn out to pray to the gods of fertility and to protect them from STIs, too. The festival arose from an ancient Japanese legend featuring a demon who hid inside the vagina of a young woman. The demon viciously attacked her partners on her two separate wedding nights. Distraught, she sought the help of a blacksmith who created an iron phallus to break the demon's teeth. You can see the phallus at the Kanayama Shrine in Kawasaki. Money from the sales of penis paraphernalia at Kanamara Matsuri now goes to fund life-saving HIV research.

One of the world's biggest celebrations of death, Día de los Muertos, takes place all over Mexico on All Saints' Day and All Souls' Day. Colorful vigils and altars are created in windows and graveyards to remember the passing of loved ones. The festival originated thousands of years ago among pre-Hispanic cultures who believed mourning was disrespectful—death was natural and loved ones should be kept alive in memory and spirit. And so, at night during Día de los Muertos, families gather around loved ones' graves to play music and sing, tell stories, and share food and drink. It's a joyous event. Expect women dressed up as the image of Catrina complete with face paint and vivid traditional dress, singing, and dancing.

Es gibt Feiern für so ziemlich *jeden* Aspekt des Lebens, doch die wichtigsten Ereignisse im Leben eines Menschen sind: Geburt und Tod. Und natürlich gibt es für beide Feste. Das vietnamesische Tet-Fest und der mexikanische Feiertag Día de los Muertos zelebrieren den Tod, das amerikanische Halloween feiert die Untoten und das Jenseits, während sich beim Kanamara-Matsuri-Fest in Japan und beim Janmashtami-Fest in vielen hinduistischen Ländern alles um Zeugung und Geburt dreht.

Kanamara Matsuri, auch als „Penis-Fest" bekannt, feiert die männliche Potenz. Besucher aus dem Ausland können sich einfach an den ungewohnt expliziten Figuren und Kostümierungen erfreuen, aber hinter den penisförmigen Lutschern und Penis-Paraden steckt eine wichtige Tradition. In Japan, einem Land, das normalerweise von züchtiger Zurückhaltung geprägt ist, ist *dies* der Moment, Sex und Fruchtbarkeit zu zelebrieren. Im April kommen in Tokio jährlich über 50 000 Menschen zusammen, um die Fruchtbarkeitsgötter um Nachwuchs (und Schutz vor Geschlechtskrankheiten) zu bitten. Das Fest basiert auf einer uralten japanischen Legende, nach der ein Dämon sich in der Vagina einer jungen Frau versteckte und in ihren Hochzeitsnächten zwei jungen Männern den Penis abbiss. Verzweifelt bat die Frau einen Schmied um Hilfe, der einen eisernen Phallus erschuf, um die Zähne des Dämons zu brechen. Dieser Eisenpenis ist heute im Kanayama-Schrein in Kawasaki zu besichtigen. Der Erlös aus dem Verkauf von Penis-Souvenirs während des Festes kommt der Aids-Forschung zugute.

Eine der größten Festlichkeiten zu Ehren des Todes, der Día de los Muertos, wird zwischen Allerheiligen und Allerseelen in ganz Mexiko begangen. In den Fenstern und auf Friedhöfen werden bunte Altäre aufgebaut, mit denen man der Verstorbenen gedenkt. Eine Ursprungstheorie besagt, dass das Fest vor Jahrtausenden von indigenen Kulturen ins Leben gerufen wurde, die Totentrauer für respektlos hielten, da der Tod etwas Natürliches ist und geliebte Menschen in der Erinnerung lebendig bleiben sollten. Daher versammeln sich am Día de los Muertos Familien an den Gräber ihrer Verstorbenen, um zu musizieren und zu tanzen, Geschichten zu erzählen und Speisen und Getränke zu sich zu nehmen. Es ist ein fröhliches Ereignis.

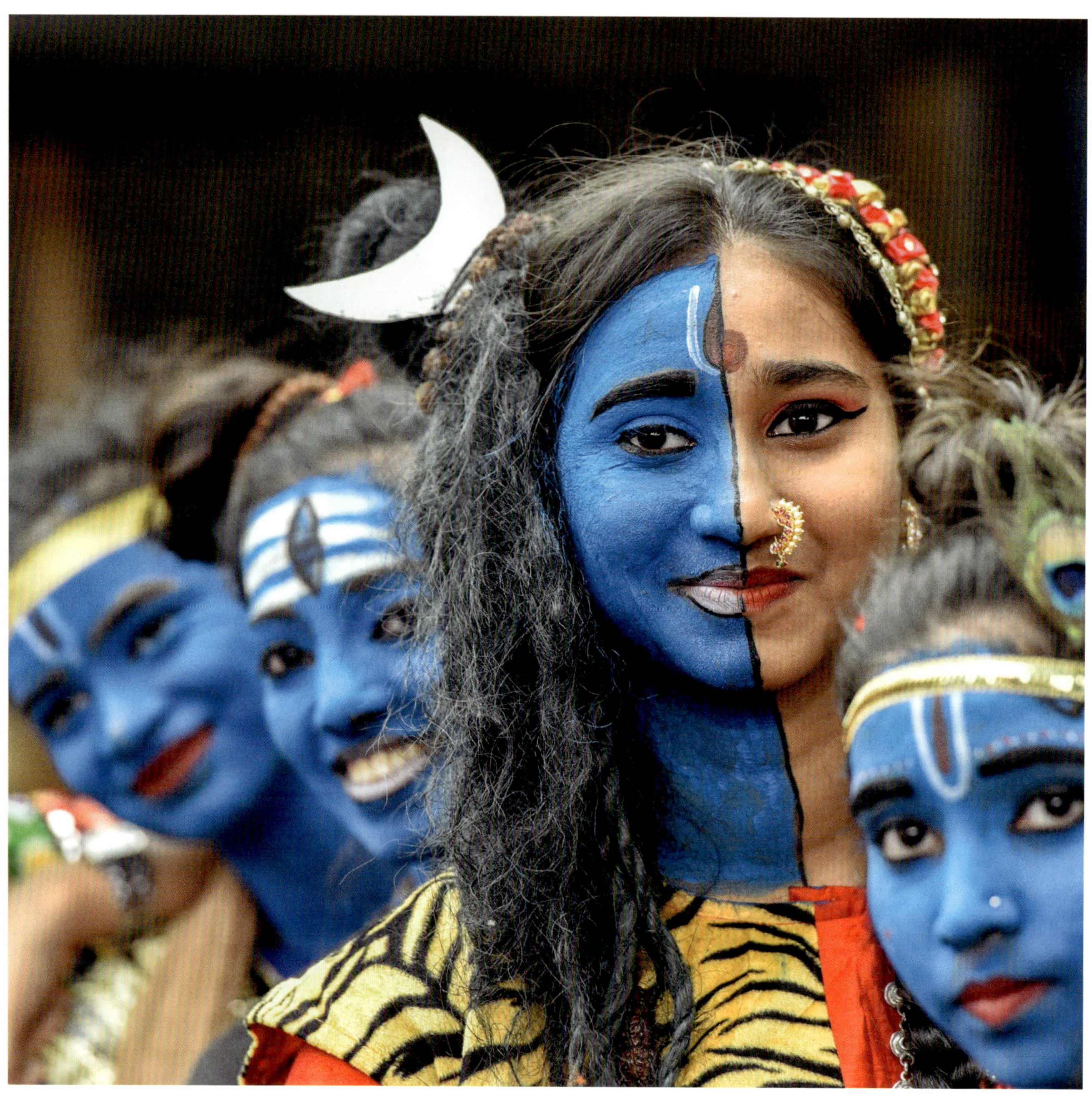

Women dress up as the Hindu gods Krishna and Shiva
during the Janmashtami Festival in Mumbai, India.

Frauen verkleiden sich auf dem Janmashtami-Fest im
indischen Mumbai als Hindu-Gottheiten Krishna und Shiva.

Devotees form a human pyramid to break an earthen pot (*handi*) filled with curd (*dahi*)
hanging above them. The ritual is called *dahi handi* and is an integral part of the
Janmashtami Festival that celebrates Krishna's birth.

Die Teilnehmer bilden eine Menschenpyramide, um ein über ihnen hängendes, mit Quark
(*dahi*) gefülltes Tongefäß (*handi*) zu zerschlagen. Dieses Ritual nennt sich *Dahi Handi* und
ist ein integraler Bestandteil des Janmashtami-Festes, das Krishnas Geburt feiert.

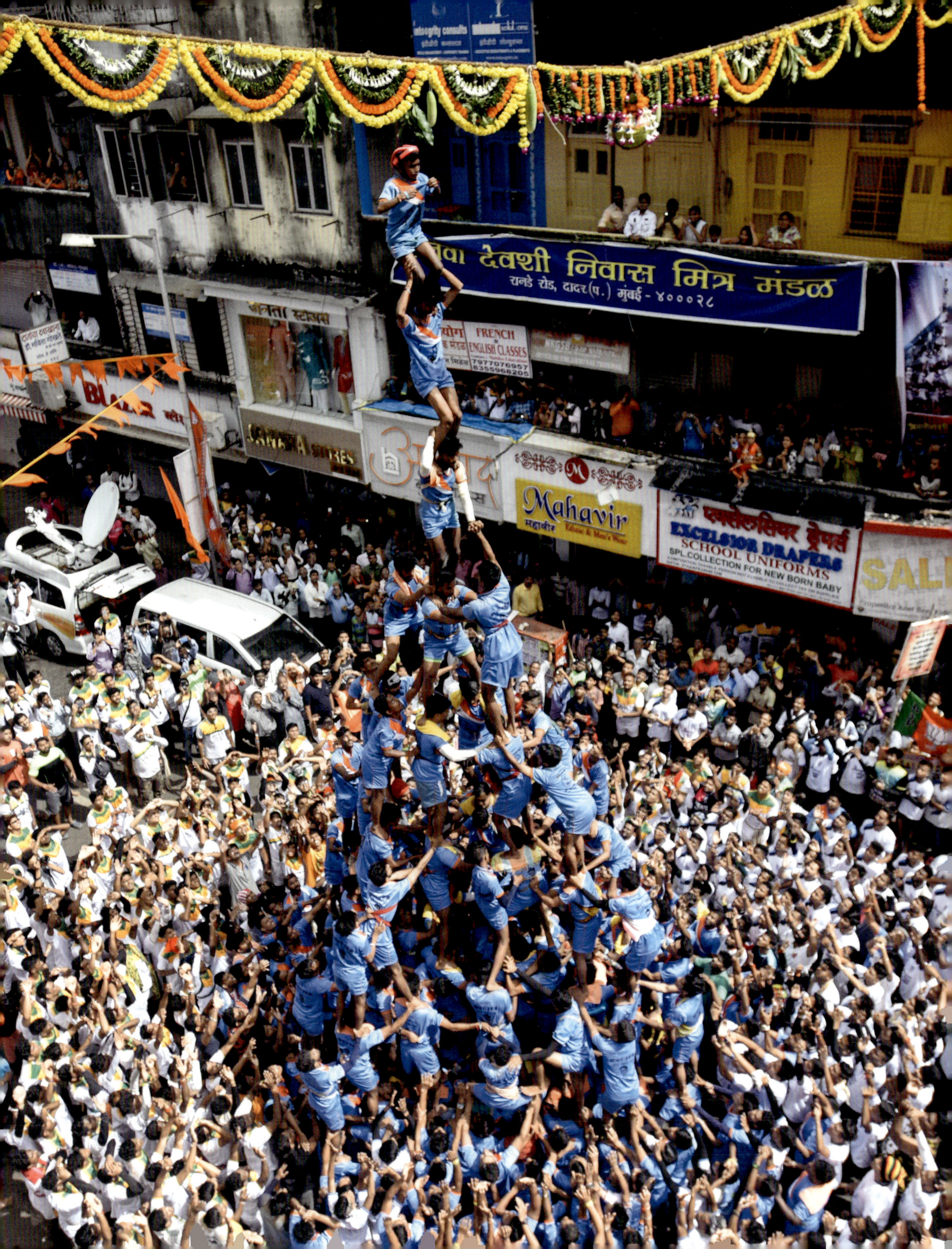
निवास मित्र मंडळ
रानडे रोड, दादर (प.) मुंबई - ४०००२८
FRENCH
ENGLISH CLASSES
7977076957
8355966205
Mahavir
Ethnic & Men's Wear
EXCELSIOR DRAPERS
SCHOOL UNIFORMS
SPL.COLLECTION FOR NEW BORN BABY
SALE

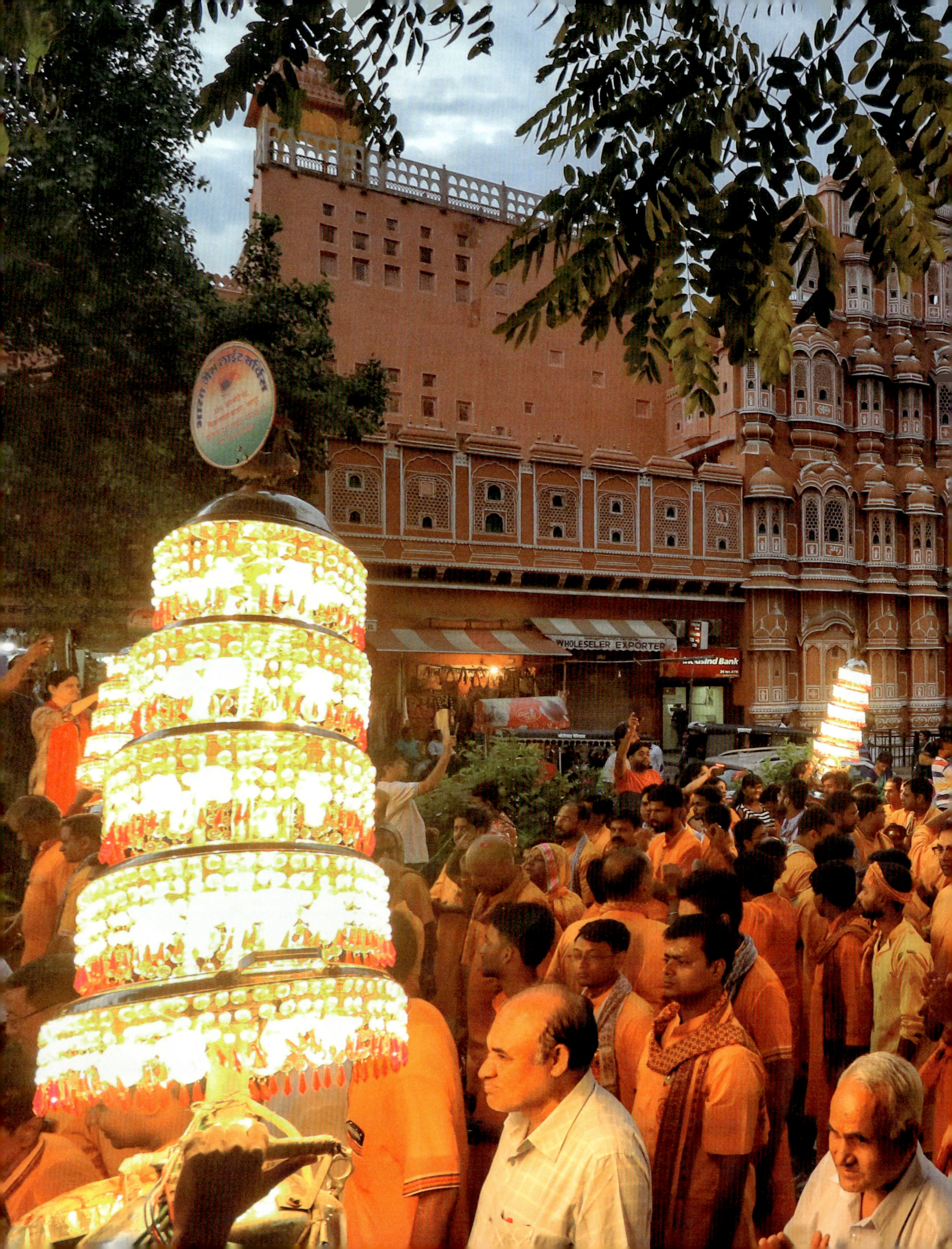

WHOLESELER EXPORTER
IndusInd Bank

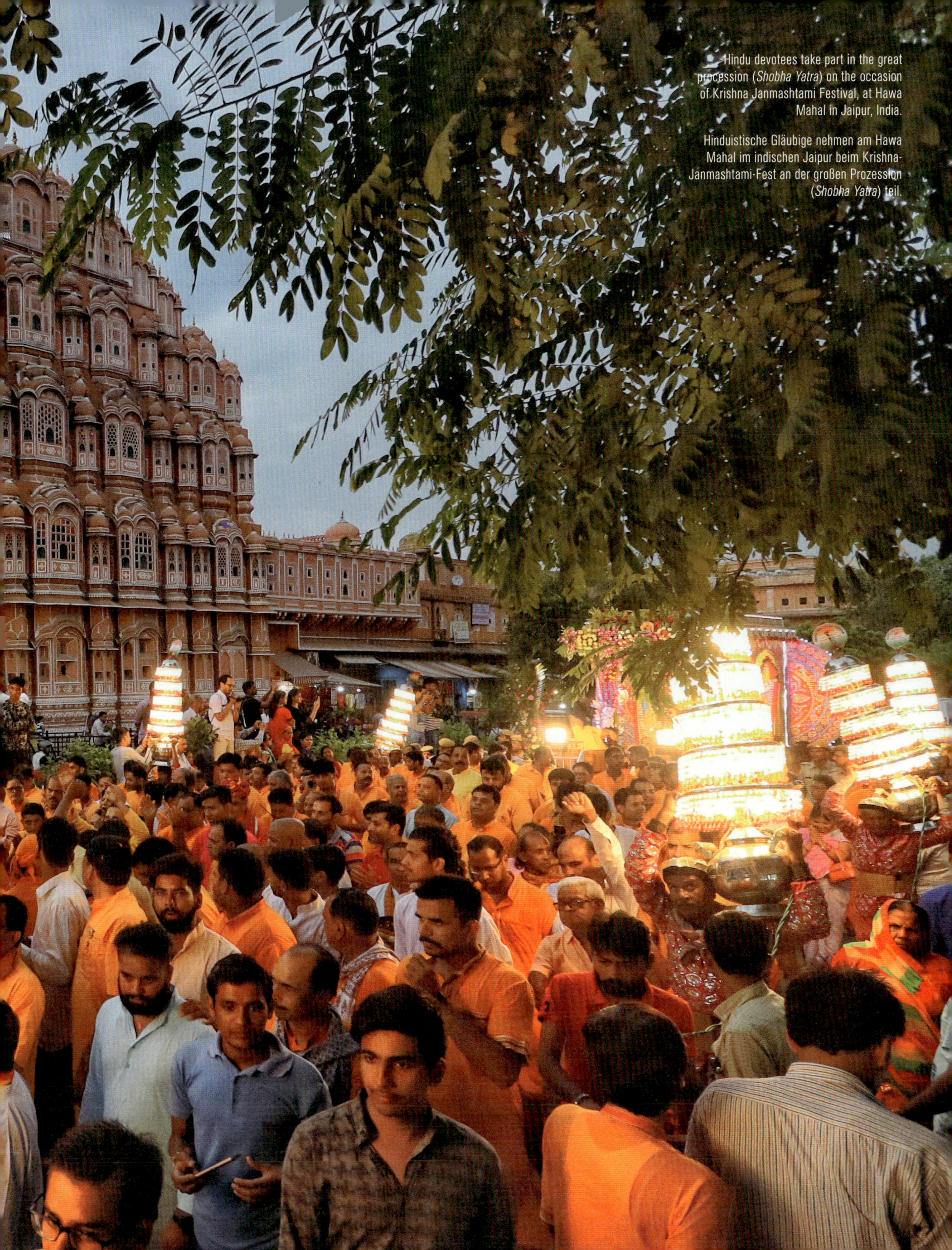

Hindu devotees take part in the great procession (*Shobha Yatra*) on the occasion of Krishna Janmashtami Festival, at Hawa Mahal in Jaipur, India.

Hinduistische Gläubige nehmen am Hawa Mahal im indischen Jaipur beim Krishna-Janmashtami-Fest an der großen Prozession (*Shobha Yatra*) teil.

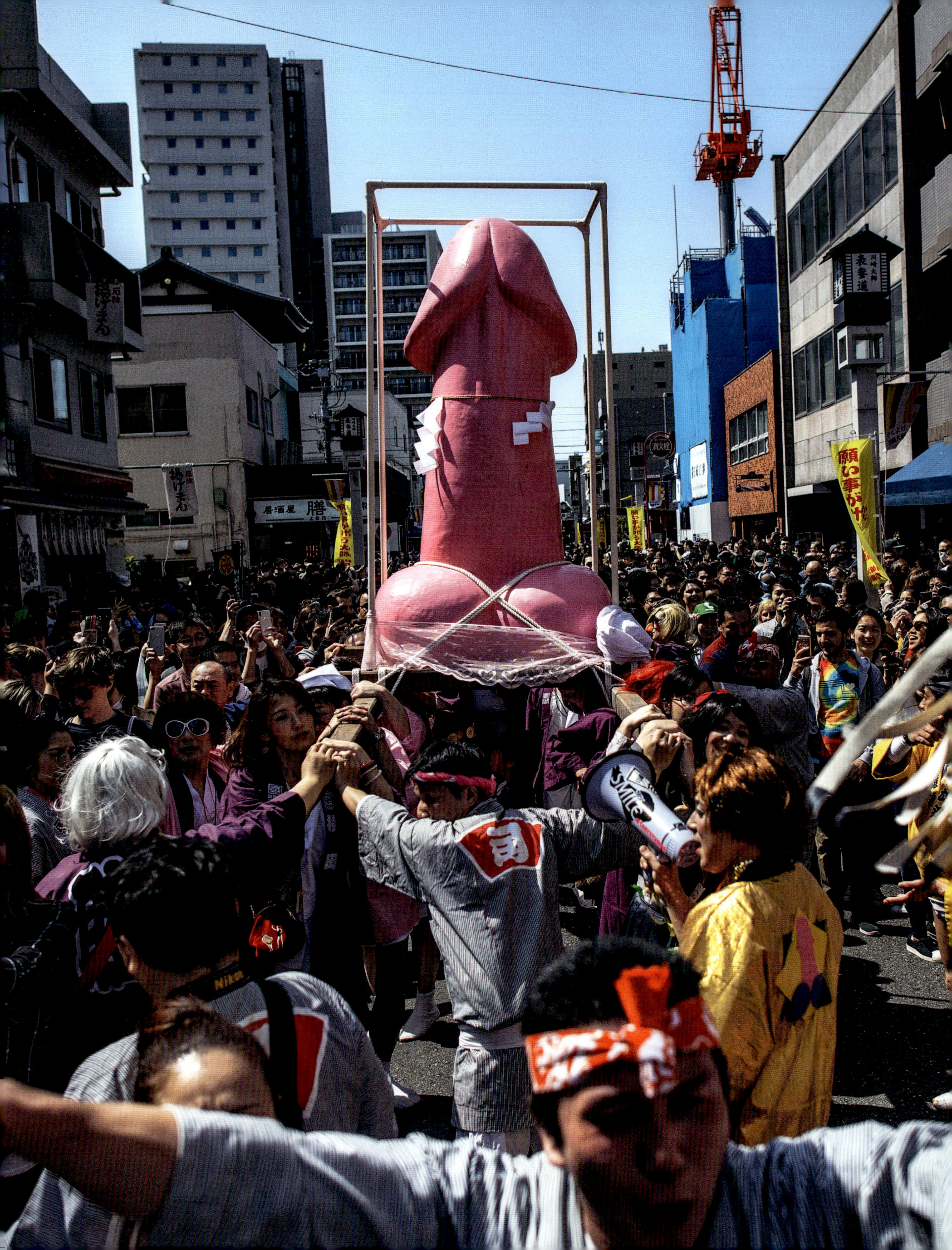

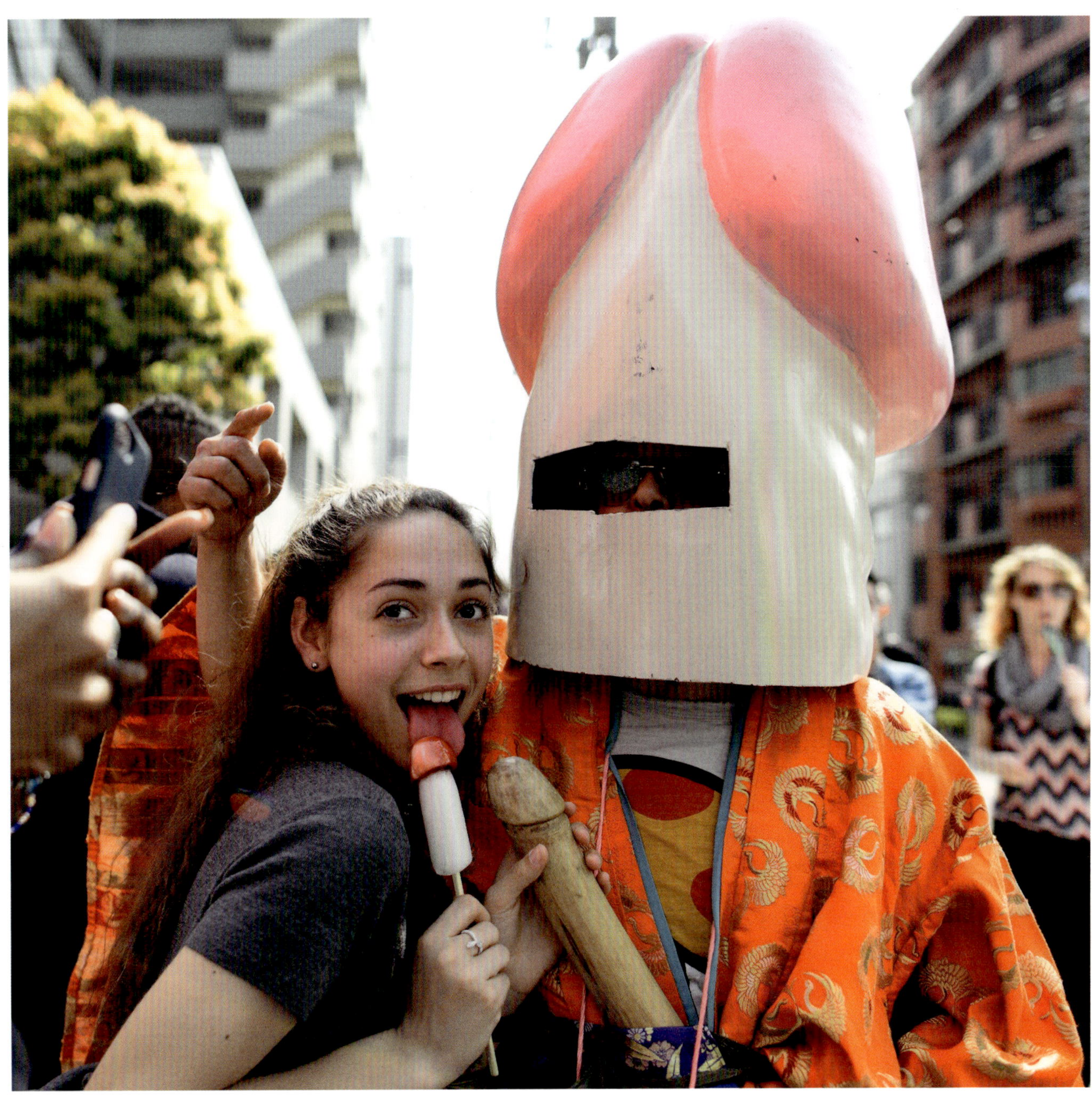

Kanamara Matsuri in Kawasaki, Japan, celebrates fertility, relationships, and business prosperity in Japan. Penis-shaped candies, key chains, trinkets, pens, chocolates, and other paraphernalia are available in abundance.

Das Fest Kanamara Matsuri im japanischen Kawasaki feiert Fruchtbarkeit, Beziehungen und geschäftliche Prosperität. Süßigkeiten, Schlüsselanhänger, Stifte und anderer Schnickschnack – alles in Penisform – ist hier omnipräsent.

A large pink phallus in a *mikoshi* (portable shrine) is paraded through the streets during Kanamara Matsuri (Festival of the Steel Phallus). The festival is dedicated to the gods who protect blacksmiths and sexuality.

Ein großer rosafarbener Phallus in einem tragbaren Schrein (*Mikoshi*) wird beim Kanamara Matsuri (Fest des stählernen Phallus) durch die Straßen getragen. Das Fest ist den Schutzgöttern der Schmiedekunst und der Sexualität gewidmet.

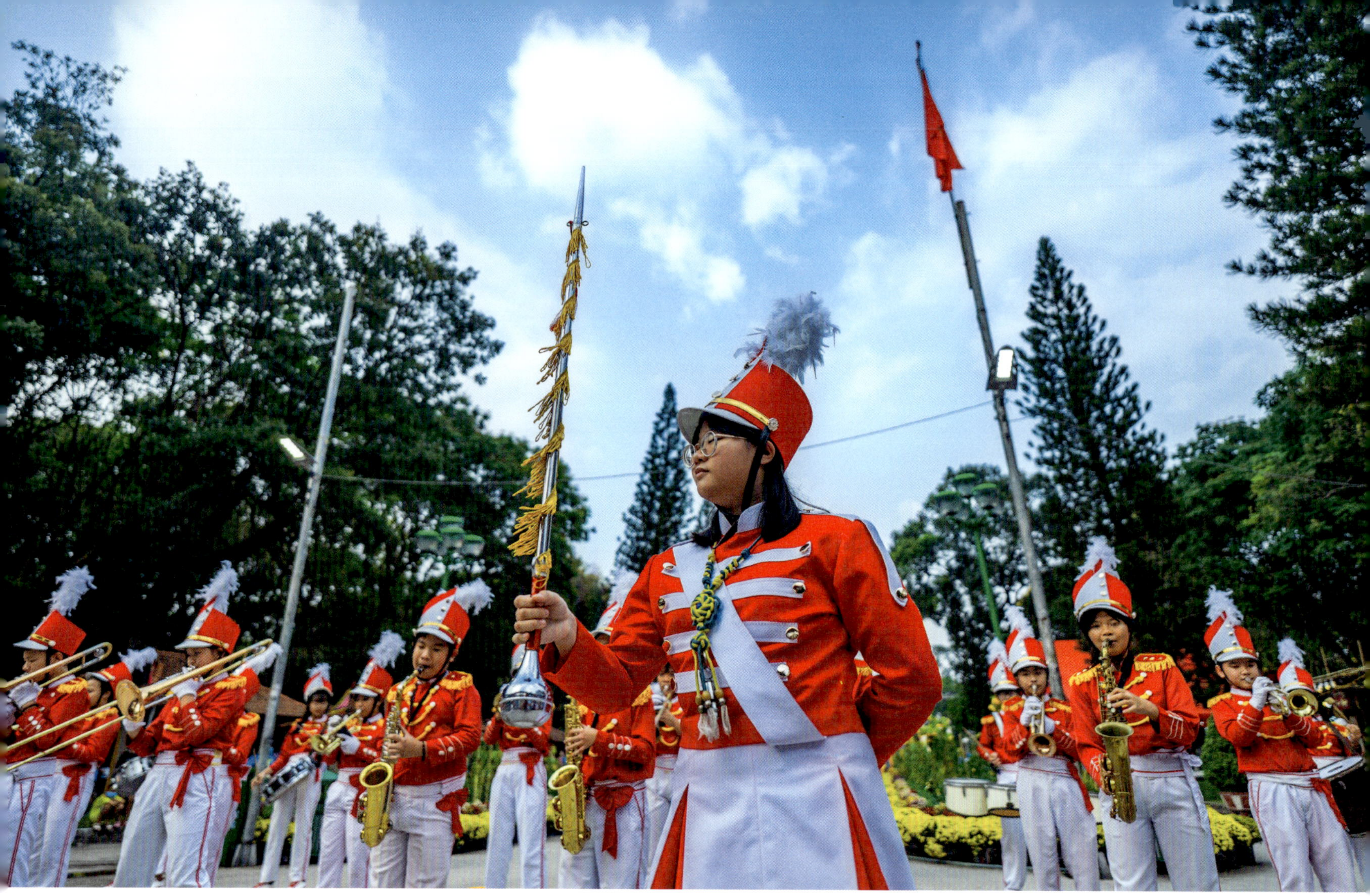

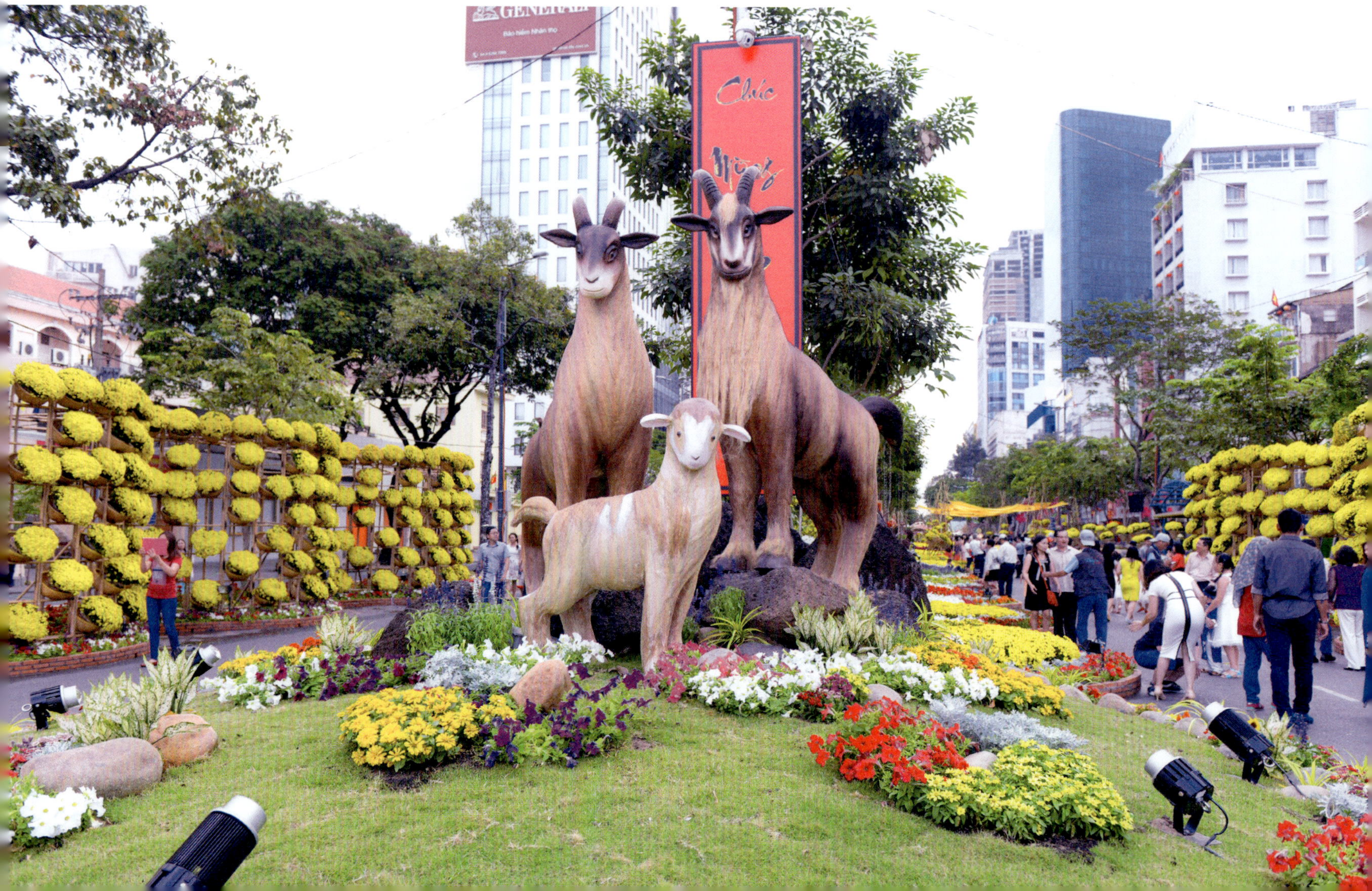

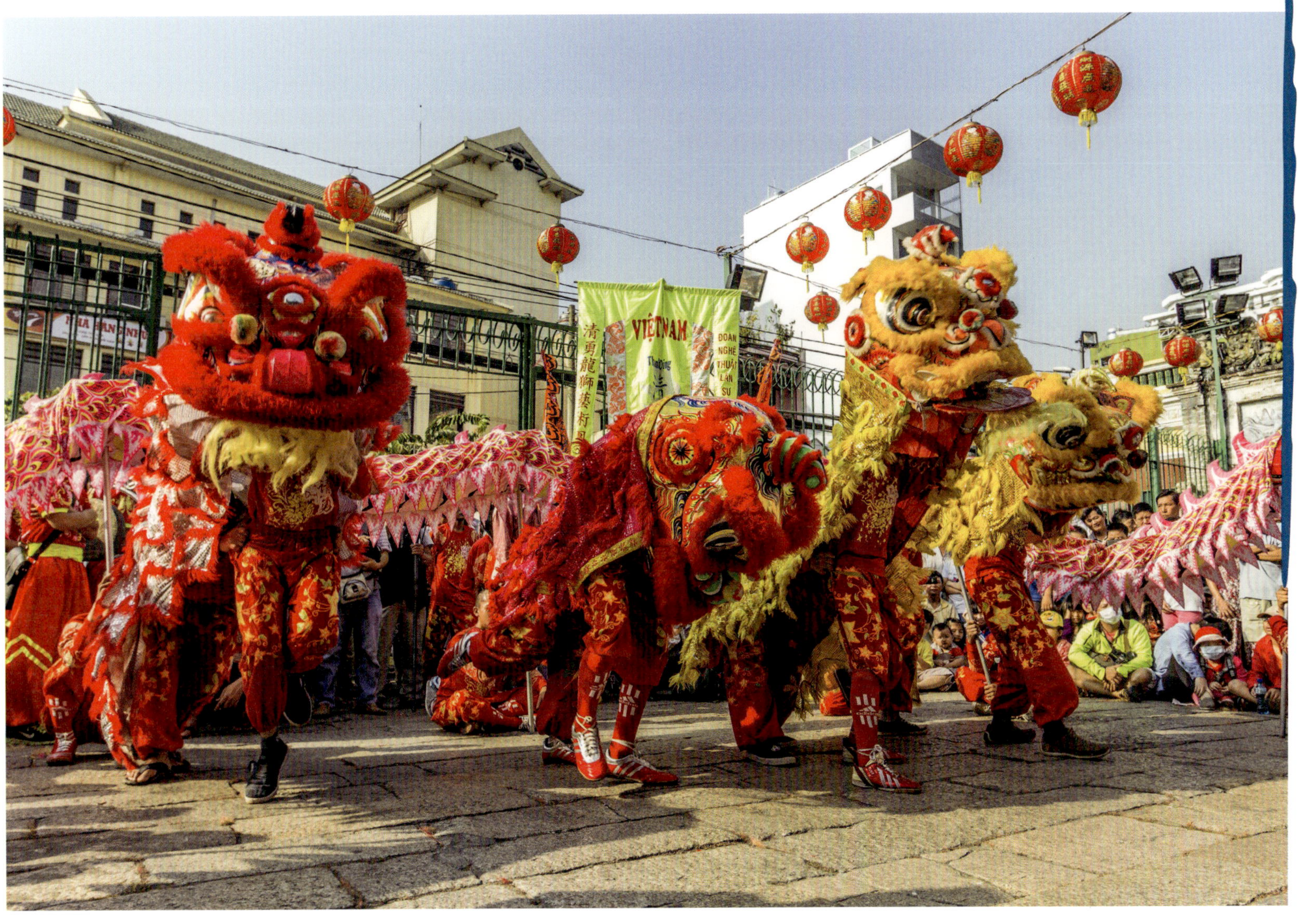

Tet (Lunar New Year) is Vietnam's most important celebration. Families come together to feast. There are also parades, music, and flower decorations.

Das Tet-Fest zum Mond-Neujahr ist die wichtigste Feier in Vietnam. Familien kommen zum Festmahl zusammen, es gibt Paraden und Musik und alles wird mit Blumen geschmückt.

The Gaelic festival of Samhain may he the origin of today's Halloween. Its cele-bration started on October 31 to welcome the cold season and new calendar year. The Celts also believed they could contact the realm of the dead on this day.

Das gälische Samhain-Fest ist möglicherweise der Ursprung von Halloween. Man fing am 31. Oktober an zu feiern, um die kalte Jahreszeit und das neue Kalender-jahr zu begrüßen. Die Kelten glaubten auch, dass sie an diesem Tag mit dem Totenreich in Verbindung treten könnten.

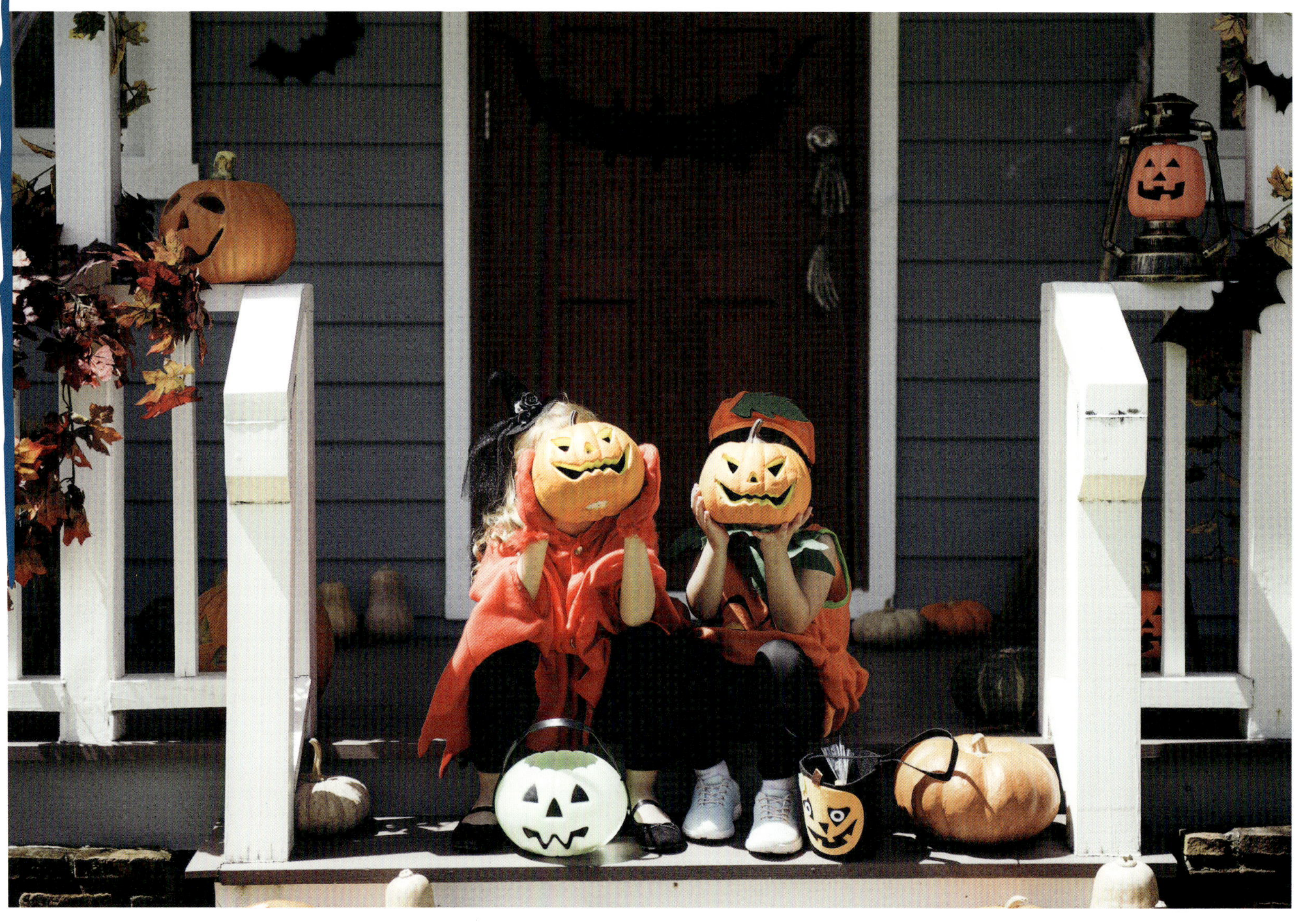

Halloween activities include attending costume parties, embellishing houses and gardens with scary decor, playing pranks, and of course trick-or-treating.

Zu den Aktivitäten an Halloween gehören Kostümpartys, das Schmücken von Haus und Garten mit Gruseldekor, Streiche spielen und natürlich – „Süßes oder Saures!" – Süßigkeiten sammeln.

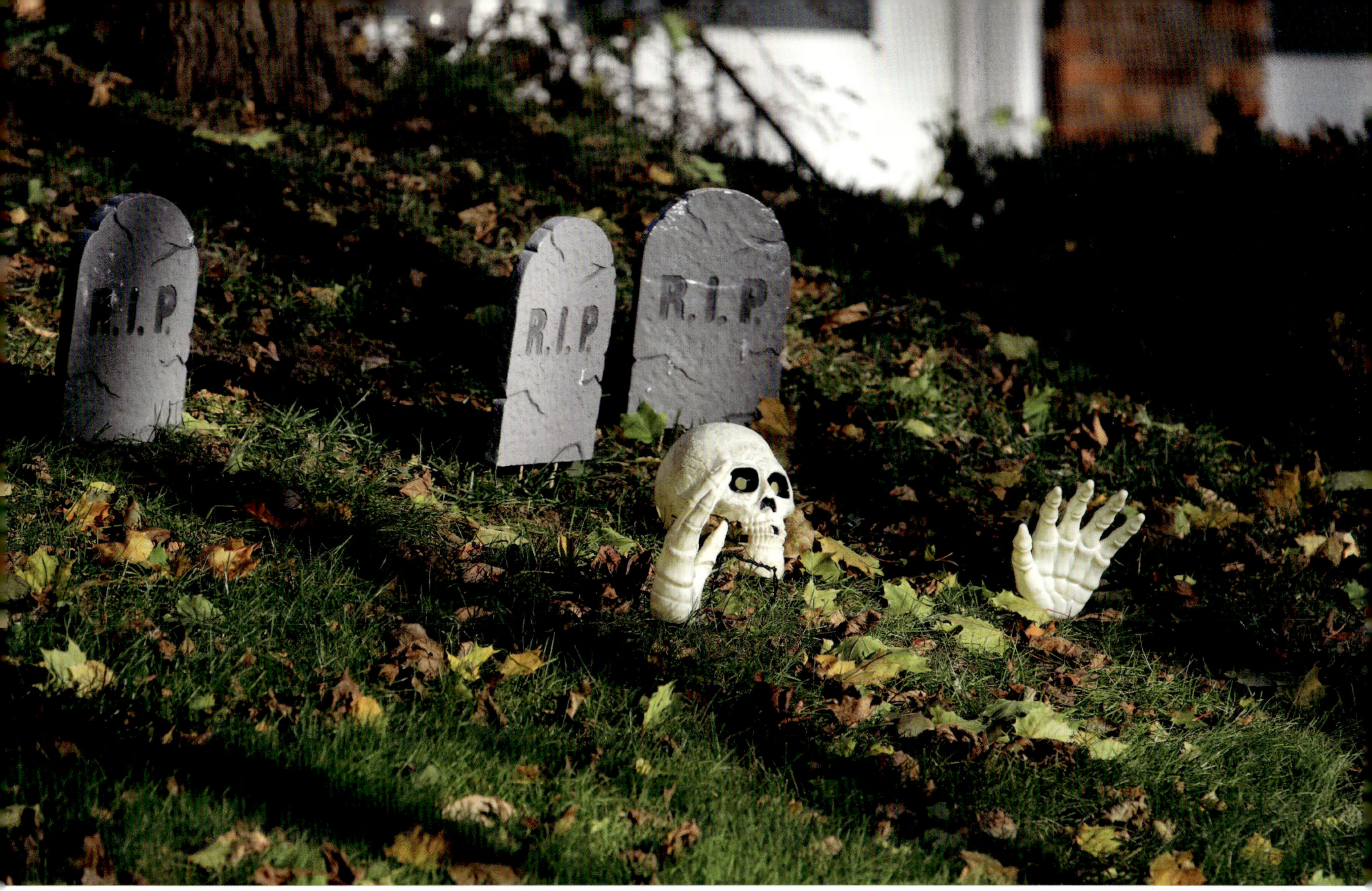

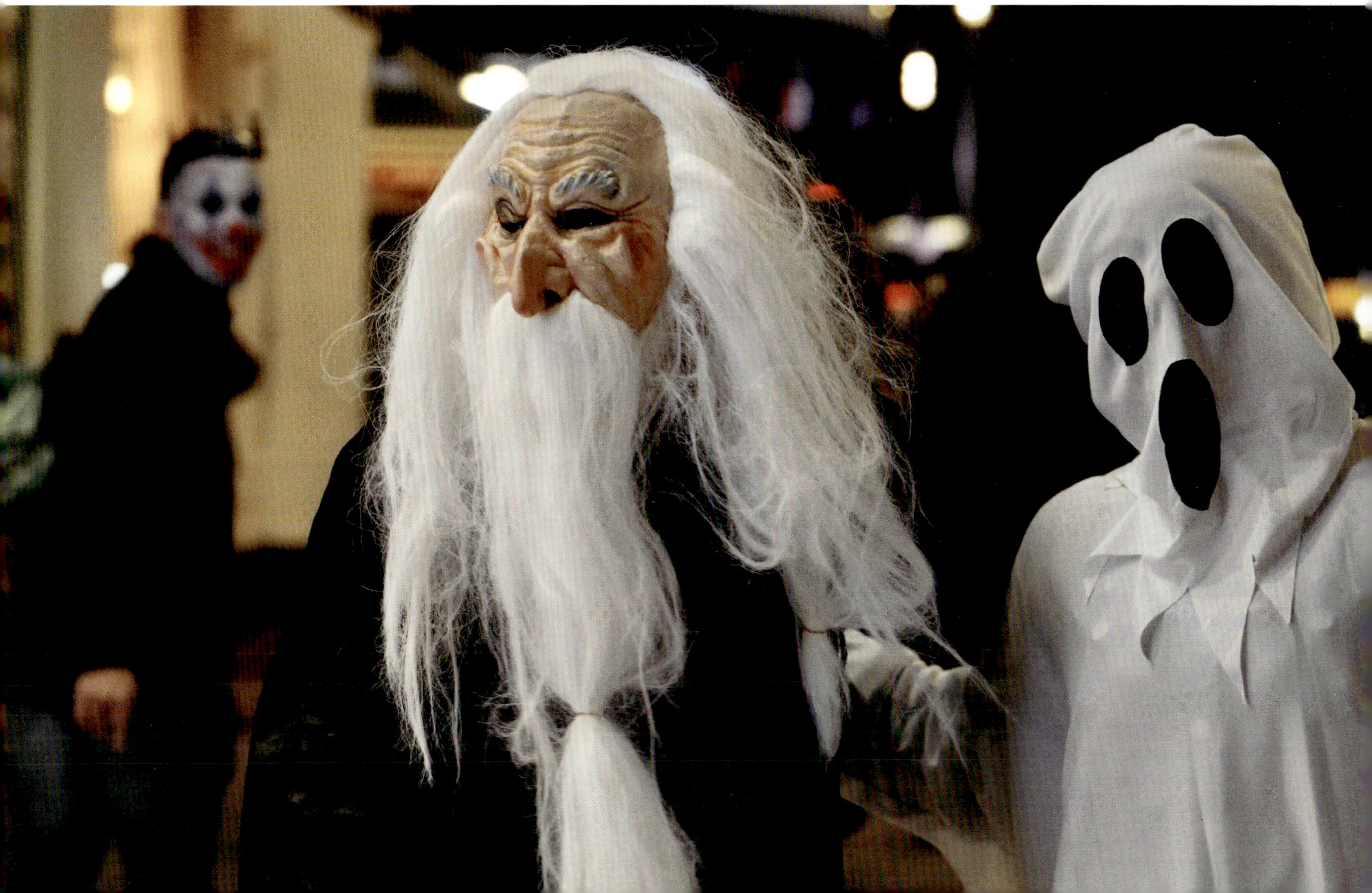

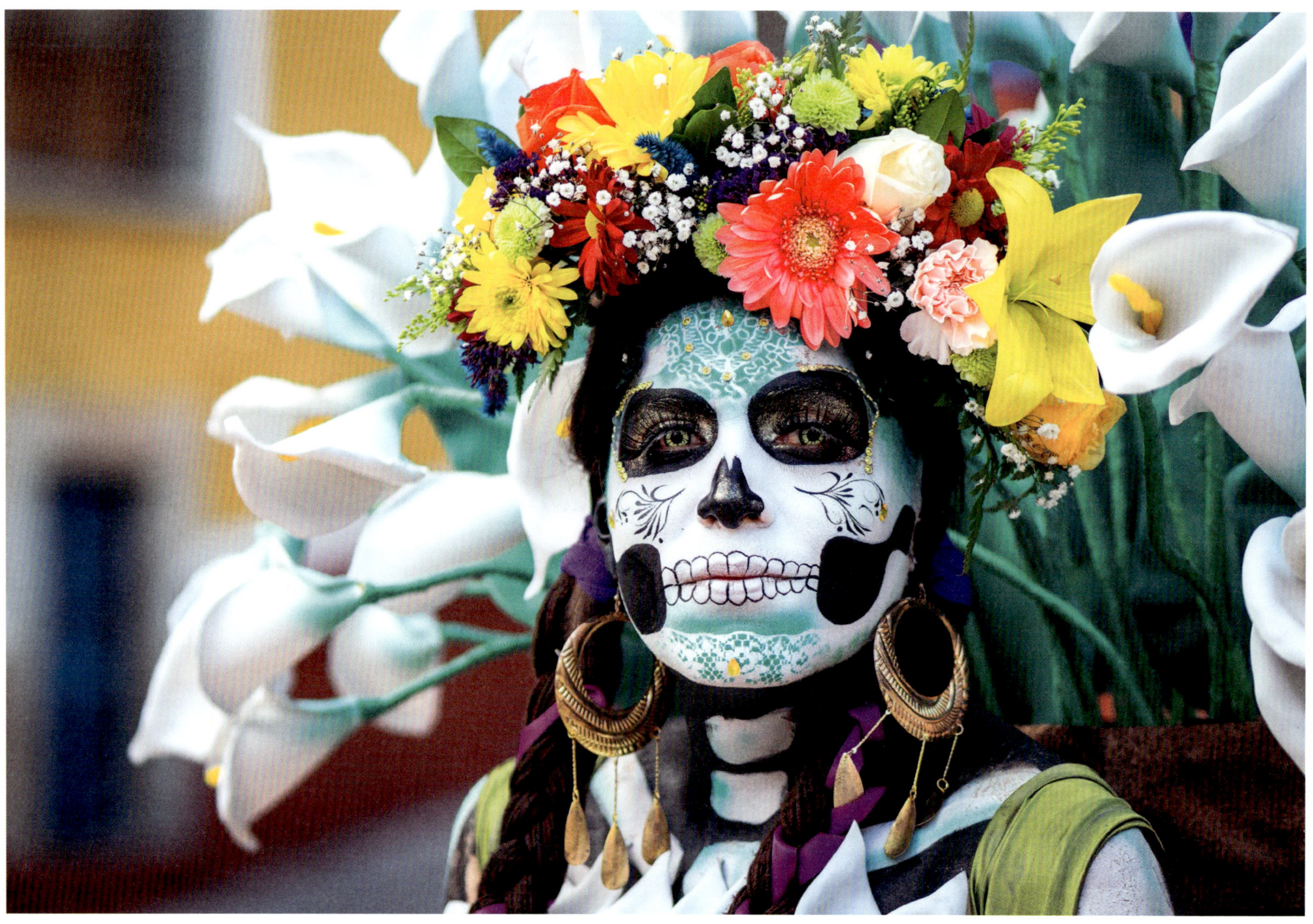

Día de los Muertos is a day of celebration, not mourning. Home altars (*ofrendas*) are built, and graves are adorned with *calavares* (edible or decorative skulls made from sugar or clay), marigolds, and the departed's favorite foods.

Am Día de los Muertos wird gefeiert, nicht getrauert. Man baut Heimaltare (*ofrendas*) und schmückt Gräber mit *calavares* (essbare oder dekorative Totenschädel aus Zucker oder Ton), Ringelblumen und den Lieblingsspeisen der Verstorbenen.

Good to know
WISSENSWERTES

Many women dress up as La Catrina—the tall female skeleton depicted by artist José Guadalupe Posada in the early 1910s—for Día de los Muertos. The image serves to remind us that we will all die in the end, no matter how fancy our lives, or our hats, may be!

Viele Frauen verkleiden sich zum Día de los Muertos als La Catrina – die große Skelettfrau, die der Künstler José Guadalupe Posada Anfang des 20. Jahrhunderts schuf. Sie erinnert uns daran, dass wir letztlich alle sterben müssen, ganz egal wie privilegiert wir sind oder wie schick unsere Hüte!

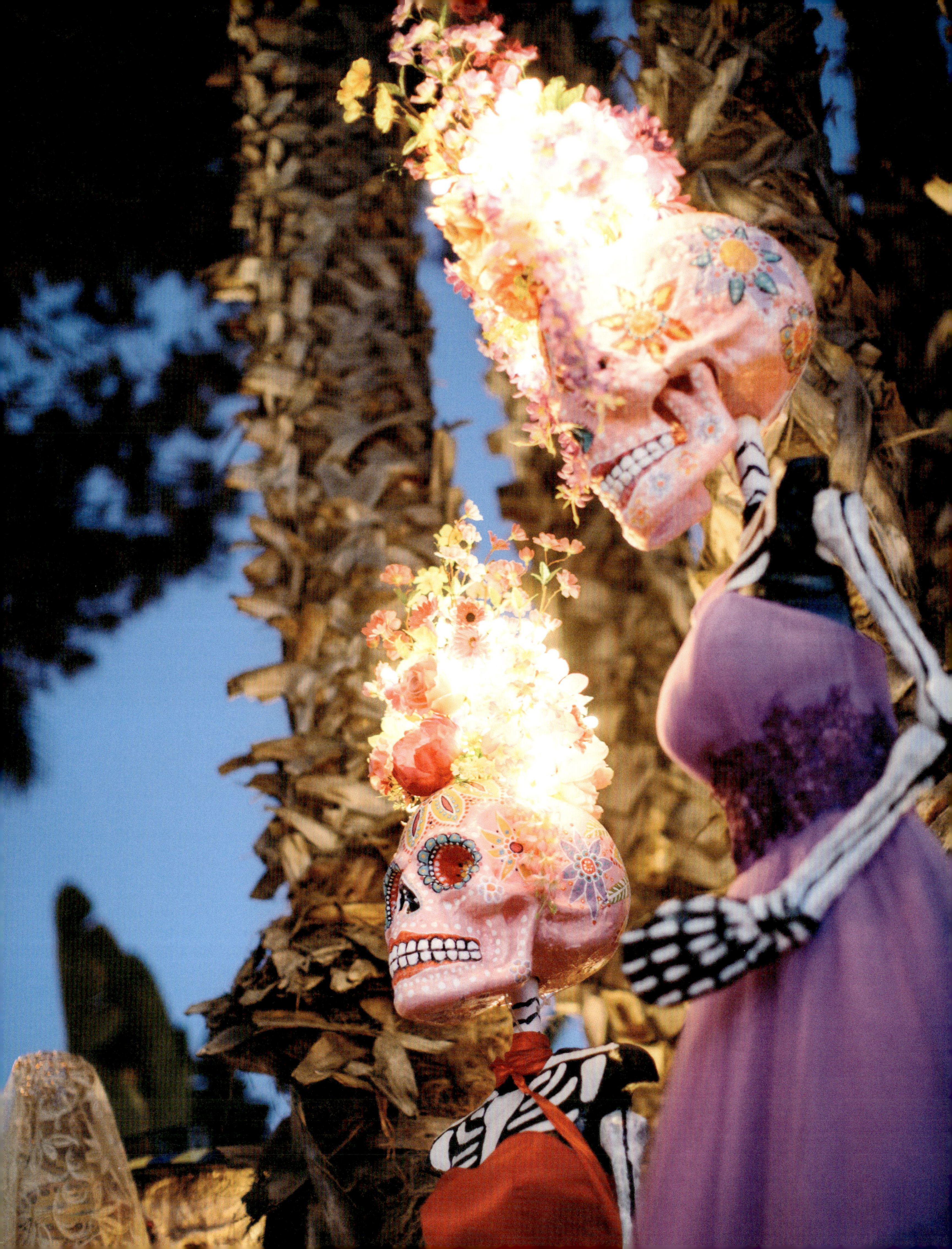

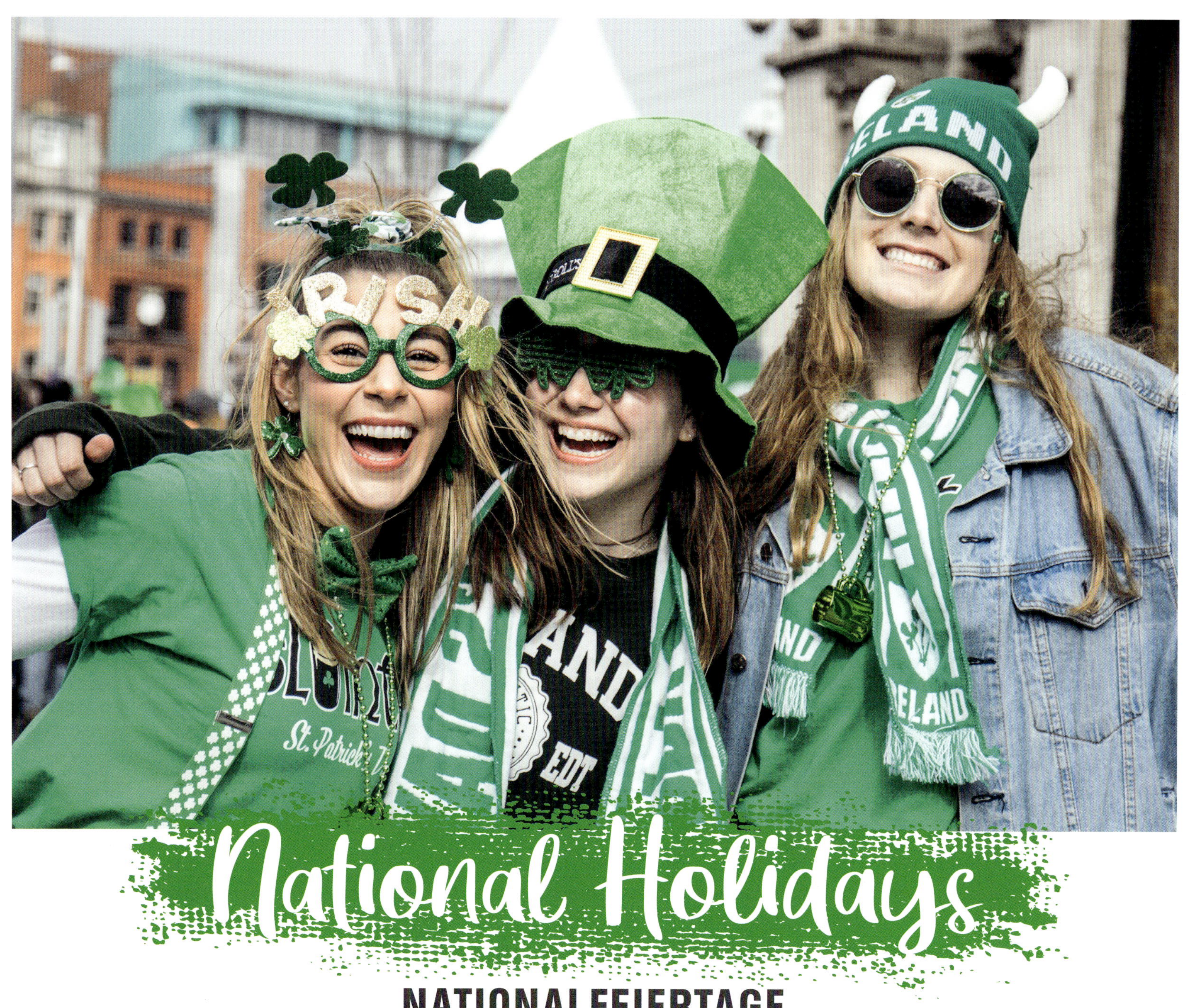

National Holidays

NATIONALFEIERTAGE

St. Patrick's Day celebration in Dublin, Ireland.

St. Patrick's Day in Dublin, Irland

In the Netherlands, King's Day or Queen's Day traditionally takes place on the birthday of the current Dutch king or queen. For the occasion, the country's sites are decorated with orange flags and many people dress completely in orange.

Der Königs- oder Königintag in den Niederlanden findet traditionell am Geburtstag des aktuellen Monarchen statt. Zu diesem Anlass lässt man orangene Fahnen wehen und viele Menschen kleiden sich von Kopf bis Fuß in der Nationalfarbe Orange.

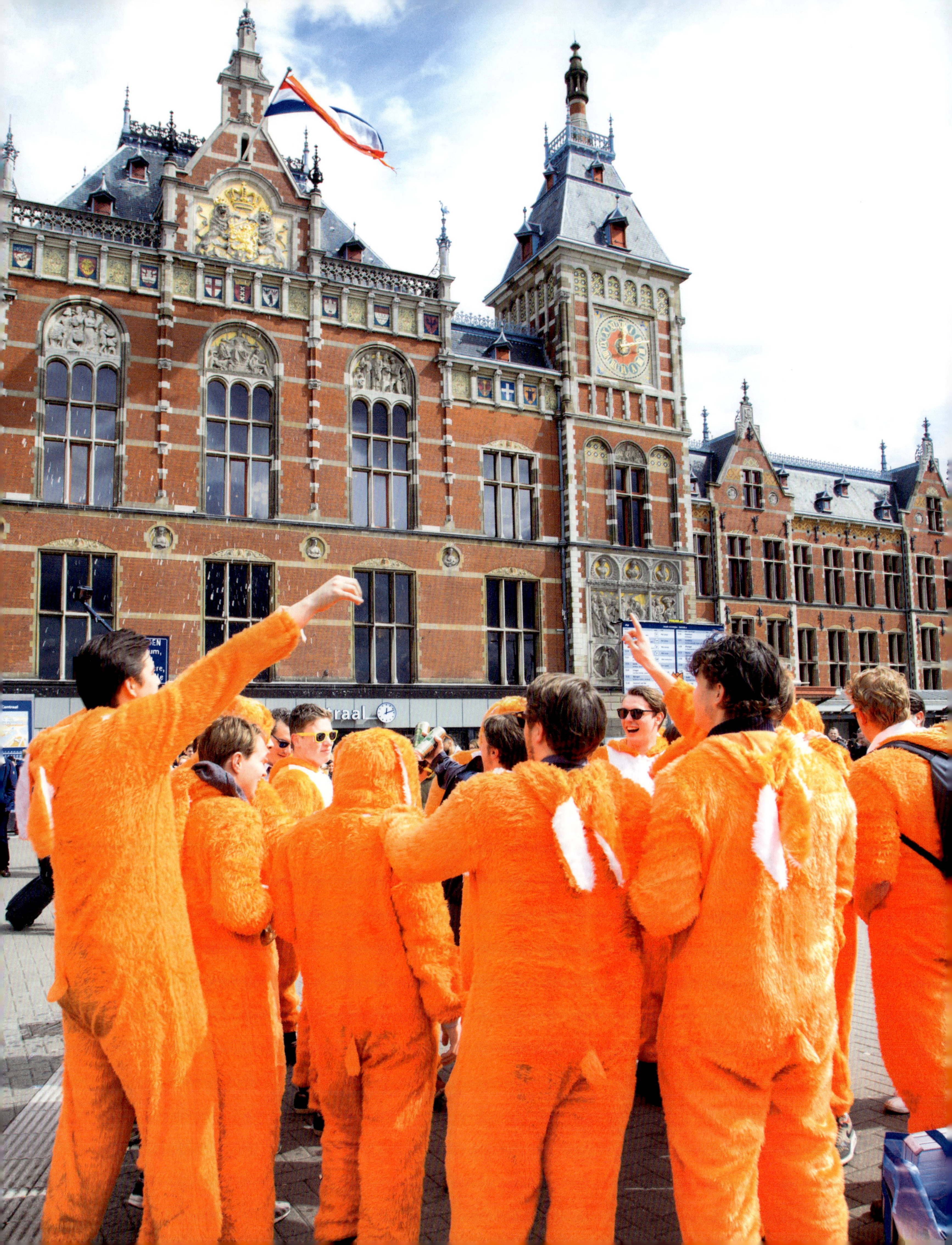

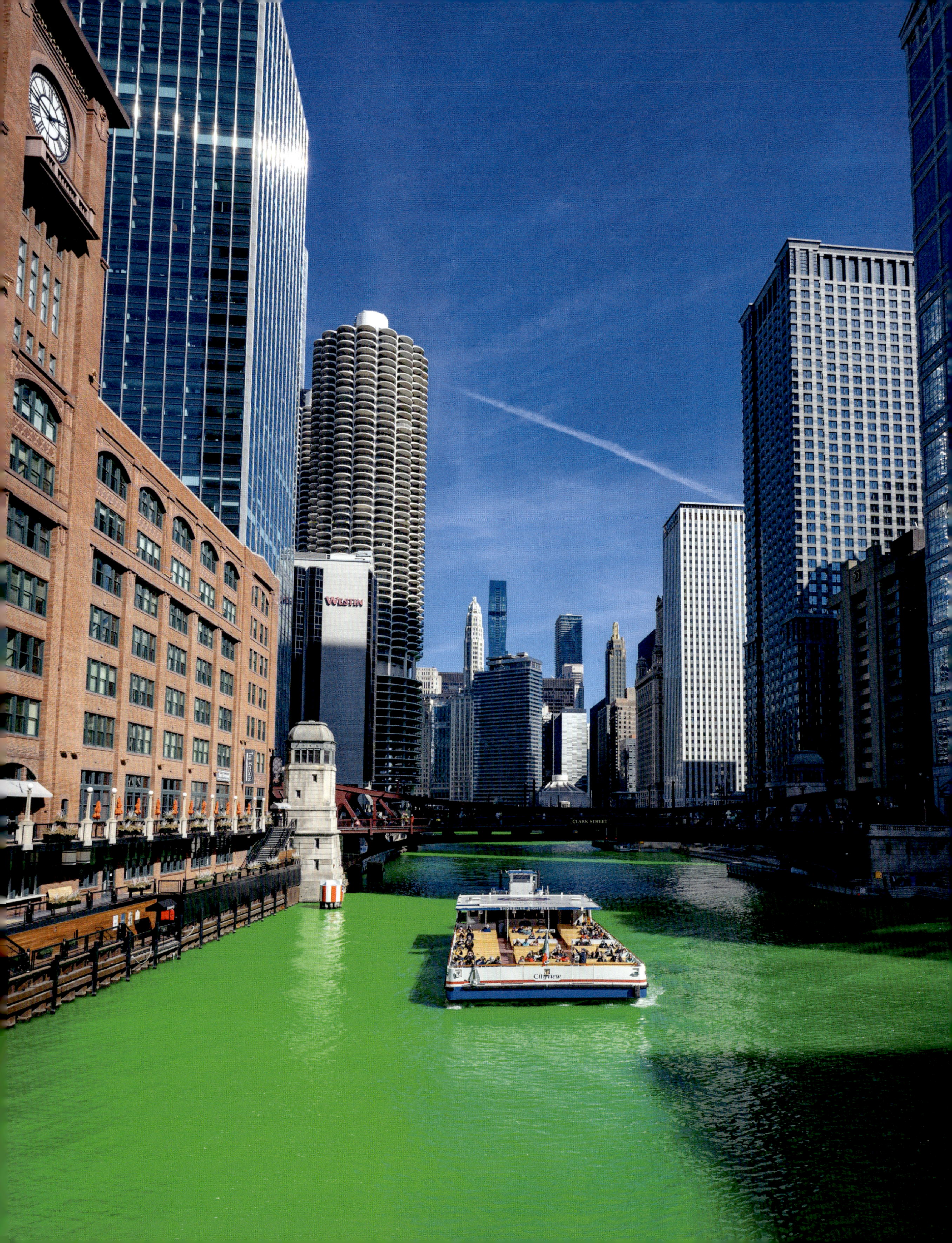

WESTIN
Cityview
CLARK STREET

*N*ational holidays are an opportunity for citizens to express their pride and appreciation for their country. Celebrations vary in size and activity depending on which country you're in.

With a significant amount of Irish expats dotted around the world, the largest national holiday has to be the Irish St. Patrick's Day. Every year on March 17, everyone becomes "a little bit Irish" to drink and party the day away. In Chicago, they even turn the Chicago River green in celebration. In London, they light up the London Eye green and there's a huge parade. And in Tokyo, they have an "I Love Ireland" festival. But the most heartfelt celebration has to be in Dublin, where they have a weeklong festival.

The Netherlands' national holiday is a bit more contained, but nevertheless still wonderful. They mark Koningsdag, or King's Day (aka Queen's Day, depending who's reigning at the time), which dates back to the 1880s in honor of the birthday of Princess Wilhelmina (it was originally called Prinsessedag, before Wilhelmina became queen in 1891). On this day, everyone wears orange, the nation's color. Music stages are set up; a citywide flea market allowing people to sell second-hand goods is a big thing; and the best parties are on the boats on the canals.

Eid is a huge celebration around the Muslim world. It marks the end of Ramadan, and it is a time to feast with family and friends to mark the end of the fast. It's a chance to show gratitude to God for the previous month of reflection. Children receive gifts, and adults share food gifts with everyone they know. In predominantly Muslim countries, like the UAE and Saudi Arabia, there are big events at mosques and in the cities in celebration.

*N*ationalfeiertage bieten Bürgern die Gelegenheit, ihr Land zu feiern und Nationalstolz zu zeigen. Die Feierlichkeiten dazu variieren von Land zu Land stark.

Aufgrund der vielen irischen Auswanderer, die auf der ganzen Welt ein neues Zuhause fanden, ist der St. Patrick's Day wohl der am globalsten gefeierte Nationalfeiertag. Jedes Jahr am 17. März wird von Iren und allen, die mitmachen wollen, feucht-fröhlich Party gemacht. In Chicago wird sogar der Chicago River grün eingefärbt. In London erscheint das Riesenrad London Eye in grünem Licht und es gibt eine riesige Parade. Sogar in Tokio gibt es ein „I Love Ireland"-Festival. Am intensivsten wird aber natürlich in Dublin gefeiert, wo die Festlichkeiten eine ganze Woche andauern.

Nicht ganz so wild, aber trotzdem wunderbar ist der niederländische Königstag (oder Königintag, je nachdem, ob gerade ein König oder eine Königin auf dem Thron sitzt). Er geht zurück auf die 1880er-Jahre, in denen der Geburtstag von Prinzessin Wilhelmina mit dem Prinsessedag gefeiert wurde (der Tag wurde umgenannt als Wilhelmina 1891 zur Königin gekrönt wurde). An diesem Tag tragen alle die Nationalfarbe Orange. Es gibt Livemusik auf zahlreichen Bühnen und die Straßen verwandeln sich in einen riesigen Flohmarkt. Die besten Partys finden auf den Kanalbooten statt.

Beim Fest des Fastenbrechens (Eid al-Fitr) feiern Muslimen auf der ganzen Welt das Ende des Fastenmonats Ramadan. Man speist mit der Familie und mit Freunden und bedankt sich bei Gott für den vorangegangenen Monat der Besinnung. Kinder erhalten Geschenke und Erwachsene überreichen allen, die sie kennen, Essensgaben. In vorwiegend muslimischen Ländern wie den VAE und Saudi-Arabien gibt es auch große Festivitäten in den Moscheen und Städten.

Royal Canadian Mounted Police ride horses through
downtown Ottawa, Ontario, in celebration of
Canada Day on July 1.

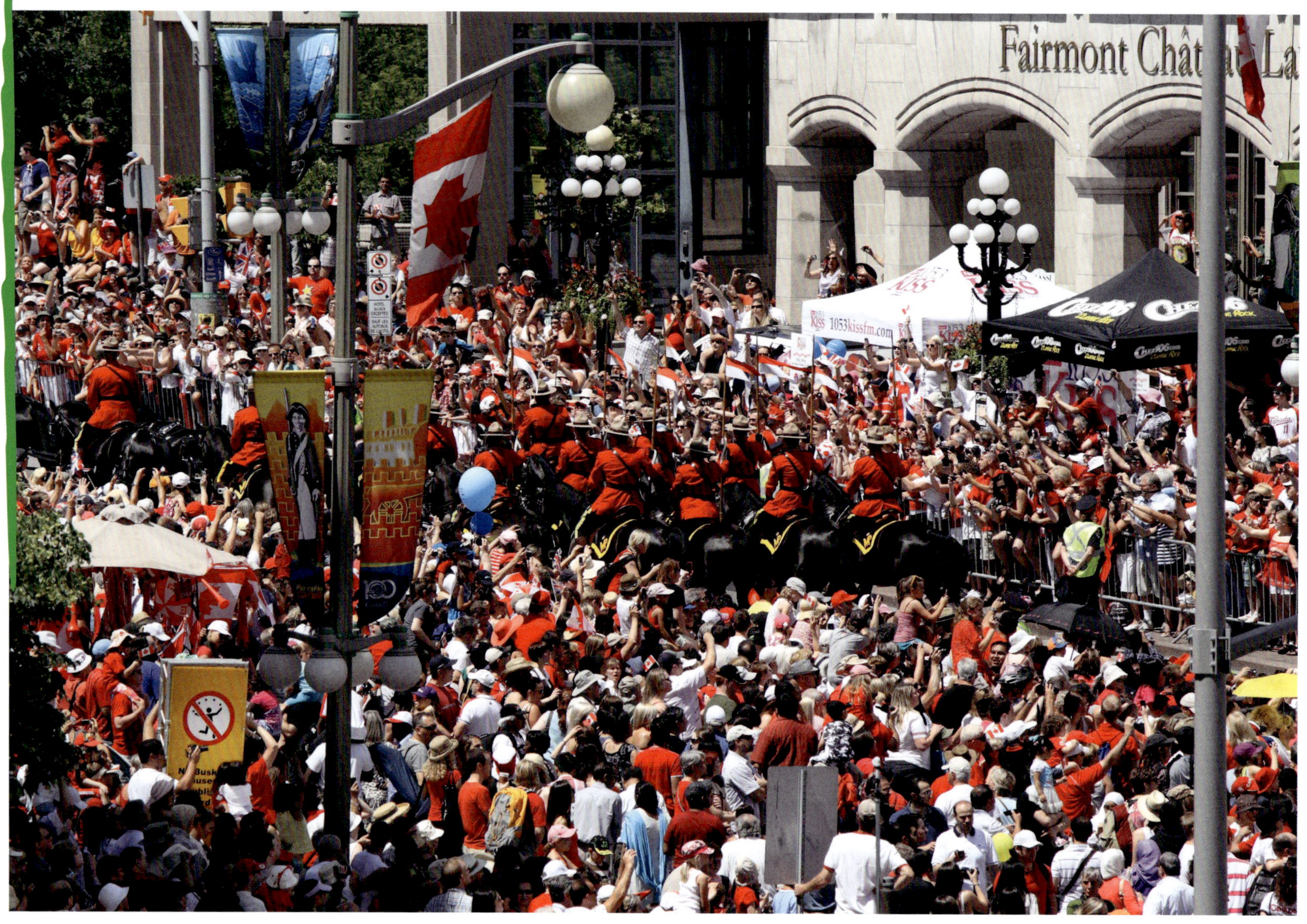

On July 4, Americans come together to parade, meet family and friends, and celebrate their Declaration of Independence
(which wasn't actually signed or declared on this exact date).
Next page: Amsterdam's canal with boats and people in orange during the celebration of the Dutch national holiday.

Am 4. Juli nehmen US-Amerikaner an Paraden teil und kommen mit Freunden und Verwandten zusammen,
um ihre Unabhängigkeitserklärung (die allerdings an diesem Datum weder verkündet noch unterschrieben wurde) zu feiern.
Nächste Seite: Auf einem Kanal in Amsterdam schippern orange gekleidete Menschen,
um den holländischen Nationalfeiertag zu begehen.

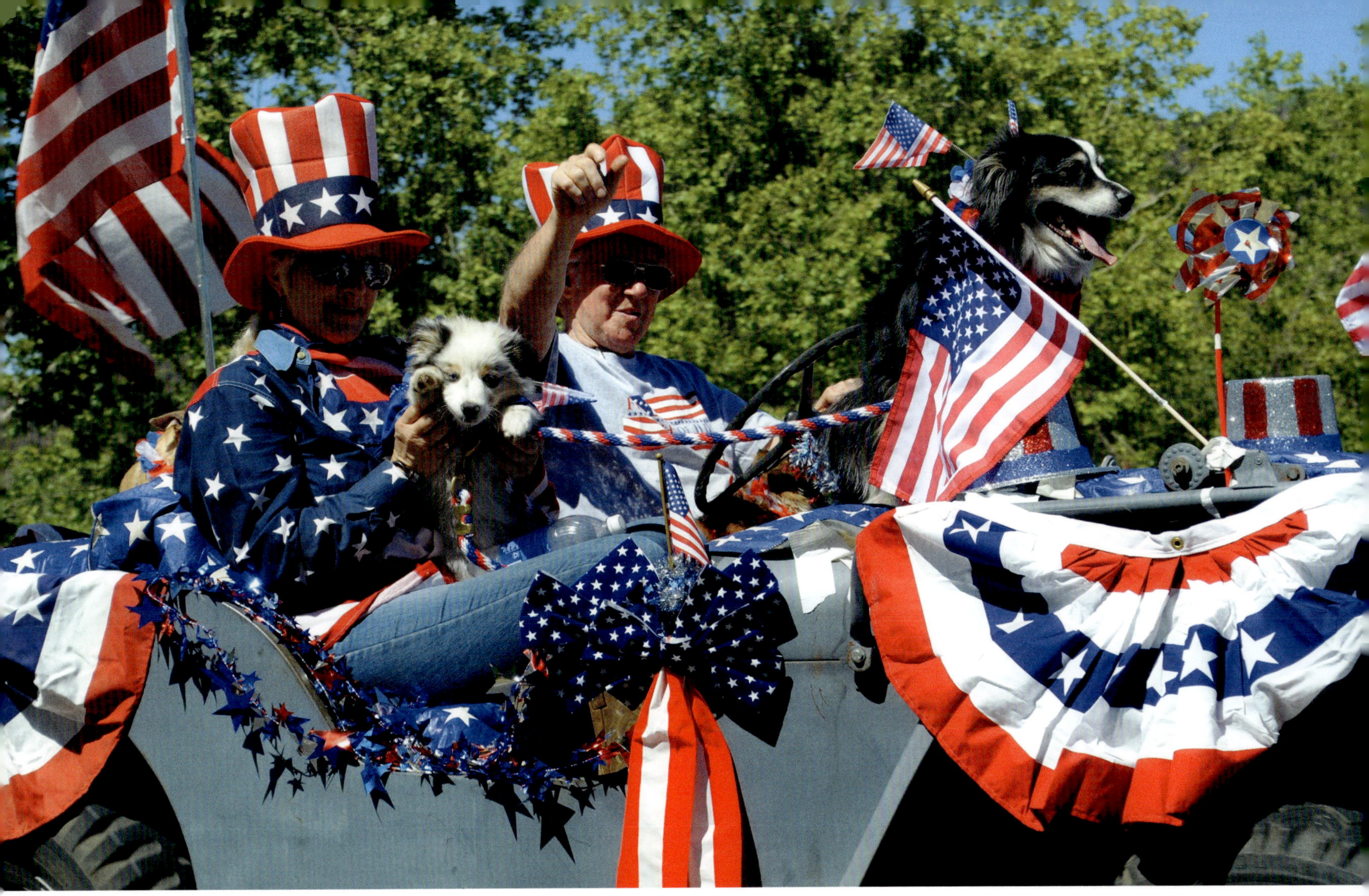

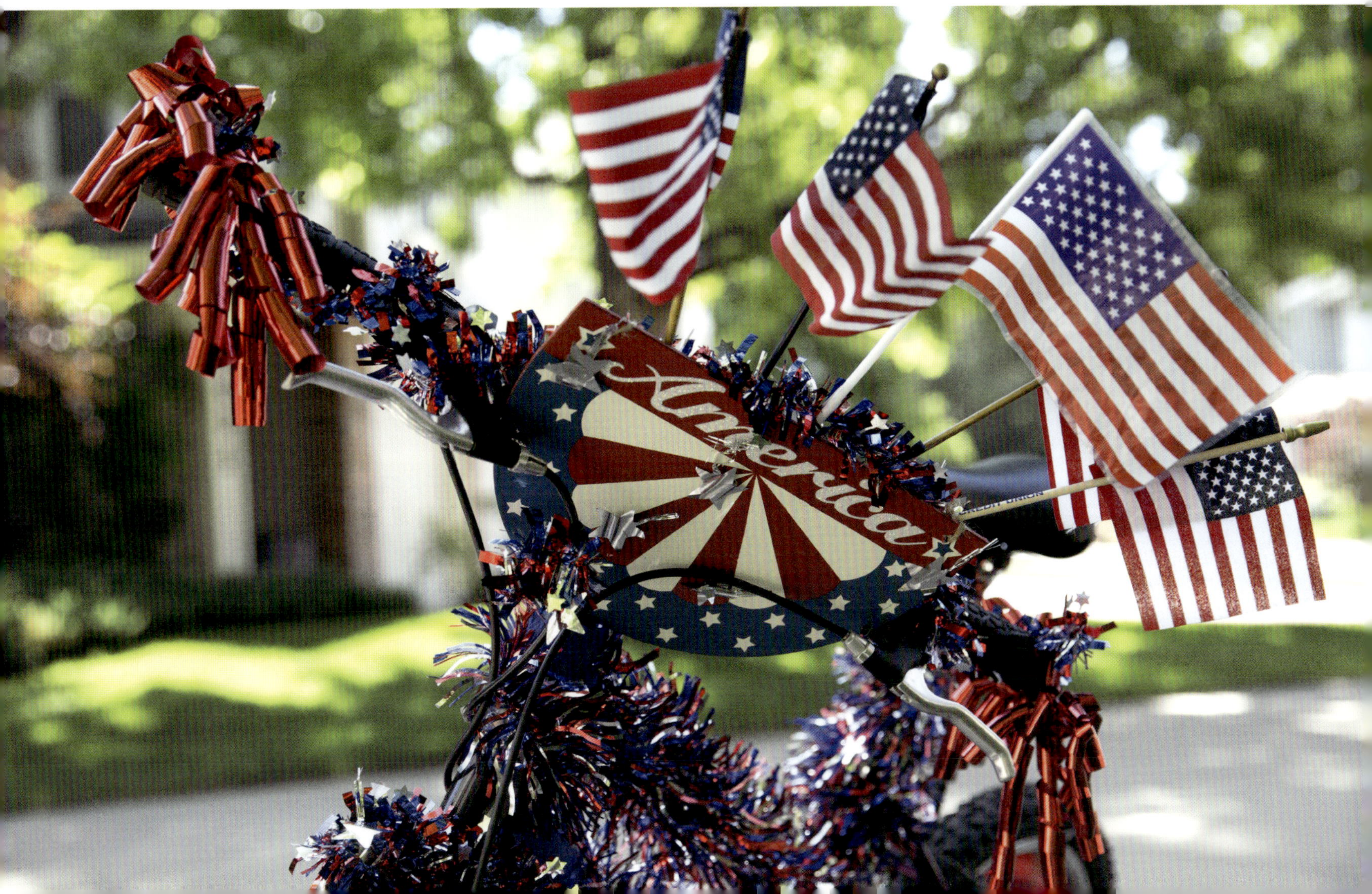

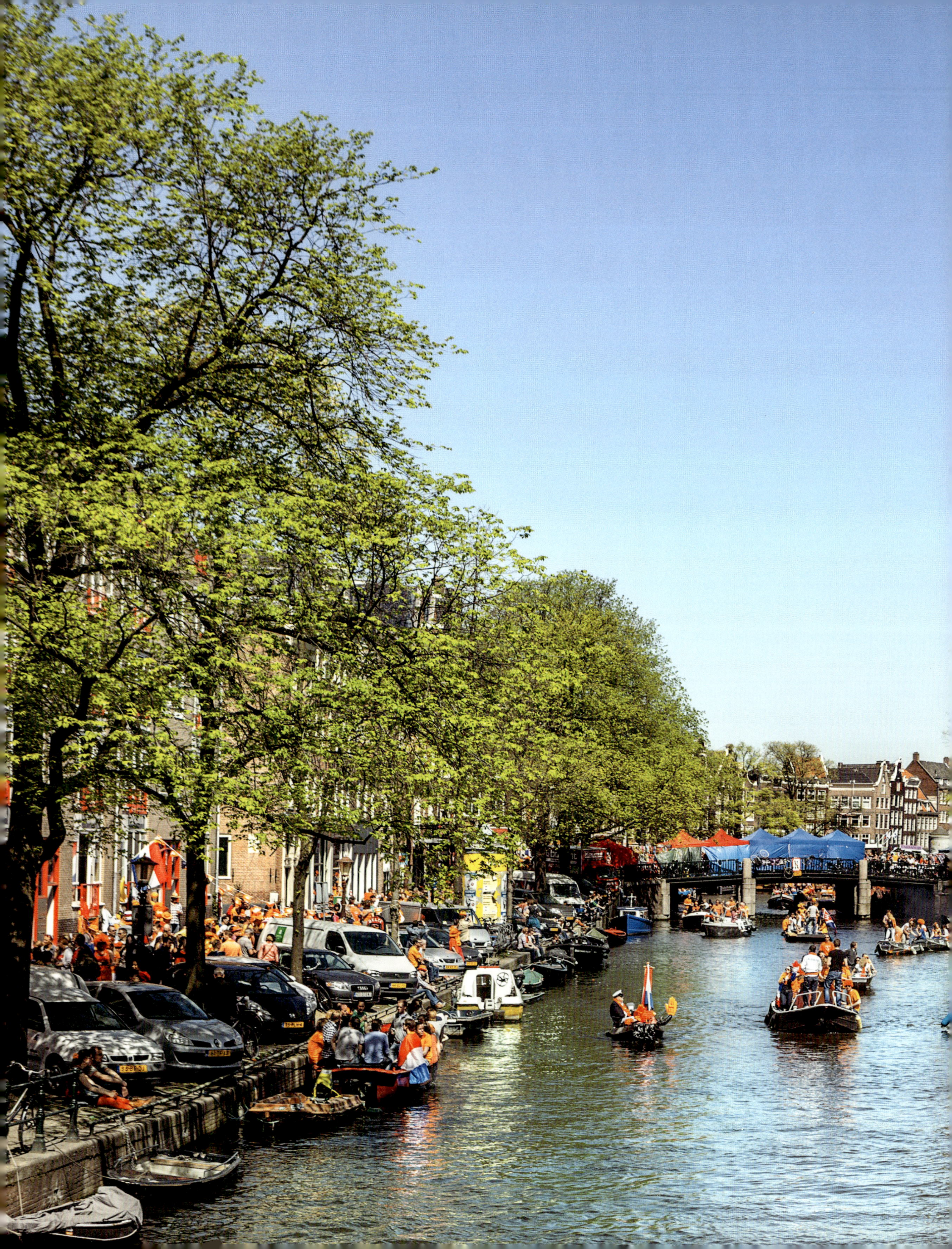

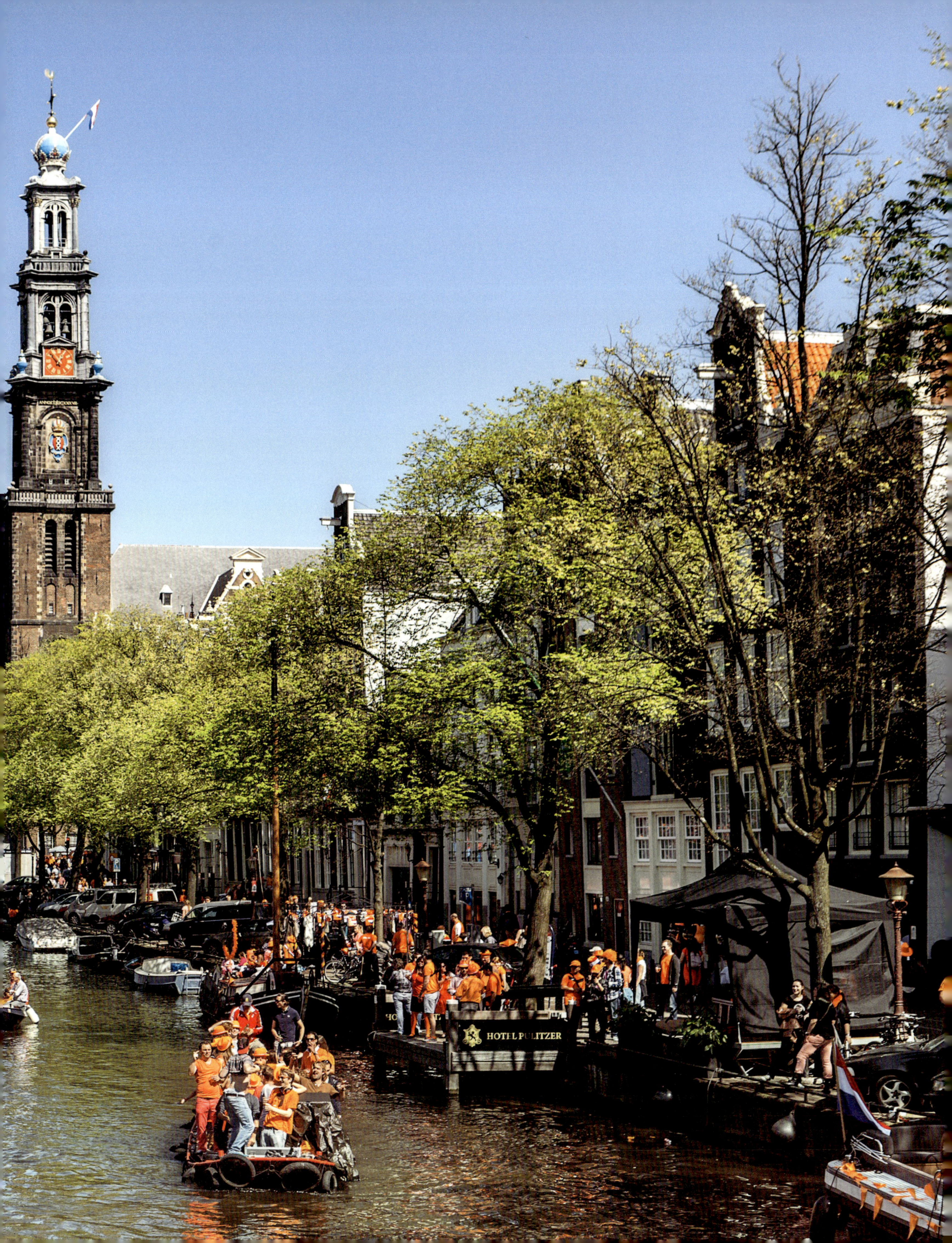
HOTEL PULITZER

La Fête Nationale, or Bastille Day, the French national holiday, hosts one of the largest military parades in Europe. The parade has been part of the celebration since 1880 and has run along the Champs-Élysées in Paris—Frances' best-known avenue—since 1918.

Am französischen Nationalfeiertag (La Fête Nationale), der an die Erstürmung der Bastille erinnert, findet in Paris eine der größten Militärparaden Europas statt. Die Parade ist seit 1880 Bestandteil der Feierlichkeiten und führt seit 1918 an Frankreichs berühmtester Straße, den Champs-Élysées, entlang.

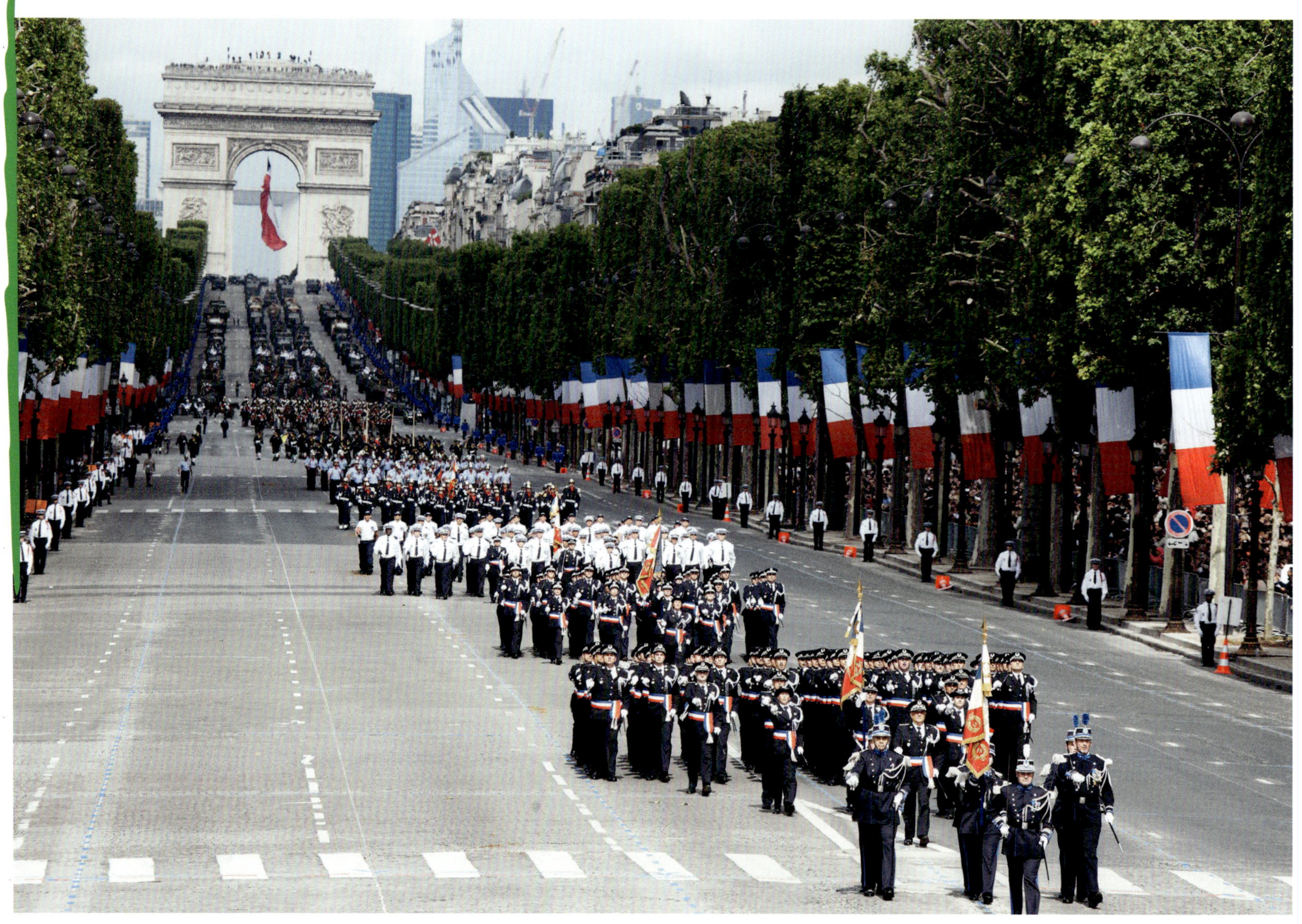

The official holiday Eid al-Fitr marks the end of Ramadan, a month of fasting, prayer, and reflection in Islam.

Der gesetzliche Feiertag Eid al-Fitr markiert das Ende des Ramadans, der im Islam ein Monat des Fastens, des Betens und der Besinnung ist.

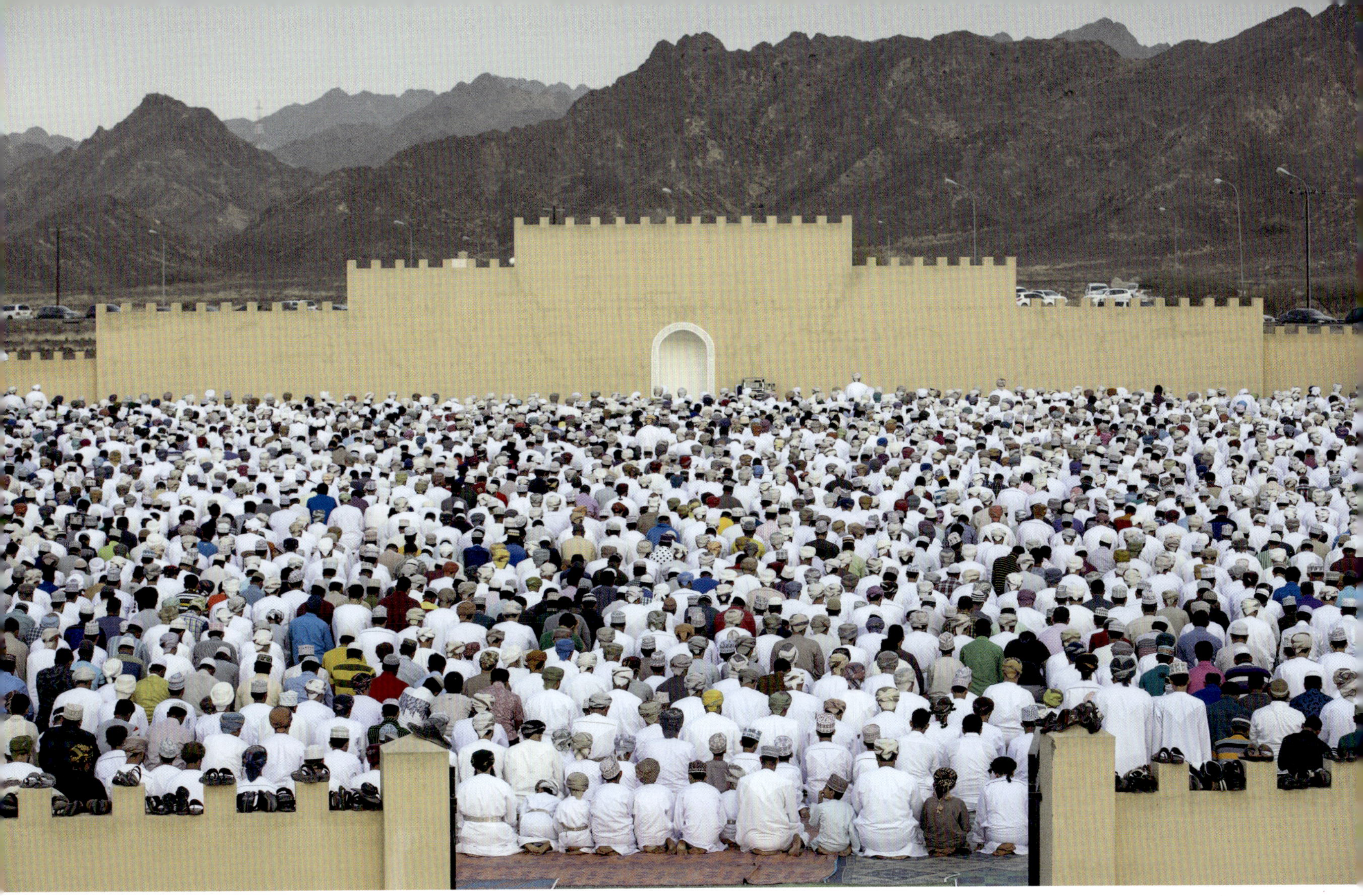

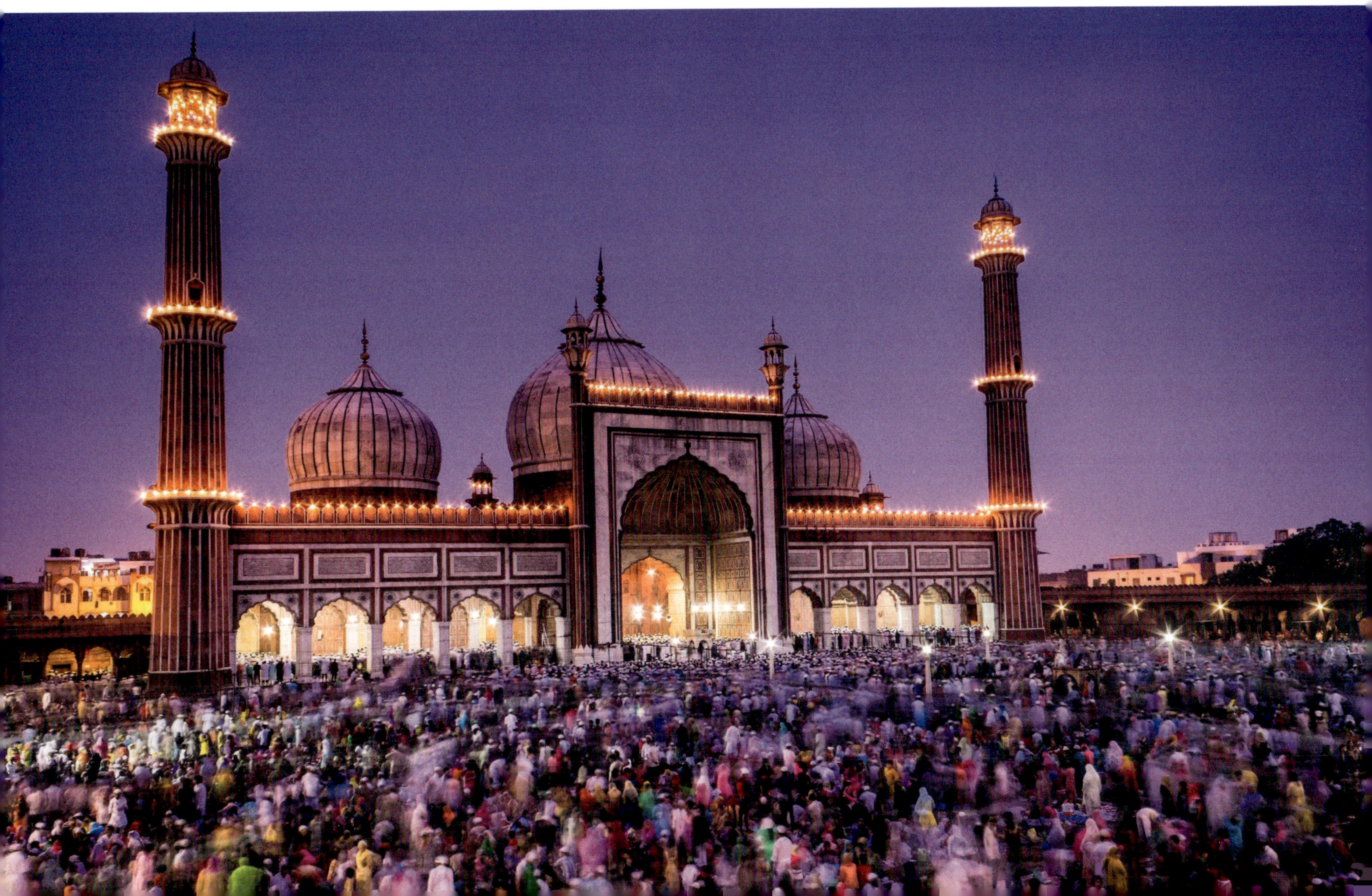

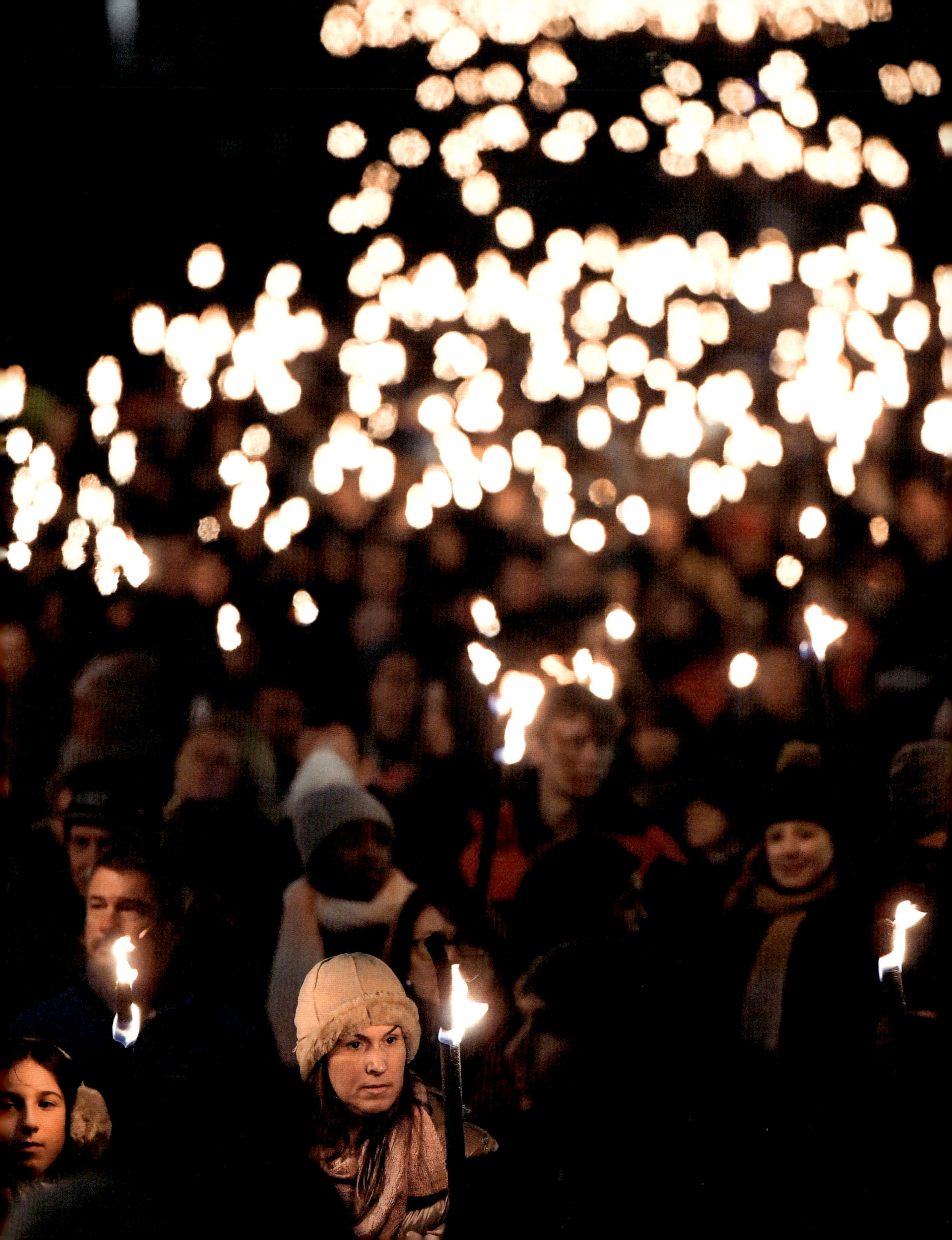

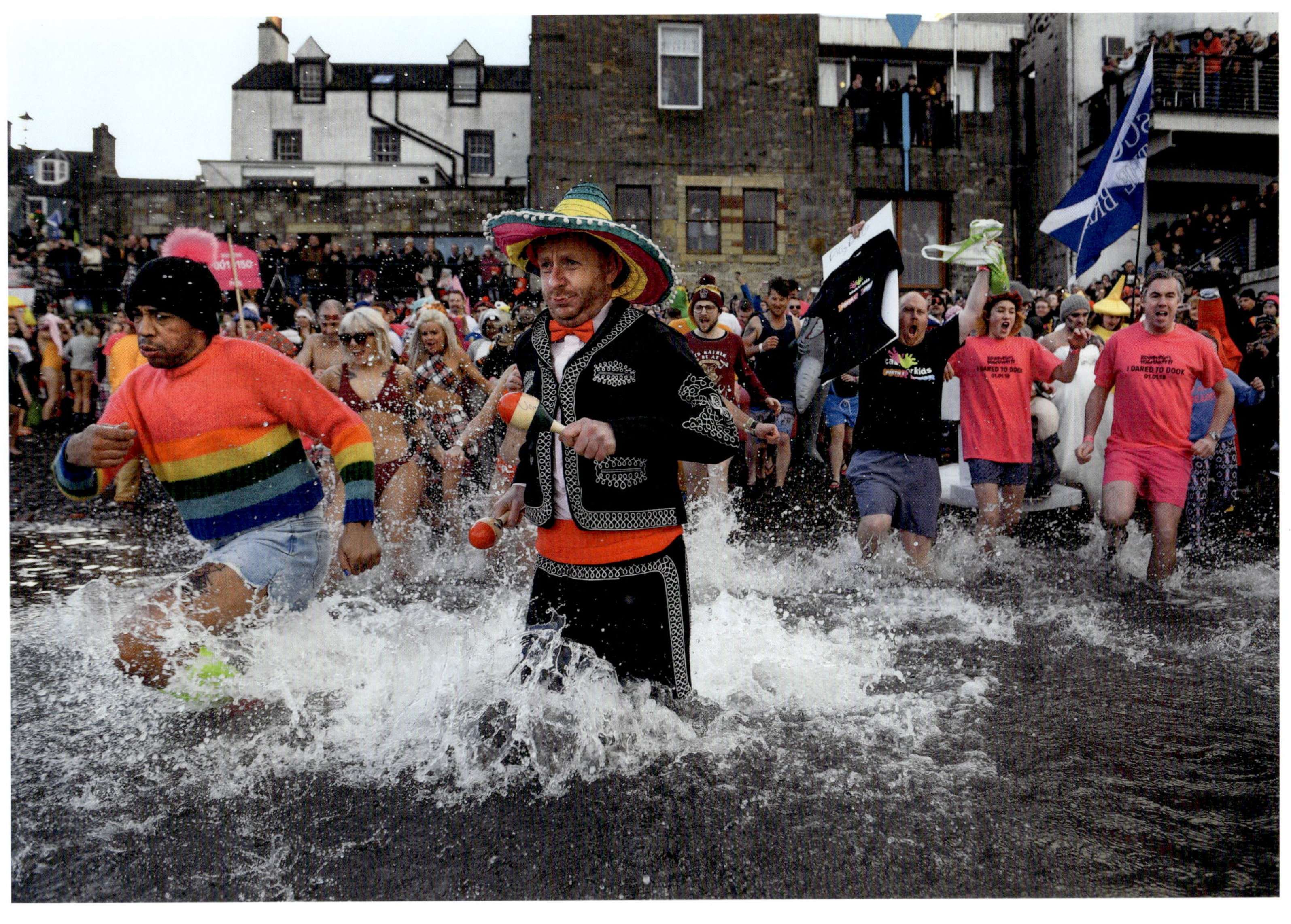

Fun Fact
SCHÖN SCHRÄG

After the New Year's Eve Hogmanay in Edinburgh, Scotland, January 1 is the Loony Dook. To join in the celebrations, you need to get your finest costume and follow the parade into the (freezing cold) water at the River Forth, into the North Sea.

Nach dem Neujahrfest Hogmanay im schottischen Edinburgh folgt am 1. Januar der Loony Dook („verrücktes Eintauchen"). Dafür muss man voll kostümiert in den (eiskalten) Firth of Forth eintauchen, der in die Nordsee mündet.

The torchlight procession as it makes its way down the Royal Mile for the start of the Hogmanay celebrations on December 30 in Edinburgh, Scotland. The traditional New Year celebrations run over three days.

Eine Fackelprozession, die am 30. Dezember im schottischen Edinburgh über die Royal Mile führt, läutet die Hogmanay-Feierlichkeiten ein. Die traditionellen Neujahrsfestivitäten erstrecken sich über drei Tage.

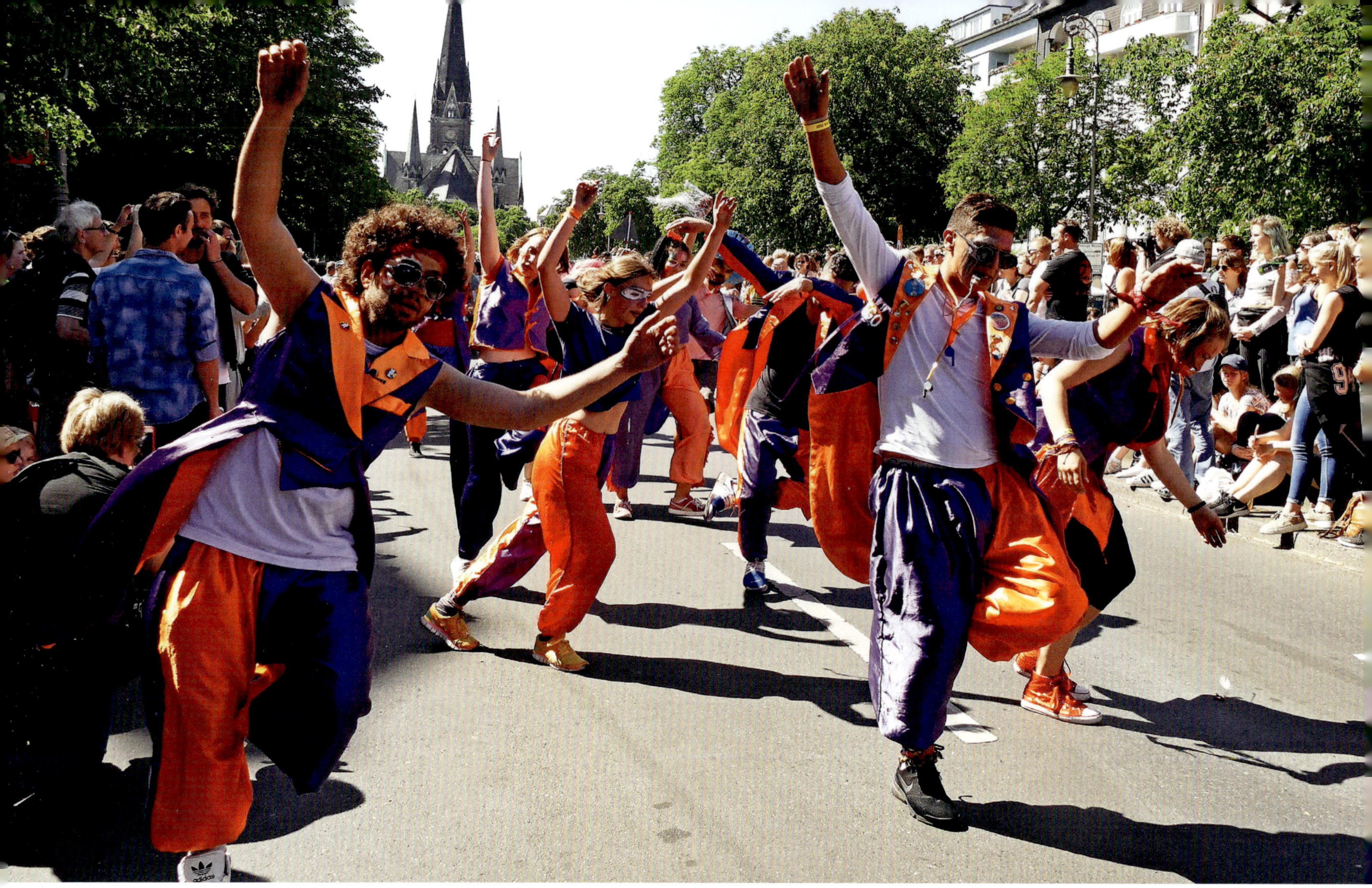

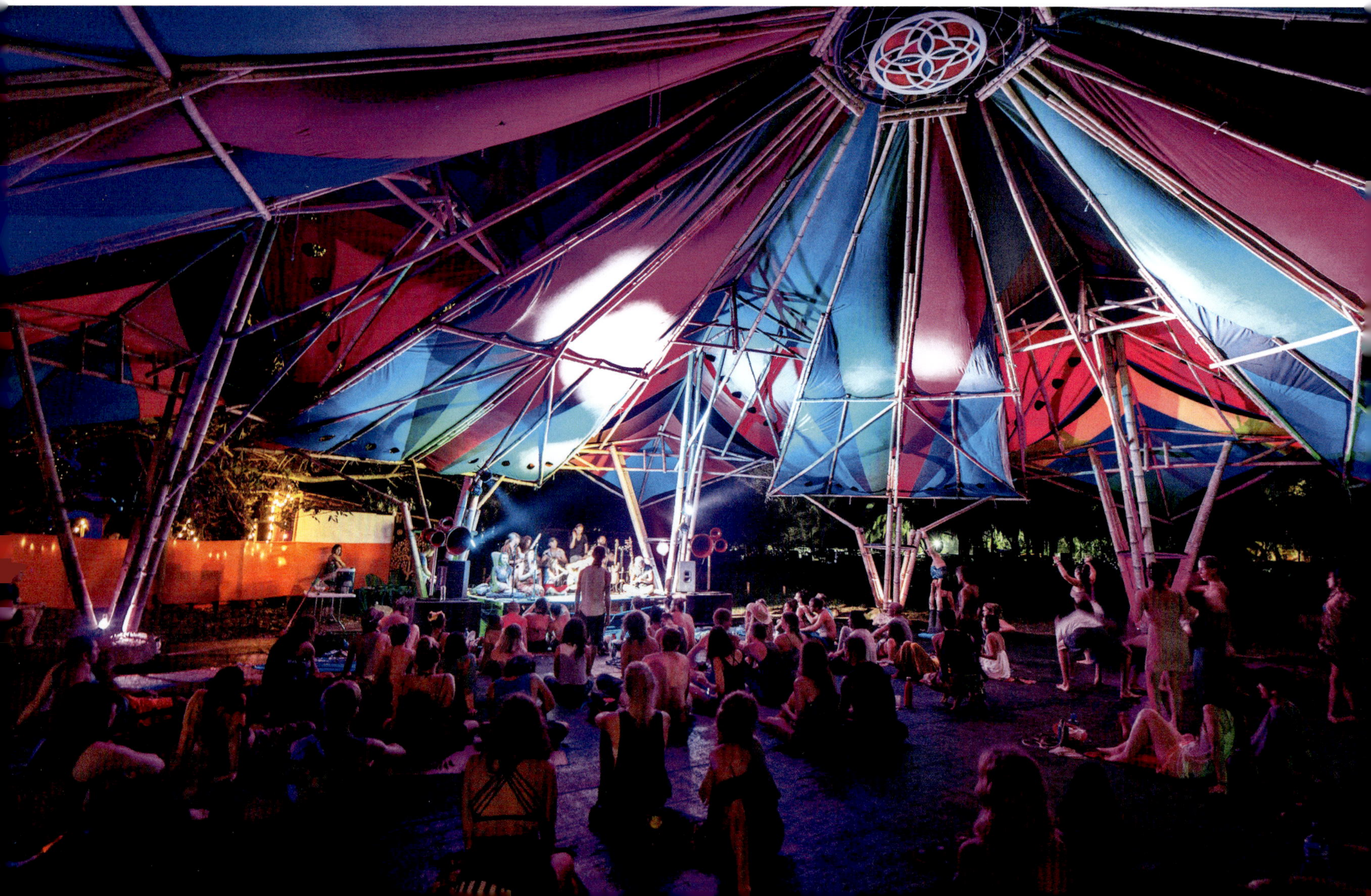

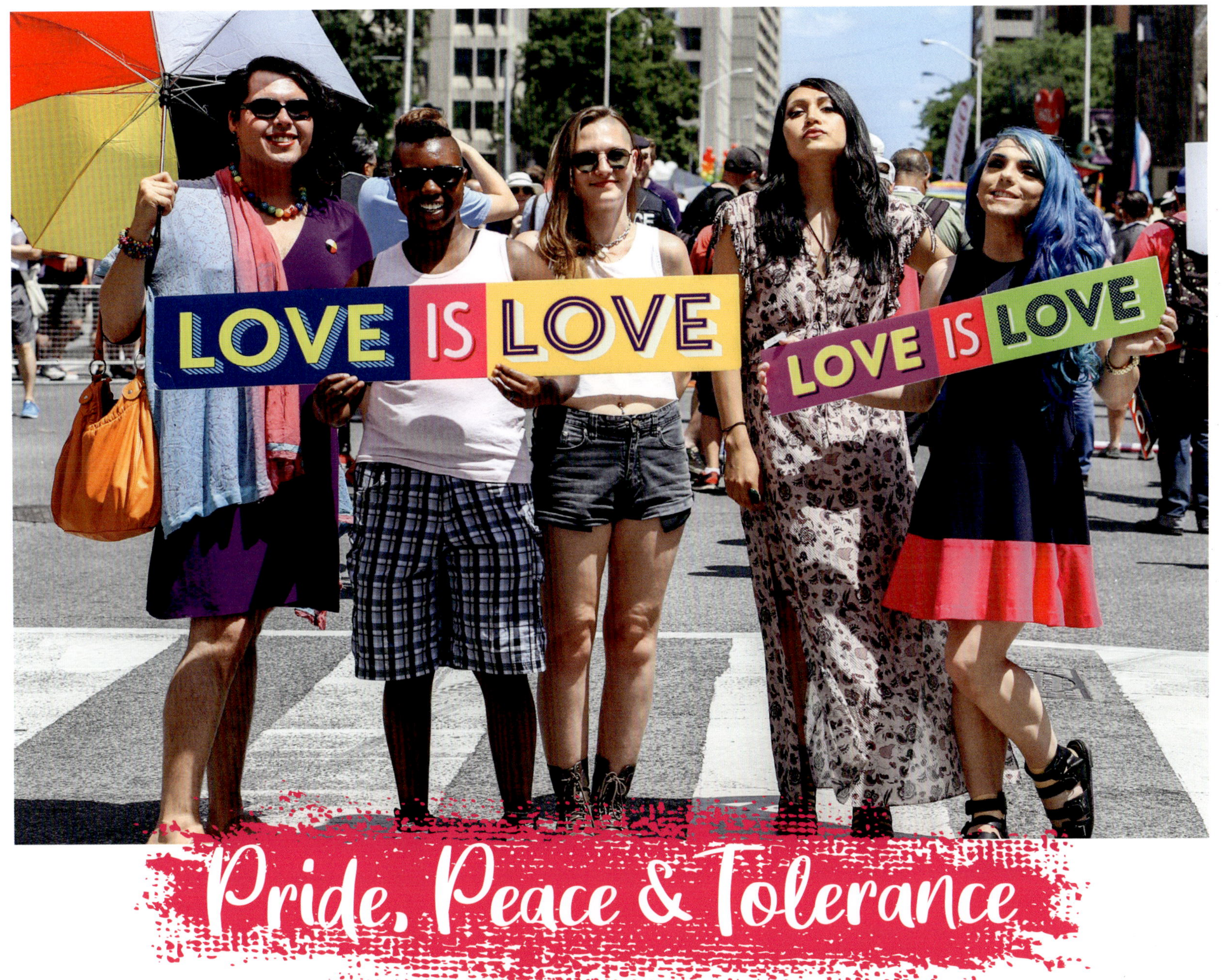

Pride, Peace & Tolerance

VIELFALT, FRIEDEN UND TOLERANZ

This page: Toronto Pride Parade.
Opposite, top: Dance performance at the Carnival of
Cultures in Berlin.

Diese Seite: Pride Parade, Toronto
Linke Seite, oben: Tänzer beim Karneval der Kulturen
in Berlin

Opposite, bottom: Concert during the Envision Festival in Uvita, Costa Rica. The festival is more than
a music festival though; it includes yoga, arts, and workshops and embraces its so-called seven pillars of
sustainability, spirituality, movement, art, music, education, and health.

Linke Seite, unten: Konzert auf dem Envision Festival in Uvita, Costa Rica. Das Festival bietet nicht nur
Musik, sondern auch Yoga, Bildende Künste und Workshops und fühlt sich sieben „Säulen" verpflichtet:
Nachhaltigkeit, Spiritualität, Bewegung, Bildende Kunst, Musik, Bildung und Gesundheit.

*P*ride marches date back to 1970, with the San Francisco Pride parade being the first. What started as a protest against the treatment of LGBTQIA+ people has now turned into a celebration for anyone who feels they don't fit into "the norm." It started with the Stonewall Riots, when the police assaulted many LGBTQIA+ at the Stonewall Inn, a bar on Christopher Street in Manhattan's Greenwich Village on June 28, 1969.

In Europe, Christopher Street Day marks the internationally celebrated Pride Week, or Pride Month as it's become. This is an important celebration of the freedom to love who you want, and it extends over many of the main European cities, with some of the largest including Madrid, London, Cologne, and Berlin.

Attend the biggest Pride event in San Francisco and you can be part of an amazing parade of confidence, acceptance, and joy. You'll see the Gay Pride rainbow painted everywhere, around 300 floats, bikes or groups, and dance stages featuring huge acts. The weekend festival is one of the biggest street parties you'll ever attend (next page).

"We are unity not division, we are acceptance not discrimination . . ." Costa Rica's Envision Festival is one of the most inclusive around. The 7 Pillars of actually going to the festival actively encourage safe spaces, sacred movements, radical self-expression, and an open mind. This is your chance to deep dive into yourself, and learn more about the human condition while enjoying the incredible Costa Rican coastline.

*D*er erste Pride-Marsch der LGBTQIA+-Community fand 1970 in San Francisco statt. Was ursprünglich ein Protest gegen die Diskriminierung von LGBTQIA+-Menschen war, ist heute ein Fest für alle, die sich nicht der „Norm" zugehörig fühlen. Es fing mit den sogenannten Stonewall Riots an, die am 28. Juni 1969 ausbrachen, nachdem die Polizei im Stonewall Inn, einer Bar auf der Christopher Street in New York City, in der homo- und transsexuelle Menschen verkehrten, eine gewalttätige Razzia veranstaltet hatte.

In Europa ist der Christopher Street Day der Höhepunkt der international begangenen Pride Week (oder manchmal sogar Pride Month). Gefeiert wird die Freiheit zu lieben, wen man will. Ein CSD findet in vielen europäischen Städten statt, die meistbesuchten darunter Köln, Berlin, Madrid und London.

Die Pride in San Francisco ist eine unglaubliche Parade aus Selbstbewusstsein, Akzeptanz und purer Freude. Überall weht die Regenbogenfahne, an dem Umzug nehmen etwa 300 Wagen sowie Motorräder und Gruppen teil, auf Bühnen treten bekannte Künstler auf. Dieses Wochenend-Festival ist eine der größten Straßenpartys der Welt und alle sind dazu eingeladen (nächste Seite).

„Wir sind Einheit, nicht Spaltung; wir sind Akzeptanz, nicht Diskriminierung …" Costa Ricas Envision Festival ist eine der inklusivsten Feiern überhaupt. Die sieben Säulen der ganzheitlichen Festival-Philosophie unterstützen auch u. a. die Freiheit zur radikalen Selbstdarstellung und Unvoreingenommenheit. Dies ist Ihre Chance, sich selbst und andere besser zu verstehen und dabei die traumhaften Strände Costa Ricas zu genießen.

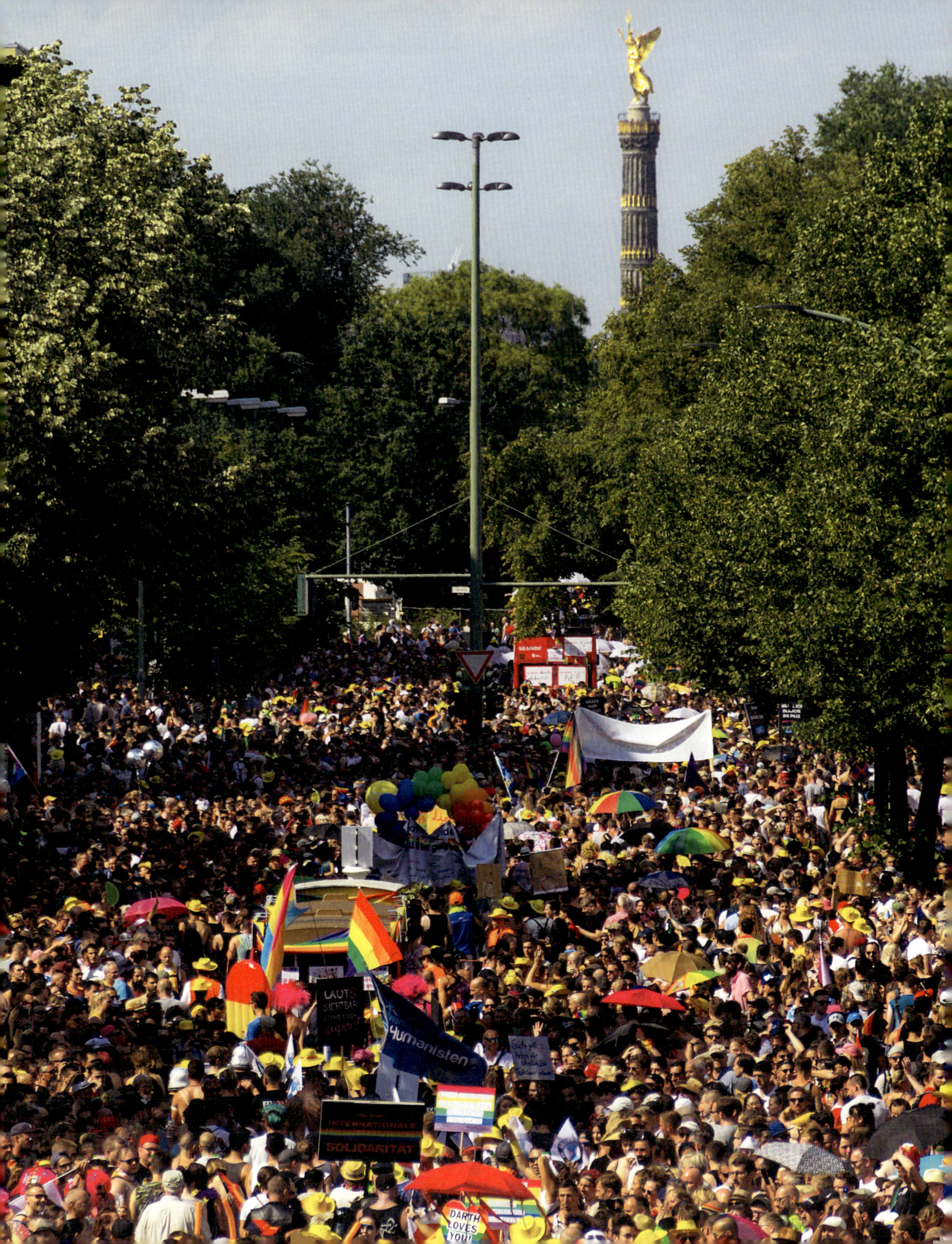

LAUT &
SICHTBAR
super
4umanisten
INTERNATIONALE
SOLIDARITÄT
DARTH
LOVES
YOU

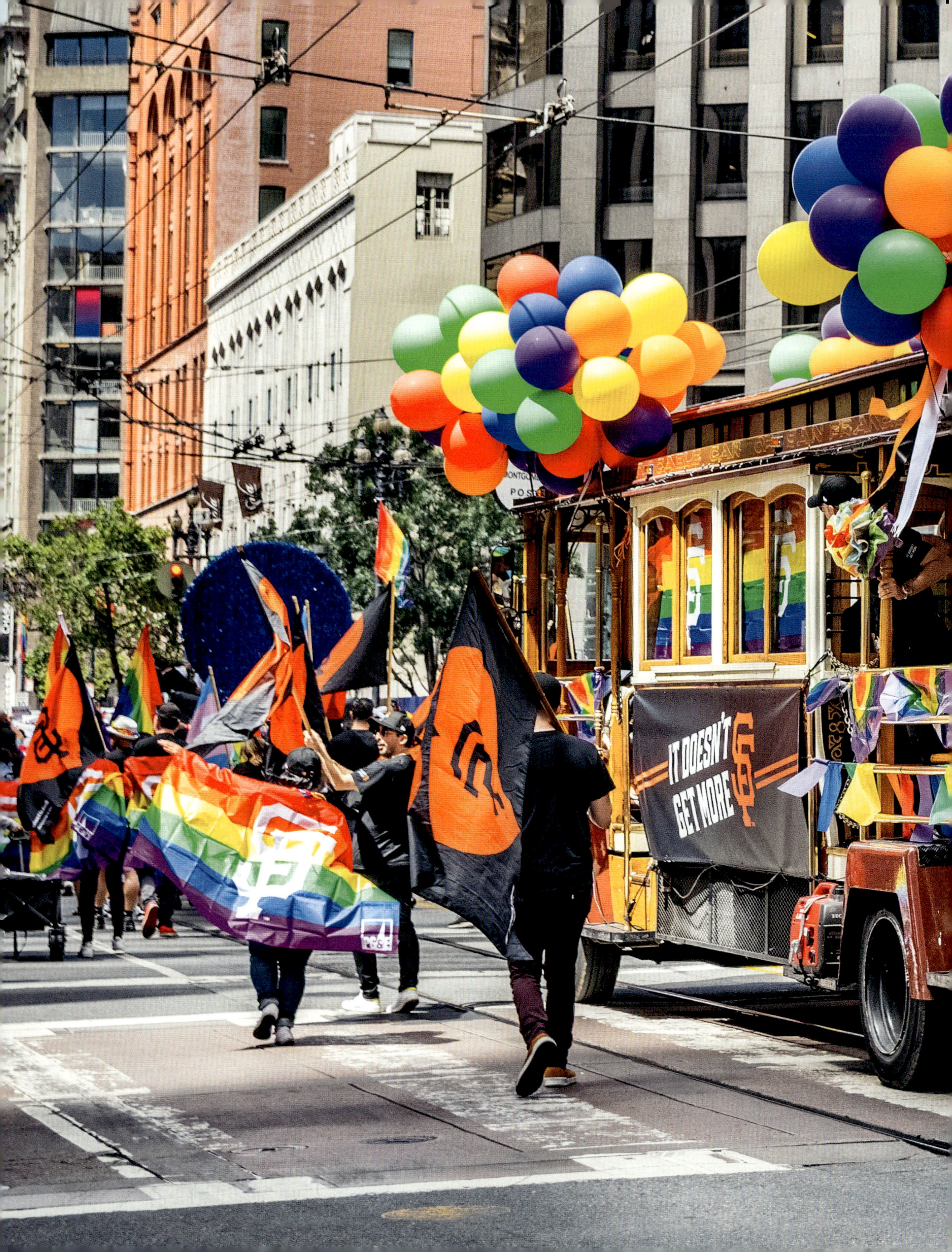
IT DOESN'T
GET MORE
SF
MUNICIPAL RAILWAY CAR OF SAN FRAN
PG&E

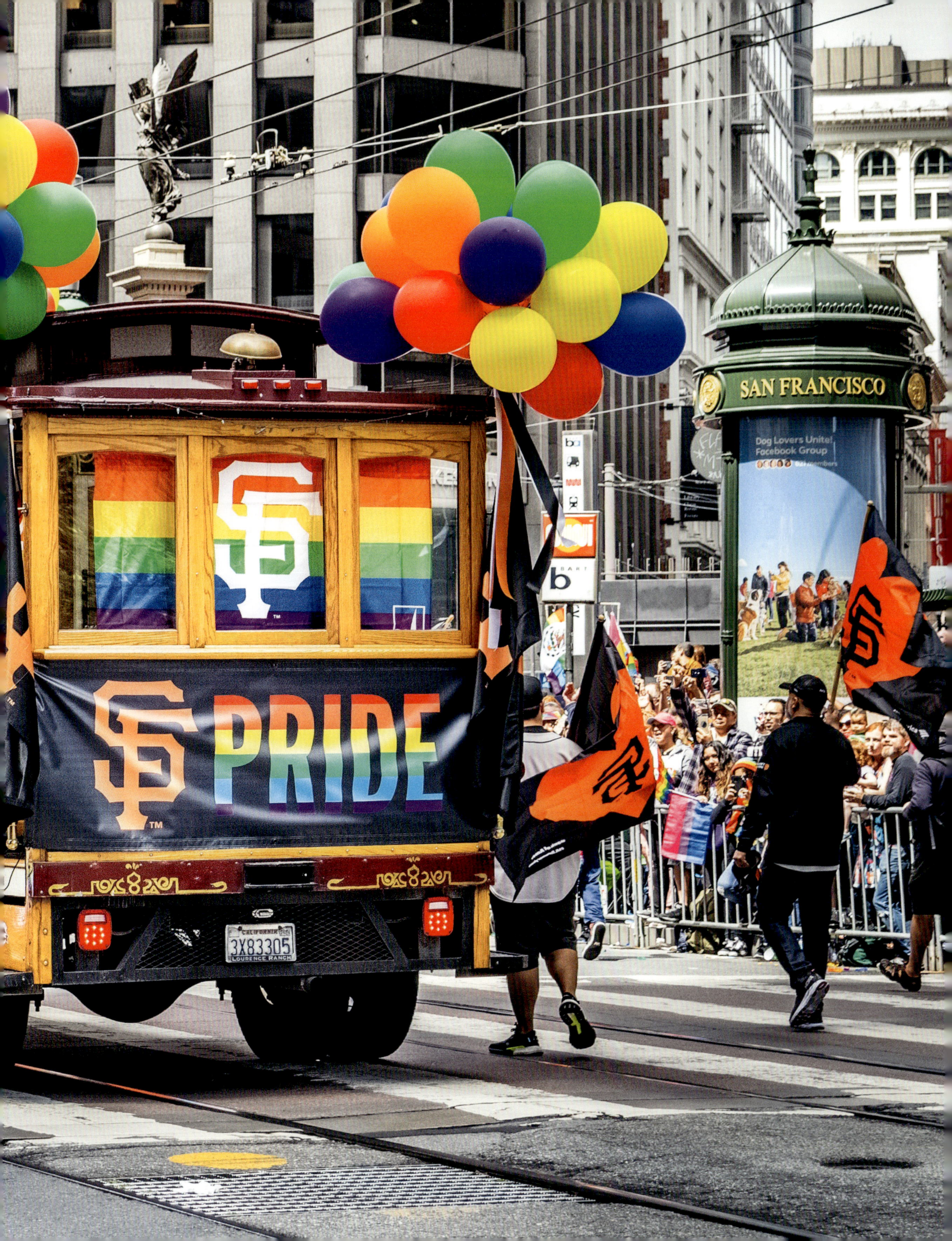

SF
SF
PRIDE
SAN FRANCISCO
Dog Lovers Unite!
Facebook Group
CALIFORNIA
3X83305
LOURENCE RANCH

About three million people participated in the São Paulo
Pride Parade, making it the largest in the world.

Etwa drei Millionen Menschen haben schon an der
Pride Parade in São Paulo teilgenommen. Sie ist damit
die größte Pride Parade weltweit.

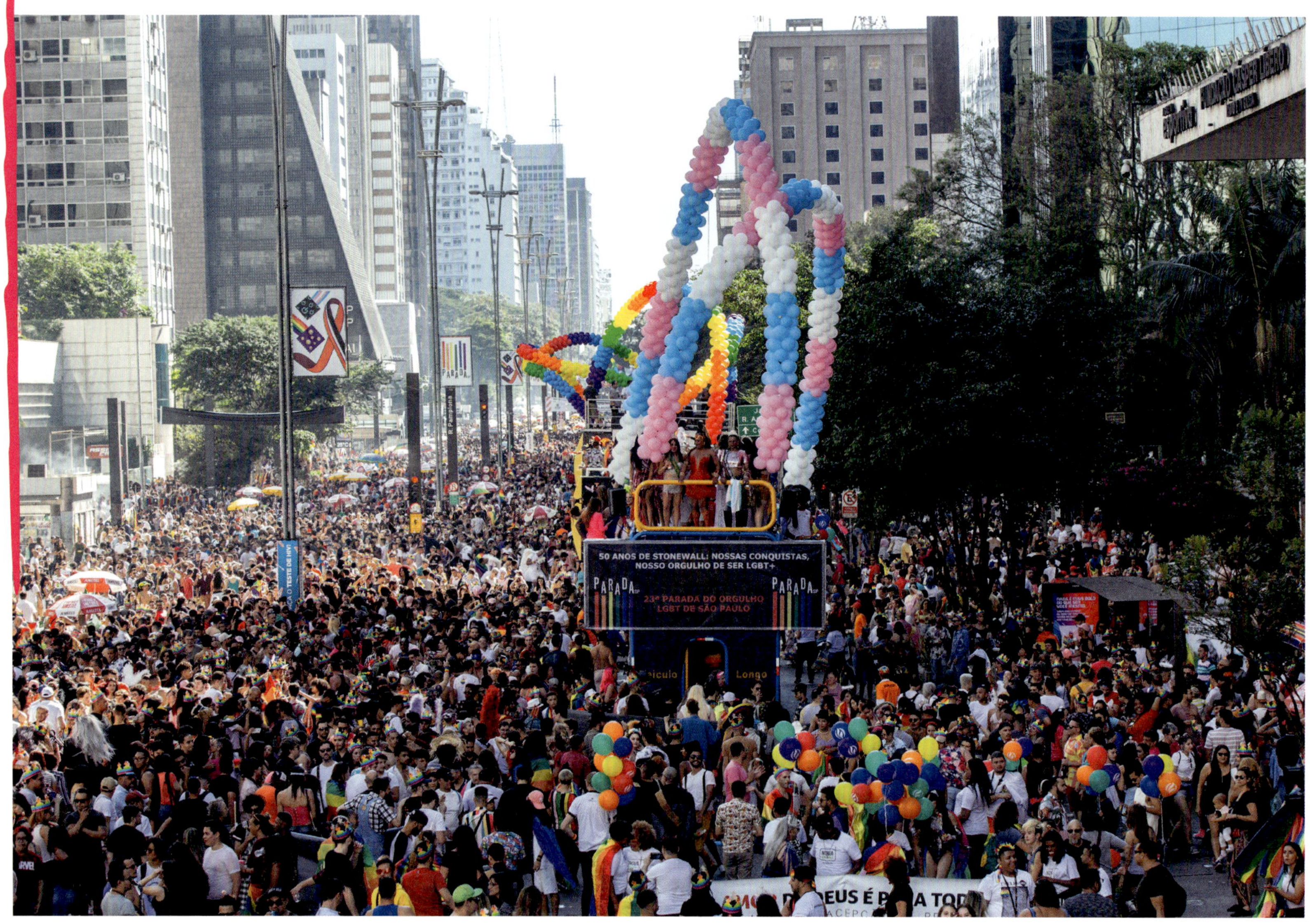

The Pride Flag was designed by Gilbert Baker for the 1978
Gay Freedom Day in San Francisco. It originally consisted of eight
symbolic colors, including pink and turquoise.

Die Pride-Fahne wurde von Gilbert Baker 1978 für den
Gay Freedom Day in San Francisco entworfen. Ursprünglich bestand
sie aus acht symbolischen Farben, darunter Pink und Türkis.

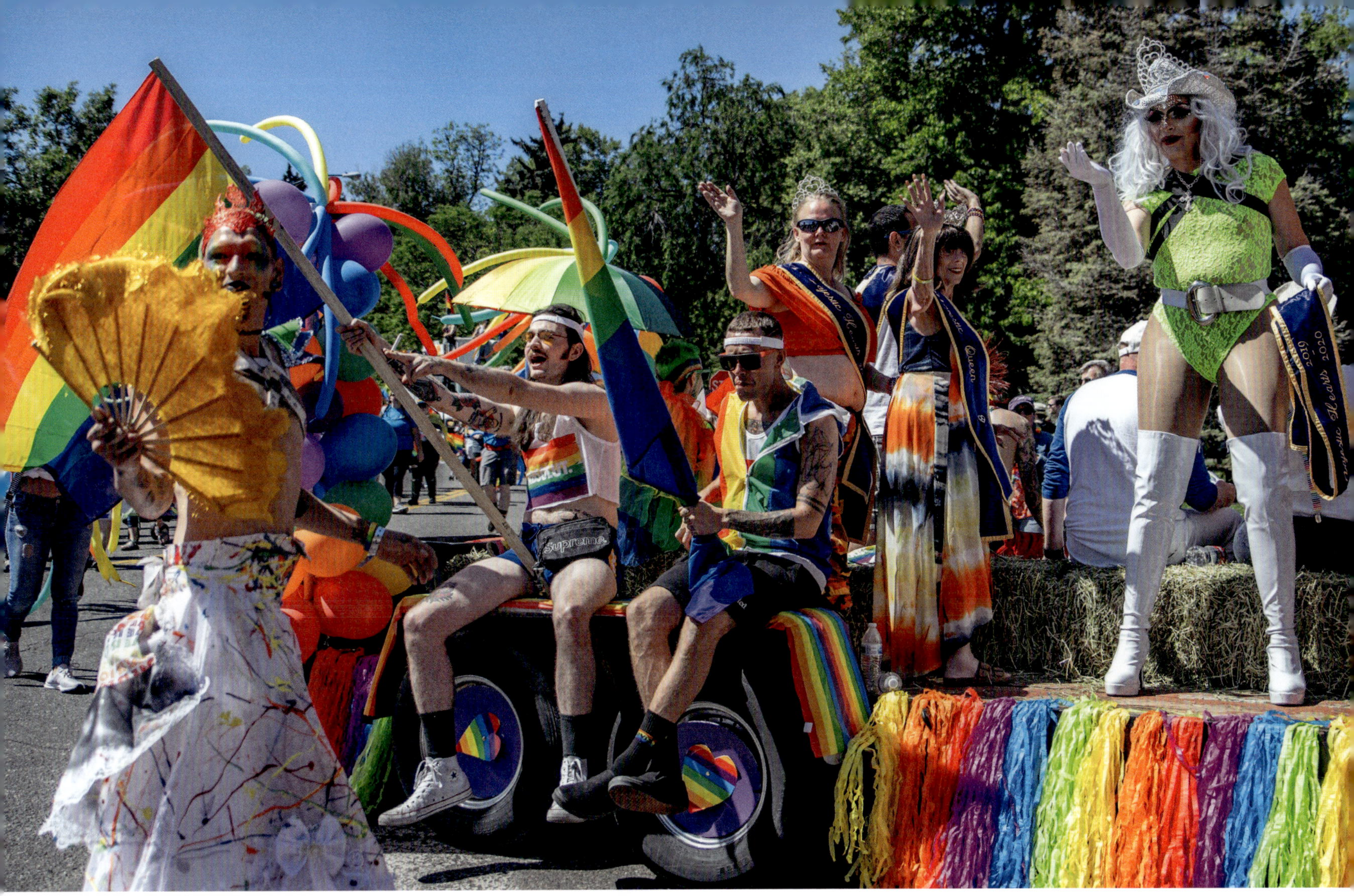

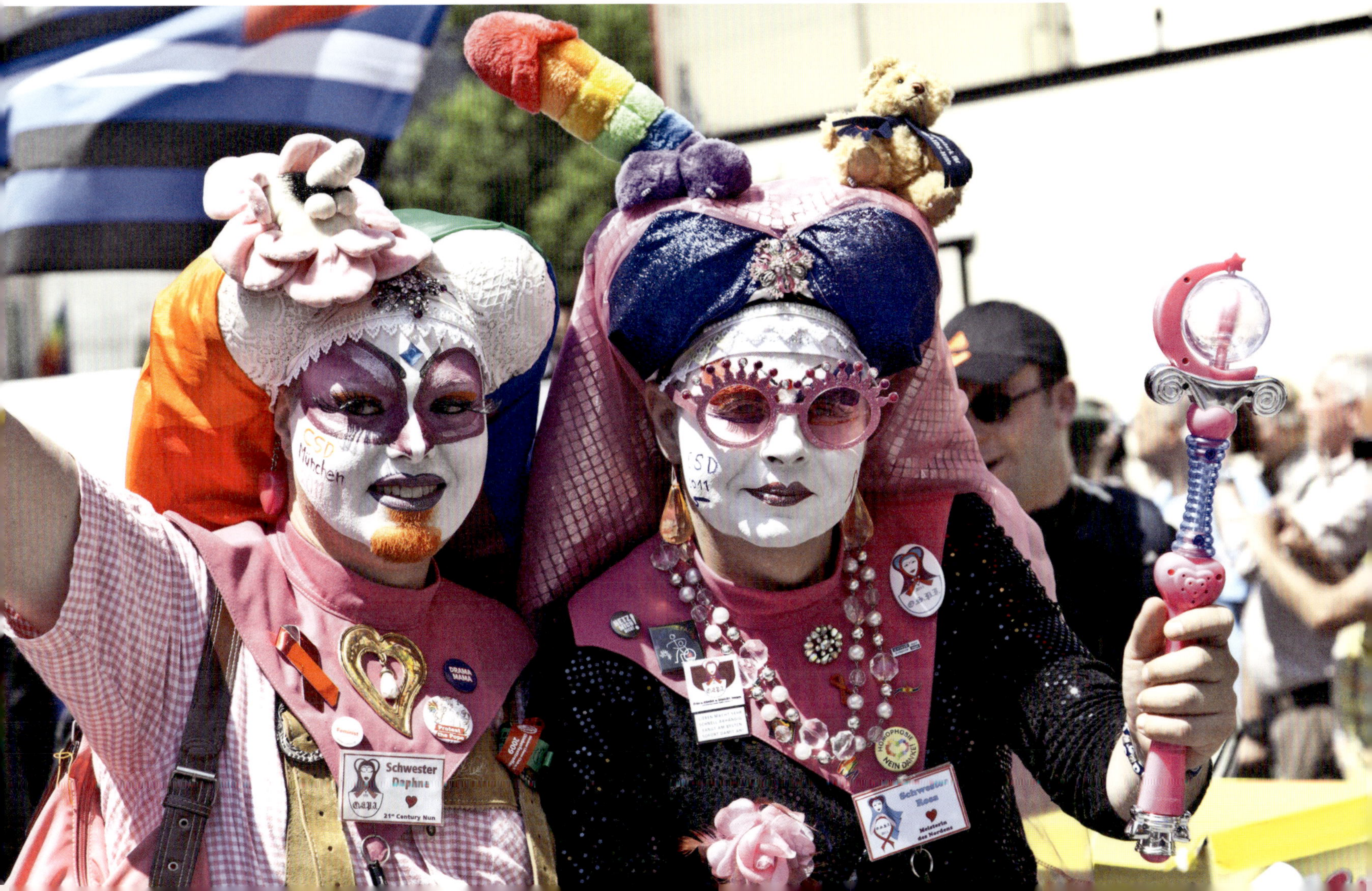

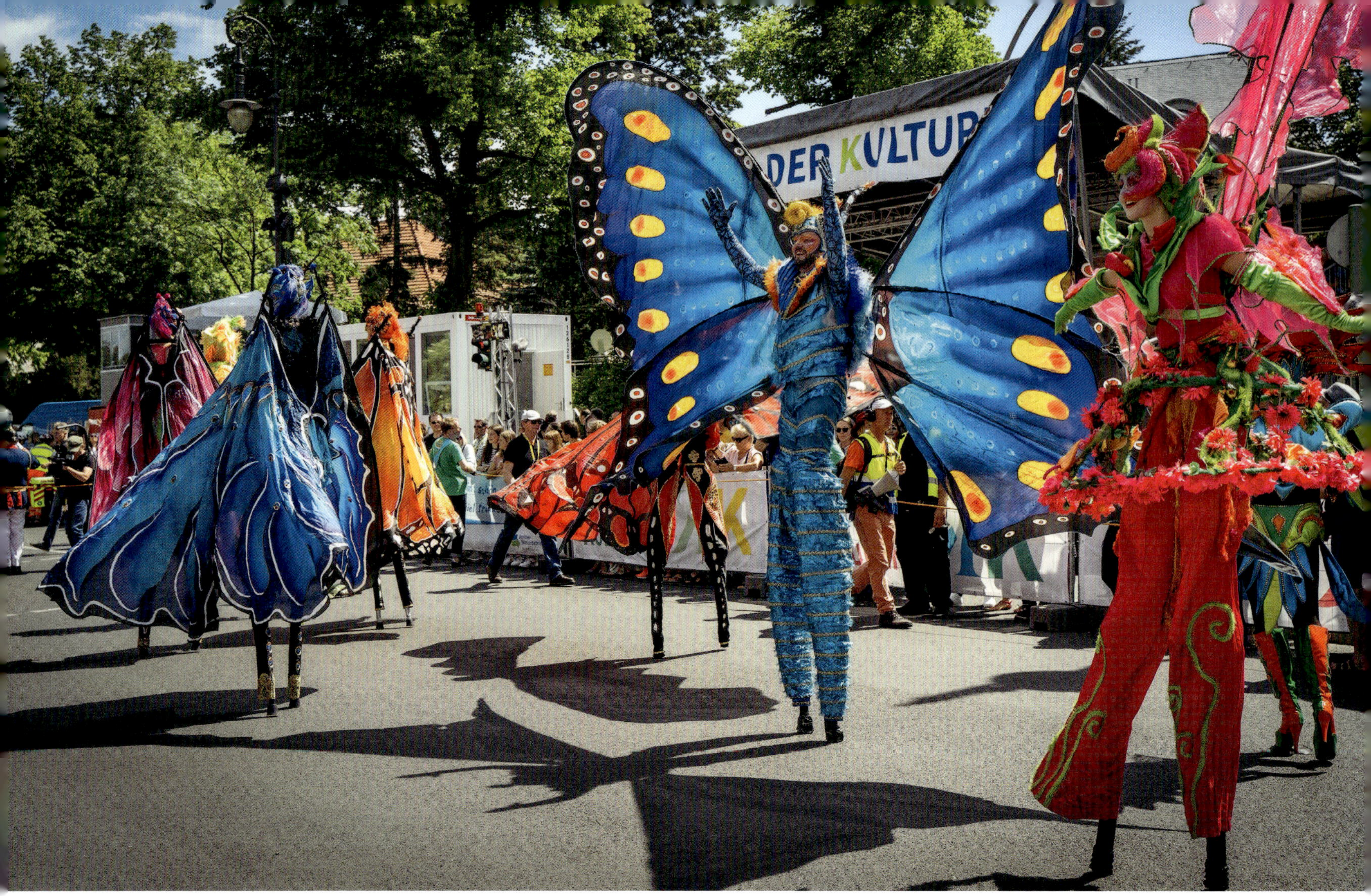
DER KULTUR

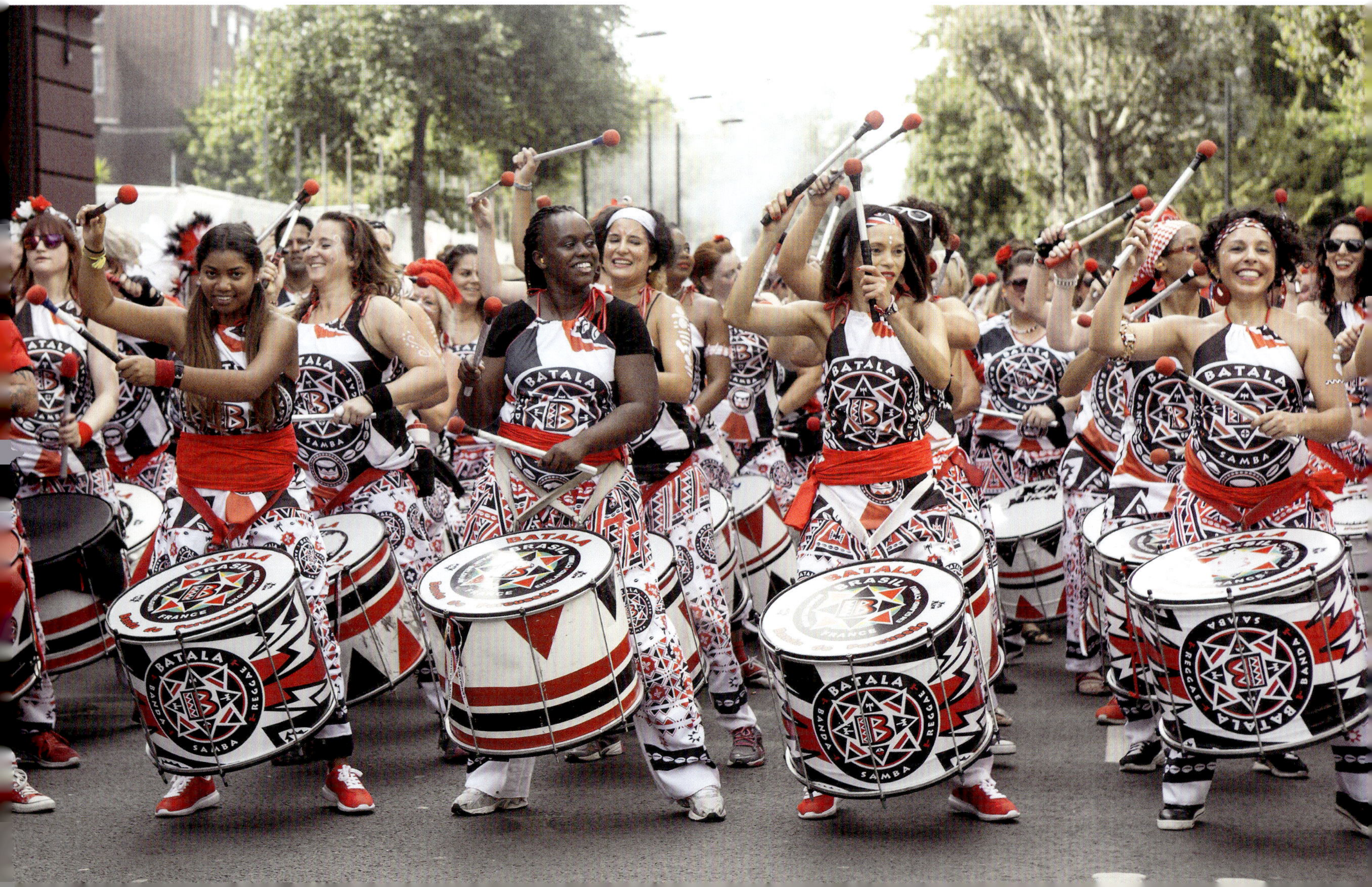
BATALA
SAMBA

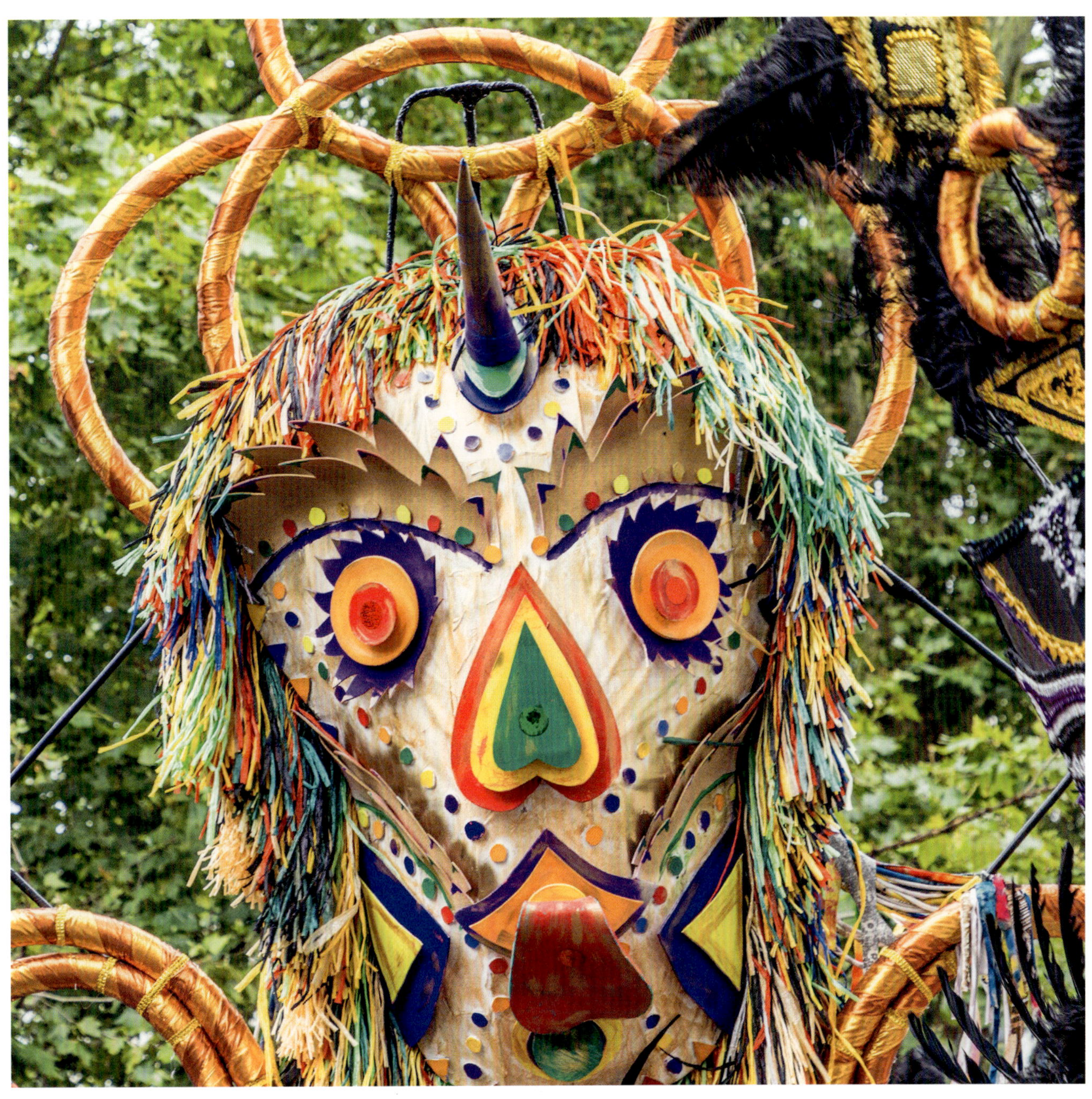

This page and opposite, bottom: The Notting Hill Carnival is an annual Caribbean carnival led by members of the British West Indian community. With two and a half million visitors each year, it is one of the world's largest street festivals.

Diese Seite und linke Seite, unten: Der Londoner Notting Hill Carnival ist ein karibisches Karnevalsfest und wurde von der aus den British West Indies stammenden Community ins Leben gerufen. Mit jährlich zweieinhalb Millionen Besuchern ist es eines der größten Straßenfeste der Welt.

Opposite, top: Numerous nationalities and ethnic groups present music, dance, performances, costumes, rituals, and acrobatics on moving floats and a street parade at the Carnival of Cultures in Berlin.

Linke Seite, oben: Beim Karneval der Kulturen in Berlin präsentieren Gruppen unterschiedlichster Nationalitäten und Ethnien auf einem Straßenumzug Musik- und Tanzperformances, Kostüme, Rituale und Akrobatik.

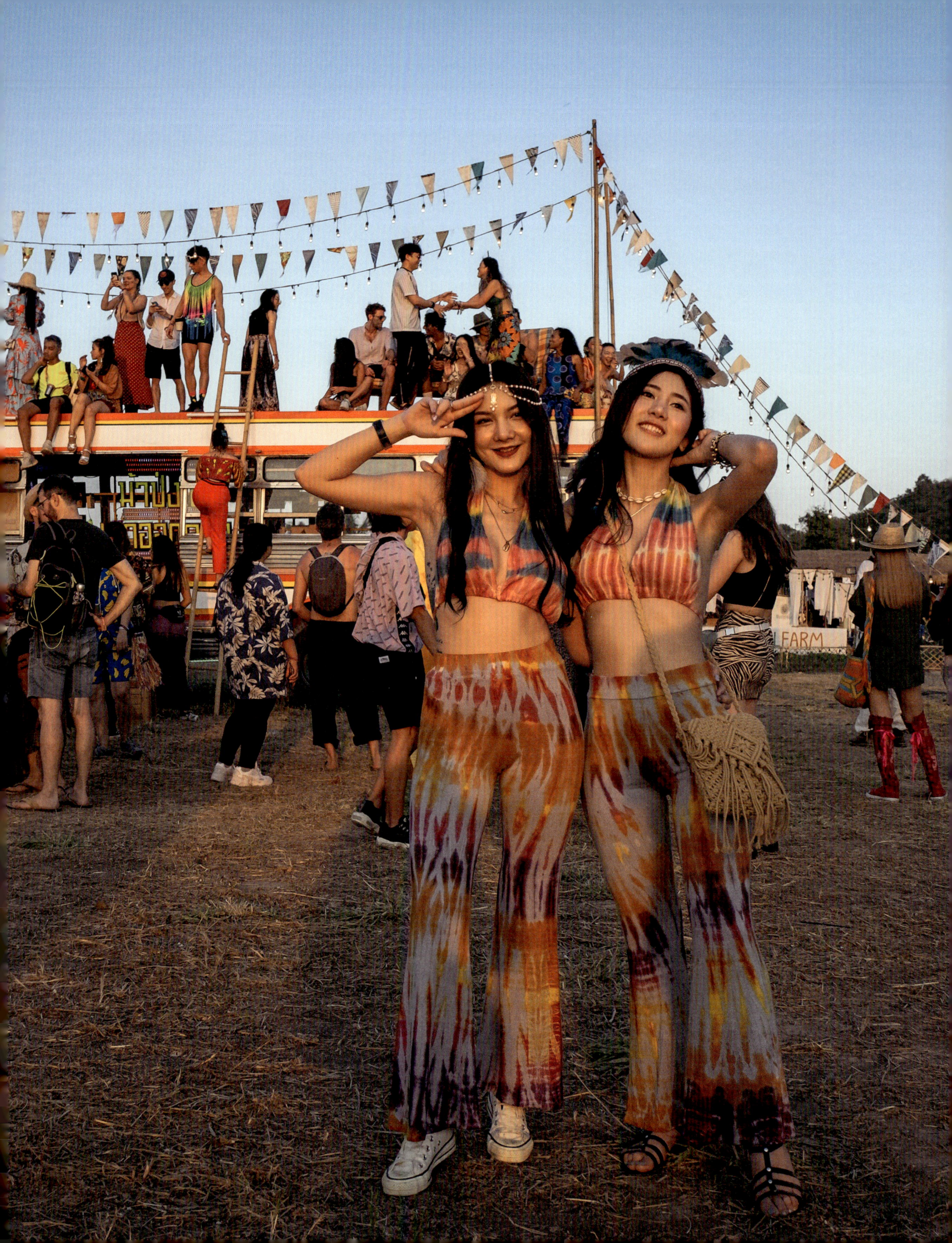

FARM

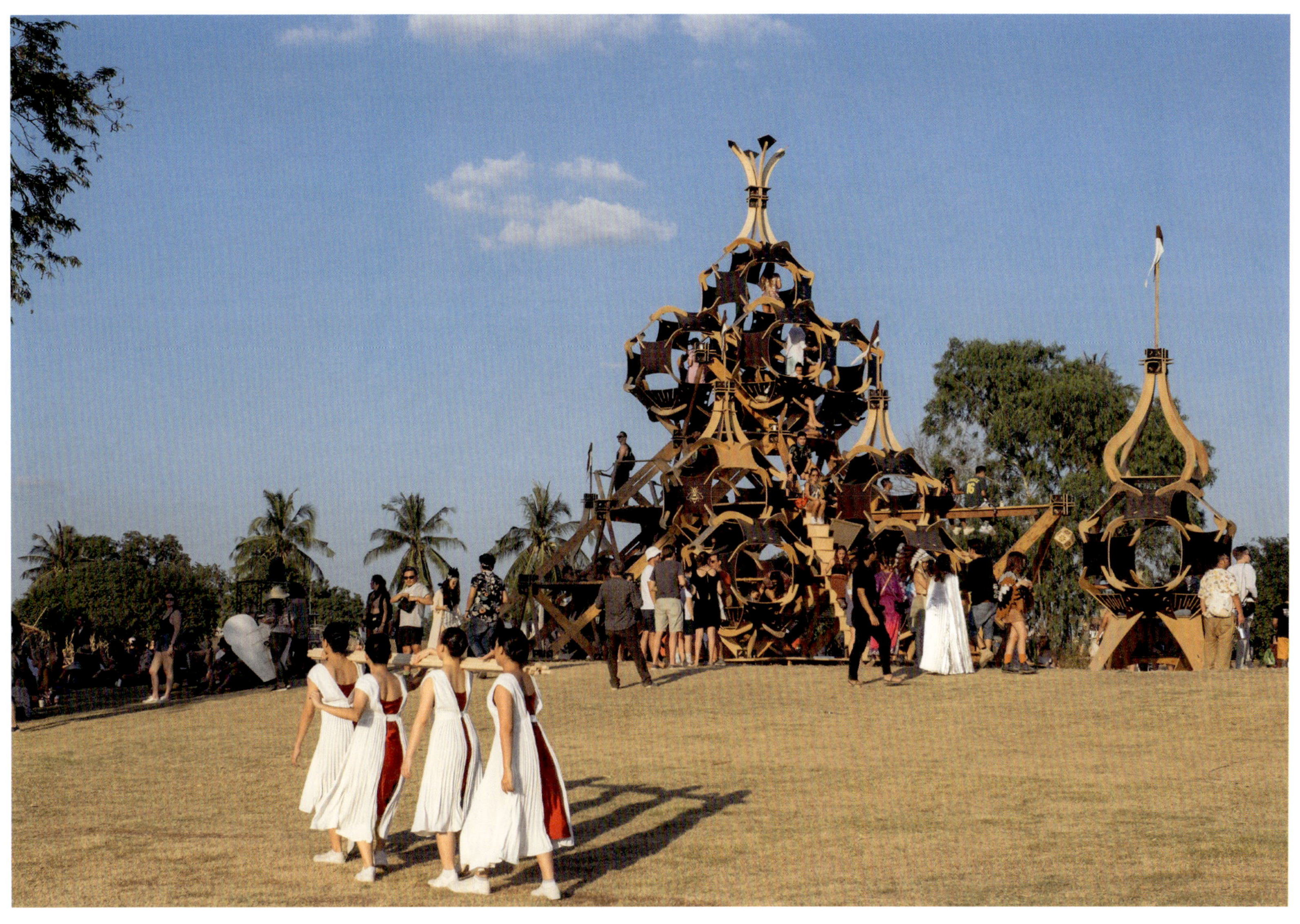

Thailand's Wonderfruit Festival is often called the "Asian Burning Man"—there are similarities, but Wonderfruit is quite spectacular in its own right.

Thailands Wonderfruit Festival wird auch oft das „asiatische Burning Man" genannt. Es gibt zwar Ähnlichkeiten mit dem US-amerikanischen Event, aber das Wonderfruit ist auf seine ganz eigene Weise spektakulär.

Good to know
WISSENSWERTES

Wonderfruit Festival in Pattaya, Thailand, promotes sustainability (e.g. no single-use plastic, stages made of bamboo), inclusion, and social responsibility through performances, art installations, workshops, and banquets. It encourages visitors to learn something new. It also features some pretty impressive music headliners, and an incredible location!

Das Wonderfuit Festival im thailändischen Pattaya legt bei seinen Performances, Kunstinstallationen, Workshops und Festmahlen Wert auf Nachhaltigkeit (Bühnen aus Bambus, keine Wegwerfbecher aus Plastik), Inklusion und soziale Verantwortung. Es ermutigt Besucher Neues zu lernen und bietet zudem einige ziemlich beeindruckende musikalische Hauptacts und eine traumhafte Location!

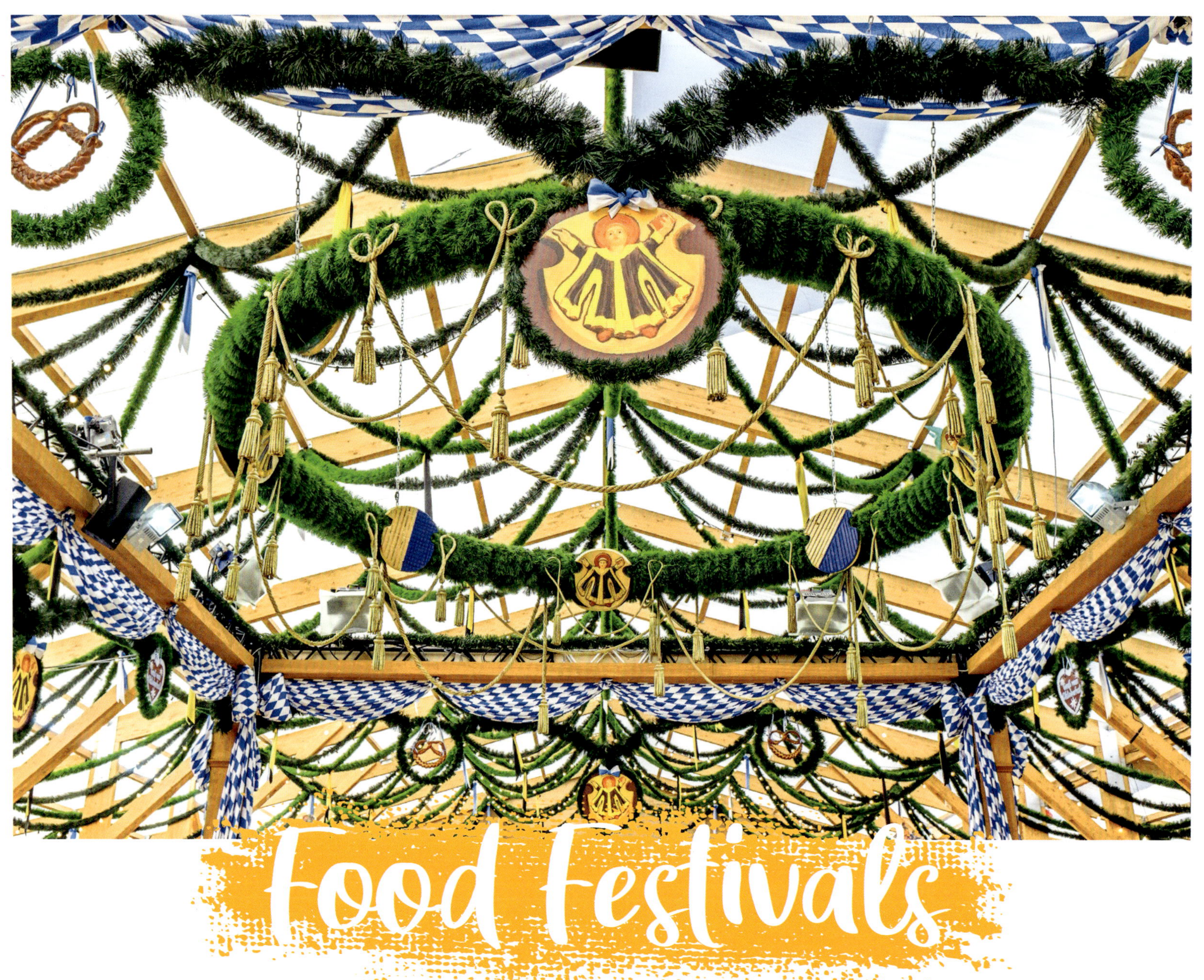

Food Festivals

WAHRHAFT NAHRHAFT

At Oktoberfest in Munich, the largest funfair in the world, an estimated 1.9 million gallons (7.5 million liters) of beer are consumed each season.

Das Oktoberfest in München ist der größte Jahrmarkt der Welt. Geschätzte 7,5 Millionen Liter Bier werden dort jedes Jahr getrunken.

Incredible floats and sculptures made of lemons and oranges can be admired during the Fête du Citron, or Lemon Festival, in Menton, France. The event is also a carnival, with a different theme each year.

Beim Zitronenfest (Fête du Citron) im französischen Menton können erstaunliche Wagen und Skulpturen aus Zitronen und Orangen bewundert werden. Das Fest ist gleichzeitig ein Karneval mit jährlich wechselndem Motto.

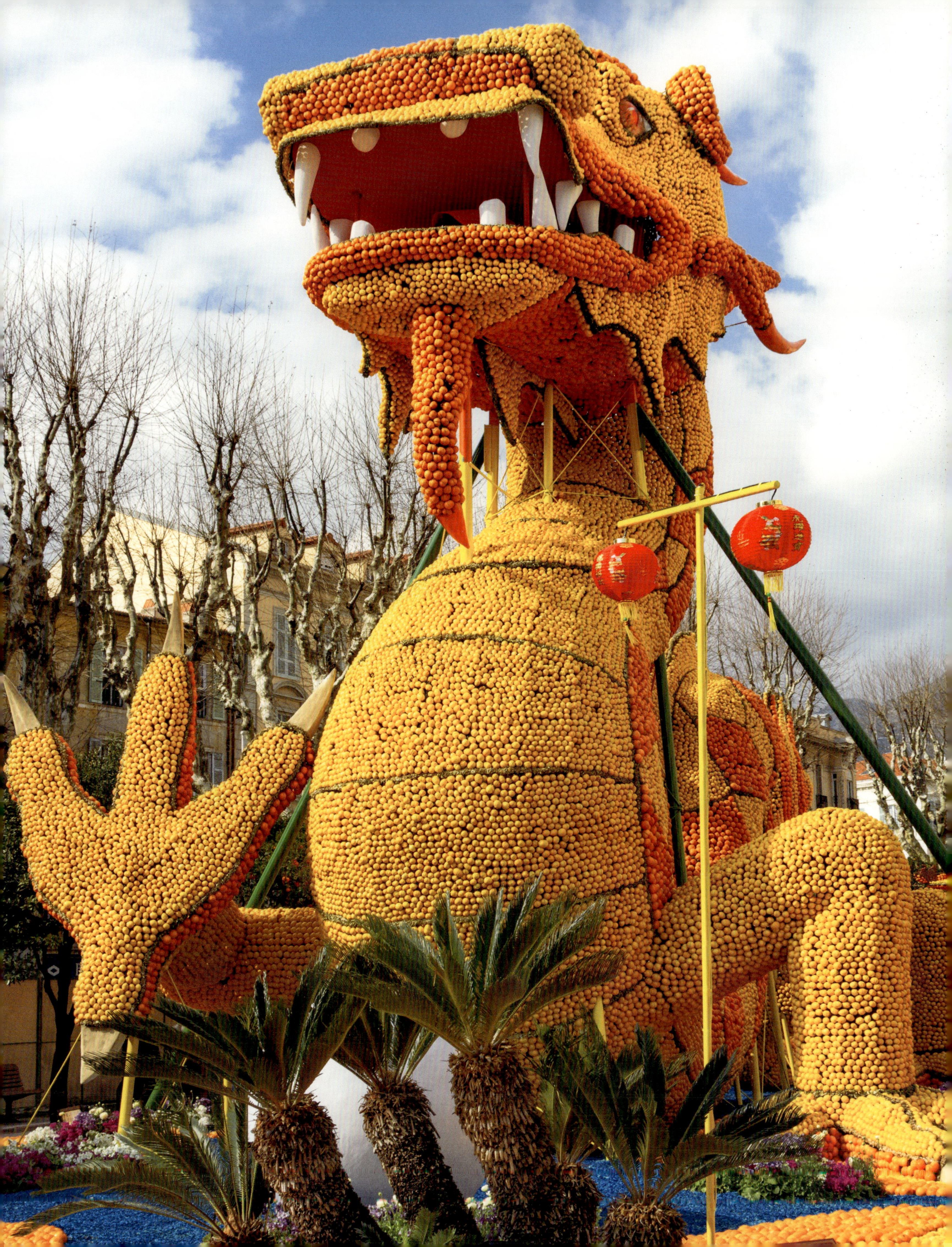

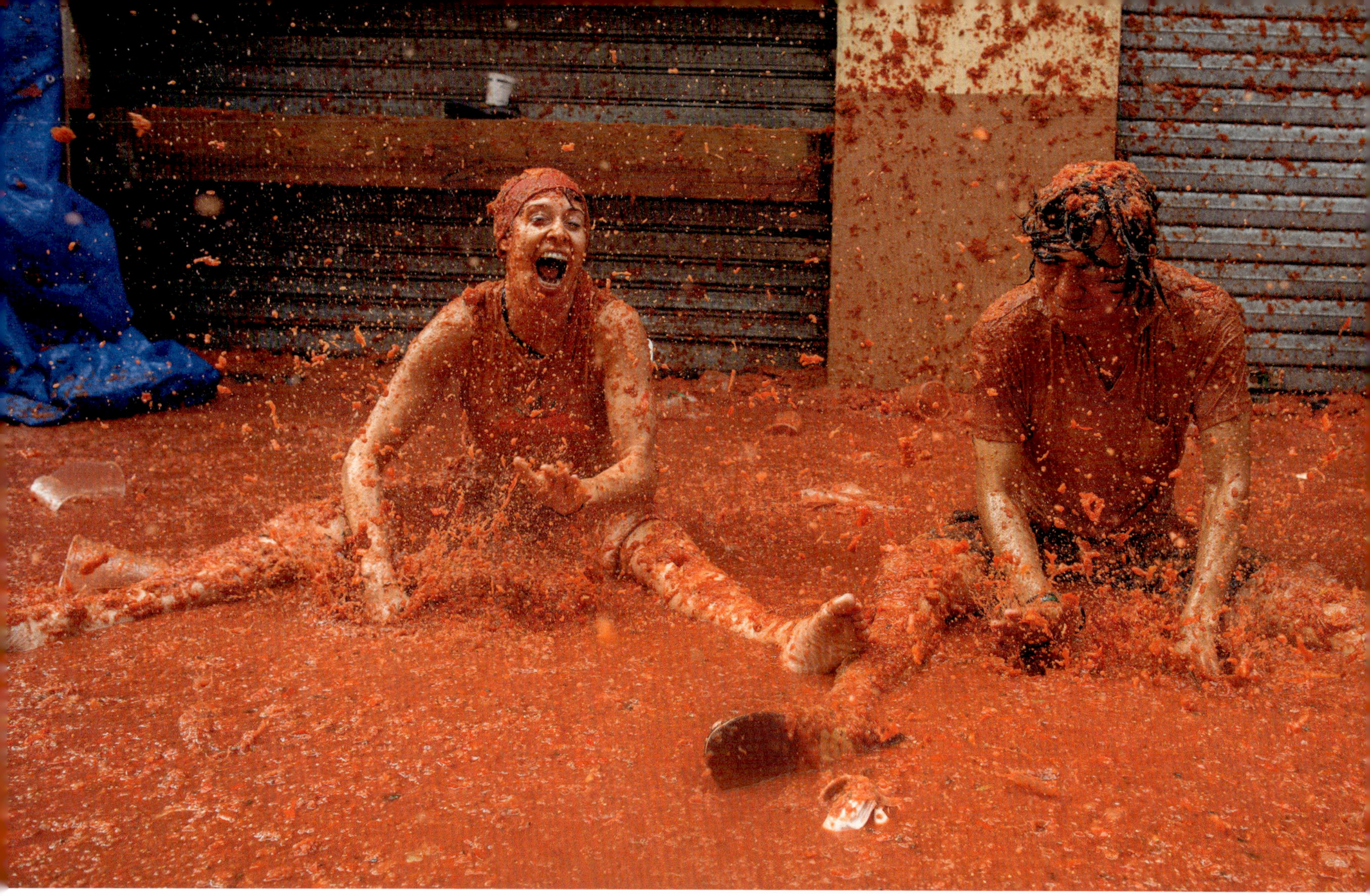

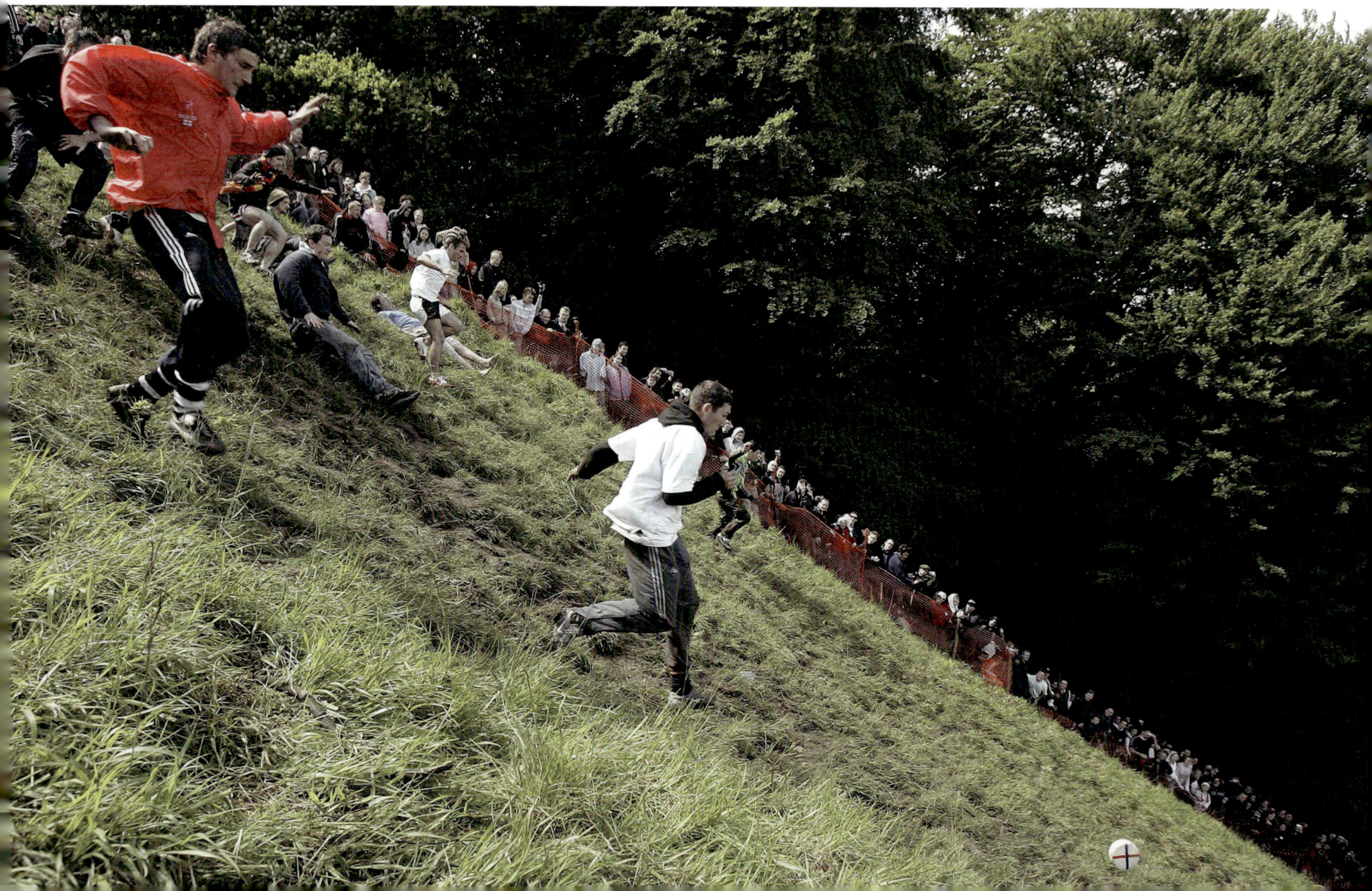

Eating is what brings us together day to day, so it absolutely makes sense to celebrate food during festivals. Around the world we welcome in the seasons with cyclical feasts and observances—they're a great way to pass on the traditions and knowledge of our ancestors in a fun way.

Out of context though, some of the world's best food festivals sound . . . bonkers.

In the UK, one of the biggest food festivals involves a race to see who can catch a 7–9 pound (3–4 kilogram) round of Double Gloucester cheese sent rolling down a hill at the Cooper's Hill Cheese-Rolling and Wake. International participants and spectators come to join in the festival, which is thought to be over 600 years old (opposite, bottom).

Food festivals are also a great way to celebrate with the food that's in abundance at the time. At Tomatina in Buñol, Spain, about 265,000 pounds (120 metric tons) of tomatoes are hurled in a two-hour session to celebrate the tomato harvest. There are a few stories around why this has become the huge tradition that it has. The most trustworthy one dates back to 1945, when two groups of youths were arguing near a vegetable stand, the dispute got physical, tomatoes were involved, and so began the great Tomatina Festival as we know it today (opposite, top).

Oktoberfest is celebrated the world over, but the biggest event is in Munich, Germany. Long table after long table of festivalgoers drinking pints of beer was all started by a horse race in 1810 to celebrate Bavarian Crown Prince Ludwig's wedding. Although, not many people know that (or even care), as now Oktoberfest centers around beer and pork knuckles, and lots of it. With live music, dancing, lederhosen, and dirndls, you can lose a few days in those beer tents!

Essen ist eine gesellige Tätigkeit, was liegt also näher, als auf Festivals Kulinarisches zu zelebrieren. Oft sind sie mit Jahreszeiten verbunden und ein wunderbarer Weg, um Traditionen und das Wissen unserer Vorfahren auf eine unterhaltsame Weise zu bewahren. Kennt man die Hintergründe nicht, hören sich einige der besten Food Festivals der Welt allerdings ziemlich schräg an.

Beim Cooper's Hill Cheese-Rolling and Wake, einem der der größten Food Festivals in Großbritannien, dreht sich alles darum, einen 3–4 Kilogramm schweren Double-Gloucester-Käse einzufangen, der einen Hügel hinunterrollt. Das skurrile Festival, das es wahrscheinlich schon seit über 600 Jahren gibt, lockt auch viele internationale Besucher an (linke Seite, unten).

Auf Food Festivals stehen oft Nahrungsmittel im Mittelpunkt, die in der jeweiligen Region und Jahreszeit gerade in Hülle und Fülle vorkommen. Auf der Tomatina im spanischen Buñol wird zwei Stunden lang mit etwa 120 Tonnen Tomaten geworfen, um die Tomatenernte zu feiern. Es kursieren mehrere Ursprungsgeschichten. Die glaubwürdigste besagt, dass sich 1945 zwei Gruppen von Jugendlichen in der Nähe eines Gemüsestandes stritten. Der Streit eskalierte, Tomaten kamen zum Einsatz und so entstand das große Tomatina-Festival, das wir heute kennen (linke Seite, oben).

Das Oktoberfest wird zwar weltweit gefeiert, ist aber natürlich in München zu Hause. An langen Tischen wird in geselligem Beisammensein eine Maß nach der anderen in Richtung trockener Kehlen gestemmt. Was viele nicht wissen: Angefangen hat alles bei einem Pferderennen im Jahr 1810 zu Ehren der Hochzeit von Kronprinz Ludwig. Heute dreht sich alles um Bier und Schweinshaxen in möglichst großen Mengen, gespickt mit Livemusik, Tanz, Lederhosen und Dirndln. O'zapft is!

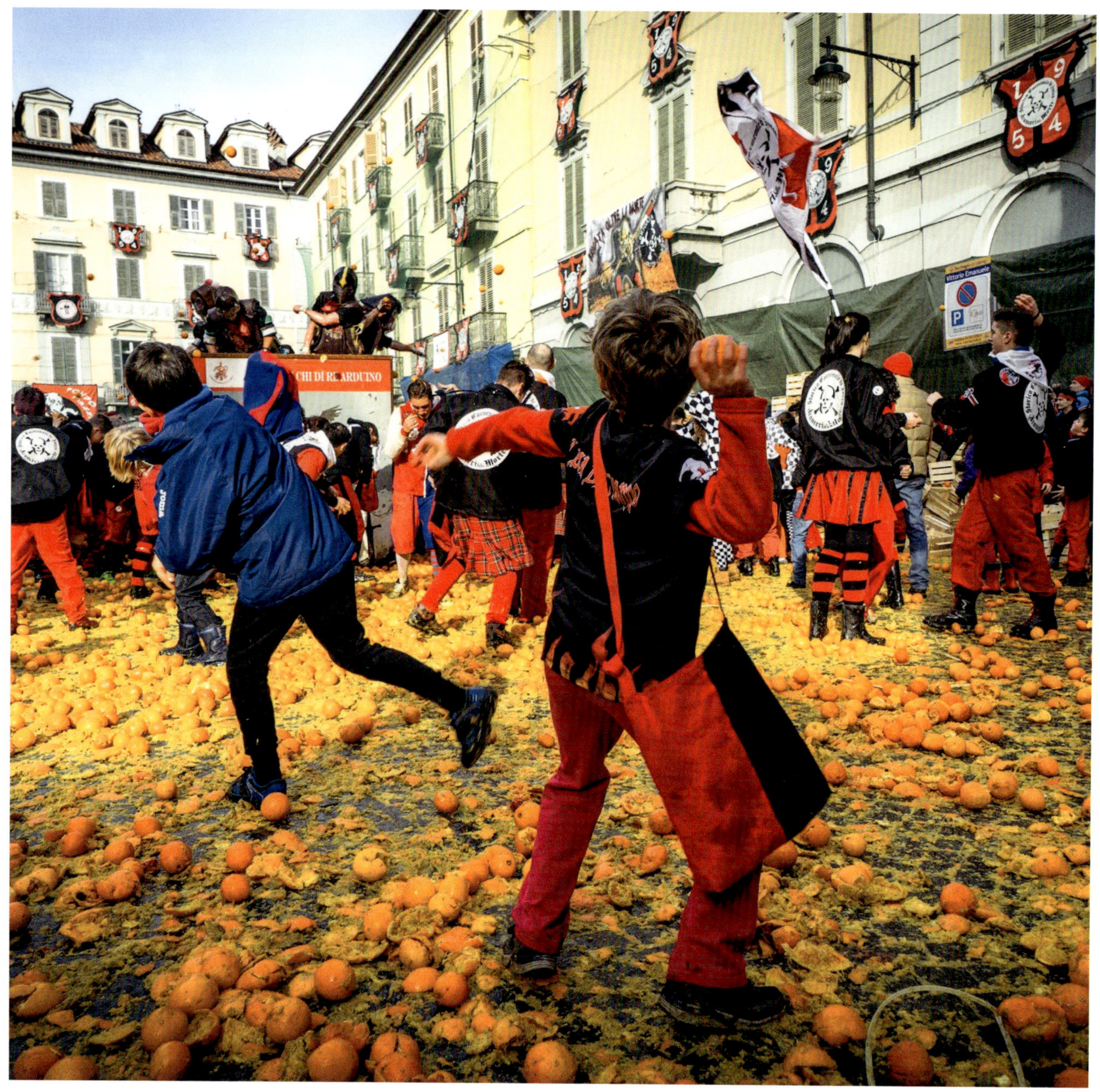

The largest food fight of Italy can be observed in Ivrea, during the
Carnival of Ivrea, which features the Battle of the Oranges.
The battle symbolizes the fight between good (the people) versus bad
(the tyrant aristocracy).

Der größte Food Fight Italiens findet während des Karnevals in Ivrea
statt. Bei der Orangenschlacht kämpfen symbolisch die Guten (das
Volk) gegen die Bösen (die tyrannische Aristokratie).

There are nine teams of *aranceri* (orange throwers) on foot,
representing the people, and *aranceri* in carts, representing the tyrants.
Each team wears different identifiers, like symbols and colors.

Neun Teams von zu Fuß gehenden *aranceri* (Orangenwerfern)
repräsentieren das Volk, in Wagen fahrende Werfer stehen für die
Tyrannen. Jedes Team hat seine eigenen Symbole und Farben.

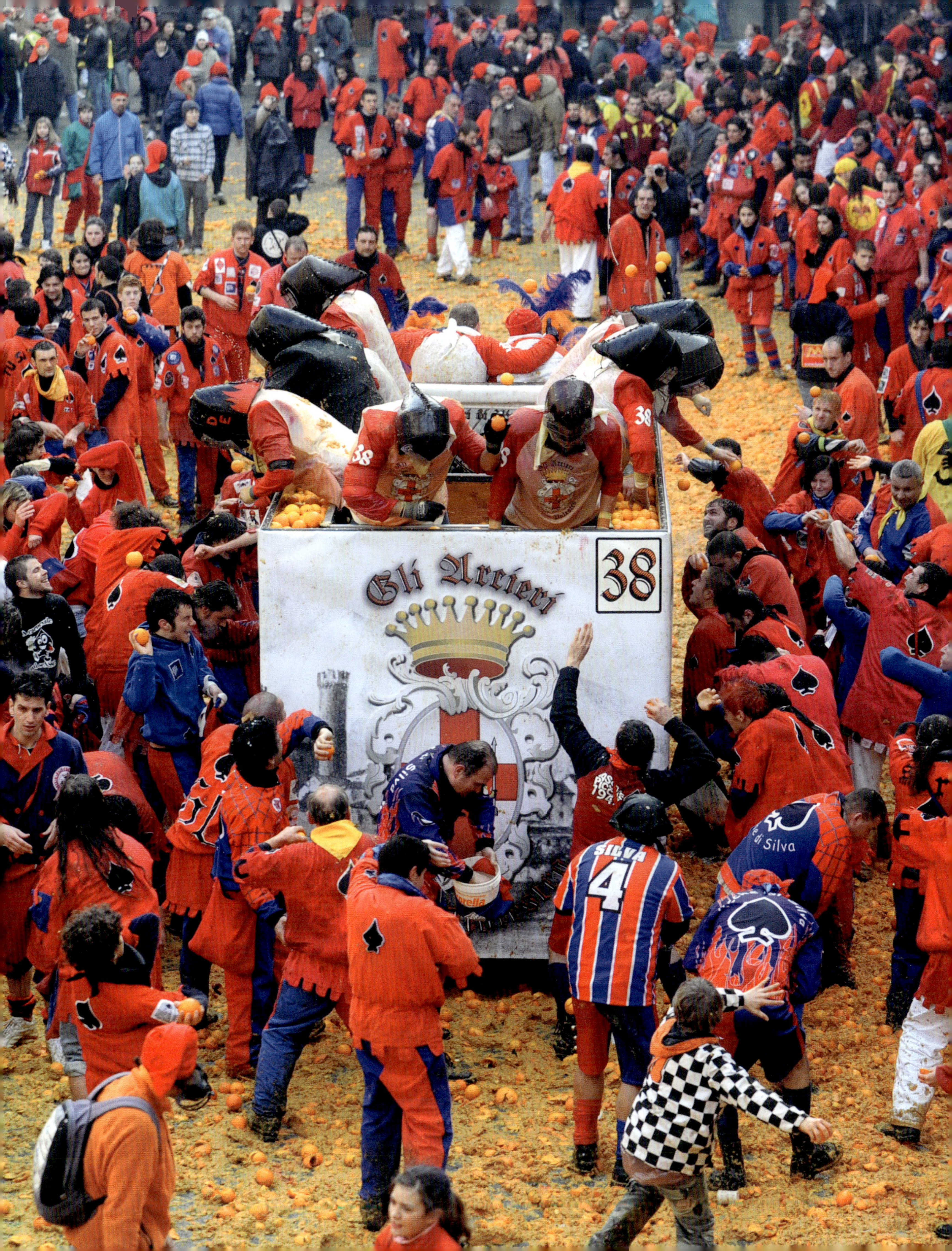
Gli Arcieri
38
38
38
SILVA
4
di Silva

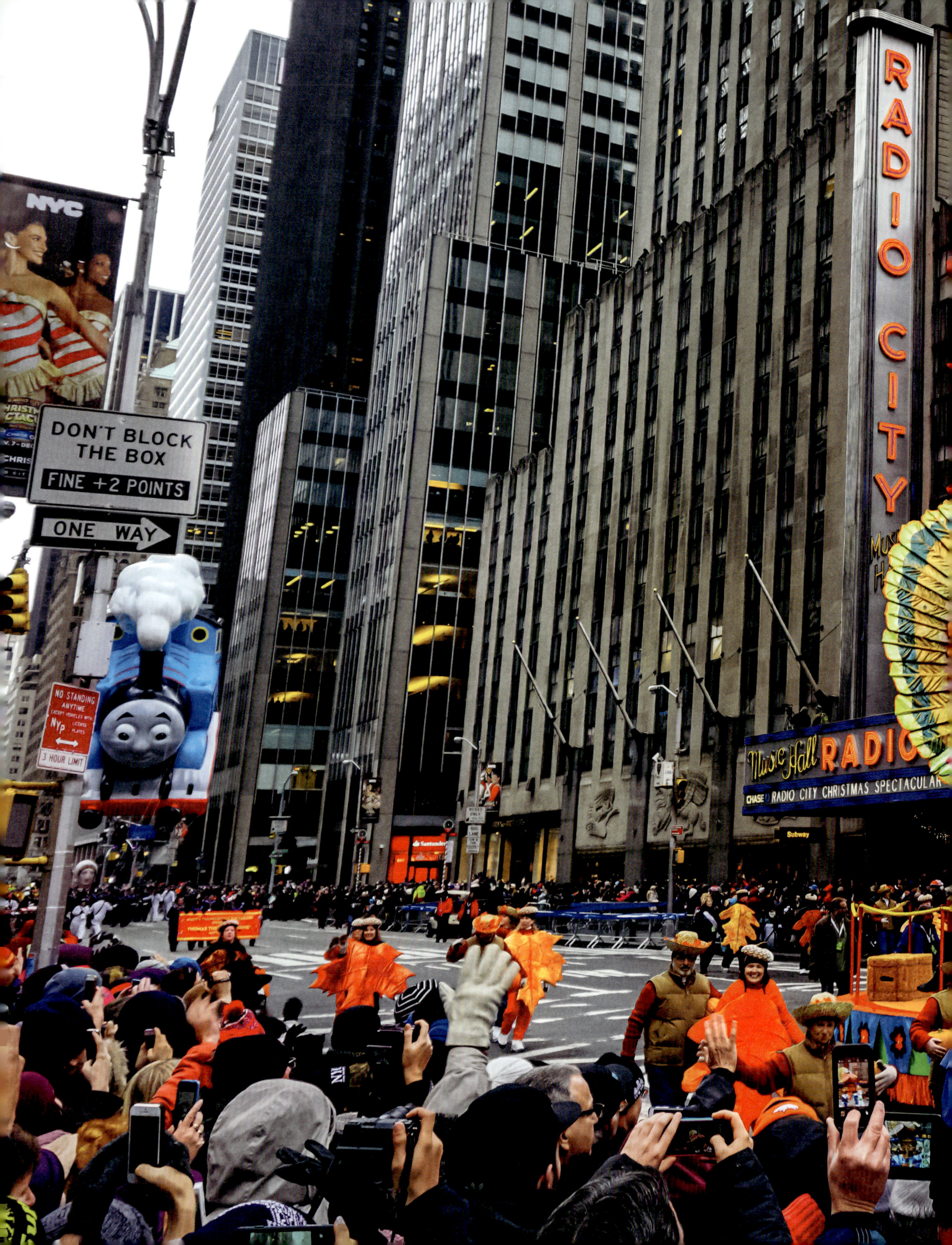

NYC
DON'T BLOCK
THE BOX
FINE +2 POINTS
ONE WAY
NO STANDING
ANYTIME
NYP
3 HOUR LIMIT
RADIO CITY
MUSIC HALL
Music Hall RADIO
CHASE RADIO CITY CHRISTMAS SPECTACULAR
Subway
Santander

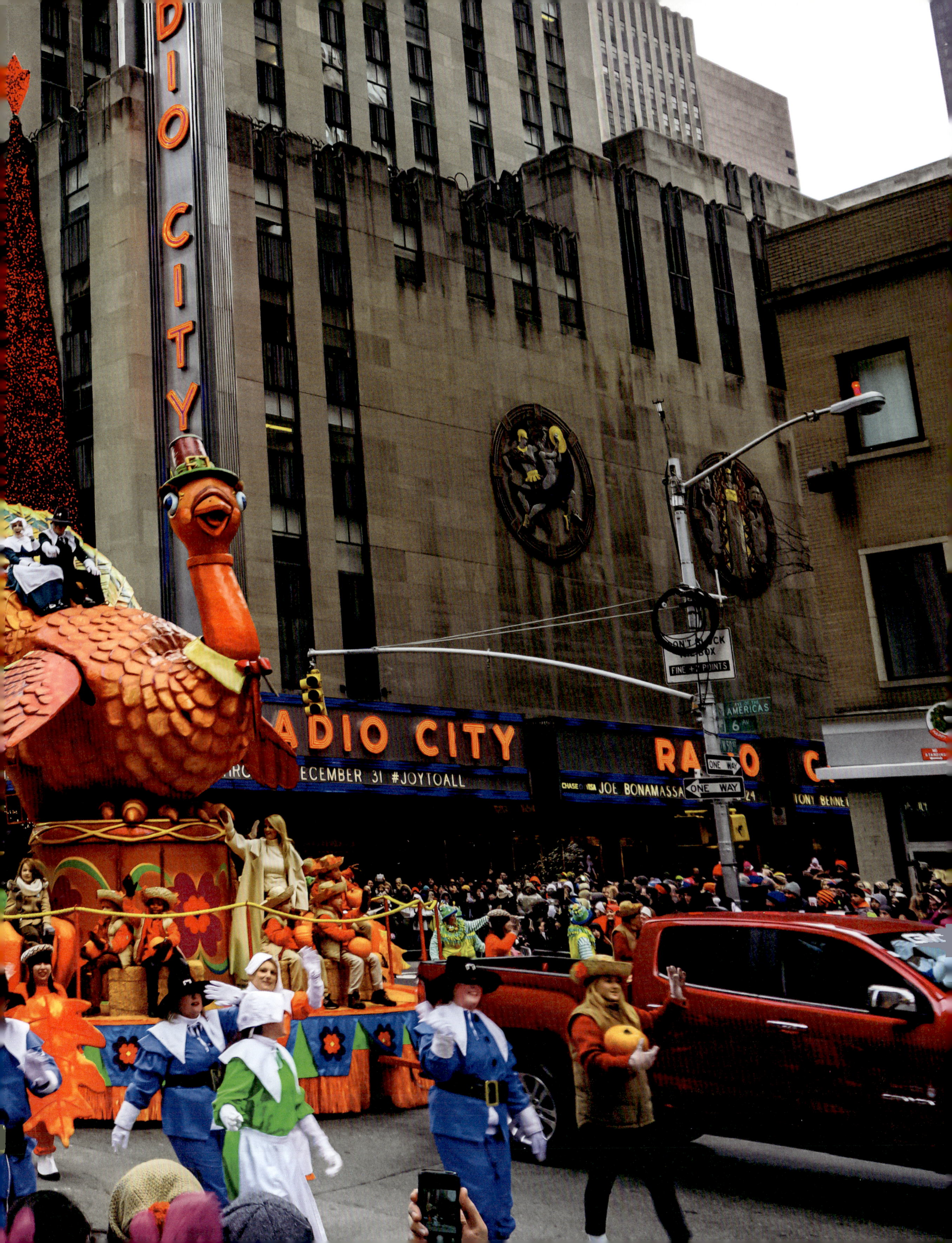

RADIO CITY
RADIO CITY
DIO CITY
RADIO C
JOE BONAMASSA
DECEMBER 31 #JOYTOALL
CHASE VISA
TONY BENNE
AVE OF THE AMERICAS
6 Av
ONE WAY
ONE WAY
DON'T BLOCK THE BOX
FINE + POINTS
NO STANDING

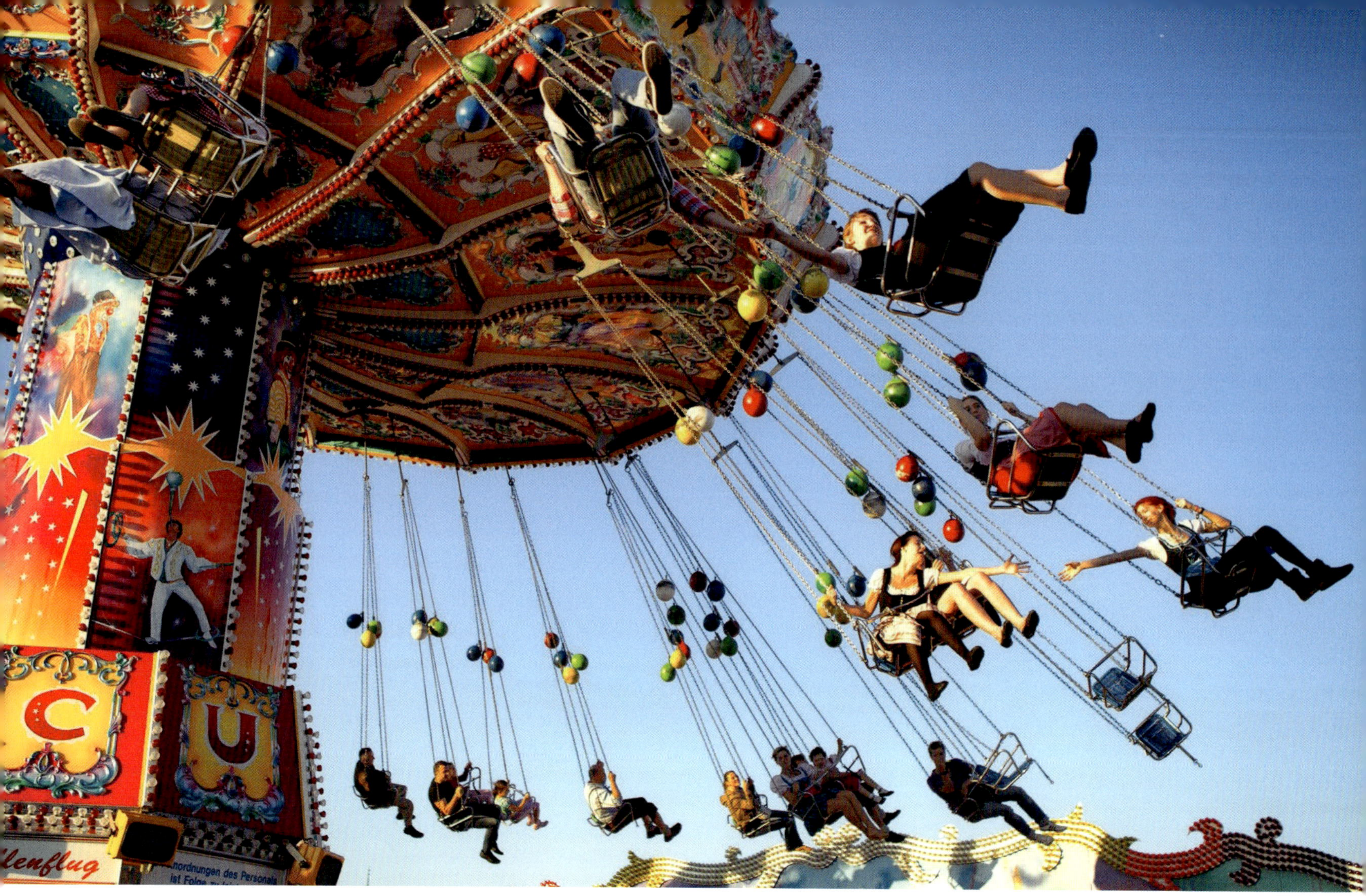

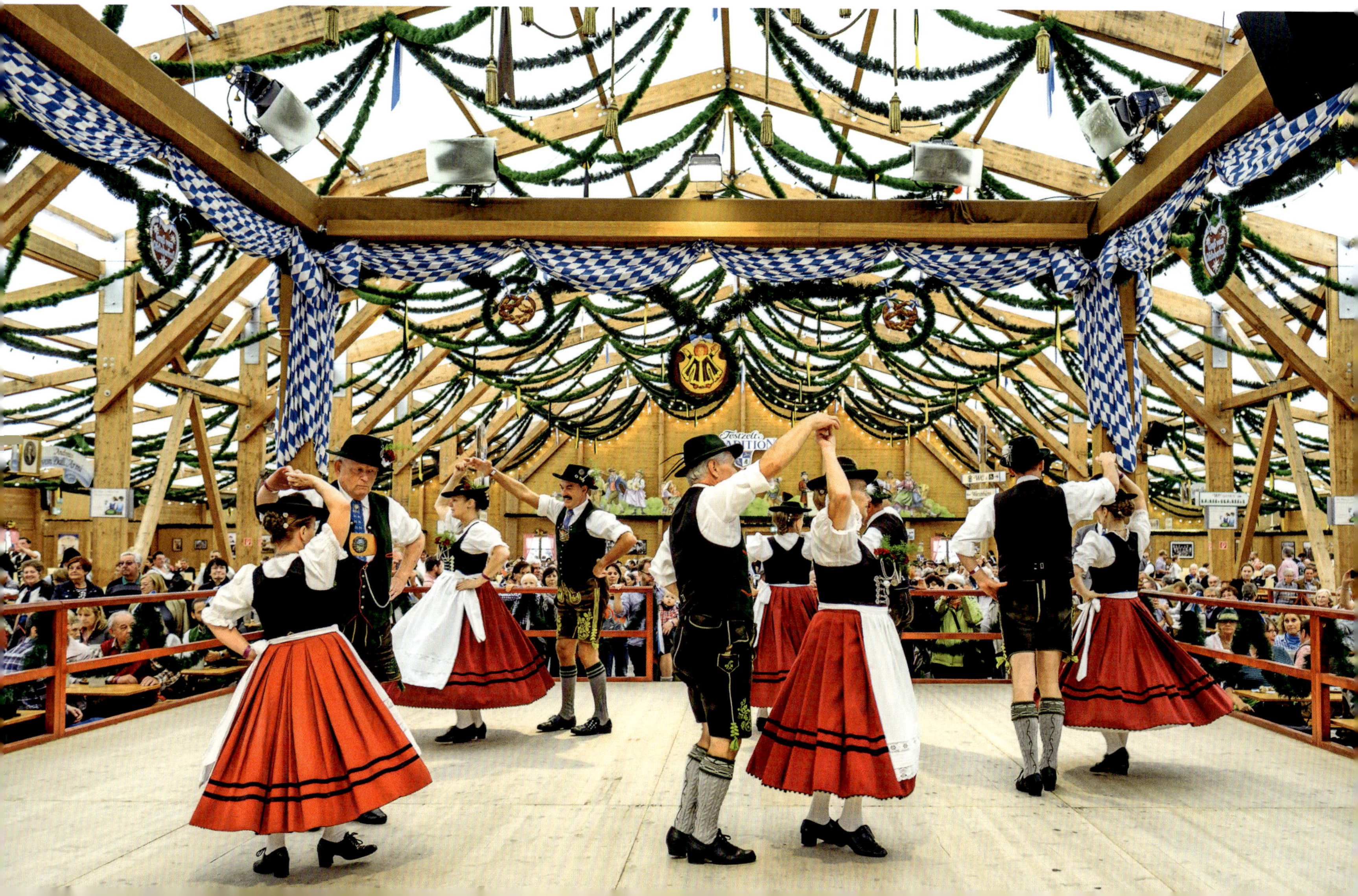

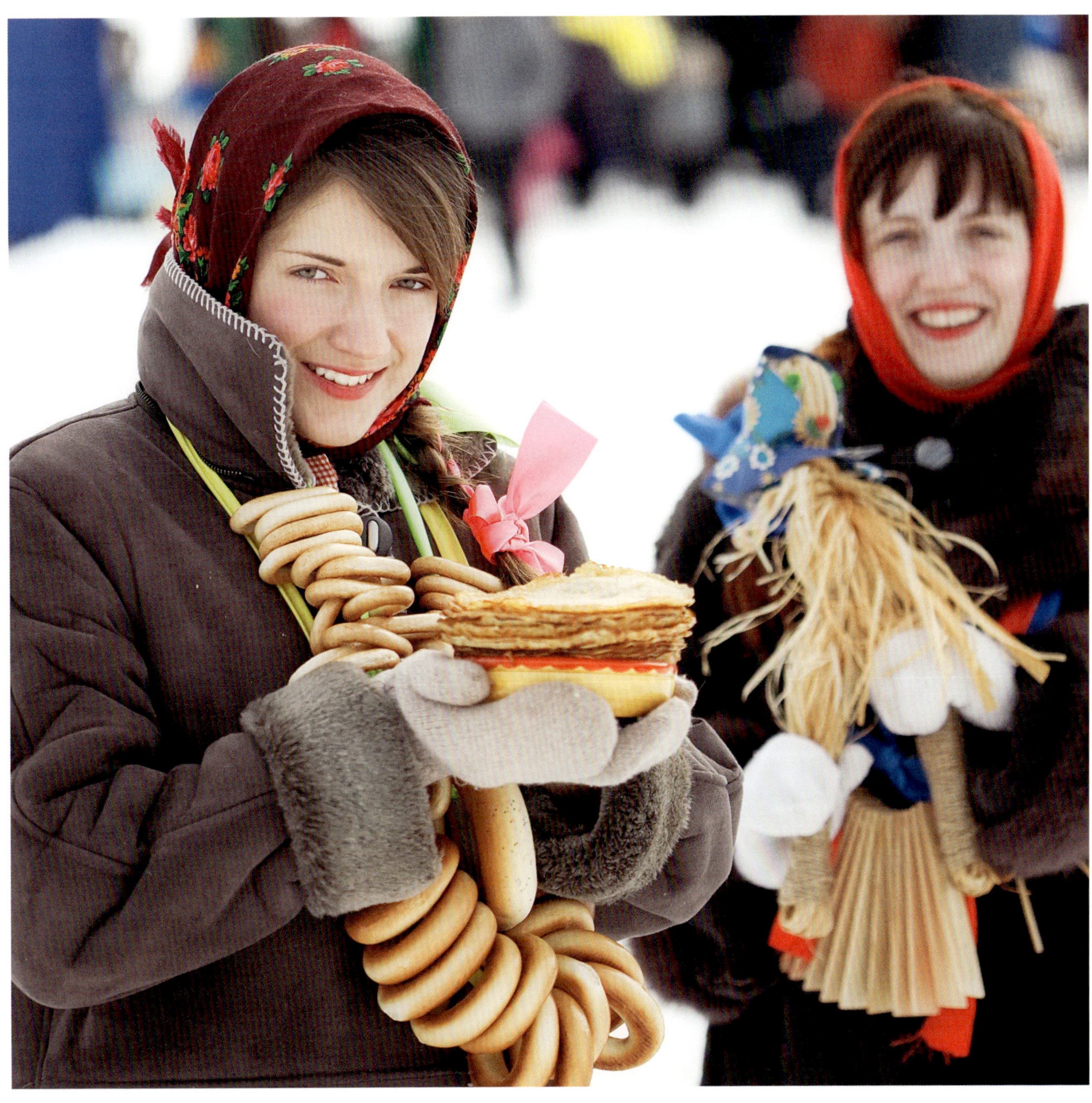

Previous page: Macy's Thanksgiving Day Parade originated in 1924. Highlights include oversized balloons paraded through the streets of Manhattan. The balloons have been featured since 1928; before that real animals were part of the parade.

Vorherige Seite: Macys Thanksgiving-Day-Parade fand 1924 erstmals statt. Zu den Highlights gehören überdimensionale Ballons, die durch die Straßen von Manhattan getragen werden. Die Ballons werden seit 1928 eingesetzt; vorher nahmen echte Tiere an der Parade teil.

Oktoberfest not only features beer and *weißwurst*, but it also offers merry-go-rounds and traditional dancing.

Zum Oktoberfest gehören nicht nur Bier und Weißwürste, sondern auch Karussells und traditionelle Tänze.

Maslenitsa, a Slavic holiday, also known as "Butter" or "Pancake Week," is celebrated the last week before the Great Lent. During this time, Orthodox Christians aren't allowed to eat meat—eggs, milk, and cheese are still permitted though, so pancakes or *blinis* it is.

Maslenitsa, ein slawischer Feiertag, den man auch „Butter-" oder „Pfannkuchenwoche" nennt, wird in der letzten Woche vor dem Beginn der orthodoxen Fastenzeit begangen. In dieser Woche dürfen orthodoxe Christen bereits kein Fleisch essen, Eier, Milch und Käse sind aber noch erlaubt – also her mit den *blinis*!

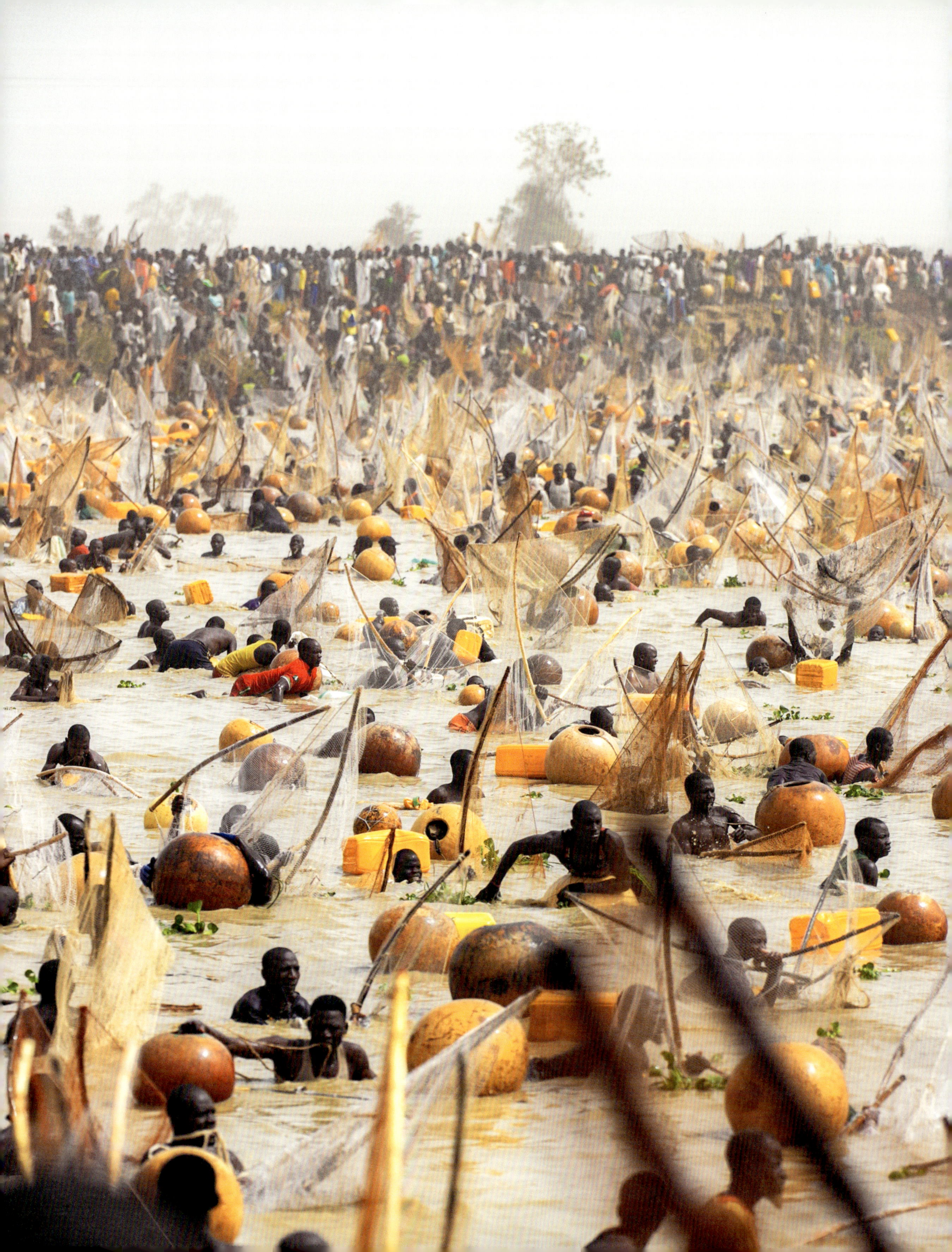

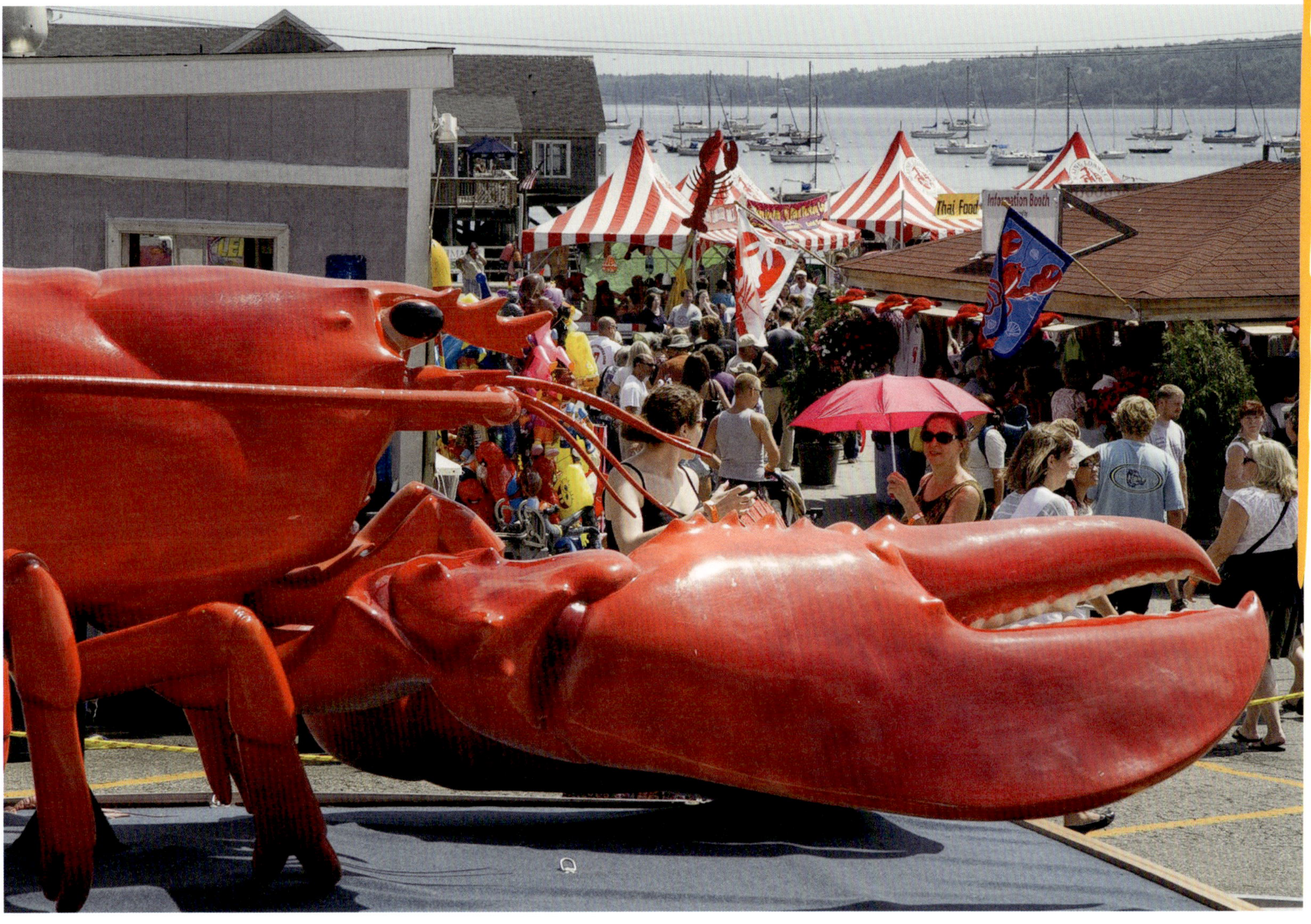

At the four-day Argungu Fishing Festival in Nigeria, activities such as canoe races, music performances, and craft showcases culminate in a competition in which thousands of participants jump into the water at the same time to catch the biggest fish.

Beim viertägigen Argungu Fishing Festival in Nigeria gibt es Kanurennen, Konzerte und Kunstgewerbe. Höhepunkt ist ein Wettbewerb, bei dem Tausende von Menschen gleichzeitig ins Wasser springen, um den größten Fisch zu fangen.

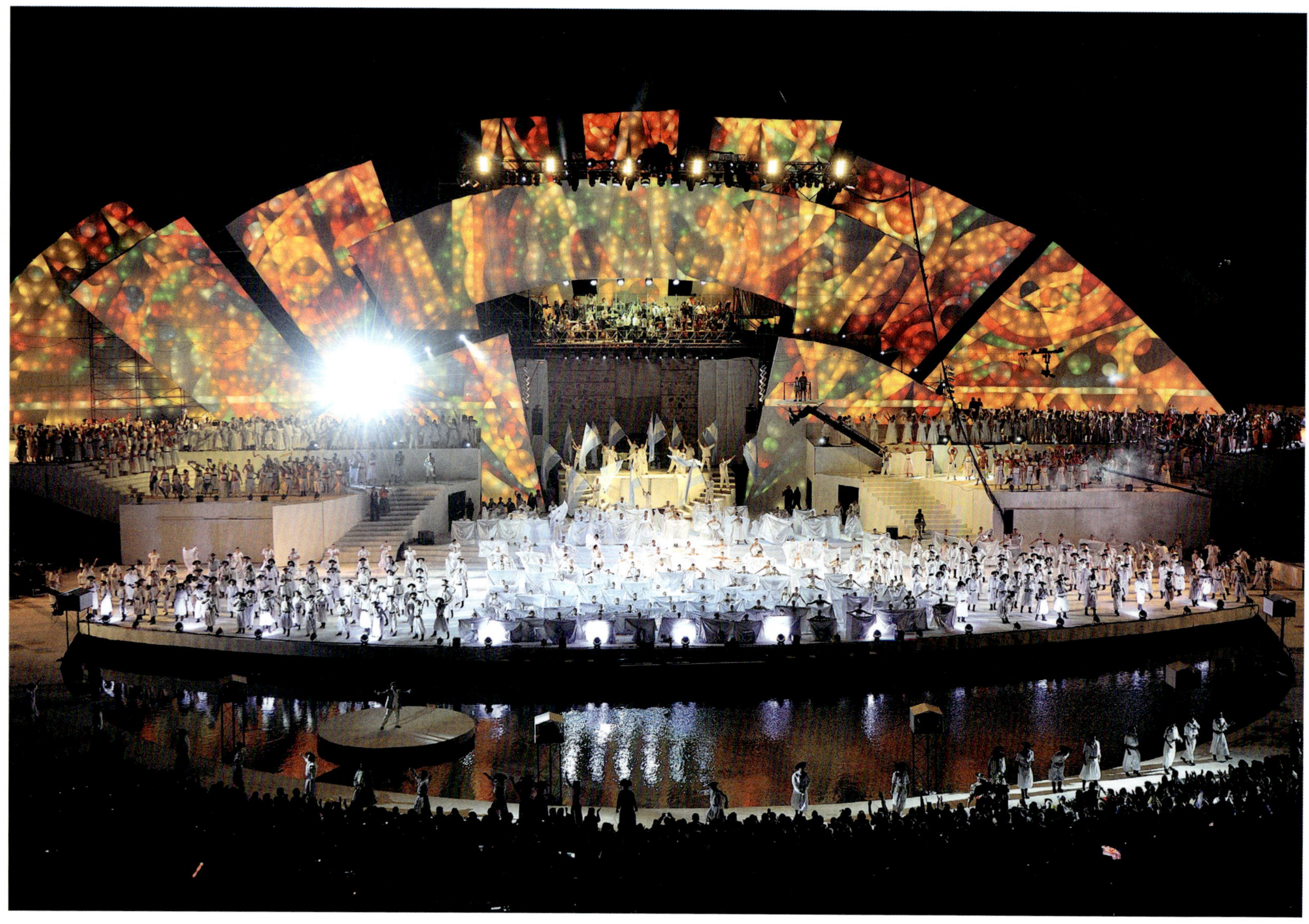

Mendoza, Argentina, is famous around the world for its wonderful wine, which is celebrated and garnered at the annual National Grape Harvest Festival. Over 1,000 performers and dancers offer a spectecular folklore music show as the *acto central*.

Die argentinische Provinz Mendoza ist berühmt für ihren wunderbaren Wein, der beim Nationalen Weinlesefest zelebriert wird. Über 1 000 Performer und Tänzer stellen beim *acto central* eine spektakuläre Folklore-Musik-Show auf die Beine.

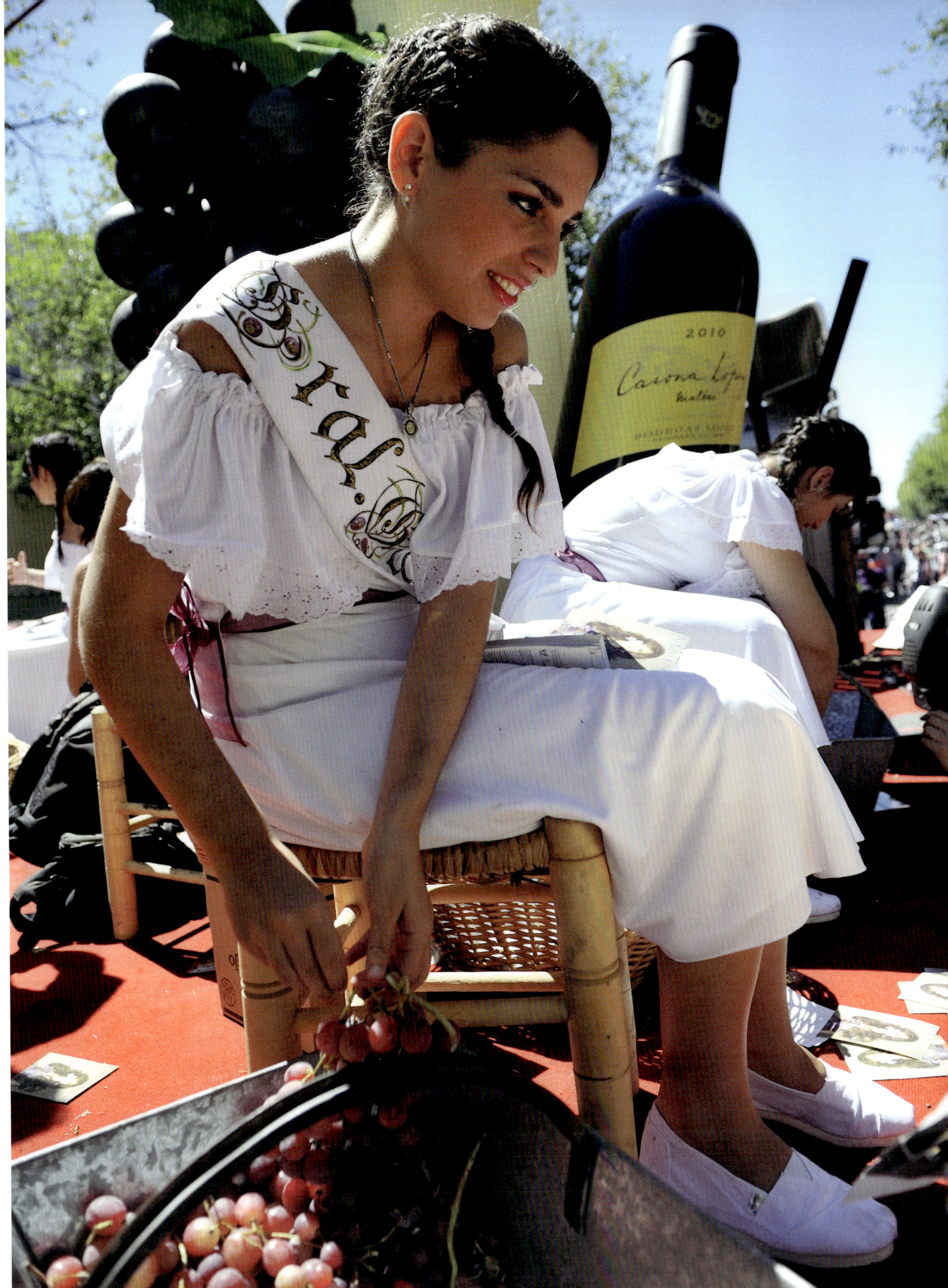

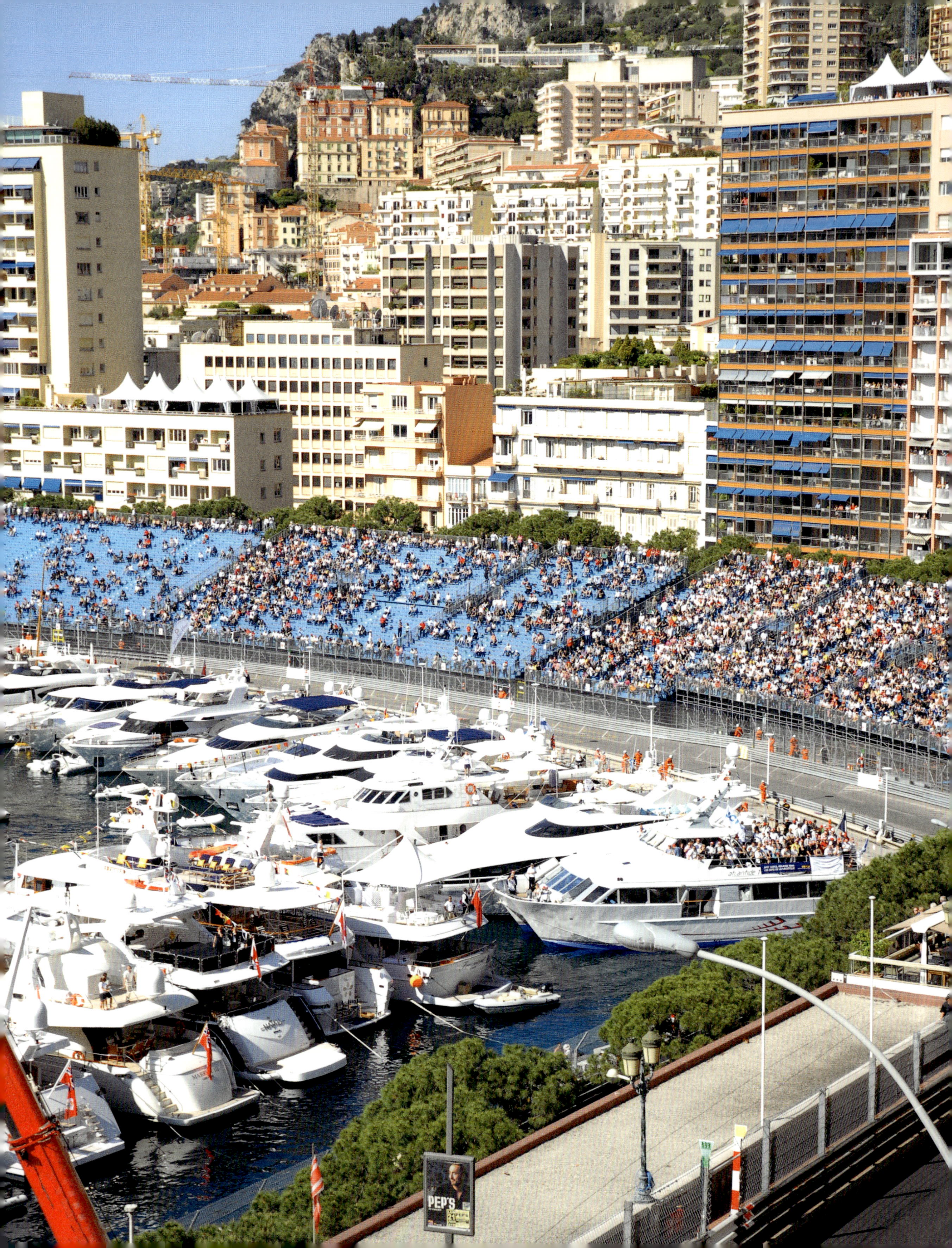

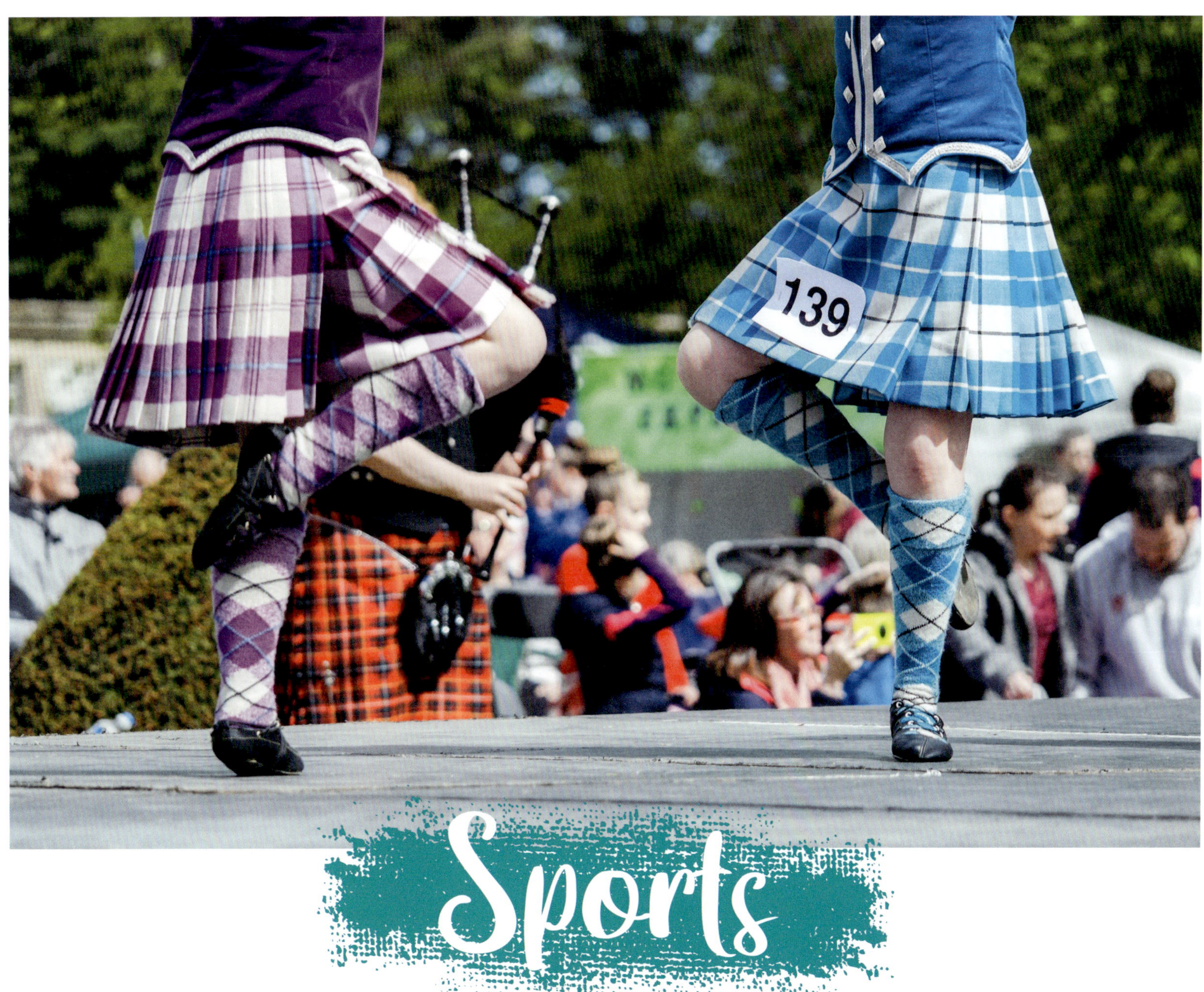

Sports

SPORTFESTE

Traditional Scottish Highland dancing competition.

Wettbewerb im traditionellen schottischen
Highland Dance

The Grand Prix de Monaco, a Formula One racing event held
on the Circuit de Monaco, in Monte Carlo, is one of the most
prestigious automobile races in the world.

Der Grandprix von Monaco, ein Formel-1-Rennen, das auf dem
Circuit de Monaco in Monte Carlo ausgetragen wird,
ist eines der prestigeträchtigsten Automobilrennen der Welt.

Sporting events and tests of strength and speed have provided us with entertainment since humans began. It's no surprise to anthropologists that humans would build up entire festivals around a sense of competition. This is a chance for the competitors to show off what they can do, for the festivalgoers to be amazed and entertained, and for festival organizers to make a bit of cash for bringing it all together.

Sports festivals are also a great way to see another nation's culture as you're traveling through. Look at the Naadam Festival, in Ulaanbaatar, Mongolia, for example. This huge event and national holiday pits competitors against each other in three traditional sports: wrestling, horseracing, and archery. It's a celebration of the nomadic way of life, and people travel with their herds through the countryside to camp out and gather for entertainment (opposite, top).

The Calgary Stampede in Canada describes itself as "The Greatest Outdoor Show on Earth." Through rodeos, this non-profit organization hopes to maintain and celebrate Calgary's heritage, culture, and community. Attend and you'll see cowboys and cowgirls showing off their skills and thoroughbreds to huge crowds by competing in barrel racing, bull riding, bareback riding, and other rodeo events amidst music, food, and a great festival atmosphere.

If you'd rather watch human strength in action, then the Highland Games in Scotland offer one of the best opportunities. The Games take place in different locations in Scotland over the summer months, and you can watch competitors in Highland Dancing, throwing the hammer (with a 16–22 pound, or 7–10 kilogram weight on the end), and tossing the caber (a traditional wooden pole) as far as possible. It's a huge celebration of Scottish and Celtic culture. The largest games, with around 30,000 attendees, is the Cowal Highland Gathering in Dunoon in August.

Sportveranstaltungen, auf denen Athleten gegeneinander antreten, gibt es schon seit Menschengedenken. So ist es aus anthropologischer Sicht wohl kaum überraschend, dass ganze Festivals auf dem Wettbewerbsgedanken basieren. Sie geben den Sportlern die Gelegenheit, ihr Können zu präsentieren, erfreuen und erstaunen die Besucher und bringen den Organisatoren Einnahmen – eine Win-Win-Win-Situation.

Doch Sportfeste bieten Reisenden auch interessante Einblicke in fremde Kulturen. Ein gutes Beispiel dafür ist das Naadam-Fest im mongolischen Ulaanbaatar. Bei diesem riesigen Fest zum Nationalfeiertag treten Wettbewerber in drei traditionellen Sportarten gegeneinander an: Ringen, Pferderennen und Bogenschießen. Zelebriert wird das nomadische Leben und die Mongolen reisen mit ihren Herden von weit her an, um sich hier unterhalten zu lassen (rechte Seite, oben).

Die Calgary Stampede in Kanada beschreibt sich selbst als „die größte Outdoor-Show der Erde". Mit der Veranstaltung von Rodeos will die Nonprofit-Organisation Calgarys Tradition Kultur und Gemeinschaft bewahren und zelebrieren. Besucher erleben, wie Cowboys und Cowgirls sich beim Fassrollen, Bullenreiten, Reiten ohne Sattel und anderen Rodeo-Disziplinen messen. Dazu gibt es Musik, Speisen und Getränke in großartiger Festival-Atmosphäre.

Wer lieber einem Kräftemessen ohne Tiere beiwohnt, kommt bei den schottischen Highland Games voll auf seine Kosten. Die Spiele finden im Sommer an verschiedenen Orten in Schottland statt. Zu den dargebotenen Wettkampfdisziplinen gehören zum Beispiel Highland Dancing, Hammerwerfen (mit 7–10 Kilogramm schweren Gewichten) und Baumstammschleudern. Das Festival feiert die schottische und keltische Kultur. Die größte Veranstaltung mit etwa 30 000 Besuchern ist das Cowal Highland Gathering in Dunoon im August.

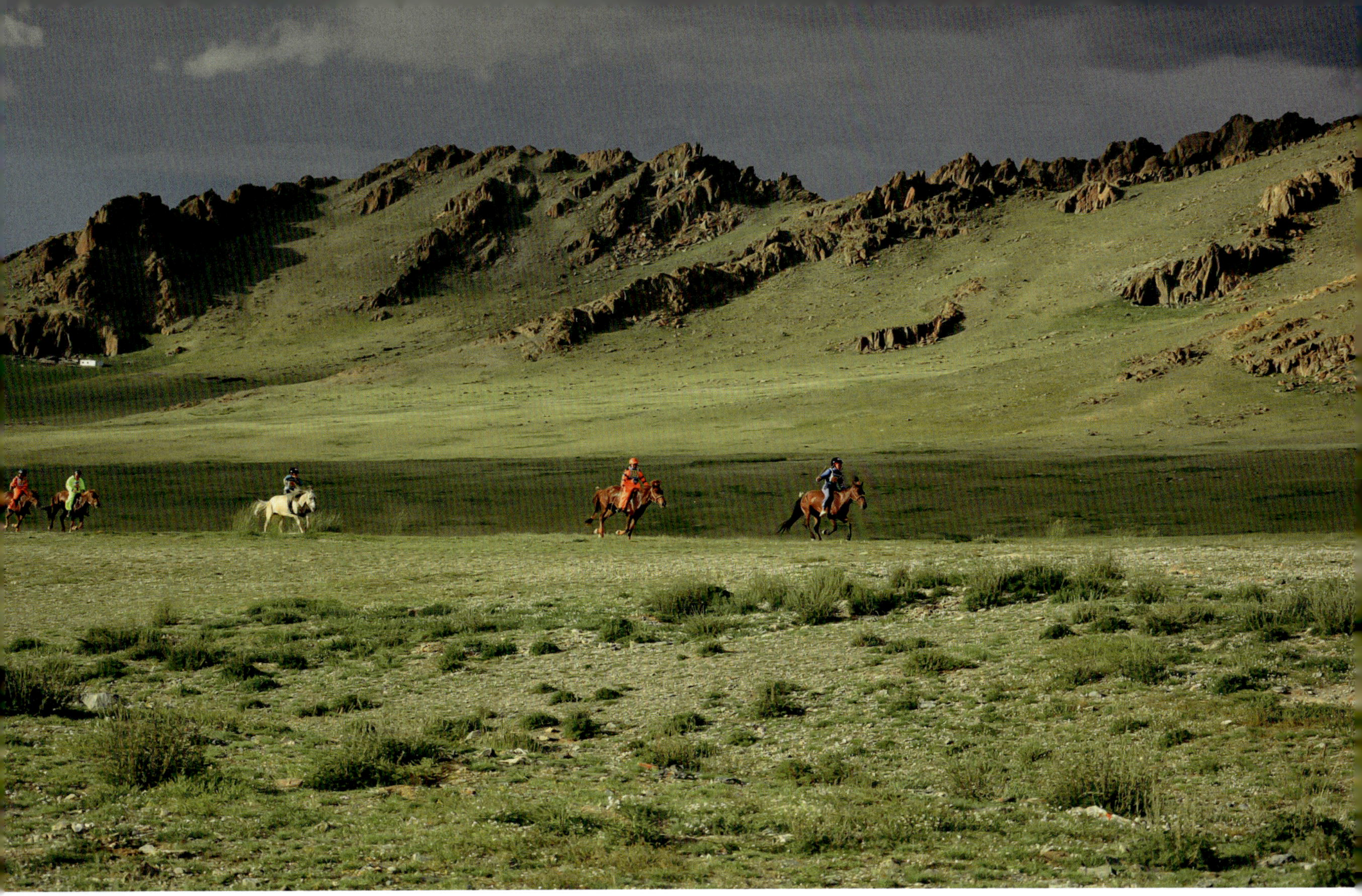

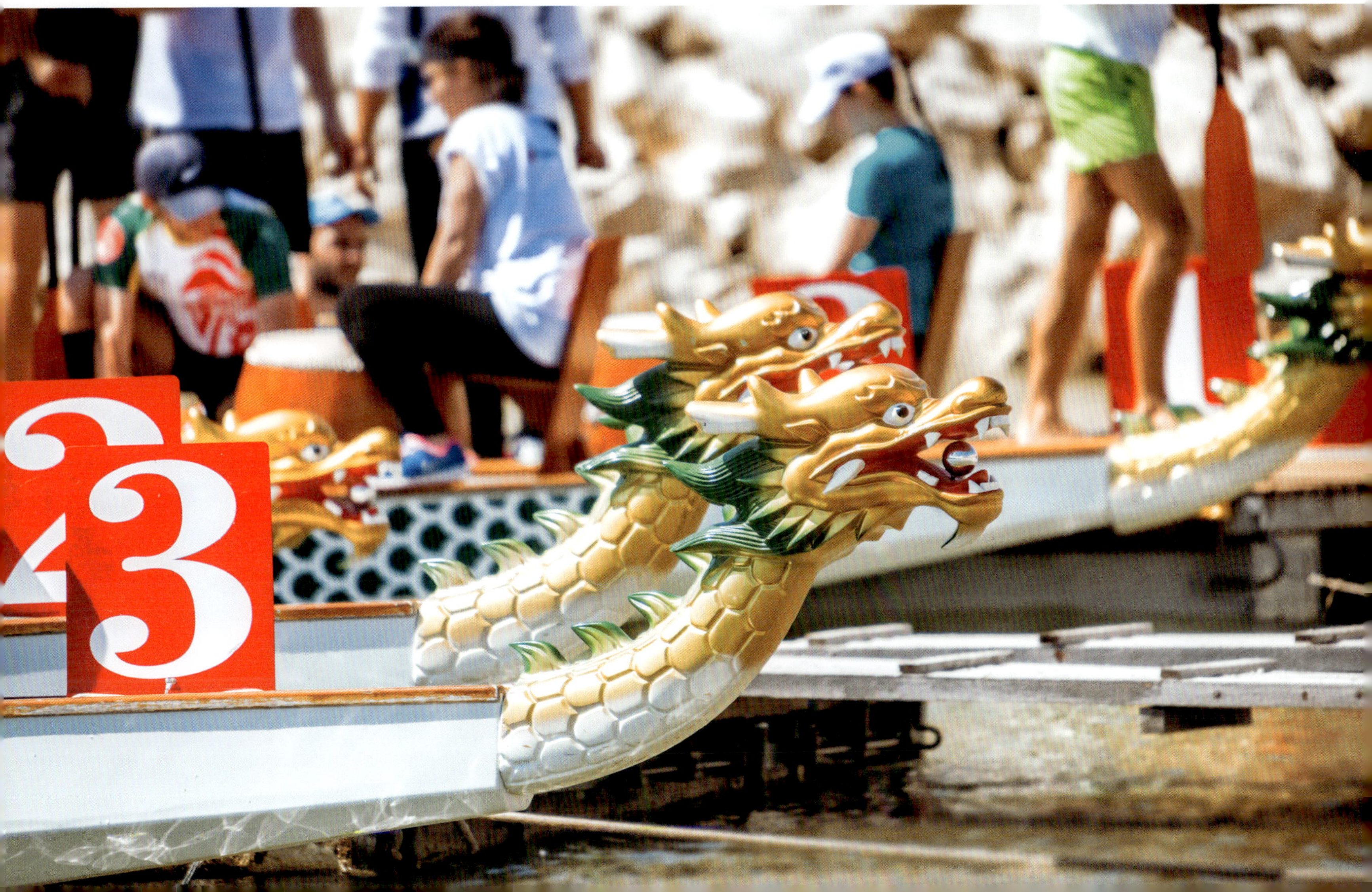

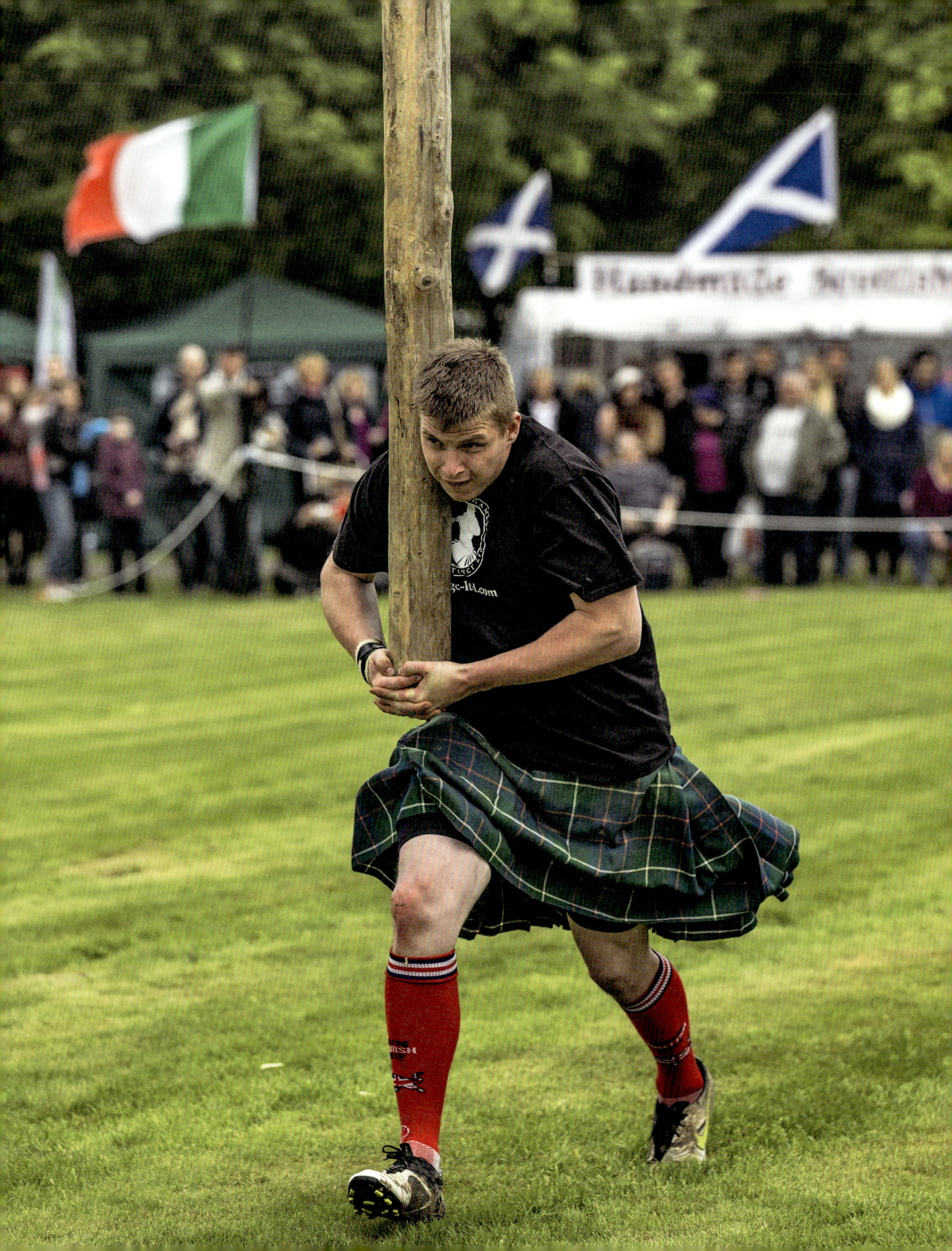

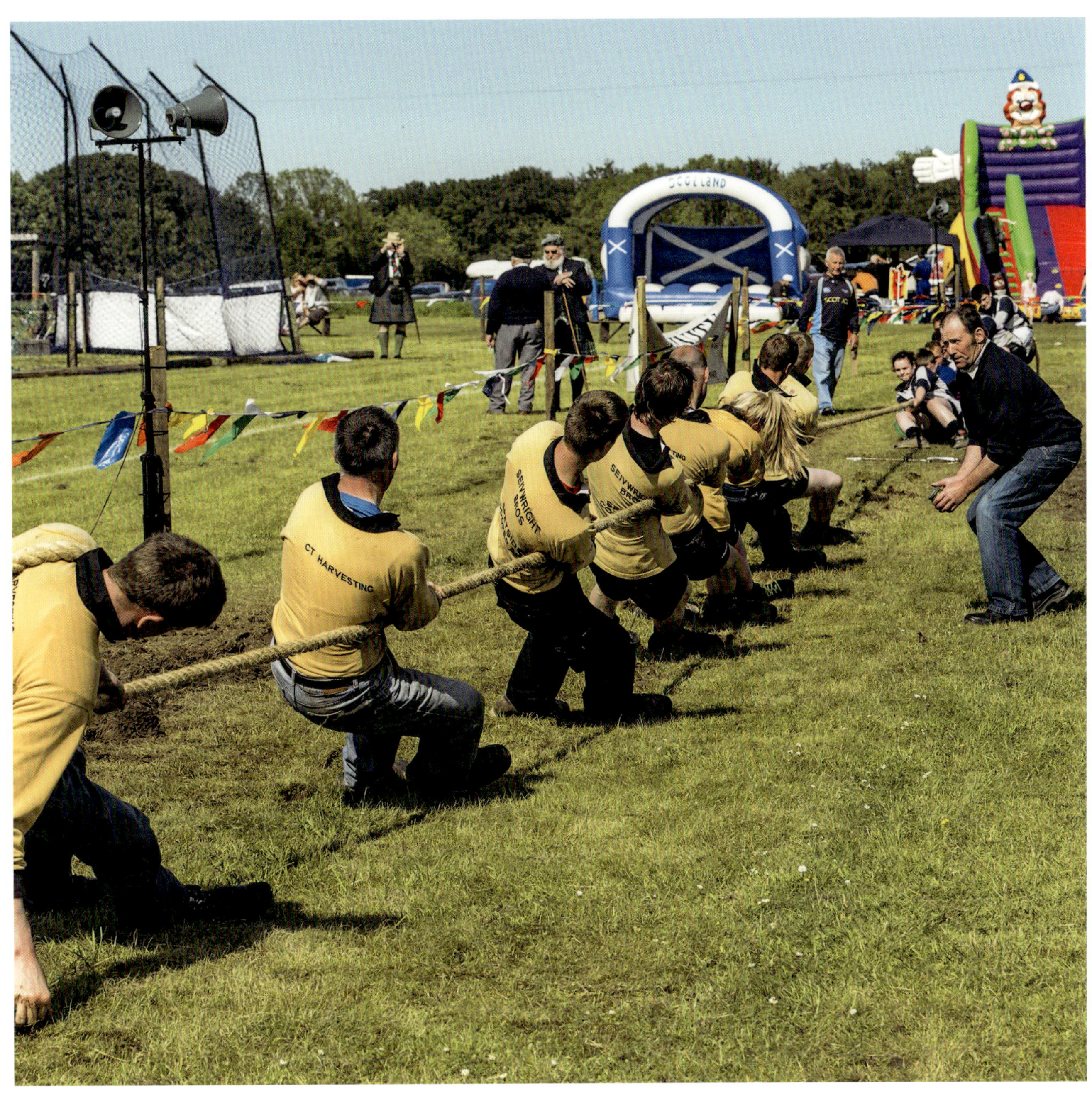

The origins of the Highland Games date back a thousand years, when the king summoned men to find out who is the strongest and fastest, to make them work for him.

Die Wurzeln der Highland Games liegen im 11. Jahrhundert, als der damalige König die schnellsten und stärksten Männer suchte, um sie anschließend für sich arbeiten zu lassen.

The Highland Games celebrate Scottish and Celtic culture. There's entertainment and competitions in piping, dancing, and athletics, such as the caber toss and tug-of-war.

Schottische und keltische Kultur steht bei den Highland Games im Vordergrund. Es gibt Wettbewerbe im Dudelsackspielen, Tanzen und Stärke beweisen, etwa beim Baumstammwerfen und Tauziehen.

Dragon boat race at the Chinese Dragon Boat Festival.
Traditional Chinese dragon boats are over 90 feet (30 meters)
long and made of wood with a colorfully decorated dragon
head and tail.

Drachenbootrennen beim chinesischen Drachenbootfest.
Traditionelle chinesische Drachenboote sind über 30 Meter
lang und aus Holz. Sie werden vorne mit einem geschnitzten
Drachenkopf verziert.

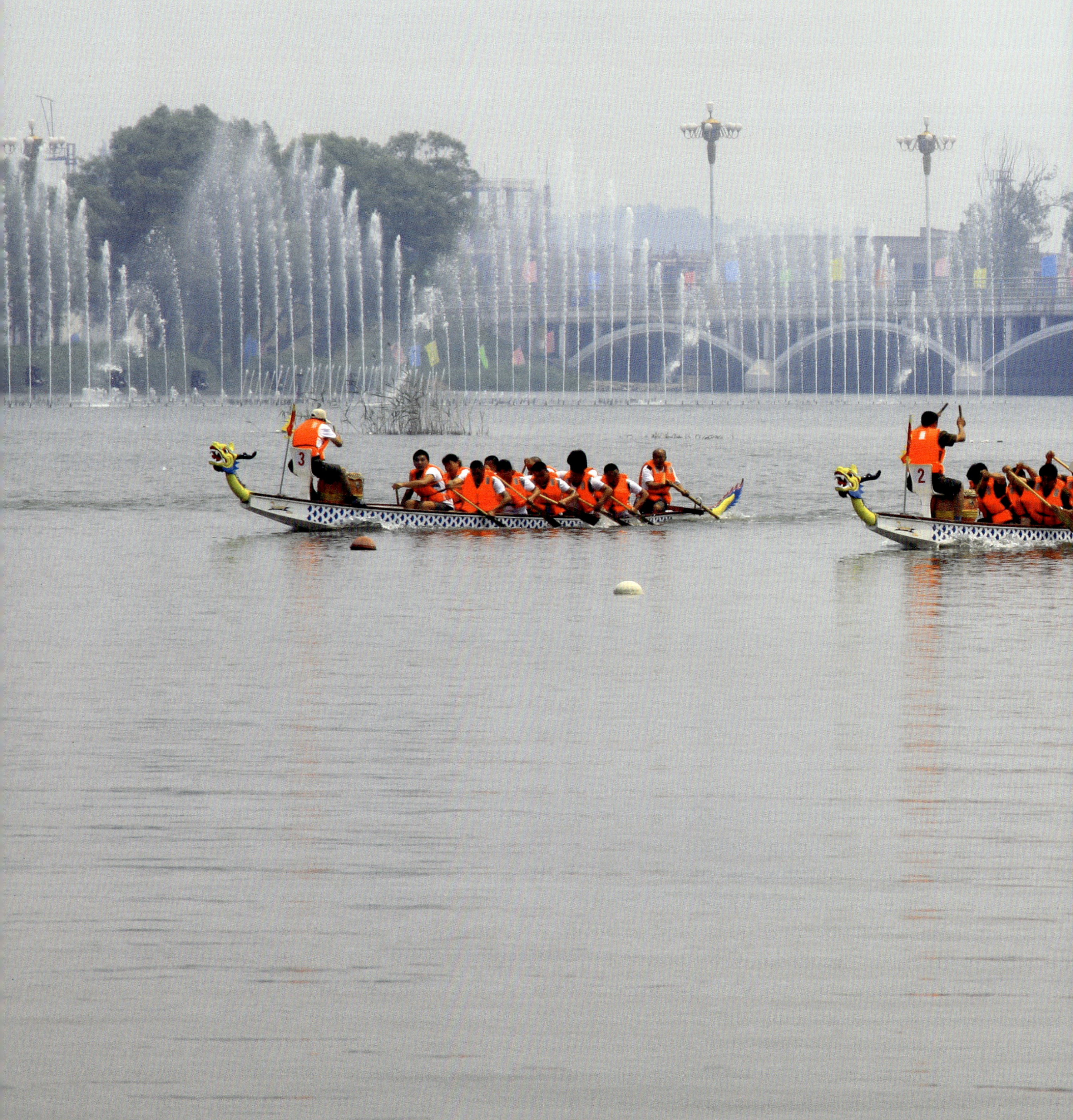

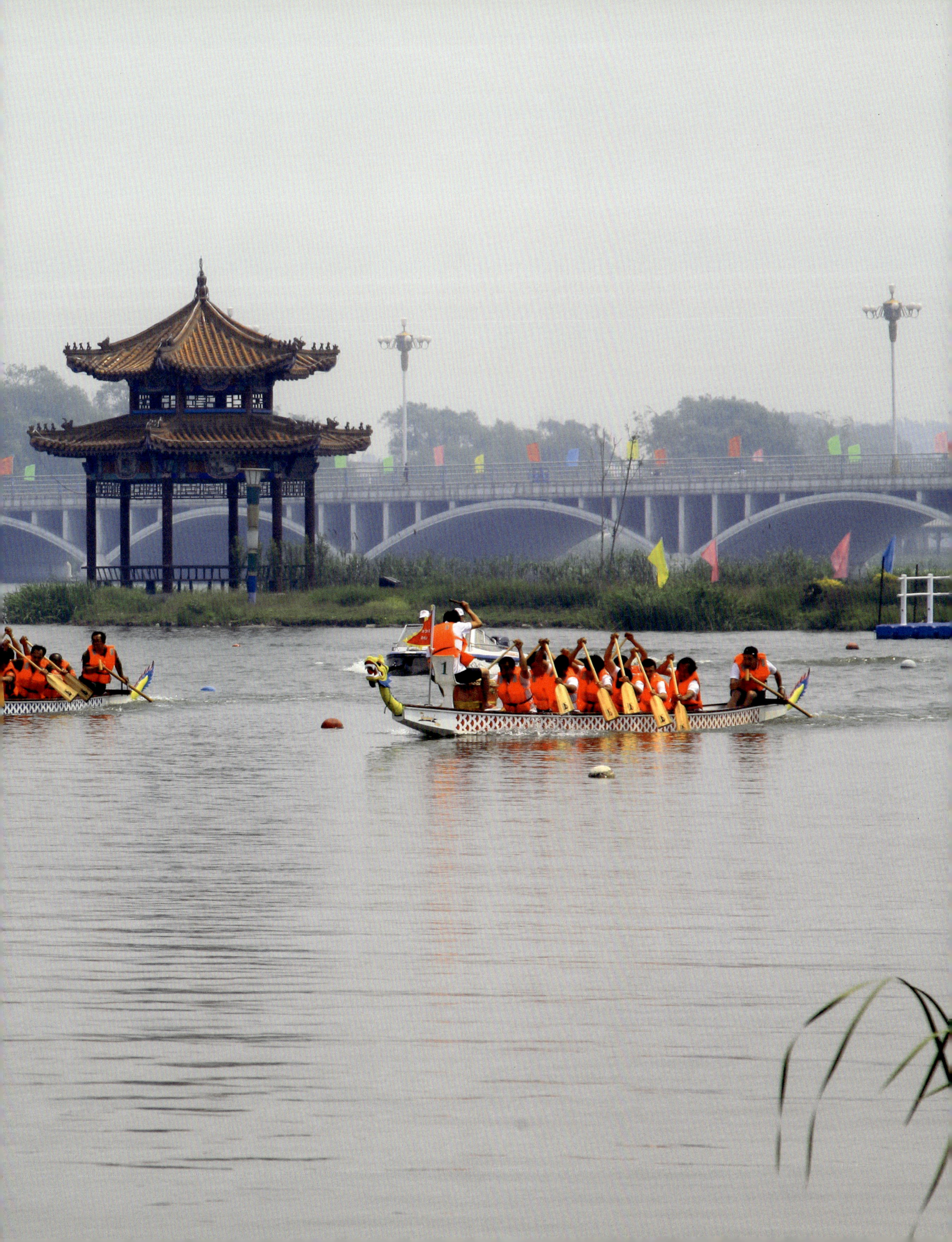

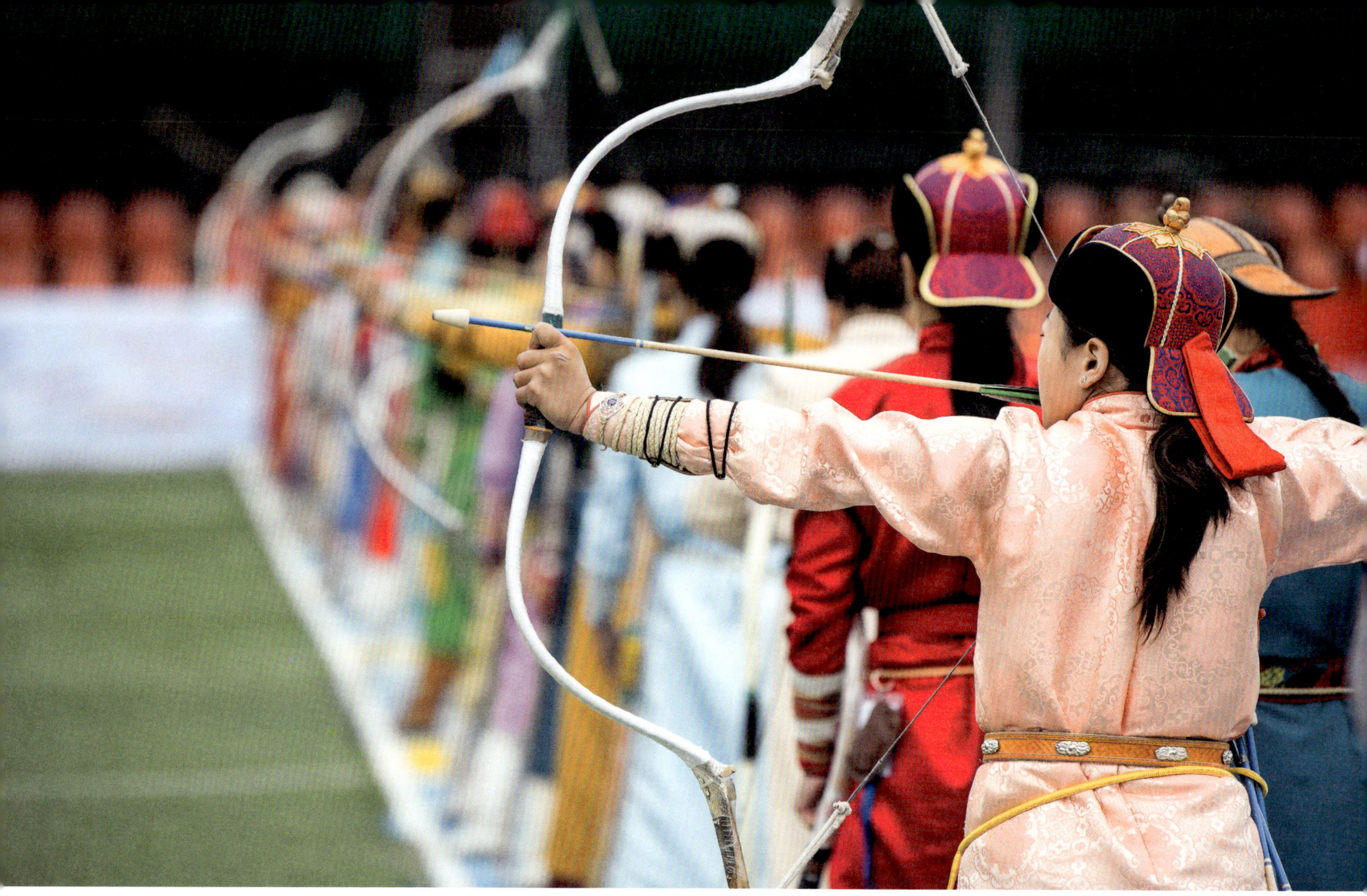

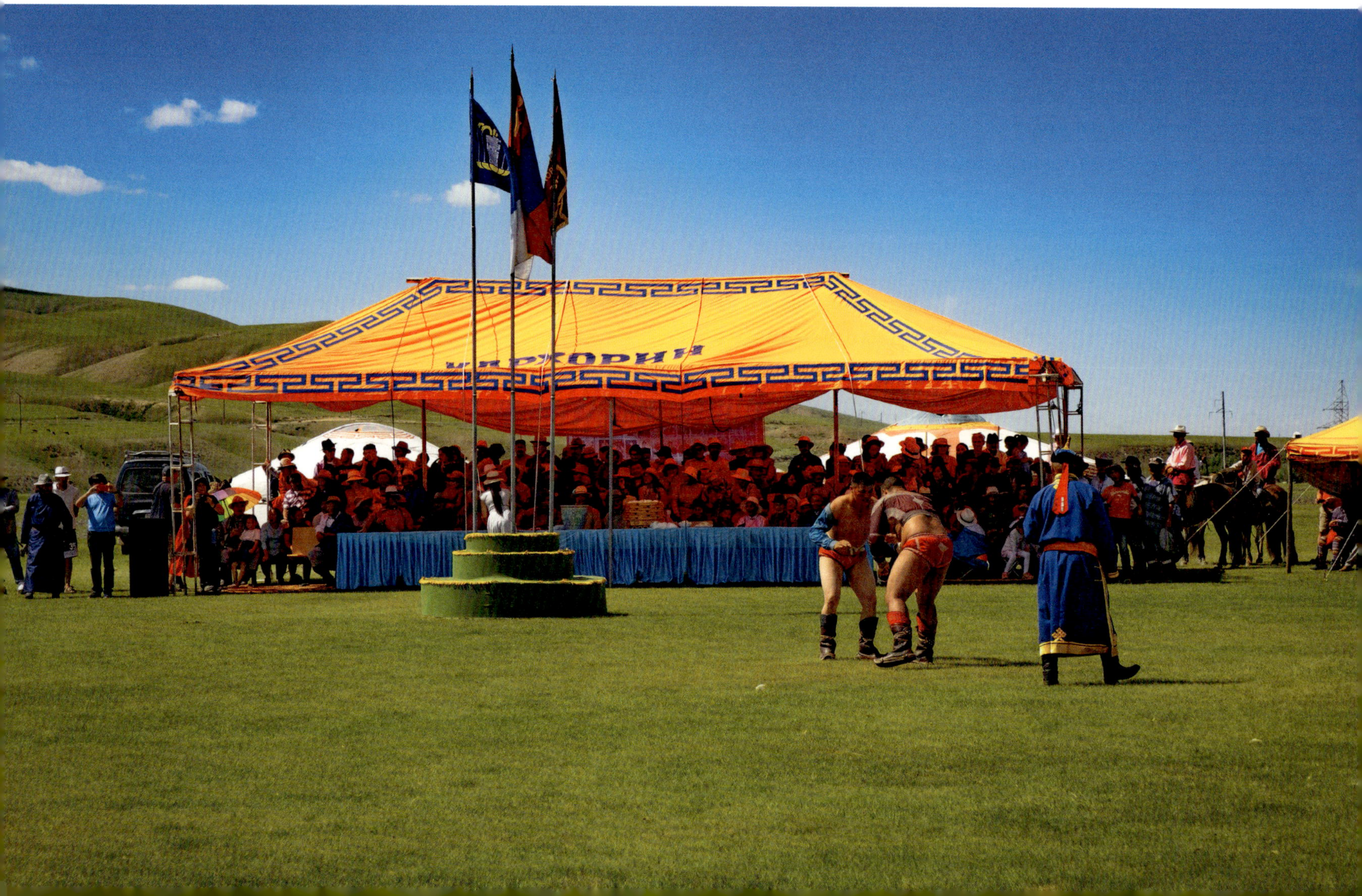

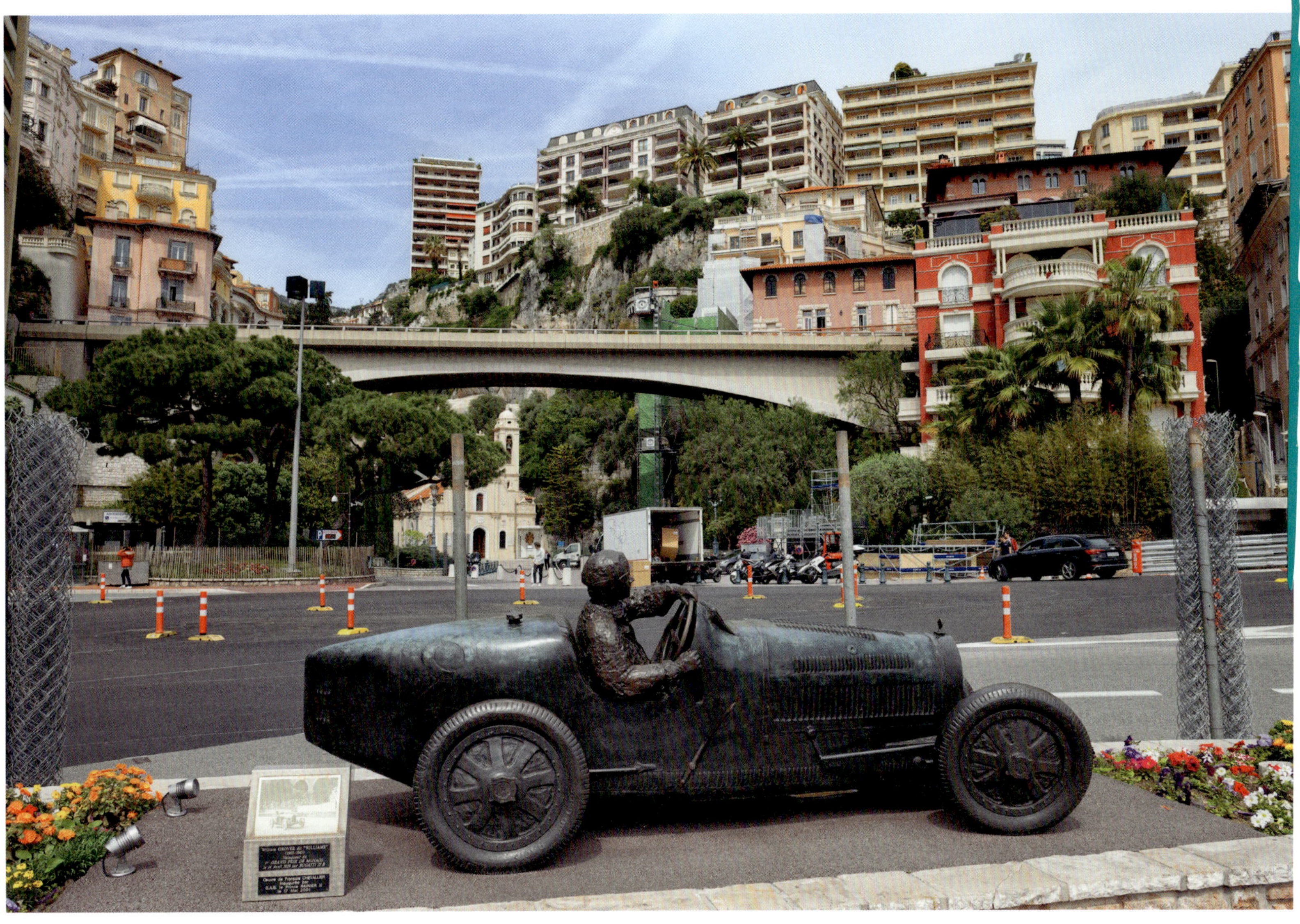

Although the traditional Mongolian festival Naadam is originally
an event for male competitors, women are nowadays participa-
ting in archery and girls in horse-racing.

Das mongolische Naadam-Fest war ursprünglich eine rein
männliche Veranstaltung. Heutzutage treten vermehrt Frauen im
Bogenschießen und Mädchen im Pferderennen an.

Indigenous peoples built a temporary teepee "village" at Calgary Stampede, Canada.

Das temporäre „Dorf aus Tipis" wird zum Anlass der Calgary Stampede in Kanada von indigenen Stämmen aufgebaut.

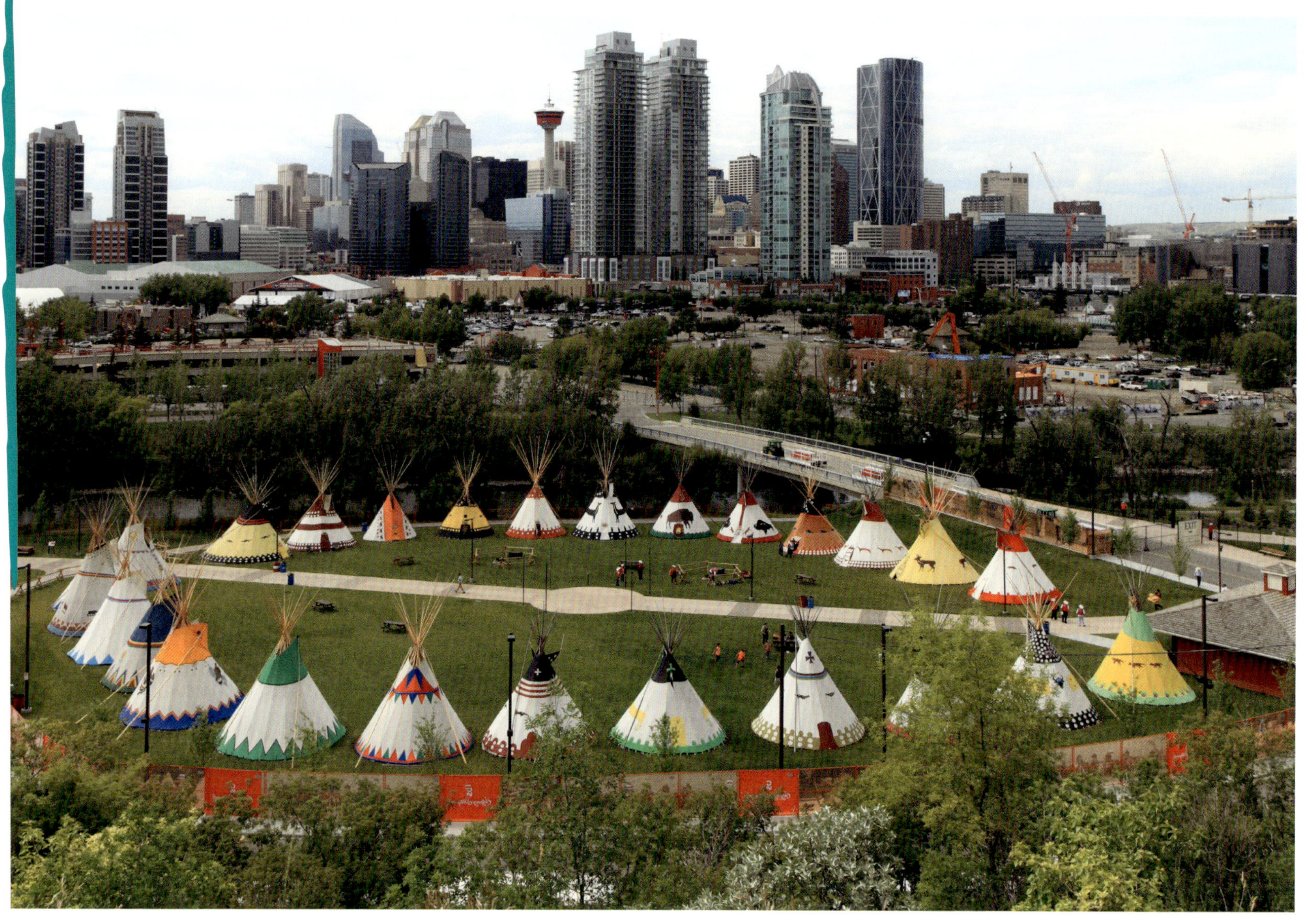

The Calgary Stampede is all about heritage, rodeos, music, and having fun.

Bei der Calgary Stampede dreht sich alles um das kulturelle Erbe, Rodeos, Musik und natürlich ums Spaß haben.

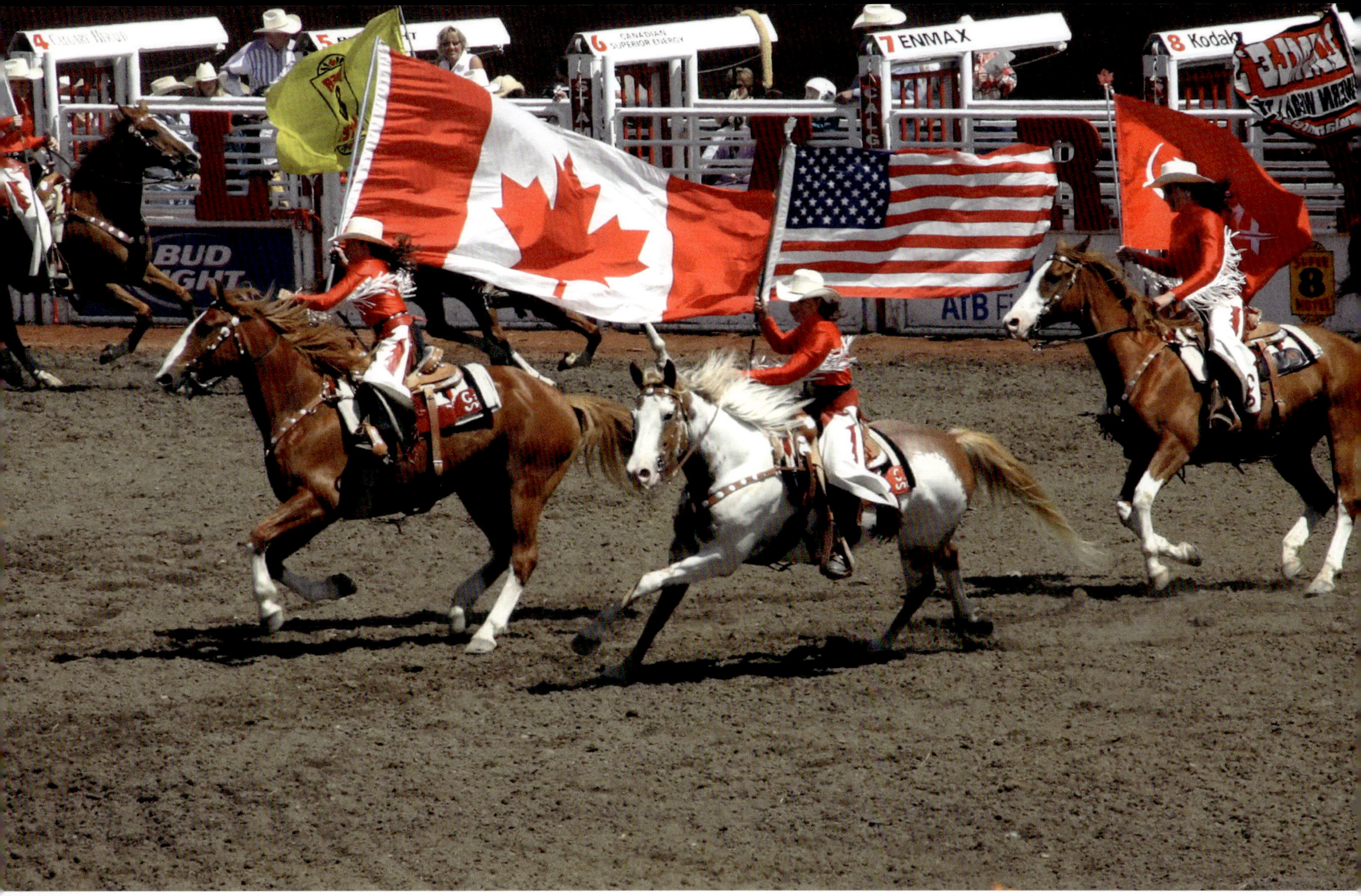
7 ENMAX
8 Kodak

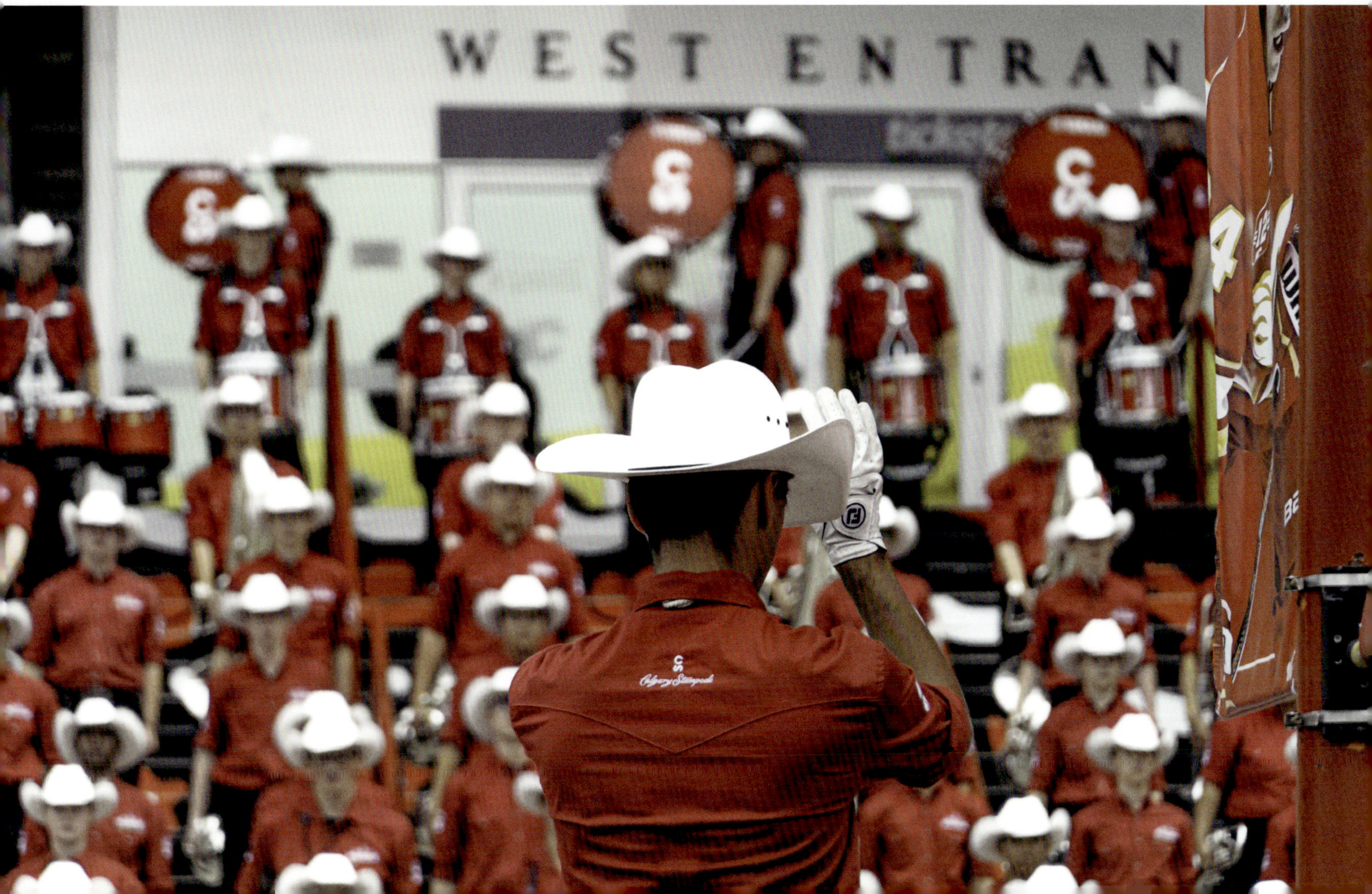
WEST ENTRAN

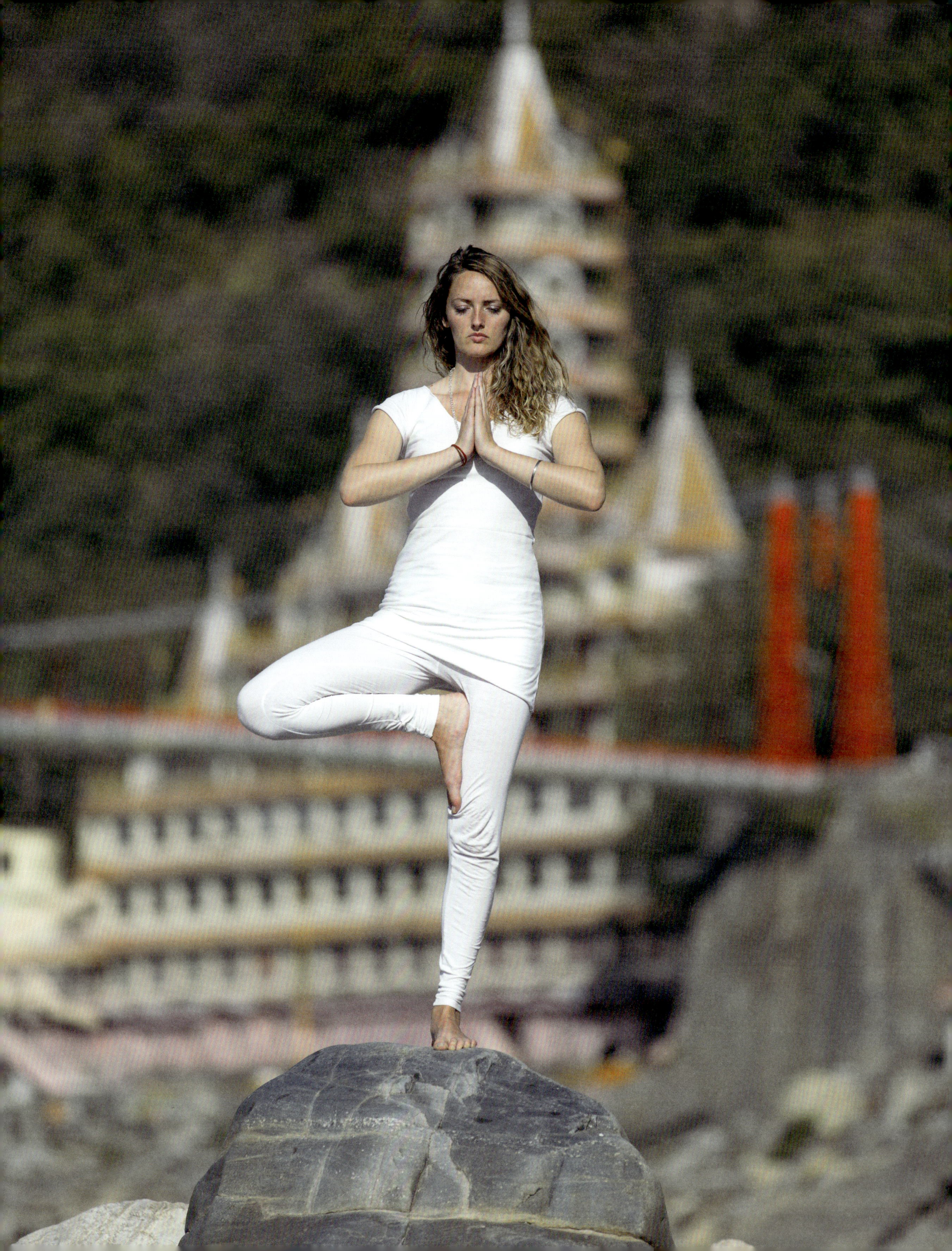

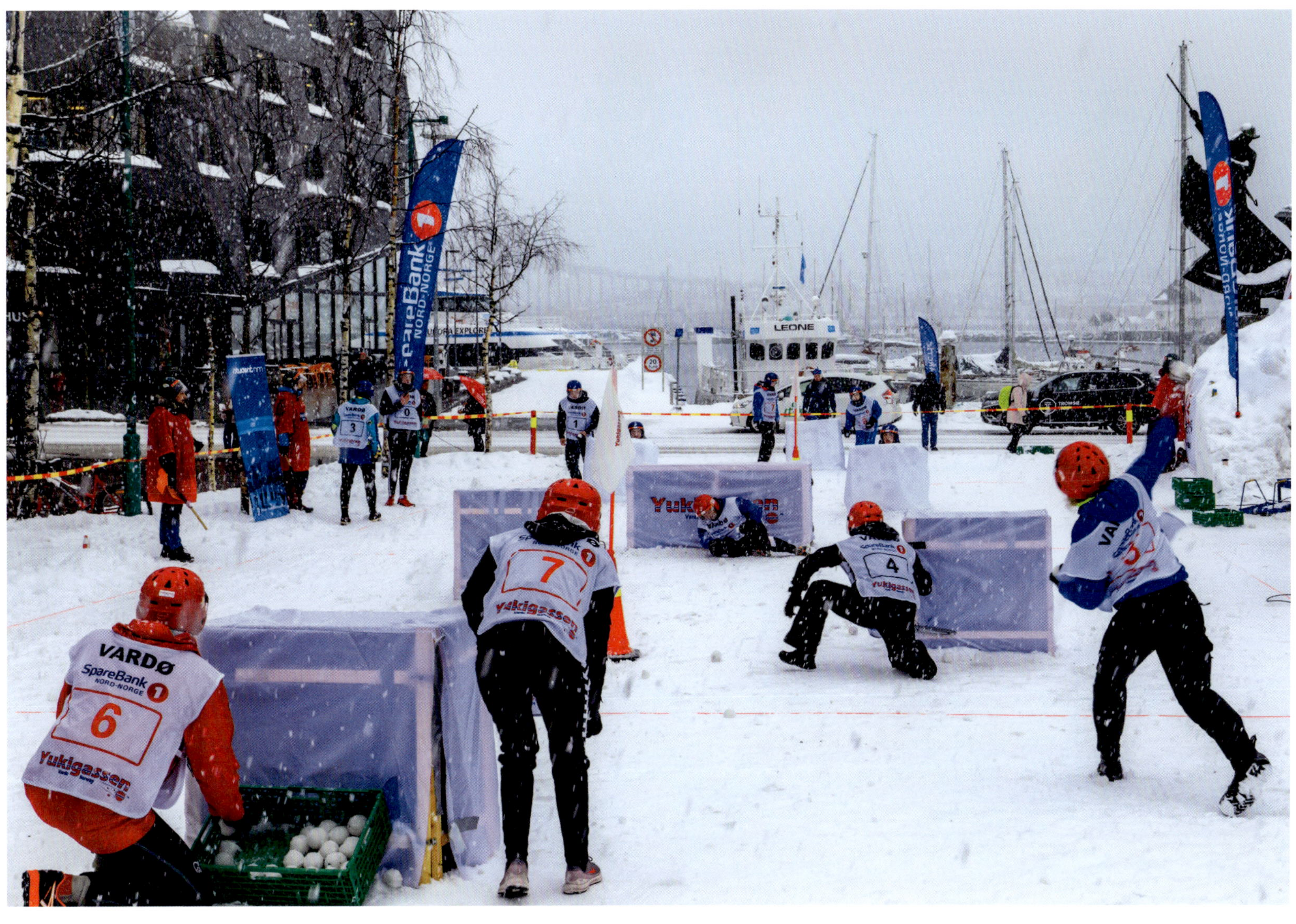

Originally a Japanese sport, Yukigassen is a popular and entertaining snowball fighting competition with annual tournaments all over the world. The rules are simple: if you're hit, you're out.

Ursprünglich ein japanischer Sport, erfreut sich Yukigassen zunehmender Beliebtheit. Die sehr unterhaltsame Schneeballschlacht wird in jährlichen Turnieren rund um die Welt ausgetragen. Dabei sind die Regeln denkbar einfach: wird man getroffen, ist man raus.

Good to know
WISSENSWERTES

Rishikesh, in India, is well known as the birthplace of yoga. It's here that you can join over 2,000 participants from more than 80 countries in the biggest celebration of yoga in the world, at the International Yoga Festival. Every different variety available!

Rishikesh in Indien gilt als der Geburtsort des Yoga. Hier können Sie mit über 2 000 Teilnehmern aus über 80 Ländern an der größten Yoga-Feier der Welt teilnehmen. Das Internationale Yoga-Festival bietet zahlreiche Stile, berühmte Yogalehrer und Klassen von früh bis spät.

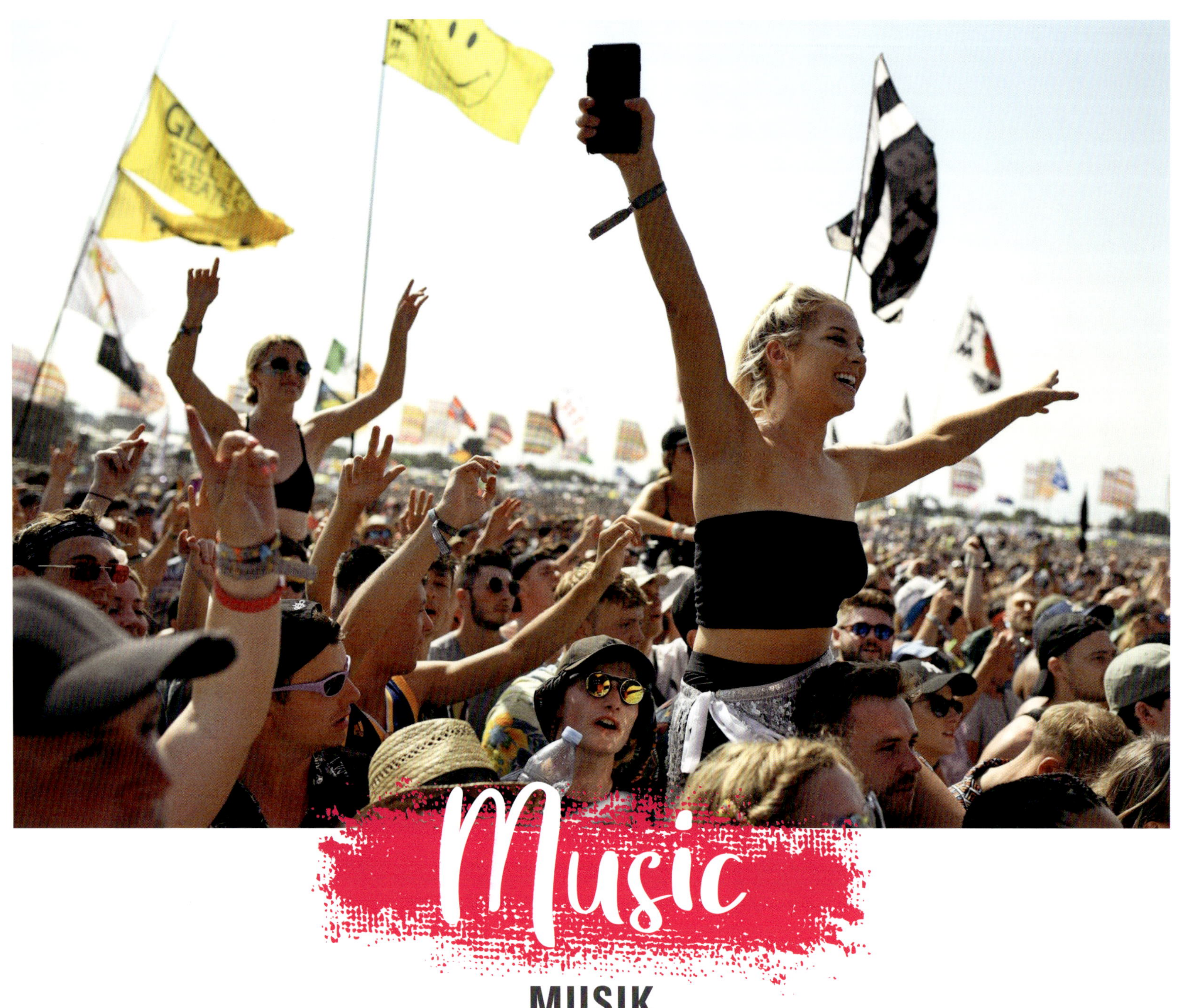

Music

MUSIK

Cheering crowd at Glastonbury Festival in England.

Jubelnde Menge beim Glastonbury-Festival in England

The EDM festival Tomorrowland, in Belgium, has won "Best Music Event" at the International Dance Music Awards five times in a row.

Das belgische EDM-Festival Tomorrowland hat bei den International Dance Music Awards fünf Mal in Folge den Preis für das „beste Music Event" gewonnen.

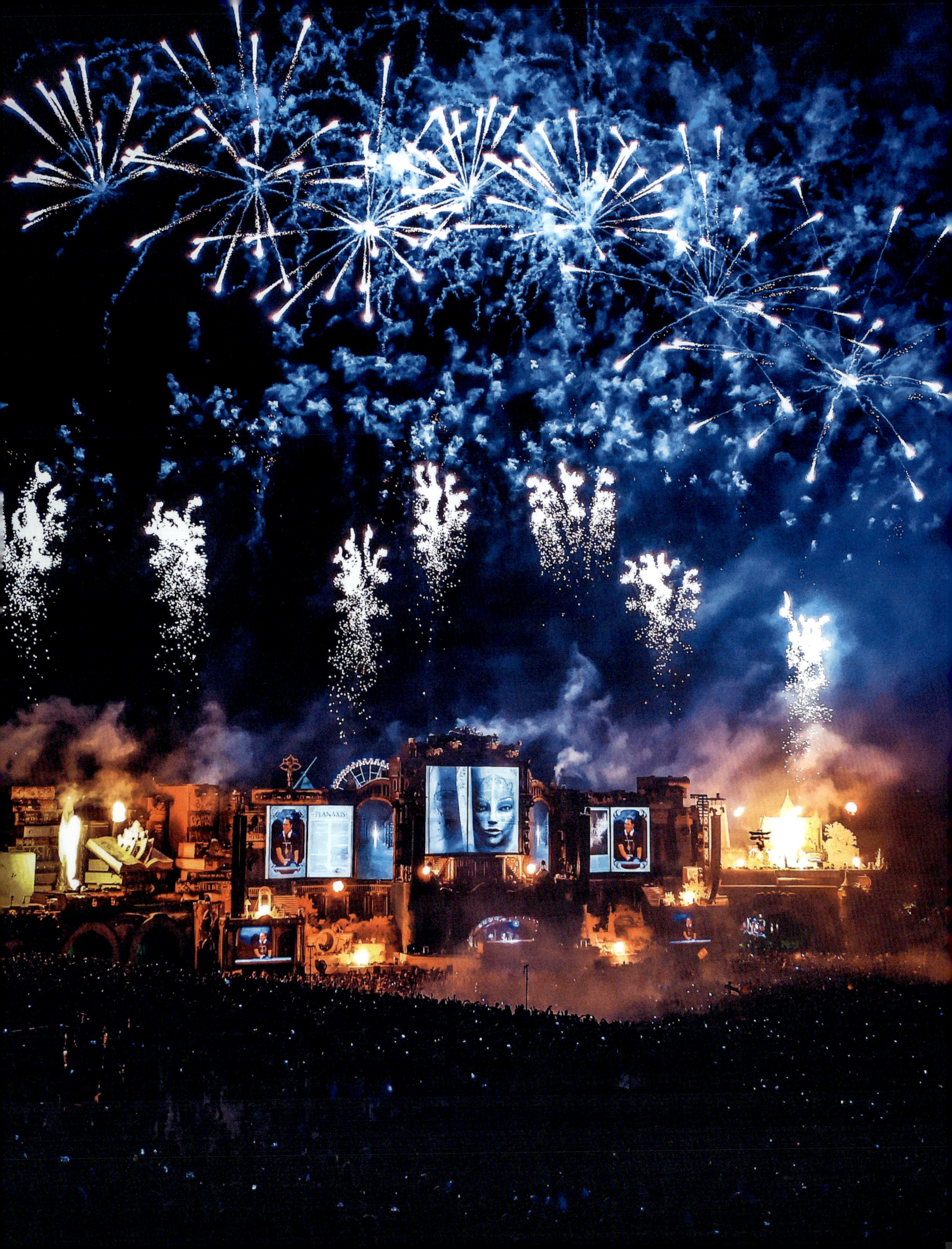

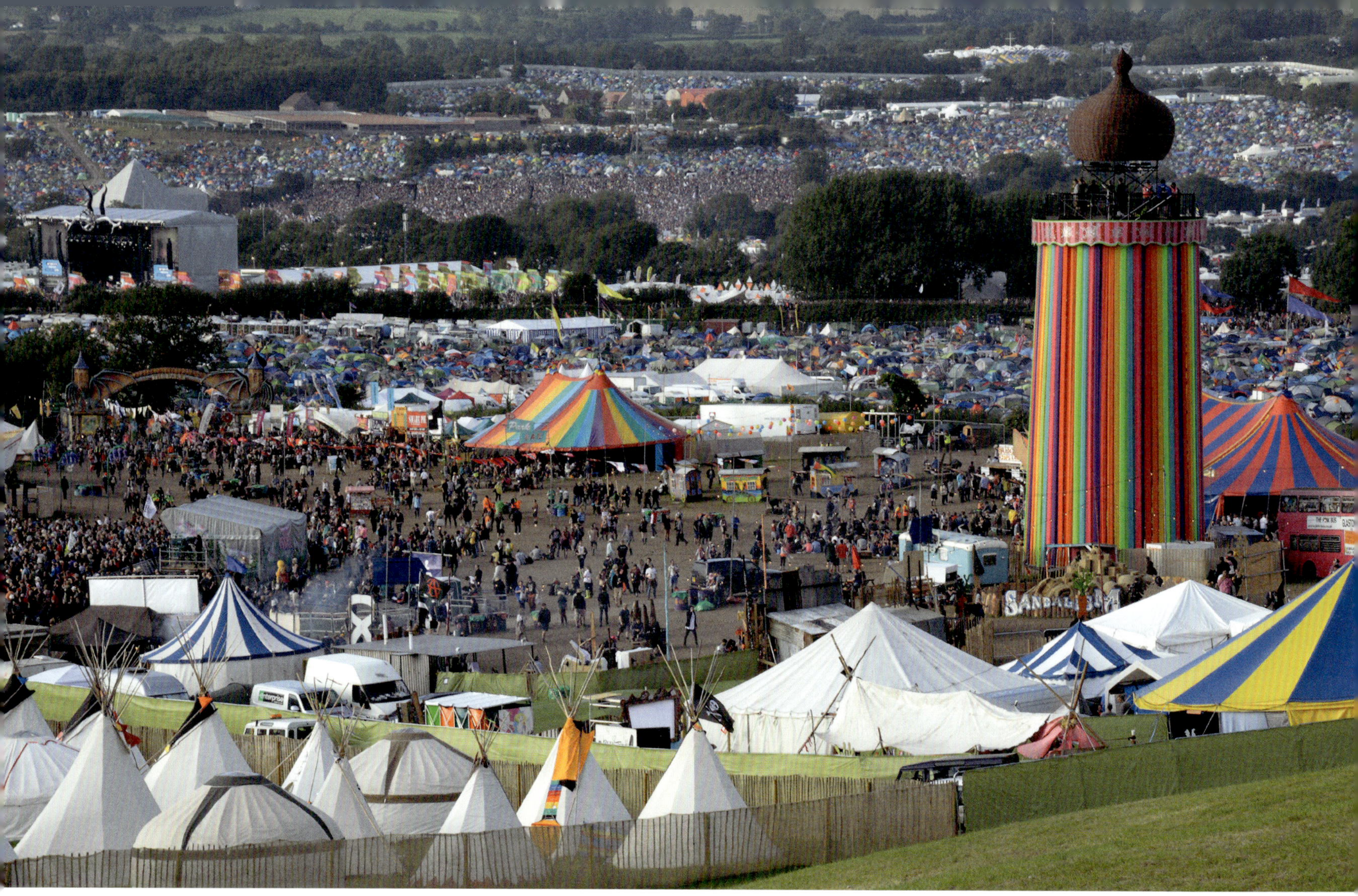

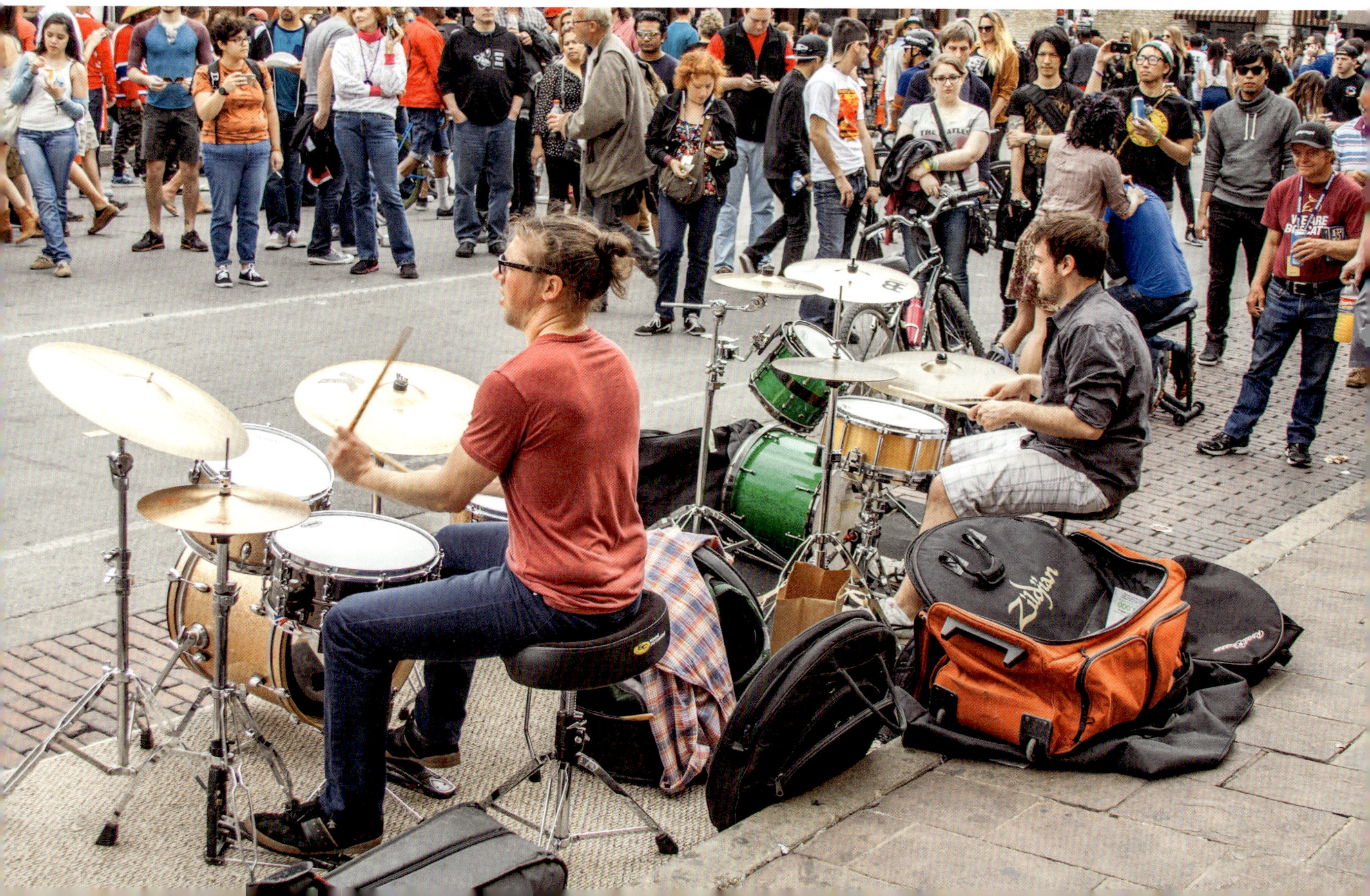

When you think of festivals, music festivals might be the first to come to mind. Standing in a field, with a pint of beer, tapping your foot to the beats coming from the stage and wondering where your friends have gone off to defines a pretty standard festival experience for many.

As much as that is part of the music festival experience, there's a lot more to them than that.

Music festivals can be transformative. They're a chance to be free of the chains of the rat race, of social and familial pressures. You can wear that glitter, pull on those colorful leggings, and dance like you've never danced before, with no judgment—just admiration.

Glastonbury Festival in the UK is the most significant field festival in the world, welcoming 170,000 lucky ticket holders to Worthy Farm every June. The Pyramid Stage has seen the biggest names in music perform, with over 100 other stages for other artists to show off their craft. The five-day festival takes place in the Vale of Avalon, an important historical and mythological area of England, which only adds to its majesty (opposite, top).

SXSW is another of the most important music festivals in the world. Taking place in Austin, Texas, it is where new artists go to be discovered—it can literally make or break a career. Go to SXSW, and in addition to discovering the latest tech, film, and innovation, you can also listen to the coolest bands in the coolest locations across Austin for ten days (opposite, bottom).

In Malawi, Africa, the Lake of Stars Festival offers a totally different music festival experience, during which you can uncover some of the most incredible Malawian and international artists on stage by Lake Malawi. It's a super friendly, small festival with a strong heart and some great music to hear. Enjoy the bands, open your mind, and make the most of this unique festival of 5,000 participants.

Wenn man an Festivals denkt, fallen einem oft zuerst Musikfestivals ein. Mit einem Glas Bier mitten in einem Feld zu stehen, zum Rhythmus der Beats auf der Bühne zu wippen und sich zu fragen, wo die Freunde geblieben sind, gehört für viele zum Standard-Festivalerlebnis. Aber da gibt es noch so viel mehr.

Musikfestivals können Besucher in eine andere Welt katapultieren. Man ist für kurze Zeit von allen Fesseln des Alltags, von sozialem und familiärem Druck befreit, kann dieses Glitzeroutfit und diese bunten Leggings tragen und hemmungslos tanzen, ohne be- und verurteilt zu werden.

Glastonbury in England ist das wichtigste Festival auf freiem Feld – jeden Juni machen 170 000 glückliche Ticketbesitzer sich zur Worthy Farm auf. Auf der Pyramid Stage haben schon die größten Acts der Musikwelt gespielt und es gibt mehr als 100 weitere Bühnen, auf denen auch etwas weniger bekannte Künstler ihr Talent zur Schau stellen können. Dass das fünftägige Festival im mythischen Avalon-Tal (dem Schauplatz der Artus-Sage) liegt, tut der Legendenbildung keinen Abbruch (linke Seite, oben).

Das Festival South by Southwest (kurz: SXSW, linke Seite, unten) im texanischen Austin gehört ebenfalls zu den wichtigsten Musikfestivals der Welt. Hier treten neben arrivierten Acts auch Künstler auf, die noch ganz groß rauskommen wollen. Besucher können sich zehn Tage lang in den coolsten Locations der Stadt die coolsten Bands anhören und nebenbei auch über die neuesten technischen Innovationen informieren.

Das Lake of Stars Festival in Malawi bietet ein Musikerlebnis der völlig anderen Art. Auf einer Bühne vor dem Malawi-See treten einige der besten malawischen und internationalen Musiker auf. Auf dem mit ca. 5 000 Teilnehmern eher kleinen Festival herrscht eine besonders herzliche Atmosphäre. Genießen Sie die fantastische Musik, öffnen Sie Ihren Geist und kosten Sie dieses einmalige Kulturereignis voll aus.

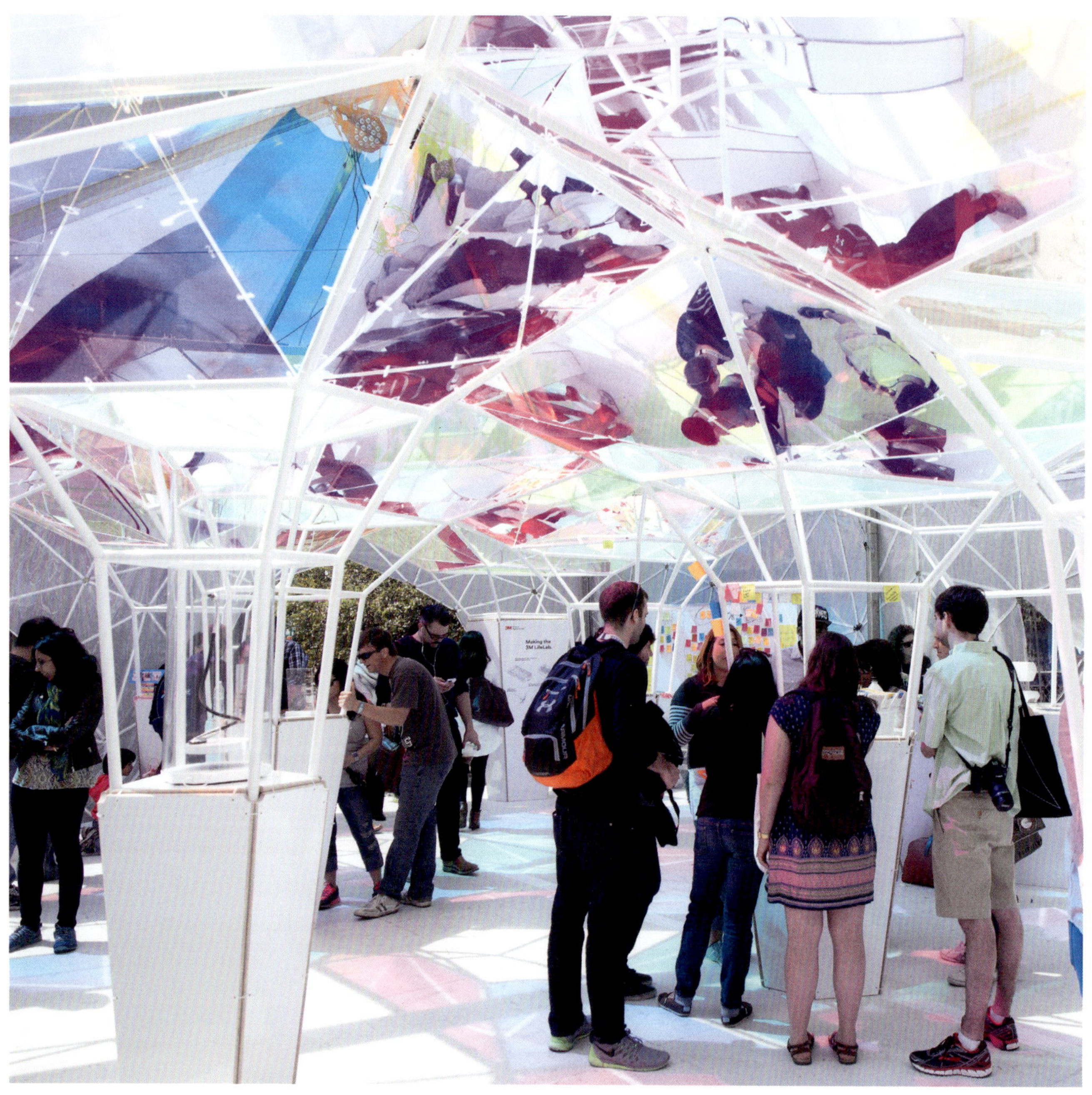

South by Southwest (SXSW) was originally a music festival. In the 1990s a film and interactive conference were added to the program.

South by Southwest (SXSW) war früher ein reines Musikfestival, ab den 1990er-Jahren wurden Konferenzen und Fachausstellungen zu Film und Interaktiven Medien ins Programm genommen.

More than 2,000 acts perform at SXSW festival and it takes over the city of Austin, in Texas, USA.

Über 2 000 Musik-Acts treten beim SXSW-Festival im amerikanischen Austin, Texas, auf.

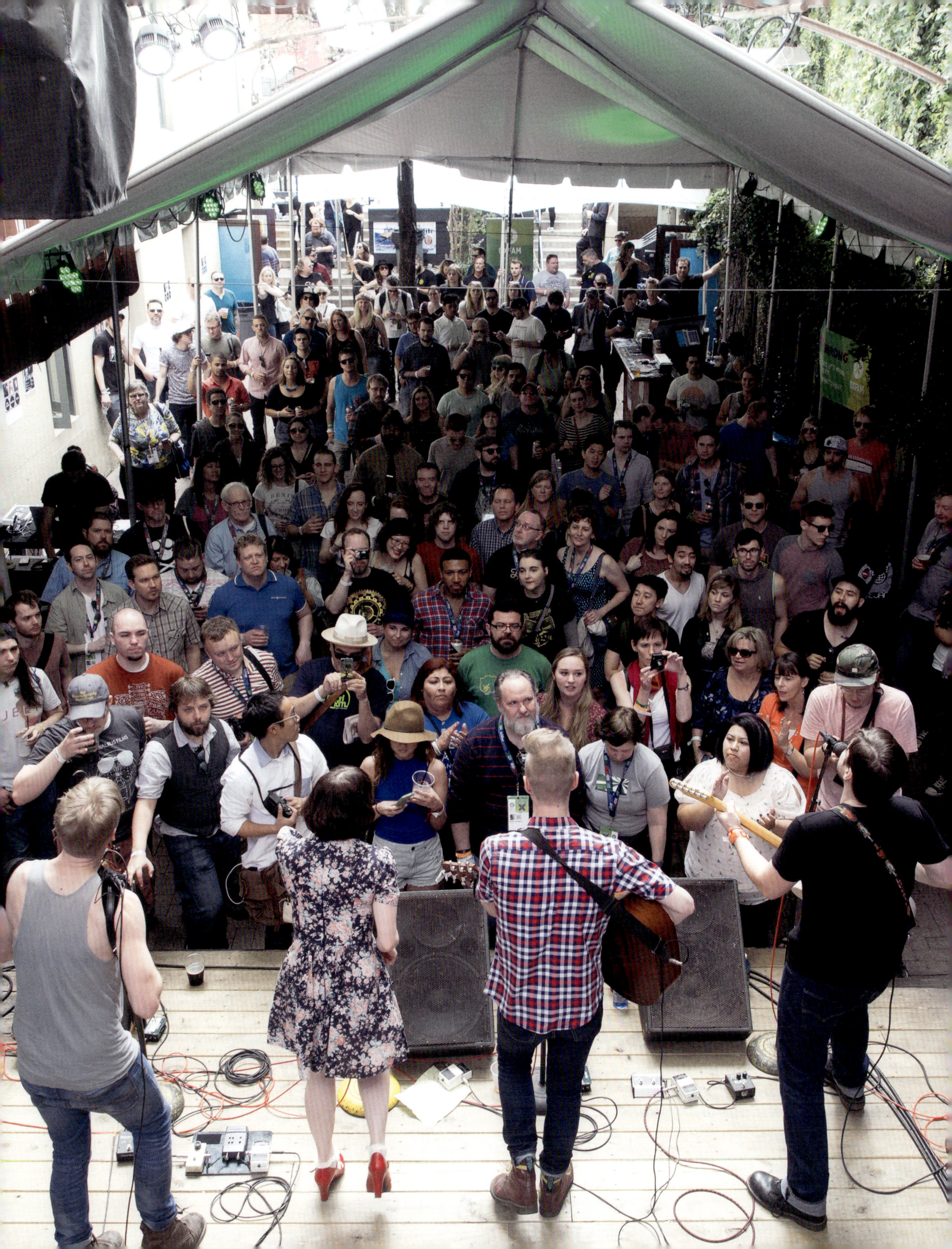

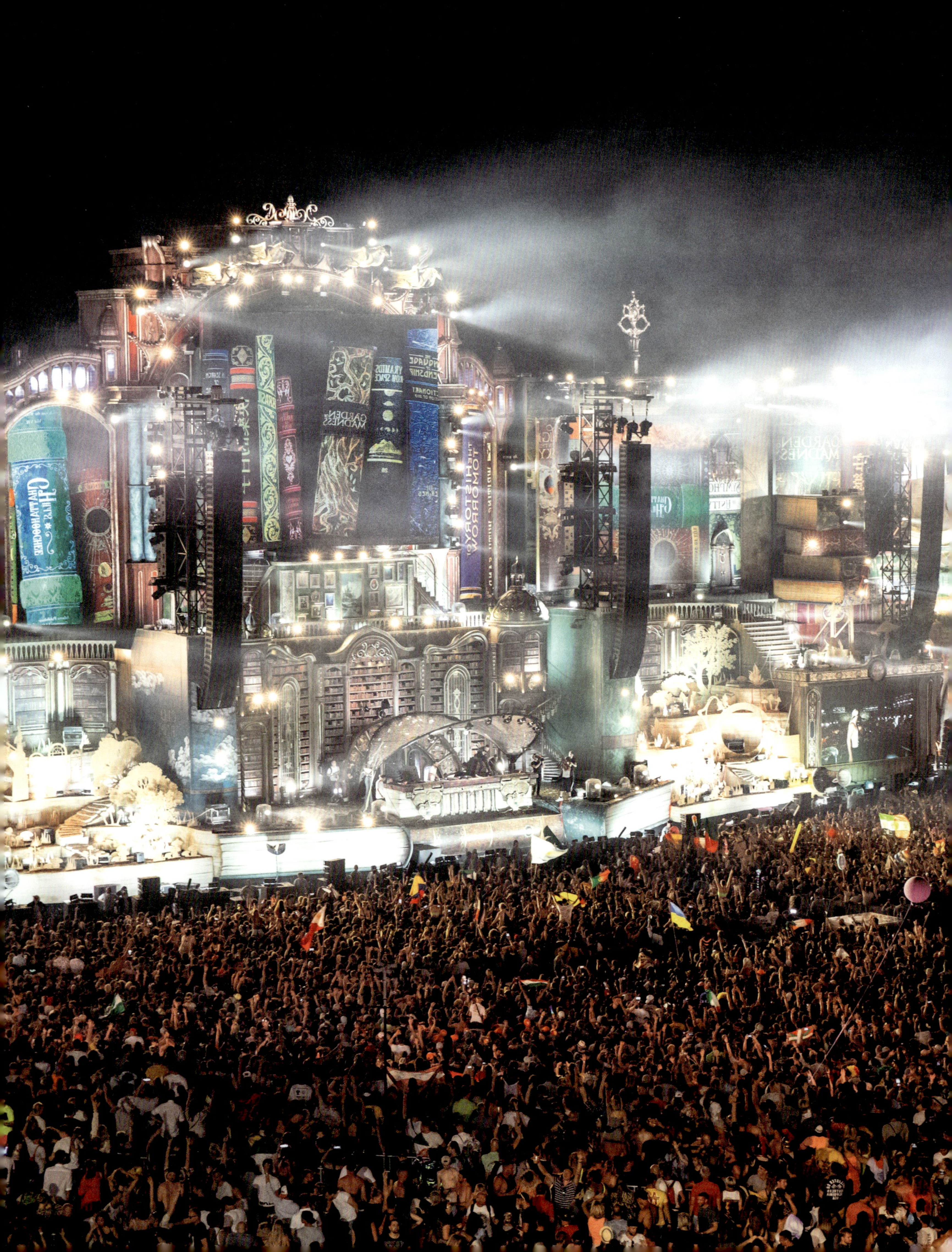

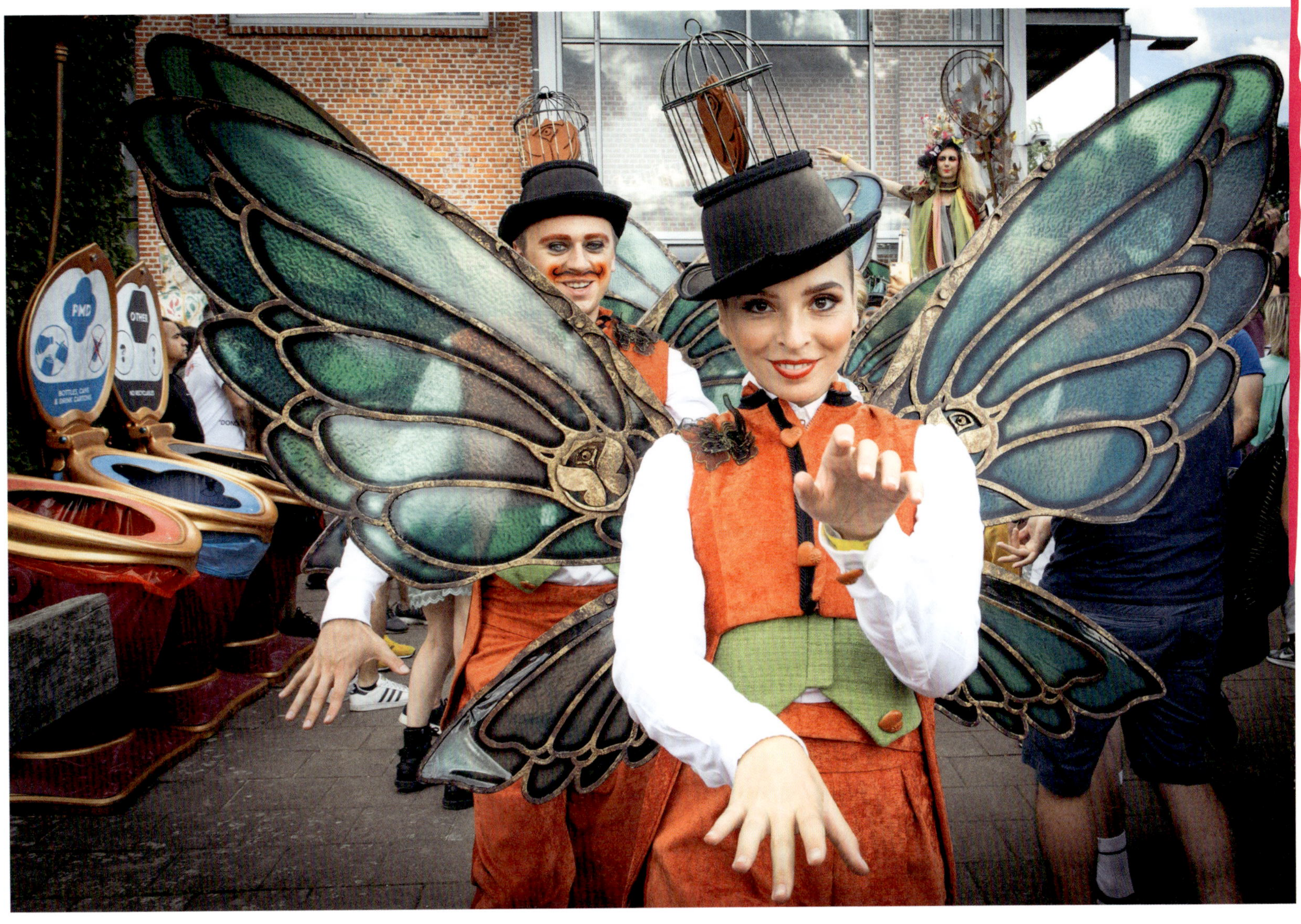

This is the biggest festival for electro and techno music
in the world.

Tomorrowland ist das größte EDM- und Techno-Musik-
festival der Welt.

At Coachella Valley Music and Arts Festival musicians from various genres perform for 250,000 people over the three-day festival held over two weekends. There are art installations, such as *Lightweaver* and *Escape Velocity*, and the dress code is hippie-inspired. H&M even launched its own Coachella collection.

Beim Coachella Valley Music and Arts Festival treten an zwei Wochenenden Musiker verschiedener Genres vor 250 000 Menschen auf. Kunstinstallationen wie *Lightweaver* und *Escape Velocity* sorgen für den Wow-Faktor, und die Kleiderordnung ist vom Hippie-Stil inspiriert. H&M brachte sogar schon eine eigene Coachella-Kollektion heraus.

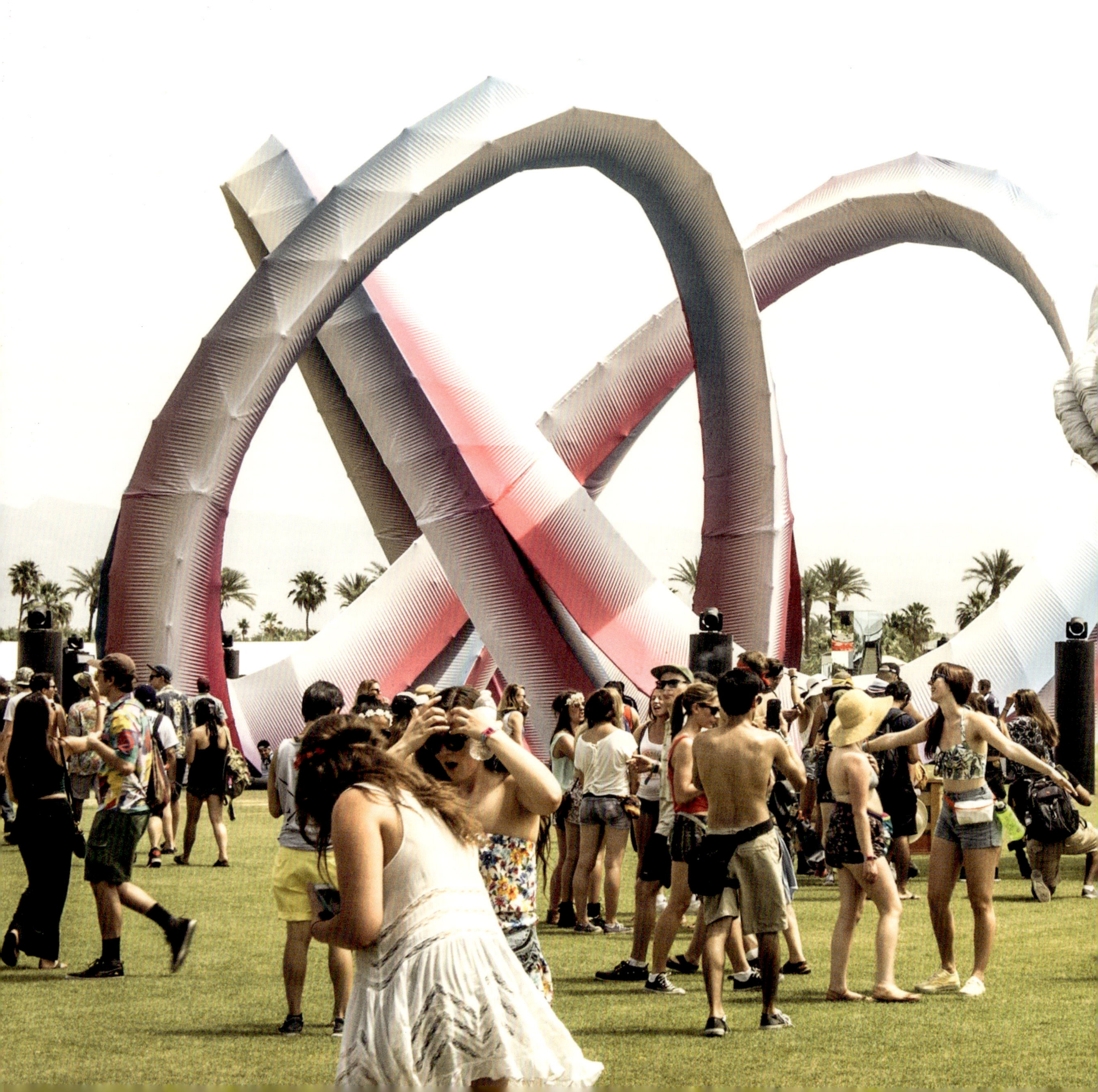

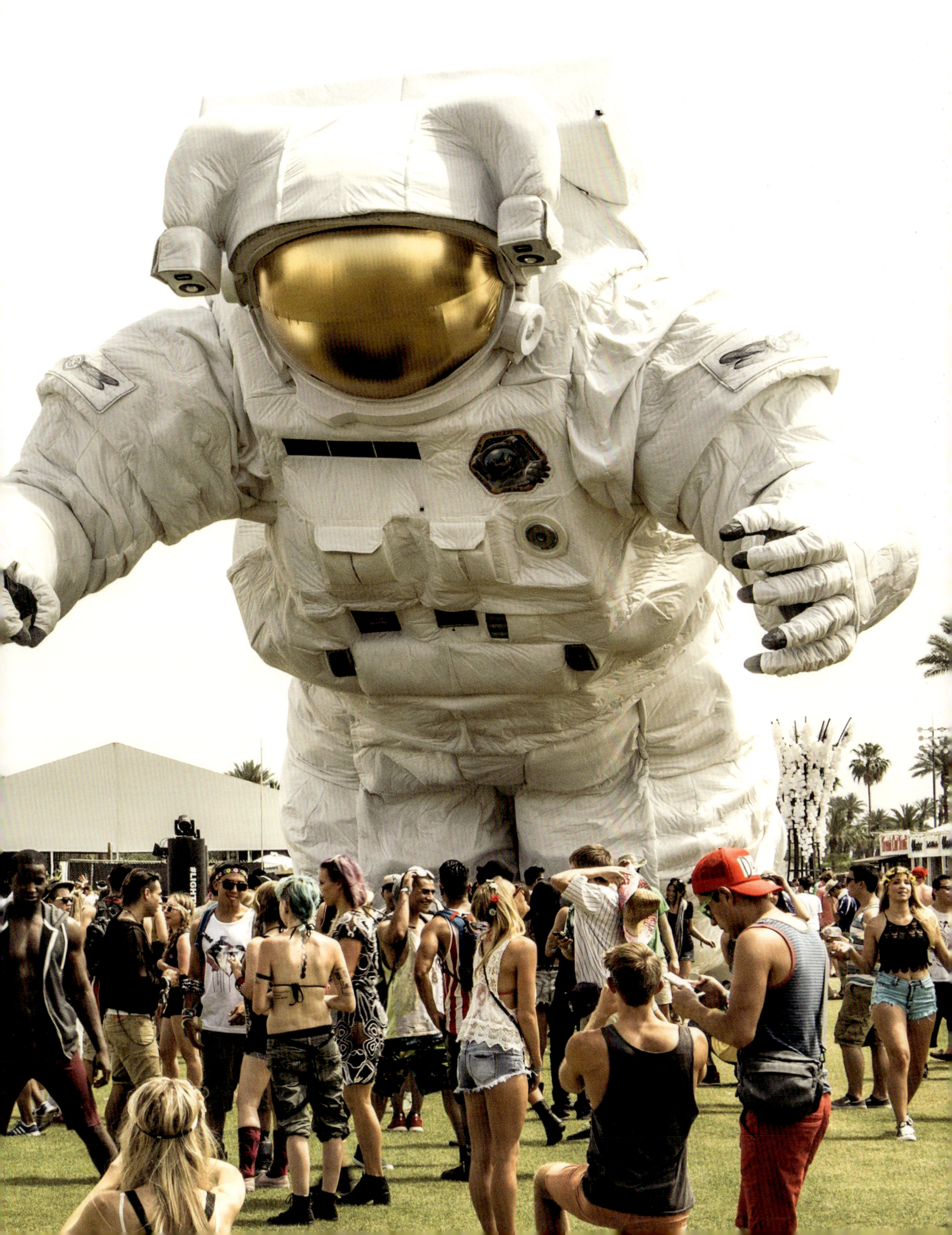

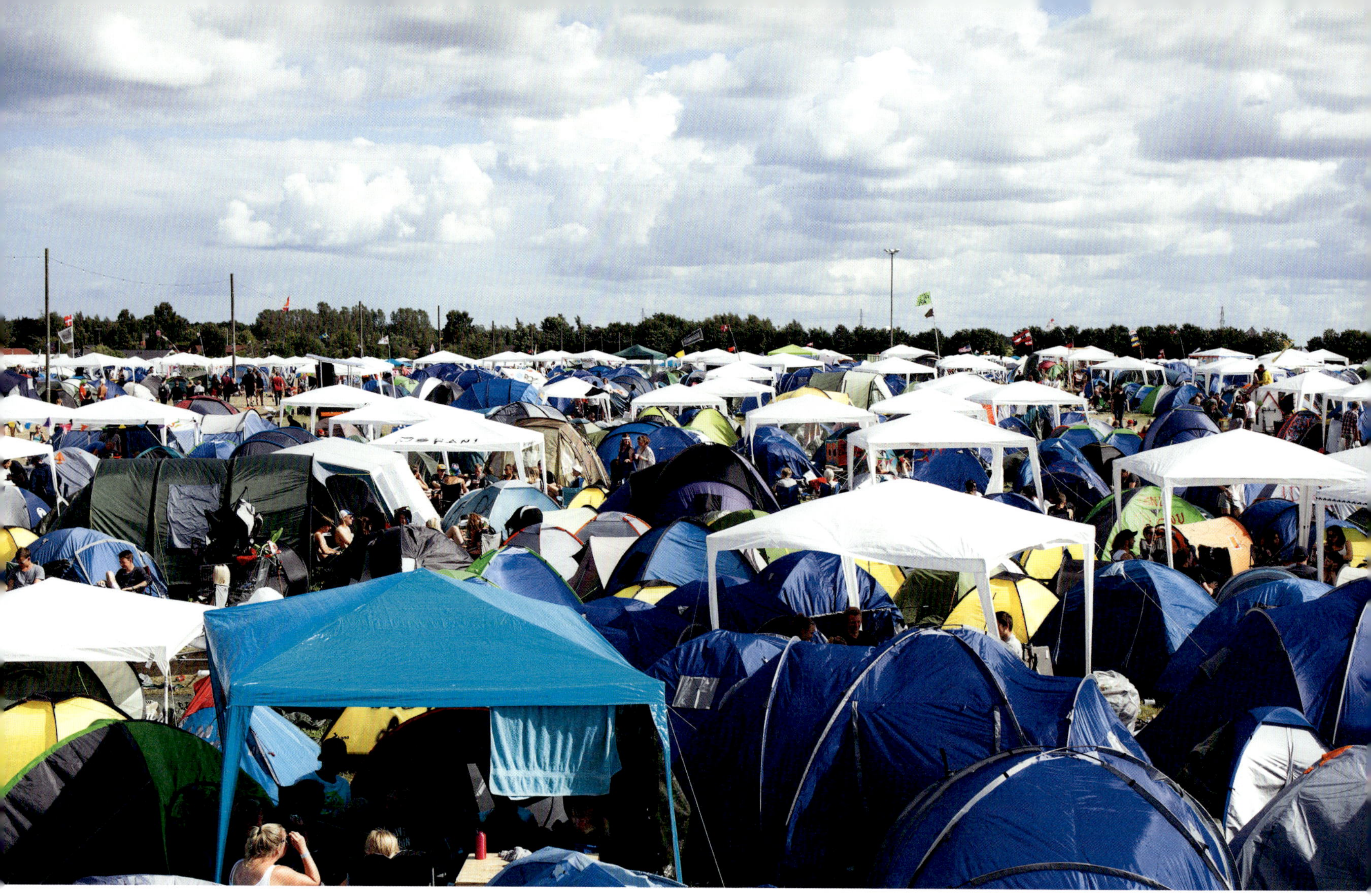

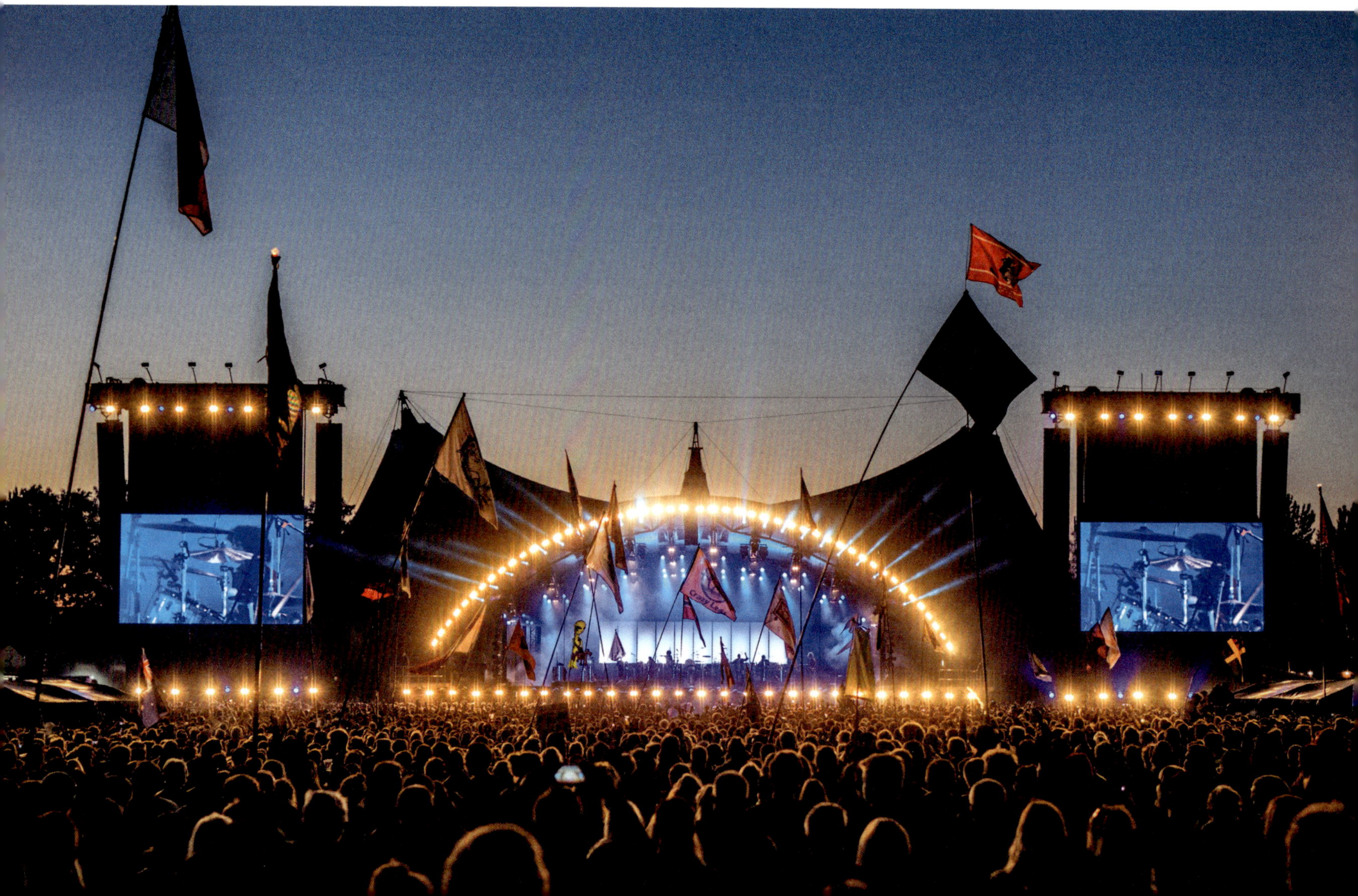

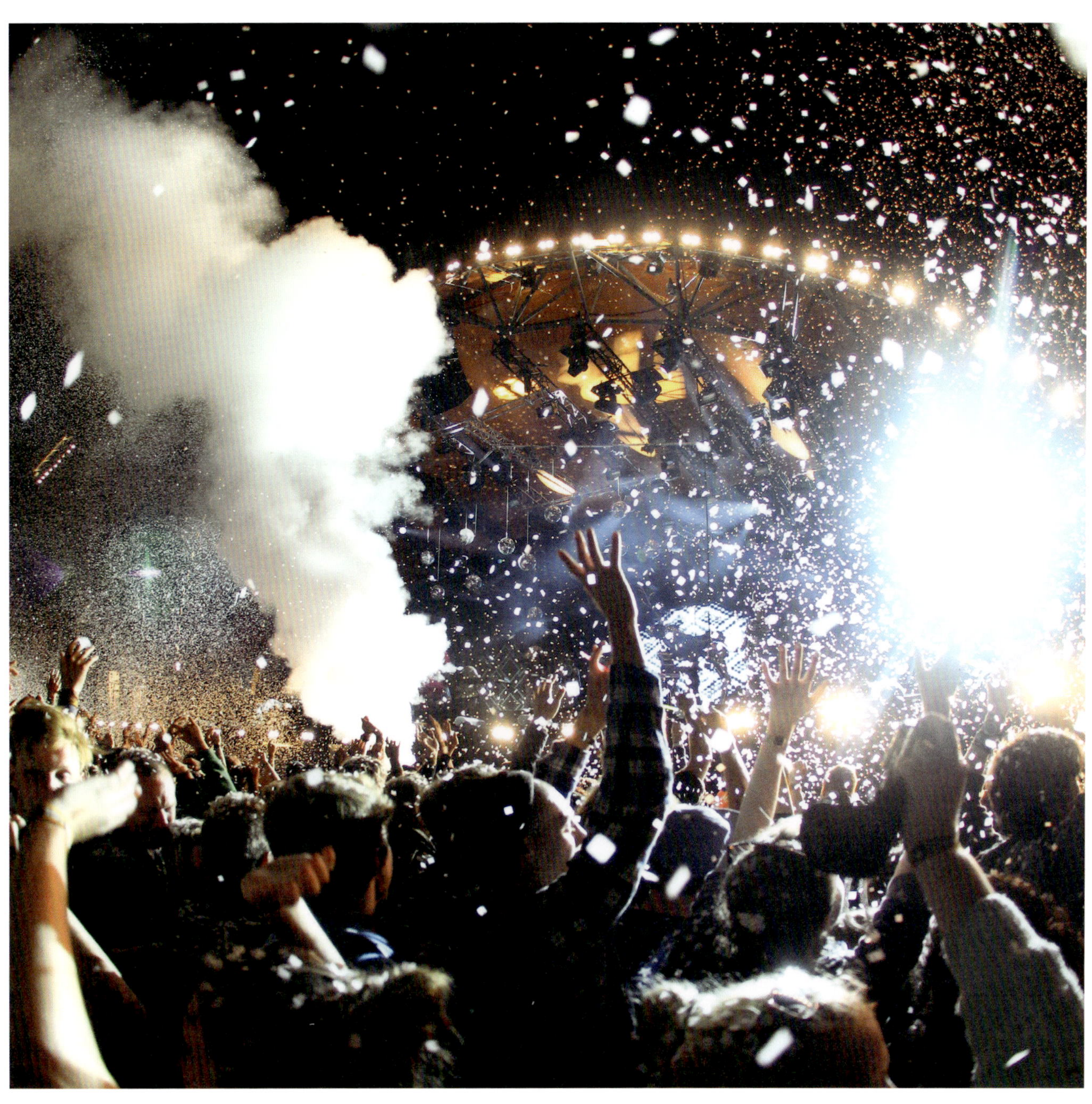

Danish Roskilde Festival is one of the longest running
music festivals, dating back to 1971.

Das dänische Roskilde-Musikfestival fand zum ersten
Mal 1971 statt und ist damit eines der
ältesten seiner Art.

Roskilde is all about community, volunteers, and humanitarian work. 30,000 volunteers work
at the festival and profits go to charities and charitable organizations, such as Amnesty
International, WWF, and Save the Children.

In Roskilde dreht sich alles um die Gemeinschaft und humanitäre Projekte.
30.000 Freiwillige arbeiten auf dem Festival und die Gewinne gehen an Wohltätigkeits-
organisationen wie Amnesty International, WWF und Save the Children.

Every year there's controversy over the crowd flags at
Glastonbury, as they block people's view, but they're an
iconic festival tradition that's impossible to stop.

In Glastonbury gehören die ikonischen Fahnen einfach
zur Festivaltradition dazu, obwohl es jedes Jahr wieder
eine Kontroverse darüber gibt, da sie den Besuchern die
Sicht versperren.

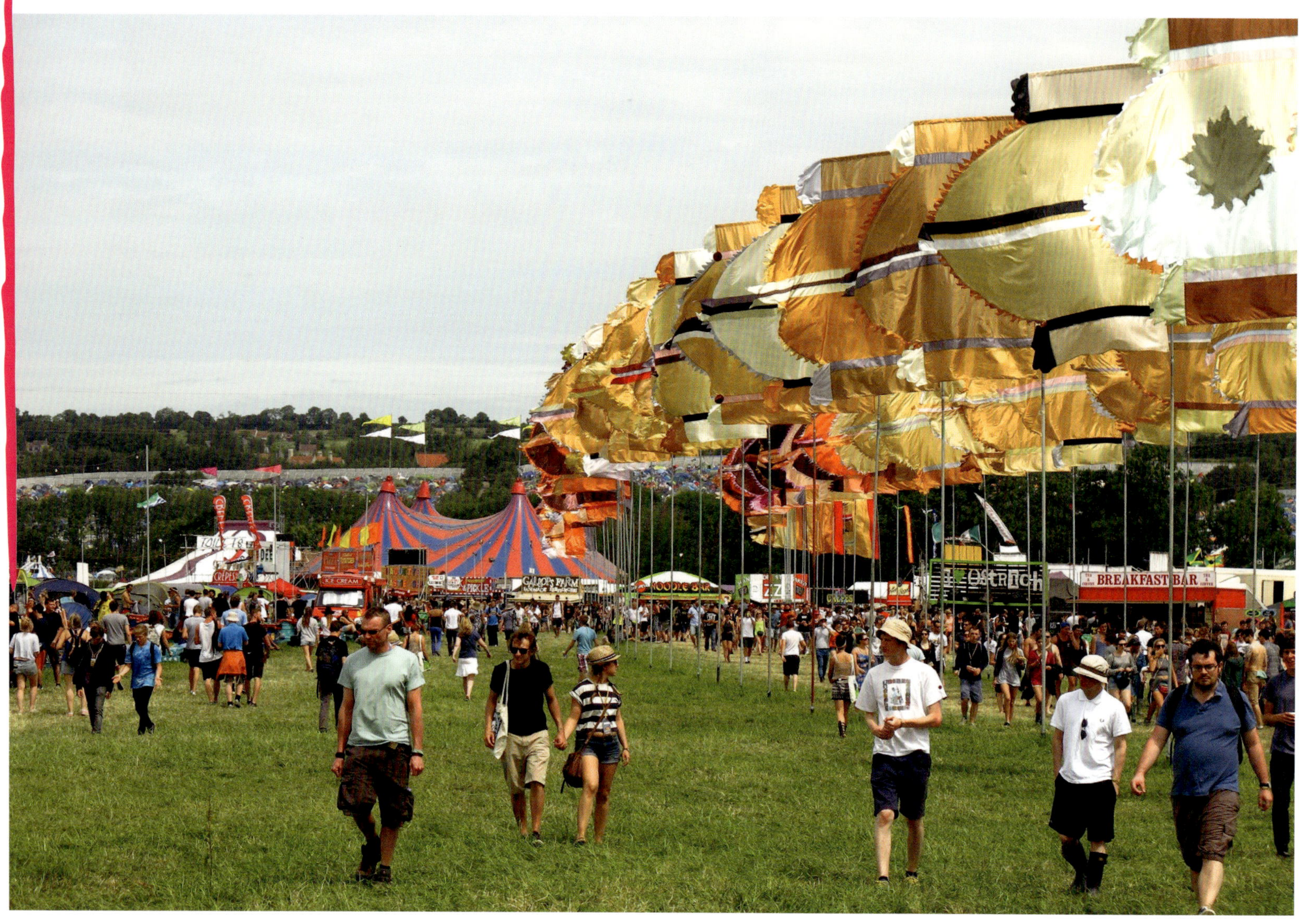

Glastonbury lasts for five days and is the hottest
ticket around. Over 170,000 tickets sold out in
33 minutes in 2019.

Das Glastonbury-Festival geht fünf Tage und
Tickets sind heißbegehrt. 2019 waren die
170 000 verfügbaren Eintrittskarten in nur
33 Minuten ausverkauft.

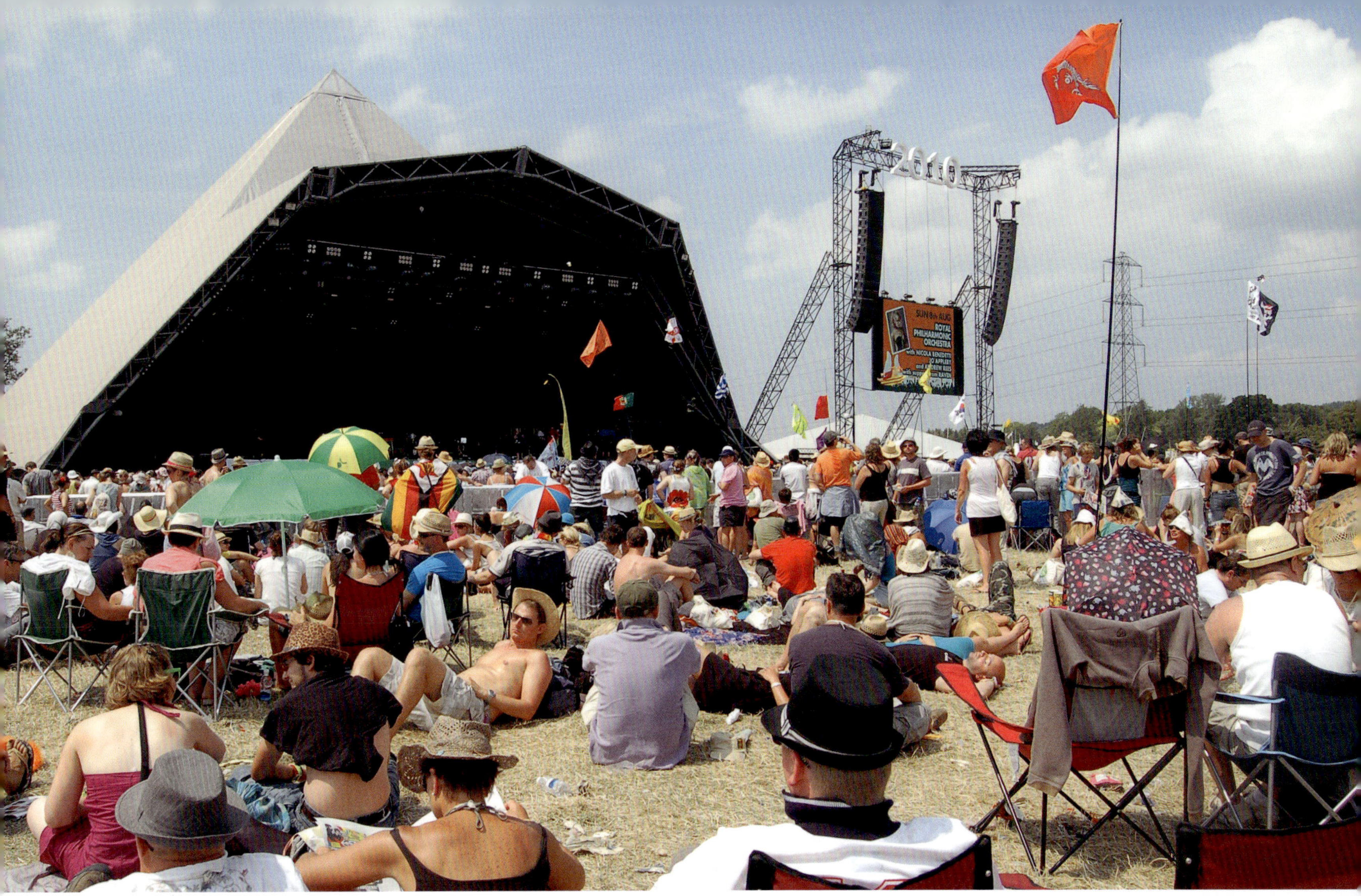

GLASTONBURY

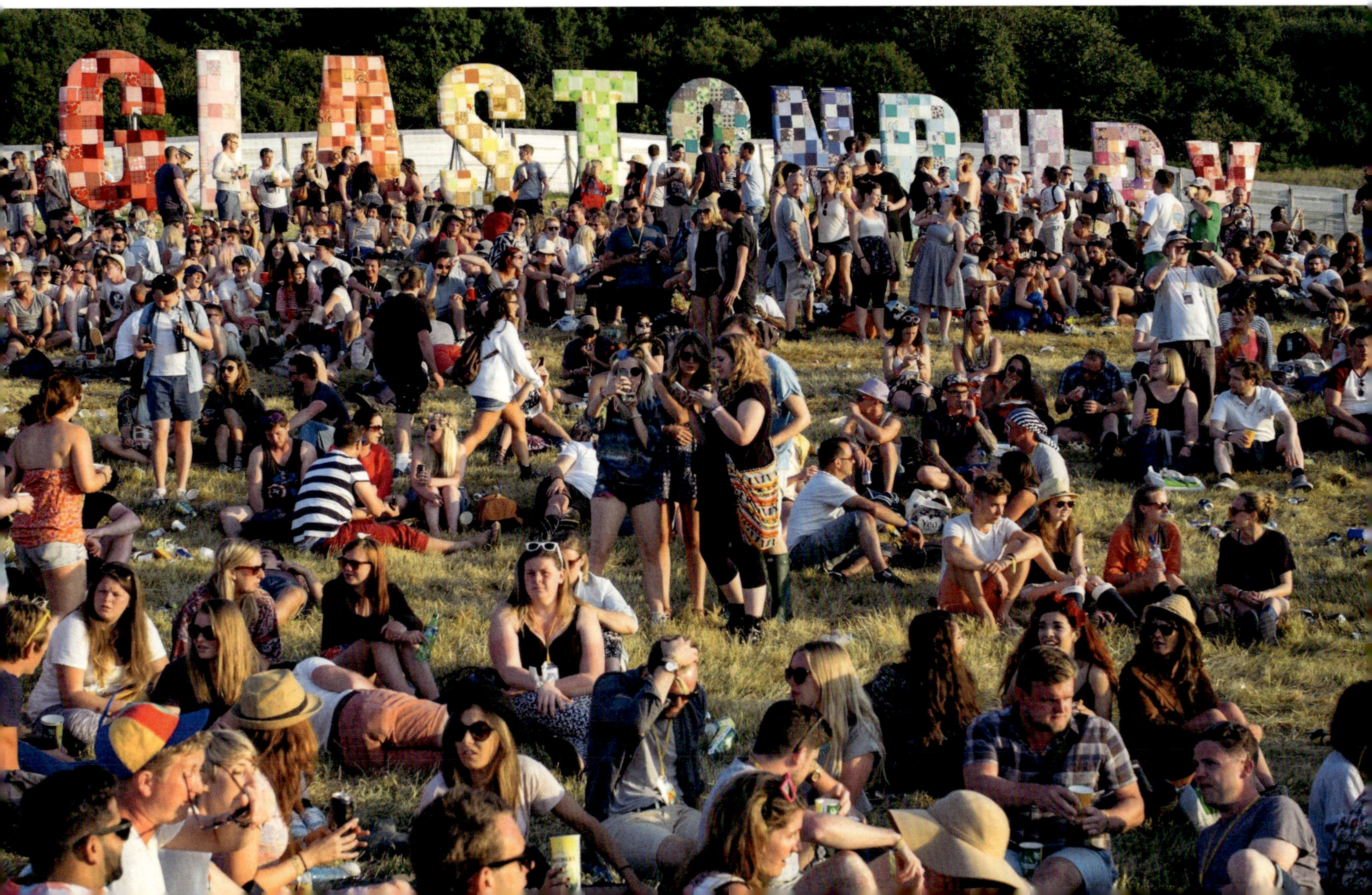

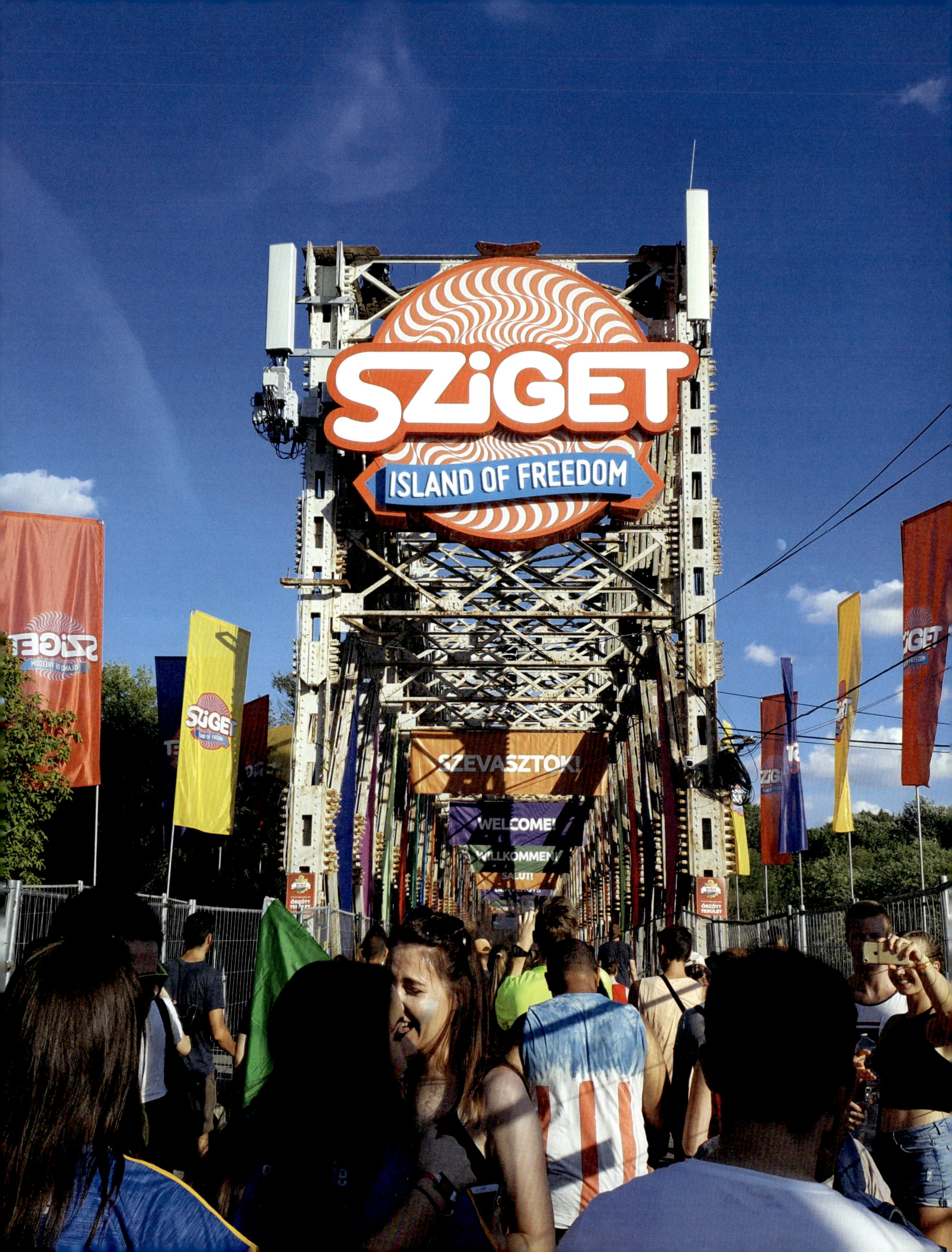

SZIGET
ISLAND OF FREEDOM
SZEVASZTOK!
WELCOME!
WILLKOMMEN!
SALUTI
ŐRZÖTT TERÜLET
ŐRZÖTT TERÜLET

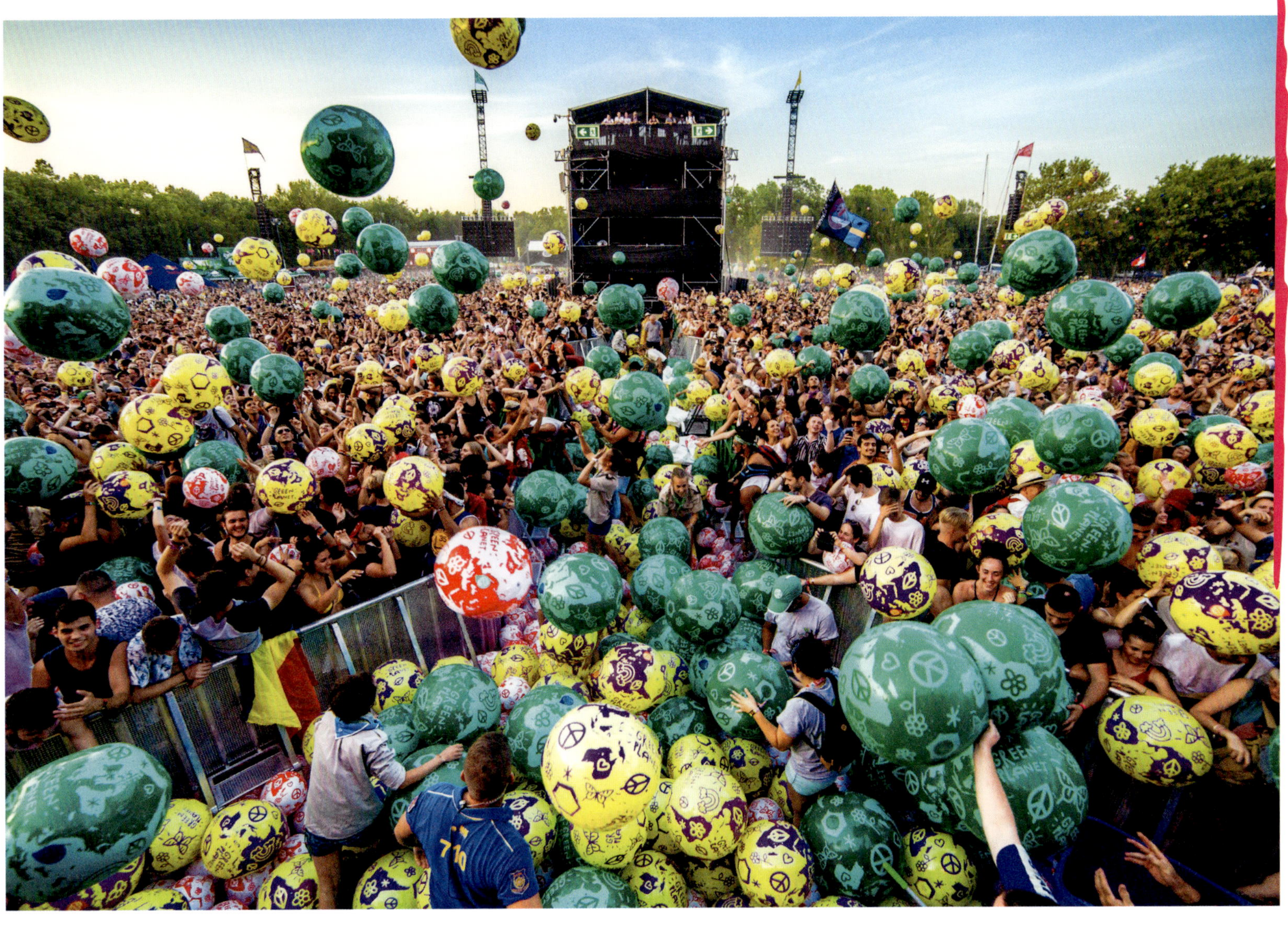

Sziget Festival is held on Óbudai-sziget, a 266-acre
(108-hectare) island on the Danube in Budapest.

Sziget-Festival findet auf Óbudai-sziget statt, einer
108 Hektar großen Insel auf der Donau in Budapest.

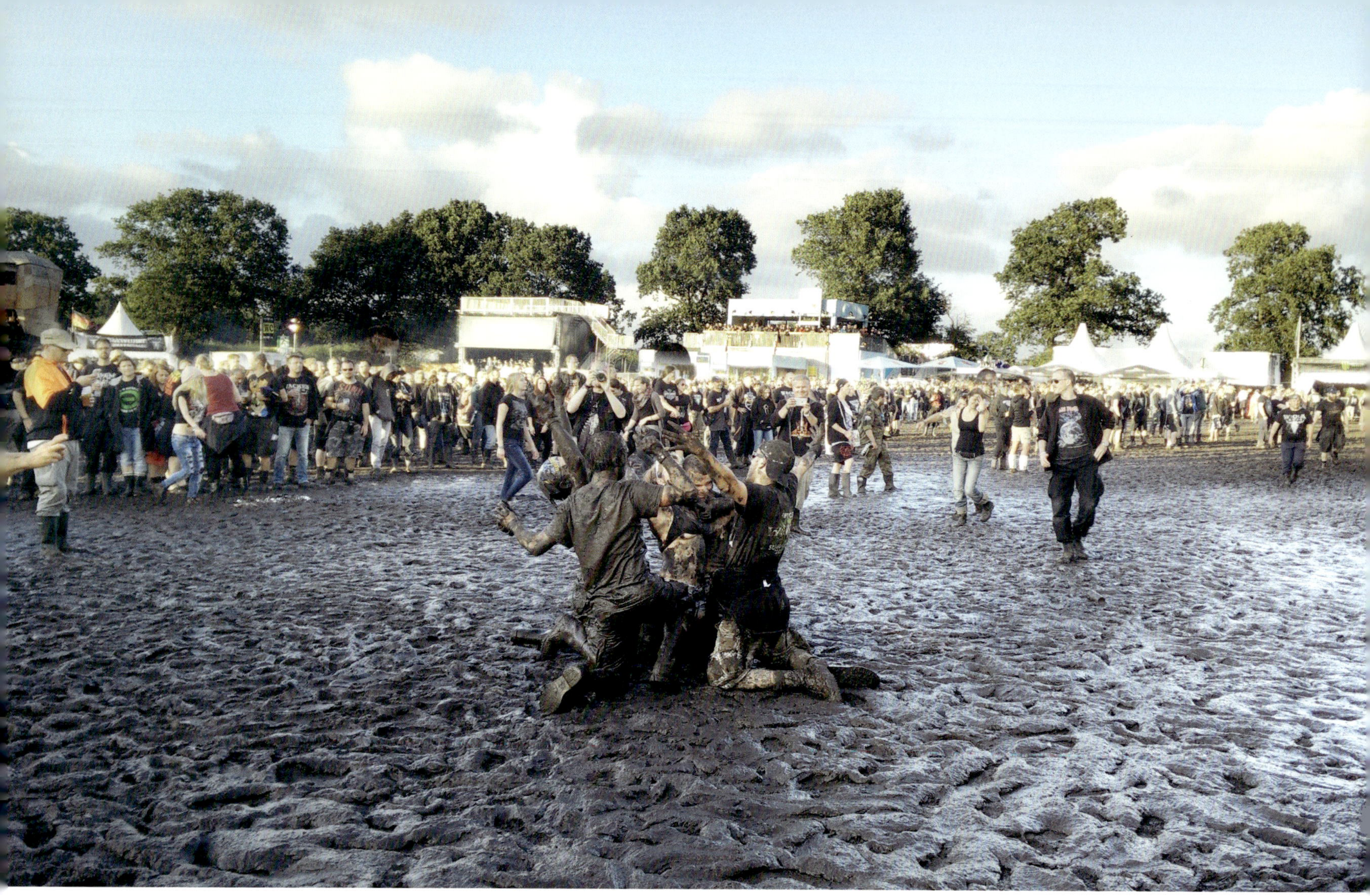

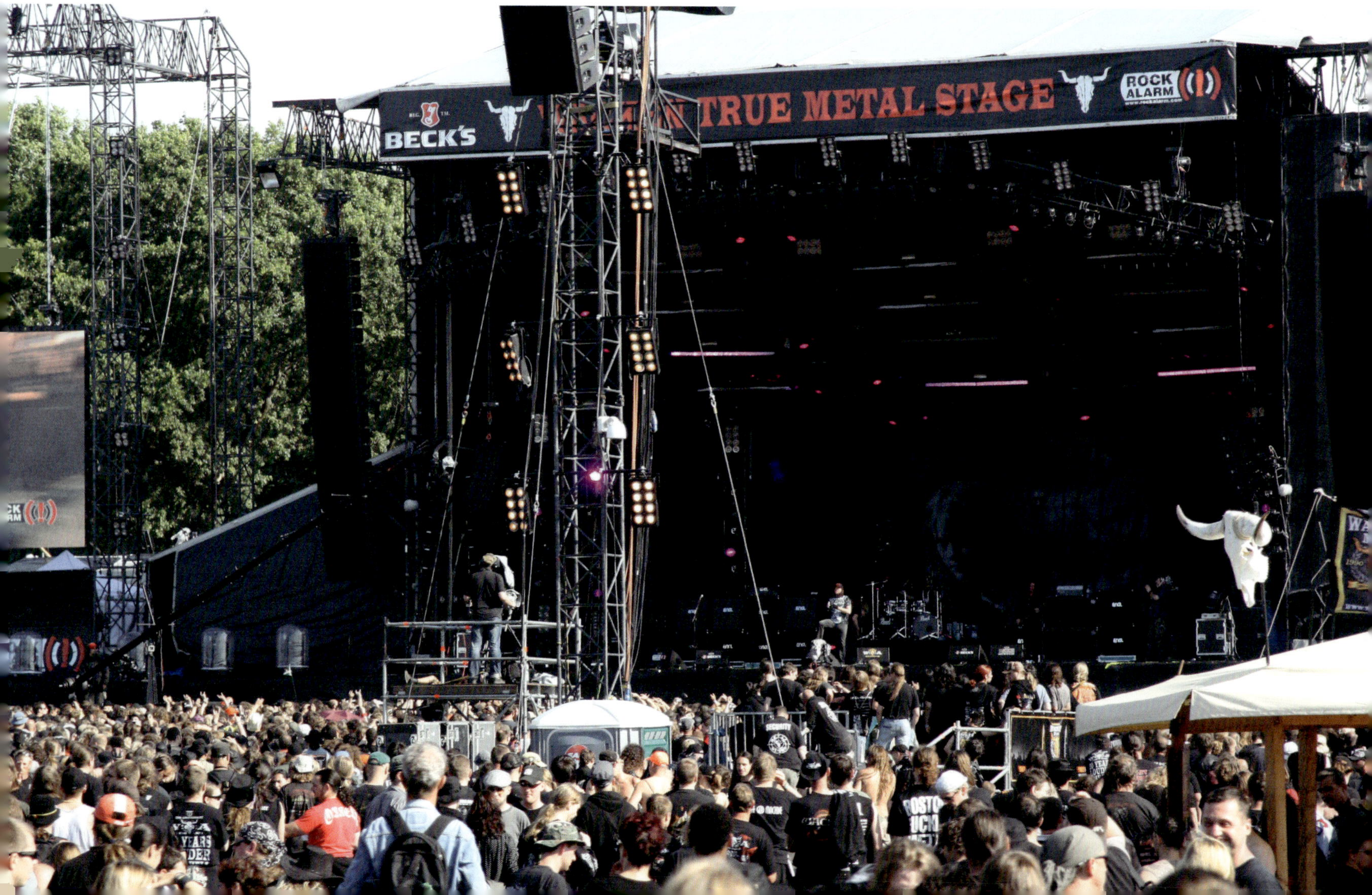

BECK'S
TRUE METAL STAGE
ROCK ALARM

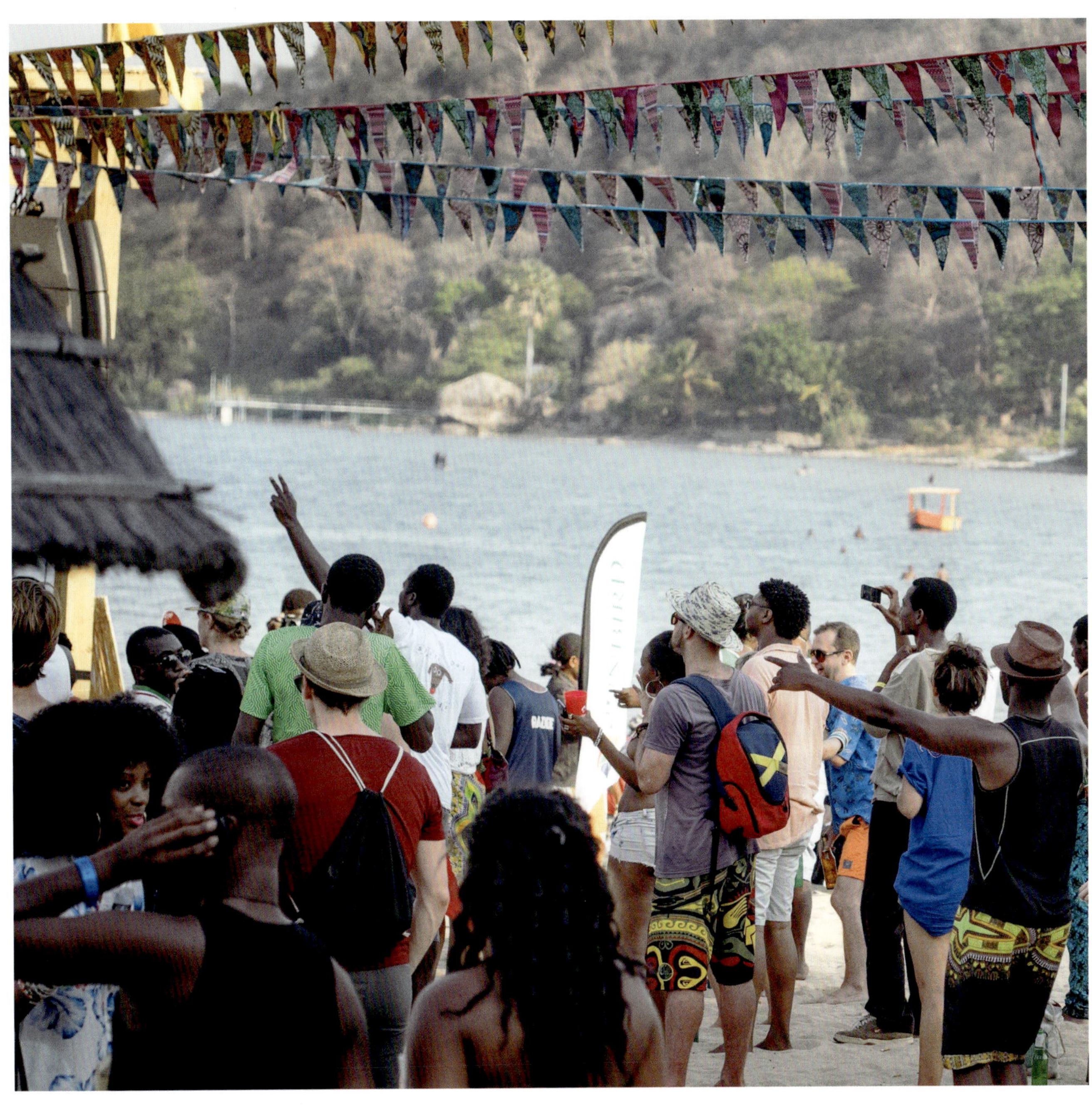

Music performances in a paradisiacal setting—this is
Lake of Stars in Malawi.

Musik in paradisischer Umgebung erleben,
beim Lake of Stars Festival in Malawi ist das möglich.

Each year, around 80,000 heavy metal fans visit the small village of Wacken,
Germany, to celebrate Wacken Open Air. Wacken's motto is "Faster, Harder,
Louder!" which are also the names of the three main stages.

Jedes Jahr pilgern rund 80 000 Heavy-Metal-Fans ins beschauliche Wacken,
um das Wacken Open Air zu feiern. Das Motto ist: schneller, härter, lauter!
Und so heißen auch die drei größten Bühnen.

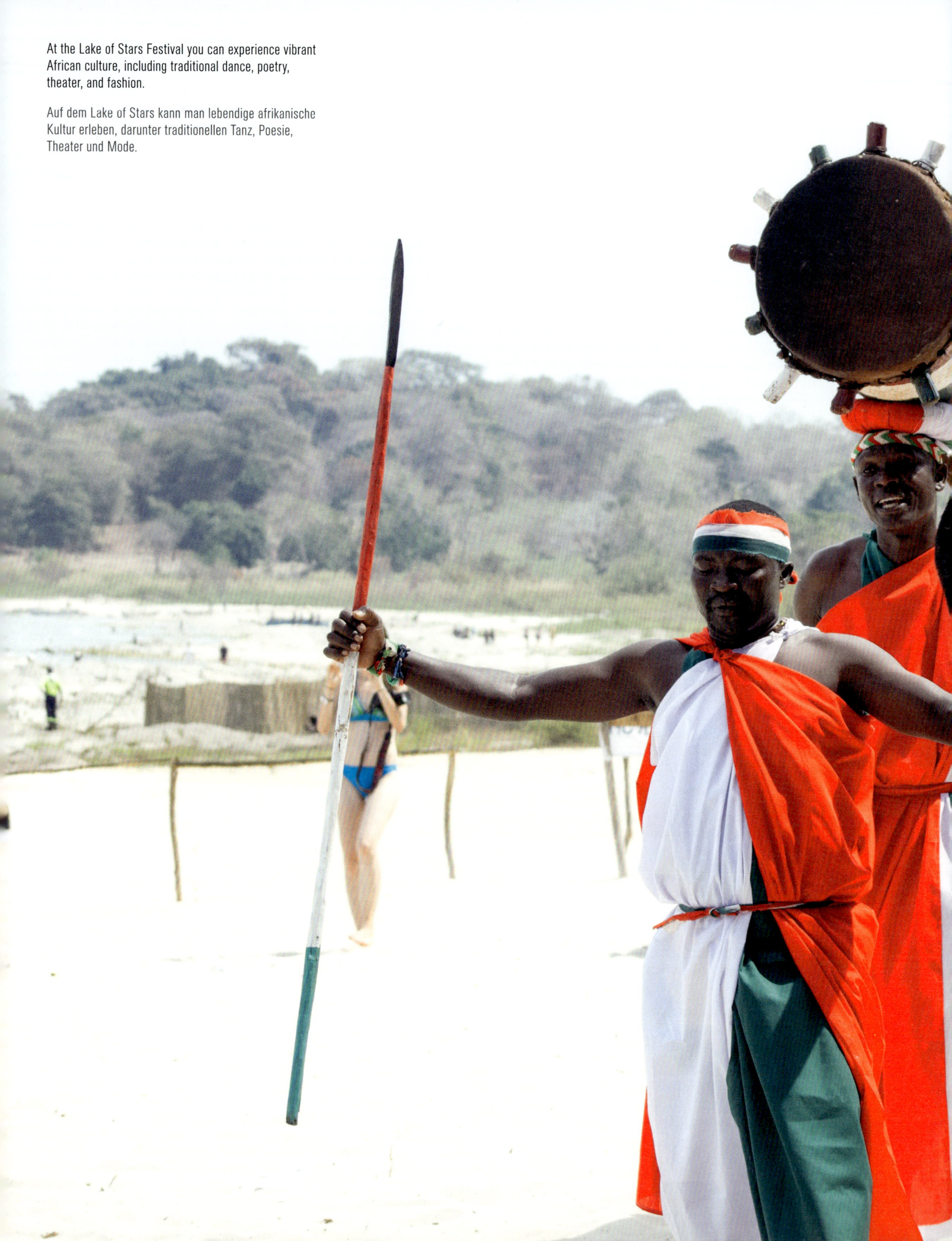

At the Lake of Stars Festival you can experience vibrant
African culture, including traditional dance, poetry,
theater, and fashion.

Auf dem Lake of Stars kann man lebendige afrikanische
Kultur erleben, darunter traditionellen Tanz, Poesie,
Theater und Mode.

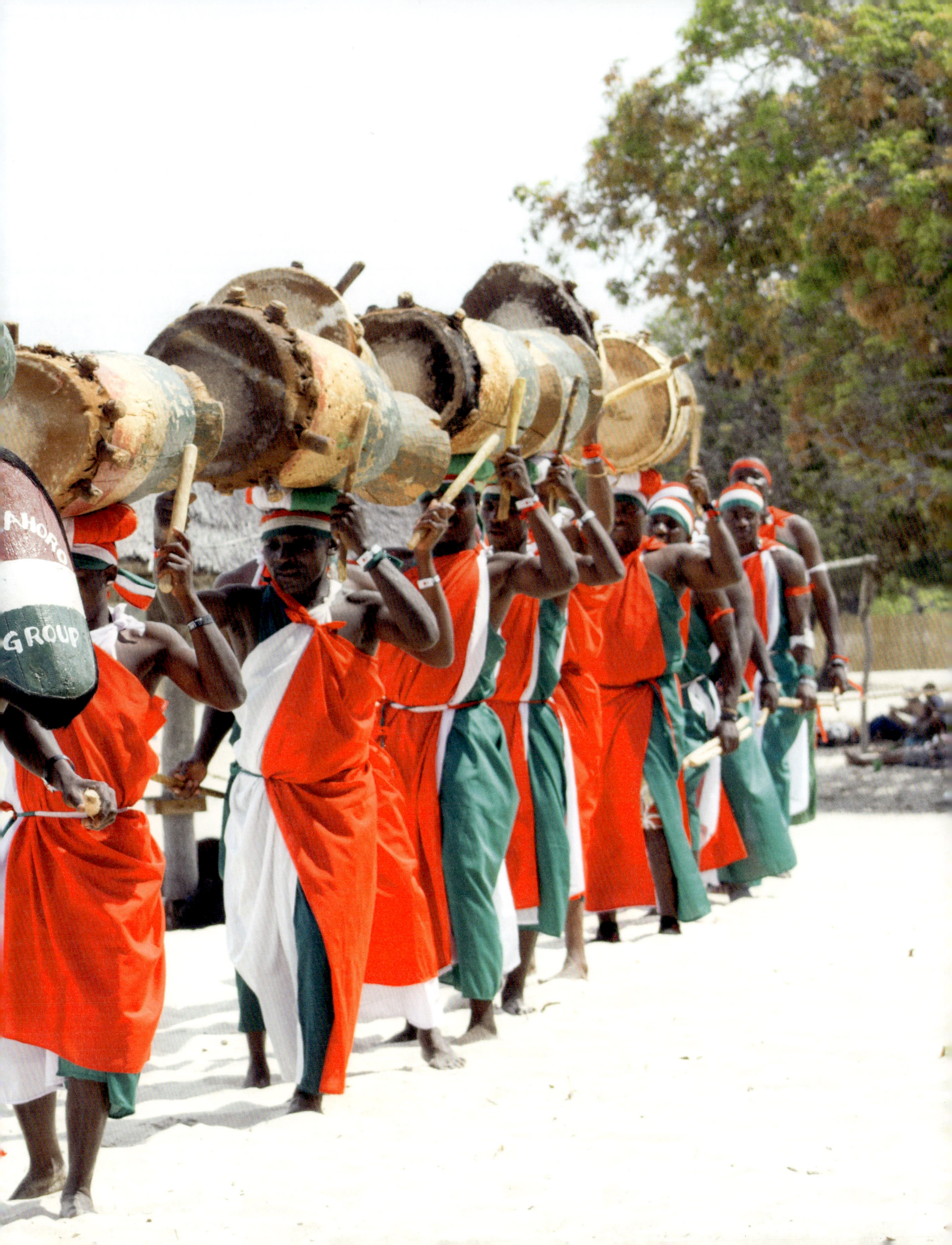
AHORO
GROUP

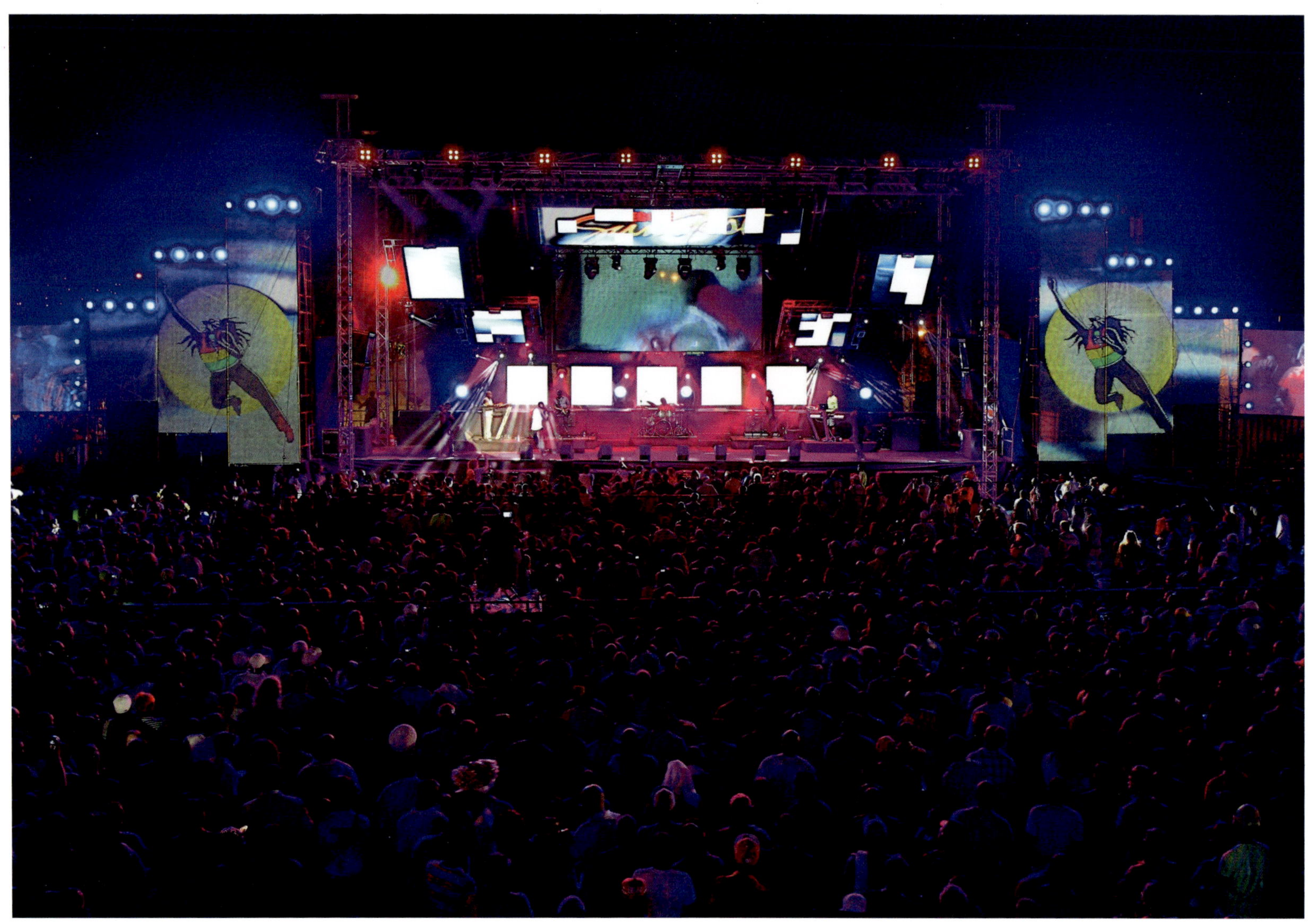

Reggae Sumfest is the largest music festival in Jamaica and the Caribbean. Running since 1993, the lineup features local reggae and dancehall artists as well as international stars.

Das Reggae Sumfest ist das größte Musikfestival in Jamaika und der Karibik. Es findet seit 1993 statt und bietet einheimischen Reggae- und Dancehall-Künstlern ebenso eine Bühne wie internationalen Stars.

Good to know
WISSENSWERTES

The Montreal Jazz Festival in Canada features over 3,000 artists from 30 countries. Around 2.5 million people come to see them in outdoor performances and inside beautiful concert halls and indoor spaces over the 11-day event. About two-thirds of the events can be visited for free!

Beim Montreal Jazz Festival in Kanada treten über 3 000 Künstler aus 30 Ländern auf. Während der 11-tägigen Veranstaltung kommen rund 2,5 Millionen Menschen, um sich die Auftritte unter freiem Himmel oder in wunderschönen Konzertsälen anzusehen. Etwa zwei Drittel der Veranstaltungen können kostenlos besucht werden!

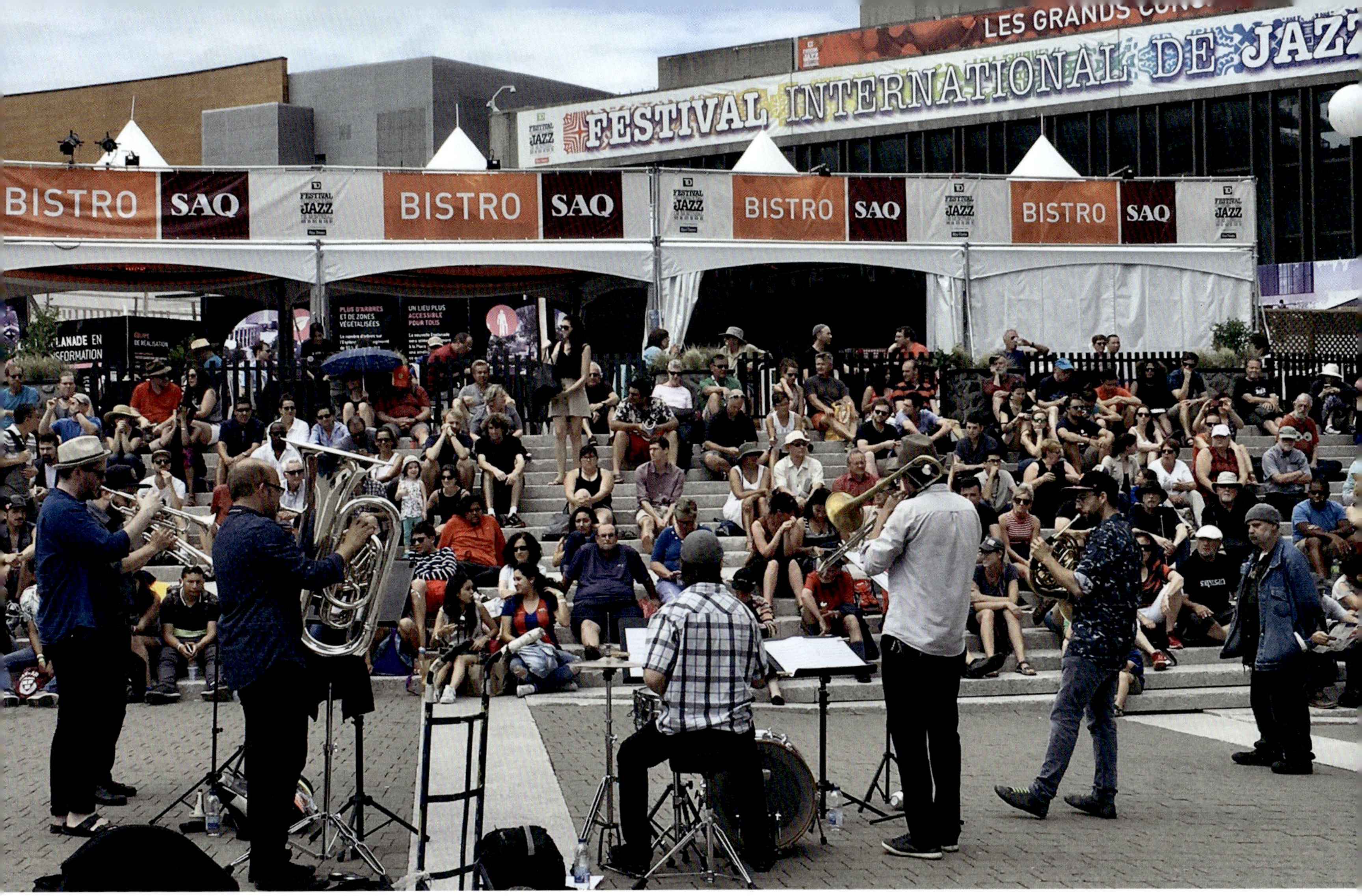

LES GRANDS CON
FESTIVAL INTERNATIONAL DE JAZZ
BISTRO SAQ 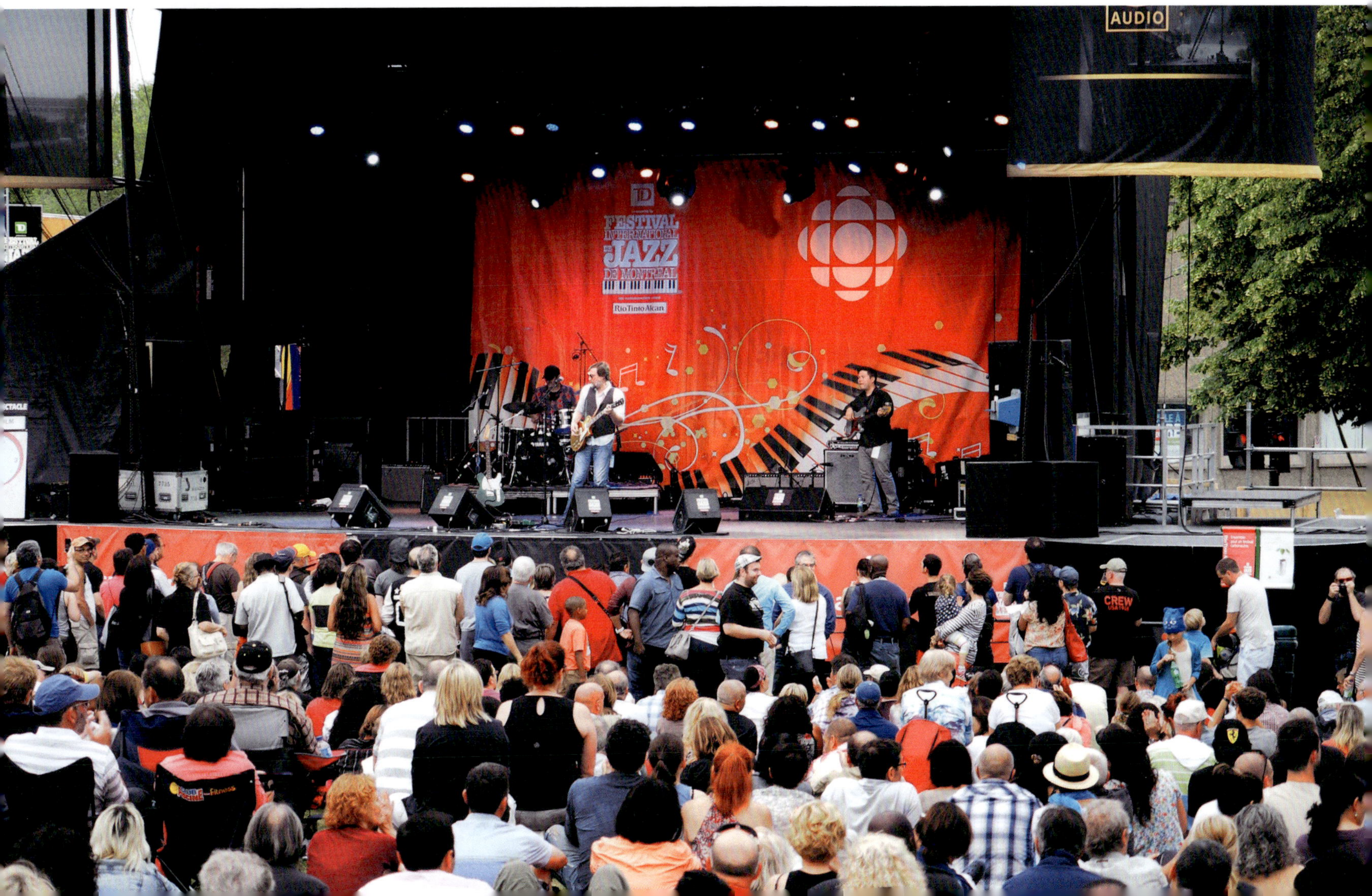
BISTRO SAQ
BISTRO SAQ
BISTRO SAQ
FESTIVAL JAZZ
PLUS D'ARBRES ET DE ZONES VÉGÉTALISÉES
UN LIEU PLUS ACCESSIBLE POUR TOUS
AUDIO
FESTIVAL INTERNATIONAL JAZZ DE MONTRÉAL
Rio Tinto Alcan
CREW

Festival Calendar

FEIERND DURCH DAS GANZE JAHR

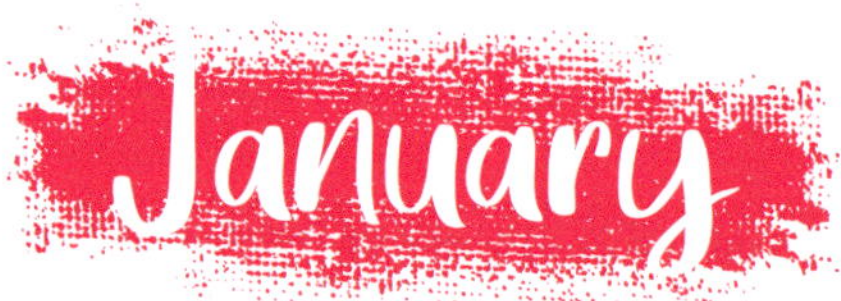

Chinese Lunar New Year, various countries, month may vary (Jan/Feb) | **Harbin International Ice and Snow Sculpture Festival**, China | **Hwacheon Sancheoneo Ice Festival**, Gangwon-do, South Korea | **Thaipusam**, various countries, month may vary (Jan/Feb) | **Timkat**, Gondar, Ethiopia | **Up Helly Aa**, Shetland, UK, *uphellyaa.org* | **Voodoo Festival**, Ouidah, Benin | **Wakakusa Yamayaki**, Nara, Japan | **Yukigassen**, various countries, Jan–Apr, *www.yukigassen-intl.com*

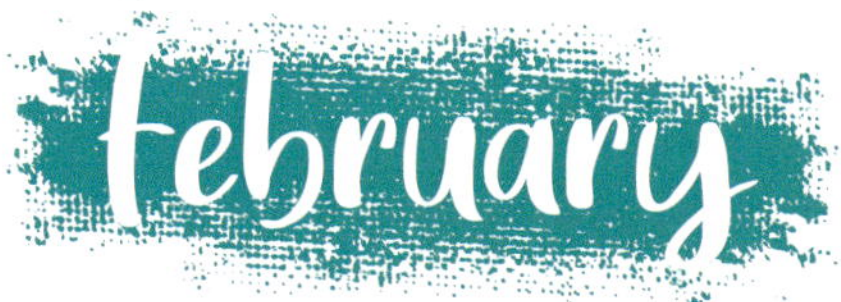

Argungu Fishing Festival, Nigeria | **Basler Fasnacht**, Switzerland, month may vary (Feb/Mar) | **Busójárás**, Mohács, Hungary | **Carnaval do Rio**, Rio de Janeiro, Brazil, month may vary (Feb/Mar) | **Carnevale di Venezia**, Venice, Italy, month may vary (Feb/Mar), *carnevale.venezia.it* | **Carnival of Ivrea** incl. **Battle of the Oranges**, Italy, month may vary (Feb/Mar) | **Chotrul Düchen** (Butter Lamp Festival), Lhasa, Tibet, month may vary (Feb/Mar) | **Envision Festival**, Uvita, Costa Rica, *envisionfestival.com* | **Fête du Citron** (Lemon Festival), Menton, France, *fete-du-citron.com* | **Fiesta Nacional de la Vendimia** (Grape Harvest Festival), Mendoza, Argentina, month may vary (Feb/Mar) | **Mardi Gras**, New Orleans, USA, month may vary (Feb/Mar), *mardigrasneworleans.com* | **Maslenitsa** (Pancake Week), Russia, month may vary (Feb/Mar) | **Rheinischer Karneval** (Rhineland carnival), various cities, Germany, month may vary (Feb/Mar) | **Sapporo Snow Festival**, Japan, *snowfes.com* | **Tet** (Lunar New Year), Vietnam

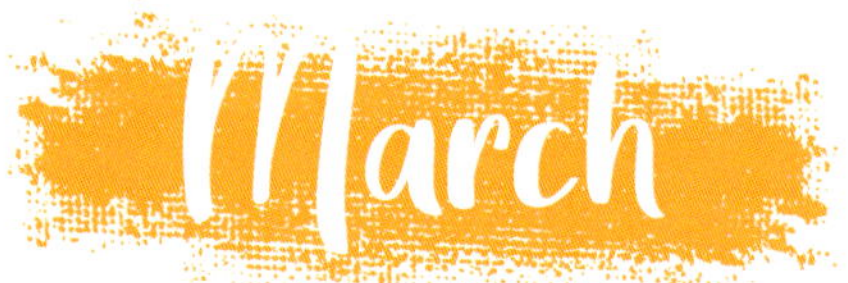

Holi, India (& other countries) | **Hola Mohalla**, Punjab, India | **International Yoga Festival**, Rishikesh, India, *internationalyogafestival.org* | **Las Fallas**, Valencia, Spain | **Paro Tshechu**, Bhutan | **Sakura Matsuri** (Cherry Blossom Festival), Japan (& other countries), Mar–May | **Semana Santa** (Holy Week), Sevilla, Spain | **Snowboxx**, Avoriaz, France, *snowboxx.com* | **Spring Equinox**, Teotihuacán, Mexico | **St. Patrick's Day**, Ireland (& other countries) | **SXSW**, Austin, Texas, USA, *sxsw.com*

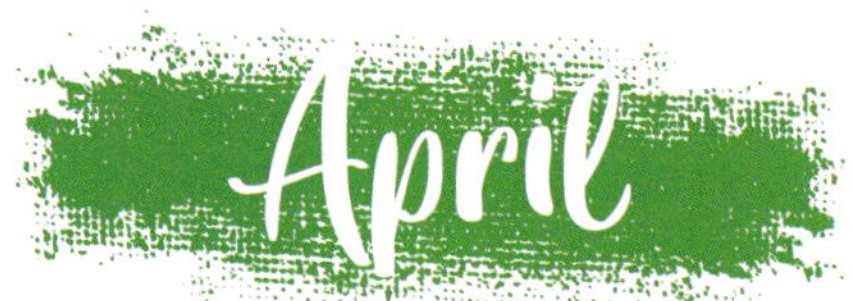

Beltane Fire Festival, Edinburgh, Scotland, *beltane.org* | **Coachella Valley Music and Arts Festival**, Indio, California, USA, *coachella.com* | **Feria de Abril**, Sevilla, Spain | **Kanamara Matsuri** (Festival of the Steel Phallus), Kawasaki, Japan | **Koningsdag**, Netherlands | **Rouketopolemos** (Rocket War), Chios, Greece | **Snowbombing**, Mayrhofen, Austria, *snowbombing.com* | **Songkran Festival**, Thailand | **Yeon Deung Hoe** (Lotus Lantern Festival), South Korea, month may vary (Apr/May)

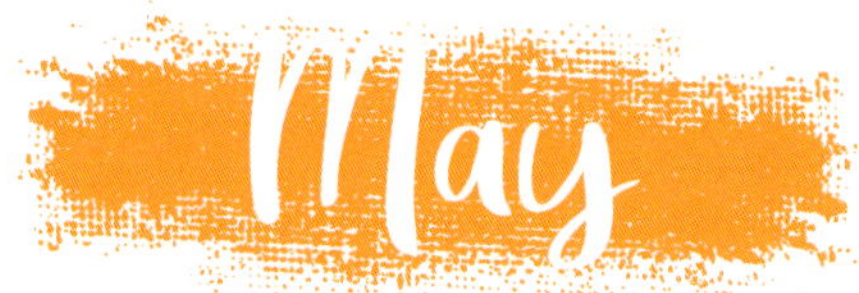

Bun Bang Fai (Rocket Festival), Yasothon, Thailand | **Cooper's Hill Cheese-Rolling and Wake**, Gloucester-shire, England | **Eid al-Fitr** (Festival of Breaking the Fast), various countries | **Formula 1 Grand Prix de Monaco**, Monte Carlo, Monaco, month may vary (May/Jun) | **Karneval der Kulturen** (Carnival of Cultures), Berlin, Germany, *karneval.berlin* | **White Nights Festival**, St. Petersburg, Russia

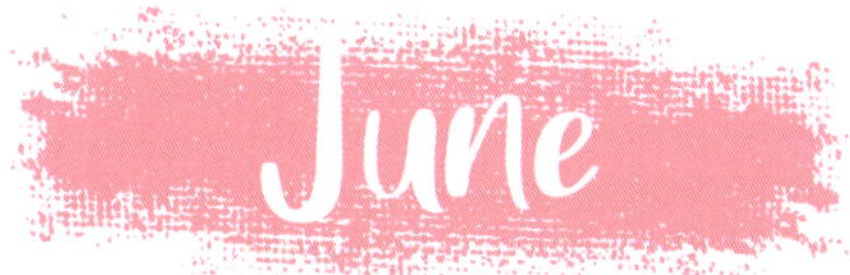

Dragon Boat Festival, China | **Glastonbury Festival**, Somerset, England, *glastonburyfestivals.co.uk* | **Highland Games**, various locations, Scotland, May–Sep | **Inti Raymi**, Cusco, Peru | **Midsommar**, Sweden | **Pride Month, Christopher Street Day and Pride Parades** in various locations worldwide | **Red Earth Festival**, Oklahoma, USA | **Roskilde Festival**, Denmark, *roskilde-festival.dk* | **Summer Solstice**, Stonehenge, Salisbury, England

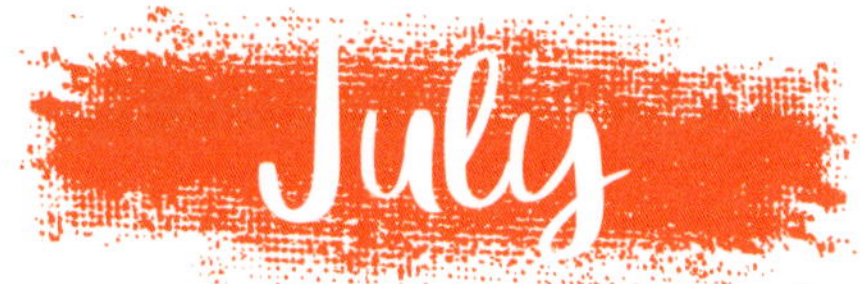

Bastille Day (Fête Nationale), France | **Boryeong Mud Festival**, South Korea, *boryeongmudfestival.com* | **Calgary Stampede**, Canada, *calgarystampede.com* | **Canada Day**, Canada | **Independence Day**, USA | **Krishna Janmashtami**, various countries, month may vary (Jul/Aug) | **Naadam Festival**, Ulaanbaatar, Mongolia, *naadamfestival.com* | **Reggae Sumfest**, Montego Bay, Jamaica, *reggaesumfest.com* | **Tomorrowland**, Boom, Belgium, *tomorrowland.com*

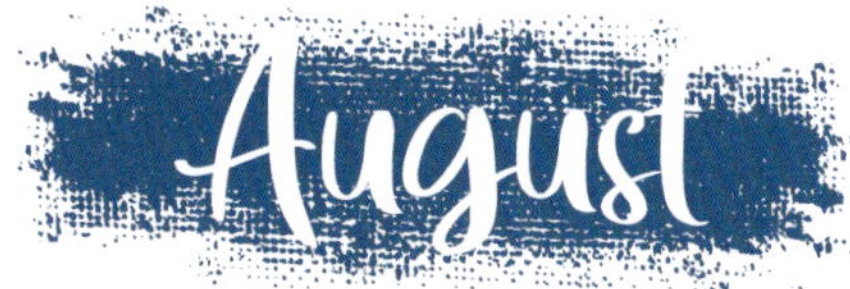

Burning Man, Black Rock Desert, Nevada, USA, *burningman.org* | **Edinburgh Festival Fringe**, Scotland, *edfringe.com* | **Garma Festival**, Gulkula, Arnhem Land, Australia, *yyf.com.au* | **La Tomatina**, Buñol, Valencia, Spain | **Maine Lobster Festival**, Rockland, USA, *mainelobsterfestival.com* | **Mount Hagen Cultural Show**, Papua New Guinea | **Notting Hill Carnival**, London, England, *nhcarnival.org* | **Sziget Festival**, Budapest, Hungary, *szigetfestival.com* | **Wacken Open Air**, Germany, *wacken.com*

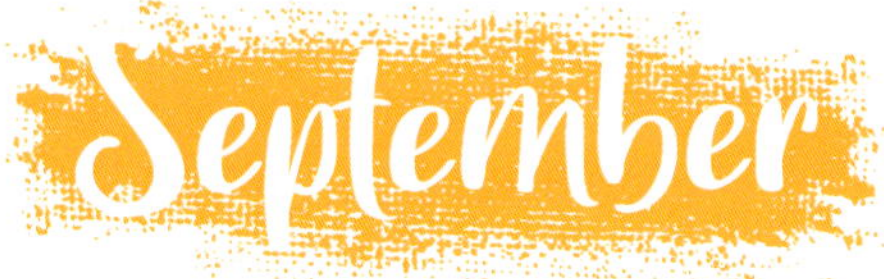

Bournemouth Air Festival, England, *bournemouthair.co.uk* | **Festival of Lights**, Berlin (& other cities around the world), *festival-of-lights.de* | **Fetu Afahye**, Cape Coast, Ghana | **Great Jack O'Lantern Blaze**, Croton-on-Hudson, New York, USA, Sep–Nov, *pumpkinblaze.org* | **Lake of Stars**, Malawi, *lakeofstars.org* | **Montreal International Jazz Festival**, Canada, *montrealjazzfest.com* | **Oktoberfest**, Munich, Germany, *oktoberfest.de* | **Snowboxx**, Cardrona, New Zealand, *snowboxx.nz* | **Summerfest**, Milwaukee, Wisconsin, USA, *summerfest.com*

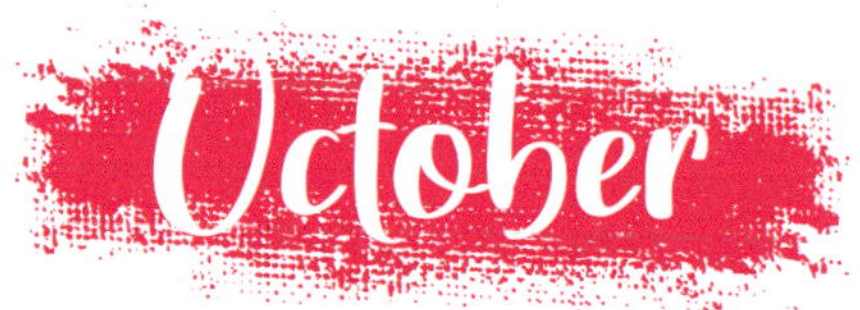

Albuquerque International Balloon Fiesta, New Mexico, USA, *balloonfiesta.com* | **Halloween**, USA |
Salem Haunted Happenings, Massachusetts, USA, *hauntedhappenings.org*

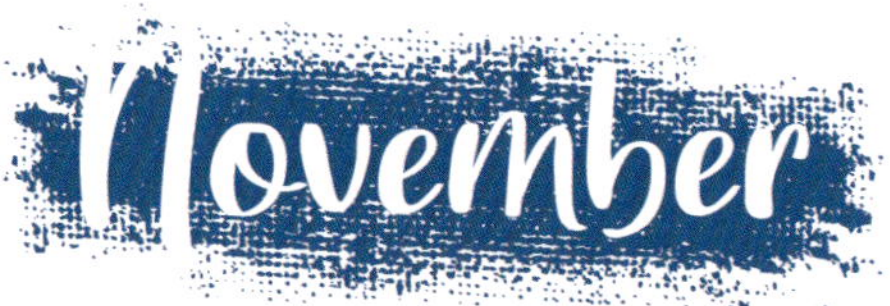

Chhath Puja, India & Nepal, month my vary (Oct/Nov) | **Día de los Muertos**, Mexico | **Diwali**, various coun-
tries, month may vary (Oct/Nov) | **Macy's Thanksgiving Day Parade**, New York City, USA, *macys.com* |
Yi Peng Festival, Chiang Mai, Thailand

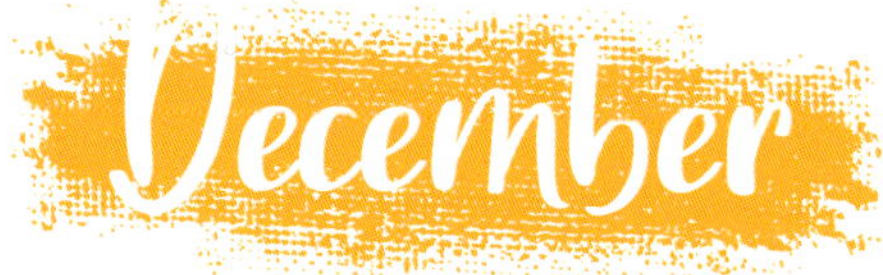

Hogmanay, Edinburgh, Scotland, *edinburghshogmanay.com* | **Krampusnacht**, Austria (& other countries) |
Los Escobazos, Jarandilla de la Vera, Spain | **Wonderfruit**, Pattaya, Thailand, *wonderfruit.co*

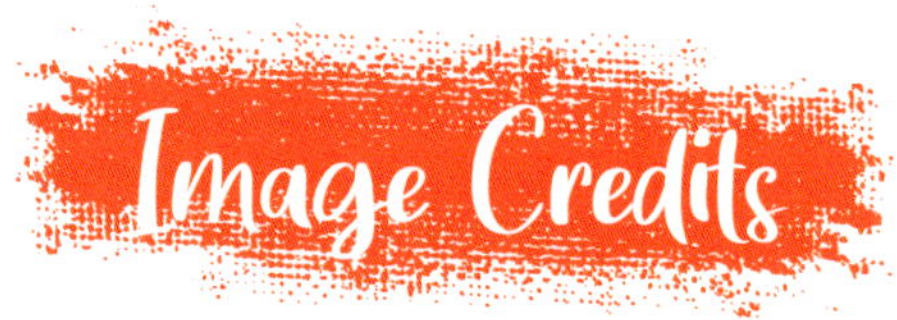

Cover: © Melinda Nagy/AdobeStock
p. 05: photo by Ugur Arpaci on Unsplash; p. 07: photo by Hitoshi Namura on Unsplash; pp. 08, 16 & 17 (top): © Raphael Dias/Getty
Images; p. 09: © emperorcosar/AdobeStock; p. 11 (top): © Anna Nahabed/Shutterstock; (bottom): © JBKC/Shutterstock; pp. 12/13:
© Suzanne C. Grim/Shutterstock; pp. 14/15: © Celso Pupo/Shutterstock; pp. 17 (bottom) & 27: photos by Terry George from United
States, CC BY-SA 2.0, via Wikimedia Commons; pp. 18 & 19: © Frank Bienewald/LightRocket via Getty Images; pp. 20 (top) & 21:
© Thomas Lohnes/Getty Images; p. 20 (bottom): © Ying Tang/NurPhoto via Getty Images; pp. 22/23: © skovalsky/Shutterstock;
pp. 24/25: © Matteo Chinellato/NurPhoto via Getty Images; p. 26: photo by Przemyslaw Smit on Unsplash; p. 28: © Greg Meland/Adobe-
Stock; p. 29 (top): © Mazur Travel/Shutterstock; (bottom left): © picture alliance/AP Photo/Daniel Ochoa de Olza; (bottom right):
© SUDONG KIM/Shutterstock; p. 30 (top): © Bule Sky Studio/Shutterstock; (bottom): © Leon Neal/Getty Images; p. 32: © Taromon/
Shutterstock; p. 33: © AndrewJ/AdobeStock; p. 34: © Roberto Ricciuti/Getty Images; pp. 35, 140, 141: © Jeff J Mitchell/Getty Images;
p. 36: © Aranami/Shutterstock; p. 37: © Gabor Kovacs Photography/Shutterstock; pp. 38/39: photo by Ian Dooley on Unsplash;
p. 40: © MrPreecha/AdobeStock; p. 41: © Martin Wildman/Shutterstock; p. 42: © Arnav Pratap Singh/AdobeStock; p. 43 (top): © Yochika
Photographer/Shutterstock; (bottom): © Chung Sung-Jun/Getty Images; p. 44 (top): © Elite Studio/Shutterstock; (bottom): © puwanai/
Shutterstock; p. 45: © Kobby Dagan/Shutterstock; p. 46 (top): © BjornBecker/Shutterstock; (bottom): © John Horsley/Photoshot/Getty
Images; p. 47: photo by Austin Neill on Unsplash; p. 49: Jan Kranendonk/Shutterstock; pp. 50/51: photo by Erica Li on Unsplash;
p. 52: photo by Jacob Buchhave on Unsplash; p. 53: © koburu/AdobeStock; p. 54: photo by Robert Metz on Unsplash; p. 55: photo by
Jones on Unsplash; pp. 56/57: © aapsky/AdobeStock; p. 58: © samshutterstock/Shutterstock; p. 59: photo by Thomas Ullrich on Pixa-
bay; p. 60: photo by Fanatic/Danny North, courtesy of Snowbombing; p. 61 (top): photo by Thelmadatter, CC BY-SA 3.0, via Wikimedia
Commons; (bottom): © Sean Pavone/Shutterstock; p. 62 (top): © Carol La Rosa/Shutterstock; (bottom): © stefanholm/AdobeStock;
p. 64: photo by Fanatic/Danny North, courtesy of Snowbombing; p. 65 (top): photo by Martin Sylvester, courtesy of Mainstage Festivals
(Snowboxx); (bottom): © Mano's/Shutterstock; pp. 66/67: © Leon Neal/Getty Images; pp. 68/69: © Alex Segre/Shutterstock; p. 70:
© Fotos593/Shutterstock; p. 71: © Pavel/AdobeStock; pp. 72/73: © John Kotlowski/Shutterstock; p. 74: © Youenn JACQUIN/AdobeStock;
p. 75 (top): © Myriam B/Shutterstock; (bottom): Roberto Epifanio/Shutterstock; pp. 76/77: © Matt Anderson Photography/Getty Images;
p. 78: © John Blanding/The Boston Globe via Getty Images; p. 79: © Inspired by Maps/Shutterstock; p. 80: © Miriam/AdobeStock; p. 81:
Nicola Simeoni/AdobeStock; p. 82 (top): © fresnel6/AdobeStock; (bottom): © diyben/Shutterstock; p. 83: © Sanket Wankhade/Hindustan
Times via Getty Images; p. 85 (top): © MudaCom/Shutterstock; (bottom): © MICHEL/AdobeStock; p. 86: © 3523studio/Shutterstock;
p. 87: © Lawrence Wee/Shutterstock; pp. 88/89: © Framalicious/Shutterstock; p. 90: © Alphorom/Shutterstock; p. 91: © Wirestock
Creators/Shutterstock; pp. 92/93, 163: © JackF/AdobeStock; p. 94: photo by Debashis RC Biswas on Unsplash; p. 95: © Yavuz Sariyildiz/
Shutterstock; p. 96: © mrallen/AdobeStock; p. 97: © mbrand85/AdobeStock; pp. 98/99: © panwasin/AdobeStock; p. 100: © Panu
Kosonen/Shutterstock; p. 101: © qingqing/Shutterstock; p. 102: © Ingo Bartussek/AdobeStock; p. 103: © luisfpizarro/AdobeStock;
p. 104 (top): © MindStorm/Shutterstock; (bottom): © Siddharth Setia/Shutterstock; p. 105: © Glenn Campbell/The Sydney Morning

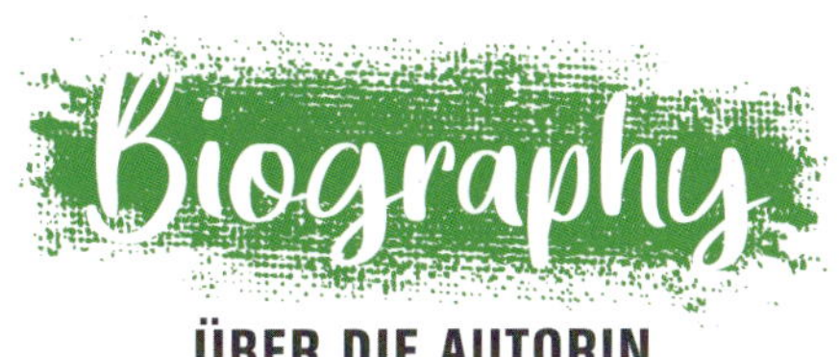
Biography
ÜBER DIE AUTORIN

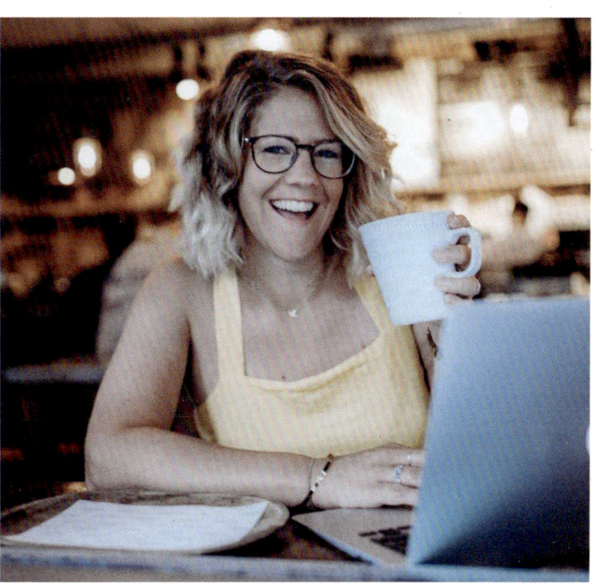

Victoria Philpott has been a travel and festival blogger at "Vicky-FlipFlop Travels" since 2012. She's been to over 60 festivals in 22 countries, with plans for many more. Her favorite festival experiences have been at Lake of Stars in Malawi, Glastonbury in the UK, and Día de los Muertos in Mexico. Visit her blog to find out more: *vickyflipfloptravels.com.*

Victoria Philpott ist seit 2012 als Reise- und Festival-Bloggerin für „VickyFlipFlip Travels" unterwegs. Sie hat über 60 Festivals in 22 Ländern besucht und bereits Reisepläne für viele weitere. Ihre schönsten Festivalerlebnisse hatte sie bei Lake of Stars in Malawi, Glastonbury in England und Día de los Muertos in Mexiko. Besuchen Sie ihren Blog, um mehr zu erfahren: *vickyflipfloptravels.com.*

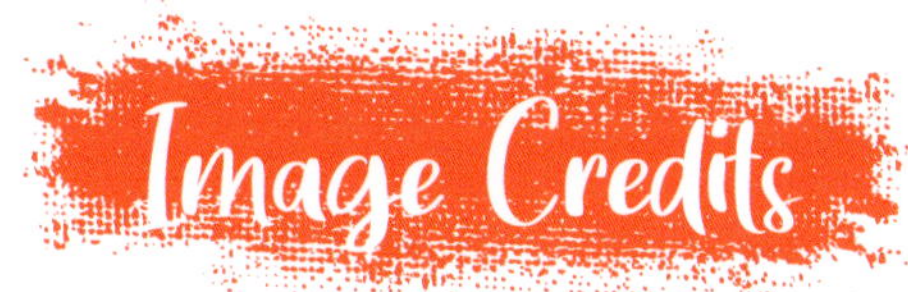
Image Credits

Imprint

© 2021 teNeues Verlag GmbH

Texts by Victoria Philpott
Translations by Ronit Jariv, derschönstesatz

Editorial Coordination by Nadine Weinhold, teNeues Verlag
Production by Sandra Jansen-Dorn, teNeues Verlag
Photo Editing, Color Separation by Jens Grundei,
 teNeues Verlag
Design by Iris van Kempen
Picture Research & Book Composition by Nadine Weinhold,
 teNeues Verlag
Copyediting by Victorine Lamothe (English),
Nadine Weinhold (German), teNeues Verlag
Proofreading by Stephanie Rebel, teNeues Verlag

ISBN: 978 3 96171-308-0 (German edition)
978-3-96171-307-3 (English edition)
Library of Congress Number: 2020935920
Printed in Slovakia by Neografia a.s.

Bibliographic information published by the Deutsche
Nationalbibliothek: The Deutsche Nationalbibliothek lists
this publication in the Deutsche Nationalbibliografie;
detailed bibliographic data are available on the Internet
at dnb.dnb.de.

Published by teNeues Publishing Group

teNeues Verlag GmbH
Werner-von-Siemens-Straße 1
86159 Augsburg, Germany

Düsseldorf Office
Waldenburger Str. 13
41564 Kaarst, Germany
e-mail: books@teneues.com

Augsburg/München Office
Werner-von-Siemens-Straße 1
86159 Augsburg, Germany
e-mail: books@teneues.com

Berlin Office
Lietzenburger Str. 53
10719 Berlin, Germany
e-mail: books@teneues.com

Press department Stefan Becht
Phone: +49-152-2874-9508 /
+49-6321-97067-99
e-mail: sbecht@teneues.com

teNeues Publishing Company
350 Seventh Avenue, Suite 301,
New York, NY 10001, USA
Phone: +1-212-627-9090
Fax: +1-212-627-9511

www.teneues.com

teNeues Publishing Group
Augsburg / München
Berlin
Düsseldorf
London
New York

teNeues

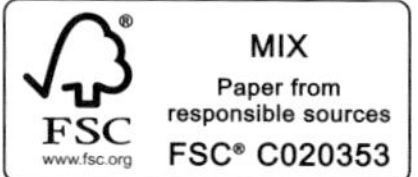

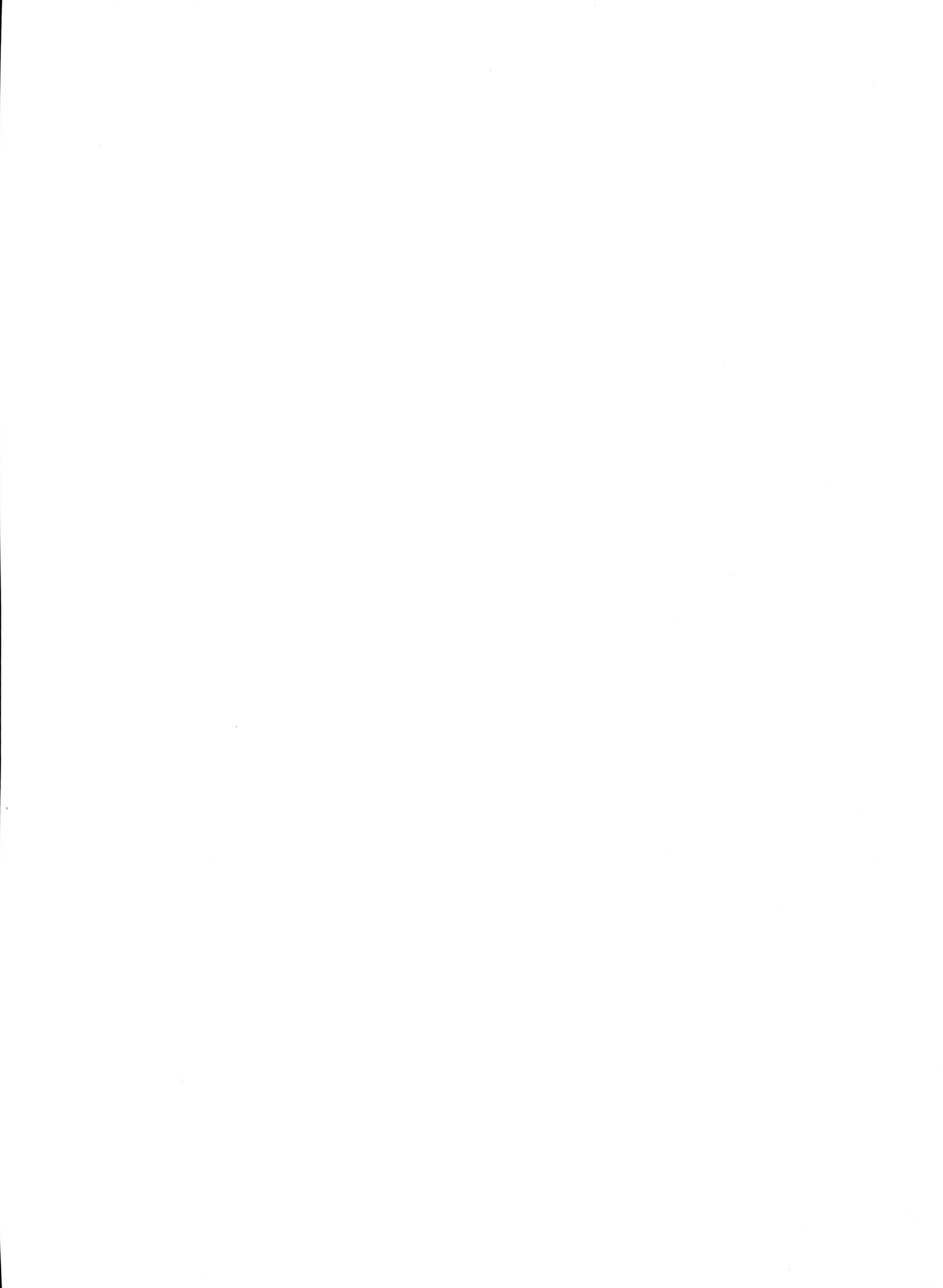